THE
unofficial **GUIDE®**
ᴛᴏ Chicago

7TH EDITION

THE *unofficial* GUIDE®
TO Chicago

7TH EDITION

DAVID HOEKSTRA *with*
ALICE VAN HOUSEN *and* LAURIE LEVY

WILEY

Please note that prices fluctuate in the course of time and that travel information changes under the impact of many factors that influence the travel industry. We therefore suggest that you write or call ahead for confirmation when making your travel plans. Every effort has been made to ensure the accuracy of information throughout this book, and the contents of this publication are believed to be correct at the time of printing. Nevertheless, the publishers cannot accept responsibility for errors or omissions, for changes in details given in this guide, or for the consequences of any reliance on the information provided by the same. Assessments of attractions and so forth are based upon the authors' own experiences; therefore, descriptions given in this guide necessarily contain an element of subjective opinion, which may not reflect the publisher's opinion or dictate a reader's own experience on another occasion. Readers are invited to write the publisher with ideas, comments, and suggestions for future editions.

Published by:
John Wiley & Sons, Inc.
111 River Street
Hoboken, NJ 07030-5774

Produced by Menasha Ridge Press

Cover design by Michael J. Freeland

Interior design by Vertigo Design

For information on our other products and services or to obtain technical support, please contact our Customer Care Department within the United States at 800-762-2974, outside the United States at 317-572-3993, or by fax at 317-572-4002.

John Wiley & Sons, Inc., also publishes its books in a variety of electronic formats. Some content that appears in print may not be available in electronic formats.

ISBN 978-0-470-04207-6

Manufactured in the United States of America

5 4 3 2 1

CONTENTS

List of Maps viii
About the Authors   ix

Introduction 1
About This Guide 3
How Information Is Organized: By Subject and Geographic Area 6

PART ONE Understanding the City 7
A Brief History of Chicago 7
FAST FACTS ABOUT THE WINDY CITY 8
Skyscrapers and the Prairie School: Chicago Architecture 16
Sculpture in the Loop 22

PART TWO Planning Your Visit 25
Seasons of Change 25
CHICAGO'S AVERAGE TEMPERATURES AND PRECIPITATION 26
Avoiding Crowds 26
How to Get More Information before Your Visit 27
Getting to Chicago 28
CHICAGO TRIP TIPS 29
A CALENDAR OF FESTIVALS AND EVENTS 29

PART THREE Accommodations 33
Deciding Where to Stay 33
Getting a Good Deal on a Room 36
Chicago Lodging for Business Travelers 41
CHAIN-HOTEL TOLL-FREE NUMBERS 43
Chicago Hotels: Rated and Ranked 44
CHICAGO HOTELS BY LOCATION 46

HOW THE HOTELS COMPARE IN CHICAGO 48–51
THE TOP 30 BEST HOTEL DEALS IN CHICAGO 52
HOTEL INFORMATION CHART 53

PART FOUR Visiting on Business 66

Convention Central, U.S.A. 66
CALENDAR OF CONVENTIONS AND SPECIAL EVENTS 68
McCormick Place Convention Center 70
Navy Pier 76
Donald E. Stephens Convention Center 77

PART FIVE Arriving and Getting Oriented 78

Coming into Chicago by Car 78
Coming into Chicago by Plane 79
HANGING OUT AT O'HARE 82
Coming into Chicago by Train 86
Getting Oriented 87
WHAT IS THE LOOP? 89
Things the Natives Already Know 92
CHICAGO'S BEST RADIO STATIONS 95

PART SIX Getting Around 100

Driving Your Car: A Really Bad Idea 100
Public Transportation 102
CHICAGO'S MAJOR CAB AND LIMOUSINE COMPANIES 106
Walking in Chicago 107

PART SEVEN Sightseeing, Tours, and Attractions 108

Touring Chicago 108
Exploring Chicago's Neighborhoods 116
Chicago for Children 133
Helpful Hints for Visitors 134
Chicago Attractions 138
Attraction Profiles 138
CHICAGO ATTRACTIONS BY TYPE 142
CHICAGO ATTRACTIONS BY LOCATION 144

PART EIGHT Dining and Restaurants 177

Dining in Chicago 177
NEWCOMERS AND OTHER RECOMMENDATIONS 178–179
Restaurants: Rated and Ranked 182
THE BEST CHICAGO RESTAURANTS 184

CHICAGO RESTAURANTS BY NEIGHBORHOOD 188
Restaurant Profiles 193

PART NINE Shopping in Chicago 255

Nothing Like It Back Home 255
Michigan Avenue: The Magnificent Mile 257
The Loop's Landmark Department Store 263
Where to Find . . . 265
Suburban Shopping Centers, Discount Malls, and Shops 308

PART TEN Exercise, Recreation, and Sports 311

Indoor Activities 311
Outdoor Activities 313
Spectator Sports 321

PART ELEVEN Entertainment and Nightlife 327

Chicago after Dark 327
Live Entertainment 328
Nightclub Profiles 344
CHICAGO NIGHTCLUBS BY LOCATION 345

Indexes and Reader Survey 357

Accommodations Index 357
Restaurant Index 359
Subject Index 363
Unofficial Guide Reader Survey 373

LIST *of* MAPS

Chicago at a Glance 2
Chicago's Best Architecture 18–19
Loop Sculpture Tour 24
Central Chicago Accommodations 34–35
McCormick Place Convention Center 71
O'Hare International Airport 80
Midway Airport 85
Downtown El and Subway Stations 104
Central Chicago Attractions 146–147
River North Dining and Nightlife 194
Loop Dining and Nightlife 195
Lincoln Park and Wrigleyville Dining and Nightlife 196–197
Wicker Park and Bucktown Dining 198
Shopping: Magnificent Mile and the Loop 259

ABOUT *the* AUTHORS

LEAD WRITER **David Hoekstra** is a staff writer and columnist at the *Chicago Sun-Times*. He won a 1987 Chicago Newspaper Guild Stick-O-Type Award for Column Writing for outstanding commentary on Chicago nightlife. He's also a contributing writer for *Playboy* and has been a contributing editor for *Chicago* magazine. His anthology of *Sun-Times* travel columns, *Ticket to Everywhere,* was published by Lake Claremont Press in 2000.

FORMER RESTAURANT CONSULTANT **Alice Van Housen** (Part Eight, Dining and Restaurants) is a writer, reviewer, and editor for a variety of food-focused publications and Web sites. She has served as Chicago editor for the print and online editions of *Zagat Survey* since 2001. She has also contributed dining chapters to *Frommer's Chicago* and *Mobil Travel Guides;* served as founding editor of *Local Palate,* a monthly foodie newspaper; and written for numerous local and national publications, including *Fast Company,* the *Los Angeles Times, Wine & Spirits, Plate, Restaurants & Institutions, Restaurant Business,* the *Chicago Tribune's* Metromix and RedEye supplements, the *Chicago Sun-Times,* the *Chicago Reader, Chicago Social,* and *Front Desk Chicago.* In addition, she has been a contributing Chicago reviewer for the Citysearch online-entertainment and dining guide since its original incarnation as Chicago Sidewalk in 1996.

JOURNALIST–FICTION WRITER **Laurie Levy** (Part Nine, Shopping in Chicago) has written locally for the *Chicago Tribune,* the *Chicago Sun-Times, The Chicago Collection, Chicago* magazine, and *Today's Chicago Woman,* among others, as well as for national publications such as *Business Traveler, Travel Agent,* and *Four Seasons Magazine.* She is the author of three nonfiction books and is an award-winning short-story writer and novelist.

INTRODUCTION

CHICAGO IS THE FRONT PORCH OF AMERICA. Few major American cities are as welcoming. Should you lose your way along North Michigan Avenue, Chicagoans will be happy to help you with directions. They will stop. They will steer the course. And if they have time, they probably will draw a map and buy you a cup of coffee. A majority of the city's residents were born and raised here; others came to Chicago from Michigan, Wisconsin, and northwest Indiana. Whether natives or transplants, they take remarkable ownership in their city.

As with any midwestern front porch, there's room for all kinds of characters. Mayor Richard J. Daley, for instance, likes to act like the crotchety patriarch, but he's really not that bad. (Sometimes he even cries at press conferences.) He's been mayor since 1989, proof that Chicagoans don't like a lot of change. Daley's father was mayor too, from 1955 until his death in 1976.

The city has witnessed tremendous growth under the current Mayor Daley. Downtown is booming after a decade of decline. New dining, shopping, and entertainment choices are enticing young people back downtown to live. Chicago has also become one of the most beautiful cities in America. Flowers and shrubs grow along city sidewalks and in median strips. Tourists consistently comment on how clean the city is.

If New York is "The Big Apple," Chicago is "Green Acres." The mayor has helped create initiatives to increase green roof usage in his goal to make Chicago "the greenest city in America." There's even a rooftop garden with more than 21,000 plants at City Hall downtown. Plus, Chicago has one of the most architecturally recognizable bridge systems in the world. The city has installed a computerized lighting system that at night illuminates 11 bridges along the main branch of the Chicago River—a river that runs backward. Chicago is quirky that way.

Sometimes, though, Mayor Daley and his pals on the front porch get a little carried away with gussying up Chicago. One alderman became famous for his proposed legislation to put diapers on carriage

chicago at a glance

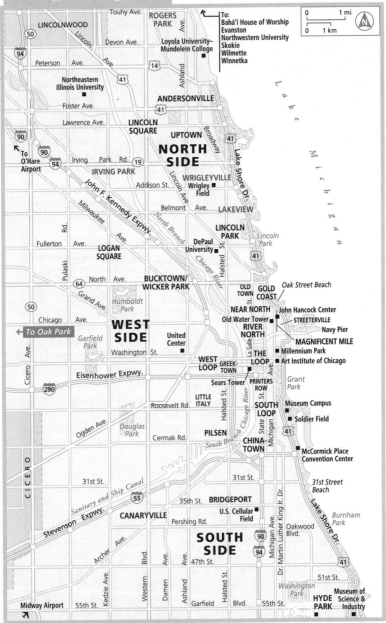

horses. The city council has also banned foie gras and kind of banned smoking in bars and restaurants, albeit with a longtime frame for compliance. The city even has its first fashion director. No, you need not wear a coat and tie to gain entrance into Chicago—the city is just trying to enhance its design-and-fashion community.

It took a long time for Chicago to change its image. For many years tourists associated the city with the rat-a-tat-tat of gangster Al Capone, the muscle of the stockyards, and the hardscrabble prose of Nelson Algren, Studs Terkel, and newspaperman Mike Royko. That gritty aura still exists, but now it's a faded tattoo under a new shirt. While leading the Bulls to six NBA titles, Michael Jordan gave Chicago a contemporary global presence. On the flip side, the numbing futility of the Cubs—who haven't won a World Series since 1908—has turned their Wrigley Field home into a carnival-like beer garden. Chicago's new face also includes talk-show queen Oprah Winfrey and trash-TV king Jerry Springer.

Visitors should keep in mind that Chicago is not big on nicknames. No one under the age of 90 calls Chicago "Chi-Town" anymore. "The Windy City" is a misnomer: Amarillo, Texas, and Wichita, Kansas, are more windy than Chicago; newspaper people coined the term for the city's blustery politicians. And Frank Sinatra's "toddlin' town" is now a world-class city.

It's also America's most livable big city. Where New York is condensed and Los Angeles is spread out, Chicago is easy to get around. Chicago Transit Authority (CTA) buses and trains are generally reliable, and city streets are laid out in an accessible grid system. Michael Jordan still keeps a home in the suburbs, while Chicago-area native Vince Vaughn lives on and off in the area. Rocker Billy Corgan of Smashing Pumpkins never left town, and Mike Ditka remains a Chicago icon, even though it's been more than 20 years since he took "Da Bears" to the Super Bowl. Chicago is a melting pot of diverse personalities, an eclectic abode of ethnic influences. The door is always open, sure to be a portal to memorable adventure.

ABOUT *this* GUIDE

WHY "UNOFFICIAL"?

MOST "OFFICIAL" GUIDES to Chicago celebrate the well-known sights, promote local restaurants and hotels indiscriminately, and leave out a lot of good stuff. This book is different. An irreverent city demands an irreverent guide.

Instead of pandering to the tourist industry, we'll tell you if a well-known restaurant's crummy food isn't worth the wait. We'll complain loudly about overpriced hotel rooms that aren't convenient to the Loop (that's the core of downtown) or the airport, and we'll guide you away from the crowds and congestion for a break now and then.

THE PROBLEM WITH GUIDEBOOKS

MOST GUIDEBOOKS ARE COLLECTIONS OF LISTS. This is true regardless of whether the information is literally presented in list form or artfully distributed through pages of prose. There is insufficient detail in a list, and prose can present tedious helpings of nonessential or marginally useful information. Such guides offer little more than departure points from which readers initiate their own quests.

Many guides are readable and well researched, but they tend to be difficult to use. To select a hotel, for example, a reader must study several pages of descriptions with only the boldface hotel names breaking up large blocks of text. Readers generally must work through all the write-ups before beginning to narrow their choices. Recommendations, if any, lack depth and conviction. These guides compound rather than solve problems by failing to narrow the average traveler's choices down to a thoughtfully considered and manageable few.

HOW *UNOFFICIAL GUIDES* ARE DIFFERENT

READERS CARE ABOUT THE AUTHOR'S OPINION. The authors care about their city. This, coupled with the fact that the traveler wants quick answers (as opposed to endless alternatives), dictates that authors should be explicit, prescriptive, and above all, direct. The *Unofficial Guide* tries to be just that. It spells out alternatives and recommends specific action. It simplifies complicated destinations and attractions and helps the traveler feel in control in even the most unfamiliar environments. The objective of the *Unofficial Guide* is not to have all the information, but, rather, the most accessible, useful information—unbiased by affiliation with any organization or industry.

Special Features

WHAT YOU'LL GET in an *Unofficial Guide:*

- Friendly introductions to Chicago's vast array of ethnic neighborhoods.
- "Best of" listings giving our well-qualified opinions on everything from bagels to pizza, four-star hotels to the best night views of Chicago.
- Listings keyed to your interests, so you can pick and choose.
- Advice on avoiding crowds, traffic, and excess expense.
- Maps that make it easy to find the places you want to visit.
- A hotel chart that helps narrow your choices with expedience.
- Compact listings that include only those restaurants, clubs, and hotels we think are worth considering.

What you *won't* get in an *Unofficial Guide:*

- Long, useless lists where everything looks the same.

- Insufficient information that gets you where you want to go at the worst possible time.
- Information without advice on how to use it.

HOW THIS GUIDE WAS RESEARCHED AND WRITTEN

MANY GUIDEBOOKS HAVE BEEN WRITTEN ABOUT CHICAGO, but few have been evaluative. Some practically regurgitate hotel and tourist promotional material. In preparing this book, nothing was taken for granted. Each museum, monument, art gallery, hotel, restaurant, shop, and attraction was evaluated and rated by trained observers according to formal criteria. Interviews were conducted to determine what tourists of all ages enjoyed most—and least—during their Chicago visit.

The trained evaluator is responsible for much more than observing and cataloging. While the average tourist may be gazing in awe from the observation deck at the Sears Tower, the professional is rating the attraction in terms of how quickly crowds move, the location of restrooms, and how well children can see over the railing in front of the plate-glass windows. The evaluator also checks out nearby attractions, alternatives if the line at a main attraction is too long, and where to find the best lunch. Observers use detailed checklists to analyze hotel rooms, restaurants, nightclubs, and attractions. Finally, evaluator ratings and observations are integrated with tourist reactions and the opinions of patrons for a comprehensive, high-quality profile of each feature and service.

LETTERS, COMMENTS, AND QUESTIONS FROM READERS

WE WANT TO LEARN FROM OUR MISTAKES, as well as from the input of our readers, and to improve with each book and edition. We encourage feedback, both positive and negative. Reader's comments and observations will be incorporated in revised editions of the *Unofficial Guide* and will contribute immeasurably to its improvement.

How to Write the Author

David Hoekstra
The Unofficial Guide to Chicago
P.O. Box 43673
Birmingham, AL 35243
ohdave@ameritech.net

Because our work often takes us out of the office for long periods of time, please bear with us if our response is delayed.

Reader Survey

AT THE BACK OF THE GUIDE you'll find a short questionnaire that you can use to express opinions concerning your Chicago visit. Clip the questionnaire along the dotted line and mail it to the above address.

How **INFORMATION** *Is* **ORGANIZED:**
By Subject and Geographic Area

TO GIVE YOU FAST ACCESS to information about the best of Chicago, we've organized material in several formats.

HOTELS Because most people visiting Chicago stay in one hotel for the duration of their trip, we've summarized our coverage of hotels in charts, maps, ratings, and rankings that allow you to quickly focus your decision-making process. We concentrate on the variables that differentiate one hotel from another: location, size, room quality, services, amenities, and cost. Comparative and informational hotel charts can be found in Part Three.

RESTAURANTS Chicago is one of the best restaurant cities in the world, and its reputation continues to grow. Because you'll probably eat a dozen or more restaurant meals during your stay, and because you can't even predict what you might be in the mood for on a Saturday night, we provide detailed profiles of the best restaurants in and around Chicago in Part Eight.

ATTRACTIONS To save you time, money, and foot ache, we've organized many of the city's sights into a handy time-saving chart divided by location. Gonna be in the Loop for dinner? Well, see what's in the area and organize your day accordingly.

ENTERTAINMENT AND NIGHTLIFE Visitors frequently try several different clubs during their stay. Because nightspots, like restaurants, are usually selected spontaneously after arriving in Chicago, we believe detailed descriptions are warranted. The best clubs and lounges are profiled in Part Eleven.

GEOGRAPHIC AREA Once you've decided where you're going, getting there becomes the next decision. To help you do that, we've divided Chicago by areas and neighborhoods:

North Side	The Loop (the core of	South Side
North Central–O'Hare	downtown)	Southern Suburbs
Airport	South Loop	Western Suburbs
Near North Side	South Central–Midway	Northwest Suburbs
	Airport	Northern Suburbs

All listings of hotels, attractions, restaurants, and nightspots include location information. For example, if you are staying at a hotel on Chicago's Magnificent Mile (North Michigan Avenue) and want to sample the latest in New American cuisine, scanning the restaurant profiles for those in Near North will get you where you want to go. Remember—in Chicago, each neighborhood is uniquely its own.

PART ONE

UNDERSTANDING *the* CITY

A **BRIEF HISTORY** *of* **CHICAGO**

THE AMERICAN SPIRIT IS EMBEDDED IN CHICAGO. You hear the sound of rebirth on any given day here. There's the rhythm of electric drills rehabbing old bungalows and the eclectic laughter of children in city parks. Street musicians play steady blues tunes, and around every corner someone is arguing about the Cubs and the White Sox.

Chicago is a true American city, one on the cusp of an eternal spring. The town was founded on a suspicious swamp and later rebuilt itself from the ashes of a tremendous fire into the nation's third-largest city. With a lakefront skyline recognized around the world, it's a town that owes its verve to generations of big shoulders. After Hurricane Katrina, Chicago took in more Gulf Coast residents (6,000) than any other city outside of the South. Muckraking journalist H. L. Mencken was charmed by the place: "I give you Chicago!" he wrote. "It is not London and Harvard. It is not Paris and buttermilk. It is American in every chitling and sparerib. It is alive from snout to tail."

It is also a cauldron of bubbling contrasts: shimmering skyscrapers and postindustrial urban decay; a long-suppressed black minority that points with pride to U.S. Senator–presidential hopeful Barack Obama and cultural icon Oprah Winfrey. Chicago is Al Capone and Michael Jordan, Jane Addams and Hugh Hefner, proletarian writer Studs Terkel and Nobel Prize winner Saul Bellow.

Chicago is a city of legends, of precious visionaries, and of quite a few scoundrels. Built on swampland at the edge of a prairie, the city has endured cycles of booms and busts. As the nation grew westward, Chicago found itself in a great geographical position to supply raw materials that fed the expansion. The city was incorporated on March 4, 1837. "Interesting women are in demand here," a lonely pioneer wrote from Chicago to the *New York Star* in 1837. The women soon arrived—and Chicago began to kick up its heels.

BEGINNINGS

TWELVE THOUSAND YEARS AGO, Lake Chicago, a larger version of Lake Michigan, covered much of what is now the Midwest. As this great glacial lake receded, it left behind a vast prairie and shoreline swamp that linked North America's two great waterways: the Mississippi River (via the Des Plaines and Illinois rivers) and the Great Lakes. The area's first residents were Native Americans, led by Chief Blackhawk—thus, the name of Chicago's hockey team the Chicago Blackhawks. They named the area *Checago* or *Checaguar,* which likely meant "wild onion" or "swamp gas," probably a reference to the pungent smell of decaying marsh vegetation that permeated the swamp. (After all, deep-dish pizza had yet to be invented.) Either way, the name implied great strength.

FIRST SETTLERS AND A MASSACRE

IN 1673 TWO FRENCH EXPLORERS were the first Europeans to set eyes on what is now Chicago: Louis Jolliet, who was searching for gold, and Father Jacques Marquette, who was searching for souls. When their Native American allies showed them the portage trail linking the Mississippi Valley and the Great Lakes, Jolliet saw Chicago's potential immediately. He predicted to Marquette, "Here some day will be found one of the world's great cities." As a token of appreciation, today the city of Joliet sits along the Illinois–Michigan Canal, 45 miles southwest of Chicago. Joliet is also on the migratory Route 66 from Chicago to Los Angeles.

In the late 18th century, the flat prairies stretching west were as empty and primeval as when the last glacier had retreated a thousand years before. Chicago's first nonnative resident, Jean-Baptiste Point du Sable, arrived in 1779 and erected a rough-hewn log house on the north bank of the Chicago River. A tall, French-speaking son of a Quebec merchant and black slave, du Sable established a trading post at what is now North Michigan Avenue. As the local Native Americans noted, "The first white man to live here was a black man."

After du Sable moved to Missouri in 1800 (leaving a handful of other traders at the mouth of the river), Chicago's first boom began. But first the frontier outpost had to endure a massacre. The Native Americans had been run out in 1795, ceding huge tracts of midwestern land—including "six miles square at the mouth of the Chickago River." The swamp turned into a speculator's dream almost overnight. The wheeling and dealing nature of Chicago was born.

Soldiers of the fledgling United States Republic arrived from Detroit in 1803 and erected Fort Dearborn near what is now the corner of lower Wacker Drive and Michigan Avenue. After evacuating the fort during the War of 1812 against the British, settlers and soldiers fleeing the fort were ambushed by Native Americans in league with the enemy; 52 men, women, and children were slain in the Fort Dearborn Massacre.

BOOM . . .

ILLINOIS BECAME A STATE IN 1818—a time when Chicago was still a struggling backwater far north of southern population centers—and in 1829 the state legislature appointed a commission to plot a canal route between Lake Michigan and the Mississippi River. Chicago was poised for a population explosion. The pace of westward development from bustling eastern seaboard cities was accelerating in the early 19th century, and pioneers roared into the Midwest. The Erie Canal opened in 1825, creating a new water route between Chicago and the East. Pioneer wagons rolled in daily, and Chicago's population swelled from around 50 in 1830 to more than 4,000 in 1837. (And not one of them was named Daley—yet.) As waves of Irish and German immigrants arrived, the town's population increased by another 100,000 in the following 30 years.

Speculators swooped in, and lots that sold for $100 in 1830 changed hands for as much as $100,000 in 1837 during a real-estate frenzy fueled by visions of wealth to be made from the planned canal. The first newspaper, the *Chicago Democrat,* was launched in 1833. The editor (and two-time mayor) was "Long John" Wentworth, who liked to carry around a jug of whiskey, allegedly to soothe the blisters on his feet. Naturally, Chicago's first brewery followed in 1836. The first policeman was hired in 1839 and no doubt had his hands full in a town brimming with saloons.

. . . AND BUST

THE BOOM WENT BUST, HOWEVER, in the Panic of 1837, one of America's first economic depressions. Work on the canal ground to a halt, and many local investors went broke. Slowly, a recovery set in, work on the canal resumed, and Chicago spawned its first ethic neighborhood.

Originally called Hardscrabble, it was an enclave of Irish laborers digging the waterway. By the time it was annexed in 1863, the South Side neighborhood was known as Bridgeport, later famous as the well-spring for generations of Irish-American politicians—including Mayor Richard J. Daley (aka "Hizzoner") and his son, Mayor Richard M. Daley. The Chicago White Sox are also based in Bridgeport.

A TRANSPORTATION HUB

ALTHOUGH THE WATERWAY WAS A BOON to commerce when it opened in 1848, it was quickly overshadowed by a new form of transportation: railroads. Soon, locomotives were hauling freight along the tracks of the Galena and Chicago Union lines, and the newly opened Chicago Board of Trade brokered commodities in what was to become the world's greatest rail hub. German and Scandinavian immigrants further swelled the city's population, and horse-drawn street railways stimulated the growth of the near suburbs. Also, in 1848, for the first time Chicago was connected with the East by telegraph.

Before growth could proceed much farther, however, the swamp-bound city had to elevate itself; streets were a quagmire most of the year. Located on the only high spot in the area, Fort Dearborn was torn down in 1868 when the land it stood on was relocated to develop what is now Randolph Street. Street grades were raised as many as a dozen feet, and first floors became basements. It was an impressive technical feat—the first of many to come.

By 1856, Chicago was the hub of ten railroad trunk lines. Lumber from nearby forests, iron ore from Minnesota, and livestock and produce from the fertile Midwest were shipped to the city and manufactured into the products that fueled America's rapid growth. Passenger rail service from New York began in 1857, cutting travel time between the two cities from three weeks to two days. The population of Chicago soared to 28,000 in 1850 and to 110,000 in 1860. Economically, Chicago was the middleman between the East and West, a role it has never ceased to play.

A PRESIDENTIAL NOMINATION AND INNOVATIVE MARKETING

BY 1860 CHICAGO WAS THE NINTH-LARGEST CITY in the United States and hosted the nominating convention of the fledgling Republican Party. "The Wigwam," a jerry-built convention hall with a capacity of 10,000, was erected at Lake and Market streets on the fringe of today's downtown Loop. The Republicans nominated Abraham Lincoln on the third ballot. (Democratic nominee Stephen A. Douglas, incidentally, was a Chicago native.) The city would host another 23 party-nominating conventions, including the controversial 1968 Democratic National Convention. In 1996 the Democrats returned to a city that was more placid and more beautiful.

Just as the city mastered politics and transportation, it shaped marketing geniuses. In 1872 Montgomery Ward opened the world's first mail-order business in the loft of a Chicago barn. Sears, Roebuck & Co. was founded in Chicago, and its influence was felt across America. (The late Roebuck "Pops" Staples of the Chicago-based Staple Singers gospel group had a brother named Sears.) Other legendary names of Chicago merchandising include Marshall Field, Potter Palmer, Samuel Carson, and John Pirie.

One of Chicago's most famous—and odorous—landmarks opened in 1865: the Union Stockyards, Chicago's largest employer for half a century. It was a city within a city, complete with its own newspaper and radio station, from 1865 until it was torn down in 1971. Bubbly Creek ran through the yards. By 1863 the city had earned the moniker "Porkopolis" by processing enough hogs to stretch all the way to New York. Gustavus Swift of meatpacking fame boasted, "We use everything but the squeal." The goat that led lambs up the ramp to the killing floor was called Judas. The darker sides of the yard—poor sanitation problems and horrific working and living conditions for its laborers—were brought to light in 1906 in Upton Sinclair's *The Jungle*. Sinclair later said he aimed at the country's heart and hit its stomach instead.

INDUSTRIAL MIGHT

THE GRITTY CITY CONTINUED TO GROW. In the years following the Civil War, Chicago ranked as the world's largest grain handler and the biggest North American lumber market. The North Side's huge McCormick plant churned out reapers and other farm equipment that were shipped around the globe. George Pullman built his first sleeping car in 1864, the nation's first steel rails came out of the North Side in 1865, and the number of sea vessels docked at Chicago in 1869 exceeded the combined number calling on New York and five other major U.S. ports.

While the swamps were a thing of the past, the city was still seeped in quagmires of different sorts. Cholera and typhoid struck regularly as Chicago fouled its Lake Michigan drinking water via the dangerously polluted Chicago River. Corruption at City Hall became rampant (it still is, in some quarters), and the city was notorious for its gambling, saloons, and 400 brothels. The most famous house of ill repute was Roger Plant's Under the Willow, which covered half a square block near Wells and Monroe streets. Plant painted some of Chicago's first graffiti on the side of his brothel: "Why Not?" Plant, a wealthy Englishman, was married with 20 children. In contrast to the luxury of Plant's bordello, hundreds of thousands of poor Chicagoans were jammed into modest pine cottages on unpaved streets without sewers. Some observers warned of dire consequences unless the city cleaned up its act.

THE GREAT CHICAGO FIRE OF 1871

THOSE WARNINGS PROVED RIGHT. Chicago in 1871 was a densely

packed city of 300,000 whose homes were built almost entirely of wood. A lengthy drought had turned the town tinder-dry, setting the stage for the most indelibly mythic event in the city's history: the Great Fire of 1871.

Legend has it that Mrs. Maureen O'Leary's cow kicked over a lantern and started the fire (supposedly, she had gone back inside her house to fetch some salt for an ailing animal). The fire spread rapidly from the O'Leary barn in the West Side, burning its way north and east through the commercial center and residential North Side. More than 17,000 buildings were destroyed, 100,000 people were left homeless, and 250 were killed. The city lay in ashes. The 100-foot-tall Chicago water works, built in 1867, was the only public building to survive and still stands today across the street from the Water Tower Place shopping mall.

Chicago was rebuilt—this time with fireproof brick. Architects, sensing unlimited opportunity, flocked to Chicago. In five years, the city's commercial core was restored with buildings erected to meet stringent fire codes, and a tradition of architectural vision was established. In 1889, the city annexed a ring of suburbs and was crowned America's Second City in the census of 1890.

The city was emerging from an era of cutthroat social Darwinism into an age of social reform. Jane Addams's Hull-House became a model for the nation's settlement-house movement. Addams and her upper-class compatriots provided fresh milk for babies, taught immigrants English, and set up day-care centers for the children of working mothers. Hull House was at ground zero of new immigration to Chicago, in a neighborhood where pathways were made of plank and streets turned to mud in the soggy spring. The crown prince of Belgium once remarked after visiting Hull House, "Such a street—no, not one—existed in Belgium."

The Columbian Exposition of 1893 was a fabulously successful World's Fair that left indelible cultural marks on the city, including the Art Institute of Chicago and the Field Museum. The era ushered in the skyscraper, a distinctly urban form created in Chicago that has reshaped the look of skylines around the world. The University of Chicago, one of the world's great research institutions, was founded in 1892 with funds from the Rockefellers.

In 1900, another architectural feat was performed when the flow of the Chicago River was reversed, much to the relief of a population in desperate need of safe drinking water from Lake Michigan—and to the consternation of populations downstream.

Architect Daniel Burnham left his mark on the city in 1909 by pursuing a plan to preserve Chicago's pristine lakefront through a creation of a series of parks and the acquisiton of a green belt of forestlands on the city's periphery. With his partner John Root, Burnham had already built 16-story skyscrapers like the Monadnock Building—the tallest masonry building in Chicago, and possibly the world, still standing at 53 West Jackson Boulevard—on floating "rafts" placed in Chicago's murky earth. "Make no little plans," Burnham urged, and today's Mayor Daley still subscribes to the "Burnham Plan." With the exception of the massive McCormick Place convention center, the lakefront remains an uncluttered recreational mecca . . . and someday they'll probably be planting gardens atop the convention center.

LABOR TROUBLES

AROUND THE TURN OF THE 19TH CENTURY, Chicago seethed with labor unrest and the threat of class warfare. Nascent labor movements argued for better working and living conditions for the city's laborers. Seven policemen were killed in the 1886 Haymarket Riot (on Randolph Street between Des Plaines and Halsted streets), who originally had been called to denounce the police shootings of four workingmen. Four anarchists were subsequently hanged. Later the Pullman Strike of 1894 was crushed by U.S. Army troops after wages were sharply cut by the sleeping-car magnate.

The lowest rung in Chicago's pecking order was reserved for blacks, who started to arrive from the South in substantial numbers, reaching 110,000 by 1920. Most of the families came from Arkansas, Louisiana, Mississippi, and Tennessee, a migration that later gave birth to Chicago blues. Segregation formed a "black belt" ghetto with buildings in poor repair—often without indoor toilets—and substantially higher rents than white housing. A six-day riot in July 1919 left 23 blacks and 15 whites dead; the governor had to send in troops to quell the uprising. But the underlying causes of the unrest weren't addressed.

Carl Sandburg celebrated the city and its tradition of hard work in verse ("Hog Butcher for the World / Tool Maker, Stacker of Wheat / Player with Railroads and the Nation's Freight Handler; / Stormy, husky, brawling, / City of the Big Shoulders"). Other pre-Depression literary giants from Chicago include Theodore Dreiser and Ben Hecht; later came James T. Farrell, Nelson Algren, Richard Wright, Saul Bellow, and Pulitzer Prize–winning newspapermen Roger Ebert and Mike Royko.

THE ROARING '20s

FOLLOWING WORLD WAR I, the focus of power shifted from industrialists to politicians; crooked pols and gangsters plundered the city. The smoke-filled room was invented in Chicago at the 1920 Republican National Convention when Warren G. Harding's nomination was dealed and sealed in Suite 804–805 at the Blackstone Hotel.

A baby-faced crook from New York named Alphonse Capone came to Chicago in 1920, right after Prohibition became national law. It was no coincidence: Chicago was soon awash in bootleg hooch, much of it illegally imported by Capone and his mob. If an alderman opposed an item on Capone's agenda, the gangster would wait outside council chambers to smack the alderman around. Capone's younger rival was Dion O'Banion, who ran a flower shop near Holy Name Cathedral. (During the 1970s, there was a Chicago punk-rock club named after the florist-criminal.) But the short, pot-bellied Capone still holds the world record for the highest gross income ever accumulated by a private citizen in a year: $105 million in 1927, when he was 28 years old.

Alas, Capone didn't pay his taxes and was put away by a group of Feds, know as the Untouchables, led by Eliot Ness. The gangster—aka "Scarface," still Chicago's best-known historical figure—served eight years in Alcatraz before dying of syphilis in 1947. During the 1930s Capone's New York compatriot "Big Jim" Colosimo ruled much of Chicago's underworld from his restaurant-showroom, Colosimo's Cafe, on Wabash Avenue. George M. Cohan was a regular guest performer when he visited Chicago. The house favorite was vaudeville singer Dale Winter, whom a newspaper reporter discovered singing in a church choir. Another Colosimo act, Texas Guinan, greeted the audience by saying, "Hello, suckers!"

ANOTHER DEPRESSION . . . AND ANOTHER FAIR

IN THE 1930S THE GREAT DEPRESSION hit Chicago like the ton of bricks it never had during the Great Chicago Fire. Out-of-work men and women marched down State Street. Businessmen went bust. Nearly 1,400 families were evicted from their homes in the first half of 1931 alone. Hardest hit were Chicago's blacks, whose population then totaled about 250,000.

Yet in 1933 the city hosted another World's Fair: the Century of Progress Exposition, which occupied 47 acres of lakefront south of the Loop. The show attracted about 39 million visitors and actually made money. Texas Guinan appeared at the fair, but the star of the show was fan dancer Sally Rand, who went on stage nude with large props—not only fans but feather boas and large balloons . . . very large balloons. Like Little Egypt at the Columbian Exposition 40 years earlier, Rand drew mobs of men to her shows and further embellished the city's randy reputation.

THE SECOND WORLD WAR

WORLD WAR II AND AN UNPARALLELED SURGE in defense spending lifted Chicago—and the rest of the country—out of the Depression. The $1.3 billion spent to build war plants in the city was unmatched anywhere else in America.

In 1942 a team at the University of Chicago, under the direction of physicist Enrico Fermi, built the world's first nuclear reactor under the stands of Stagg Field, named after the university's football coach, Amos Alonzo Stagg. The school's ability to control the energy of the atom provided critical technology for the development of nuclear power and allowed the nation to embark on the ambitious Manhattan Project, which led to the creation of the atomic bomb. Today the portentous site at Stagg Field is marked by a squat, brooding Henry Moore sculpture.

A NEW ERA

CHICAGO REACHED ITS PEAK POPULATION of 3.6 million in 1950, a year that marked the beginning of a long slide of urban dwellers moving to surrounding suburbs. Following eras of settlement, growth, booms, busts, depression, and war, Chicago moved into one last period: the 21-year-rule of Mayor Richard J. Daley, a power-monger who left another indelible mark on the city.

Daley was born in Bridgeport, the only child of immigrant Irish-Catholic parents. He was elected mayor in 1955 with 708,222 votes—a number he used on a vanity license plate for his limousine during his years in office. Under Daley, Chicago's motto was "I Will." And Daley did. He shut down gambling houses and scolded aldermen who talked while city council was in session. He bulldozed neighborhoods, built segregated walls of high-rise public housing, and constructed an elaborate system of freeway exchanges in the heart of the city. Critics said the maze of highways cut the hearts out of flourishing neighborhoods and provided accessible corridors for suburban flight. One way or the other, Daley had earned the nickname "Da Boss."

In the summer of 1966, Dr. Martin Luther King Jr. and a young preacher named Jesse Jackson confronted the Daley machine when Dr. King tried to encourage racial integration of Chicago's immigrant neighborhoods—including Marquette Park, near the South Side area that Daley grew up in. Daley opposed any power base, black or white, that was not Chicago controlled. King's efforts in Chicago were largely unsuccessful, which became a setback for the civil-rights movement.

Daley was a kingmaker for presidents, delivering the winning—though slim—margin to John F. Kennedy in 1960. In 1968, at the peak of the Vietnam conflict, Daley unleashed his police on antiwar protesters at the Democratic National Convention. Some called it a police riot; Crosby, Stills, Nash, and Young sang about it in "Chicago." Hizzoner pugnaciously scowled at news cameras and growled, "Duh policemen isn't dere to create disorder, duh policemen is dere to *preserve* disorder." The whole world was watching. Not all of it understood.

POSTINDUSTRIAL CHICAGO

DALEY PASSED AWAY IN 1976 WHILE STILL MAYOR. At this point, computer operators outnumbered steel-mill workers, and postindustrial Chicago shuffled along. The Gold Coast and the Magnificent Mile were glitzier than ever, and the Playboy Club was hopping. Chicago's work force—what was left of it—was learning to survive in a service economy. More people fled for greener horizons beyond city limits, trading deteriorating schools and racial strife for safer neighborhoods.

But Chicago hung on. In the 1970s and 1980s, a forest of new skyscrapers shot up on the city's skyline, including the Sears Tower, the world's third-tallest building. The Loop survived an attempt (from 1979 to 1996) to prevent automobiles on State Street's ill-fated outdoor shopping mall. After Daley's death, the city saw its first woman mayor, Jane Byrne, who moved into a housing project for a spell, and its first black mayor, Harold Washington, a grandfatherly figure who died in office in 1987. The city entered the 21st century with Mayor Richard "Richie" Daley, son of Hizzoner, solidly in office with his heart still in the South Side—even though he left Bridgeport for the South Loop. Although the city has been leaking population for decades, 2.84 million people still live in Chicago.

"A REAL CITY"

TODAY, CHICAGO COMPRISES 228 SQUARE MILES, with 30 miles stretching along Lake Michigan's shores. It's 550 parks, eight forest preserves, 29 beaches, 250 good restaurants (many of them world-class), 2,000 lousy restaurants, and dozens of stands selling the best hot dogs around. It's a city where football is serious business and politics is a game. It's heaven for symphony lovers, nirvana for jazz buffs, and the alternative-rock center of America. Come to Chicago, and within a half hour someone will tell you it's "a city of neighborhoods." Sprinkled with curiosities, the city's ethnic districts offer visitors a flavor of the old world and a chance for discovery.

And the Loop? It's back in a big way. Lines form for theaters and steakhouses, a ripple effect from the new Millennium Park. Similarily, the United Center gave rebirth to West Madsion Street, where new eateries and hipster taverns stand on the site of a 1970s skid row.

Walk along Michigan Avenue late on a Friday afternoon, and watch the lights wink on in the skyscrapers overhead. Take a carriage ride. Hear the voices that build into a choir of character. There will be a warm moment when you will feel at home—and then you will understand the resilient spirit of Chicago.

SKYSCRAPERS *and the* PRAIRIE SCHOOL: *Chicago Architecture*

THOUGH NO ONE SERIOUSLY ARGUES Chicago's status as the Second City—even the most avid boosters concede New York's status as America's leading city in population, culture, and finance—the Windy City lays claim to one superlative title that remains undisputed: the world capital of modern architecture.

And it's not just that the skyscraper was born here. A visit to Chicago is a crash course in the various streams of architecture that have helped shape the direction of 20th-century building design. Even folks with an otherwise casual interest in architecture are bedazzled by the architectural heritage displayed here. Chicago is the world's largest outdoor museum of modern architecture.

A BOVINE BEGINNING

A SUBSTANTIAL AMOUNT OF THE CREDIT for Chicago's status in the world of architecture can be laid at the feet of a cow—if it's true that Mrs. O'Leary's cow kicked over a lantern, starting an inferno of mythic proportions. The Great Chicago Fire of 1871 destroyed four square miles of the central city, and architects from around the world flocked to Chicago—not unlike Sir Christopher Wren, who rushed to London after a great fire leveled much of that city in the late 17th century.

Several other factors figured in Chicago's rise to preeminence in building design in the decades after the fire. The rapidly rising value of real estate in the central business district motivated developers to increase building heights as much as they could. Advances in elevator technology freed designers from vertical constraints; easily rentable space no longer needed to be an easy climb from street level.

But most important was the development of the iron-and-steel skeletal frame, which relieved the walls of the burden of carrying a building's weight. For the first time, a structure's exterior walls didn't need to grow thicker as the building grew taller. New technology also allowed for larger windows.

THE CHICAGO SCHOOL

AS NEW TECHNOLOGY TOOK HOLD, many architects felt a building's external form should be equally innovative. The result was a style of architecture with a straightforward expression of structure. A masonry grid covered the steel structure beneath, while projecting bay windows created a lively rhythm on the facade. Any ornamentation was usually subordinated to the overall design and often restricted to the top and bottom thirds of the building, creating a kind of classical column effect. Collectively, the style came to be known as the Chicago School of Architecture.

Early skyscrapers that flaunt the technological innovations that made Chicago famous include the 15-story **Reliance Building** (32 North State Street; Burnham and Root, 1890) and the 12-story structure that until recently housed the **Carson Pirie Scott & Company** department store (1 South State Street; Adler and Sullivan, 1899). These show-off buildings, held up by thin tendons of steel, are close in spirit to the modernist architecture that was to follow.

CLASSICAL DESIGNS BY THE LAKE

DANIEL BURNHAM, WHO DEVELOPED CHICAGO'S urban plan and designed some of its most innovative buildings, also organized the 1893 World's Columbian Exposition. Yet the formal Beaux Arts style used in the major structures that remain were designed by East Coast

chicago's best architecture

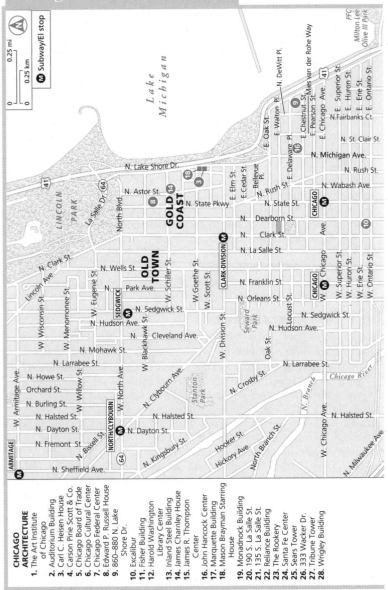

CHICAGO ARCHITECTURE
1. The Art Institute of Chicago
2. Auditorium Building
3. Carl C. Heisen House
4. Carson Pirie Scott & Co.
5. Chicago Board of Trade
6. Chicago Cultural Center
7. Chicago Federal Center
8. Edward P. Russell House
9. 860–880 N. Lake Shore Dr.
10. Excalibur
11. Fisher Building
12. Harold Washington Library Center
13. Inland Steel Building
14. James Charnley House
15. James R. Thompson Center
16. John Hancock Center
17. Marquette Building
18. Mason Brayman Starring House
19. Monadnock Building
20. 190 S. La Salle St.
21. 135 S. La Salle St.
22. Reliance Building
23. The Rookery
24. Santa Fe Center
25. Sears Tower
26. 333 Wacker Dr.
27. Tribune Tower
28. Wrigley Building

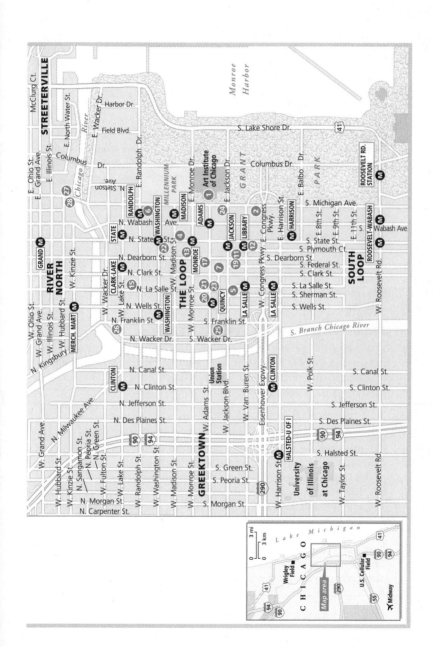

architects. As a result, cultural institutions such as the **Art Institute** (Michigan Avenue at Adams Street; Shepley, Rutan & Coolidge, 1892) and the **Chicago Cultural Center** (78 East Washington Street; Shepley, Rutan & Coolidge, 1897) have their underlying structures disguised in white, neoclassical historical garb.

THE PRAIRIE SCHOOL

YET NOT ALL OF CHICAGO'S ARCHITECTURAL innovations pushed upward or aped the classical designs of the past. In the early 1900s, Frank Lloyd Wright and his contemporaries were developing a modern style that's now called the Prairie School. The break from historically inspired Victorian house designs is highlighted by low, ground-hugging forms, hovering roofs with deep eaves, and bands of casement windows. Interiors feature open, flowing floor plans, centrally located hearths, natural woodwork, and uniform wall treatments.

Truly shocking in their day, Wright's designs now dot Chicago and its suburbs. The flowing horizontal planes sharply contrast with the upward thrust of skyscrapers in the Loop and convey a feeling of peace and calm. The largest groups of Prairie School houses are found in Oak Park, where Forest Avenue and nearby streets are lined with houses designed by Wright and his disciples.

1920s PROSPERITY AND ART DECO

THE PROSPERITY OF THE 1920S resulted in a building boom; the construction of the Michigan Avenue Bridge encouraged developers to look for sites north of the Chicago River. It was the "heroic age" for the city's skyline, and designers borrowed heavily from European sources. The **Wrigley Building** (400 and 410 North Michigan Avenue; Graham, Anderson, Probst & White, 1922) is a dazzling white terra cotta–clad lollipop of a building that's strikingly well lighted from the opposite shore of the river; the clock tower remains one of Chicago's most distinctive landmarks.

The **Tribune Tower** (435 North Michigan Avenue; Hood & Howells, 1925) is a neo-Gothic tower (considered "retro" when built) that soars upward like a medieval cathedral. At **333 North Michigan Avenue** stands Chicago's first Art Deco skyscraper, designed by Holabird & Root in 1928. More of the Art Deco impulse is displayed south of the river at the **Chicago Board of Trade Building** (141 West Jackson Boulevard; Holabird & Root, 1930), which anchors La Salle Street's financial canyon and is topped with a 30-foot aluminum statue of Ceres, the Roman goddess of grain.

THE INTERNATIONAL STYLE

WHEN THE DEPRESSION HIT, most construction ground to a halt and didn't resume until after World War II. But after the postwar economic recovery arrived, German-born Ludwig Mies van der Rohe (who fled Nazi persecution before the war and later taught architecture at the

Illinois Institute of Technology) found Chicago a receptive canvas for his daring designs.

Mies's motto was "Less is more," and the result was the sleek and unadorned International Style (often called the Second Chicago School). He was concerned with structural expression and the use of new technology as much as his predecessors in the 1890s, and Chicago boasts some of his most famous designs: the **Illinois Institute of Technology** (State Street between 31st and 35th streets, 1940–1958), the **Federal Center Complex** (Dearborn Street between Jackson Boulevard and Adams Street, 1964–1975), and his last major design, the **IBM Building** (330 North Wabash, 1971).

Mies's signature style is the high-rise with an open colonnaded space around a solid shaft; the glass-and-steel skin is carefully detailed to represent the steel structure within. The designs are macho, strong, and sinewy, with great care given to proportion, play of light, and simplicity. Detractors sniff and call them "glass boxes."

POSTMODERNISM

INEVITABLY, REBELLION BEGAN, and the result was postmodernism, a catchall term describing anything outside the realm of mainstream modernist design. Often the postmodernists overturned modernist beliefs while echoing the Chicago aesthetic of the past in new, often graceful designs. Macho and cold is out; whimsy and colorful are in. The starkness of Mies-inspired architecture gave way to purely decorative elements in designs that are still unmistakably modern.

Arguably the most graceful of the newer buildings in Chicago, **333 North Wacker Drive** (Kohn Pedersen Fox–Perkins and Will, 1983) features a curved facade of glass that reflects the Chicago River in both shape and color. Another stunner is **150 North Michigan Avenue** (A. Epstein & Sons, 1984), whose sloping glass roof slices diagonally through the top ten floors.

Tipping its hat to the past is the **Harold Washington Library Center** (400 South State Street; Hammond, Beeby & Babka, 1991), which references numerous city landmarks. A red-granite base and brick walls pay tribute to the Rookery and Manadnock buildings (two Burnham and Root gems), while the facade and pediments along the roof recall the Art Institute. Even more retro is the **NBC Tower** (455 North Cityfront Plaza; Skidmore, Owings & Merrill, 1989), a 38-story Art Deco tower that successfully mines the architectural past.

One of Chicago's most controversial buildings is the **State of Illinois Center** (100 West Randolph Street; C. F. Murphy/Jahn Associates and Lester B. Knight & Associates, 1983). It's a 17-story glass-and-steel interpretation of the traditional government office building created by the bad boy of Chicago architecture, Helmut Jahn. Inside, 13 floors of balconied offices encircle a 332-foot central rotunda that's topped with a sloping glass skylight 160 feet in diameter. You've got to see it to believe it. The controversy? Some people loathe it—and state employees often endure blistering heat in the summer and freezing cold in the winter.

SCRAPING THE SKY

ANOTHER HARD-TO-IGNORE ELEMENT in recent downtown Chicago designs is height: Chicago claims several of the world's ten tallest buildings, including the 1,454-foot **Sears Tower** (233 South Wacker Drive; Skidmore, Owings & Merrill, 1974). The world's third-tallest building is a set of nine square tubes bundled together to give strength to the whole; seven tubes drop away as the building ascends, and only two go the distance.

Yet the 1,127-foot **John Hancock Center** (875 North Michigan; Skidmore, Owings & Merrill, 1969) usually gets higher marks from critics for its tapered form that's crisscrossed by diagonal wind bracing; locals say the view from the top is better, too. The Hancock Center is the world's 14th-tallest building, but the world's 13th-tallest is also in Chicago: the 80-story, 1,136-foot **AON Center** (200 East Randolph Street; E. D. Stone/Perkins and Will, 1974). New white-granite cladding on the AON Center replaced a Carrera marble skin that couldn't stand up to Chicago's wind and temperature extremes.

AN OUTDOOR MUSEUM

MOST OF CHICAGO'S LANDMARK BUILDINGS—and we've only described a few—are located in and around the Loop, making a comfortable walking tour the best way to explore this outdoor museum of modern architecture. If you've got the time and the interest, we strongly recommend taking one of the **Chicago Architecture Foundation**'s two-hour walking tours of the Loop (info at (312) 922-3432 or **www.architecture.org**). It's by far the best way to gain a greater appreciation of one of the world's great architectural mosaics.

SCULPTURE *in the* LOOP

CHICAGO, THE WORLD LEADER IN MODERN ARCHITECTURE, also boasts one of the finest collections of public art in the United States. Major pieces by such 20th-century greats as Picasso, Chagall, Calder, Miró, Moore, Oldenburg, Nevelson, and Noguchi are scattered throughout the Loop.

It's a cornucopia of postmodern masterpieces—although some might take a little getting used to. After Picasso's untitled abstract sculpture in the Civic Center plaza was unveiled by Mayor Richard J. Daley in 1967, one Chicago alderman introduced a motion in the city council that it be removed and replaced by a monument to Cubs baseball hero Ernie Banks. Nothing came of the motion, and now the sculpture is a beloved city landmark. Here's an informal tour of some of the Loop's best (see map on page 24 for these and other works):

1. *Untitled* (1967, Pablo Picasso); Richard J. Daley Plaza (West Washington Street between North Dearborn and North Clark streets); Cor-Ten steel.

2. *Flamingo* (1974, Alexander Calder); Federal Center (219 South Dearborn Street between West Adams Street and West Jackson Boulevard); painted steel.

3. *Chicago* (1967, Joan Miró; installed 1981); Chicago Temple (69 West Washington Street at North Clark Street); bronze, concrete, tile.

4. *The Four Seasons* (1975, Marc Chagall); First National Plaza (West Monroe Street between South Clark and South Dearborn streets); hand-chipped stone, glass fragments, brick.

5. *Monument with Standing Beast* (1985, Jean Dubuffet); State of Illinois Center (100 West Randolph Street at North Clark Street); fiberglass.

6. *Ceres* (1930, John Storrs); atop Chicago Board of Trade Building (141 West Jackson Boulevard at South La Salle Street); aluminum.

7. *Batcolumn* (1977, Claes Oldenburg); Social Security Administration Building Plaza (600 West Madison Street at North Clinton Street); painted steel.

8. *Dawn Shadows* (1983, Louise Nevelson); Madison Plaza (200 West Madison Street at North Wells Street); steel.

9. *The Universe* (1974, Alexander Calder); Lobby, Sears Tower (233 South Wacker Drive); painted aluminum.

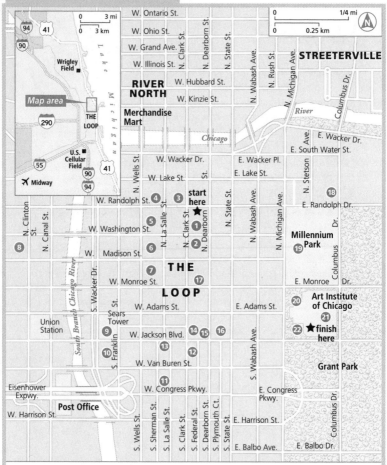

loop sculpture tour

1. *Untitled ("The Picasso")*, Pablo Picasso (1967)
2. *Chicago*, Joan Miró (1981)
3. *Monument with Standing Beast*, Jean Dubuffet (1984)
4. *Freeform*, Richard Hunt (1993)
5. *Flight of Daedalus and Icarus*, Roger Brown (1990)
6. *Dawn Shadows*, Louise Nevelson (1983)
7. *Loomings and Knights and Squires*, Frank Stella
8. *Batcolumn*, Claes Oldenburg (1977)
9. *The Universe*, Alexander Calder (1974)
10. *Gem of the Lakes*, Raymond Kaskey (1990)
11. *San Marco II*, Ludovico de Luigi (1986)
12. *The Town-Ho's Story*, Frank Stella (1993)
13. *Ceres*, John Storrs (1930)
14. *Ruins III*, Nita K. Sutherland (1978)
15. *Flamingo*, Alexander Calder (1974)
16. *Lines in Four Directions*, Sol Lewitt (1985)
17. *The Four Seasons*, Marc Chagall (1974)
18. *Untitled Sounding Sculpture*, Harry Bertoia (1975)
19. *Cloud Gate*, Anish Kapoor (2004)
20. *Large Interior Form*, Henry Moore (1983)
21. *Celebration of the 200th Anniversary of the Founding of the Republic*, Isamu Noguchi (1976)
22. *The Fountain of the Great Lakes*, Lorado Taft (1913)

PART TWO

PLANNING *your* VISIT

SEASONS *of* CHANGE

CHICAGO IS ONE TOWN THAT WON'T LET YOU DOWN—unless you're talking about the weather, which can change with the snap of a finger. During the mid-1800s, some well-intentioned journalists founded the *Chicago Magazine of Fashion, Music, and Home Reading* in an attempt to introduce Culture to the grizzly midwestern homestead. They wrote, in part: "The uncertainty and inclemency of the spring weather interferes sadly with the permanency of a new toilet, since, if one day is warm enough for a parasol, the next demands a resume of cloak and furs."

These lifestyle pioneers may have meant *toilet* in the sense of grooming and clothes, but their point still holds true today: Chicago's weather is flush with change. In January and February, the climate is often distinguished by a bone-chilling combination of subfreezing temperatures and howling winds. Late Chicago native Lou Rawls sang about these winds as "The Hawk." The average winter snowfall is 40 inches. The less said about that, the better.

The summer months of June, July, and August, on the other hand, are noted for high temperatures (and high humidity) that can approach triple digits. Though the combination can make for miserably hot and sticky summer afternoons, breezes off of Lake Michigan are often a mitigating factor that can make a stroll through Lincoln Park bearable.

Temperature-wise, spring and fall are the most docile times of year. Many people, in fact, say autumn is their favorite Chicago season. Evening temperatures in October and

unofficial **TIP**
In any season, Chicago's lakefront location and its position in a major west-to-east weather path make atmospheric conditions highly changeable (and, as you'll discover during your stay, difficult to predict). Temperatures in the suburbs often differ from those by the lake. Plan accordingly on all-day outings by bringing along appropriate rain gear and/or extra clothing.

CHICAGO'S AVERAGE TEMPERATURES AND PRECIPITATION		
MONTH	AVERAGE DAILY TEMPERATURE (MINIMUM/MAXIMUM, IN DEGREES FAHRENHEIT)	AVERAGE MONTHLY PRECIPITATION
January	18°/34°	1.6"
February	20°/36°	1.3"
March	29°/45°	2.6"
April	40°/58°	3.7"
May	49°/70°	3.2"
June	59°/81°	4.1"
July	65°/86°	3.6"
August	65°/85°	3.5"
September	56°/76°	3.4"
October	45°/65°	2.3"
November	32°/49°	2.1"
December	22°/36°	2.1"

November may dip into the 40s, but the days are usually warm. Starting in mid-October, the fall foliage creates a pastiche of color that tempts thousands of folks to jump in their cars for day trips north of the city along scenic Sheridan Road or longer journeys to Galena, near the Mississippi River in the northwest corner of Illinois.

For visitors enjoying Chicago's museums, galleries, shopping, restaurants, and other attractions, any season is okay—the city goes full blast all year. While winter may be the least desirable time of the year to visit Chicago, it's the cultural season: theater, music, and museum programs are plentiful. In recent years, the city and the convention and tourism bureau have offered considerable hotel discounts to coincide with special winter festivals. It's also fun to check out everyone in their winter gear of wacky hats, scarves, and ear warmers.

AVOIDING CROWDS

THE SUMMER MONTHS—mid-June through mid-August, when school is out—are the busiest times at most tourist attractions. Weekends are busier than weekdays, and Saturdays are busier than Sundays. Most major Chicago attractions offer free admission one day a week; this day is usually the most crowded.

Driving during rush hour should be avoided—whether you're a tourist or native. The traffic will drive you crazy for a number of reasons. For one thing, nearly 3 million people live in Chicago and another 8 million in the surrounding area. For another, Chicago has an antiquated expressway system, not to mention more wide-eyed gapers than Los Angeles or New York. Massive tie-ups are routine on the main arteries leading in and out of the city, as well as major expressways that connect the suburbs. And because that temperamental Chicago weather takes its toll on local streets and highways, there generally is some kind of road construction going on somewhere.

If you must drive, stay off the road before 9 a.m. and after 4 p.m. so you'll miss the worst rush-hour traffic.   Likewise, if you're driving to Chicago or planning to get from the airport to downtown by car or cab, avoid arriving during rush hour (especially on Friday afternoon). The drive from O'Hare to the Loop can take up to four hours as all the high-rise office buildings release legions of office workers eager to get home for the weekend. Don't get in their way. And stay off your cell phone—it is now illegal to use one while driving within Chicago city limits.

*un*official **TIP**
On weekdays during the school year, places such as the Art Institute of Chicago, the Field Museum, and the Lincoln Park Zoo are besieged by scores of school buses. If you'd rather tour when things are a little more mellow, come back in the afternoon. The buses are needed at the end of the school day, so kids are typically whisked back to class by 1:30 p.m.

In contrast, getting around by car on weekends and holidays is a breeze, although you may run into an occasional backup on the Eisenhower (heading west to Naperville) or Kennedy (heading north to Milwaukee) Expressway, the two major highways that lead in and out of downtown.

HOW *to* GET MORE INFORMATION *before your* VISIT

FOR INFORMATION ON ENTERTAINMENT, sightseeing, maps, shopping, dining, and lodging in the Chicago area, call or write:

Chicago Office of Tourism, Chicago Cultural Center
78 East Washington Street
Chicago, Illinois 60602
☎ 877-CHICAGO or 312-744-2964 (TDD); **www.877chicago.com**

Also visit the **Chicago Convention and Tourism Bureau** at **www.choosechicago.com.**

In addition, three visitor-information centers are centrally located: in the Historic Water Tower on the Magnificent Mile (on North Michigan Avenue, across from the Water Tower Place shopping mall); in the Chicago Cultural Center (downtown on South Michigan at Washington Street); and in the Explore Chicago kiosk inside the Sears on State store (2 North State Street, in the Loop). All are open daily, offer help planning itineraries, and feature plenty of free information and maps. Chicago's hotels also have some of the best-informed concierges in America.

GETTING *to* CHICAGO

FOLKS PLANNING A TRIP TO CHICAGO have several options: plane, train, bus, or automobile. Your distance from the city—and your tolerance for such hassles as traffic congestion and endless waits in holding patterns—will probably determine which mode of transportation you ultimately choose.

unofficial **TIP**
Truly creative travelers are taking advantage of **Mitchell International Airport,** 75 miles north of Chicago in Milwaukee. An Amtrak station has opened here in an attempt to lure Chicago passengers away from O'Hare. There are seven round trips daily from Union Station in Chicago to the Milwaukee airport.

FLYING

IF YOU'RE COMING TO CHICAGO from the East, the West, the Gulf Coast, Europe, Asia, South America, or any other place that's more than a 12-hour drive away, you'll likely arrive the way most folks do: by plane into **O'Hare International Airport,** the world's busiest—and often most frustrating—airfield. A 24-hour subway line connects O'Hare with downtown.

But a growing number of domestic fliers avoid the hassles of O'Hare by using less-congested **Midway Airport,** which has been expanded and remodeled in recent years. If you have a choice, fly in here. (See Part Five, Arriving and Getting Oriented, for maps of O'Hare and Midway.) About 15 miles southwest of the Loop, Midway is on a subway line (but the last train out of the airport is 12:55 a.m. daily) and is only about 20 minutes from downtown (longer during rush hour).

TAKING THE TRAIN

JUST AS O'HARE IS A MAJOR HUB between the East and West coasts of the United States, Chicago's **Union Station** is the major rail station between the two coasts. Though long-distance travel by train can be tedious, it enables people who live in the Midwest to come into Chicago without fear of getting stuck in a holding pattern over O'Hare or trapped in a traffic snarl on the Eisenhower Expressway.

Cities closest to Chicago with Amtrak passenger-train service are Milwaukee (1½ hours one way) and Indianapolis (4½ hours). Other cities offering daily rail service to Union Station include St. Louis (5 hours), Detroit (5 hours), Cincinnati (7 hours, three days a week); Cleveland (6 hours), Kansas City (8½ hours), Omaha (9 hours), and Minneapolis (8 hours). For schedules and reservations, call Amtrak at ☎ 800-872-7245 or visit **www.amtrak.com.**

HOP ON THE BUS, GUS

A COMMERCIAL BUS TRIP is always filled with interesting surprises, but the **Greyhound** station in Chicago is not as seedy as it used to be. A new station opened in 1991 at 630 West Harrison on the Near South Side, two blocks southwest of the Clinton

CHICAGO TRIP TIPS

- To avoid problems booking a room, time your trip to avoid major conventions (see Part Four, page 68).

- Don't drive—parking is a pain, public transportation is good, and cabs are plentiful.

- Fly into Midway (it's closer and easier than O'Hare).

- Chicago's weather is highly changeable—dress accordingly. Depending on the season, take a rain jacket, umbrella, or sweater on outings.

- To avoid busloads of schoolchildren on field trips, plan your weekday museum and zoo outings in the afternoons; the kids head back to school by 1:30 p.m.

stop on the El line to O'Hare (☎ 312-408-5800; **www.greyhound.com**). Travelers from Cleveland, Detroit, Indianapolis, and other nearby cities have also used the new no-frills **Megabus** that is popular in Europe (**www.megabus.com**). If you plan early enough, you can ride Megabus for $1 using the Internet. There's no station for Megabus passengers— the bus picks people up next to Union Station on the east side of South Canal Street, between Jackson Boulevard and Adams Street—but it's one of the cheapest ways to get to Chicago.

DRIVING

IF YOU LIVE CLOSE TO CHICAGO and driving is an option, think carefully. Why? Not only does traffic never let up, but parking is tough, too. Convenient, affordable, and/or secure places to leave your car are rare luxuries. Cops are eager to give tickets. A new automated system can issue a ticket that shows up weeks later. Instead of enduring traffic and parking stress, use Chicago's extensive and generally effective public-transportation system and abundance of taxis. Airport vans also transport visitors to and from downtown hotels. For more information about travel in Chicago without a car, see "Public Transportation" in Part Six, Getting Around.

unofficial **TIP**
If you must drive, make sure your hotel offers on-site or nearby off-street parking. Don't arrive during rush hour. Never leave anything of value in your car—hide it in your trunk. Be flexible about using public transportation. It often makes more sense to leave the car parked and take a bus, the El, or a cab.

A CALENDAR *of* FESTIVALS *and* EVENTS

January

CHICAGO BOAT, SPORTS, AND RV SHOW McCormick Place. Hands-on displays of sporting goods, boats, motor homes, and recreational vehicles. Admission: $10 adults, $4 ages 13–15, free for ages 12 and under. ☎ 312-946-6200; **www.chicagoboatshow.com.**

CHICAGO PARK DISTRICT HOLIDAY FLOWER SHOW Garfield Park Conservatory and Lincoln Park Conservatory. Through the first week of January. Free. ☎ 312-746-5100 (Garfield Park), ☎ 312-742-7737 (Lincoln Park).

February

CHINESE NEW YEAR PARADE Chinatown. Parade complete with firecrackers and a "dragon" dancing in the streets. Free. ☎ 312-225-0303.

NATIONAL AFRICAN AMERICAN HISTORY MONTH Various locations. A month-long city-wide celebration of black Americans' lives, times, and art. Free. ☎ 773-256-0149 (South Shore Cultural Center).

March

CHICAGO FLOWER AND GARDEN SHOW Navy Pier, 600 East Grand Avenue. Displays featuring gardening, demonstrations, tablescapes, family and children's activities and entertainment. Free. ☎ 312-222-5086.

ST. PATRICK'S DAY PARADE Columbus Drive from Balbo Avenue to Monroe Street. Forty pounds of vegetable dye turns the Chicago River green, and everyone is Irish for the day. The parade starts at noon and features floats, marching bands, and hundreds of thousands of spectators. Free. ☎ 312-744-3315.

April

CHICAGO LATINO FILM FESTIVAL Various locations. ☎ 312-431-1330.

May

ART CHICAGO Navy Pier. Art, both past and present, offered for sale by prestigious art galleries. Admission: $15. **www.artchicago.com.**

POLISH CONSTITUTION DAY PARADE Dearborn Street from Wacker Drive to Van Buren Street. Free. ☎ 773-282-6700.

WRIGHT PLUS Oak Park. The only chance to tour the interiors of ten homes designed by Frank Lloyd Wright and his contemporaries. Admission: $85; tickets go on sale on March 1, and the event usually sells out by mid-April. The all-day tour is held on the third Saturday in May. ☎ 708-848-1976; **www.wrightplus.org.**

June

ANDERSONVILLE MIDSUMMER FEST Neighborhood festival on Clark Street from Foster to Catalpa avenues. Free. ☎ 773-665-4682.

CHICAGO BLUES FESTIVAL Petrillo Music Shell, Grant Park. Fabulous music, food, and dozens of artists from Chicago and beyond. Free. ☎ 312-744-3315.

GAY AND LESBIAN PRIDE PARADE Starts at Halsted Street and Belmont Avenue. Free. ☎ 773-348-8243.

RAVINIA FESTIVAL Highland Park from late June to late August. A 12-week season of the Chicago Symphony Orchestra; dance, jazz, ballet, folk, and comedy in a picnic setting. Admission: $10 to $20 lawn; pavilion tickets vary from about $20 to about $75. ☎ 847-266-5100; **www.ravinia.org.**

TASTE OF CHICAGO Grant Park. In the week preceding Independence Day more than 100 restaurants serve Chicago-style and ethnic cuisine at this alfresco food festival; musical entertainment. ☎ 312-744-3315.

WELLS STREET ART FAIR North Wells between North and Division. Free. ☎ 773-868-3010.

July

CONCERTS IN THE PARKS Various locations. More than 80 concerts performed in 64 Chicago parks in July and August. Free. ☎ 312-742-7529; **www.chicagoparkdistrict.com.**

INDEPENDENCE DAY CONCERT AND FIREWORKS Petrillo Music Shell, Grant Park. A classical concert kicks off Chicago's traditional Fourth of July celebration. Free. ☎ 312-744-3370.

IRISH AMERICAN HERITAGE FESTIVAL Irish American Heritage Center, 4626 North Knox Avenue. Three days of continuous entertainment, 40 Irish bands, food, Irish step dancing, and museum and art gallery tours. ☎ 773-282-7035.

SHEFFIELD GARDEN WALK AND FESTIVAL Corner of Sheffield Avenue and Webster Street at St. Vincent's Church. Self-guided walking tour of private gardens, garage sales, food, and entertainment. Admission: $6 to $10. ☎ 773-929-9255.

August

BUD BILLIKEN PARADE King Drive to Washington Park. The South Side African American community's fun-filled event for kids and grown-ups. Free. ☎ 312-225-2400, ext. 142.

CHICAGO JAZZ FESTIVAL Petrillo Music Shell, Grant Park. A jazz marathon over Labor Day weekend; the world's largest free jazz festival featuring the greats from traditional and swing to bebop, blues, and avant-garde. Free. ☎ 312-744-3370.

CONCERTS IN THE PARKS Various locations. More than 80 concerts performed in 64 Chicago parks in July and August. Free. ☎ 312-742-7529; **www.chicagoparkdistrict.com.**

GINZA HOLIDAY FESTIVAL Midwest Buddhist Temple, 435 West Menomonee Street. A celebration of Japanese culture featuring food, dance, mime, martial arts, music, origami, painting, and sculpture. Admission: $4 adults, $3 seniors and students, free for ages 12 and under. ☎ 312-943-7801.

GOLD COAST ART FAIR Between Ontario, Huron, Franklin, and State streets. For three days, 350 artists display and sell high-quality paintings, photographs, and hand-crafted fine art. Free. ☎ 847-444-9600.

September

OKTOBERFEST Adams Street between State and Dearborn streets. Long-running street party with beer tents, bands, and dancing. ☎ 312-427-3170.

"VIVA CHICAGO" Petrillo Music Shell, Grant Park. Latin Music Festival. Free. ☎ 312-744-3315.

October

CHICAGO INTERNATIONAL FILM FESTIVAL Screenings at various theaters throughout the city. Exciting new international films, directors, and stars. Admission: $10. ☎ 312-683-0121.

COLUMBUS DAY PARADE Dearborn Street from Wacker Drive to Congress Parkway. Free. ☎ 708-450-9050.

HISTORIC PULLMAN DISTRICT'S ANNUAL HOUSE TOUR Historic Pullman Center, 614 East 113th Street. Annual fall tour of homes and historic buildings; refreshments available. Admission: $15 advance, $18 at the door. ☎ 773-785-8901.

November–December

CANDLELIGHT TOURS OF PRAIRIE AVENUE HOUSES Near McCormick Place. Authentic period Christmas decorations; docents talk about the history of Christmas traditions in Chicago. Admission: $15. ☎ 312-326-1480.

CHRISTMAS AROUND THE WORLD Museum of Science and Industry. A grand ethnic festival, plus entertainment. Admission: $9. ☎ 773-684-1414; **www.msichicago.org.**

MAGNIFICENT MILE FESTIVAL OF LIGHTS North Michigan Avenue from the Chicago River to Oak Street. The kickoff of Chicago's traditional holiday shopping season features stage shows, a parade, fireworks, and 300,000 lights on Michigan Avenue and Oak Street. Free. ☎ 312-642-3570.

THANKSGIVING DAY PARADE State Street from Congress to Randolph. ☎ 312-781-5681.

PART THREE

ACCOMMODATIONS

▌DECIDING WHERE *to* STAY

THOUGH CHICAGO SPRAWLS FOR MILES NORTH and south along Lake Michigan, and threatens on the west side to realize some suburban manifest destiny by creeping all the way to the Iowa border, the city is as focused and anchored as Manhattan. Chicago is defined by its city center. Downtown Chicago is not simply the heart of the city, it is the heart of the Midwest. As American as Valley Forge and as foreign as Warsaw, downtown Chicago is a magnet. If you visit Chicago, downtown is where you want to be.

The Chicago hotel scene reflects the dynamism and power of the city's bustling core. By and large, Chicago hotels are big, huge even, soaring 20, 30, and more stories above the lake. Although there are hotels near Midway and O'Hare airports and in smaller towns that have expanded to surround the great city, the majority of Chicago's nearly 77,000 rooms are situated in a narrow strip bordered by Lake Michigan on the east, Clark Street on the west, North Avenue on the north, and Roosevelt Road on the south. All told, the area is about three miles north to south and less than a mile wide.

Though some of the finest hotels in the world are in Chicago, finding comfortable lodging for less than $100 a night is easier here than in New York. Chicago is not cheap, but the quality standards for hotels are generally high. In Chicago, unlike in Boston, Atlanta, or Washington, D.C., the option of booking a less expensive hotel in the suburbs and commuting to downtown is impractical. The commute is long, the suburban hotels few, and the savings insignificant to nonexistent.

Finally, Chicago is the busiest convention city in the United States. If your visit to Chicago coincides with one or more major conventions or trade shows, hotel rooms will be both scarce and expensive. If, on the other hand, you are able to schedule your visit to avoid big meetings, you will have a good selection of hotels at surprisingly

central chicago accommodations

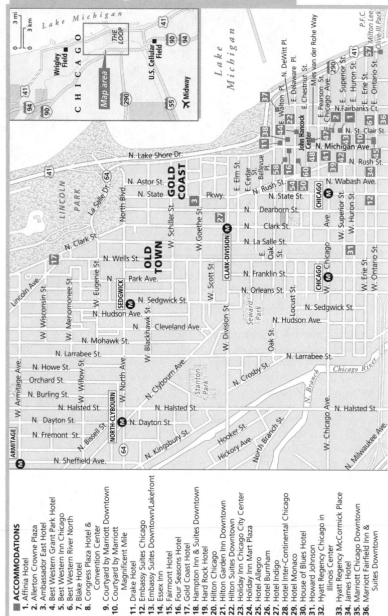

ACCOMMODATIONS

1. Affinia Hotel
2. Allerton Crowne Plaza
3. Ambassador East Hotel
4. Best Western Grant Park Hotel
5. Best Western Inn Chicago
6. Best Western River North
7. Blake Hotel
8. Congress Plaza Hotel & Convention Center
9. Courtyard by Marriott Downtown
10. Courtyard by Marriott Magnificent Mile
11. Drake Hotel
12. Embassy Suites Chicago
13. Embassy Suites Downtown/Lakefront
14. Essex Inn
15. Fairmont Hotel
16. Four Seasons Hotel
17. Gold Coast Hotel
18. Hampton Inn & Suites Downtown
19. Hard Rock Hotel
20. Hilton Chicago
21. Hilton Garden Inn Downtown
22. Hilton Suites Downtown
23. Holiday Inn Chicago City Center
24. Holiday Inn Mart Plaza
25. Hotel Allegro
26. Hotel Burnham
27. Hotel Indigo
28. Hotel Inter-Continental Chicago
29. Hotel Monaco
30. House of Blues Hotel
31. Howard Johnson
32. Hyatt Regency Chicago in Illinois Center
33. Hyatt Regency McCormick Place
34. James Hotel
35. Marriott Chicago Downtown
36. Marriott Fairfield Inn & Suites Downtown

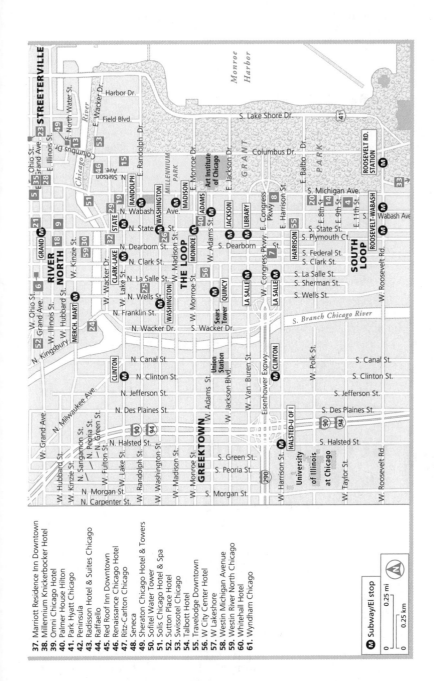

37. Marriott Residence Inn Downtown
38. Millennium Knickerbocker Hotel
39. Omni Chicago Hotel
40. Palmer House Hilton
41. Park Hyatt Chicago
42. Peninsula
43. Radisson Hotel & Suites Chicago
44. Raffaello
45. Red Roof Inn Downtown
46. Renaissance Chicago Hotel
47. Ritz-Carlton Chicago
48. Seneca
49. Sheraton Chicago Hotel & Towers
50. Sofitel Water Tower
51. Solis Chicago Hotel & Spa
52. Sutton Place Hotel
53. Swissotel Chicago
54. Talbott Hotel
55. Travelodge Downtown
56. W City Center Hotel
57. W Lakeshore
58. Westin Michigan Avenue
59. Westin River North Chicago
60. Whitehall Hotel
61. Wyndham Chicago

Ⓜ Subway/El stop

competitive prices. If you happen to be attending one of the big conventions, book early and use some of the tips listed below to get a discounted room rate. To assist in timing your visit, we have included a convention and trade-show calendar in Part Four, Visiting on Business (page 68).

SOME CONSIDERATIONS

1. When choosing your Chicago lodging, make sure your hotel is situated in a location convenient to your recreation or business needs, and that it is in a safe and comfortable area. Please note that although it is not practical to walk to McCormick Place (the major convention venue) from any of the downtown hotels, larger conventions and trade shows provide shuttle service.

2. Find out how old the hotel is and when the guest rooms were last renovated. Request that the hotel send you its promotional brochure. Ask if brochure photos of guest rooms are accurate and current.

3. If you plan to take a car, inquire about the parking situation. Some hotels offer no parking at all, some charge dearly for parking, and a few offer free parking.

4. If you are not a city dweller, or perhaps are a light sleeper, try to book a hotel on a more quiet side street. Ask for a room off the street and high up.

5. The Chicago skyline is quite beautiful, as is the lake. If you are on a romantic holiday, ask for a room on a higher floor with a view.

6. If shopping is high on your agenda, try to book a hotel near Michigan Avenue between Oak Street and East Wacker Drive.

7. When you plan your budget, remember that Chicago's combined room and sales tax is a whopping 15.39%.

GETTING *a* GOOD DEAL
on a ROOM

SPECIAL WEEKEND RATES

ALTHOUGH WELL-LOCATED CHICAGO HOTELS are tough for the budget conscious, it's not impossible to get a good deal, at least relatively speaking. For starters, most downtown hotels that cater to business, government, and convention travelers offer special weekend discount rates that range from 15 to 40% below normal weekday rates. You can find out about weekend specials by calling individual hotels or your travel agent.

GETTING CORPORATE RATES

MANY HOTELS OFFER DISCOUNTED corporate rates (5 to 20% off rack rate). Usually you do not need to work for a large company or have a special relationship with the hotel to obtain these rates. Simply call the hotel of your choice and ask for their corporate rates. Many hotels will guarantee you the discounted rate on the phone when you make your reservation. Others may make the rate conditional on your providing some sort of bona fides, for instance a fax on your company's letterhead requesting the rate, or a company credit card or business card on check-in. Generally, the screening is not rigorous.

HALF-PRICE PROGRAMS

THE LARGER DISCOUNTS ON ROOMS (35 to 60%), in Chicago or anywhere else, are available through half-price hotel programs, often called travel clubs. Program operators contract with an individual hotel to provide rooms at deep discounts, usually 50% off rack rate, on a "space available" basis. Space available generally means that you can reserve a room at the discounted rate whenever the hotel expects to be at less than 80% occupancy. A little calendar sleuthing to help you avoid city-wide conventions and special events will increase your chances of choosing a time when the discounts are available.

Most half-price programs charge an annual membership fee or directory subscription charge of $25 to $125. Once enrolled, you are mailed a membership card and a directory listing participating hotels. Examining the directory, you will notice immediately that there are many restrictions and exceptions. Some hotels, for instance, "black out" certain dates or times of year. Others may offer the discount only on certain days of the week, or require you to stay a certain number of nights. Still others may offer a much smaller discount than 50% off rack rate.

Programs specialize in domestic travel, international travel, or both. More established operators offer members between 1,000 and 4,000 hotels to choose from in the United States. All of the programs have a heavy concentration of hotels in California and Florida, and most have a very limited selection of participating properties in New York City or Boston. Offerings in other cities and regions of the United States vary considerably. The programs with the largest selections of Chicago hotels are **Encore, Travel America at Half Price** (Entertainment Publications), **International Travel Card,** and **Quest.** Each of these programs lists between four and 50 hotels in the greater Chicago area.

Encore Travel Club	☎ 800-638-0930
Entertainment Publications	☎ 800-285-5525
International Travel Card	☎ 800-342-0558
Quest	☎ 800-638-9819

One problem with half-price programs is that not all hotels offer a full 50% discount. Another slippery problem is the base rate against which the discount is applied. Some hotels figure the discount on an exaggerated rack rate that nobody would ever have to pay. A few participating hotels may deduct the discount from a supposed "superior" or "upgraded" room rate, even though the room you get is the hotel's standard accommodation. Though hard to pin down, the majority of participating properties base discounts on the rate published in the *Hotel & Travel Index* (a quarterly reference work used by travel agents) and work within the spirit of their agreement with the program operator. As a rule, if you travel several times a year, your room rate savings will easily compensate for program membership fees.

A noteworthy addendum: Deeply discounted rooms through half-price programs are not commissionable to travel agents. In practical terms, this means that you must ordinarily make your own inquiry calls and reservations. If you travel frequently, however, and run a lot of business through your travel agent, he or she will probably do your legwork, lack of commission notwithstanding.

PREFERRED RATES

IF YOU CANNOT BOOK THE HOTEL of your choice through a half-price program, you and your travel agent may have to search for a lesser discount, often called a preferred rate. A preferred rate could be a discount made available to travel agents to stimulate their booking activity, or a discount initiated to attract a certain class of traveler. Most preferred rates are promoted through travel industry publications and are often accessible only through an agent.

We recommend sounding out your travel agent about possible deals. Be aware, however, that the rates shown on travel agents' computerized reservations systems are not always the lowest rates obtainable. Focus on a couple of hotels that fill your needs in terms of location and quality of accommodations, and then have your travel agent call the hotel for the latest rates and specials. Hotel reps almost always respond to travel agents because travel agents represent a source of additional business. As discussed earlier, there are certain specials that hotel reps will disclose only to travel agents. Travel agents also come in handy when the hotel you want is supposedly booked. A personal appeal from your agent to the hotel's director of sales and marketing will get you a room more than half of the time.

WHOLESALERS, CONSOLIDATORS, AND RESERVATION SERVICES

IF YOU DO NOT WANT TO JOIN A PROGRAM or buy a discount directory, you can take advantage of the services of a wholesaler or consolidator. Wholesalers and consolidators buy rooms, or options on rooms (room blocks), from hotels at a low, negotiated rate. They then resell the rooms at a profit through travel agents, tour packagers, or directly to the public. Most wholesalers and consolidators have a provision for returning unsold rooms to participating hotels, but are not inclined to do so. The wholesaler's or consolidator's relationship with any hotel is predicated on volume. If they return rooms unsold, the hotel may not make as many rooms available to them the next time around. Thus wholesalers and consolidators often offer rooms at bargain rates, anywhere from 15 to 50% off rack, occasionally sacrificing their profit margins in the process to avoid returning the rooms to the hotel unsold.

When wholesalers and consolidators deal directly with the public, they frequently represent themselves as "reservation services." When you call, you can ask for a rate quote for a particular hotel, or alternatively ask for their best available deal in the area where you prefer to stay. If there is a maximum amount you are willing to pay, say so. Chances are the service will find something that will work for you, even if they have to shave a dollar or two off their own profit. Sometimes you will have to pay for your room with a credit card when you make your reservation. Other times you will pay as usual, when you check out. Two such services are **Hotel Reservations Network** (☎ 800-964-6835) and **Hot Rooms** (☎ 773-468-7666).

ALTERNATIVE LODGING

B&BS **Chicago Bed & Breakfast Association** at ☎ 800-375-7084 is a reservation service for guest houses and furnished apartments primarily in the downtown area. Rates usually range from $95 to $295 for guest houses and from $185 to $1,000 for furnished apartments. For more information, visit **www.chicago-bed-breakfast.com.**

CONDOS If you want to rent a condo for a week in Chicago, you are out of luck. Local law stipulates a minimum rental period of 30 days. If you are planning an extended stay and are interested in a condo, your best bet is to shop realtors in the area where you prefer to stay. If they don't handle rentals, they can refer you to someone who does.

HOW TO EVALUATE A TRAVEL PACKAGE

HUNDREDS OF CHICAGO PACKAGE VACATIONS are offered to the public each year. Packages should be a win-win proposition for both the buyer and the seller. The buyer has to make only one phone call and deal with a single salesperson to set up the whole vacation: transportation, rental car, lodging, meals, attraction admissions, and even golf and tennis. The seller, likewise, has to deal with the buyer only once, eliminating the need for separate sales, confirmations, and billing. In addition to streamlining sales, processing, and administration, some packagers also buy airfares in bulk on contract like a broker playing the commodities market. Buying a large number of airfares in advance allows the packager to buy them at significant savings from posted fares. The same practice is also applied to hotel rooms. Because selling vacation packages is an efficient way of doing business, and because the packager can often buy individual package components (airfare, lodging, etc.) in bulk at discount, savings in operating expenses realized by the seller are sometimes passed on to the buyer, so that, in addition to convenience, the package is also an exceptional value. In any event, that is the way it is supposed to work.

All too often, in practice, the seller cashes in on discounts and passes none on to the buyer. In some instances, packages are loaded additionally with extras that cost the packager next to nothing but inflate the retail price sky-high. As you may expect, the savings to be passed along to customers remain somewhere in Fantasyland.

When considering a package, choose one that includes features you are sure to use. Whether you use all the features or not, you will most certainly pay for them. Second, if cost is of greater concern than convenience, make a few phone calls and see what the package would cost if you booked its individual components (airfare, rental car, lodging, etc.) on your own. If the package price is less than the à la carte cost, the package is a good deal. If the costs are about the same, the package is probably worth buying just for the convenience.

If your package includes a choice of rental car or airport transfers (transportation to and from the airport), take the transfers unless you are visiting Chicago for the weekend. During the weekend, with the exception of some sections of Michigan Avenue, it is relatively easy to get around. During the week, forget it. Also, if you take the car, be sure to ask if the package includes free parking at your hotel.

HELPING YOUR TRAVEL AGENT HELP YOU

WHEN YOU CALL YOUR TRAVEL AGENT, ask if he or she has been to Chicago. If the answer is no, be prepared to give your travel agent some direction. Do not accept any recommendations at face value. Check out the location and rates of any suggested hotel and make certain that the hotel is suited to your itinerary.

Because some travel agents are unfamiliar with Chicago, your agent may try to plug you into a tour operator's or wholesaler's preset package. This essentially allows the travel agent to set up your whole trip with a single phone call and still collect an 8 to 10% commission. The problem with this scenario is that most agents will place 90% of their Chicago business with only one or two wholesalers or tour operators. In other words, it's the line of least resistance for them, and not much choice for you.

Travel agents will often use wholesalers who run packages in conjunction with airlines. Because of the wholesaler's relationship with the carrier, these trips are very easy for travel agents to book. However, they will probably be more expensive than a package offered by a high-volume wholesaler who works with a number of airlines in a primary Chicago market.

To help your travel agent get you the best possible deal, do the following:

1. Determine where you want to stay in Chicago, and if possible choose a specific hotel. This can be accomplished by reviewing the hotel

information provided in this guide, by writing or calling hotels that interest you, and by doing research online.

2. Check out the hotel deals and package vacations advertised in the Sunday travel sections of the *Chicago Tribune* and *Chicago Sun-Times* newspapers. Often you will be able to find deals that beat the socks off anything offered in your local paper. See if you can find specials that fit your plans and include a hotel you like.

3. Call the hotels, wholesalers, or tour operators whose ads you have collected. Ask any questions you have concerning their packages, but do not book your trip with them directly.

4. Tell your travel agent about the deals you find and ask if he or she can get you something better. The deals in the paper will serve as a benchmark against which to compare alternatives proposed by your travel agent.

5. Choose from the options that you and your travel agent uncover. No matter which option you select, have your travel agent book it. Even if you go with one of the packages in the newspaper, it will probably be commissionable (at no additional cost to you) and will provide the agent some return on the time invested on your behalf. Also, as a travel professional, your agent should be able to verify the quality and integrity of the deal.

IF YOU MAKE YOUR OWN RESERVATION

AS YOU POKE AROUND TRYING TO FIND A GOOD DEAL, there are several things you should know. First, always call the specific hotel as opposed to the hotel chain's national toll-free number. Quite often, the reservationists at the national toll-free number are unaware of local specials. Always ask about specials before you inquire about corporate rates. Do not be reluctant to bargain. If you are buying a hotel's weekend package, for example, and want to extend your stay into the following week, you can often obtain at least the corporate rate for the extra days. Do your bargaining, however, before you check in, preferably when you make reservations.

CHICAGO LODGING *for* BUSINESS TRAVELERS

THE PRIMARY CONSIDERATIONS FOR BUSINESS TRAVELERS are affordability and proximity to the place where you will transact your business. Identify the area(s) where your business will take you, and then use the Chicago Hotels by Location chart later in this chapter (page 46) to find hotels located there. (The Central Chicago Accommodations map, pages 34–35, can also help.) Once you have developed a short list of possible hotels that are conveniently located, fit your budget, and offer the standard of accommodation you require, you (or your travel agent) can make use of the cost-saving suggestions discussed earlier to obtain the lowest rate.

LODGING CONVENIENT TO McCORMICK PLACE

IF YOU ARE ATTENDING A MEETING or trade show at McCormick Place, the most convenient lodging is downtown Chicago, though none of the hotels, practically speaking, are within walking distance. From most downtown hotels, McCormick Place is a 5- to 14-minute cab or 10- to 30-minute shuttle ride away. Parking is available at the convention center, but it is expensive and not all that convenient. We recommend that you leave your car at home and use shuttles and cabs. The **Hyatt Regency McCormick Place** has 800 rooms and is connected to McCormick's Grand Concourse.

Commuting to McCormick Place from the suburbs or the airports during rush hour is something to be avoided, if possible. If you want a room downtown, book early . . . *very* early. If you screw up and need a room at the last minute, try a wholesaler or reservation service, or one of the strategies listed in the next section.

CONVENTION RATES: HOW THEY WORK AND HOW TO DO BETTER

IF YOU ARE ATTENDING A MAJOR CONVENTION or trade show, it is probable that the meeting's sponsoring organization has negotiated "convention rates" with a number of hotels. Under this arrangement, hotels reserve a certain number of rooms at an agreed-on price for conventioneers. Sometimes, as in the case of a small meeting, only one hotel is involved. In the event of a large "citywide" convention at McCormick Place, however, almost all downtown and airport hotels will participate in the room block.

Because the convention sponsor brings a lot of business to the city and reserves a large number of rooms, it usually can negotiate a volume discount on the room rates, a rate that should be substantially below rack rate. The bottom line, however, is that some conventions and trade shows have more bargaining clout and negotiating skill than others. Hence, your convention sponsor may or may not be able to obtain the lowest possible rate.

Once a convention or trade show sponsor has completed negotiations with participating hotels, it will send its attendees a housing list that includes all the hotels serving the convention, along with the special convention rate for each. When you receive the housing list, you can compare the convention rates with the rates obtainable using the strategies covered in the previous section. If the negotiated convention rate doesn't sound like a good deal, you can try to reserve a room using a half-price club, a consolidator, or a tour operator. Remember, however, that many of the deep discounts are available only when the hotel expects to be at less than 80% occupancy, a condition that rarely prevails when a big convention is in town.

CHAIN-HOTEL TOLL-FREE NUMBERS

Best Western	☎ 800-780-7234 U.S. and Canada
	☎ 800-528-2222 TDD
Comfort Inn	☎ 800-228-5150 U.S.
Courtyard by Marriott	☎ 888-236-2427 U.S.
Days Inn	☎ 800-329-7466 U.S.
DoubleTree	☎ 800-222-TREE U.S.
Econo Lodge	☎ 800-424-4777 U.S.
Embassy Suites	☎ 800-362-2779 U.S. and Canada
Fairfield Inn by Marriott	☎ 800-228-2800 U.S. & Canada
Hampton Inn	☎ 800-426-7866 U.S. and Canada
Hilton	☎ 800-445-8667 U.S. ☎ 800-368-1133 TDD
Holiday Inn	☎ 800-465-4329 U.S. and Canada
Howard Johnson	☎ 800-654-2000 U.S. and Canada
	☎ 800-654-8442 TDD
Hyatt	☎ 800-233-1234 U.S. and Canada
Loews	☎ 800-23-LOEWS U.S. and Canada
Marriott	☎ 800-228-9290 U.S. and Canada
	☎ 800-228-7014 TDD
Quality Inn	☎ 800-228-5151 U.S. and Canada
Radisson	☎ 800-333-3333 U.S. and Canada
Ramada Inn	☎ 800-272-6232 U.S. ☎ 800-228-3232 TDD
Renaissance Hotel	☎ 800-468-3571 U.S. and Canada
Residence Inn by Marriott	☎ 800-331-3131 U.S.
Ritz-Carlton	☎ 800-241-3333 U.S.
Sheraton	☎ 800-325-3535 U.S. and Canada
Wyndham	☎ 877-999-3223 U.S. and Canada

Strategies for Beating Convention Rates

There are several tactics for getting around convention rates:

1. **Reserve early.** Most big conventions and trade shows announce meeting sites one to three years in advance. Get your reservation booked as far in advance as possible using a half-price club. If you book well ahead of the time the convention sponsor sends out the housing list, chances are the hotel will accept your reservation.

2. **Compare your convention's housing list with the list of hotels presented in this guide.** You may be able to find a suitable hotel that is not on the housing list.

3. **Use a local reservations agency or consolidator.** This is also a good strategy to employ if, for some reason, you need to make reservations

at the last minute. Local reservations agencies and consolidators almost always control some rooms, even in the midst of a huge convention or trade show.

CHICAGO HOTELS:
Rated and Ranked

WHAT'S IN A ROOM?

EXCEPT FOR CLEANLINESS, STATE OF REPAIR, and decor, most travelers do not pay much attention to hotel rooms. There is, of course, a discernible standard of quality and luxury that differentiates Motel 6 from Holiday Inn, Holiday Inn from Marriott, and so on. In general, however, hotel guests fail to appreciate the fact that some rooms are better engineered than others.

Contrary to what you might suppose, designing a hotel room is (or should be) much more complex than picking a bedspread to match the carpet and drapes. Making the room usable to its occupants is an art, a planning discipline that combines both form and function.

Decor and taste are important, certainly. No one wants to spend several days in a room whose decor is dated, garish, or even ugly. But beyond the decor, several variables determine how "livable" a hotel room is. In Chicago, for example, we have seen some beautifully appointed rooms that are simply not well designed for human habitation. The next time you stay in a hotel, pay attention to the details and design elements of your room. Even more than decor, these will make you feel comfortable and at home.

HOTEL RATINGS

OVERALL QUALITY To distinguish properties according to relative quality, tastefulness, state of repair, cleanliness, and size of standard rooms, we have grouped the hotels and motels into classifications with an overall rating denoted by stars. Star ratings in this guide apply to Chicago-area properties only and do not necessarily correspond to stars awarded by Mobil, AAA, or other travel critics. Because stars carry little weight when awarded in the absence of common standards of comparison, we have linked our ratings to expected levels of quality established by specific American hotel corporations.

Star ratings describe the property's standard accommodations. For most hotels, a "standard accommodation" is a room with either one king bed or two queen beds. In an all-suite property, the standard accommodation is either a one- or two-room suite. In addition to standard accommodations, many hotels offer luxury rooms and special suites not rated here. Star ratings are assigned without regard to whether a property has restaurant(s), recreational facilities, entertainment, or other extras.

★★★★★	Superior	Tasteful and luxurious by any standard
★★★★	Extremely Nice	What you would expect at a Hyatt Regency or Marriott
★★★	Nice	Holiday Inn or comparable quality
★★	Adequate	Clean, comfortable, and functional without frills (like a Motel 6)
★	Budget	Spartan, not aesthetically pleasing, but clean

ROOM QUALITY In addition to stars (which delineate broad categories), we also employ a numerical rating system. Our rating scale is 0 to 100, with 100 as the best possible rating, and zero (0) as the worst. Numerical ratings are presented to show the difference we perceive between one property and another. Rooms at the Westin Michigan Avenue, Millennium Knickerbocker Hotel, and the Radisson O'Hare are all rated as three and a half stars (★★★½). In the supplemental numerical ratings, the Westin is rated an 82, the Knickerbocker an 80, and the Radisson a 76. This means that within the three-and-a-half-star category, the Knickerbocker is nicer than the Radisson, and the Westin has an edge over both.

COST Cost estimates are based on the hotel's published rack rates for standard rooms. Each "$" represents $60. Thus, a cost symbol of "$$$" means a room (or suite) at that hotel will cost about $180 a night.

LOCATION The location column identifies the neighborhood where you will find a particular property (see chart next page).

unofficial **TIP**
This just in: The **House of Blues Hotel** on Dearborn Street will reopen in May 2007 as the upscale **Hotel Sax Chicago,** and the **Gold Coast Hotel** on Clark Street will reopen in July 2007 as the **Park View.** We'll include updated ratings for both in future editions.

HOW THE HOTELS COMPARE

ON PAGES 48–51 IS A HIT PARADE of the nicest rooms in town. We've focused strictly on room quality and excluded any consideration of location, services, recreation, or amenities. In a few instances, a suite can be had for the same price or less than that of a standard hotel room.

If you use subsequent editions of this guide, you will notice that many of the ratings and rankings have changed. In addition to the inclusion of new properties, these changes also consider guest-room renovations or improved maintenance and housekeeping. A failure to properly maintain guest rooms or a lapse in housekeeping standards can negatively affect the ratings.

Although unusual, it is certainly possible that the rooms we randomly inspect are not representative of the majority of rooms at a particular hotel. Another possibility is that the rooms we inspect in a given hotel are representative but that by bad luck a reader is assigned

Chicago Hotels by Location

NORTH SIDE

Best Western Hawthorne Terrace

Days Inn Lincoln Park North

Gold Coast Hotel

Willows Hotel

NORTH CENTRAL– O'HARE

Best Western O'Hare

Candlewood Suites O'Hare

Carleton of Oak Park

Crowne Plaza Chicago O'Hare

DoubleTree O'Hare Rosemont

Embassy Suites O'Hare

Four Points Sheraton O'Hare

Hampton Inn O'Hare

Hilton O'Hare

Holiday Inn Express O'Hare

Holiday Inn Select O'Hare

Hyatt Regency O'Hare

Hyatt Rosemont

Marriott O'Hare

Marriott Suites O'Hare

Motel 6 O'Hare East

Quality Inn O'Hare

Radisson O'Hare

Residence Inn by Marriott O'Hare

Sheraton Gateway Suites O'Hare

Sofitel Chicago O'Hare

Travelodge Chicago O'Hare

Westin Hotel O'Hare

Wyndham Garden Hotel O'Hare

Wyndham O'Hare

NEAR NORTH SIDE

Affinia Hotel

Allerton Crowne Plaza

Ambassador East Hotel

Best Western Inn Chicago

Best Western River North

Courtyard by Marriott Downtown

Courtyard by Marriott Magnificent Mile

Drake Hotel

Embassy Suites Chicago

Embassy Suites Downtown/ Lakefront

Four Seasons Hotel

Hampton Inn & Suites Downtown

Hilton Garden Inn Downtown

Hilton Suites Downtown

Holiday Inn Chicago City Center

Holiday Inn Mart Plaza

Hotel Indigo

Hotel Inter-Continental Chicago

House of Blues Hotel

Howard Johnson

James

Marriott Chicago Downtown

Marriott Fairfield Inn & Suites Downtown

Marriott Residence Inn Downtown

Millennium Knickerbocker Hotel

Omni Chicago Hotel

Park Hyatt Chicago

Peninsula

Radisson Hotel & Suites Chicago

Raffaello

Red Roof Inn Downtown

Ritz-Carlton Chicago

Seneca

a room that is inferior. The key to avoiding disappointment is to snoop around in advance. We recommend that you look on the Web, ask for a photo of a hotel's standard guest room before you book, or at least get a copy of the hotel's promotional brochure. Alas, some hotel chains use the same guest-room photo in their promotional literature for all their properties; a specific guest room may not resemble the brochure photo. Find out how old the property is and when your guest room was last renovated. If you arrive and are assigned an inferior room, demand to be moved.

Sheraton Chicago Hotel & Towers

Sofitel Water Tower

Sutton Place Hotel

Talbott Hotel

W Lakeshore

Westin Michigan Avenue

Westin River North Chicago

Whitehall Hotel

Wyndham Chicago

THE LOOP

Fairmont Hotel

Hard Rock Hotel

Hotel Allegro

Hotel Burnham

Hotel Monaco

Hyatt Regency Chicago in Illinois Center

Palmer House Hilton

Renaissance Chicago Hotel

Solis Chicago Hotel & Spa

Swissotel Chicago

W City Center Hotel

SOUTH LOOP

Best Western Grant Park Hotel

Blake

Congress Plaza Hotel & Convention Center

Essex Inn

Hilton Chicago

Hyatt Regency McCormick Place

Travelodge Downtown

SOUTHERN SUBURBS

Hampton Inn Midway Bedford Park

Hampton Inn Westchester/ Chicago

Sleep Inn Midway Airport

Wyndham Drake Hotel Oak Brook

WESTERN SUBURBS

Comfort Inn Downers Grove

Courtyard by Marriott Oakbrook Terrace

DoubleTree Downers Grove

DoubleTree Hotel Chicago Oak Brook

Embassy Suites Lombard

Hilton Garden Inn Oakbrook Terrace

Hilton Suites Oakbrook Terrace

Holiday Inn Express Downers Grove

Holiday Inn Oakbrook Terrace

La Quinta Inn Oakbrook Terrace

Marriott Oak Brook

Marriott Suites Downers Grove

Red Roof Inn Downers Grove

Renaissance Oakbrook Hotel

NORTHWEST SUBURBS

Comfort Inn Elk Grove Village

Courtyard by Marriott Wood Dale

Holiday Inn Elk Grove Village

NORTHERN SUBURBS

Best Western University Plaza

Hilton Garden Inn Evanston

Holiday Inn North Shore

North Shore Skokie Hotel

Orrington Hotel Evanston

Purple Hotel

TOP 30 HOTEL DEALS IN CHICAGO

HAVING LISTED THE NICEST ROOMS IN TOWN, let's reorder the list to rank the best combinations of quality and value in a room. The rankings are made without consideration of location or the availability of restaurant(s), recreational facilities, entertainment, or amenities. See page 52 for the full list.

How the Hotels Compare in Chicago

HOTEL	OVERALL RATING	ROOM QUALITY RATING	COST ($ = $60)	LOCATION
Peninsula	★★★★★	99	$$$$$$$	Near North Side
Park Hyatt Chicago	★★★★★	97	$$$$$$$$+	Near North Side
Raffaello	★★★★★	97	$$$$+	Near North Side
James	★★★★½	95	$$$$$$+	Near North Side
Westin River North Chicago	★★★★½	95	$$$$$	Near North Side
Affinia Hotel	★★★★½	94	$$$$	Near North Side
W Lakeshore	★★★★½	93	$$$$$$+	Near North Side
Hard Rock Hotel	★★★★½	92	$$$$	The Loop
Hotel Burnham	★★★★½	92	$$$$–	The Loop
Hotel Inter-Continental Chicago	★★★★½	92	$$$$$$	Near North Side
Hotel Monaco	★★★★½	92	$$$+	The Loop
Renaissance Chicago Hotel	★★★★½	92	$$$$$$$	The Loop
Ritz-Carlton Chicago	★★★★½	92	$$$$$$$$	Near North Side
W City Center Hotel	★★★★½	92	$$$$$$$$$$	The Loop
Hilton Chicago	★★★★½	91	$$$–	South Loop
Omni Chicago Hotel	★★★★½	91	$$$$$$$	Near North Side
Westin Michigan Avenue	★★★★½	91	$$$$$$+	Near North Side
Blake	★★★★½	90	$$$+	South Loop
DoubleTree O'Hare Rosemont	★★★★½	90	$$–	North Central–O'Hare
Drake Hotel	★★★★½	90	$$$$$–	Near North Side
Sheraton Chicago Hotel & Towers	★★★★½	90	$$$$+	Near North Side
Hotel Allegro	★★★★	89	$$$–	The Loop
Hyatt Regency Chicago in Illinois Center	★★★★	89	$$$$+	The Loop
Orrington Hotel Evanston	★★★★	89	$$$$–	Northern Suburbs
Sheraton Gateway Suites O'Hare	★★★★	89	$$$–	North Central–O'Hare
Sofitel Water Tower	★★★★	89	$$$$+	Near North Side
Solis Chicago Hotel & Spa	★★★★	89	$$$$$–	The Loop
Embassy Suites Downtown/ Lakefront	★★★★	88	$$$$$+	Near North Side
Hilton Suites Downtown	★★★★	88	$$$$$$$	Near North Side
Hotel Indigo	★★★★	88	$$$+	Near North Side

HOTEL	OVERALL RATING	ROOM QUALITY RATING	COST ($ = $60)	LOCATION
House of Blues Hotel	★★★★	88	$$$$$$	Near North Side
Marriott Suites O'Hare	★★★★	88	$$	North Central–O'Hare
Residence Inn by Marriott O'Hare	★★★★	88	$$$	North Central–O'Hare
Four Seasons Hotel	★★★★	87	$$$$$$$$	Near North Side
Hilton Suites Oakbrook Terrace	★★★★	87	$$+	Western Suburbs
Marriott Suites Downers Grove	★★★★	87	$$	Western Suburbs
Palmer House Hilton	★★★★	87	$$$$+	The Loop
Wyndham Chicago	★★★★	87	$$$$$$	Near North Side
Fairmont Hotel	★★★★	86	$$$$$$–	The Loop
Hilton Garden Inn Downtown	★★★★	86	$$$	Near North Side
Hyatt Regency McCormick Place	★★★★	86	$$$	South Loop
Renaissance Oakbrook Hotel	★★★★	86	$$	Western Suburbs
Swissotel Chicago	★★★★	86	$$$$$$$$	The Loop
Westin Hotel O'Hare	★★★★	86	$$+	North Central–O'Hare
Embassy Suites Lombard	★★★★	85	$$$–	Western Suburbs
Embassy Suites O'Hare	★★★★	85	$$$–	North Central–O'Hare
Marriott Chicago Downtown	★★★★	85	$$$$$	Near North Side
Sofitel Chicago O'Hare	★★★★	85	$$$$–	North Central–O'Hare
Sutton Place Hotel	★★★★	85	$$$$$$–	Near North Side
Talbott Hotel	★★★★	85	$$$+	Near North Side
Candlewood Suites O'Hare	★★★★	84	$$–	North Central–O'Hare
Courtyard by Marriott Downtown	★★★★	84	$$$$+	Near North Side
Courtyard by Marriott Magnificent Mile	★★★★	84	$$$$+	Near North Side
Four Points Sheraton O'Hare	★★★★	84	$$+	North Central–O'Hare
Hampton Inn & Suites Downtown	★★★★	84	$$$	Near North Side
North Shore Skokie Hotel	★★★★	84	$$$–	Northern Suburbs
Whitehall Hotel	★★★★	84	$$$$$+	Near North Side
DoubleTree Downers Grove	★★★★	83	$+	Western Suburbs
Embassy Suites Chicago	★★★★	83	$$$$$	Near North Side

How the Hotels Compare in Chicago (continue

HOTEL	OVERALL RATING	ROOM QUALITY RATING	COST ($ = $60)	LOCATION
Hilton Garden Inn Evanston	★★★★	83	$$+	Northern Suburbs
Hyatt Regency O'Hare	★★★★	83	$$$+	North Central–O'Hare
Hyatt Rosemont	★★★★	83	$$–	North Central–O'Hare
Marriott Residence Inn Downtown	★★★★	83	$$$	Near North Side
Radisson O'Hare	★★★★	83	$$–	North Central–O'Hare
Allerton Crowne Plaza	★★★½	82	$$$$$	Near North Side
Ambassador East Hotel	★★★½	82	$$$$	Near North Side
Carleton of Oak Park	★★★½	82	$$+	North Central–O'Hare
Courtyard by Marriott Oakbrook Terrace	★★★½	82	$$–	Western Suburbs
Courtyard by Marriott Wood Dale	★★★½	82	$$+	Northwest Suburbs
Holiday Inn Elk Grove Village	★★★½	82	$$–	Northwest Suburbs
Holiday Inn Select O'Hare	★★★½	82	$$	North Central–O'Hare
Marriott O'Hare	★★★½	82	$$–	North Central–O'Hare
Crowne Plaza Chicago O'Hare	★★★½	81	$$$$$$+	North Central–O'Hare
DoubleTree Hotel Chicago Oak Brook	★★★½	81	$$–	Western Suburbs
Hilton Garden Inn Oakbrook Terrace	★★★½	81	$$$–	Western Suburbs
Hilton O'Hare	★★★½	81	$$$–	North Central–O'Hare
Millennium Knickerbocker Hotel	★★★½	81	$$$$+	Near North Side
Seneca	★★★½	81	$$$$	Near North Side
Holiday Inn Express O'Hare	★★★½	80	$$	North Central–O'Hare
Radisson Hotel & Suites Chicago	★★★½	80	$$$$–	Near North Side
Wyndham Drake Hotel Oak Brook	★★★½	80	$$$	Southern Suburbs
Hampton Inn O'Hare	★★★½	79	$$–	North Central–O'Hare
Marriott Oak Brook	★★★½	79	$$	Western Suburbs
Wyndham O'Hare	★★★½	79	$$$	North Central–O'Hare
Holiday Inn Mart Plaza	★★★½	78	$$$+	Near North Side
Holiday Inn North Shore	★★★½	78	$$+	Northern Suburbs
Best Western University Plaza	★★★½	77	$$$–	Northern Suburbs
Best Western River North	★★★½	76	$$$	Near North Side

HOTEL	OVERALL RATING	ROOM QUALITY RATING	COST ($ = $60)	LOCATION
Hampton Inn Westchester/ Chicago	★★★½	76	$$–	Southern Suburbs
Best Western Inn Chicago	★★★	74	$$$$	Near North Side
Comfort Inn Elk Grove Village	★★★	74	$$–	Northwest Suburbs
Holiday Inn Oakbrook Terrace	★★★	74	$$–	Western Suburbs
Wyndham Garden Hotel O'Hare	★★★	74	$$	North Central–O'Hare
Hampton Inn Midway Bedford Park	★★★	73	$$–	Southern Suburbs
Marriott Fairfield Inn & Suites Downtown	★★★	73	$$+	Near North Side
Willows Hotel	★★★	73	$$$–	North Side
Best Western O'Hare	★★★	72	$$$–	North Central–O'Hare
Holiday Inn Chicago City Center	★★★	72	$$$$	Near North Side
Holiday Inn Express Downers Grove	★★★	72	$$–	Western Suburbs
Best Western Hawthorne Terrace	★★★	71	$$$	North Side
Comfort Inn Downers Grove	★★★	71	$$	Western Suburbs
Purple Hotel	★★★	71	$$–	Northern Suburbs
Best Western Grant Park Hotel	★★★	70	$$$–	South Loop
Quality Inn O'Hare	★★★	70	$+	North Central–O'Hare
Red Roof Inn Downers Grove	★★★	70	$	Western Suburbs
La Quinta Inn Oakbrook Terrace	★★★	69	$+	Western Suburbs
Red Roof Inn Downtown	★★★	69	$$	Near North Side
Essex Inn	★★★	68	$$$$	South Loop
Motel 6 O'Hare East	★★★	67	$	North Central–O'Hare
Congress Plaza Hotel & Convention Center	★★★	66	$$$	South Loop
Howard Johnson	★★½	64	$$+	Near North Side
Sleep Inn Midway Airport	★★½	64	$$$–	Southern Suburbs
Days Inn Lincoln Park North	★★½	62	$$–	North Side
Travelodge Downtown	★★½	60	$$+	South Loop
Gold Coast Hotel	★★½	58	$$$	North Side
Travelodge Chicago O'Hare	★★½	58	$+	North Central–O'Hare

The Top 30 Best Hotel Deals in Chicago

HOTEL	OVERALL RATING	QUALITY RATING	COST ($ = $60)	LOCATION
1. DoubleTree Downers Grove	★★★★	83	$+	Western Suburbs
2. DoubleTree O'Hare Rosemont	★★★★½	90	$$–	North Central–O'Hare
3. Radisson O'Hare	★★★★	83	$$–	North Central–O'Hare
4. Candlewood Suites O'Hare	★★★★	84	$$–	North Central–O'Hare
5. Motel 6 O'Hare East	★★★	67	$	North Central–O'Hare
6. Red Roof Inn Downers Grove	★★★	70	$	Western Suburbs
7. Hyatt Rosemont	★★★★	83	$$–	North Central–O'Hare
8. DoubleTree Hotel Oak Brook	★★★½	81	$$–	Western Suburbs
9. Hampton Inn O'Hare	★★★½	79	$$–	North Central–O'Hare
10. Marriott Suites O'Hare	★★★★	88	$$	North Central–O'Hare
11. Marriott Suites Downers Grove	★★★★	87	$$	Western Suburbs
12. Renaissance Oakbrook Hotel	★★★★	86	$$	Western Suburbs
13. Courtyard Oakbrook Terrace	★★★½	82	$$–	Western Suburbs
14. Holiday Inn Elk Grove Village	★★★½	82	$$–	Northwest Suburbs
15. Marriott O'Hare	★★★½	82	$$–	North Central–O'Hare
16. Hilton Chicago	★★★★½	91	$$$–	South Loop
17. Hilton Suites Oakbrook Terrace	★★★★	87	$$+	Western Suburbs
18. La Quinta Inn Oakbrook Terrace	★★★	69	$+	Western Suburbs
19. Hampton Inn Westchester	★★★½	76	$$–	Southern Suburbs
20. Four Points Sheraton O'Hare	★★★★	84	$$+	North Central–O'Hare
21. Holiday Inn Select O'Hare	★★★½	82	$$	North Central–O'Hare
22. Quality Inn O'Hare	★★★	70	$+	North Central–O'Hare
23. Westin Hotel O'Hare	★★★★	86	$$+	North Central–O'Hare
24. Marriott Oakbrook	★★★½	79	$$	Western Suburbs
25. Holiday Inn Express O'Hare	★★★½	80	$$	North Central–O'Hare
26. Sheraton Gateway Suites O'Hare	★★★★	89	$$$–	North Central–O'Hare
27. Hilton Garden Inn Evanston	★★★★	83	$$+	Northern Suburbs
28. Comfort Inn Elk Grove Village	★★★	74	$$–	Northwest Suburbs
29. Courtyard by Marriott Wood Dale	★★★½	82	$$	Northwest Suburbs
30. Embassy Suites O'Hare	★★★★	85	$$$–	North Central–O'Hare

Hotel Information Chart

Affinia Hotel ★★★★½
166 East Superior Street
Chicago 60611
☎ 312-787-6000
TOLL FREE ☎ 800-367-7701
www.affinia.com

ROOM QUALITY	94
COST ($ = $60)	$$$$
LOCATION	Near North Side
NO. OF ROOMS	140
PARKING	Valet, $38
ROOM SERVICE	•
BREAKFAST	—
ON-SITE DINING	•
POOL	•
SAUNA	—
EXERCISE FACILITIES	•

Allerton Crowne Plaza ★★★½
701 North Michigan Avenue
Chicago 60611
☎ 312-440-1500
TOLL FREE ☎ 800-227-6963
www.allertonchi.crowneplaza.com

ROOM QUALITY	82
COST ($ = $60)	$$$$$
LOCATION	Near North Side
NO. OF ROOMS	443
PARKING	Valet $40
ROOM SERVICE	•
BREAKFAST	—
ON-SITE DINING	•
POOL	—
SAUNA	—
EXERCISE FACILITIES	•

Ambassador East Hotel ★★★½
1301 North State Parkway
Chicago 60610
☎ 312-787-7200
TOLL FREE ☎ 888-506-3471
www.theambassadoreasthotel.com

ROOM QUALITY	82
COST ($ = $60)	$$$$
LOCATION	Near North Side
NO. OF ROOMS	285
PARKING	Valet, $36
ROOM SERVICE	•
BREAKFAST	—
ON-SITE DINING	•
POOL	—
SAUNA	—
EXERCISE FACILITIES	—

Best Western Grant Park Hotel ★★★
1100 South Michigan Avenue
Chicago 60605
☎ 312-922-2900
TOLL FREE ☎ 800-472-6875
www.bestwestern.com

ROOM QUALITY	70
COST ($ = $60)	$$$–
LOCATION	South Loop
NO. OF ROOMS	172
PARKING	Valet, $24 (cars only)
ROOM SERVICE	•
BREAKFAST	—
ON-SITE DINING	•
POOL	•
SAUNA	—
EXERCISE FACILITIES	•

Best Western Hawthorne Terrace ★★★
3434 North Broadway Street
Chicago 60657
☎ 773-244-3434
TOLL FREE ☎ 888-860-3400
www.hawthorneterrace.com

ROOM QUALITY	71
COST ($ = $60)	$$$
LOCATION	North Side
NO. OF ROOMS	59
PARKING	Valet, $18
ROOM SERVICE	—
BREAKFAST	Continental
ON-SITE DINING	—
POOL	—
SAUNA	—
EXERCISE FACILITIES	•

Best Western Inn Chicago ★★★
162 East Ohio Street
Chicago 60611
☎ 312-787-3100
TOLL FREE ☎ 800-557-2378
www.bestwestern.com

ROOM QUALITY	74
COST ($ = $60)	$$$$
LOCATION	Near North Side
NO. OF ROOMS	357
PARKING	Self, $26; valet, $28
ROOM SERVICE	—
BREAKFAST	—
ON-SITE DINING	—
POOL	—
SAUNA	—
EXERCISE FACILITIES	•

Best Western O'Hare ★★★
10300 West Higgins Road
Rosemont 60018
☎ 847-296-4471
TOLL FREE ☎ 800-528-1234
www.bestwesternohare.com

ROOM QUALITY	72
COST ($ = $60)	$$$–
LOCATION	North Central–O'Hare
NO. OF ROOMS	143
PARKING	Lot, free
ROOM SERVICE	•
BREAKFAST	—
ON-SITE DINING	•
POOL	•
SAUNA	—
EXERCISE FACILITIES	•

Best Western River North ★★★½
125 West Ohio Street
Chicago 60610
☎ 312-467-0800
TOLL FREE ☎ 800-704-6941
www.rivernorthhotel.com

ROOM QUALITY	76
COST ($ = $60)	$$$
LOCATION	Near North Side
NO. OF ROOMS	150
PARKING	Lot, free
ROOM SERVICE	•
BREAKFAST	—
ON-SITE DINING	•
POOL	•
SAUNA	—
EXERCISE FACILITIES	•

Best Western University Plaza ★★★½
1501 Sherman Avenue
Evanston 60201
☎ 847-491-6400
TOLL FREE ☎ 800-381-2830
www.bestwestern.com

ROOM QUALITY	77
COST ($ = $60)	$$$–
LOCATION	Northern Suburbs
NO. OF ROOMS	159
PARKING	Self, $10
ROOM SERVICE	—
BREAKFAST	—
ON-SITE DINING	—
POOL	•
SAUNA	—
EXERCISE FACILITIES	•

Hotel Information Chart (continued)

Blake ★★★★½
500 South Dearborn Street
Chicago 60605
☎ 312-344-4966
TOLL FREE ☎ 800-233-1234
www.hotelblake.com

ROOM QUALITY	90
COST ($ = $60)	$$$+
LOCATION	South Loop
NO. OF ROOMS	162
PARKING	Valet, $36
ROOM SERVICE	•
BREAKFAST	—
ON-SITE DINING	•
POOL	—
SAUNA	—
EXERCISE FACILITIES	•

Candlewood Suites O'Hare ★★★★
4021 North Mannheim Road
Schiller Park 60176
☎ 847-671-4663
TOLL FREE ☎ 888-CANDLEWOOD
www.candlewoodsuites.com

ROOM QUALITY	84
COST ($ = $60)	$$–
LOCATION	North Central–O'Hare
NO. OF ROOMS	160
PARKING	Self, $5
ROOM SERVICE	—
BREAKFAST	—
ON-SITE DINING	—
POOL	—
SAUNA	—
EXERCISE FACILITIES	•

Carleton of Oak Park ★★★½
1110 Pleasant Street
Oak Park 60302
☎ 708-848-5000
TOLL FREE ☎ 888-CARLETON
www.carletonhotel.com

ROOM QUALITY	82
COST ($ = $60)	$$+
LOCATION	North Central–O'Hare
NO. OF ROOMS	150
PARKING	Lot, free
ROOM SERVICE	•
BREAKFAST	—
ON-SITE DINING	•
POOL	—
SAUNA	—
EXERCISE FACILITIES	—

Courtyard by Marriott Downtown ★★★★
30 East Hubbard Street
Chicago 60611
☎ 312-329-2500
TOLL FREE ☎ 800-321-2211
www.marriott.com

ROOM QUALITY	84
COST ($ = $60)	$$$$+
LOCATION	Near North Side
NO. OF ROOMS	337
PARKING	Valet, $39
ROOM SERVICE	•
BREAKFAST	—
ON-SITE DINING	•
POOL	•
SAUNA	•
EXERCISE FACILITIES	•

Courtyard by Marriott Magnificent Mile ★★★★
165 East Ontario
Chicago 60611
☎ 312-573-0800
TOLL FREE ☎ 800-321-2211
www.marriott.com

ROOM QUALITY	84
COST ($ = $60)	$$$$+
LOCATION	Near North Side
NO. OF ROOMS	306
PARKING	Self, $26; valet, $36
ROOM SERVICE	•
BREAKFAST	—
ON-SITE DINING	•
POOL	•
SAUNA	—
EXERCISE FACILITIES	•

Courtyard by Marriott Oakbrook Terrace ★★★½
6 Transam Plaza Drive
Oakbrook Terrace 60181
☎ 630-691-1500
TOLL FREE ☎ 800-321-2211
www.marriott.com

ROOM QUALITY	82
COST ($ = $60)	$$–
LOCATION	Western Suburbs
NO. OF ROOMS	147
PARKING	Lot, free
ROOM SERVICE	—
BREAKFAST	—
ON-SITE DINING	•
POOL	•
SAUNA	•
EXERCISE FACILITIES	•

DoubleTree Downers Grove ★★★★
2111 Butterfield Road
Downers Grove 60515
☎ 630-971-2000
TOLL FREE ☎ 800-222-TREE
www.doubletree.com

ROOM QUALITY	83
COST ($ = $60)	$+
LOCATION	Western Suburbs
NO. OF ROOMS	247
PARKING	Lot, free
ROOM SERVICE	•
BREAKFAST	—
ON-SITE DINING	•
POOL	•
SAUNA	—
EXERCISE FACILITIES	•

DoubleTree Hotel Chicago Oak Brook ★★★½
1909 Spring Road
Oak Brook 60523
☎ 630-472-6000
TOLL FREE ☎ 800-222-TREE
www.doubletree.com

ROOM QUALITY	81
COST ($ = $60)	$$–
LOCATION	Western Suburbs
NO. OF ROOMS	427
PARKING	Garage, free
ROOM SERVICE	•
BREAKFAST	—
ON-SITE DINING	•
POOL	•
SAUNA	—
EXERCISE FACILITIES	•

DoubleTree O'Hare Rosemont ★★★★½
5460 North River Road
Des Plaines 60018
☎ 847-292-9100
TOLL FREE ☎ 800-222-TREE
www.doubletree.com

ROOM QUALITY	90
COST ($ = $60)	$$–
LOCATION	North Central–O'Hare
NO. OF ROOMS	369
PARKING	Self, $11; valet, $24
ROOM SERVICE	•
BREAKFAST	—
ON-SITE DINING	•
POOL	•
SAUNA	—
EXERCISE FACILITIES	•

Comfort Inn Downers Grove ★★★
3010 Finley Road
Downers Grove 60515
☎ 630-515-1500
TOLL FREE ☎ 800-228-5150
www.comfortinn.com

ROOM QUALITY	71
COST ($ = $60)	$$
LOCATION	Western Suburbs
NO. OF ROOMS	120
PARKING	Lot, free
ROOM SERVICE	–
BREAKFAST	Continental
ON-SITE DINING	–
POOL	–
SAUNA	–
EXERCISE FACILITIES	•

Comfort Inn Elk Grove Village ★★★
2550 Landmeier Road
Elk Grove Village 60007
☎ 847-364-6200
TOLL FREE ☎ 877-424-6423
www.comfortinnchicago.com

ROOM QUALITY	74
COST ($ = $60)	$$–
LOCATION	Northern Suburbs
NO. OF ROOMS	100
PARKING	Lot, free
ROOM SERVICE	–
BREAKFAST	Continental
ON-SITE DINING	•
POOL	–
SAUNA	–
EXERCISE FACILITIES	•

Congress Plaza Hotel & Convention Center ★★★
520 South Michigan Avenue
Chicago 60605
☎ 312-427-3800
TOLL FREE ☎ 800-635-1666
www.congressplazahotel.com

ROOM QUALITY	66
COST ($ = $60)	$$$
LOCATION	South Loop
NO. OF ROOMS	886
PARKING	Self, 27; valet, $32
ROOM SERVICE	•
BREAKFAST	•
ON-SITE DINING	•
POOL	–
SAUNA	–
EXERCISE FACILITIES	•

Courtyard by Marriott Wood Dale ★★★½
900 North Wood Dale Road
Chicago 60191
☎ 630-766-7775
TOLL FREE ☎ 800-321-2211
www.marriott.com

ROOM QUALITY	82
COST ($ = $60)	$$+
LOCATION	Northern Suburbs
NO. OF ROOMS	149
PARKING	Lot, free
ROOM SERVICE	–
BREAKFAST	–
ON-SITE DINING	•
POOL	•
SAUNA	–
EXERCISE FACILITIES	•

Crowne Plaza Chicago O'Hare ★★★½
5440 North River Road
Rosemont 60018
☎ 847-671-6350
TOLL FREE ☎ 888-642-7344
www.chi-ohare.crowneplaza.com

ROOM QUALITY	81
COST ($ = $60)	$$$$$$+
LOCATION	North Central– O'Hare
NO. OF ROOMS	503
PARKING	Self, $18
ROOM SERVICE	•
BREAKFAST	–
ON-SITE DINING	•
POOL	•
SAUNA	•
EXERCISE FACILITIES	•

Days Inn Lincoln Park North ★★½
644 West Diversey Parkway
Chicago 60614
☎ 773-525-7010
TOLL FREE ☎ 888-LPN-DAYS
www.lpndaysinn.com

ROOM QUALITY	62
COST ($ = $60)	$$–
LOCATION	North Side
NO. OF ROOMS	124
PARKING	Valet, $20
ROOM SERVICE	–
BREAKFAST	Continental
ON-SITE DINING	–
POOL	–
SAUNA	–
EXERCISE FACILITIES	–

Drake Hotel ★★★★½
140 East Walton Place
Chicago 60611
☎ 312-787-2200
TOLL FREE ☎ 800-55-DRAKE
www.thedrakehotel.com

ROOM QUALITY	90
COST ($ = $60)	$$$$$$–
LOCATION	Near North Side
NO. OF ROOMS	537
PARKING	Valet, $41
ROOM SERVICE	•
BREAKFAST	–
ON-SITE DINING	•
POOL	–
SAUNA	–
EXERCISE FACILITIES	•

Embassy Suites Chicago ★★★★
600 North State Street
Chicago 60610
☎ 312-943-3800
TOLL FREE ☎ 800-EMBASSY
www.embassysuites.com

ROOM QUALITY	83
COST ($ = $60)	$$$$$
LOCATION	Near North Side
NO. OF ROOMS	365
PARKING	Valet, $36
ROOM SERVICE	•
BREAKFAST	Full
ON-SITE DINING	•
POOL	•
SAUNA	–
EXERCISE FACILITIES	•

Embassy Suites Downtown/ Lakefront ★★★★
511 North Columbus Drive
Chicago 60611
☎ 312-836-5900
TOLL FREE ☎ 800-EMBASSY
www.embassysuites.com

ROOM QUALITY	88
COST ($ = $60)	$$$$$+
LOCATION	Near North Side
NO. OF ROOMS	455
PARKING	Self, $34; valet, $39
ROOM SERVICE	•
BREAKFAST	Full
ON-SITE DINING	•
POOL	•
SAUNA	–
EXERCISE FACILITIES	•

Hotel Information Chart (continued)

Embassy Suites Lombard ★★★★
707 East Butterfield Road
Lombard 60148
☎ 630-969-7500
TOLL FREE ☎ 800-EMBASSY
www.embassysuites.com

ROOM QUALITY	85
COST ($ = $60)	$$$–
LOCATION	Western Suburbs
NO. OF ROOMS	262
PARKING	Lot, free
ROOM SERVICE	•
BREAKFAST	Cooked to order
ON-SITE DINING	•
POOL	•
SAUNA	–
EXERCISE FACILITIES	•

Embassy Suites O'Hare ★★★★
5500 North River Road
Rosemont 60018
☎ 847-678-4000
TOLL FREE ☎ 800-EMBASSY
www.embassysuites.com

ROOM QUALITY	85
COST ($ = $60)	$$$–
LOCATION	North Central–O'Hare
NO. OF ROOMS	293
PARKING	Self, $18; valet, $25
ROOM SERVICE	•
BREAKFAST	Continental
ON-SITE DINING	•
POOL	•
SAUNA	–
EXERCISE FACILITIES	•

Essex Inn ★★★
800 South Michigan Avenue
Chicago 60605
☎ 312-939-2800
TOLL FREE ☎ 800-621-6909
www.essexinn.com

ROOM QUALITY	68
COST ($ = $60)	$$$$
LOCATION	South Loop
NO. OF ROOMS	254
PARKING	Valet, $21
ROOM SERVICE	–
BREAKFAST	•
ON-SITE DINING	•
POOL	•
SAUNA	•
EXERCISE FACILITIES	•

Gold Coast Hotel ★★½
1816 North Clark Street
Chicago 60614
☎ 312-664-3040
www.thegoldcoasthotel.com

ROOM QUALITY	58
COST ($ = $60)	$$$
LOCATION	North Side
NO. OF ROOMS	196
PARKING	Self, $17.50
ROOM SERVICE	–
BREAKFAST	–
ON-SITE DINING	–
POOL	–
SAUNA	–
EXERCISE FACILITIES	•

Hampton Inn & Suites Downtown ★★★★
33 West Illinois Street
Chicago 60610
☎ 312-832-0330
TOLL FREE ☎ 800-HAMPTON
www.hamptoninn.com

ROOM QUALITY	84
COST ($ = $60)	$$$
LOCATION	Near North Side
NO. OF ROOMS	230
PARKING	Valet, $36
ROOM SERVICE	•
BREAKFAST	Full
ON-SITE DINING	–
POOL	•
SAUNA	–
EXERCISE FACILITIES	•

Hampton Inn Midway Bedford Park ★★★
6540 South Cicero Avenue
Bedford Park 60638
☎ 708-496-1900
TOLL FREE ☎ 800-HAMPTON
www.hamptoninn.com

ROOM QUALITY	73
COST ($ = $60)	$$–
LOCATION	Southern Suburbs
NO. OF ROOMS	170
PARKING	Lot, free
ROOM SERVICE	•
BREAKFAST	Full
ON-SITE DINING	•
POOL	•
SAUNA	–
EXERCISE FACILITIES	•

Hilton Chicago ★★★★½
720 South Michigan Avenue
Chicago 60605
☎ 312-922-4400
TOLL FREE ☎ 800-HILTONS
www.hilton.com

ROOM QUALITY	91
COST ($ = $60)	$$$–
LOCATION	South Loop
NO. OF ROOMS	1,544
PARKING	Self, $38; valet, $41
ROOM SERVICE	•
BREAKFAST	–
ON-SITE DINING	•
POOL	•
SAUNA	–
EXERCISE FACILITIES	•

Hilton Garden Inn Downtown ★★★★
10 East Grand Avenue
Chicago 60611
☎ 312-595-0000
TOLL FREE ☎ 877-STAY-HGI
www.hiltongardenchicago.com

ROOM QUALITY	86
COST ($ = $60)	$$$
LOCATION	Near North Side
NO. OF ROOMS	357
PARKING	Self, $22; valet, $36
ROOM SERVICE	•
BREAKFAST	Full
ON-SITE DINING	•
POOL	•
SAUNA	–
EXERCISE FACILITIES	•

Hilton Garden Inn Evanston ★★★★
1818 Maple Avenue
Evanston 60201
☎ 847-475-6400
TOLL FREE ☎ 877-782-9444
www.hiltongardeninn.com

ROOM QUALITY	83
COST ($ = $60)	$$+
LOCATION	Northern Suburbs
NO. OF ROOMS	178
PARKING	Self, $10
ROOM SERVICE	•
BREAKFAST	–
ON-SITE DINING	•
POOL	•
SAUNA	–
EXERCISE FACILITIES	•

Fairmont Hotel ★★★★
200 North Columbus Drive
Chicago 60601
☎ 312-565-8000
TOLL FREE ☎ 800-257-7544
www.fairmont.com

ROOM QUALITY	86
COST ($ = $60)	$$$$$$–
LOCATION	The Loop
NO. OF ROOMS	692
PARKING	Valet, $45
ROOM SERVICE	•
BREAKFAST	–
ON-SITE DINING	•
POOL	–
SAUNA	–
EXERCISE FACILITIES	•

Four Points Sheraton O'Hare ★★★★
10249 West Irving Park Road
Schiller Park 60176
☎ 847-671-6000
TOLL FREE ☎ 800-323-1239
www.starwoodhotels.com

ROOM QUALITY	84
COST ($ = $60)	$$+
LOCATION	North Central–O'Hare
NO. OF ROOMS	295
PARKING	Lot, free
ROOM SERVICE	•
BREAKFAST	–
ON-SITE DINING	–
POOL	•
SAUNA	•
EXERCISE FACILITIES	•

Four Seasons Hotel ★★★★
120 East Delaware Place
Chicago 60611
☎ 312-280-8800
TOLL FREE ☎ 800-819-5053
www.fourseasons.com

ROOM QUALITY	87
COST ($ = $60)	$$$$$$$$
LOCATION	Near North Side
NO. OF ROOMS	343
PARKING	Self, $26; valet, $36
ROOM SERVICE	•
BREAKFAST	–
ON-SITE DINING	•
POOL	•
SAUNA	•
EXERCISE FACILITIES	•

Hampton Inn O'Hare ★★★½
3939 North Mannheim Road
Schiller Park 60176
☎ 847-671-1700
TOLL FREE ☎ 800-446-4656
www.hamptoninnohare.com

ROOM QUALITY	79
COST ($ = $60)	$$–
LOCATION	North Central–O'Hare
NO. OF ROOMS	150
PARKING	Lot, free
ROOM SERVICE	•
BREAKFAST	Continental
ON-SITE DINING	–
POOL	–
SAUNA	–
EXERCISE FACILITIES	•

Hampton Inn Westchester/Chicago ★★★½
2222 Enterprise Drive
Westchester 60154
☎ 708-409-1000
TOLL FREE ☎ 800-HAMPTON
www.hamptoninn.com

ROOM QUALITY	76
COST ($ = $60)	$$–
LOCATION	Southern Suburbs
NO. OF ROOMS	112
PARKING	Lot, free
ROOM SERVICE	–
BREAKFAST	Full
ON-SITE DINING	–
POOL	–
SAUNA	–
EXERCISE FACILITIES	•

Hard Rock Hotel ★★★★½
230 North Michigan Avenue
Chicago 60601
☎ 312-345-1000
TOLL FREE ☎ 866-966-5166
www.hardrockhotelchicago.com

ROOM QUALITY	92
COST ($ = $60)	$$$$
LOCATION	The Loop
NO. OF ROOMS	381
PARKING	Valet, $38
ROOM SERVICE	•
BREAKFAST	–
ON-SITE DINING	•
POOL	–
SAUNA	–
EXERCISE FACILITIES	•

Hilton Garden Inn Oakbrook Terrace ★★★½
1000 Drury Lane
Oakbrook Terrace 60181
☎ 630-941-1177
TOLL FREE ☎ 877-STAY-HGI
www.hilton.com

ROOM QUALITY	81
COST ($ = $60)	$$$–
LOCATION	Western Suburbs
NO. OF ROOMS	128
PARKING	Garage, free
ROOM SERVICE	•
BREAKFAST	–
ON-SITE DINING	•
POOL	•
SAUNA	–
EXERCISE FACILITIES	•

Hilton O'Hare ★★★½
O'Hare International Airport
Chicago 60666
☎ 773-686-8000
TOLL FREE ☎ 800-HILTONS
www.hilton.com

ROOM QUALITY	81
COST ($ = $60)	$$$–
LOCATION	North Central–O'Hare
NO. OF ROOMS	858
PARKING	Valet, $38
ROOM SERVICE	•
BREAKFAST	–
ON-SITE DINING	•
POOL	•
SAUNA	–
EXERCISE FACILITIES	•

Hilton Suites Downtown ★★★★
198 East Delaware Place
Chicago 60611
☎ 312-664-1100
TOLL FREE ☎ 800-222-TREE
www.hilton.com

ROOM QUALITY	88
COST ($ = $60)	$$$$$$$
LOCATION	Near North Side
NO. OF ROOMS	345
PARKING	Valet, $40
ROOM SERVICE	•
BREAKFAST	–
ON-SITE DINING	•
POOL	•
SAUNA	–
EXERCISE FACILITIES	•

Hotel Information Chart (continued)

Hilton Suites Oakbrook Terrace ★★★★
10 Drury Lane
Oakbrook Terrace 60181
☎ 630-941-0100
TOLL FREE ☎ 800-HILTONS
www.hilton.com

ROOM QUALITY	87
COST ($ = $60)	$$+
LOCATION	Western Suburbs
NO. OF ROOMS	211
PARKING	Lot, free
ROOM SERVICE	•
BREAKFAST	–
ON-SITE DINING	•
POOL	•
SAUNA	–
EXERCISE FACILITIES	•

Holiday Inn Chicago City Center ★★★
300 East Ohio Street
Chicago 60611
☎ 312-787-6100
TOLL FREE ☎ 800-HOLIDAY
www.chicc.com

ROOM QUALITY	72
COST ($ = $60)	$$$$
LOCATION	Near North Side
NO. OF ROOMS	500
PARKING	Self, $30
ROOM SERVICE	•
BREAKFAST	–
ON-SITE DINING	•
POOL	•
SAUNA	•
EXERCISE FACILITIES	•

Holiday Inn Elk Grove Village ★★★½
1000 Busse Road
Elk Grove Village 60007
☎ 847-434-1142
TOLL FREE ☎ 800-972-2494
www.ichotelsgroup.com

ROOM QUALITY	82
COST ($ = $60)	$$–
LOCATION	Northern Suburbs
NO. OF ROOMS	160
PARKING	Lot, free
ROOM SERVICE	•
BREAKFAST	–
ON-SITE DINING	•
POOL	•
SAUNA	•
EXERCISE FACILITIES	•

Holiday Inn North Shore ★★★½
5300 West Touhy Avenue
Skokie 60077
☎ 847-679-8900
TOLL FREE ☎ 888-221-1298
www.holiday-inn.com

ROOM QUALITY	78
COST ($ = $60)	$$+
LOCATION	Northern Suburbs
NO. OF ROOMS	244
PARKING	Lot, free
ROOM SERVICE	•
BREAKFAST	–
ON-SITE DINING	•
POOL	•
SAUNA	•
EXERCISE FACILITIES	•

Holiday Inn Oakbrook Terrace ★★★
17 West 350 22nd Street
Oakbrook Terrace 60181
☎ 630-833-3600
TOLL FREE ☎ 800-325-3535
www.ichotelsgroup.com

ROOM QUALITY	74
COST ($ = $60)	$$–
LOCATION	Western Suburbs
NO. OF ROOMS	222
PARKING	Lot, free
ROOM SERVICE	•
BREAKFAST	–
ON-SITE DINING	•
POOL	•
SAUNA	–
EXERCISE FACILITIES	•

Holiday Inn Select O'Hare ★★★½
10233 West Higgins Road
Rosemont 60018
☎ 847-954-8600
TOLL FREE ☎ 800-HOLIDAY
www.holiday-inn.com

ROOM QUALITY	82
COST ($ = $60)	$$
LOCATION	North Central–O'Hare
NO. OF ROOMS	366
PARKING	Lot, free
ROOM SERVICE	•
BREAKFAST	–
ON-SITE DINING	•
POOL	•
SAUNA	•
EXERCISE FACILITIES	•

Hotel Inter-Continental Chicago ★★★★½
505 North Michigan Avenue
Chicago 60611
☎ 312-944-4100
TOLL FREE ☎ 800-628-2112
www.intercontinental.com

ROOM QUALITY	92
COST ($ = $60)	$$$$$$
LOCATION	Near North Side
NO. OF ROOMS	879
PARKING	Valet, $41
ROOM SERVICE	•
BREAKFAST	–
ON-SITE DINING	•
POOL	•
SAUNA	•
EXERCISE FACILITIES	•

Hotel Monaco ★★★★½
225 North Wabash Avenue
Chicago 60601
☎ 312-960-8500
TOLL FREE ☎ 866-610-0081
www.monaco-chicago.com

ROOM QUALITY	92
COST ($ = $60)	$$$+
LOCATION	The Loop
NO. OF ROOMS	192
PARKING	Valet, $36
ROOM SERVICE	•
BREAKFAST	–
ON-SITE DINING	•
POOL	–
SAUNA	–
EXERCISE FACILITIES	•

House of Blues Hotel ★★★★
333 North Dearborn
Chicago 60610
☎ 312-245-0333
TOLL FREE ☎ 877-569-3742
www.houseofblueshotel.com

ROOM QUALITY	88
COST ($ = $60)	$$$$$$
LOCATION	Near North Side
NO. OF ROOMS	367
PARKING	Valet, $34
ROOM SERVICE	•
BREAKFAST	–
ON-SITE DINING	•
POOL	–
SAUNA	–
EXERCISE FACILITIES	•

Holiday Inn Express Downers Grove ★★★
3031 Finley Road
Downers Grove 60515
☎ 630-810-9500
TOLL FREE ☎ 800-HOLIDAY
www.ichotelsgroup.com

ROOM QUALITY	72
COST ($ = $60)	$$–
LOCATION	Western Suburbs
NO. OF ROOMS	133
PARKING	Lot, free
ROOM SERVICE	–
BREAKFAST	Continental
ON-SITE DINING	–
POOL	–
SAUNA	–
EXERCISE FACILITIES	–

Holiday Inn Express O'Hare ★★★½
6600 North Mannheim Road
Rosemont 60018
☎ 847-544-7500
TOLL FREE ☎ 800-972-2494
www.ichotelsgroup.com

ROOM QUALITY	80
COST ($ = $60)	$$
LOCATION	North Central–O'Hare
NO. OF ROOMS	305
PARKING	Self, $14
ROOM SERVICE	•
BREAKFAST	Full
ON-SITE DINING	–
POOL	•
SAUNA	–
EXERCISE FACILITIES	•

Holiday Inn Mart Plaza ★★★½
350 North Orleans Street
Chicago 60654
☎ 312-836-5000
TOLL FREE ☎ 800-HOLIDAY
www.ichotelsgroup.com

ROOM QUALITY	78
COST ($ = $60)	$$$+
LOCATION	Near North Side
NO. OF ROOMS	521
PARKING	Self, $25; valet, $35
ROOM SERVICE	•
BREAKFAST	–
ON-SITE DINING	–
POOL	•
SAUNA	•
EXERCISE FACILITIES	•

Hotel Allegro ★★★★
171 West Randolph Street
Chicago 60601
☎ 312-236-0123
TOLL FREE ☎ 866-672-6143
www.allegrochicago.com

ROOM QUALITY	89
COST ($ = $60)	$$$–
LOCATION	The Loop
NO. OF ROOMS	483
PARKING	Self, $16–$25; valet $36
ROOM SERVICE	•
BREAKFAST	–
ON-SITE DINING	•
POOL	–
SAUNA	–
EXERCISE FACILITIES	•

Hotel Burnham ★★★★½
1 West Washington Street
Chicago 60602
☎ 312-782-1111
TOLL FREE ☎ 866-690-1986
www.burnhamhotel.com

ROOM QUALITY	92
COST ($ = $60)	$$$$–
LOCATION	The Loop
NO. OF ROOMS	122
PARKING	Valet, $35
ROOM SERVICE	•
BREAKFAST	–
ON-SITE DINING	•
POOL	–
SAUNA	–
EXERCISE FACILITIES	•

Hotel Indigo ★★★★
1244 North Dearborn Parkway
Chicago 60610
☎ 312-787-4980
TOLL FREE ☎ 866-521-6950
www.goldcoastchicagohotel.com

ROOM QUALITY	88
COST ($ = $60)	$$$+
LOCATION	Near North Side
NO. OF ROOMS	167
PARKING	Self and valet, $35
ROOM SERVICE	–
BREAKFAST	–
ON-SITE DINING	•
POOL	–
SAUNA	–
EXERCISE FACILITIES	•

Howard Johnson ★★½
720 North La Salle Street
Chicago 60610
☎ 312-664-8100
TOLL FREE ☎ 800-446-4656
www.hojo.com

ROOM QUALITY	64
COST ($ = $60)	$$+
LOCATION	Near North Side
NO. OF ROOMS	71
PARKING	Lot, free
ROOM SERVICE	–
BREAKFAST	–
ON-SITE DINING	•
POOL	–
SAUNA	–
EXERCISE FACILITIES	–

Hyatt Regency Chicago in Illinois Center ★★★★
151 East Wacker Drive
Chicago 60601
☎ 312-565-1234
TOLL FREE ☎ 800-233-1234
www.hyatt.com

ROOM QUALITY	89
COST ($ = $60)	$$$$+
LOCATION	The Loop
NO. OF ROOMS	2,019
PARKING	Valet, $41
ROOM SERVICE	•
BREAKFAST	–
ON-SITE DINING	•
POOL	–
SAUNA	–
EXERCISE FACILITIES	•

Hyatt Regency McCormick Place ★★★★
2233 Martin Luther King Drive
Chicago 60616
☎ 312-567-1234
TOLL FREE ☎ 800-233-1234
www.hyatt.com

ROOM QUALITY	86
COST ($ = $60)	$$$
LOCATION	South Loop
NO. OF ROOMS	800
PARKING	Self, $24; valet, $29
ROOM SERVICE	•
BREAKFAST	–
ON-SITE DINING	•
POOL	•
SAUNA	•
EXERCISE FACILITIES	•

Hotel Information Chart (continued)

Hyatt Regency O'Hare
★★★★
9300 West Bryn Mawr Avenue
Chicago 60018
☎ 847-696-1234
TOLL FREE ☎ 800-233-1234
www.ohare.hyatt.com

ROOM QUALITY	83
COST ($ = $60)	$$$+
LOCATION	North Central–O'Hare
NO. OF ROOMS	1,099
PARKING	Self, $17; valet, $28
ROOM SERVICE	•
BREAKFAST	—
ON-SITE DINING	•
POOL	•
SAUNA	—
EXERCISE FACILITIES	•

Hyatt Rosemont ★★★★
6350 North River Road
Rosemont 60018
☎ 847-518-1234
TOLL FREE ☎ 800-233-1234
www.rosemont.hyatt.com

ROOM QUALITY	83
COST ($ = $60)	$$–
LOCATION	North Central–O'Hare
NO. OF ROOMS	204
PARKING	Garage, free
ROOM SERVICE	•
BREAKFAST	—
ON-SITE DINING	•
POOL	—
SAUNA	—
EXERCISE FACILITIES	•

James ★★★★½
55 East Ontario
Chicago 60611
☎ 312-337-1000
TOLL FREE ☎ 877-526-3755
www.jameshotels.com

ROOM QUALITY	95
COST ($ = $60)	$$$$$$+
LOCATION	Near North Side
NO. OF ROOMS	297
PARKING	Self, $32; valet, $42
ROOM SERVICE	•
BREAKFAST	—
ON-SITE DINING	•
POOL	•
SAUNA	•
EXERCISE FACILITIES	•

Marriott O'Hare ★★★½
8535 West Higgins Road
Chicago 60631
☎ 773-693-4444
TOLL FREE ☎ 800-228-9290
www.marriott.com

ROOM QUALITY	82
COST ($ = $60)	$$–
LOCATION	North Central–O'Hare
NO. OF ROOMS	681
PARKING	Self, $20; valet, $25
ROOM SERVICE	—
BREAKFAST	—
ON-SITE DINING	•
POOL	•
SAUNA	•
EXERCISE FACILITIES	•

Marriott Oak Brook
★★★½
1401 West 22nd Street
Oak Brook 60523
☎ 630-573-8555
TOLL FREE ☎ 800-228-9290
www.marriott.com

ROOM QUALITY	79
COST ($ = $60)	$$
LOCATION	Western Suburbs
NO. OF ROOMS	347
PARKING	Lot, free
ROOM SERVICE	
BREAKFAST	Pastries
ON-SITE DINING	•
POOL	•
SAUNA	—
EXERCISE FACILITIES	•

Marriott Residence Inn Downtown ★★★★
201 East Walton Place
Chicago 60611
☎ 312-943-9800
TOLL FREE ☎ 800-331-3131
www.marriott.com

ROOM QUALITY	83
COST ($ = $60)	$$$
LOCATION	Near North Side
NO. OF ROOMS	221
PARKING	Valet, $38
ROOM SERVICE	•
BREAKFAST	Buffet
ON-SITE DINING	—
POOL	—
SAUNA	—
EXERCISE FACILITIES	•

Motel 6 O'Hare East ★★★
9408 West Lawrence Avenue
Schiller Park 60176
☎ 847-671-4282
TOLL FREE ☎ 800-4-MOTEL6
www.motel6.com

ROOM QUALITY	67
COST ($ = $60)	$
LOCATION	North Central–O'Hare
NO. OF ROOMS	143
PARKING	Lot, free
ROOM SERVICE	—
BREAKFAST	—
ON-SITE DINING	—
POOL	—
SAUNA	—
EXERCISE FACILITIES	—

North Shore Skokie Hotel
★★★★
9599 Skokie Boulevard
Chicago 60077
☎ 847-679-7000
www.skokieillinoishotel.com

ROOM QUALITY	84
COST ($ = $60)	$$$–
LOCATION	Northern Suburbs
NO. OF ROOMS	367
PARKING	Lot, free
ROOM SERVICE	•
BREAKFAST	—
ON-SITE DINING	•
POOL	•
SAUNA	—
EXERCISE FACILITIES	•

Omni Chicago Hotel
★★★★½
676 North Michigan Avenue
Chicago 60611
☎ 312-944-6664
TOLL FREE ☎ 800-843-6664
www.omnihotels.com

ROOM QUALITY	91
COST ($ = $60)	$$$$$$$
LOCATION	Near North Side
NO. OF ROOMS	347
PARKING	Valet, $40
ROOM SERVICE	•
BREAKFAST	—
ON-SITE DINING	•
POOL	•
SAUNA	—
EXERCISE FACILITIES	•

La Quinta Inn Oakbrook Terrace ★★★
1 South 666 Midwest Road
Oakbrook Terrace 60181
☎ 630-495-4600
TOLL FREE ☎ 800-531-5900
www.lq.com

ROOM QUALITY	69
COST ($ = $60)	$+
LOCATION	Western Suburbs
NO. OF ROOMS	152
PARKING	Lot, free
ROOM SERVICE	–
BREAKFAST	Continental
ON-SITE DINING	–
POOL	•
SAUNA	–
EXERCISE FACILITIES	•

Marriott Chicago Downtown ★★★★
540 North Michigan Avenue
Chicago 60611
☎ 312-836-0100
TOLL FREE ☎ 800-228-9290
www.marriott.com

ROOM QUALITY	85
COST ($ = $60)	$$$$$
LOCATION	Near North Side
NO. OF ROOMS	1,192
PARKING	Self, $26; valet, $35
ROOM SERVICE	–
BREAKFAST	–
ON-SITE DINING	•
POOL	•
SAUNA	•
EXERCISE FACILITIES	•

Marriott Fairfield Inn & Suites Downtown ★★★
216 East Ontario Street
Chicago 60611
☎ 312-787-3777
TOLL FREE ☎ 800-228-2800
www.marriott.com

ROOM QUALITY	73
COST ($ = $60)	$$+
LOCATION	Near North Side
NO. OF ROOMS	185
PARKING	Valet, $38
ROOM SERVICE	–
BREAKFAST	Continental
ON-SITE DINING	–
POOL	–
SAUNA	–
EXERCISE FACILITIES	•

Marriott Suites Downers Grove ★★★★
1500 Opus Place
Downers Grove 60515
☎ 630-852-1500
TOLL FREE ☎ 800-228-9290
www.marriott.com

ROOM QUALITY	87
COST ($ = $60)	$$
LOCATION	Western Suburbs
NO. OF ROOMS	254
PARKING	Lot, free
ROOM SERVICE	–
BREAKFAST	–
ON-SITE DINING	•
POOL	•
SAUNA	•
EXERCISE FACILITIES	•

Marriott Suites O'Hare ★★★★
6155 North River Road
Chicago 60018
☎ 847-696-4400
TOLL FREE ☎ 800-228-9290
www.marriott.com

ROOM QUALITY	88
COST ($ = $60)	$$
LOCATION	North Central–O'Hare
NO. OF ROOMS	256
PARKING	Self, $18
ROOM SERVICE	–
BREAKFAST	–
ON-SITE DINING	•
POOL	•
SAUNA	•
EXERCISE FACILITIES	•

Millennium Knickerbocker Hotel ★★★½
163 East Walton Place
Chicago 60611
☎ 312-751-8100
TOLL FREE ☎ 866-866- 8086
www.milleniumhotels.com

ROOM QUALITY	81
COST ($ = $60)	$$$$+
LOCATION	Near North Side
NO. OF ROOMS	305
PARKING	Valet, $39
ROOM SERVICE	•
BREAKFAST	–
ON-SITE DINING	•
POOL	–
SAUNA	–
EXERCISE FACILITIES	•

Orrington Hotel Evanston ★★★★
1710 Orrington Avenue
Evanston 60201
☎ 847-866-8700
TOLL FREE ☎ 888-677-4648
www.hotelorrington.com

ROOM QUALITY	89
COST ($ = $60)	$$$$–
LOCATION	Northern Suburbs
NO. OF ROOMS	269
PARKING	Valet, $20
ROOM SERVICE	•
BREAKFAST	–
ON-SITE DINING	•
POOL	–
SAUNA	•
EXERCISE FACILITIES	•

Palmer House Hilton ★★★★
17 East Monroe Street
Chicago 60603
☎ 312-726-7500
TOLL FREE ☎ 800-HILTONS
www.hilton.com

ROOM QUALITY	87
COST ($ = $60)	$$$$+
LOCATION	The Loop
NO. OF ROOMS	1,544
PARKING	Self, $30; valet, $38
ROOM SERVICE	•
BREAKFAST	–
ON-SITE DINING	•
POOL	•
SAUNA	–
EXERCISE FACILITIES	•

Park Hyatt Chicago ★★★★★
800 North Michigan Avenue
Chicago 60611
☎ 312-335-1234
TOLL FREE ☎ 800-233-1234
www.hyatt.com

ROOM QUALITY	97
COST ($ = $60)	$$$$$$$$+
LOCATION	Near North Side
NO. OF ROOMS	202
PARKING	Valet, $39
ROOM SERVICE	•
BREAKFAST	–
ON-SITE DINING	•
POOL	•
SAUNA	–
EXERCISE FACILITIES	•

Hotel Information Chart (continued)

Peninsula ★★★★★
108 East Superior Street
Chicago 60611
☎ 312-337-2888
TOLL FREE ☎ 866-288-8889
www.peninsula.com

ROOM QUALITY	99
COST ($ = $60)	$$$$$$$$
LOCATION	Near North Side
NO. OF ROOMS	339
PARKING	Valet, $26
ROOM SERVICE	•
BREAKFAST	—
ON-SITE DINING	•
POOL	•
SAUNA	—
EXERCISE FACILITIES	•

Purple Hotel ★★★
4500 West Touhy Avenue
Lincolnwood 60712
☎ 847-677-1234
TOLL FREE ☎ 800-272-6232
www.purplehotel.com

ROOM QUALITY	71
COST ($ = $60)	$$–
LOCATION	Northern Suburbs
NO. OF ROOMS	293
PARKING	Lot, free
ROOM SERVICE	•
BREAKFAST	•
ON-SITE DINING	•
POOL	•
SAUNA	•
EXERCISE FACILITIES	•

Quality Inn O'Hare ★★★
3801 North Mannheim Road
Schiller Park 60176
☎ 847-678-0670
TOLL FREE ☎ 877-424-6423
www.choicehotels.com

ROOM QUALITY	70
COST ($ = $60)	$+
LOCATION	North Central–O'Hare
NO. OF ROOMS	144
PARKING	Lot, free
ROOM SERVICE	•
BREAKFAST	Continental
ON-SITE DINING	•
POOL	•
SAUNA	—
EXERCISE FACILITIES	•

Red Roof Inn Downers Grove ★★★
1113 Butterfield Road
Downers Grove 60515
☎ 630-963-4205
TOLL FREE ☎ 800-RED-ROOF
www.redroof.com

ROOM QUALITY	70
COST ($ = $60)	$
LOCATION	Western Suburbs
NO. OF ROOMS	135
PARKING	Lot, free
ROOM SERVICE	—
BREAKFAST	—
ON-SITE DINING	—
POOL	—
SAUNA	—
EXERCISE FACILITIES	—

Red Roof Inn Downtown ★★★
162 East Ontario Street
Chicago 60611
☎ 312-787-3580
TOLL FREE ☎ 800-RED-ROOF
www.redroof.com

ROOM QUALITY	69
COST ($ = $60)	$$
LOCATION	Near North Side
NO. OF ROOMS	195
PARKING	Off site $26-$31
ROOM SERVICE	—
BREAKFAST	—
ON-SITE DINING	•
POOL	—
SAUNA	—
EXERCISE FACILITIES	—

Renaissance Chicago Hotel ★★★★½
1 West Wacker Drive
Chicago 60601
☎ 312-372-7200
TOLL FREE ☎ 800-228-9290
www.marriott.com

ROOM QUALITY	92
COST ($ = $60)	$$$$$$$
LOCATION	The Loop
NO. OF ROOMS	553
PARKING	Self and valet, $39
ROOM SERVICE	•
BREAKFAST	•
ON-SITE DINING	•
POOL	•
SAUNA	•
EXERCISE FACILITIES	•

Seneca ★★★½
200 East Chestnut Street
Chicago 60611
☎ 312-787-8900
TOLL FREE ☎ 800-800-6261
www.senecahotel.com

ROOM QUALITY	81
COST ($ = $60)	$$$$
LOCATION	Near North Side
NO. OF ROOMS	268
PARKING	Valet, $38–$40
ROOM SERVICE	—
BREAKFAST	—
ON-SITE DINING	•
POOL	—
SAUNA	—
EXERCISE FACILITIES	•

Sheraton Chicago Hotel & Towers ★★★★½
301 East North Water Street
Chicago 60611
☎ 312-464-1000
TOLL FREE ☎ 877-242-2558
www.sheratonchicago.com

ROOM QUALITY	90
COST ($ = $60)	$$$$+
LOCATION	Near North Side
NO. OF ROOMS	1,209
PARKING	Self, $16–$25; valet $26–$35
ROOM SERVICE	•
BREAKFAST	—
ON-SITE DINING	•
POOL	•
SAUNA	•
EXERCISE FACILITIES	•

Sheraton Gateway Suites O'Hare ★★★★
6501 North Mannheim Road
Rosemont 60018
☎ 847-699-6300
TOLL FREE ☎ 800-325-3535
www.sheraton.com

ROOM QUALITY	89
COST ($ = $60)	$$$–
LOCATION	North Central–O'Hare
NO. OF ROOMS	297
PARKING	Self, $12
ROOM SERVICE	•
BREAKFAST	—
ON-SITE DINING	•
POOL	•
SAUNA	•
EXERCISE FACILITIES	•

Radisson Hotel & Suites Chicago ★★★½
160 East Huron Street
Chicago 60611
☎ 312-787-2900
TOLL FREE ☎ 800-333-3333
www.radisson.com

ROOM QUALITY	80
COST ($ = $60)	$$$$–
LOCATION	Near North Side
NO. OF ROOMS	350
PARKING	Valet, $39
ROOM SERVICE	•
BREAKFAST	–
ON-SITE DINING	•
POOL	•
SAUNA	–
EXERCISE FACILITIES	•

Radisson O'Hare ★★★★
1450 East Touhy Avenue
Des Plaines 60018
☎ 847-296-8866
TOLL FREE ☎ 800-333-3333
www.radisson.com

ROOM QUALITY	83
COST ($ = $60)	$$–
LOCATION	North Central–O'Hare
NO. OF ROOMS	246
PARKING	Lot, free
ROOM SERVICE	•
BREAKFAST	–
ON-SITE DINING	•
POOL	•
SAUNA	–
EXERCISE FACILITIES	•

Raffaello ★★★★★
201 East Delaware Place
Chicago 60611
☎ 312-601-8610
TOLL FREE ☎ 800-983-7870
www.raffaellochicago.com

ROOM QUALITY	97
COST ($ = $60)	$$$$+
LOCATION	Near North Side
NO. OF ROOMS	174
PARKING	Valet, $41
ROOM SERVICE	•
BREAKFAST	–
ON-SITE DINING	•
POOL	•
SAUNA	–
EXERCISE FACILITIES	•

Renaissance Oak Brook Hotel ★★★★
2100 Spring Road
Oak Brook 60523
☎ 630-573-2800
TOLL FREE ☎ 800-228-9290
www.renaissancehotels.com

ROOM QUALITY	86
COST ($ = $60)	$$
LOCATION	Western Suburbs
NO. OF ROOMS	168
PARKING	Self, free; valet, $5
ROOM SERVICE	–
BREAKFAST	–
ON-SITE DINING	•
POOL	•
SAUNA	–
EXERCISE FACILITIES	•

Residence Inn by Marriott O'Hare ★★★★
7101 Chestnut Street
Rosemont 60018
☎ 847-375-9000
TOLL FREE ☎ 800-331-3131
www.marriott.com

ROOM QUALITY	88
COST ($ = $60)	$$$
LOCATION	North Central–O'Hare
NO. OF ROOMS	192
PARKING	Lot, free
ROOM SERVICE	–
BREAKFAST	Buffet
ON-SITE DINING	•
POOL	•
SAUNA	–
EXERCISE FACILITIES	•

Ritz-Carlton Chicago ★★★★½
160 East Pearson Street
Chicago 60611
☎ 312-266-1000
TOLL FREE ☎ 800-621-6906
www.fourseasons.com

ROOM QUALITY	92
COST ($ = $60)	$$$$$$$$
LOCATION	Near North Side
NO. OF ROOMS	435
PARKING	Self, $25; valet, $36
ROOM SERVICE	•
BREAKFAST	–
ON-SITE DINING	•
POOL	•
SAUNA	•
EXERCISE FACILITIES	•

Sleep Inn Midway Airport ★★½
6650 South Cicero Avenue
Bedford Park 60638
☎ 708-594-0001
TOLL FREE ☎ 877-424-6423
www.choicehotels.com

ROOM QUALITY	64
COST ($ = $60)	$$$–
LOCATION	Southern Suburbs
NO. OF ROOMS	120
PARKING	Lot, free
ROOM SERVICE	–
BREAKFAST	Continental
ON-SITE DINING	–
POOL	–
SAUNA	–
EXERCISE FACILITIES	•

Sofitel Chicago O'Hare ★★★★
5550 North River Road
Rosemont 60018
☎ 847-678-4488
TOLL FREE ☎ 800-763-4835
www.sofitel.com

ROOM QUALITY	85
COST ($ = $60)	$$$$–
LOCATION	North Central–O'Hare
NO. OF ROOMS	300
PARKING	Self, $18; valet, $28
ROOM SERVICE	•
BREAKFAST	–
ON-SITE DINING	•
POOL	•
SAUNA	•
EXERCISE FACILITIES	•

Sofitel Water Tower ★★★★
20 East Chestnut Street
Chicago 60611
☎ 312-324-4000
TOLL FREE ☎ 800-763-4835
www.sofitel.com

ROOM QUALITY	89
COST ($ = $60)	$$$$+
LOCATION	Near North Side
NO. OF ROOMS	415
PARKING	Valet, $39
ROOM SERVICE	•
BREAKFAST	–
ON-SITE DINING	•
POOL	–
SAUNA	–
EXERCISE FACILITIES	•

Hotel Information Chart (continued)

Solis Chicago Hotel & Spa ★★★★
71 East Wacker Drive
Chicago 60601
☎ 312-346-7100
TOLL FREE ☎ 800-621-4005
www.solischicago.com

ROOM QUALITY	89
COST ($ = $60)	$$$$$$–
LOCATION	The Loop
NO. OF ROOMS	454
PARKING	Valet, $39
ROOM SERVICE	•
BREAKFAST	–
ON-SITE DINING	•
POOL	–
SAUNA	–
EXERCISE FACILITIES	•

Sutton Place Hotel ★★★★
21 East Bellevue Place
Chicago 60611
☎ 312-266-2100
TOLL FREE ☎ 800-606-8188
www.suttonplace.com

ROOM QUALITY	85
COST ($ = $60)	$$$$$$–
LOCATION	Near North Side
NO. OF ROOMS	246
PARKING	Valet, $29–$39
ROOM SERVICE	•
BREAKFAST	–
ON-SITE DINING	•
POOL	–
SAUNA	–
EXERCISE FACILITIES	•

Swissotel Chicago ★★★★
323 East Wacker Drive
Chicago 60601
☎ 312-565-0565
TOLL FREE ☎ 800-637-9477
www.swissotelchicago.com

ROOM QUALITY	86
COST ($ = $60)	$$$$$$$$
LOCATION	The Loop
NO. OF ROOMS	632
PARKING	Valet, $41
ROOM SERVICE	•
BREAKFAST	–
ON-SITE DINING	•
POOL	•
SAUNA	• (fee)
EXERCISE FACILITIES	• (fee)

W City Center Hotel ★★★★½
172 West Adams Street
Chicago 60603
☎ 312-332-1200
TOLL FREE ☎ 888-625-5144
www.whotels.com

ROOM QUALITY	92
COST ($ = $60)	$$$$$$$$$$
LOCATION	The Loop
NO. OF ROOMS	369
PARKING	Valet, $38
ROOM SERVICE	•
BREAKFAST	–
ON-SITE DINING	•
POOL	–
SAUNA	–
EXERCISE FACILITIES	•

W Lakeshore ★★★★½
644 North Lakeshore Drive
Chicago 60611
☎ 312-943-9200
TOLL FREE ☎ 888-625-5144
www.starwoodhotels.com

ROOM QUALITY	93
COST ($ = $60)	$$$$$$+
LOCATION	Near North Side
NO. OF ROOMS	520
PARKING	Valet, $41
ROOM SERVICE	•
BREAKFAST	–
ON-SITE DINING	•
POOL	•
SAUNA	–
EXERCISE FACILITIES	•

Westin Hotel O'Hare ★★★★
6100 River Road
Rosemont 60018
☎ 847-698-6000
TOLL FREE ☎ 800-228-3000
www.westinohare.com

ROOM QUALITY	86
COST ($ = $60)	$$+
LOCATION	North Central–O'Hare
NO. OF ROOMS	525
PARKING	Self, $18; valet, $27
ROOM SERVICE	•
BREAKFAST	–
ON-SITE DINING	•
POOL	•
SAUNA	•
EXERCISE FACILITIES	•

Willows Hotel ★★★
555 West Surf Street
Chicago 60657
☎ 773-528-8400
TOLL FREE ☎ 800-787-3108
www.cityinns.com

ROOM QUALITY	73
COST ($ = $60)	$$$–
LOCATION	North Side
NO. OF ROOMS	55
PARKING	Self, $22
ROOM SERVICE	–
BREAKFAST	Continental
ON-SITE DINING	–
POOL	–
SAUNA	–
EXERCISE FACILITIES	–

Wyndham Chicago ★★★★
633 North St. Clair Street
Chicago 60611
☎ 312-573-0300
TOLL FREE ☎ 800-WYNDHAM
www.wyndham.com

ROOM QUALITY	87
COST ($ = $60)	$$$$$$$
LOCATION	Near North Side
NO. OF ROOMS	417
PARKING	Valet, $39
ROOM SERVICE	•
BREAKFAST	–
ON-SITE DINING	•
POOL	•
SAUNA	•
EXERCISE FACILITIES	•

Wyndham Drake Hotel Oak Brook ★★★½
2301 York Road
Oak Brook 60523
☎ 630-574-5700
TOLL FREE ☎ 800-996-3426
www.wyndham.com

ROOM QUALITY	80
COST ($ = $60)	$$$
LOCATION	Southern Suburbs
NO. OF ROOMS	160
PARKING	Self and valet, free
ROOM SERVICE	•
BREAKFAST	Continental
ON-SITE DINING	•
POOL	•
SAUNA	–
EXERCISE FACILITIES	•

Talbott Hotel ★★★★
20 East Delaware Place
Chicago 60611
☎ 312-944-4970
TOLL FREE ☎ 800-TALBOTT
www.talbotthotel.com

ROOM QUALITY	85
COST ($ = $60)	$$$+
LOCATION	Near North Side
NO. OF ROOMS	149
PARKING	Valet, $32
ROOM SERVICE	•
BREAKFAST	–
ON-SITE DINING	•
POOL	–
SAUNA	–
EXERCISE FACILITIES	•

Travelodge Chicago O'Hare ★★½
3003 Mannheim Road
Des Plaines 60018
☎ 847-296-5541
TOLL FREE ☎ 800-578-7878
www.travelodge.com

ROOM QUALITY	58
COST ($ = $60)	$+
LOCATION	North Central–O'Hare
NO. OF ROOMS	94
PARKING	Lot, free
ROOM SERVICE	–
BREAKFAST	Continental
ON-SITE DINING	–
POOL	•
SAUNA	–
EXERCISE FACILITIES	–

Travelodge Downtown ★★½
65 East Harrison Street
Chicago 60605
☎ 312-427-8000
TOLL FREE ☎ 800-578-7878
www.travelodge.com

ROOM QUALITY	60
COST ($ = $60)	$$+
LOCATION	South Loop
NO. OF ROOMS	250
PARKING	Self, $20–$26
ROOM SERVICE	•
BREAKFAST	–
ON-SITE DINING	•
POOL	–
SAUNA	–
EXERCISE FACILITIES	–

Westin Michigan Avenue ★★★★½
909 North Michigan Avenue
Chicago 60611
☎ 312-943-7200
TOLL FREE ☎ 800-228-3000
www.westinmichiganave.com

ROOM QUALITY	91
COST ($ = $60)	$$$$$+
LOCATION	Near North Side
NO. OF ROOMS	774
PARKING	Valet, $38
ROOM SERVICE	•
BREAKFAST	–
ON-SITE DINING	•
POOL	–
SAUNA	–
EXERCISE FACILITIES	•

Westin River North Chicago ★★★★½
320 North Dearborn Street
Chicago 60610
☎ 312-744-1900
TOLL FREE ☎ 800-WESTIN-1
www.westinchicago.com

ROOM QUALITY	95
COST ($ = $60)	$$$$$
LOCATION	Near North Side
NO. OF ROOMS	424
PARKING	Valet, $36–$45
ROOM SERVICE	•
BREAKFAST	–
ON-SITE DINING	•
POOL	–
SAUNA	–
EXERCISE FACILITIES	•

Whitehall Hotel ★★★★
105 East Delaware Place
Chicago 60611
☎ 312-944-6300
TOLL FREE ☎ 800-948-4255
www.thewhitehallhotel.com

ROOM QUALITY	84
COST ($ = $60)	$$$$$+
LOCATION	Near North Side
NO. OF ROOMS	221
PARKING	Valet, $34–$50
ROOM SERVICE	•
BREAKFAST	–
ON-SITE DINING	•
POOL	–
SAUNA	•
EXERCISE FACILITIES	•

Wyndham Garden Hotel O'Hare ★★★
8201 West Higgins Road
Chicago 60631
☎ 773-693-2323
TOLL FREE ☎ 877-999-3223
www.wyndham.com

ROOM QUALITY	74
COST ($ = $60)	$$
LOCATION	North Central–O'Hare
NO. OF ROOMS	122
PARKING	Lot, free
ROOM SERVICE	•
BREAKFAST	–
ON-SITE DINING	•
POOL	•
SAUNA	•
EXERCISE FACILITIES	•

Wyndham O'Hare ★★★½
6810 North Mannheim Road
Rosemont 60018
☎ 847-297-1234
TOLL FREE ☎ 800-333-3333
www.wyndham.com

ROOM QUALITY	79
COST ($ = $60)	$$$
LOCATION	North Central–O'Hare
NO. OF ROOMS	467
PARKING	Self, $14
ROOM SERVICE	•
BREAKFAST	Continental and buffet
ON-SITE DINING	•
POOL	•
SAUNA	•
EXERCISE FACILITIES	•

PART FOUR

VISITING *on* BUSINESS

CONVENTION CENTRAL, U.S.A.

CHICAGO, THE HEART OF THE MIDWEST and the third-largest city in the United States, attracts more than 7 million overnight pleasure visitors a year. Tourists from all over the world come to enjoy the city's fabled attractions, take in the legendary skyline and enjoy the endless summer season's free lakefront festivals. Summer is short in Chicago, but the summer spirit is long.

The **Shedd Aquarium** and the **Museum of Science and Industry,** Chicago's most popular fee-charging attractions, drew 1.8 million visitors each in 2005, and the **Taste of Chicago** attracts 3.6 million outdoor fun-seekers annually around the Fourth of July weekend. **Navy Pier** is Chicago's top attraction with a mind-boggling 8.6 million visitors in 2005.

Yet not everyone visiting Chicago arrives with a tourist agenda. Because of its central location, Chicago bills itself as the Convention Capital of the World, hosting more top trade shows than any other city in the country. In 2005 Chicago attracted a record 13.78 million business travelers. There are 7,000 restaurants and 67,000 hotel rooms to accommodate nearly 5 million tradeshow and convention visitors annually.

The Windy City also boasts an unparalleled location to house all those exhibitions: **McCormick Place Convention Center,** the largest convention hall in North America. Located on the shores of Lake Michigan a mile or so south of downtown, McCormick Place is a sprawling 27-acre venue with 2.2 million square feet of exhibit space, a 4,000-seat theater, and ceilings up to 50 feet high. A $987 million expansion of McCormick Place included the construction of the 840,000-square-foot South Building (near the intersection of the Stevenson Expressway and Lake Shore Drive), a glass-enclosed Grand Concourse linking the three buildings that make up the convention center, a five-acre landscaped park, and renovations to existing facilities.

In 2007, the newest addition to McCormick Place will open—the West Building, which will add about 470,000 square feet of exhibit space and 250,000 square feet of meeting space (including a 100,000-square-foot ballroom).

OTHER BUSINESS VISITORS

IN ADDITION TO CONVENTIONEERS and trade-show attendees who are bound for McCormick Place or another convention hall, other people come to conduct business at the city's wide array of manufacturing and financial firms (many of which are located in Chicago's suburbs). In addition to Chicago's four major financial exchanges (**Chicago Mercantile Exchange, Chicago Stock Exchange, Chicago Board of Trade,** and **Chicago Board Options Exchange**), the Windy City is also home to many blue-chip public companies, including Sears, Amoco, Motorola, Allstate, Sara Lee, and Caterpillar.

The city's large number of higher learning institutions (including the **University of Chicago, Northwestern University,** the **University of Illinois at Chicago, DePaul University,** the **Illinois Institute of Technology,** and **Loyola University**) attract a lot of visiting academics, college administrators, and students and their families.

HOW THE *UNOFFICIAL GUIDE* CAN HELP

IN MANY WAYS, THE PROBLEMS facing business visitors and conventioneers on their first trip to Chicago don't differ much from the problems of tourists intent on seeing Chicago's best-known attractions. Business visitors need to locate a convenient hotel, want to avoid the worst of the city's traffic, face the same problems of navigating a huge city, must figure out the public transportation system, and want to pinpoint Chicago's best restaurants. This book can help.

For the most part, though, business visitors aren't nearly as flexible about the timing of their visit as people who pick Chicago as a vacation destination. While we advise that the best times for visiting the city are spring and fall, the necessities of business may dictate that you pull into the Windy City in hot and humid August—or even worse, January, a month when cold temperatures and stiff winds off Lake Michigan often create double-digit negative windchill readings.

Yet much of the advice and information presented in the *Unofficial Guide* is as valuable to business visitors as it is to tourists. As for our recommendations on seeing the city's many sights . . . who knows? Maybe you'll be able to squeeze a morning or an afternoon out of your busy schedule, grab this book, and spend a few hours exploring some of the attractions that draw more than 6 million tourists each year.

CONVENTION OVERLOAD

BUSINESS VISITORS HAVE A HUGE IMPACT ON CHICAGO when, say, 70,000 exhibitors and trade-show attendees come into town and snatch up literally every hotel room within a 100-mile radius of the Loop.

Calendar of Conventions and Special Events

DATE	EVENT	LOCATION	ATTENDANCE
2007			
Mar 8–10	Big Ten Conference—Men's Basketball Tournament	United Center	Public
Mar 11–13	Int'l. Home & Housewares Show	McCormick	60,000
Mar 16–18	Big Ten Conference—NCAA Men's Basketball Championship First & Second Rounds	United Center	Public
Apr 17–20	Coverings, The Ultimate Tile & Stone Experience	McCormick South	30,000
Apr 27–30	Chicago Antiques Fair	Merchandise Mart	Public
May 1–Nov 30	Farmer's Market	Daley Center Plaza	400,000
May 6–8	Food Marketing Institute	McCormick North	35,000
May 6–8	9th Spring Fancy Food Show	McCormick North	20,000
May 19–22	National Restaurant Assoc.	McCormick South	75,000
Jun 1–3	Chicago Gospel Festival	Millennium Park	175,000
Jun 1–5	American Society of Clinical Oncology	McCormick	30,000
Jun 7–10	Chicago Blues Festival	Grant Park	175,000
Jun 11–13	NeoCon—World's Trade Fair 2007	Merchandise Mart	58,000
Jun 15–17	U.S. Volleyball Assoc.—ASICS Junior Nat'l. Volleyball Championships	McCormick North	40,000
Jun 19–21	NXTcomm 2007	McCormick	20,000
Jun 29–Jul 8	Taste of Chicago	Grant Park	175,000
Jun 30–Jul 1	Chicago Country Music Festival	Grant Park	175,000
Jul 14–15	Mayor's Cup Youth Soccer Tournament	Grant Park	175,000
Jul 17–Aug 28	Chicago Outdoor Film Festival	Grant Park	500,000
Jul 22–25	Chicago Market: Living & Giving	Merchandise Mart	21,000
Jul 28–29	Venetian Night	Grant Park	175,000
Jul 28–Aug 1	Institute of Food Technologists	McCormick South	25,000
Aug 18–19	Chicago Air & Water Show	Grant Park	175,000
Aug 25–26	Viva! Chicago Latin Music Festival	Grant Park	175,000
Aug 30–Sep 2	Chicago Jazz Festival	Grant Park	175,000
Sep 9–12	GRAPH EXPO PackPrint	McCormick South	31,000
Sep 15–16	Celtic Fest Chicago	Grant Park	175,000
Oct 5–6	LaSalle Bank Chicago Marathon Health & Fitness Expo	McCormick North	Public
Oct 7	LaSalle Bank Chicago Marathon	Grant Park	33,000

DATE	EVENT	LOCATION	ATTENDANCE
2007			
Oct 12–31	Halloween Pumpkin Plaza	Daley Center Plaza	175,000
Oct 20	Halloween Happenings	Daley Center Plaza	175,000
Oct 24–27	Worldwide Food Expo	McCormick	33,500
Nov 7–10	Nat'l. Assoc. for Education of Young	McCormick	32,000
Nov 11–14	FABTECH International	McCormick	35,000
Nov 22–Dec 24	Daley Plaza Santa's House	Daley Center Plaza	600,000
Nov 23	Holiday Tree Lighting Ceremony	Daley Center Plaza	175,000
Nov 25–30	RSNA - Scientific Assembly	McCormick	60,000
Dec 28–30	Holiday Sports Festival	McCormick South	175,000
Dec 31	New Year's Eve Fireworks	Grant Park	175,000
2008			
Jan 16–20	Chicago Boat, RV & Outdoors Show	McCormick North	Public
Jan 26–29	Chicago Gift & Home Market	Merchandise Mart	25,000
Feb 1–10	Chicago Auto Show	Lakeside Center at McCormick	Public
Feb 22–24	Chicago Dental Society	McCormick West	30,000
Mar 16–18	Int'l. Home & Housewares Show	McCormick	59,000
Mar 29–31	American College of Cardiology	McCormick South	28,000
Apr 11–13	Kitchen/Bath Industry Show	McCormick South	60,000
May 31–Jun 3	American Society of Clinical Oncology	McCormick	33,000
Jun 9–11	NeoCon—World's Trade Fair	Merchandise Mart	40,000
Jun 10–12	SUPERCOMM 2008	McCormick South	22,000
Jul 16–20	Nat'l. Sports Collectors Convention	Donald E. Stephens Convention Center	Public
Sep 8–13	Int'l. Manufacturing Technology Show	McCormick	92,000
Sep 23–25	Motivation Show	McCormick	20,000
Oct 5–7	Nat'l. Assoc. of Convenience Stores	McCormick	35,000
Oct 12	LaSalle Bank Chicago Marathon	Grant Park	40,000
Oct 26–29	GRAPH EXPO	McCormick South	40,000
Nov 9–13	PACK EXPO Int'l. 2008	McCormick	75,000
Nov 30–Dec 5	RSNA—Scientific Assembly	McCormick	60,000
2009			
Jan 12-15	Material Handling Industry of America	McCormick South	42,000
Jan 26–28	Int'l. AHR Expo	McCormick South	60,000

Finding a place to sleep can be nearly impossible when all the radiologists in the United States converge on Chicago for their national convention.

The good news: The large trade shows register no discernible effect on the availability of cabs and restaurant tables, or on traffic congestion; it seems that only hotel rooms and rental cars become scarce when a big convention hits town. Consult our Calendar of Conventions and Special Events on page 68 when planning your trip to Chicago.

McCORMICK PLACE CONVENTION CENTER

IT'S BIG . . .

THE LARGEST EXHIBITION AND MEETING FACILITY in North America is Chicago's **McCormick Place** (2301 South Lake Shore Drive; ☎ 312-791-7000; fax 312-791-6543; **www.mccormickplace.com**). With 2.2 million square feet of exposition space (1.3 million on one level), 345,000 square feet of meeting, banquet, and ballroom space, as well as three theaters (including the 4,249-seat **Arie Crown Theater**), McCormick Place is the 800-pound gorilla of Chicago convention venues.

The original McCormick Place was the brainchild of Col. Robert R. McCormick, a former owner of the *Chicago Tribune*. It opened in 1960 and enjoyed seven years of success before being destroyed by fire in 1967. A more comprehensive structure (**Lakeside Center**) replaced it in 1971 and, along with the **North Building** (added in 1986) and the **South Building** (completed in 1996), compose today's McCormick Place.

. . . AND IT HAS ITS DRAWBACKS

MCCORMICK PLACE IS HUGE, and its drawbacks are varied. The convention center's location on Lake Michigan destroys any vestiges of an open, uncluttered Chicago lakefront; a formidable tangle of ramps and viaducts connects the Stevenson Expressway (I-55) to Lake Shore Drive. For weary conventioneers looking for a respite from crowded exhibition halls, there is nothing—repeat, nothing—within walking distance of the huge complex that can provide distractions—with the possible exception of a stroll along the bike path that follows the shoreline of placid Lake Michigan.

As one spokesman for the giant hall once commented, McCormick Place is "totally business oriented. There is no lounge area in the lobby. There aren't even any clocks in this place. The reason this place is popular with exhibitors is once a guy is here, he's stuck." Though we spotted a few clocks in Lakeside Center, the rest of the statement remains essentially true: the closest hotels and restaurants (with the exception of eating places inside the center) are a $5 cab ride away. Even the food court in the South Building offers relatively few dining options—and with $7 hamburgers and $3 fries, it's overpriced.

mccormick place convention center

Soldier Field Lot

Burnham Park Lot

Lake Michigan

North Building

Lakeside Center

Michigan Ave.

Indiana Ave.

Prairie Ave.

Cermak Rd.

M. L. King Lot

23rd St.

Cottage Grove

South Building

McCormick Place Underground Garage

24th Pl.

55

Stevenson Expwy.

25th St.

26th St.

MLK Jr. Drive

McCormick Place 31st Street Lot

Lake Shore Dr.

41

31st St.

THE LAYOUT

MCCORMICK PLACE'S THREE SEPARATE CONVENTION venues—
Lakeside Center, the North Building, and the South Building—are connected by the Grand Concourse, which serves as a unified entrance to
McCormick Place and a link between the three. The spectacular 100-
foot-high, 900-foot-long pedestrian walkway includes visitor lobbies, a
business center, cafes, coffee shops, specialty shops, and fountains. The
glass-enclosed multilevel concourse also crosses Lake Shore Drive to
provide a seamless connection with the Lakeside Center and allows the
South and North buildings' exhibit halls to be combined for a total of
1.3 million square feet of exhibition space on one level.

Finding Your Way

Exhibit halls are named by consecutive letters. The South Building
contains exhibit hall A; the North Building houses exhibit halls B
(level 3) and C (level 1); and the Lakeside Center contains exhibit
halls D (level 3), E (level 2), and F (level 1). Sometimes halls may be
divided, for example: D1 and D2.

All meeting-room numbers begin with either E, N, or S and stand
for Lakeside Center (formerly the East Building), North Building,
and South Building. The next numeral (1, 2, 3, or 4) indicates the
level, and the last two digits specify the exact room. To avoid confu-
sion, no room numbers are duplicated among the three buildings.
Rooms 1 through 25 are located in the South Building, 26 through 49
are in the North Building, and 50 through 75 are found in the Lakeside Center. Some meeting rooms with divider walls can create
several smaller meeting rooms; these will have an "a," "b," "c," or
"d" suffix following the number. Thus, meeting room N126b is
located on the first level of the North Building, room 26.

Lakeside Center

Located east of South Lake Shore Drive on the shores of Lake Michigan,
the Lakeside Center (formerly the East Building) has a business center,
cafe/bar, and gift shop. It's about to operate independently of the rest of
McCormick Place, separating smaller and midsized events from the huge
shows taking place in the North and South buildings across Lake Shore
Drive. The building contains more than a half-million square feet of exhibit areas and a 2,100-space underground parking garage.

Level 2, the lobby and mezzanine level, features the 283,000-square-
foot **Hall E1,** the building's second-largest major exhibit area (which has
its own loading docks). Also located on this level is the **Arie Crown Theater,** a site for major entertainment productions, corporate meetings,
and convention keynote addresses; it's the largest theater in Chicago.

The 75,000-square-foot lobby on Level 2 accommodates registration
and includes private show management offices and a press facility. The
McCormick Place Business Center (☎ 312-791-6400; fax 312-791-6501) offers a wide array of services, including faxing, photocopying, equipment

rentals, shipping, secretarial services, office supplies, foreign currency exchange on show management request, and more. There's also an additional 10,000 square feet of meeting rooms on this level.

Level 3 contains a 45,000-square-foot **Grand Ballroom and Lobby** that's divisible into two 22,500-square-foot rooms. Hall D, with a north-south divider wall, can be divided into two 150,000-square-foot exhibition spaces for midsized shows. Two meeting rooms add another 58,000 square feet of space. The Grand Concourse connects Lakeside Center with the North and South buildings across Lake Shore Drive. Loading docks are located at the north end of the building.

Level 1 offers **Hall F1,** a 60,000-square-foot room for extra exhibits, meetings, or registration; restaurants; two meeting rooms totaling nearly 5,000 square feet; and a coffee shop. Also located on this level are the McCormick Place administrative offices and an office of the **Chicago Convention and Tourism Bureau.** Level 4, the small upper level, contains three meeting rooms totaling 35,000 square feet.

The North Building

The North Building boasts 188,000 square feet of exhibit space, additional escalators, a business center, and a gift shop. Level 1, the lower level, contains **Hall C1,** a 148,500-square-foot exhibition space that can be used independently or in conjunction with the larger upper level hall; and **Hall C2,** a 61,000-square-foot extension area that can be used for additional exhibit space or crate storage. The lower-level lobby has dedicated taxi space and areas for bus loading/unloading, 15 meeting rooms, and direct access to 4,000 outside parking spaces.

Level 3, the upper level, contains **Hall B1,** a 369,000-square-foot exhibition hall with an adjoining 127,000 square feet of space (**Hall B2**) that can be used for exhibits or crate storage; both halls can be combined with exhibition space in the South Building for a total of 1.3 million square feet of space on one level. A suspended-roof design provides virtually column-free exhibition space and allows for clear ceiling heights of up to 40 feet. Loading docks are located at the north end of the building. The Grand Concourse connects the North Building with the South Building and the Lakeside Center.

Level 2, the mezzanine level, provides easy access to both the upper- and lower-level exhibition halls, as well as eight meeting rooms, two restaurants, and service areas. Over 50,000 square feet of lobby space is available for registration. Level 4 has two meeting rooms totaling 14,555 square feet.

The South Building

The South Building provides 840,000 square feet of exhibition space and 45 meeting rooms totaling another 170,000 square feet. It also boasts the 22,000-square-foot Vista Room and the 33,000-square-foot **Grand Ballroom.** Behind the scenes, the building has 170,000 square feet of indoor crate storage and full in-floor utilities. The South Building has 65 concealed truck docks and a special ramp for oversized exhibits. The weather-protected west entrance faces five-acre McCormick Square, featuring lighted 75-foot pylons, fountains, and landscaping.

Level 3 contains **Hall A1** and **Hall A2,** which, when combined, total 840,000 square feet. Loading docks are located on the east and south ends of the building. Across the Grand Concourse is Level 3 of the North Building and another half-million square feet of exhibition space.

Level 1 features the main entrance and lobby, the Grand Ballroom, and six meeting rooms; Level 2.5 contains a food court, a restaurant, a business center, a first-aid station, access to Metra commuter trains, and retail stores; Level 4 has five meeting rooms totaling about 24,000 square feet and the two-story, 22,000-square-foot **Vista Room;** Level 5 contains five meeting rooms with nearly 19,000 square feet of space.

PARKING AT McCORMICK PLACE

OUR ADVICE TO CHICAGO VISITORS is the same whether you're vacationing or attending a convention at McCormick Place: Don't drive. Not only is the traffic congestion of epic proportions, but finding a place to put your car is equally frustrating—and expensive. While McCormick Place has 6,000 adjacent parking spaces and an underground parking garage ($12 a day for private cars), save yourself the expense and bother of fighting the traffic and leave the car at home.

In fact, so many people fly into Chicago for conventions that McCormick Place officials claim parking is a major problem (read: nearly impossible) only during large public shows that attract local residents. Example: The world's largest car show, held at McCormick Place each February, draws 1.1 million auto buffs.

EXHIBITOR MOVE-IN AND MOVE-OUT

THOUGH IT'S EXPENSIVE, WE RECOMMEND shipping your display as opposed to hauling it yourself. McCormick Place is not really set up to accommodate smaller exhibitors who want to bring in their own displays. If you elect to move yourself in and out, the easiest way is to arrive at McCormick Place in a cab. If you have too much stuff to fit in a cab, you can try to fight your way into one of the tunnels servicing the loading docks. (Access to the 65 loading docks serving the South Building should be easier—they're above ground and accessible from Martin Luther King Jr. Drive.) Because move-in and set-up usually take place over two- to three-day periods, getting in is less of a problem than getting out (when everyone wants to leave at the same time). In any event, be prepared to drag your exhibit a long way. Try to pack everything into cases with wheels or bring along some sort of handcart or dolly.

GETTING TO AND FROM McCORMICK PLACE

LARGE CONVENTIONS PROVIDE BUS SHUTTLE SERVICE from major downtown hotels to McCormick Place. On weekends, the shuttle service operates pretty smoothly. On weekdays, however, when the buses must contend with Chicago traffic, schedules break down and meeting attendees must wait a long time. To compound the problem, neither police nor convention authorities seem able to control the taxi cabs that constantly block the buses from getting to their convention center loading zones. The predictable result of this transportation anarchy is gridlock. If you depend on shuttle buses or cabs, prepare for long queues. Give yourself an hour to get to McCormick Place in the morning and two hours to get back to your hotel at night. If you want to take a cab to an outside restaurant for lunch, go before noon or after 1:30 p.m.

A preferable option to shuttle buses and cabs is to take the commuter train, accessible from the Grand Concourse. Each train can accommodate several thousand conventioneers at once. At most shows, we recommend using the shuttle buses in the morning to go to the convention center and returning in the evening by train. To commute to downtown hotels from McCormick Place, take the northbound train three stops to the Randolph Station at the end of the line. You will emerge from the station in the Loop area, a reasonably safe part of Chicago just south of the Chicago River. From here you can take a cab or walk to most downtown hotels in about 15 minutes. On weekdays, the trains run frequently enough that you don't really need to consult a schedule. On weekends, however, the trains run up to 45 minutes apart.

In 2002 a dedicated busway was created that allows charter buses to bypass local traffic on an exclusive two-lane 2.5-mile roadway. This decreases travel times and subsequently busing costs, for transporting attendees between their hotels and the convention center. The free busway runs from Randolph Street (downtown) to 25th Street at Martin Luther King Jr. Drive, parallel to Michigan Avenue. Entrance and exits are on Lower Randolph, just east of Columbus, and just south of McCormick Place at 25th Street. For a map and more information, visit **www.choosechicago.con/meeting/busway.**

GETTING TO AND FROM THE AIRPORT

Airport Express (☎ 888-284-3826) offers van service to and from McCormick Place and O'Hare and Midway airports. The vans depart from the main entrance at the new Grand Concourse. The fare to O'Hare is $25 one-way; the ride to Midway is $27.

Cab fare to O'Hare is about $30, and $35 to Midway; actual fares vary depending on traffic conditions and don't include a tip. However, the cost will be the same regardless of the number of passengers.

LUNCH ALTERNATIVES AT McCORMICK PLACE

EATING AT MCCORMICK PLACE IS A REAL HASSLE. There are too few food-service vendors for the size of the facility, and even fewer table areas where you can sit and eat your hard-won victuals. Almost without exception, you must wait in one queue to obtain your food and in another to pay for it.

If you are an exhibitor, a small cooler should be an integral part of your booth. Ice frozen in a gallon milk jug lasts for days to keep drinks cold. Both exhibitors and nonexhibitors should eat breakfast before going to the show. After breakfast, but before you catch your shuttle, stop at one of the many downtown delis and pick up a sandwich, chips, fruit, and some drinks for lunch as well as for snacking throughout the day. If you want to leave campus for lunch, get in the cab queue before 11:30 a.m. or after 1:30 p.m. Getting back to McCormick Place by cab after lunch will not be a problem. For a rundown on the best restaurants for a quiet business lunch, see Part Eight, Dining and Restaurants (page 177).

NAVY PIER

IN THE SUMMER OF 1995, NAVY PIER, a Chicago landmark jutting out nearly a mile into Lake Michigan, was reopened after a $200-million face-lift. (The pier first opened in 1916.) Today, it's a year-round tourist attraction and convention center for exhibitions, meetings, and special events. **Festival Hall,** located near the east end of the pier, contains 170,000 square feet of exhibit space and 65,000 square feet of meeting rooms designed for small- and medium-sized shows. The hall is surrounded by dining spots, cruise boats, a 150-foot Ferris wheel, a shopping mall, and a drop-dead view of Chicago's skyline.

Unlike visitors to McCormick Place, conventioneers and trade-show attendees at Festival Hall have access to 13,000 hotel rooms located within a few blocks, enclosed parking for 1,900 cars (which still isn't enough; we recommend either walking, public transportation, or cabs to reach Festival Hall), and on-the-pier restaurants and catering providing choices ranging from fast food to elegant dining with skyline and waterfront views. Plus, Chicago's best hotels, shopping, and restaurants are only a few blocks away. Navy Pier is literally within walking distance of the Magnificent Mile and the Loop. For more information on Navy Pier, see its profile in Part Seven, Sightseeing, Tours, and Attractions (page 169).

NAVY PIER CONVENTION FACILITIES

FESTIVAL HALL FEATURES MORE THAN 170,000 square feet of exhibit space divisible into two areas of 113,000 square feet (**Hall A**) and 56,000 square feet (**Hall B**). Taking maximum advantage of the pier's lakefront setting, the halls boast ceiling heights of up to 60 feet (30 feet minimum) and a full range of electrical and telecommunication amenities for exhibitors' needs.

The main halls are located on the second level; small exhibitors can carry or roll show material from the public parking area on the first level. Loading docks are located on the second (main hall) level at the west end of Festival Hall. The ramp to the loading docks is reached from the drive along the north side of Navy Pier.

Meeting rooms divisible into as many as 36 separate areas total more than 48,000 square feet and are located on a mezzanine overlooking the exhibition floor and on the exhibition level. The 18,000-square-foot **Grand Ballroom,** featuring an 80-foot domed ceiling and panoramic water views, continues to serve banquet, performance, and special exhibit functions as it has since the pier first opened in 1916.

DONALD E. STEPHENS CONVENTION CENTER

LOCATED NORTHWEST OF DOWNTOWN CHICAGO and five minutes from O'Hare International Airport, the **Donald E. Stephens Convention Center** (5555 N. River Road, Rosemont; ☎ 847-692-2220; fax 847-696-9700; **www.rosemont.com**) is an exhibition venue offering convenience for fly-in exhibitors and trade-show attendees—but not much else. Unfortunately, the location on the far fringe of Chicago's suburbs is strictly nowheresville in terms of easy access to the attractions, restaurants, nightlife, and ethnic diversity that make the Windy City a world-class travel destination.

Stephens is, however, a clean, modern facility offering 840,000 square feet of flexible convention space that can accommodate a continuous 250,000-square-foot space containing up to 1,150 booths. A 5,000-space parking garage and more than 3,000 nearby hotel rooms (in the **Sofitel Chicago** and **Hyatt Regency O'Hare**) are connected by a 7,000-linear-foot enclosed pedestrian Skybridge Network. Heated in the winter and air-conditioned in the summer, it's very nice when the weather is nasty outside and you want to get to your car or one of the nearby hotels.

Stephens handles a wide variety of both public and trade shows, ranging from the Chicago Midwest Bicycle Show (trade) to public ski shows. The center's six halls feature ceiling heights ranging from 16 to 26 feet and five drive-in freight doors. The conference center offers an additional 52,000 square feet of floor space in 34 meeting rooms located on two levels.

Other hotels close to Stephens include the **Westin Hotel O'Hare** (525 rooms), **Ramada Plaza Hotel O'Hare** (723 rooms), **Holiday Inn O'Hare International** (507 rooms), and **Sheraton Gateway Suites O'Hare** (325 suites). For places to eat that rise above standard hotel dining rooms, see Part Eight, Dining and Restaurants (page 177).

Getting to downtown Chicago from Stephens takes about 20 minutes by car (except during rush hours) and about 45 minutes by train. To drive, take I-90 (the Kennedy Expressway) east. You can board the CTA O'Hare Line train to downtown at either O'Hare or River Road in Rosemont (which has parking).

PART FIVE

ARRIVING *and* GETTING ORIENTED

COMING *into* CHICAGO *by* CAR

ONE WORD OF ADVICE: RELAX.

The major north–south route into Chicago is **Interstate 90/94** (better known as the **Dan Ryan Expressway** south of downtown and the **Kennedy Expressway** to the north). Make sure your camera is nearby. Each expressway has magnificent views of the downtown skyline, and you'll have ample time to take a snapshot. These expressways are usually backed up—the Dan Ryan is in the midst of a two-year construction project, the largest road rehabilitation in the city's history. People are cryin' on the Ryan, and we aren't lyin'.

South of the city, I-90/94 links with **I-80,** a major east–west route that connects Chicago to South Bend, Indiana; Toledo and Cleveland, Ohio; and New York City to the east and Davenport and Des Moines, Iowa; Omaha, Nebraska; and other points to the west. I-90/94 also joins I-57, which continues south through Illinois to Kankakee, Champaign, and eventually Memphis, Tennessee, on a historic migratory path

North of downtown, I-90/94 changes names to become the Kennedy Expressway; it veers northwest toward O'Hare International Airport before splitting. I-90 (now called the **Northwest Tollway**) continues northwest past the airport to Madison, Wisconsin, where it meets I-94. Got it?

The **Stevenson Expressway** (I-55) enters Chicago near McCormick Place from the southwest; this interstate begins in New Orleans and goes north through Memphis and

unofficial **TIP**
The Dan Ryan Expressway is the Chicago area's busiest and most accident-plagued highway. About 320,000 vehicles travel it every day. Interstate 90/94, which runs roughly north to south through Chicago (paralleling Lake Michigan), features express lanes (without exits) and local lanes (with exits). All in all, it's a helter-skelter system guaranteed to exasperate first-time visitors.

St. Louis before crossing I-80 and passing Midway Airport to its terminus in the city at Lake Shore Drive. From the west, the **Eisenhower Expressway** (I-290) comes into the Loop from **I-88** (the East–West Tollway) and De Kalb.

West of the city limits, two highways run north and south through Chicago's suburbs to link the major roads coming into Chicago from the south, west, and north; the highways serve as "beltways" in otherwise beltway-less Chicago. **I-294** (the Tri-State Tollway) starts at I-80 south of the city and crosses the Stevenson Expressway, the Eisenhower Expressway, and the Kennedy Expressway near O'Hare. North of Chicago it merges with I-94 en route to Milwaukee.

A few miles west of I-294, the newer **US 355** (the North–South Tollway) connects I-55 and I-88 to I-290 west of O'Hare; I-290 goes north to I-90, the Northwest Tollway that links Madison and Chicago.

US 41, a popular route also known as the **Edens Expressway,** links I-90/94 on Chicago's North Side (north of the Chicago River) with the densely populated northern suburbs of Skokie and Highland Park before merging with I-94 south of the Wisconsin state line. As if all this isn't goofy enough, the Edens Expressway is named after William G. Edens, a local banker—who never drove a car. Farther south into the city, US 41 becomes **Lake Shore Drive,** which follows Lake Michigan south past downtown and into Indiana.

unofficial **TIP**
Don't discount US 41 South as an option when the Dan Ryan Expressway is backed up.

COMING *into* CHICAGO *by* PLANE

OVER THE PAST COUPLE OF YEARS, the title of world's busiest airport has gone back and forth between **O'Hare International Airport** and Hartsfield-Jackson Atlanta International Airport. These statistical flip-flops are easier to take than the holding pattern you can experience in the air at O'Hare, which in 2005 handled 76 million people— 11 million of them international visitors. The airport is 17 miles northwest of downtown Chicago. That means there are usually enough travelers on hand to turn the huge facility into its own city when lousy weather snarls air traffic and strands travelers by the thousands.

Yet O'Hare isn't the only game in town. **Midway Airport,** a long 15 miles southwest of downtown, handles about one-tenth the passenger traffic of its big brother to the north, making it a more hassle-free point of arrival and departure for many visitors to Chicago.

O'HARE INTERNATIONAL AIRPORT

OPENED IN 1955 AND NAMED FOR Congressional Medal of Honor winner Edward O'Hare, a Navy pilot killed in the Battle of Midway, this

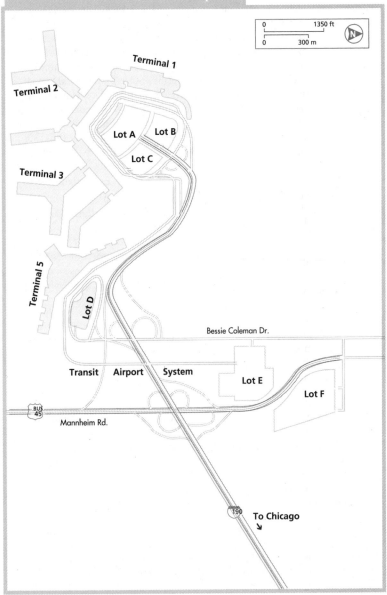

o'hare international airport

sprawling airport includes four terminals connected by passenger walkways, moving sidewalks, and a "people mover," an automated transit system that covers 2.7 miles of airport property. Statistics at O'Hare are impressive. For decades, it has been the commercial-aviation capital of the world, providing service to all 50 states and many foreign countries. The mammoth airport alternates with its Atlanta rival for the greater number of passengers and flights served (in 2005 O'Hare handled 970,000 flights, Hartsfield-Jackson about 980,197). Nearly 200,000 passengers pass through O'Hare each day, and an average of 100 aircraft arrive or depart each hour. Covering 7,700 acres, the airport regularly serves about 60 commercial, commuter, and cargo airlines.

The airport is connected to Chicago's subway system—albeit a long walk—and is close to I-90 (the Kennedy Expressway), which goes downtown to the Loop. Although O'Hare is renowned for its holding patterns in the air, on the ground it boasts a modern international terminal, is easy to get around, and is still growing. More than $700 million in improvements (including new runways and a new Terminal 6) are planned over the next few years.

The Layout

The "core" of O'Hare contains Terminals 1, 2, and 3, where most domestic flights come and go. Terminal 2 lies in the center of the horseshoe-shaped arrangement and faces the O'Hare Hilton, a parking garage, and parking lots. Don't look for Terminal 4—there is none. Terminal 5 handles international flights. Located south of the core, it is reached via the Airport Transit System (or "people mover"). In the three main terminals, the second-floor departure level features fast-food eateries, bars, shops, newsstands, and a "restaurant rotunda" between Terminals 2 and 3. From the gate, arriving passengers follow signs to the baggage-claim area on the lower level.

The People Mover

If you need to get from, say, Terminal 1 to Terminal 3 or your destination is the long-term parking area, take the "people mover" train. Escalators and elevators in front of the ticket counters take you over the roadway, where departing passengers are dropped off. The people mover is free, and a train comes every few minutes.

unofficial **TIP**
If you've got some time to kill before your flight, explore the people mover. This mini-El of a transportation system is fun to ride, and you'll be treated to some nice views of the airfield.

Getting Downtown

CABS AND SHUTTLES Visitors who fly into Chicago have to make a choice when it comes to getting downtown. If your final destination is a major hotel near the Loop or the Magnificent Mile (which is where most of them are), **Airport Express** (☎ 888-284-3826) is the cheapest and easiest way to go—unless you're not schlepping luggage (take the train) or in a group (take a cab). Just inquire at the Airport Express

HANGING OUT AT O'HARE

Unbeknownst even to natives, O'Hare is now a city unto itself. Additions in recent years have included, for example, a satellite of Chicago's landmark **Berghoff Café** on Concourse C in Terminal 1 and **Wolfgang Puck's** in Terminal 3. If you're stuck overnight in O'Hareland, here's a tip: international Terminal 5 has the airport's only 24-hour restaurants. O'Hare orphans can get hot dogs, frozen yogurt, and assorted snacks there. In addition, Terminal 5's food court has cheaper prices and is usually less crowded overall than food courts in other terminals.

The **O'Hare Hilton** hotel is connected to the airport through an underground tunnel and outdoor walkway. The underground passage includes a bookstore, clothing shop, currency exchange, and dentist (with limited hours). The Hilton features a sports-themed restaurant and bar and a basement athletic club with a dry sauna and pool. Even Traveler's Aid will suggest that if you need to freshen up, buy a one-day membership at the club for $10 and take a quick shower there.

If you have time to explore, wander through the hotel lobby, at the west end of which sits the last **Gaslight Club** in America. The Gaslight started in 1953 as a private club on Chicago's Gold Coast. Cofounder Burton Browne set out to re-create a 1920s speakeasy with Dixieland jazz and servers dressed in skimpy flapper outfits. Browne's concept was a prototype for Hugh Hefner's Playboy Clubs. The dimly lit O'Hare Gaslight Club, which opened in 1973, is a separate operation from the Hilton.

desk in the baggage-claim areas of O'Hare or Midway, and ask if the van goes to your hotel. It's also a good idea to ask if your hotel is one of the first or last stops the van makes.

The service operates vans to major downtown hotels from 5:15 a.m. to 11:30 p.m. daily that leave about every 10 to 15 minutes. Ticket counters are in the baggage-claim areas of all four O'Hare terminals. One-way fares are $25; round-trip fares are $46. Figure on a 45-minute ride to your hotel during non–rush hour traffic. Call to make reservations for a pickup from your downtown hotel, or for a guaranteed seat, on the day before you leave; last-minute reservations can be made up to an hour before departure on a space-available basis.

If your hotel isn't served by Airport Express, taxis, buses, hotel vans, and rental-car pickups are located outside the lower-level baggage areas. Cab fares to downtown run about $35 to $40 one-way for the normal travel time of 30 minutes; share-the-ride cabs cost $20 per person for a taxi shared by two to four passengers headed downtown. Allow at least an hour and a half during rush hour, and expect to pay a higher fare for the longer cab ride.

PUBLIC TRANSPORTATION If you're traveling light, the Chicago Transit Authority (CTA) **Blue Line** train terminal is located in front of and beneath Terminal 2 (follow the signs that read "Trains to Downtown"); it's about a 40-minute trip to the Loop that costs $1.75

one-way. Trains leave about every 10 minutes weekdays and about every 15 minutes early evenings and weekends. Unfortunately, there's no place to store luggage on the rapid-transit trains (although one piece of luggage is usually manageable, as many airline employees attest). For more information, call the CTA at ☎ 312-836-7000.

DRIVING If you're renting a car and driving, getting to the Loop is pretty easy. Follow signs out of the airport to I-90 east, which puts you on the Kennedy Expressway; it's a straight 18-mile ride to downtown that takes about a half hour (longer during rush hour; Friday afternoons are the worst). As you approach the city, Chicago's distinctive skyline, anchored by the John Hancock Center on the left and the Sears Tower on the right, comes into view—if it's not raining.

If you're headed for the Loop, move into the right lane as you approach the tunnel (just before the city center) and get ready to exit as you come out of the tunnel. Take the Ohio Street exit to get to the north-downtown area. The last of four exits to downtown is the **Congress Parkway** (where I-290 west, aka the Eisenhower Expressway, meets the Kennedy Expressway) to South Loop; miss it and you're on your way to Indiana. Taking the Congress Parkway exit scoots you through the U.S. Post Office building to the south edge of the Loop; South Michigan Avenue and South Lake Shore Drive lie straight ahead. For more information on getting around Chicago, see Part Six, Getting Around (page 100).

Visitor Services

Twenty-six multilingual information specialists are on hand to provide information and translation assistance to travelers. Five information booths are located throughout the airport on the lower levels of Terminals 1, 2, and 3 and on the lower and upper levels of Terminal 5. The booths are open daily from 8:15 a.m. to 8 p.m. For more information, call the main airport number (☎ 773-686-2200).

The **U.S. Postal Service** operates an office in Terminal 2 on the upper level. Hours are 7 a.m. to 7 p.m. weekdays. Teletext phones for the hearing impaired can be found next to the information booths in the three domestic terminals (lower level) and outside the customs area in the international terminal. More teletext phones are located in phone banks throughout the airport; ☎ 773-601-8333.

Foreign-currency exchanges are located in Terminals 1, 3, and 5. Hours are 8 a.m. to 8 p.m. daily.

A duty-free shop, located in Terminal 5 in the center court on the upper level, offers a wide range of merchandise. Hours vary; the shop frequently stays open later than normal to serve international flights. Satellite shops are also located in Terminal 1 near gate C18 and in Terminal 3 across from gate K11; hours vary according to flight times.

ATMs are located on the upper levels of Terminals 1, 2, and 3 near the concourse entrances (airside) and on the upper and lower levels of Terminal 5.

Lost stuff? For items lost near a ticket counter, in a gate area, or on a plane, contact the airline. For items lost in the public areas of the terminals, contact Chicago Police at ☎ 773-686-2385. For items lost in a food-service location, call ☎ 773-686-6148. Don't lose these numbers.

Kids on the Fly is an exhibit for youngsters operated by the Chicago Children's Museum. Centrally located in Terminal 2 (near the security checkpoint), the 2,205-square-foot interactive playground lets children ages 1 to 12 burn off excess energy as they explore a kid-sized air-traffic-control tower, a ceiling-high model of the Sears Tower, a cargo plane, a luggage station (enjoy the fun of waiting!), and a fantasy helicopter. It's free and open to all visitors during regular flight hours and to ticketed passengers after 10 p.m.

Parking

O'Hare provides more than 12,000 spaces in short- and long-term parking lots and a garage (☎ 773-686-7530; for maps and detailed information, visit **www.ohare.com/ohare/parking**). There's even valet parking; $10 for the first hour, then $32 a day. Short-term parking in the first level of the garage is $3 for the first hour, $21 for the next four hours (and another $21 after that), and finally $50 for 9 to 24 hours. Parking on Levels 2 to 6 of the parking garage and inside lots B and C costs $3 for an hour or less, with a maximum fee of $26 for 24 hours. Rates in short-term Lot D (next to the international terminal) are $3 for an hour or less and $30 for 13 to 24 hours. Long-term parking in the faraway Lot E (served by the "people mover") is $13 per day.

MIDWAY AIRPORT

TUCKED AWAY IN A CLASSIC CHICAGO bungalow community 15 miles southwest of downtown Chicago, this airport is everything O'Hare isn't: small, convenient, and relatively uncongested. If you can get a direct flight into Midway, take it. Why fight the hassles of O'Hare?

The homespun airport was once owned by the Chicago Board of Education. In fact, until 1955 an elementary school was on the property, just 100 yards from an active runway what was then the world's busiest airport.

Southwest Airlines is the most popular carrier at Midway (American and United ended all scheduled service here in 2006). The new terminal at Midway has six concourses. From your gate, follow signs to the baggage area to pick up your luggage. Passenger pick-up and drop-off, taxis, buses, car rental, and the CTA **Orange Line** train station are right outside the door. (The last train out is at 12:55 a.m.) Free shuttles to the long-term economy-parking lot arrive every 15 minutes.

midway airport

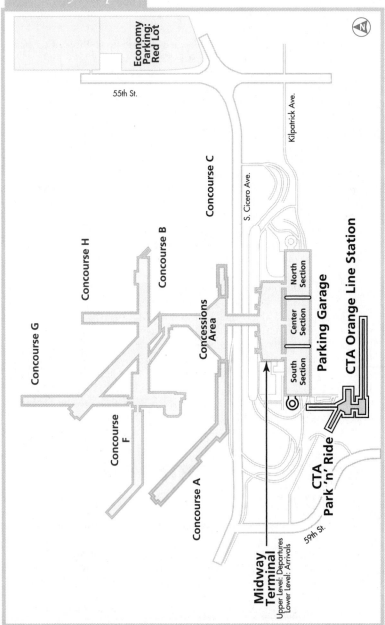

Economy Parking: Red Lot

55th St.

Kilpatrick Ave.

Concourse C

S. Cicero Ave.

Concourse H

Concourse B

Concourse G

Concessions Area

North Section

Center Section

Parking Garage

CTA Orange Line Station

South Section

Concourse F

Concourse A

CTA Park 'n' Ride

59th St.

Midway Terminal
Upper Level: Departures
Lower Level: Arrivals

Cab fares from Midway to downtown run about $40, and the ride does not show the best side of Chicago. It's not dangerous, just ugly. The trip takes between 20 minutes and a half hour (figure on a higher fare during heavy traffic and/or bad weather).

Share-the-ride cabs let you split the trip with up to three other passengers going downtown; the cost is $10 per person.

Airport Express (☎ 888-284-3826) offers van service to and from downtown hotels; the fare is $18 one-way for adults and $8.50 for children under age 12 with an adult. The trip takes about 30 minutes, and vans depart every 15 to 20 minutes. Round-trip fare for adults is $30. For a return reservation, call a day in advance. Last-minute reservations can be made up to an hour before departure as space allows.

CTA's **Orange Line** connects Midway to downtown, and its trains offer plenty of room for luggage. The fare is $1.75 one-way; the ride lasts 35 minutes. Trains run every day from 5 a.m. to 11 p.m. weekdays and Saturdays, and 7:30 a.m. to 11 p.m. Sundays and holidays. Trains run every six to eight minutes during rush hour and every ten minutes the rest of the time. Weekday-morning rush-hour bus service to downtown is via the **#99M Midway Express** (do not take this bus in the evening). Pick it up at the airport's center entrance. The **#62 Archer bus** provides 24-hour service to downtown. Fares are $1.75 for both buses.

If you're renting a car and driving downtown, take South Cicero Avenue north a few miles to I-55 (the Stevenson Expressway) east. The highway ends at Lake Shore Drive and the McCormick Place complex; take Lake Shore Drive north to get downtown or places farther north.

As you bear left onto Lake Shore Drive, you're treated to a great view of the Chicago skyline and Lake Michigan. After passing the Field Museum on the right, turn left onto Balbo Avenue to reach Michigan Avenue, the Loop, and I-290 (the Eisenhower Expressway). Or continue straight along the lake across the Chicago River to reach the Magnificent Mile, Navy Pier, and other points north. From Midway, the 15-mile drive to downtown takes about 20 minutes (longer during rush hour).

COMING *into* CHICAGO *by* TRAIN

CHICAGO'S HISTORIC **Union Station** (210 South Canal, across the Chicago River) is a hub for **Amtrak** rail service and **Metra** commuter trains. Unfortunately, the train station's location makes it rather inconvenient, unless you are connecting to the Chicago suburbs. If you have time, take a close look at this grand old dame. Union Station was built between 1913 and 1925 as a palace commemorating Chicago's hub as a transportation center. Today, the only part of the original station that remains is the so-called Great Hall (the rest was razed and remodeled in 1969). The Great Hall waiting room, which covers a city block, is aglow with a 90-foot-high skylighted ceiling, pink Tennessee-marble floors, and bronze torches. The barreled and vaulted ceiling is said to be patterned after an early Roman bath. This main waiting room harkens back to the golden days of railroading. The only drawback is that napping is difficult on the Great Hall's hard wooden benches.

Union Station is not particularly close to anything such as major hotels or subway stations (the John Hancock Center is a couple of blocks east), and its layout is confusing. Amtrak trains arrive on the concourse level of the station. After picking up your baggage, head for the taxi stand near the north concourse (Adams Street exit). The "El" train is several blocks to the east—too far to walk if you're carrying luggage. The only public-transportation option is the **#151 bus**—also not a good idea if you're lugging a suitcase or two—which you can catch outside Canal Street. The bus goes through the Loop and up North Michigan Avenue. To sum up: if you're not being picked up by someone in a car, a cab is your best option for getting out of Union Station.

GETTING ORIENTED

THE OPERATIVE WORD FOR CHICAGO, the nation's third-largest city, is *big.*

New York City is bigger, Los Angeles more spread out. Chicago is midwestern muscle. Located a third of the way between the East and West coasts, Chicago covers 227 square miles and stretches 33 miles along the southwestern coastline of Lake Michigan (the second largest of the five Great Lakes, after Lake Superior). With a population of just under 3 million—in a metropolitan area of over 6 million—Chicago is not only the largest city in Illinois, it's the de facto economic and cultural capital of the Midwest. (But it's not the capital of the state; that distinction belongs to Springfield, 200 miles south.)

A GEOGRAPHY LESSON

CHICAGO IS IN THE NORTHEAST CORNER OF ILLINOIS, a very large midwestern state bordered by (starting clockwise southeast of the city), Indiana, a bit of Kentucky, Missouri, Iowa, and Wisconsin; Michigan is to the east and north across the lake. Most of the land that surrounds the city is flat—like most of the Midwest—a fact, theorists say, that may explain the city's passion for tall buildings and the easily recognizable skyline.

To the southeast, just past the city line on the southern tip of Lake Michigan, lies the gritty industrial town of **Gary, Indiana** (birthplace of Michael, Janet, and various other Jacksons). North along the lake, the city merges with the comfortable suburban enclave of **Evanston** (home of Northwestern University); farther north, but still within commuting range of Chicago, are **Highland Park** (near where Michael Jordan still keeps a home) and **Waukegan**. The Wisconsin state line lies about 40 miles north of the **Loop,** the heart of downtown Chicago.

The closest major city is **Milwaukee,** a blue-collar beer-drinking town on Lake Michigan, 90 miles to the north. Other midwestern cities arrayed around Chicago are **Detroit** (290 miles to the east), **Indianapolis** (180 miles to the southeast), **St. Louis** (300 miles to the southwest), **Des Moines** (360 miles to the west), and **Minneapolis–St. Paul** (410 miles to the northwest).

CHICAGO'S LAYOUT

River and Lake

The other major geographic feature of Chicago is the narrow **Chicago River,** which meets **Lake Michigan** downtown along the carefully preserved lakefront (which is lined with parks and a wildly popular bike and jogging trail, not factories and wharves). The direction of the river was reversed in 1900. Today it flows away from Lake Michigan downstate to the Illinois River, which connects with the Mississippi River, forming a major shipping route to the Gulf of Mexico. Boat tours on the Chicago offer some of the best views of the city's fabled architecture.

The Loop and Grant Park

Tucked south and east of a bend in the river is the **Loop,** Chicago's downtown core of government buildings, financial and trading institutions, office buildings, hotels, and retail establishments.

A couple of blocks east of the Loop and hugging Lake Michigan is **Grant Park,** a barrier of green where millions of Chicagoans and visitors flock each summer to enjoy outdoor events and music festivals, including concerts at the **Jay Pritzker Pavilion** in the new Millennium Park. Grant Park also provides a campuslike setting for some of the city's largest museums, colorful **Buckingham Fountain,** and many softball fields. The view of the Chicago skyline from the park is spectacular.

Lake Shore Drive

Running north and south through Grant Park and along Lake Michigan is **Lake Shore Drive.** "LSD," as locals call it, opened in 1937 as Leif Erickson Drive, which sounds more like a Minneapolis byway than a Chicago highway. Although the multilane road's high speeds and congestion usually result in a scary driving experience for first-time visitors, a cruise along the highway provides cool vistas of the Chicago skyline, yacht basins, parks full of trees and greenery, beaches, and oceanlike Lake Michigan stretching east to the horizon. (The views at night are even more mind-boggling. In 1971 the nocturnal sights were the subject of a regional pop hit, "Lake Shore Drive," by Alliota, Haynes, and Jeremiah.) Lake Shore Drive is also a major north–south corridor through the city, which is longer than it is wide.

WHAT IS THE LOOP?

You'll see the Loop mentioned a lot in this book. So what exactly is it?

The Loop is what locals call downtown Chicago. It gets its name from the elevated train tracks ("the El") that circle the central business district—the second largest downtown in the United States after Midtown Manhattan.

Over the years, the Loop's definition has expanded beyond the El tracks. Some say the Loop goes as far west as the Chicago River and as far south as Roosevelt Road—an area that only recently has become known as the South Loop. But real Chicagoans know that the real Loop is downtown, surrounded by the El. And that's the scoop on the Loop.

In late 1996 Lake Shore Drive was relocated to the west of the **Field Museum** and **Soldier Field.** In 1997 the old lanes to the east were demolished and transformed into ten acres of new parkland, creating a traffic-free "Museum Campus" for the Field Museum, the **Adler Planetarium,** and the **Shedd Aquarium.** With its paths, bikeways, a pedestrian concourse under Lake Shore Drive that serves as a gateway to the Museum Campus, and extensive landscaping, this new lakefront park provides Chicagoans and visitors with another place to stroll, bike, run, and relax as they take in the views. For drivers, an extensive system of new directional signs was installed.

Near North

North of the Chicago River are two areas popular with out-of-town visitors: the **Magnificent Mile,** a glitzy strip of North Michigan Avenue full of the city's toniest shops and galleries (Oprah Winfrey has an apartment in this neighborhood), and **River North** (one of Chicago's premier nightclub and restaurant districts). Renovated and reopened in 1995 and jutting out into Lake Michigan is **Navy Pier,** featuring amusement rides, a shopping mall, clubs, a theater, restaurants, and convention space. The pier is popular with tourists; locals don't go there except for special events. Farther north are the **Gold Coast,** an enclave of exclusive homes (and a great walking destination), and **Lincoln Park.** Surrounded by a residential neighborhood of young urban professionals and high-rises, the park is the site of the most visited zoo in the United States.

South and West of the Loop

South of the Loop along the lake is the sprawling **McCormick Place,** North America's largest convention venue. Farther south are the **Museum of Science and Industry** and **Hyde Park,** home of the regal **University of Chicago** campus (and more museums). The West Loop is booming, thanks in part to Oprah Winfrey opening **Harpo Studios,** her TV-production house, at 1058 West Washington Boulevard in 1988. In the late 1960s and early 1970s, West Washington was off skid row; today it has several good restaurants and a few boutiques. Move farther west, past such landmarks as the **United Center,** and things get a little iffy. Still, there are some not-to-be-missed attractions west of the Loop, including **Hull-House** (where Nobel Prize winner Jane Addams gave turn-of-the-19th-century immigrants a leg up on the American dream), ethnic restaurants in **Greektown** and **Little Italy,** the beautiful **Garfield Park Conservatory,** and, just west of the city line, **Oak Park** (hometown of famed architect Frank Lloyd Wright and equally famous Nobel-laureate novelist Ernest Hemingway).

Scattered throughout the city to the north, west, and south of downtown are a wide array of urban neighborhoods featuring shops, museums, and dining that honor the ethnic diversity of Chicago; see "Exploring Chicago's Neighborhoods" in Part Seven, Sightseeing, Tours, and Attractions, for descriptions and locations. Beyond the city limits are more attractions worth the drive: the **Brookfield Zoo, Chicago Botanic Garden,** and **Morton Arborteum** are all less than an hour from downtown Chicago (allow more time in rush-hour traffic).

THE MAJOR HIGHWAYS

THE MAJOR INTERSTATE ROUTES TO Chicago's Loop are **I-90/94** (better known to Chicagoans as the **Dan Ryan Expressway** south of downtown and the **Kennedy Expressway** to the north and west), **I-290** (the **Eisenhower Expressway**), and **I-55** (the **Stevenson Expressway,** which ends about a mile south of downtown at McCormick Place).

West of the city, **I-294** (the **Tri-State Tollway**) parallels Lake Michigan through Chicago's suburbs as it heads north and links I-80 (a major transcontinental route south of the city) to I-90 (which goes to Milwaukee). I-294 also skirts **O'Hare International Airport,** where it intersects with I-90 (which links Chicago to Madison, Wisconsin).

A Word about Driving: Don't

With four major interstates converging downtown at or near the Loop, entering the city makes for a very interesting driving experience, especially if it's your first visit to Chicago . . . and it's rush hour.

unofficial **TIP**
Our advice: if you're staying at a downtown hotel, don't drive.

The congestion in America's third-largest city is unrelenting: morning and evening rush-hour traffic reports endlessly list backups, accidents, and delays occurring throughout the metropolitan area. And parking? Forget it. Chicago is notorious for its lack of convenient and affordable places to park.

Whether you're in town for business or pleasure, spare yourself the frustration of battling traffic, lanes that change direction depending on the time of day, and a tangle of highways. Instead, ride Chicago's extensive public-transportation systems, take airport vans to and from downtown hotels, and take advantage of an abundance of taxis to get around town. (For more information on how to negotiate Chicago without a car, see "Public Transportation" in Part Six, Getting Around, page 102.)

FINDING YOUR WAY AROUND CHICAGO

CHICAGO'S SHEER SIZE CAN BE OVERWHELMING, but here's a tip for visitors: the city is a "right angle" town, a characteristic that's invaluable in finding your way around. Except for the rare diagonal street, Chicago is laid out numerically on a grid, with **State and Madison streets** (in the Loop) intersecting at the zero point. This is another reason Chicago is called "The City That Works."

And it works like this: North Side Chicago is north of Madison Street, and South Side is south of it. The West Side, logically enough, is west of State Street. And the East Side? It hardly exists; most of what could be termed "East Side" is Lake Michigan, since State Street is only a few blocks west of the lakefront.

Street numbers run in increments of 100 per block, with eight blocks to the mile. (Folks can spend their spare time figuring distances using street addresses.) Generally speaking, North Side streets and north–south streets on the South Side have names (Michigan Avenue, Erie Street, Chicago Avenue), while east–west streets on the South Side are usually numbered (for example, the popular Museum of Science and Industry is on 57th Street at Lake Shore Drive; Chicago blues legends migrated to East 43rd Street in the 1940s and 1950s).

After you've tried it a few times, navigating Chicago's grid can be fun—at least on weekends, when traffic is relatively light. Locating, say, the **Balzekas Museum of Lithuanian Culture** is a snap. The address, 6500 South Pulaski Road, tells you the museum is at the corner of South Pulaski and 65th Street. It also helps that many (but not all) major avenues traverse the entire city from north to south. Like old friends, names such as Western, Cermak, Halsted, and Clark crop up over and over as you explore the city.

unofficial **TIP**
To stay oriented when exploring Chicago, just remember this: If the street numbers are going up, you're headed away from downtown. If they're going down, you're moving to the center of the city.

WHERE TO FIND TOURIST INFORMATION IN CHICAGO

IF YOU'RE SHORT ON MAPS OR YOU NEED MORE information on sightseeing, hotels, shopping, and other activities in and around Chicago, there are several places to pick up maps and brochures:

- In downtown Chicago, the **Visitor Information Center** in the Randolph Lobby of the Chicago Cultural Center (78 East Washington Street at Michigan Avenue; ☎ 312-744-2400) dispenses literature and advice to tourists. Orientations with videos and displays are provided just off the lobby. Open Monday through Friday, 10 a.m. to 6 p.m.; Saturday, 10 a.m. to 5 p.m.; and Sunday, 11 a.m. to 5 p.m. Closed on major holidays.

- On the Magnificent Mile north of the Loop, the **Chicago Water Works Visitor Center** at Pearson Street and Michigan Avenue (you can't miss it—the tower is one of two structures that survived the Great Fire of 1871) provides tourist information, maps, hotel reservations, and advice. In addition, the center stocks plentiful info on tourist attractions throughout Illinois. Open daily, 7:30 a.m. to 7 p.m.; closed Thanksgiving and Christmas; ☎ 312-744-8783.

- In the Loop, the **Explore Chicago** kiosk inside the Sears on State store (2 North State Street) is open Monday through Saturday, 10 a.m. to 6 p.m.; and Sunday, noon to 5 p.m.

- In suburban Oak Park, visitors interested in touring the former residences of Frank Lloyd Wright and Ernest Hemingway should make their first stop at the **Oak Park Visitors Bureau** (158 Forest Avenue; ☎ 888-OAK-PARK or 708-848-1500). Visitors can park free in the adjacent parking garage on weekends, and can purchase tickets and pick up free maps in the visitor center. Open daily, 10 a.m. to 5 p.m.

THINGS *the* NATIVES *already* KNOW

CHICAGO CUSTOMS AND PROTOCOL

CHICAGOANS HAVE EARNED A WELL-DESERVED reputation for friendliness yet often display a degree of forwardness that can put off foreigners and visitors from more formal parts of our country. (Do ya got a problem with dat?) Sometimes the locals come off as brash or blunt, since many value getting directly to the point: Chicagoans don't have time to waste. In this respect, Chicago can be a Puritan city. And that's mostly good news for tourists, who can count on plenty of help finding a destination when riding a crowded rush-hour bus, for example. The moral is, don't hesitate to ask a native for assistance. Even if he's wearing a Bears sweatshirt—and Bears stocking cap—and Bears warm-up jacket . . .

Eating in Restaurants

By and large, *casual* is the byword when dining in Chicago. Only the most chichi eateries require men to wear a jacket or prohibit ladies from wearing shorts or tank tops. Even swank spots such as the Ritz-Carlton downtown have ceased requiring men to wear ties at dinner. Although people tend to dress up more for dinner downtown, you'll still find plenty of casual restaurants (the ones at Navy Pier, for example). Just about all ethnic restaurants beyond downtown have nonexistent dress codes.

unofficial **TIP**
If you're not sure how to dress before you go out to eat, call ahead—or dress "chic casual": relaxed but put together, not sloppy (no T-shirts or running shoes).

Tipping

Is the tip you normally leave at home appropriate in Chicago? Yes. Just bear in mind that a tip is a reward for efficient service. Here are some guidelines.

PORTERS AND SKYCAPS A dollar a bag, more if the bags are cumbersome.

CAB DRIVERS Almost everything depends on service and courtesy. If the fare is less than $8, give the driver the change and a dollar. Example: if the fare is $4.50, give the cabbie 50 cents and a buck. If the fare is more than $8, give the driver the change and $2. If you ask the cabbie to take you only a block or two, the fare will be small, but you should tip large ($3 to $5) to make up for his or her wait in line and to partially compensate him or her for missing a better-paying fare. Add an extra dollar to your tip if the driver handles a lot of luggage.

PARKING For a valet, $2 is correct if he or she is courteous and demonstrates some hustle. A dollar will do if the service is just okay. Pay only when you check your car out, not when you leave it. Especially around the Gold Coast area, valets have been under scrutiny in recent years.

BELLMEN AND DOORMEN When a bellman greets you at your car with a rolling luggage cart and handles all your bags, $6 is about right. The more luggage you carry yourself, the less you should tip. Add $1 or $2 if the bellman opens your room. For calling a taxi, tip the doorman $1.

WAITERS Whether you eat at a coffee shop, dine at an upscale eatery, or order room service from the hotel kitchen, the standard gratuity hovers around 20% of the tab before sales tax. At buffets or brunches where your serve yourself, leave $1 per diner for the bussers. Some restaurants, however, have adopted the European custom of automatically adding gratuity to the bill, so check before leaving a cash tip. Thousands of Chicago coffee shops now have a tip cup near the register. Staff often don't expect a tip, but leave $ 1 or more if the service is extraordinary.

unofficial **TIP**
Veteran Chicago bartenders and cocktail waiters frown on loose change. They're often pressed for time and don't like picking up three quarters, two dimes, and a nickel off the bar.

SOMMELIER Tips aren't required, but if the sommelier has excelled, Chicagoans often leave 15% of the cost of the first bottle of wine.

COCKTAIL WAITERS AND BARTENDERS Here you tip by the round: for two people, $1 a round; for more than two, $2 a round. For a large group, use your judgment. Is everyone drinking beer, or is the order long and complicated? Tip accordingly.

HOTEL MAIDS On checking out, leave a dollar or two per day for each day of your stay, provided the service was good.

How to Look and Sound Like a Native

Chicagoans are tough. They're mostly down-to-earth realists who take a sort of pride in their city's legendarily crooked politicians, horrible winters, and screwy traffic jams. Because the city shuns phoniness, visitors who want to blend in only need be themselves. But if it's important to you not to look like a tourist, we offer the following advice.

1. Don't call Chicago the "Windy City." Natives don't do that. That would be like San Franciscans calling their elegant city "San Fran."

2. Don't crash-diet. Except for razor-thin fashion victims haunting the boutiques along the Magnificent Mile, Chicagoans disdain the frou-frou sveltness that's the norm in New York or Los Angeles. Being overweight in Chicago isn't a social faux pas—this is after all, a town known for its pizza, steaks, Italian beef and sausage sandwiches, and many other kinds of artery-clogging, waistband-expanding delicacies. And when Chicagoans are feeling too fat, they just head 90 miles north to Milwaukee, where they always fit in.

3. Be obsessive about the Bears. Pick either the Cubs or White Sox in baseball—you can't root for both. (By the way, never, ever call the Cubs the "Cubbies." They're a sad enough operation without sounding like something rescued from an animal shelter.) Talk about Jerry Sloan, Norm Van Lier, and Chet Walker in the days before the Bulls had Michael Jordan. No one talks about the Blackhawks anymore.

4. Talk through your nose. Master the flat phonetics of the Midwest: give the letter *A* a harsh sound and throw in a few *dem*s and *dose*s when attempting to converse with natives.

5. Occasionally, for no apparent reason, erupt in your best attempt at a Chicago accent: "Yah, but the city works." Or "Da Bears."

6. Do not, under any circumstances, put ketchup on a Chicago-style hot dog.

7. Read the *Sun-Times* on a bus or the El. Read the *Tribune* on a train to the suburbs.

PUBLICATIONS FOR VISITORS

CHICAGO HAS TWO MAJOR DAILY NEWSPAPERS, the *Chicago Sun-Times* and the *Chicago Tribune*. Both are morning papers that cover local, national, and international news; both also have Friday editions with up-to-the-minute information on entertainment for the weekend. A more comprehensive source for entertainment and arts listings is in the weekly *Chicago Reader,* a free alternative newspaper that shows up on downtown newsstands (as well as at a variety of clubs, bars, bookstores, cafes, and shops) on Thursday afternoons.

The weekly *Time Out Chicago* magazine is also popular with tourists. It's published by the same folks who created *Time Out New York* and *Time Out London*. The Chicago edition has gobs of bar, restaurant, and entertainment recommendations. *Chicago* is a slightly stuffy monthly magazine (owned by the *Tribune*) that's strong on lists (top 20 restaurants, and so on) and provides a calendar of events, dining information, and feature articles.

Windy City Sports is a free monthly guide to fitness and outdoor recreation that highlights seasonal sports such as skiing, bicycling, running, inline skating, and sailboarding. Look for it at bike shops and outdoors outfitters.

Chicago Scene highlights Chicago's beautiful people and visiting celebs as they scarf canapes at the town's top social events; the free monthly also contains articles on dining and fashion. Pick up a copy at swank shops, hair salons, and cafes up and down the Gold Coast. At the other end of the social spectrum, *Street Wise,* published twice monthly, is sold by homeless and formerly homeless men and women for $1 (look for identifying vendor badges). The newspaper includes features, a calendar of events, sports, poetry, and film reviews.

CHICAGO ON THE AIR

ASIDE FROM THE USUAL BABBLE OF FORMAT ROCK, talk, easy listening, and country music, Chicago is home to a few radio stations that really stand out for high-quality broadcasting. Tune in to what hip Chicagoans listen to, as listed below.

CHICAGO'S BEST RADIO STATIONS		
FORMAT	FREQUENCY	STATION
NPR, News	91.5 FM	WBEZ
Progressive Rock	93.1 FM	WXRT
Jazz	95.5 FM	WNUA
Classic Rock	97.1 FM	WDRV
Classical	98.7 FM	WFMT

ACCESS FOR THE DISABLED

LIKE MOST LARGE AMERICAN. CITIES, Chicago tries to make itself accessible to people with physical disabilities. Most museums and restaurants, for example, feature wheelchair access. At the **Art Institute of Chicago,** wheelchair access is through the Columbus Drive (east) entrance, and a limited number of wheelchairs and strollers are available free at both main entrances. Most public areas associated with the **Chicago History Museum** are accessible to the disabled, and a limited number of wheelchairs are also available. Parking for disabled visitors is provided in the parking lot adjacent to the building.

The **Field Museum** has wheelchairs available on the ground level near the West Entrance and first-floor North Door, and the **Adler Planetarium** has wheelchair-accessible restrooms on the first floor (down the vending machine hallway). Elevators are available for folks in wheelchairs, parents with strollers, and those with other special needs.

The **Chicago Botanic Garden** has wheelchairs available at the Information Desks in the Gateway and Education centers. Accessible parking is located in parking lots 1, 2, and 3. The garden's Orientation Center is equipped with assistive-listening devices, closed-caption monitors, and signs in Braille. The **Brookfield Zoo** provides assistive-listening devices in the Administration Building near the South Gate and in the Discovery Center near the North Gate. A telecommunications device for the deaf (TDD and TTY) is also available in the Administration Building.

Services for the Disabled

The **City of Chicago Department on Disability** offers information and reference: ☎ 312-744-6673 or 312-744-4964 (TDD).

Handicapped visitors can arrange door-to-door transportation from the airport or train station to their hotel, as well as transportation anywhere in the city in special vans; the rate is $1.50 each time you board. Call the **Chicago Transportation Authority Special Services Division** at ☎ 312-432-7025 or 312-432-7116 (TDD) for more information.

The **Chicago Transit Authority (CTA)** operates 112 routes with lift-equipped buses; look for the blue wheelchair symbol displayed on the first bus–last bus chart on the CTA map. For routes, fares, schedules, and a copy of the latest transit map, call ☎ 312-836-7000 from 5 a.m. to 1 a.m. The TDD number is ☎ 888-282-8891. Some (but not all) train stations are wheelchair accessible. Here's the list; call ☎ 312-836-7000 for hours of operation:

- **Blue Line** (O'Hare-Congress-Douglas): O'Hare, Rosemont, Cumberland, Harlem-Higgins, Jefferson Park, Logan Square, Western, Clark-Lake (Lake transfer), Jackson, UIC–Halsted-Morgan, Polk, 18th, Cicero-Cermak, Medical Center (Damen entrance), Kedzie-Homan, and Forest Park.

- **Brown Line** (Ravenswood): Kimball, Western, Clark-Lake, Washington-Wells, and Merchandise Mart.

- **Green Line** (Lake Street–Jackson Park): Ashland-63rd, Halsted, East 63rd–Cottage Grove, 51st, 47th, 43rd, 35th-Bronzeville-ITT, King Drive, Roosevelt, Clark-Lake, Clinton, Ashland-Lake, California, Kedzie, Conservatory–Central Park Drive, Pulaski, Cicero, Laramie, Harlem-Lake (Marion entrance), and Central.

- **Orange Line** (Midway): All stations between Midway Airport and Roosevelt; also Clark-Lake and Washington-Wells.

- **Pink Line** (54th-Loop): 54th-Cermak, Cicero, Kostner, Pulaski, Central Park, Kedzie, California, Western, Damen, 18th, Polk, Clark-Lake, Library-State–Van Buren, and Washington-Wells.

- **Purple Line** (Evanston): Linden, Davis, Merchandise Mart, Clark-Lake, Library-State–Van Buren, and Washington-Wells.

- **Red Line** (Howard–Dan Ryan): Loyola, Granville, Addison, Chicago, Lake, Washington, Jackson, Roosevelt, and Sox-35th, 79th, 95th–Dan Ryan.

- **Yellow Line** (Skokie).

TIME ZONE

CHICAGO IS IN THE CENTRAL TIME ZONE, which puts the city one hour behind New York, two hours ahead of the West Coast, an hour ahead of the Rocky Mountains, and six hours behind Greenwich Mean Time.

PHONES

THE CHICAGO AREA IS SERVED BY FIVE AREA CODES: ☎ 312 for the Loop and downtown, ☎ 773 for the rest of the city, ☎ 630 for the far-western suburbs, ☎ 708 for the near-western and southern suburbs, and ☎ 847 for the northern suburbs. Calls from pay phones are 50¢. To dial out of Chicago to the suburbs, dial 1, then the appropriate area code, then the phone number you want to reach. While the initial call to the suburbs costs the same as an intracity call, keep some change handy. On longer calls, you may have to plug in more coins or get disconnected. If you're calling into the city from the suburbs, dial 1, then ☎ 312 or ☎ 773, then the number.

LIQUOR, TAXES, SMOKING, AND PIGEONS

IN CHICAGO THE LEGAL DRINKING AGE IS 21, and no store may sell alcoholic beverages before noon on Sundays. The local sales tax is 9%; the combined sales and hotel-room tax is 15.39%. Chicago now bans smoking in most public places. Nightclubs and restaurants with freestanding bars are exempt until July 1, 2008, when the law kicks in for real; in addition, smoking is prohibited on public transportation. Chicago is also the only major American city that has banned racing pigeons.

CRIME IN CHICAGO

FOR MOST OBSERVERS, CHICAGO AND CRIME go together like Bonnie and Clyde. The image is mostly left over from the Prohibition era, when bootlegger Al Capone and arch-gangster John Dillinger earned the city worldwide notoriety. Mention Chicago almost anyplace in the world, and the response is likely to be a pantomimed machine gun with a "rat-a-tat-tat" flourish.

The truth is, Chicago wasn't all that dangerous for John Q. Public in the 1920s. Only 75 hoodlums went down in gang warfare in 1926—about 10% of today's annual murder count. Sadly, although metropolitan Chicago has about the same population that it did in the Roaring '20s, the average person today is more likely to become a crime statistic.

Places to Avoid

Like virtually all large U.S. cities, Chicago has its ghettos. Until recently, one of the most infamous was **Cabrini-Green,** a high-rise public-housing complex that came to be a national symbol of the failure of mid-20th-century urban planning. Over the last couple of years, the Near North neighborhood in which Cabrini-Green once stood has undergone dramatic changes because of the real estate boom. There's even a farmer's market at the once-dangerous corner of Division Street and Clybourn Avenue.

While this area is becoming gentrified, much of the South and Near West sides contain areas that most visitors should avoid (exceptions include **Chinatown, Hyde Park,** and **Pullman** on the Far Southeast Side). On the North Side, glitzy neighborhoods are often next door to dicier areas, so don't wander too far afield. Here's some more advice: the city has been installing cameras on light posts in high-crime neighborhoods, so if you see a box with a blinking blue light, it's best to vamoose. (For more information on crime in the city, visit **www.chicagocrime.org**.)

unofficial **TIP**
Often in Chicago, relative safety is a question of day or night. The lakefront, public parks, the Loop, and River North are active during the day but are deserted at night except around restaurants and clubs. Take a cab or drive to nighttime destinations in these areas.

Safe areas at virtually any time of day or night include the Magnificent Mile and Oak, Rush, and Division streets in the Gold Coast community. Just stay within well-lighted areas, and keep your eyes peeled for shady-looking characters who may have sinister designs on your purse or billfold. Never look tentative. Pickpockets, by the way, are especially active in downtown shopping crowds during the holiday season and on subway trains to and from O'Hare airport.

Even with these recommendations, though, keep in mind that crime can happen anywhere. Chicago, unfortunately, is an innovator when it comes to new ways of victimizing people; this is where carjacking and "smash and grab"—that is, breaking a car window and snatching a purse off the seat—first gained national notoriety.

Taxicab Safety

unofficial **TIP**
If you need to catch a cab at the train station or one of the airports, always choose one from the official queue. These taxis are properly licensed and regulated. Never accept an offer for a cab or limo from a stranger in the terminal or baggage-claim area. At best, you will be significantly overcharged for the ride; at worst, you may be abducted.

When hailing a cab, you are somewhat vulnerable. Particularly after dusk, call a reliable taxi company and wait for your cab inside. When it arrives, check out the driver's certificate, which must by law be posted on the dashboard. Address the cabbie by his or her last name, or mention the cab number. If your driver knows you've made a point of remembering him or her, not only will you be safer, but the cabbie will think twice about running up the fare.

If you are comfortable reading maps, familiarize yourself with the most direct route to your destination ahead of time, or go over it with the concierge at your hotel. If you can say "Piper's Alley movie theater on North Wells via State Street," the driver is less likely to take a longer—and more expensive—route.

Carjackings

Special precautions are also in order when you're the one doing the driving. Stay alert in traffic. Keep doors locked and windows rolled up. Watch out for people offering to wash your windshield on the Near West and South sides. Leave enough space in front of your car that you can make a U-turn in case someone approaches and starts beating on your windows or otherwise acts threatening. Store your purse or briefcase under your knees or your seat rather than on the seat beside you.

PART SIX

GETTING AROUND

DRIVING YOUR CAR:
A Really Bad Idea

FOUR MAJOR INTERSTATES, ROAD CONSTRUCTION, unpredictable weather, and rush-hour traffic jams of mythic proportions are some of the sober realities faced by drivers who venture into downtown Chicago on any day but Sunday. Throw in a dearth of on-street parking, astronomical rates at most parking garages, and the in-your-face driving style of most Chicago drivers, and you've got a recipe for meltdown.

Yet as the traffic congestion attests, lots of people continue to brave the streets of Chicago by car every day—and that includes visitors. What if you're one of them?

TIME OF DAY

FIRST-TIME CHICAGO DRIVERS who are staying downtown should map out their routes in advance, avoid arriving or departing during rush hour (7 to 9:30 a.m. and 3 to 7 p.m. weekdays), and then plan on leaving the car parked in their hotel garage during most of their stay. Exceptions to the don't-drive rule are weekday evenings, weekends, and holidays.

PARKING

CHICAGO'S LACK OF ON-STREET PARKING is legendary. And watch for towing signage in certain lots. The "Lincoln Park Pirates" are a towing company that was popularized in song by the late folk singer Steve Goodman. They are expensive. Moreover, they are not friendly. If you decide to try your luck at finding a space, however, bring lots of quarters—most meters demand 50¢ for 15 minutes, with a two-hour limit (which isn't much time for sightseeing or attending a business meeting). Some metered spots are now taking credit cards.

The fine for parking at an expired meter, by the way, is $50. Within 15 feet of a fire hydrant? That's $100, and the police *will* measure the 15 feet. (Chicago traffic cops are notoriously efficient at handing out tickets and towing illegally parked cars.)

While the chances of finding an on-street spot in the Loop on weekdays are virtually nil, you'll have better luck east of the **Loop** on **Congress Parkway** between **Lake Shore Drive** and **South Michigan Avenue** (behind the Art Institute, facing the lake). Be patient, and be prepared to do a lot of circling before snagging a space. A better idea: head south of the Loop for one of the many outside commercial parking lots along **State** and **Wabash** streets south of Congress Parkway. After about 9:30 a.m., you can park for about $6 a day. On weekends, finding on-street parking in and around the Loop is a bit easier—but more young people are moving downtown to live.

Parking near the Magnificent Mile is another magnificent headache. Street parking is virtually impossible—and that includes evenings and weekends. Most major area hotels have under- or above-ground parking garages; be sure to check when making a hotel reservation. Spaces can be tight, so leave your SUV at home.

The farther you are from downtown, the easier it generally is to find a parking spot, although exceptions abound. For example, in popular and hip Old Town near Second City, forget about finding street parking on a Friday or Saturday night; even the garages fill up. Same thing goes for the nightlife area around Wrigley Field. It doesn't matter if the Cubs are in town or it's the middle of November. Wrigleyville, as locals call it, is the new Rush Street. In addition, the most popular neighborhoods have resident-only parking rules that prohibit visitors from grabbing scarce spaces in the evenings. During snowstorms, locals observe a storied Chicago tradition: placing lawn furniture and assorted household items on the street to mark their parking spots. Don't mess with this stuff, either.

A final note: when you do find a space, don't leave your valuables in your car or trunk.

INSIDER TIPS FOR DRIVERS

MANY NATIVE CHICAGOANS who own cars routinely use public transportation or taxis to get downtown. The hassle and expense of parking just aren't worth it. This is especially true during the holidays, when out-of-towners and suburbanites converge on the city to shop—and parking the car for a long evening of shopping and enjoying the lights can cost $15. Yet because Chicago is fairly easy to navigate and traffic levels drop off significantly after rush hour and on weekends, sometimes driving makes sense—at

unofficial **TIP**
Some out-of-the-way museums offer convenient parking. The **Museum of Science and Industry** in Hyde Park is one example, and there's a secret lot just north of the **Chicago History Museum** (formerly the Chicago Historical Society) on Clark Street.

least if you've already got a car. For example, if you're going out to dinner, call ahead and see if the restaurant offers valet parking or is close to a commercial lot.

SUBTERRANEAN CHICAGO

ADVENTUROUS DRIVERS CAN EXPLORE SUBTERRANEAN **Lower Wacker Drive** and **Lower Michigan Avenue** (actually, they're at lake level; Chicago's downtown streets were elevated before the Civil War). They're generally less congested than their surface counterparts, but they are a bit scary for drivers making the descent for the first time. You'll pass the legendary **Billy Goat Tavern,** which is 40 feet below ground level despite its aboveground address of 430 North Michigan. Drawbacks include lots of truck traffic, poor signage, and underground murkiness. Pluses include quick access to the Eisenhower Expressway, nice scenes of the river, and views of locations used in popular films such as *The Untouchables* and *Code of Silence.* The city has also cleared out most of the homeless population that used to reside on Lower Wacker.

PUBLIC TRANSPORTATION

THE CTA

WHILE NATIVE MOAN ABOUT BUS, subway, and train service, out-of-towners are usually impressed by the extensive public-transportation system operated by the **Chicago Transit Authority.** It's so cool, in fact, it was the original name of the rock band Chicago. True, much of the system's infrastructure is aging, but many CTA routes run 24 hours a day, crisscrossing the city and providing service to a number of bordering suburbs. And consider the alternative: battling Chicago's endless traffic jams in a car. For the most part, CTA service is clean and dependable, even though it's an uneven mix of the sleek and the seedy as some routes get upgraded while others are bypassed. Most routes take visitors to places they want to be—or at least within a few blocks. (A notable exception is the lack of train service to McCormick Place, although now charter buses can get there nonstop on a dedicated busway.)

unofficial **TIP**
Warning: After 10 p.m., don't take a chance with public transportation in any form. Either drive or take a cab.

THE EL

FOR VISITORS, THE MOST IMPORTANT and easiest-to-master segment of the CTA service is rapid transit—what is usually called "the subway" in other cities. But in Chicago, it's called **"the El"** (for "elevated"), although large parts of the train system do run underground or down the middle of expressways. Never mind: the entire train system is known as the El, and you'll have an 'ell of a good time. CTA ridership in 2005—492 million rides—reached the highest point since 1992. You might make a new friend!

Chicago currently boasts eight train routes that run north, northeast, east, southeast, west, and south from downtown. The newest of these is the **Pink Line (54th–Loop),** a name that beefy, muscular Chicagoans have had a hard time getting used to. Opened in 2006, it runs from the Loop elevated and on the surface to the West Side and Near West suburbs, and comprises the Lake branch, Paulina connector, and Cermak (Douglas) branch. The **Red (Howard–Dan Ryan), Blue (O'Hare-Congress-Douglas**), and **Yellow (Skokie)** trains run underground or on the surface. The **Brown (Ravenswood), Purple (Evanston**), and **Orange (Midway Airport)** lines are elevated. The **Green Line** is an elevated line linking Jackson Park (south), the Loop, and Lake Street (east).

Downtown, the El defines the Loop as it circles Chicago's core financial and retail district, and it's obvious that this part of the system is more than 100 years old as the trains rattle, shake, and roar overhead. The aging, peeling structures that hold the trains up don't inspire much confidence in most first-time visitors. Just think of the rickety setup as Chicago's answer to Coney Island.

Fares

Cash fares for the train are $1.75 (85¢ for children ages 7 to 11). The CTA has been eliminating attendants in favor of Transit Card vending machines, so it's not a bad idea to bring exact change. Transfers cost 25¢ (15¢ for children), must be purchased when you pay your fare, and allow two more rides within two hours—but not on the route you started on. They also allow transfers to a bus route (and vice versa).

unofficial **TIP**
It's very wise to visit **www.transitchicago.com** before you plan to brave the El or bus system. It will save you lots of hassles.

If you plan to use the El or buses a lot during your stay, consider purchasing a one-, two-, three-, or five-day visitor pass for unlimited rides. The passes range in price from $5 (one day) to $18 (five days) and are sold at both airports, Amtrak at Union Station, visitor-information centers, Hot Tix, and most museums and major attractions.

Another option is the electronic-fare-card system that allows you to buy $1.75 to $100 worth of rides on the system's trains and buses, with a bonus $1 worth for every $10 purchased. You can buy the fare cards at Transit Card machines installed in the stations as well as from the locations mentioned above.

Train-line Names

The eight El lines currently in operation are color coded, such as the Red Line. Watch out, though—some signs at stations and on the trains themselves were never changed to show the color names. So it's good to know that the Red Line is also called the Howard–Dan Ryan line (the names identify the two ends of the line).

downtown el and subway stations

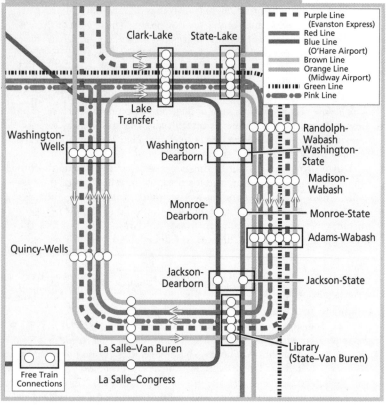

The Red Line travel time is also the slowest of all CTA rail lines. On a good day, trains run every 3 to 12 minutes during rush hour; every 6 to 15 minutes midday, early evenings, and weekends; and every 6 to 20 minutes in the later evening. From 1:30 to 4:30 a.m., only four lines operate: the Red Line (every 15 minutes), the Purple Line (every 30 to 45 minutes), and the Blue and Green lines (every 30 to 60 minutes). There is 24-hour service out of O'Hare International Airport, but Midway Airport passengers should know that the last train leaves there at 12:55 a.m.

Riding the El

In the Loop, finding the stations is easy: just look up. Then climb the stairs up to the platform, pay the fare, and enjoy the weather and sights as you await the next train—the elevated stations are partially covered but not enclosed. To determine the direction of the train you want, use the maps displayed and the signs posted overhead and on columns.

Taking the Plunge in the Loop

Figuring out which lines are elevated and which ones are underground—and how they all interconnect—is a headache-inducing experience in the Loop, where all the El lines converge. Here's a tip: on the elevated lines circling the Loop, as you face north, the Orange Line to Midway runs counterclockwise and the Brown Line to Ravenswood runs clockwise; at the Clark-Lake, State-Lake, Adams-Wabash, and La Salle–Van Buren stations, riders can transfer free to other lines, including the underground Blue Line to O'Hare and the Red Line to the North Side. Sounds complicated, but it's not as bad as Tokyo.

Our advice: to get familiar with the system, take the plunge and board the elevated Brown (Ravenswood) El in the Loop. The views as you circle the downtown area are spectacular. Next, the train passes the Merchandise Mart near the river and continues northwest.

If it's a nice day, continue north to the Diversey station; get off the train and reboard the next one south. The postcard view of the approaching skyline that unfolds as you return downtown should not be missed. At $1.75, the ride is one of the best tourist bargains in town. If you haven't had your fill of aerial views of Chicago, board the Orange Line and take the elevated train to Midway Airport and back (a half-hour ride one-way).

To reach the platform at underground stations, riders descend a set of narrow stairs to the (often-seedy) stations. After paying the fare, descend to the next level and the platform, which is usually narrow, not climate controlled, and noisy when a train comes through. No one makes eye contact down here. The trains themselves, however, are usually clean and free of litter and graffiti.

BUSES

BUS FARES ARE $1.75 (85¢ for children ages 7 to 11); a transfer is 25¢. Unlike the El, you need either exact change or a token to ride the bus; dollar bills are okay, but the drivers don't make change. If you need a transfer, buy it when you board. (You can use the transfer to enter the El system or board a bus on a different route twice within two hours.) Chicago bus drivers are friendly and will answer any questions you have about reaching your intended destination.

Depending on the route and the time of day, fellow passengers are another matter. It's usually best to steer clear. Two more warnings about riding Chicago's buses: first, rush-hour crowds, especially along hectic Michigan Avenue, are

unofficial **TIP**
Though it's not a long walk to the below-ground Red Line train station at State Street and Chicago Avenue from hotels on North Michigan Avenue, it's often more convenient to grab one of the buses going up and down the Magnificent Mile. This is especially true on days when it's cold, raining, windy, snowing, or any combination of brazen Chicago weather.

mind-boggling, and you'll often have to wait for a bus that's not packed full. Second, after the evening rush hour, you should either drive or take a cab for safety's sake.

Chicago's bus system is massive and complicated . . . and ultimately best left to commuters. Buses are also much slower than trains, especially in Chicago's dense traffic. Yet a few bus lines that follow relatively unconvoluted routes are invaluable to visitors staying downtown— particularly those lodging in hotels along the subway-less Magnificent Mile. We don't recommend that visitors on vacation use the bus system exclusively when in town, but we do think using it judiciously can save tourists, business travelers, and conventioneers a lot of walking, not to mention cab fares and/or parking fees.

Buses **#145, #146,** and **#151** (among others) provide quick, easy access south to the Loop and attractions such as the Field Museum along Lake Michigan. The **#36** bus that goes north along State and Clark streets provides easy access to Lincoln Park, the Lincoln Park Zoo, and Old Town. The **#6** express bus, which can be boarded at State and Lake streets in the Loop, quickly traverses the South Side to the Museum of Science and Industry (which does not have an El station). The **#56** bus heads out Milwaukee Avenue through Chicago's extensive Polish neighborhoods. It's a measured look at Old Chicago. Buses **#29, #56, #65,** and **#66** stop at Navy Pier, Chicago's most popular tourist attraction.

Which Bus?

To get exact, efficient directions for the bus and El routes, check with your hotel concierge or call ☎ 312-836-7000 from anywhere in the Chicago area between 5 a.m. and 1 a.m. daily. CTA personnel who answer the phones are generally polite and helpful; just tell them where you are and where you want to go, and they'll give you precise directions on routes and transfers (if needed). Make sure you have a pen and paper handy to write down the directions. If you have more lead time, you can get extensive route maps and directions from the CTA's Web site, **www.transitchicago.com.**

TAXIS

IN CHICAGO, cabs are plentiful and constitute one of the primary modes of transportation in this spread-out city. Along major thoroughfares it's easy to hail a taxi, with the possible exception of rush hour and when the weather has turned nasty (and everyone needs one). You'll also find cab stands in front of major hotels.

Chicago's taxi-fare system is straightforward and similar to New York City's. It's based on both distance and time—which means a $5 fare during non–rush hours can double when traffic is slow and heavy. The basic charge is $1.60 for the first mile and $1.40 for each mile after. A three-mile jaunt downtown from a hotel along the Magnificent Mile or from McCormick typically will run about $8 (non–rush hour). If

CHICAGO'S MAJOR CAB AND LIMOUSINE COMPANIES	
American United Cab	☎ 773-248-7600
Checker Cab	☎ 312-243-2537
Chicago Limousines	☎ 800-543-5466
Crown Cars and Limousines	☎ 800-876-7725
RightChoice Limousine Service	☎ 312-654-5466
Wolley	☎ 312-225-5411
Yellow Cab	☎ 312-TAXI-CAB

you need a cab, ask your hotel doorman or call a taxi company that offers 24-hour service. Tips for all involved are virtually mandatory.

WALKING *in* CHICAGO

WHILE CHICAGO IS A HUGE PRAIRIE CITY stretching about 30 miles north and south along Lake Michigan and 15 miles to the west, the major areas of interest to visitors are concentrated in a few fairly compact areas: the Loop, the Magnificent Mile along North Michigan Avenue (also called Streeterville), Grant Park (a campuslike setting that's home to some of the city's best museums), and the Near North Side (which offers a wide range of shopping, dining, and nightlife options). There isn't a hill for miles around. Given good weather and a relaxed schedule, walking is the best mode of discovering the city.

unofficial **TIP**
Here's a secret: find the block-long **Alta Vista Terrace,** between Grace and Byron streets, a block north of Wrigley Field. It's an easy walk, and the early-1900s row houses—replicas of those found in London's Mayfair district—make this street unlike any other in Chicago.

Great places to take a walk or a stroll include the **Loop; Grant Park** (great views of the skyline and the lake); nearby **Millennium Park;** the **Gold Coast** (where Chicago's richest citizens have lived since the 1890s); and, just west of the city line, **Oak Park** (with 25 homes, churches, and fountains designed by Frank Lloyd Wright). Chicago's varied ethnic neighborhoods, such as **Andersonville** on the Far North Side (a charming mix of Swedish and Middle Eastern), are also fine walking destinations.

PEDWAYS

IN ADDITION, DOWNTOWN IS HONEYCOMBED with an underground system of pedestrian walkways that make Chicago a lot easier to negotiate when the weather is bad. The "pedways" link train stations and major buildings (such as the State of Illinois Center, Macy's, the Chicago Cultural Center, and the Hyatt Regency in Illinois Center). Visitors seeking a mole's-eye view of the city will even find shops and cafes as they explore the still-growing pedway system.

PART SEVEN

SIGHTSEEING, TOURS, *and* ATTRACTIONS

TOURING CHICAGO

A VISIT TO CHICAGO WILL KEEP YOU ON YOUR TOES—no one is a passive participant. Not only does Chicago offer a wide selection of world-class museums, but the city itself is a museum. The Loop and the lakefront, for example, encompass the world's largest collection of outdoor modern architecture. Turn any corner, and you're confronted with yet another aesthetic or technical innovation in building design.

There's more. Tourists, professionals, and residents jam Chicago's downtown streets year-round to absorb its muscular skyline, lakefront, art, history, shopping, cultural attractions, and festivals—which run every weekend during the summer. Inevitably, out-of-towners rub big shoulders with the city's outspoken (and often-humorous) natives, most of whom are remarkably friendly to visitors and take pride in their city. Here are some tips to assist first-time visitors in discovering this sprawling, dynamic place.

TAKING AN ORIENTATION TOUR

VISITORS CAN'T MISS THE regular procession of open-air tour buses—"motorized trolleys" might be a more accurate term—that prowl Michigan Avenue, the Loop, and the museums and attractions along the lakeshore. The **Chicago Trolley Co.** (☎ 773-648-5000; **www.coachusa.com/chicagotrolley**) runs regularly scheduled shuttle buses that drop off and pick up paying customers along a route that incorporates the town's most popular attractions. Between stops, passengers listen to a tour guide talk about the city's cataclysmic fire of 1871, machine gun–toting gangsters, and spectacular architecture.

The guides also suggest places to eat and drop tidbits of interesting information—such as the best places to go for an Oprah sighting (her studio on the Near West Side and the Crate & Barrel on North Michigan

Avenue). You will be riding amid Chicago tradition. Dating back to the horseless carriages of the late 1800s, Chicago's level topography has created a fertile landscape for streetcars, buses, and trolleys.

If this is your first visit to Chicago, take one of the tours early in your trip. Here's why: Chicago is on a plot of land 228 miles square. Seen from the air, the city is surprisingly contained. Its towers rise up from the lakeside with a stunning vertical thrust but then give way to the prairie flatness that characterizes the Midwest. Yet once on the ground, visitors discover that the city is too vast to take in—and that includes its downtown. Although it's possible to embark on a walking tour that includes River North, the Magnificent Mile, the Loop, Grant Park, and Chicago's major museums, you'll murder your feet—and your enthusiasm for touring—in the process.

Chicago trolley tickets are $22.50 for adults, $18 for seniors (age 65 and over), and $9 for children ages 3 to 11. Youngsters can use their ticket to ride the trolley free the next day; a two-day ticket for adults is $30 (Sunday through Thursday only), and a family package for two adults and two children under age 12 runs $57.50. Approach these narrated tours as a basic educational system that not only gets you to the most well-known attractions but also provides a timely education on the city's history and scope. (One quibble: the references to Roaring '20s gangsters are clichéd.)

Tour buses run every 20 minutes, and boarding locations include the city's most popular downtown attractions. You can board at any stop on the route and pay the driver. The complete tour lasts about two hours. Heated in the winter and open air in the summer, the trolleys operate rain or shine, from 9 a.m. to 5 p.m. daily (longer hours in the summer).

The tour buses make 13 stops: **Wacker Drive South,** the **Art Institute,** the **Field Museum,** the **Millennium Park Theater District,** the **Hilton Towers and Hotel, Sears Tower,** the **John Hancock Center,** the historic **Water Tower, North Pier, Navy Pier, Wacker Drive North,** the **Magnificent Mile,** and the **River North** shopping district.

ARCHITECTURE AND BOAT TOURS

IT'S OFTEN SAID THAT IN CHICAGO, architecture is a spectator sport. While an introductory bus tour of downtown Chicago gives first-time visitors a sense of the city's layout and a glimpse of Chicago architecture, things look different from the Chicago River. Don't miss it. During the warmer months, riverboats glide down the river for a dockside view of downtown architecture and historical sites. And the Loop takes on a new perspective after embarking on a walking tour with a docent pointing out and explaining the modern architectural trends on display in Chicago's ever-changing downtown.

Boat Tours

Not so long ago, everyone made fun of the first Mayor Daley's dream of people someday fishing in the Chicago River, which he loved inordinately.

unofficial **TIP**
Tours offered by the **Chicago Architecture Foundation** emphasize the city's buildings and Chicago's role as a leader in modern urban architecture. If you're not that big of a culture vulture and you don't need to hear another word about Louis Sullivan, you'll probably get more out of a generalist tour from an operator such as **Mercury Tours** or **Wendella Sightseeing Boats.** Can't make up your mind? Pick the cruise that best fits your schedule.

Every St. Patrick's Day he had it dyed green, a tradition that continues today. Once scorned as a sewage canal, the Chicago River has been cleaned up. The now-resplendent river offers outstanding views of the city's best buildings, including the Sears Tower, the Civic Opera Building on Wacker Drive, the IBM Building (Mies van der Rohe's last major Chicago structure), and the NBC Tower, built in 1989.

On downtown boat tours, guides weave history and technology as they tell the story of the Great Chicago Fire of 1871 and the role of the structural iron frame in rebuilding the city. The result was the skyscraper and a truly modern style unencumbered by any allegiance to the past.

CHOOSING A BOAT TOUR Visitors can choose from several boat-touring companies that sail on 90-minute narrated cruises up the Chicago River or out on Lake Michigan for a view of the city's fabled skyline. All the modern, motorized ships are enclosed and air-conditioned, and they offer beverage services while en route; the cruises are offered spring through fall.

Chicago Architecture Foundation Tours

The **Chicago Architecture Foundation** (CAF) offers 86 different tours by foot, bus, and boat. Each tour is led by a volunteer from a fleet of about 450 docents (tour guides). The tour leaders ae witty, incredibly informed, and enthusiastic about Chicago architecture. Go on at least one Foundation tour during your visit. Better yet, take a walking tour of the Loop *and* an architectural boat tour. You won't regret it.

BY BOAT *Chicago's First Lady* and *Chicago's Little Lady* depart from Riverside Gardens at the southwest corner of Michigan Avenue and Wacker Drive for the **CAF Architecture River Cruise.** The yachts, which offer outdoor seating on the upper deck and air-conditioned interior seating, depart three to nine times daily from late April until mid-November (five times daily on weekends); tickets are $25 on weekdays, $27 on weekends and holidays. Cruises board 15 minutes before departure; advance reservations are highly recommended.

In addition to the unique river perspective on Chicago architecture, you'll see where Chicago's Trump International Hotel and Tower is being built, on the site of the former *Chicago Sun-Times* building. In the summer of 2004, the *Little Lady* scored a notch in Chicago lore when a bus driver for the Dave Matthews Band illegally dumped 800 pounds of raw sewage onto unsuspecting upper-deck passengers enjoying the scenery near the Merchandise Mart. Even though that was a once-in-a-lifetime glitch, it's a good idea to bring headgear, as cruises depart rain or shine. For more information, visit **www.cruisechicago.com.** For reservations, call Ticketmaster at ☎ 312-902-1500.

BY FOOT Two-hour walking tours of the Loop and bus excursions to Chicago's neighborhoods start at the CAF's headquarters and gift shop at 224 South Michigan Avenue (across from the Art Institute of Chicago). The walking tours complement the boat tour, allowing you to observe the buildings from street level as well as catch some lobbies that are every bit as spectacular as the buildings' exteriors. Tours cost $12 per person and are offered daily on a varying schedule throughout the year. For more information, visit **www.architecture.org.** For reservations, call Ticketmaster at ☎ 312-902-1500.

MORE CAF TOURS In addition to Loop walking tours and boat cruises, CAF offers the three-and-a-half-hour **Chicago Architecture Highlights by Bus** tour (March to November, every Saturday, Sunday, and Wednesday at 9:30 a.m; $37 per person) and **Frank Lloyd Wright by Bus** tours (May to October, first Saturday of the month at 9:30 a.m.; $40). For more information, visit **www. architecture.org.** For reservations, call ☎ 312-922-3432.

Historical and Architectural Lake and River Cruises from North Pier

Tours from the **Lake** (☎ 312-527-1977; **www.chicagoline.com**) are different from the CAF in that the Lake is a little less formal in its approach to architecture, and coffee, lemonade, cookies, and muffins are served during cruises. There's also a 6 p.m. cocktail cruise. Boat tours depart from North Pier daily May through September for cruises on the Chicago River and Lake Michigan. On the historical cruise, visitors pass the spot where du Sable first established a trading post among the local Native Americans and where Fort Dearborn stood to protect the community. The tour also passes through the heart of the city, where the fire of 1871 reduced buildings to ash at a rate of 65 acres an hour.

On Lake Michigan, the boat passes **Buckingham Fountain,** where the Columbian Exposition of 1893 left its legacy of the **Field Museum, Shedd Aquarium, Adler Planetarium,** and **Museum of Science and Industry.** When you hear someone talk about the "Museum Campus," this is it. But the highlight of the cruise is a view of the magnificent skyline of Chicago, a profile recognized around the world.

Architectural cruises take visitors downtown for up-close views of Chicago's most recognized buildings, including the **Tribune Tower,** the **Merchandise Mart, Lake Point Tower** (where Sammy Sosa once lived), and of course, the **Sears Tower,** the third-tallest office building in the world. Visitors also see the spot near the **Kinzie Street Bridge** where the Chicago River flooded an old railroad freight tunnel in April 1991, shutting down the Loop and causing hundreds of millions of dollars in damage. The 90-minute cruises leave North Pier daily on the hour, 9 a.m. to 4 p.m. from May to September and on a reduced schedule in October. Prices are $28 for adults, $26 for seniors, and $16 for children and students ages 7 to 18. For more information and reservations (recommended), call ☎ 312-527-1977.

Other Boat Cruises

Mercury Tours (☎ 312-332-1353) offers architectural, historical, and maritime-sights tours May through September from the lower level and southeast corner of the Michigan Avenue Bridge over the Chicago River (at Wacker Drive). Cruises range from one to two hours in length, each with continuous commentary. Tours depart throughout the day from morning to late evening; prices are $19 for adults and $9 for children; kids under age 3 are admitted free. Tickets go on sale an hour before the cruise (no reservations necessary).

   Wendella Sightseeing Boats (☎ 312-337-1446; **www.wendellaboats .com**). Wendella is the city's throwback boat tour with a history that dates back to 1935. The company was founded by Albert "Bo" Borgstrom, a Swedish immigrant who refurbished a 65-foot-long wooden yacht named *Wendela* (it was spelled with one *L* until the 1950s) and began offering 30-minute guided boat tours from Navy Pier. Today a beautiful fleet hosts cruises on the Chicago River and along the lakefront mid-April to mid-October. Lake and river tours (which go through the Chicago Lock) last 90 minutes and cost $19 for adults, $17 for seniors age 62 and older, and $10 for children under age 11. Tours leave throughout the day and evening from the base of the Wrigley Building, at the northwest corner of the Michigan Avenue Bridge over the Chicago River. During the spring and summer, commuters also take the popular **Wendella River Bus** from stops near Union Station to Michigan Avenue. Tickets are $2 one-way and $13 for ten rides.

Bridgehouse Tours

The **Friends of the Chicago River** is a nonprofit organization that has been a force in cleaning up and revitalzing the waterway since 1979. It has also developed the new **McCormick Tribune Bridgehouse and Chicago River Museum** (376 North Michigan; ☎ 312-977-0227; **www.bridgehouse museum.org**). After viewing the historic bridgeworks, visitors can climb to the top of the tower to see river views. Exhibits detail the history of bridges in Chicago, the styles and designs that were created in Chicago, and how the Michigan Avenue bridge itself works. The museum is open daily from June until August 31; September 1 to 30, Wednesday to Sunday. Tickets are $3 per person; kids under age 5 are admitted free.

SPECIALIZED TOURS

American Sightseeing (☎ 312-251-3100; 800-621-4153; **www.american sightseeing.org**) offers general-interest tours (as opposed to the CAF tours, which focus on architecture) around the city, plus special tours on architectural highlights and Chicago neighborhoods (such as the two-hour **North Side Tour;** $22 for adults and $11 for children ages 5 to 14). The **Grand Tour** takes visitors to Chicago's parks and most scenic spots as well as the Loop, the Magnificent Mile, Wrigley Field, Lincoln Park Conservatory, the Adler Planetarium, the University of Chicago campus, and the Museum of Science and Industry. The tour also makes periodic stops at sites such as the Botanic Gardens on the North Side, where visitors can briefly debark and explore on their own. The cost of the four-hour tour is $35 for adults and $17.50 for children. American Sightseeing bus tours start at the **Palmer House** hotel in the Loop (17 East Monroe Street). Unlike the hard benches on the "trolley" tours, the buses feature comfortable reclining seats, overhead lights, and air-conditioning.

Gangsters and Ghosts

Chicago has scores of spooky sights (not including the haunted grounds of Wrigley Field), and **Supernatural Tours** (☎ 708-499-0300; **www.ghosttours.com**) does a super job with the supernatural. Even locals take in owner Richard Crowe's 70-passenger coach and bus tours, which highlight the city's heritage of ghost stories and folklore, bizarre tales, murder sites, cemeteries, gangsters, pubs, and restaurants. In 1973 Crowe became the Midwest's first full-time ghost hunter. You'll see and learn about Al Capone's grave site, the John Dillinger death site near the Biograph Theatre, and the "Hanged Man Ghost of the Water Tower." You'll learn why the alley next to the Gene Siskel Film Center downtown is known as "Death Alley" (125 people jumped to their deaths there during the 1903 Iroquis Theater fire). Tours are scheduled on select weekends from 7 to 11 p.m; the cost is $37 per person, and reservations are required. Don't even think about going on Halloween night unless you book weeks ahead. The trips depart from the **Goose Island Brewery,** 1800 North Clybourn (not the Goose Island by Wrigley Field—too scary).

The folks at **Untouchable Tours** (☎ 773-881-1195 or 800-660-8824; **www.gangstertour.com**) go directly for the jugular: Chicago's gangster history. Friendly actors in pinstripe suits and fedoras escort vistors on a two-hour bus tour of Chicago's creepy past, including the site of Al Capone's former headquarters, the Biograph Theatre, and the site of the St. Valentine's Day Massacre on Clark Street. The tour is historically correct and a crowd-pleaser, appealing to youngsters. It begins at the **Rock 'n' Roll McDonald's** on North Clark Street (look for the black bus). Guns not permitted. In addition to daily tours at 10 a.m., tours are scheduled on Thursday at 1 p.m., Friday at 1 p.m. and 7:30 p.m., Saturday at 1 p.m. and 5 p.m., and Sunday at 1 p.m. The cost is $25 for adults and $19 for children; reservations are recommended. Guests get free gangster gags as a souvenir.

Dining on Lake Michigan

While not guided tours, Lake Michigan cruises on the *Odyssey* feature fine dining, live music, dancing, and memorable views of

Chicago's skyline. Cruising on the elegant 850-passenger ship is a great way to see the city, and the operation is top-notch. (No *Gilligan's Island*/Jimmy Buffett shenanigans allowed.) There's a dress code; men should wear jackets. Best bet: a sunset dinner cruise. Second best bet: the midnight jazz cruise. Three-hour dinner cruises start at $114 per person standard base (including tax and gratuity), but vary a little per day; two-hour lunch cruises start at $54.53, weekdays, $62.50 on Saturday, and $66.50 on Sunday. *Odyssey II* departs from Navy Pier throughout the year. (There are also *Odyssey*s in Washington, D.C., and Boston.) For more information and reservations, call ☎ 888-741-0282, or visit **www.odysseycruises.com**.

CARRIAGE RIDES

AN EASY AND ROMANTIC WAY TO SEE downtown Chicago is by horse and buggy. The **Noble Horse** (☎ 312-266-7878), at the southwest corner of Michigan and Chicago avenues, provides horse-drawn carriage rides weekdays from 10 a.m. to 4 p.m. and 7 p.m. to midnight, and weekends from 10 a.m. to 1 a.m. The cost is $35 per half hour for up to four adults (maximum) and $5 extra for each additional adult. Reservations are not necessary.

The **Antique Coach & Carriage Company** (☎ 773-735-9400; **www.antiquecoach-carriage.com**) offers rides daily from the southeast corner of Michigan Avenue and Huron Street. Hours are 6:30 p.m. to 1 a.m. Monday through Thursday, 6:30 p.m. to 2 a.m. Friday, 1 p.m. to 2 a.m. Saturday, and 1 p.m. to 1 a.m. Sunday. The cost is $40 per 30 minutes of riding.

TOURING ON YOUR OWN: OUR FAVORITE ITINERARIES

IF YOUR TIME IS LIMITED and you want to experience the best of Chicago in a day or two, here are some game plans. The schedules assume you're staying downtown, have already eaten breakfast, and are ready to hit the streets around 9 a.m.

Day One

1. Tour downtown on one of the open-air shuttle-bus services with unlimited reboarding privileges for the day. If the weather's clear, get off at the **Sears Tower** and check out the view. Then catch the next shuttle.

2. Pick one: explore the **Shedd Aquarium** or the **Adler Planetarium** (they're close together on the "Museum Campus"). Then get back on the bus.

3. Next stop: **Navy Pier** and lunch at the **Navy Pier Beer Garden** or **Charlie's Ale House,** featuring 38 different types of beer.

4. Take a deep breath of cool Chicago air, and climb aboard for a scenic 30-minute **skyline cruise on Lake Michigan** that leaves Navy Pier every half hour in warm weather.

5. After the boat ride, take the shuttle bus to the **Historic Water Tower** on North Michigan Avenue. Explore the shops along Michigan, one of

the world's great shopping streets, and check out the **Museum of Contemporary Art** (with one of the city's most eclectic gift shops).

6. Grab dinner at a restaurant in **River North.** Afterward, catch some live music and shake your moneymaker at **Blue Chicago** (736 North Clark Street; ☎ 312-642-6261), a blues bar with a dignified roster of Chicago musicians.

7. Finish the evening with a visit to the **John Hancock Center Observatory** for an excellent view of the city and beyond.

Day Two

1. Sleep in—but not too late. You don't want to miss the 10 a.m. **Chicago Architecture Foundation** walking tour of the Loop.

2. Wander over for lunch at the **Billy Goat Tavern,** a longtime Chicago journalists' hangout that was popularized by John Belushi on *Saturday Night Live* ("cheezburger, cheezburger"). You know what to order. Then jump on the **Ravenswood El** for a ride around the Loop; take it north past the huge **Merchandise Mart,** and catch the next train back (south) for some teriffic views of the city.

3. Explore the **Art Institute of Chicago.** Try to catch the free tour that begins daily at 1 p.m. near the Grand Staircase.

4. Reward the kids with a trip to the **Chicago Children's Museum** at Navy Pier. Or explore the other Navy Pier attractions, including multiple views of the skyline. Take a ride on the pier's Ferris wheel for one of the most intimate views of the city.

5. Take in an evening of improvisational comedy at **The Second City** (1616 North Wells Street; ☎ 312-664-4032).

6. Dump the kids and have a postcomedy coffee at the 24-hour **Starbucks** on North Wells, directly south of The Second City. The coffee shop is one of the most kinetic spots on the North Side. If you want something a little more authentic and moody, head across the street to the **Old Town Ale House** at 219 West North Avenue, which is open until 5 a.m. on Saturday and 4 a.m. weekdays.

If You've Got More Time . . .

If you're spending more than two days in town, or if you're a return visitor, consider some of these options for an in-depth Chicago experience:

1. Explore one of Chicago's many neighborhoods beyond downtown. Suggestions: **Hyde Park** (South Side) has the **University of Chicago** and several museums; shop and eat lunch in **Chinatown** (Near South Side). **Andersonville** (North Side) features an eclectic mix of Swedish and Middle Eastern shops and inexpensive ethnic restaurants.

2. **Oak Park,** just west of the city line, boasts two famous native sons: architect Frank Lloyd Wright and Nobel Prize–winning novelist Ernest Hemingway. Spend a morning or afternoon learning about them. There's also a grand old movie theater that shows first-run flicks in downtown Oak Park.

3. Hit two Chicago museums that are so large, each requires a full day: the **Field Museum** and the **Museum of Science and Industry.**

4. Stretch your legs along the **Gold Coast,** where Chicago's wealthiest residents have made their homes for more than a century; it's just north of the Magnificent Mile. Or rent a bike and ride the path along **Lake Michigan.**

5. **Go to a play.** Chicago boasts well more than 100 active theater companies.

6. Kick back and enjoy a festival in **Grant Park** or a concert in new **Millennium Park.**

7. Spend a few hours browsing the art galleries in **River North.**

8. Check out **Macy's** on State Street. This used to be **Marshall Field's,** and the name change rankled most longtime Chicagoans. (For more info, see Part Nine, Shopping in Chicago.)

9. Attend a concert by the **Chicago Symphony Orchestra,** consistently rated as one of the best orchestras in the world.

10. Hop on a train or rent a car to west-suburban **Naperville,** named in 2006 by *Money* magazine as the second-best place to live in America. (Fort Collins, Colorado, was first.) Several Chicago chefs have opened restaurants in downtown Naperville, and the Riverwalk is reminiscent of San Antonio's.

11. Root for the **Cubs** at **Wrigley Field,** the **White Sox** at **U.S. Cellular Field** (locals call it "The Cell"), or the **Bulls** or **Blackhawks** at the **United Center.** Minor-league hockey is also huge in Chicago: the **Wolves** play at **Allstate Arena** in Rosemont, near O'Hare International Airport.

EXPLORING CHICAGO'S NEIGHBORHOODS

NEIGHBORHOODS FORM THE PERSONAL SCALE that makes a city work. The nearly 3 million people of Chicago form a quilt of nearly 3 million colorful threads, and you will find vitality and warmth within this quilt. Chicago's rich architectural history and cultural diversity are embraced in the city's many communities, some ethnically mixed and some not.

What follows is not a comprehensive guide to Chicago's neighborhoods, since the city officially claims 77 in all, but our suggestions for dipping in and sampling the remarkably vibrant array of individualistic architecture, cuisine, history, and culture that defines Chicago. In so many ways, Chicago is 77 little cities wrapped into one. Taking an extended ride on the **Ravenswood El** lets you survey the spectacle of Chicago's neighborhoods—and back porches and rooftop graffiti—without getting your feet wet. (For route and fare information on CTA and Metra, call ☎ 312-836-7000.)

unofficial **TIP**
Apart from a bike ride along the lakefront, Chicago is a city best explored on foot. You can use the El, the bus system, or a car to get around, but in most cases we recommend stepping out for a stroll to get the feel and flavor of these neighborhoods.

Our sampling tour of Chicago neighborhoods starts in the north and generally flows south along the lake, with several excursions to the northwest and southwest.

ANDERSONVILLE

YOU MAY BE SURPRISED AT THE NOTION of "Swede Town" in Chicago, but amble north along Clark Street from Foster and you'll see Swedish flags flying; you might even hear a little ABBA. Check out the **Swedish American Museum** (5211 North Clark Street), and savor excellent coffeecakes and pastries at the **Swedish Bakery** (5348 North Clark) or Swedish pancakes and limpa bread at **Svea Restaurant** (5236 North Clark). The cinnamon rolls from **Ann Sather's Restaurant** (5207 North Clark) are known across Chicago. Buy a dozen to take home—if they last that long.

In spite of its Scandinavian influence, Andersonville, like most Chicago neighborhoods, is a mixing and melting pot. The well-kept redbrick "two-flats" (long, narrow buildings with one apartment stacked atop another) on the streets fanning east from Clark have become the city's newest mecca for gays and lesbians. The Clark Street strip features a number of feminist stores and shops, such as **Women & Children First Bookstore** (5233 North Clark), with its wide selection of progressive books by women. Along Clark, you'll also find some cool thrift shops. Gays and straights alike flock to **Reza's,** a Persian/ Mediterranean restaurant with huge portions (5255 North Clark), as well as **Angel's** (5403 North Clark), which has heavenly *chilaquiles.* Wash it all down at the **Hopleaf Bar** (5148 North Clark), which carries more than 200 beers, many of them from Belgium. Chicago isn't known for its delis, but you'll find one of the best here: **Erickson's Delicatessen** (5250 North Clark) has great flatbread and the only frozen lingonberries in Chicago, along with food from Denmark and Norway. Open seven days a week (but not at night), Erickson's ships anywhere in the country.

TO GET THERE Take the CTA Red Line (Howard) to the Berwyn station, and then walk west on Foster about four blocks. Or transfer to the #92 Foster bus at the station.

By car from the Loop, drive north on Lake Shore Drive to the Foster exit, and head west to Clark Street. There's metered parking along Clark and free parking on side streets.

DEVON AVENUE

ON A FRIDAY NIGHT ALONG DEVON AVENUE, you're likely to see Orthodox Jews in dark suits and black hats heading home from synagogue on the same sidewalks as Indians in bright, flowing saris. Mixed among the kosher butchers, Bangladeshi vendors, and Pakistani groceries on the stretch from Western (2400 West Devon Avenue) to the north branch of the Chicago River (3200 West Devon Avenue) is a newer sprinkling of Thai and

unofficial **TIP**
Don't ask how to get to "DEE-von Avenue." Locals pronounce it "duh-VON."

Korean shops and restaurants. This makes for one of the most colorful neighborhoods on the North Side of Chicago.

You can pick up a yarmulke at **Rosenblum's World of Judaica** (2906 West Devon) or check out the colorful saris at **Taj Sari Palace** (2553 West Devon). **Gitel's Kosher Pastry Shop** (2745 West Devon) and **Tel Aviv Kosher Bakery** (2944 West Devon) sell traditional Sabbath challah. For decent kosher restaurants, try **Mi Tsu Yun** (yes, it's kosher *and* Chinese; 3010 West Devon) or **Jerusalem Kosher Restaurant** (3014 West Devon). **Viceroy of India** (2518 West Devon) is highly rated for

unofficial **TIP**
Note that many stores on Devon Avenue close early on Friday night and remain closed on Saturday for the Jewish Sabbath.

its curries and breads. **Ebner's Kosher Meat Market** (2649 West Devon) has been a staple of the neighborhood since 1966. Everything is kosher in this authentic Chicago butcher shop, even the attitude. Chicago hipsters check out **Reel Subcontinent** (2541 West Devon), a video-rental store that also carries hard-to-find Indian and Pakistani CDs. The video shop is also known for its wide selection of ethnic soap operas and cricket matches.

TO GET THERE Take the CTA Red Line (Howard) north to Loyola, and then transfer to a westbound #155 Devon Avenue bus.

By car from the Loop, drive north on Lake Shore Drive. At its northern end, take Ridge (west) to Devon and turn left (west); or take the Kennedy Expressway (I-90/94) north, then merge onto the Edens Expressway (I-94), exit at Petersen heading east, and turn north (left) on Kedzie to Devon.

UPTOWN

HANDS DOWN, UPTOWN IS ONE OF CHICAGO'S most interesting neighborhoods.

After World War II, Uptown attracted European immigrants, laborers from the Deep South, and Midwest transplants. This was one of the only Chicago neighborhoods where landlords did not require long-term leases or security deposits, which was attractive to the thrifty urban pioneers. During the mid-1960s, Uptown had the largest concentration of Southern whites in the northern United States.

At one time Uptown had two major movie palaces within one block of each other—the **Uptown** and the **Riviera**—and a grand dance hall, the **Aragon.** The Uptown is shuttered, but the Riviera (4746 North Racine) is still used for rock concerts, and the Aragon (1106 West Lawrence) is vital with live rock and salsa concerts, live boxing, and other events.

Uptown is coming back after a long period of seedy transition. Pockets of elegance have been restored in the huge homes that line **Hutchinson Street** and **Castlewood Terrace,** and a Borders bookstore would have been unheard of a few years ago. The community near Broadway and Argyle, often called **New Chinatown,** is in fact, a brimming mix of Vietnamese, Laotian, Chinese, Cambodian, and Thai immigrants. You'll find Asian groceries, bakeries, and gift shops; some of Chicago's top chefs buy ingredients here. Naturally, there's a profusion of restaurants. Try **Ha Mien** (4920 North Sheridan Road) for excellent Vietnamese fare or **Furama** (4936 North Broadway) for dim sum.

unofficial **TIP**
If you stray from the Broadway–Argyle axis, you'll quickly see the funkier parts of Uptown: don't try it alone or on foot after dark.

Former rock musician Rick Adee is the unofficial mayor of Uptown. Check out his used-book store, **Shake Rattle & Read** (4812 North Broadway), a local treasure in the shadow of the old Uptown Theater. The shop has been in the same location for 20 years, and the large inventory reflects its sedentary nature: 15,000 paperbacks; 10,000 hardcover books; 10,000 magazines; and 5,000 jazz, soul, and country albums. He's obviously not moving anytime soon. A few doors down, the **Green Mill Jazz Club** (4802 North Broadway) offers jazz and Sunday-night poetry slams of national renown each week.

TO GET THERE The CTA Red Line (Howard) stops at Argyle Street, where there's a $100,000 pagoda over the station.

By car from the Loop, drive north along Lake Shore Drive, exit at Lawrence (4800 North), head west to Broadway, and then go north to Argyle.

LINCOLN SQUARE

IN 1998 THE LEGENDARY **Old Town School of Folk Music** (students included Steve Goodman, John Prine, and Roger McGuinn of the Byrds) moved into an old library at 4544 North Lincoln Avenue in the heart of Lincoln Square. A statue of Abraham Lincoln presides over the intersection of Lincoln, Lawrence, and Western avenues. (He wasn't Greek.)

The centerpiece of Lincoln Square is the small shopping area—virtually a pedestrian mall—along the 4700 block of Lincoln Avenue. Many stores feature Tyrolean clothes, and **Meyer's Delicatessen** (4750 North Lincoln Avenue)—where the first language is often German—gives the place a decided European feel. Stop by **Merz Apothecary** (4716 North Lincoln Avenue), in the neighborhood for nearly a century, for imported soaps or any homeopathic remedies you might need. If you have kids or are a repressed kid yourself, don't miss **Quake Collectibles** (4628

unofficial **TIP**
Don't confine yourself to just the square area: it's safe to walk around here.

North Lincoln), packed to the walls with action figures, vintage board games, and old lunch boxes. It's like walking into Pee Wee's Playhouse.

Check out the glorious Louis Sullivan facade of the **Kelmscott Building** (4611 North Lincoln Avenue) and the periodicals section—and modern design—of the **Conrad Sulzer Library** (4455 North Lincoln). A large **wall mural** at 4662 North Lincoln depicts scenes from the German countryside.

Some of the best Thai food on the North Side is found at **Siam Country** (4637 North Damen), under the El's Damen Brown Line stop. The spring rolls (not fried) are a must.

Lincoln Square's German residents are nestled against **Greektown** west of the mall along Lawrence Avenue between Talman and Maplewood. **St. Demetrios Orthodox Church,** a 1928 basilica-style structure at 2727 West Winona, serves the Greek community. **St. Matthias,** an 1887 German church, is at 2310 West Ainslie.

TO GET THERE   Take the CTA Brown Line (Ravenswood) to the Western Avenue stop (Monday through Saturday until midevening; on Sunday, take the Red Line to Belmont and transfer to the Brown Line there) or the #11 bus, which connects the Loop with Lincoln Square, though it is a very long ride.

By car, take Lake Shore Drive north, exit at Lawrence Avenue (4800 North), and head west to Western Avenue (2400 West). There's metered parking on Lincoln Avenue and a lot at Leland next to the El station.

LAKEVIEW-WRIGLEYVILLE

THE LEGENDARY **Wrigley Field** is the centerpiece of this neighborhood, which has replaced Rush Street and Division Street as Chicago's top nightlife district. Wrigley Field—home of baseball's hapless Cubs—opened in 1914 on the grounds that formerly housed the Chicago Lutheran Theological Seminary. Cubs fans are devout, but generations of them have never seen a world championship in this ballpark.

So very sad.

That's why this neighborhood parties hard.

There is a bar and/or restaurant in just about every storefront south of Wrigley Field (at the corner of Addison and Clark). The most storied stops are **Murphy's Bleachers** (3655 North Sheffield, across from the bleacher entrance), **The Cubby Bear** (1059 West Addison), and **Bernie's Tavern** (3644 North Clark), and they all have dozens of TVs for watching sports year-round. The city's most popular reggae bar is the **Wild Hare,** just a block south of the ballpark (3530 North Clark).

Wrigley Field is a real neighborhood ballpark where fans stream in from the Addison El stop and others pay premium prices to watch from the roofs of nearby three-flats. (Don't be afraid to try for day-of-game tickets at the window.) It's common to see tourists wandering by Wrigley in the dead of winter just to take a picture of this landmark. A 2005 ballpark renovation also incorporated a sidewalk peephole in the right-field corner so pedestrians can look in and check out the team's annual rebuilding plans.

So very sad.

The mansions along **Hawthorne Place** (a one-way street heading east between Broadway and Sheridan Road) exude a stately lakeside grandeur. The facing rows of townhouses on **Alta Vista Terrace**

(1054 West between Byron and Grace streets north of Wrigley Field) are mirror images.

Locals flock to **Ann Sather's Restaurant** (929 West Belmont Avenue, a branch of the Andersonville store), drawn by the irresistible lure of addictive cinnamon rolls and well-prepared, moderately priced food. You'll find thrift shops, hip shops, bookstores, and espresso on nearly every corner, including the pungent smell of beans roasting at the **Coffee & Tea Exchange** (3311 North Broadway), one of the city's finest purveyors of coffee and equipment for making it. Now 25 years old, **Unabridged Books** (3251 North Broadway) is one of the staunch independents holding out against the invasion of Borders and Barnes & Noble. You'll find the city's largest cluster of gay bars along Halsted and Broadway between Belmont and Addison and an eclectic variety of stores selling things antique to antic along the commercial strips of Belmont, Diversey, Broadway, Halsted, and Clark.

TO GET THERE From the Loop, take the CTA Red Line (Howard) or Brown Line (Ravenswood) to Belmont or the #151 bus along Michigan Avenue north to Belmont, and then walk west. The #22 Clark Street bus, a quicker option, puts you in the heart of Lakeview-Wrigleyville.

By car, drive north on Lake Shore Drive to the Belmont exit, and head west on Belmont. Wrigley Field is about five blocks north of Belmont. (There's a CTA Red Line stop at Addison, near the ballpark.)

MILWAUKEE AVENUE

CHICAGO IS KNOWN AS AMERICA'S SECOND CITY, but it is also a City of Second Chances due to its influx of immigrants during the early 20th century. Nowhere is this more apparent than the long and winding road that is Milwaukee Avenue.

The heart of the city's Polish community was once at Milwaukee and Division but has since angled north to the neighborhood called **Avondale,** although Milwaukee Avenue, especially between Central Park and Pulaski, remains a primary Polish corridor. On weekend afternoons, this section teems with shoppers and diners, all gossiping—in Polish—and talking about the Pope.

Your best bet is to stroll along the avenue, taking in the sights and sounds. Step into **Andy's Deli** (5442 North Milwaukee Avenue) to gape at the 25 varieties of sausage lining the back wall and choose among packaged pierogi, *gulasz,* and Polish comic books. At the Polish department store **Syrena** (3044 North Milwaukee), you can snap up that missing tuxedo for your children in white or black.

For a sit-down meal from which you'll struggle to rise, consider the buffet at **Red Apple** (two locations, 3123 North Milwaukee and 6474 North Milwaukee). Owner Czerwone Jabluszko is known across the Northwest Side for huge portions of Wiener schnitzel, cheese blintzes, and gonzo potato pancakes.

St. Hyacinth's Roman Catholic Church (3636 West Wolfram) looms over the tidy bungalows and two-flats wedged on the side streets angling off Milwaukee. The church, built in ornate Renaissance Revival style, draws up to 1,000 people at a time for Polish-language masses.

TO GET THERE The CTA #56 Milwaukee Avenue bus takes the *s-l-o-w* scenic route through some of Chicago's oldest—and now graying—immigrant communities. Yet it is one of the most compelling bus rides in the city. You'll see Polish, Serbian, German, and Hispanic residents. Board at Randolph and Michigan or along Madison in the Loop. For a quicker, but not as interesting, ride, take the CTA Blue Line (O'Hare) to Logan Square, and transfer to a northbound #56 Milwaukee Avenue bus.

By car from the Loop, take the Kennedy Expressway (I-90/94) north to the Kimball (Belmont) or Addison exits, and head west (left) to Milwaukee Avenue.

WICKER PARK AND BUCKTOWN

IF YOU WANT TO SEE HIPSTER CHICAGO and hang out where slacker attitude prevails, head for Wicker Park and Bucktown. Adjoining neighborhoods stretching from Division on the south to Fullerton on the north, between the Kennedy Expressway and Western Avenue, these formerly Polish, currently Puerto Rican communities have seen significant incursions by artists and yuppies of all stripes. Near **Wicker Park** itself, a small triangle at Schiller and Damen, are the late-1800s stone mansions of beer barons lining Pierce, Hoyne, Oakley, and Damen. Chicago author Nelson Algren once lived along here, which is why Evergreen Avenue is also called Nelson Algren Avenue. Note the gingerbread house at **2137 West Pierce.**

The cradle of the flourishing arts scene is the **Coyote Building** at 1600 North Milwaukee Avenue and its across-the-street landmark counterpart, the **Flatiron Building** (1579 North Milwaukee). Each year in September, the galleries and studios hold a celebratory open house called Around the Coyote. Nearby is **Pentimento** (1629 North Milwaukee), featuring clothes by local designers.

Damen Avenue has become a mecca for small bistros, such as chef-owned **Le Bouchon** (1958 North Damen Avenue). Neighborhood stalwart **The Northside** (1635 North Damen) has an outdoor patio and a lively crowd.

Steep yourself in the late-night music scene at the **Double Door** (1572 North Milwaukee) or the supreme funk parlor called **Red Dog** (1958 West North).

TO GET THERE From the Loop, take the CTA Blue Line (O'Hare) to the Damen Avenue stop, which places you right at the confluence of Damen, North, and Milwaukee avenues in the heart of Bucktown. The #56 Milwaukee Avenue bus also takes you through Wicker Park and Bucktown.

By car from the Loop, drive north on the Kennedy Expressway (I-90/94) to the Division Street or North Avenue exits, and head west.

UKRAINIAN VILLAGE

UKRAINIAN VILLAGE IS MORE AUTHENTIC than Wicker Park, its gentrified neighbor to the north. On any given morning, you can still see old-world Ukrainians sweeping their sidewalks in front of the gingerbread cutouts and stained glass on their homes in this cozy neighborhood. (During the same morning in Wicker Park, you'll see trust-fund kids staggering home after a night on the town.)

Ukrainian Village stretches west along Chicago Avenue beween Ashland and Western and north to Division. Locals now call it "East Village" (east of Damen Avenue) and "West Town," which runs from Damen Avenue west to California Avenue.

The neighborhood's spiritual center is the **St. Nicholas Ukrainian Catholic Church,** at the corner of Oakley and Roice. The 13 copper-clad domes are modeled after those of the Basilica of St. Sophia in Kiev. But the real jewel is the much smaller **Russian Orthodox Holy Trinity Cathedral** (1121 North Leavitt at Haddon Street), designed by Louis Sullivan in 1901 and bearing his characteristic stenciling and ornamentation. Locals and longtime residents congregate for coffee and pastries at the **Village Cafe** (2304 West Chicago Avenue), which is connected to **Violet Berk's Flower Shop** (2300 West Chicago Avenue), a neighborhood staple for many years.

The hipster Wicker Park influence is evident in many new bars and restaurants that have opened up along Chicago Avenue. Younger people congregate at the **High Dive** (1938 West Chicago Avenue), where old-school soul plays loudly over the jukebox. Down the street, the **Continental** (2801 West Chicago Avenue) has a 4 a.m. weekday/5 a.m. Saturday liquor license, plus some of the city's best DJs. Next door to the Continental is **Feed** (2803 West Chicago Avenue), which serves Southern-style rotisserie chicken and catfish at affordable prices. At **Tommy's Rock 'n' Roll Cafe, Guitars, and Collectibles** (2548 West Chicago Avenue), you can buy one of more than 300 hundred electric guitars hanging on the wall while waiting for breakfast or lunch. Rocker Tom Petty did.

Thursday through Sunday, stop in at the **Ukrainian National Museum of Chicago** (2249 West Superior Street), featuring exhibits of traditional folk art, a rare-book library, and an archive chronicling the history of the city's Ukrainian community (see profile on page 175). **RR # 1 Chicago** (814 North Ashland at Chicago Avenue) carries handmade soaps, herbal teas, and hundreds of kitschy gifts. The shop is housed in a 1940s drugstore with more than 100 evenly cut oak medicine drawers and faded phamaceutical-art prints. The staff is accommodating, and there's usually a friendly dog wandering around the store.

TO GET THERE By public transportation, take the CTA Blue Line (O'Hare) northbound to Chicago Avenue, transfer to a westbound

#66 bus, and travel to Damen or Ashland. Or get on the #66 bus westbound near Water Tower Place at Chicago and Michigan.

By car from the Loop, drive north on Michigan Avenue to Chicago Avenue. Turn left (west) and continue to Ukrainian Village. This is one of the closest working-class neighborhoods to the Loop.

GOLD COAST AND OLD TOWN

BEHIND THE HIGH-RISES STRETCHING NORTH of Michigan Avenue aloing Lake Shore Drive are some of the most elegant townhouses and stately mansions in Chicago. It costs a fortune to live here, thus the name "Gold Coast," but it costs nothing to stroll along Astor Street or its neighbors from Division to North Avenue. Along the way, imagine urbane life in the former **Patterson-McCormick Mansion** (20 East Burton), which has since been divided into condominiums, or count the chimneys at **1555 North State Parkway,** the official residence of Chicago's Catholic archbishop.

Consider treating yourself to lunch at the **Pump Room** in the **Ambassador East Hotel** (1301 North State Parkway), which was Frank Sinatra's home away from home when he visited Chicago.

Old Town, which stretches west along North Avenue, was once a bohemian haven for artists, folkies, jazz clubs, and strip joints. Now the rehabbed townhomes and coach houses have made it quieter (and costlier), with upscale boutiques and trendy shops along Wells. Many children of the city's blue-blood families enroll at the private **Latin School** (59 West North Avenue).

Conversely, you'll find a young, beery crowd at some of the bars along Division. When the young ones get old and bitter, they graduate to the legendary **Old Town Ale House** (219 West North Avenue). The most authentic place to eat in Old Town is **Twin Anchors**, established in 1932 off the beaten path at 1655 North Sedgwick. It's known for its ribs, lots of Sinatra on the jukebox, and long waits. But it's worth it. (See profile in Part Eight, Dining and Restaurants.)

TO GET THERE Street parking is at a premium on the Gold Coast, so consider walking north from Michigan Avenue or taking the #151 bus and getting off anywhere between Oak Street and North Avenue. Walk west one block. For Old Town, there's a large parking garage next to the Piper's Alley theaters on North Avenue; you can also take the #22 or #36 buses heading north (board downtown along Dearborn) into the heart of the area.

CHINATOWN

CHICAGO'S TRADITIONAL CHINATOWN is a crowded, bustling area along the Wentworth Avenue corridor, its formal entrance marked by the ornate **Oriental arch** at Wentworth and Cermak. Walk south along Wentworth and note the templelike **On Leong Building** (2216 South Wentworth), the cornerstone of the commercial district, where immigrant bachelors in years past rented space in apartments on the second floor. (Plans call for the building to be converted into a youth center.) Wentworth offers a lively, teeming mix of restaurants, shops, groceries, even a wholesale-noodle company. The Chinatown branch of the **Chicago Public Library** (2353 South Wentworth) circulates more books and cassettes (many in Chinese) than any other in the city. Newer shopping areas have spilled out across Cermak Road and Archer Avenue, and newer Chinese and Asian neighborhoods have evolved on the Far North Side near Argyle Street, but for the sights and smells most of us expect in Chinatown, this is where you'll find them.

TO GET THERE From the Loop, take the CTA southbound Red Line (Dan Ryan) from State Street to the Cermak-Chinatown stop. The #24 Wentworth bus heads south from Clark and Randolph in the Loop, and the #62 Archer Avenue bus travels south along State Street (get off at Cermak and Archer, and walk one block east).

By car from the Loop, drive south on Michigan Avenue to 22nd Street (Cermak Road), turn right, and drive five blocks to a public parking lot at Wentworth and Cermak. Or drive south on the Dan Ryan Expressway and take the 22nd Street–Canalport turnoff, which leads to Chinatown.

TAYLOR STREET AND LITTLE ITALY

ONCE THE HEART OF ITALIAN CHICAGO, **Taylor Street** was severely altered by the construction of the University of Illinois at Chicago campus in the early 1960s, which displaced thousands of residents. Still, the Taylor Street area has undergone a renaissance, with new townhouses being built and coffeehouses and fern bars offering proximity to the Loop with the lure of the university. Combine a tour of the area with a visit to the **Jane Addams Hull-House Museum** (800 South Halsted Street; see attraction profile, 160) as well as the celebrated **Chicago Fire Academy** (558 West DeKoven), built on the spot where the Great Chicago Fire allegedly started.

For a taste of Taylor Street, try **Al's No. 1 Italian Beef** (1079 West Taylor Street)—so famous that tour buses stop here—followed by an Italian ice at **Mario's Lemonade Stand** on Taylor between Aberdeen and Carpenter (open only in summer; you'll have to wait in line or wend your way through cars parked three abreast). For Italian provisions, don't miss the **Conte di Savoia** deli (1438 West Taylor) or the **Ferrara Original Bakery** (2210 West Taylor). A classic neighborhood stop is **Tufano's Restaurant,** also known as the **Vernon Park Tap** (1073 West Vernon Park Place, across from the park). Opened in 1931 as a social club, the tap was discovered in the 1960s by author Nelson Algren, who would stop in on his way to White Sox games at Old Comiskey Park.

One of the city's best-kept secrets—even some locals don't know about it—is the **Little Italy** strip, on Oakley south of Taylor. Residents here don't like to be compared to Taylor Street: many Little Italy families have roots in northern Italy, while Taylor Street residents are mostly of Sicilian descent.

Taylor Street is roughly surrounded by 16th Street, Western Avenue, the Stevenson Expressway, and the south branch of the Chicago River. There are several storefront restaurants and delis; one of the best is **Bruna's Ristorante** (2424 South Oakley), which has been in the quiet neighborhood since the 1930s. Little Italy, meanwhile, has opened its big arms to **Mila's Restaurant and Bakery** (2401 South Oakley), a popular Polish stomping ground that also serves Italian cannoli and tiramisu.

North on Polk Street, between Laflin and Loomis, you can see some turn-of-the-19th-century homes built in the style prevalent before the Great Fire of 1871. **Bishop Street** between Taylor and Polk and **Ada Street** between Flournoy and Columbus Park also give a great feel to the neighborhood. **St. Basil Greek Orthodox Church,** at Ashland and Polk, bears witness to the neighborhood's ethnic evolution from Jewish to Greek to Italian—the church was once a synagogue, and a Hebrew inscription is still visible on the exterior.

TO GET THERE Take any CTA Blue Line train heading west to the UIC-Halsted stop or the Racine stop. During the week you can take the #37 bus southbound on Wells through the Loop.

By car from the Loop, drive west on the Eisenhower Expressway (I-290) to the Ashland exit, and head south to Taylor Street. To get to Little Italy, take the Western exit until the 2400 block, and turn left on Oakley.

PILSEN–LITTLE VILLAGE

CALL THESE CHICAGO'S BARRIOS—home to the largest population of Mexican Americans in the Midwest—where the signs are in Spanish and the smells are enticing. **Pilsen** lies principally along 18th Street between Canal and Damen. **Little Village,** considered somewhat more prosperous and stable, opens with its own pink-stucco gateway arch at 26th Street and Albany and unwinds in boisterous fashion west along 26th to Kostner. Get your kicks on 26th.

Once the province of Bohemians and Poles, Pilsen is now home to thousands of Mexicans. It also has a thriving artist's colony and is home to the **Mexican Fine Arts Center Museum** (1852 West 19th Street). The museum, which opened in 1987 in the converted Harrison Park Boat Craft Shop, strives to showcase the wealth and breadth of Mexican art in its exhibitions. Works from legends such as Diego Rivera and David Siquieros are part of the museum's permanent collection. Find time to survey some of the 20 **hand-painted murals** depicting various cultural, religious, and political themes scattered throughout Pilsen (at 1305 West 18th Street, 18th and Racine, 18th and Wood, and lining the concrete wall along the tracks at 16th and Allport). When you visit, notice the elaborate cornices and roofs of some of the 19th-century storefronts and two-flats along 18th Street west of Halsted. The **Providence of God Church** (717 West 18th Street) is the focal point for many celebrations, including a powerful Via Crucis (Way of the Cross) procession on Good Friday.

A favorite gathering place is the **Cafe Jumping Bean** (1439 West 18th Street), where you are sure to run into neighborhood artists and teachers drinking coffee or enjoying a hot focaccia sandwich. Local art is also featured on the walls. "The Bean," as locals call the cafe, is on the first floor of the most breathtaking structure on 18th Street, a three-story building constructed in 1907. An aqua dome sits on top, creating a castlelike ambience.

Plenty of taquerias, bakeries, and taverns line the strip. Check out **Panaderia Nuevo Leon** (1634 West 18th Street) for sweets or **Carnitas Uruapan** (1725 West 18th Street) for barbecued pork, *chicharrones* (fried pork rinds), and spicy salsa.

The neighborhood's favorite (and safest) tavern is **Skylark** (2149 South Halsted), where a fine selection of beer is accented by Southern-style comfort food. The atmosphere is deep 1960s, with green-leather couches and groovy lighting. Chicago foodies are also flocking to the new **Mundial Cocina Mestiza** (1640 West 18th Street) for its made-to-order tortillas and made-from-scratch tamales. Don't miss the grilled salmon with caramelized mangoes.

Little Village has its own colorful wall murals, such as the **"Broken Wall"** mural in the back of Los Comales Restaurant next to McDonald's (26th and Kedzie). You'll find others at 26th and Homan, 25th and St. Louis, and 25th and Pulaski. Here, too, the neighborhood pulses along the commercial strip of 26th. Consider selecting a piñata from the many styles found at **La Justicia Grocery** (Millard and 26th), and try the dependable Mexican fare at **Lalo's** (4126 West 26th Street).

TO GET THERE For Pilsen: by public transportation, board the westbound CTA Blue Line at Dearborn in the Loop, and get off at the 18th Street stop in the heart of Pilsen. By car, drive south on the Dan Ryan Expressway (I-90/94), exit at 18th Street, and head west.

For Little Village: by public transportation, board the #60 Blue Island–26th Street bus westbound on Adams in the Loop. By car from Pilsen, continue west along 18th Street to Western, go south (left) to 26th Street, and proceed west past the Cook County Courthouse and the turrets marking the perimeter of the Cook County Jail to the arch at Albany.

BRIDGEPORT

IF YOU REALLY WANT TO KNOW CHICAGO, get to know Bridgeport. Just south of Chinatown, it's the home of the White Sox and the bar with the oldest liquor license in town (now that the original **Berghoff** has closed). Bridgeport has also supplied the city with its bodacious mayors, except for a brief respite between 1979 and 1989. In a city where politics is played at Super Bowl level (with the occasional quarterback sneak), the shrines to

Chicago's leaders are what you would expect: the family home, the neighborhood pub, and the ward organization office—or, in an earlier era, what might have irreverently been called "the machine shop."

First stop on the pilgrimage, then, is **3536 South Lowe,** the former home of the late Mayor Richard J. and Eleanor "Sis" Daley, parents of the current mayor, Richard M. Daley. The modest redbrick bungalow is distinguished from its neighbors only by a flagpole. At the end of the block is a police station whose handy placement was arranged by Hizzoner. A few years ago, when the younger Mayor Daley left the neighborhood for the South Loop, it made front-page news locally.

A few blocks to the west and south, you'll find the other two neighborhood shrines right across the street from each other, at 37th Street and Halsted: the **11th Ward Democratic Organization** and **Schaller's Pump** (3714 South Halsted), licensed to sell liquor longer than any other tavern in Chicago: 125 years. The Pump's dim lights and tin ceiling warmed many of the elder Mayor Daley's victory celebrations. During the 1940s and 1950s, workers from the nearby Union Stockyards lunched here. Today Schaller's is a popular postgame hangout for White Sox fans, but it retains its sense of history. The Schaller family might even tell you how Bridgeport got its name: a port was built because a low bridge at Ashland Avenue and the Chicago River forced the unloading and reloading of barges in order to pass.

The walk around Bridgeport is remarkable. You'll see longtime residents sitting on their bungalow stoops and families playing boccie in the park. Have a meal at the **Polo Cafe** (3322 South Morgan), where pasta, salads, and fish are served in the Old Eagle Room, a converted 1914 nickelodeon that, in its former incarnation as the Eagle Theater, was popular with Lithuanian immigrants.

Stroll north along Halsted to sample the changing flavor of Bridgeport. You'll see Chinese, Mexican, Italian, and Lithuanian establishments all within a few blocks. Above all, don't miss **Healthy Food Restaurant** (3236 South Halsted Street), where slim waitresses in flowing skirts dish out ample portions of hearty Lithuanian *kugelis* and mushroom soup to the music of Tchaikovsky.

TO GET THERE Take the CTA Red Line (Dan Ryan) to the new 35th Street stop at U.S. Cellular Field (from there it's a bit of a hike to Halsted, or you can transfer to a #35 bus westbound). Or board a #44 bus southbound on State Street in the Loop.

By car, drive south on Lake Shore Drive to the 31st Street exit and then west on Halsted, or drive south on the Dan Ryan Expressway to the 35th Street exit and then west to Halsted.

HYDE PARK–KENWOOD

THIS IS THE PLACE FOR BIG HOMES, big ideas, and a great cluster of cultural institutions. Drive along Ellis, Greenwood, and Woodlawn between 47th and East Hyde Park Boulevard (5100 South) in **Kenwood,** and you'll marvel at the number of grand mansions on large lots. Years ago, these were homes of titans of industry; today they more than likely harbor faculty from the nearby **University of Chicago,** a hotbed of Nobel Laureates that anchors **Hyde Park** with its cerebral gray presence between 57th Street and the Midway Plaisance, a wide, grassy boulevard created for the 1893 Columbian Exposition. Descend the stairs to the **Seminary Co-op Bookstore** (5757 South University), and you can't help but feel like a scholar yourself. At the **Reynolds Club** (57th Street and University), you can survey the eternal student scene at Hutchinson Commons from behind one of the nouveau 'zines free for the taking.

Hyde Park is also one of the city's better integrated communities. The late Mayor Harold Washington used to live here, and the Fifth Ward is considered one of the city's most liberal. **K.A.M. Isaiah Israel** (1100 East Hyde Park Boulevard), the Midwest's oldest Jewish congregation, is here as well. Good shopping can be found at the bustling commercial strips along 53rd and 57th streets and at **Harper Court** shopping center (52nd and South Harper). You'll certainly shed the tourist label if you tip back a brew at **Woodlawn Tap** (1172 East 55th Street) or eat at **Valois** (1518 East 53rd Street), a cafeteria hangout for cops, cabbies, and students of urban life where the motto is "See Your Food."

TO GET THERE Be prepared for a lot of walking (not recommended after dark), or plan to tour the avenues by car. If you want to use public transportation, take the #6 Jeffrey express bus (30¢ surcharge) southbound from State Street to 57th, and walk to the University of Chicago. Or take the slower #1 Indiana–Hyde Park bus east on Jackson from Union Station, then south on Michigan to East Hyde Park Boulevard for a tour of Kenwood.

Metra electric trains also serve Hyde Park. Board underground at Randolph and Michigan or at Van Buren and Michigan, and exit at the 53rd and Lake Park stop, the combined 55th-56th-57th Street stop, or the University of Chicago stop at 59th Street and Harper. (The fare is $2.05 one-way.)

By car from the Loop, drive south on Lake Shore Drive to the 57th Street exit. Pass in front of the Museum of Science and Industry, and follow the signs for the University of Chicago. Or take the 47th Street exit, drive west, and then turn south on Woodlawn or Greenwood for a look at the mansions.

*uno*fficial **TIP**
The **Chicago Architecture Foundation** (☎ 312-922-3432) offers two-hour walking tours of Kenwood in May, June, September, and October.

BRONZEVILLE

KNOWN AS "THE BLACK METROPOLIS" in the early 20th century (and immortalized in poet Gwendolyn Brooks's *A Street in Bronzeville*), this South Side community is on the rebound in the early 21st century. Luminaries such as Louis Armstrong, Nat

"King" Cole, and boxer Joe Louis lived in Bronzeville in its heyday; the neighborhood is coming back in their spirit. The boundaries of Bronzeville are roughly 22nd Street (just south of McCormick Place) south to 51st Street, east to the lake, and west to the Dan Ryan Expressway. The **Bronzeville Walk of Fame,** along the eastern sidewalk of King Drive near 22nd Street, features markers honoring past residents such as singers Sam Cooke and Howlin' Wolf.

The hub of activity is near the **Harold Washington Cultural Center** (4701 South King Drive), which presents concerts in a 1,000-seat theater and features rotating exhibits. Across the street from the cultural center, residents gather for coffee at the **Spoken Word Cafe** (4655 South King Drive) and peruse the more than 9,000 titles next door at the **Afrocentric Bookstore** (4655 South King Drive). Enjoy live jazz and remarkable soul food at the **Negro League Café** (301 East 43rd Street) or stand-up comedy at a new club called **Jokes and Notes** (4641 South King Drive). And you haven't been to the South Side until you've tried spicy **Harold's Chicken.** Harold's #7 (108 East 47th) has been in Bronzeville forever. New to the neighborhood is the **Bronzeville Information Center,** in the Supreme Life Building (35th Street and King Drive).

Over the years, Bronzeville has had its share of notable residents. **Louis Armstrong** lived at 421 East 44th Street until 1931, when the trumpet legend relocated to California. Bluesman **Muddy Waters** built a small studio in the basement of his house near Lake Michigan at 4339 South Lake Park, where he lived from 1954 to 1974. Crooner **Nat "King" Cole** once called 4023 South Vincennes home. Even the **Marx Brothers** lived in the neighborhood around 1910 (at 4512 South King Drive) while playing the Chicago vaudeville circuit. They cooked up some story about being farmers on the South Side, but in truth Groucho, Chico, Harpo, Zeppo, and Gummo slacked off while watching baseball at nearby Comiskey Park.

TO GET THERE The CTA Green Line Stop at 47th Street is still funky and dangerous, so it's best to drive or take a taxi. Take the Dan Ryan Expressway south to 47th Street, and turn left (east) to King Drive.

SOUTH SHORE

LOCATED BETWEEN 67TH and 79th streets and reaching from Lake Michigan on the east to Stony Island Avenue on the west, South Shore has been home to Chicagoans for more than 100 years. Today, many affluent African Americans dwell in some of the large, elegant homes lining South Euclid, Constance, and Bennett streets between East 67th and East 71st at Jeffrey. Though the commercial strip along East 71st has suffered, the South Shore Bank (71st and Jeffrey) has become a national leader in innovative financing for community-development projects.

The **South Shore Country Club,** at the intersection of 71st Street and South Shore, remains a gem. Once the scene of South Side society gatherings, the stucco Spanish-style structure fell on hard times until the Chicago Park District purchased it 20 years ago. Now restored and open to the public, the club has a golf course, stables for Chicago Police Department horses, and up-close lakefront views. In the winter you'll see a few solitary cross-country skiers; in the summer, there's picnicking and lakeside play.

The massive **Church of St. Philip Neri** (2132 East 72nd Street), one of Chicago's largest, has an exquisite sequence of mosaics depicting the Stations of the Cross. Another impressive house of worship is the **Masjid Honorable Elijah Muhammad** (7351 South Stony Island Avenue), an Islamic mosque that occupies what was once the largest Greek Orthodox church in North America.

To experience local cuisine, try **Army & Lou's** for soul food (422 East 75th Street) or **Alexander's Steak House and Cocktail Lounge** (3010 East 79th Street), where they've been dishing out prime rib and jazz at night for more than 50 years. **Salaam Restaurant & Bakery,** (700 West 79th Street) is a showcase community investment by the Nation of Islam.

TO GET THERE The CTA #6 Jeffrey express bus goes southbound on State Street to 71st Street and Jeffrey (30¢ surcharge). A quicker option is the Metra electric train from Randolph and Michigan—the station is underground—which stops at Bryn Mawr (71st Street and Jeffrey; the fare is $2.05 one-way).

By car from the Loop, drive south along Lake Shore Drive through Jackson Park to South Shore.

OTHER NEIGHBORHOODS OF INTEREST

Rogers Park

The city's northernmost conglomeration of cultures and lifestyles, Rogers Park mixes well-preserved lakeside condos with 1960s hippie holdovers and ethnic groups ranging from Russian to Jamaican to Pakistani. Visit the **Heartland Café** (7000 North Glenwood) for vegetarian food served with radical politics. Sip espresso at **No Exit Café** (6970 North Glenwood) or **Ennui** (6981 North Sheridan Road).

unofficial **TIP**
Rogers Park sprawls pretty far, and it's probably best not to wander alone or travel on foot after dark.

Lincoln Park–DePaul

This section, sandwiched between Old Town and Lakeview, may have the city's largest concentration of young white urban professionals (aka "Trixies" and "Todds")—or at least the loudest and most visible. Students at **DePaul University,** the large Catholic institution renowned for its Blue Demons basketball team, probably can't afford to live here after graduation unless they double up in one of the two- or three-flats along Bissel or Sheffield whose back porches face the El tracks.

It's fun to roam the pleasant, tree-lined streets and check out the gentrified townhomes. Lincoln Park was one of the first North Side neighborhoods to turn over a new leaf in the 1960s and 1970s. The most majestic homes line Fullerton Parkway as you head west from the lake, but a walk along any of the side streets, such as Hudson, Cleveland, Belden, and Fremont, will provide ample viewing pleasure.

Oz Park, at Webster and Orchard, is a favorite playground for kids and adults. The nearby **Glascott's Saloon** (2158 North Halsted) is a favorite playground for adults acting like kids. The shops, galleries, boutiques, and restaurants clustered along Halsted, Armitage, and Clark are fun for browsing and spending. With the recent closing of Demon Dogs underneath the El tracks, the most venerable restaurant in the neighborhood is now **Geja's Cafe** (340 West Armitage), a romantic fondue hideaway that opened in Old Town in 1965 and moved to Lincoln Park a few years later. Live classical and flamenco guitarists accompany the best fondue in the Midwest. It is, however, pricier than Demon Dogs.

TO GET THERE The CTA Brown Line (Ravenswood) stops at Armitage or Fullerton; the Red Line (Howard) also goes to Fullerton (the stop closest to DePaul, where Demon Dogs was). The #151 bus is a beautiful ride through Lincoln Park, while the #22 or #36 buses (board north along Dearborn) put you closer to the shopping district.

By car, drive north on Lake Shore Drive to the Fullerton exit, and then head west. Or take the North Avenue exit to Stockton, and drive through Lincoln Park.

Humboldt Park–Logan Square

Originally settled by Polish and Russian Jews, then by Scandinavians, Ukrainians, and Eastern Europeans, Humboldt Park and Logan Square are now home to a large number of Hispanic residents, along with young artists and musicians getting bargains on spacious apartments and condos.

A tour here opens the door to an earlier era of residential gentility. Many elegant graystones line the grand boulevards of Humboldt, Palmer, Kedzie, and Logan (one of the city's widest). **Logan Square** was the northwesternmost point of Daniel Burnham's 1909 Chicago Plan, which mixed dense green landscaping with affordable housing for immigrants. The hot dining spot here is **Lula** (2537 North Kedzie), known for fabulous breakfasts with natural ingredients (see profile in Part Eight, Dining and Restaurants). Sometimes, though, you can cut the "hip" factor with a knife. In addition, Logan Square has Chicago's most unusual intersection—a traffic circle with a massive marble column commemorating the centennial of Illinois statehood. Some of the areas off the boulevards are dicey but improving. Still, be careful.

TO GET THERE The CTA Blue Line (O'Hare) stops at Logan Square. By car, drive west along North Avenue to Humboldt Boulevard and then north to Palmer Square.

Pullman

Originally a company town built by George Pullman to house workers at his railroad-car factory, this area is now a historic district, with more than 80% of the original 1,800 buildings still standing. Start your tour at the **Historic Pullman Foundation,** housed in the Florence Hotel (named for Pullman's daughter) at 11141 South Cottage Grove Avenue (☎ 773-785-8901; **www.pullmanil.org**). The neighborhood harbors architecturally unique mansions—once the executives' houses—and far more modest two-story attached row houses in muted Queen Anne style.

TO GET THERE Pullman is on the Far Southwest Side, almost at the city's southern boundary. By public transportation, take the Metra Electric train ($2.75 one-way) from the station under Randolph and Michigan to the Pullman stop at 111th and Cottage Grove (it's one block to the Florence Hotel) or to the Kensington stop at 115th, which has more frequent service.

By car, drive south on the Dan Ryan Expressway (I-90/94); continue south on the Calumet Expressway (I-94), and exit at 111th Street. Head west a few blocks to South Forrestville.

FINAL NOTE

AS RICH AS CHICAGO IS IN ARCHITECTURE, history, culture, and ethnic diversity, it is a major American city—which is to say, it is grappling with problems of unemployment, decaying infrastructure (especially the so-called expressways), crime, and beseiged public schools. Many areas of the city's West Side still have not recovered from the fires and looting that followed the assassination of Martin Luther King Jr. in 1968. You need only drive west on 47th Street after touring the mansions of Kenwood to see the once-stately buildings on Drexel Boulevard now boarded up and barren, or glance across the Dan Ryan Expressway from U.S. Cellular Field to the forlorn hulks of Stateway Gardens and the Robert Taylor Homes (the largest public-housing complex in the world). In such juxtapositions of wealth and poverty, you will recognize the challenges facing Chicago. But as you get to know Chicago, you will know the city can stand up to the task.

CHICAGO *for* CHILDREN

QUESTION: BESIDES THE REQUISITE TRIP to the top of the Sears Tower, what else is there to entertain kids on a Chicago vacation?

Answer: A lot. Chicago offers plenty of fun-filled places to visit and things to do that will satisfy the most curious—and fidgety—kids. Their folks will have fun, too.

The *Unofficial Guide* rating system for attractions includes an Appeal by Age Group category ranging from one star (★), meaning don't bother, to five stars (★★★★★), meaning not to be missed. To get you started, we've provided a list of the attractions in and around Chicago that are most likely to appeal to children. (Also look for the

"Kids" icon next to kid-friendly listings in our main attraction profiles, starting on page 138.)

MORE THINGS TO DO WITH CHILDREN

CHICAGO HAS MORE FOR KIDS TO ENJOY than museums, zoos, and tall buildings. Some ideas: swimming in Lake Michigan at **Oak Street Beach** and **North Avenue Beach;** roller skating at **United Skates of America** (Rainbow Entertainment Center, 4836 North Clark Street; ☎ 773-271-5668); and browsing at **NikeTown,** a high-tech shoe store (669 North Michigan Avenue; ☎ 312-642-6363), or the hugely popular three-level **American Girl Place** (111 East Chicago Avenue; ☎ 312-943-9400), with a cafe, a photo salon, and even a beauty shop for dolls. Another sure hit is *That's Weird, Grandma,* a collection of skits performed and written by Barrel of Monkeys, a group of Chicago public-school children. The popular show is staged every Monday night at the **Neo-Futurarium** (5153 North Ashland Avenue; ☎ 773-275-5255).

PRO SPORTS AND A REALLY BIG AMUSEMENT PARK

DEPENDING ON THE SEASON and ticket availability, take the gang to a **Bears, Blackhawks, Bulls, Cubs,** or **White Sox** game. In the summer, don't forget **Buckingham Fountain** in Grant Park: computer-controlled water displays send 14,000 gallons of water a minute through 133 jets. Colorful displays can be seen nightly from dusk to 11 p.m.

unofficial **TIP**
Six Flags Great America gets packed—go early in the day during the week, and avoid weekends.

Farther afield (if you've got a car), take a drive to **Six Flags Great America,** a monster amusement park north of Chicago with more than 100 rides (including 13 roller coasters), shops, stage shows, and special theme sections representing different eras in American history. The park is open from May through October with varying hours; admission is $54.99 for adults, $34.99 for children. With prices like these, plan on spending the day. For more information and directions, call ☎ 847-249-INFO.

Other neat activities kids will enjoy: bicycling or Rollerblading on the bike path along Lake Michigan or taking the **Untouchables Tour** and exploring the old haunts of Chicago's gangsters (for more information, call ☎ 773-881-1195).

HELPFUL HINTS *for* VISITORS

HOW TO GET INTO MUSEUMS FOR HALF PRICE

SAVE MORE THAN $30 WHEN you visit Chicago's most popular museums and attractions with a **CityPass,** a book of tickets that cuts the price of admission in half at the Art Institute of Chicago, Field

Museum, Adler Planetarium and Astronomy Museum, Shedd Aquarium, and Hancock Observatory.

The passes cost $49.50 for adults and $39 for children ages 4 to 11. Ticket books are sold at participating attractions and are good for nine days, beginning with the first day you use them. Don't remove the individual tickets from the booklet; just present the CityPass at each attraction. The clerk at the site removes the ticket, and you walk on in (usually without waiting in line to buy a ticket). For more information, visit **www.citypass.com.**

WHEN ADMISSION IS FREE

MANY CHICAGO MUSEUMS that usually charge admission open their doors at no charge one day a week. If you'd like to save a few bucks during your visit, use our list when planning your touring itinerary.

In addition, a few worthy attractions around town are free to the public all the time. Here's the list:

- Chicago Botanic Garden ($12 parking)
- Chicago Cultural Center
- Garfield Park Conservatory (donation requested during flower shows)
- Harold Washington Library Center
- Jane Addams Hull-House Museum
- Lincoln Park Conservatory
- Lincoln Park Zoo
- Mexican Fine Arts Center Museum
- Oriental Institute Museum
- Polish Museum of America ($5 donation requested)
- Smart Museum of Art
- Smith Museum of Stained Glass

Other Free-admission Days

MONDAY

Adler Planetarium

Chicago History Museum

Museum of Science and Industry (fall and winter, except December)

TUESDAY

Adler Planetarium

Art Institute of Chicago

Brookfield Zoo (October–March; $8 parking)

International Museum of Surgical Science

Museum of Contemporary Art (evenings only)

Museum of Science and Industry (fall and winter, except December)

THURSDAY

Brookfield Zoo (October–March; $8 parking)

Chicago Children's Museum (evenings)

SUNDAY

DuSable Museum of African American History

SCENIC DRIVES

THOUGH WE RECOMMEND THAT VISITORS to Chicago forgo driving and rely on airport vans, taxis, and public transportation, not everyone will heed our advice. In addition, rental cars are plentiful in Chicago, and traffic gets downright manageable on weekends. If you've got access to a set of wheels and you feel the urge to roam, here are a few ideas.

Around Town

The best views of the city unfold anywhere along **Lake Shore Drive.** For an urban exploration beyond the lakefront, tour Chicago's boulevards and greenways, a series of wide streets laid out in the 19th century that link seven parks along what once was the city's western border.

Heading North

For a quick and scenic escape from the city, head north on Lake Shore Drive until it becomes **Sheridan Road.** This pleasant drive meanders along the lakeshore and passes through affluent neighborhoods full of gorgeous homes and mansions. In Evanston, Sheridan skirts the beautiful campus of **Northwestern University** and, in Wilmette, the breathtaking **Bahá'í House of Worship.**

unofficial **TIP**
Enjoy the scenery along Lake Shore Drive, but for safety's sake, don't get too distracted by the sights as you navigate this busy highway.

Farther north along Sheridan Road in Glencoe is the **Chicago Botanic Garden**—worth a stop in any season—and, in Highland Park, the **Ravinia Festival,** where evening summertime performances range from Joan Baez to the Chicago Symphony Orchestra.

GREAT VIEWS

NOBODY COMES TO THE MIDWEST for the views, right? Wrong—at least in Chicago. Here's a list of ten great spots that offer breathtaking vistas of skyline, Lake Michigan, and the city stretching toward the horizon.

1. The observation decks atop the **Sears Tower** and the **John Hancock Center** offer stupendous vistas from vantage points over 1,000 feet high. Go on a clear day; better yet, go at night. We prefer the Hancock Center, which is closer to the lake and usually not very crowded.

2. **Lake Shore Drive** offers dramatic views of the Chicago skyline and the lake all along its length. We especially like the vantage point looking

north where the Stevenson Expressway joins Lake Shore Drive (at McCormick Place).

3. **Grant Park** is a great place to walk and look up at Chicago's downtown. *Note:* Unless there is a summer festival going on, consider the park unsafe at night.

4. The view of downtown from the **Shedd Aquarium** is a knockout, especially at dusk as the lights begin to wink on.

unofficial **TIP**
A drive along Sheridan Road is especially popular with Chicagoans in the fall when the leaves change. To avoid the worst of the traffic, go early in the day.

5. The **Michigan Avenue Bridge** over the Chicago River offers a heart-stopping view of downtown buildings, especially at night, when the Wrigley Building and Tribune Tower are both illuminated.

6. Starting around Thanksgiving, the **Festival of Lights** along North Michigan Avenue features more than 300,000 white lights for the holidays.

7. The **Ravenswood El** has surprises around every corner as it encircles the Loop. Don't get off—take it north, then grab the next train toward downtown for more views of the city.

8. **Montrose Harbor** offers a spectacular view of the Chicago skyline, especially at night. You'll need a car: the harbor is near the northern end of Lincoln Park on a finger of land jutting out into Lake Michigan; get there from Lake Shore Drive.

9. As a lot of Chicago runners and bicyclists know, a stunning sunrise is a frequent reward on an early morning jaunt on the **Lakefront Trail** along Lake Michigan.

10. Or try this not-to-be-forgotten scene from anywhere on the lakefront (if the heavens cooperate on your trip): moonrise over **Lake Michigan.**

OPRAH'S ON!

THE UNOFFICIAL GUIDE TO CHICAGO IS WRITTEN BY NATIVES. And these natives are restless that more people ask about getting into **The Oprah Winfrey Show**—the number-one talk show in America—than getting into the Art Institute of Chicago. Still, lots of people visit the city just to see Oprah. If you're one of them, here's what to do:

For audience reservations, call ☎ 312-591-9222 at least one month before your visit. A better bet is to visit **www.oprah.com** for last-minute e-mail reservations. There's no charge, and reservations are accepted for up to four people (who must be age 18 or older). **Harpo Studios** (*Harpo* is *Oprah* spelled backward), where the shows are taped twice daily (early and late morning, frontward) on Tuesdays, Wednesdays, and Thursdays, is a couple of blocks west of the Loop at 1058 West Washington Boulevard. The show goes on hiatus from late June to late August and again from mid-December through mid-January, when Oprah usually takes her staff on a highfalutin vacation.

Jer-ry! Jer-ry! Jer-ry!

Can't get a ticket to *Oprah*? There's always the classy consolation prize of **The Jerry Springer Show.** Call at least one month in advance. Tickets are free, and parties are (sensibly) limited to six people; shows are usually taped at 10 a.m. and 1 p.m. on Mondays, Tuesdays, and Wednesdays, and on Tuesday evenings at 6 and 8 p.m. (No shows are taped in July—there are enough fireworks as it is.) The studios are located at the NBC Tower (454 North Columbus Drive, north of the Loop and just east of Michigan Avenue; ☎ 312-321-5365). Jerry's Web site (**www.jerryspringertv.com**) also has reservation forms and lists of tasteful upcoming topics. If you strike out here, you could move on to *Judge Mathis*. The reality-based court show tapes on Thursdays and Fridasy from April through mid-July, also at the NBC Tower (☎ 866-362-8447 or 866-837-3428).

CHICAGO ATTRACTIONS

THE FOLLOWING PROFILES PROVIDE YOU with a comprehensive guide to Chicago's top attractions. We give you enough information so that you can choose the places you want to see, based on your own interests. Each attraction includes a location description so you can plan your visit logically without spending a lot of valuable time crisscrossing the city.

ATTRACTIONS BY TYPE AND LOCATION

BECAUSE OF THE WIDE RANGE OF ATTRACTIONS in and around Chicago—from an unparalleled collection of French Impressionist paintings in the Art Institute to America's tallest building—we provide the following charts to help you prioritize your touring at a glance. You'll find attractions organized by type and neighborhood, complete with authors' ratings from one star (skip it) to five stars (not to be missed). Individual attraction profiles follow the charts, organized alphabetically by attraction name.

ATTRACTION PROFILES

Adler Planetarium and Astronomy Museum ★★½

APPEAL BY AGE	PRESCHOOL ★	GRADE SCHOOL ★★★★	TEENS ★★★
YOUNG ADULTS ★★★		OVER 30 ★★★	SENIORS ★★★

LOCATION **South Loop; 1300 South Lake Shore Drive; ☎ 312-922-STAR; www.adlerplanetarium.org**

Type of attraction Narrative sky shows in a domed theater, a slide presentation, and exhibits on astronomy and space exploration; a self-guided tour. **Admission** *Daily:* $16 adults; $14 children ages 4–17; $15 seniors (age 65 and over), for 1 show and audio tour; 2 shows, add $4; additional shows, $5 each. Free museum admission on Monday and Tuesday, January 9–February 28 and September 11–December 19. Shows are an additional cost. Monday and Tuesday, free; admission includes 1 sky-show exhibit. **Hours** Daily, 9:30 a.m.–4:30 p.m. (summer until 6 p.m.); first Friday of each month, 9:30 a.m.–10 p.m.; closed Thanksgiving and Christmas. **When to go** Anytime. **Special comments** The comfortable, high-backed seats in the theater almost guarantee you won't get a stiff neck from watching the show on the domed ceiling. Some fascinating stuff on display, but the low-key planetarium show is geared to younger viewers and hard-core space cadets. **How much time to allow** 40 minutes for the show and at least half an hour to view the exhibits.

DESCRIPTION AND COMMENTS The Adler Planetarium was the first in the country when it opened in 1930. The 12-sided pink granite building that houses the Sky Theater was funded by a Sears, Roebuck & Company executive who had the Zeiss projector imported from Germany. In addition to the narrated sky shows (which change throughout the year), visitors can explore a wide range of exhibits on topics that include telescopes, the planets, man-made satellites, the moon, optics, and navigation. It's a modern, informative place that will delight youngsters and adults who read Carl Sagan. In early 1997, the Adler embarked on a $40-million expansion and renovation program that added 60,000 square feet of new space.

TOURING TIPS Enter the planetarium through the glass building that faces the planetarium, not via the granite steps. On Friday nights (when the planetarium is open until 10 p.m.) visitors can tour the Doane Observatory and see its 20-inch telescope. Visit the planetarium late in a day of hard sightseeing; relaxing in a comfortable, high-backed chair for 40 minutes is nirvana even if you don't give a hoot about the cosmos. The view of the city skyline on the promontory leading to the building is spectacular, especially at sunset when the skyscrapers begin to light up.

OTHER THINGS TO DO NEARBY The John G. Shedd Aquarium and the Field Museum of Natural History are both within easy walking distance on the traffic-free Museum Campus. Bad news if you're hungry: getting something to eat beyond a hot dog requires flagging a cab or grabbing a bus downtown.

Art Institute of Chicago ★★★★★

| APPEAL BY AGE | PRESCHOOL ★ | GRADE SCHOOL ★★★ | TEENS ★★★ |
| YOUNG ADULTS ★★★★ | OVER 30 ★★★★★ | SENIORS ★★★★★ |

LOCATION **The Loop; 111 South Michigan Avenue; ☎ 312-443-3600; www.artic.edu**

Type of attraction Internationally acclaimed collections of paintings and sculptures housed in a complex of neoclassical buildings erected for the World's Columbian Exposition of 1893; guided and self-guided tours. **Admission** $12 adults, $7 students and seniors; children ages 12 and under free; free admission on Thursday and Friday evenings, 5–9 p.m., through Labor Day, and Thursday evenings, 5–8 p.m., throughout the year, every day February 1–February 21;

checkroom, $1 per item. **Hours** *Through Labor Day:* Monday–Wednesday, 10:30 a.m.–5 p.m.; Thursday and Friday, 10:30 a.m.–9 p.m.; Saturday and Sunday, 10 a.m.–5 p.m. *After Labor Day:* Monday–Wednesday and Friday, 10:30 a.m.–5 p.m.; Thursday, 10:30 a.m.–8 p.m.; Saturday and Sunday, 10 a.m.–5 p.m.; closed Christmas, New Year's Day, and Thanksgiving. **When to go** During the school year, the museum is often besieged by groups of schoolchildren on field trips in the mornings; afternoons are usually less crowded. **Special comments** The first floor is the only level that connects the three buildings that compose the Art Institute. It also provides access to Michigan Avenue (west) and Columbus Drive (east), food, restrooms, and water fountains. Disabled access is at the Columbus Drive entrance. The best of a handful of attractions that elevate Chicago to world-class status. Not to be missed. **How much time to allow** At least 2 hours for a brief run-through, all day for art lovers. Better yet, try to visit the Art Institute more than once—the place is huge.

DESCRIPTION AND COMMENTS The massive classical-Renaissance–style home of the Art Institute of Chicago was completed in 1892, just in time for the 1893 World's Columbian Exposition. Located on the edge of Grant Park near the Loop, the museum is easily identified by the two bronze lions standing guard on Michigan Avenue.

It's a world-class museum especially renowned for its Impressionist collection, which includes five of the paintings in Monet's haystack series, Caillebotte's *Paris, a Rainy Day,* and, perhaps the museum's best-known painting, Seurat's pointillist masterpiece *Sunday Afternoon on the Island of La Grande Jatte.* The large museum shop features calendars, books, cards, gifts (mugs, scarves, posters, CDs), and a huge collection of art books (some at reduced prices).

TOURING TIPS The second-floor gallery of European art is arranged chronologically from late medieval to post-Impressionist, with paintings and sculptures arranged in skylight-brightened rooms; prints and drawings are hung in corridor galleries.

OTHER THINGS TO DO NEARBY The Loop is a block west; Grant Park and Lake Michigan are behind the Art Institute. Walking tours of downtown Chicago start across the street at the Chicago Architecture Foundation; no visit to the Windy City is complete until you've taken at least one. Culture vultures in search of more art (but with a modern slant) can cross Michigan Avenue to the Museum of Contemporary Photography, on the grand floor of Columbia College, 600 North Michigan Avenue. It's the only museum of its kind in the Midwest and features rotating exhibits of modern photography. It's free and open weekdays 10 a.m. until 5 p.m. (until 8 p.m. on Thursdays) and Saturdays noon to 5 p.m.; ☎ 663-5554; **www.mocp.org.** For lunch, Michigan Avenue has several fast-food places nearby, or try the Euro-deli next to the Chicago Architecture Foundation shop.

Balzekas Museum of Lithuanian Culture ★★

APPEAL BY AGE GROUP	PRESCHOOL ★★	GRADE SCHOOL ★★	TEENS ★★
YOUNG ADULTS ★★	OVER 30 ★★		SENIORS ★★★

LOCATION **South Central–Midway Airport; 6500 South Pulaski Road;**
☎ **773-582-6500; www.lithaz.org/museums/balzekas**

Type of attraction An eclectic collection of exhibits on Lithuanian history and culture; a self-guided tour. **Admission** $5 adults, $4 seniors and students, $2 children. **Hours** Daily, 10 a.m.–4 p.m.; closed Thanksgiving, Christmas, and New Year's Day. **When to go** Anytime. **Special comments** Call in advance for information on special exhibits and programs. All exhibits are located on the ground floor. Although there's some interesting stuff here, it's a small museum that lacks coherence. **How much time to allow** 30 minutes to an hour.

DESCRIPTION AND COMMENTS   Inside this small museum you'll find items ranging from a suit of armor to press clippings from World War II—and everything in between: old photos of immigrants, folk art (including dolls, toys, leather items, wooden household utensils), photos of rural Lithuania, genealogical information, a playroom for children (with a poster depicting the ancient kings of Lithuania), glass cases full of old prayer books, swords, rare books, jewelry, native costumes, coins, stamps. . . . There's a lot on display here, but it's all in a jumble.

TOURING TIPS   Visitors can watch a short video about Lithuania that primes them for a tour of the museum.

OTHER THINGS TO DO NEARBY   Not much. If you're flying in or out of Midway, it's only a few blocks away. Oak Park, the hometown of Frank Lloyd Wright and Ernest Hemingway, is about five miles to the north, just off the Eisenhower Expressway (I-290).

kids Brookfield Zoo ★★★★

APPEAL BY AGE	PRESCHOOL ★★★★★	GRADE SCHOOL ★★★★★	TEENS ★★★★
YOUNG ADULTS ★★★★	OVER 30 ★★★★		SENIORS ★★★★

LOCATION **Southern Suburbs; First Avenue and 31st Street, Brookfield (14 miles west of the Loop). By car, take I-55 (Stevenson Expressway), I-290 (Eisenhower Expressway), or I-294 (Tri-State Tollway) and watch for signs. By train, take the Burlington/Metra Northern Line to the Zoo Stop at the Hollywood Station. For information on reaching the zoo by bus, call ☎ 312-836-7000 (city) or 800-972-7000 (suburbs); ☎ 800-201-0784; www.brookfieldzoo.org**

Type of attraction A zoo featuring 2,500 animals and more than 400 species spread throughout 215 acres of naturalistic habitat; a self-guided tour. **Admission** $10 adults, $6 seniors and children ages 3–11; free admission on Tuesdays and Thursdays in January, February, October, November, and December. Saturdays and Sundays are free in January and February. (Free admission is good only during normal zoo hours; admission fees apply to Holiday Magic.) **Hours** Memorial Day–Labor Day daily, 9:30 a.m.–6 p.m.; rest of year 10 a.m.–5 p.m. **When to go** On weekdays in the spring and fall; go after 1:30 p.m. to avoid large school groups. **Special comments** Telecommunications devices for the deaf (TDD) are available in the administration building. Widely separated buildings, well-landscaped grounds, and a campuslike setting make for a pleasant (not spectacular) zoo. **How much time to allow** 2 hours to half a day.

Chicago Attractions by Type

ATTRACTION | ZONE | AUTHOR'S RATING

GARDENS, PARKS, AND ZOOS

Brookfield Zoo | Southern Suburbs | ★★★★

Chicago Botanic Garden | Northern Suburbs | ★★★★

Garfield Park Conservatory | North Central–O'Hare Airport | ★★★

Lincoln Park Zoo | North Side | ★★★

Morton Arboretum | Western Suburbs | ★★★½

MUSEUMS

Art Institute of Chicago | The Loop | ★★★★★

Balzekas Museum of Lithuanian Culture | South Central–Midway Airport | ★★

Chicago Children's Museum | Near North Side | ★★

Chicago History Museum | North Side | ★★★

David and Alfred Smart Museum of Art | South Side | ★★★

DuSable Museum of African American History | South Side | ★★★½

Field Museum of Natural History | South Loop | ★★★★★

Hemingway Museum | North Central–O'Hare Airport | ★★

International Museum of Surgical Science | Near North Side | ★★½

Jane Addams Hull-House Museum | South Central–Midway Airport | ★★½

Mexican Fine Arts Center Museum | South Central–Midway Airport | ★★★½

Museum of Contemporary Art | Near North Side | ★★★★½

Museum of Holography | North Central–O'Hare Airport | ★★½

DESCRIPTION AND COMMENTS   Attractions at this lush wooded park include bottlenosed dolphins, walruses, re-creations of steamy rain forests featuring exotic animals, and an "African waterhole" populated by giraffes, zebras, and topi antelope. More traditional sights include lions, tigers, snow leopards, reptiles, and elephants. The Australia House features a variety of unusual animals from Down Under.

Although the zoo is spread out, visitors don't necessarily have to hoof it from exhibit to exhibit. Motor Safari, an open-air tram that operates from late spring to early fall, lets you get off and reboard four times along its route; the trams run every 5 to 15 minutes. The fee is $3 for adults and $2 for seniors and children ages 3 to 11.

TOURING TIPS   The most popular exhibits at Brookfield Zoo are the dolphin show at the 2,000-seat Seven Seas Panorama ($3 for adults, $2.50 for

ATTRACTION | ZONE | AUTHOR'S RATING

MUSEUMS (CONTINUED)

Museum of Science and Industry | South Side | ★★★★★

National Vietnam Veterans Art Museums | South Loop | ★★★

Oriental Institute Museum | South Side | ★★★★

Peace Museum | North Central–O'Hare Airport | Not rated

Peggy Notebaert Nature Museum | North Side | ★★★

Polish Museum of America | North Central–O'Hare Airport | ★★½

Swedish American Museum Center | North Side | ★★½

Ukrainian National Museum of Chicago | North Central–O'Hare Airport | ★

SKYSCRAPERS

John Hancock Center Observatory | Near North Side | ★★★★★

Sears Tower Skydeck | The Loop | ★★★★★

TOURIST LANDMARKS

Adler Planetarium and Astronomy Museum | South Loop | ★★½

Chicago Cultural Center | The Loop | ★★★½

Frank Lloyd Wright Home and Studio | North Central–O'Hare Airport | ★★★★

Harold Washington Library Center | The Loop | ★★★

Hemingway's Birthplace | North Central–O'Hare Airport | ★½

John G. Shedd Aquarium | South Loop | ★★★★★

Navy Pier | Near North Side | ★★★★

children; for show times, check at zoo kiosks or the Seven Seas ticket booth; it's free anytime to watch the sea mammals underwater through plate-glass windows), Tropic World (a huge indoor rain forest containing gorillas, monkeys, free-flying tropical birds, waterfalls, rocky streams, and big trees), Habitat Africa, "The Swamp" (a replica of a Southern cypress swamp), and summertime elephant demos. The zoo's wolf woods features a pack of five male gray wolves on a 2.1-acre site.

First-time visitors can catch a free slide presentation at the Discovery Center that runs every 15 minutes (longer intervals in the winter). Finally, when planning a visit to the zoo, keep in mind that the most pleasant weather occurs in the spring and fall, animals are most active in the mornings and late afternoons, and the zoo is least crowded on rainy, chilly days.

Chicago Attractions by Location

ATTRACTION	DESCRIPTION	AUTHOR'S RATING
NORTH SIDE		
Chicago History Museum	Chicago, U.S. history	★★★
Lincoln Park Zoo	Urban animal park	★★★
Peggy Notebaert Nature Museum	Interactive kids' museum	★★★
Swedish American Museum Center	Swedish-immigrant story	★★½
NORTH CENTRAL–O'HARE AIRPORT		
Frank Lloyd Wright Home and Studio	Famous architect's home	★★★★
Garfield Park Conservatory	Botanical gardens	★★★
Hemingway Museum	Writer's memorabilia	★★
Hemingway's Birthplace	Victorian house	★½
Museum of Holography	3D photo gallery	★★½
Peace Museum	Exhibits on nonviolence	Not rated
Polish Museum of America	Ethnic art and history	★★½
Ukrainian National Museum of Chicago	Folk art	★
NEAR NORTH SIDE		
Chicago Children's Museum	High-tech playground	★★
International Museum of Surgical Science	History of surgery	★★½
John Hancock Center Observatory	94th-floor view	★★★★★
Museum of Contemporary Art	Avant-garde art	★★★★½
Navy Pier	All-purpose tourist mecca	★★★★
THE LOOP		
Art Institute of Chicago	Highbrow art palace	★★★★★
Chicago Cultural Center	Art, architecture, tourist info	★★★½
Harold Washington Library Center	Largest library in U.S., art	★★★
Sears Tower Skydeck	View from America's tallest building	★★★★★

ATTRACTION	DESCRIPTION	AUTHOR'S RATING
SOUTH LOOP		
Adler Planetarium and Astronomy Museum	Star show and space exhibits	★★½
Field Museum of Natural History	Nine acres of natural history	★★★★★
John G. Shedd Aquarium	Largest indoor fish emporium	★★★★★
National Vietnam Veterans Art Museums	Emotionally powerful art	★★★
SOUTH CENTRAL–MIDWAY AIRPORT		
Balzekas Museum of Lithuanian Culture	Lithuanian culture and history	★★
Jane Addams Hull-House Museum	Birthplace of social work	★★½
Mexican Fine Arts Center Museum	Mexican art and culture	★★★½
SOUTH SIDE		
David and Alfred Smart Museum of Art	Highbrow art gallery	★★★
DuSable Museum of African American History	African American art and culture	★★★½
Museum of Science and Industry	Technology, hands-on exhibits	★★★★★
Oriental Institute Museum	Near East archaeology	★★★★
SOUTHERN SUBURBS		
Brookfield Zoo	Campuslike animal park	★★★★
WESTERN SUBURBS		
Morton Arboretum	1,500 acres of trees, shrubs	★★★½
NORTHERN SUBURBS		
Chicago Botanic Garden	Formal, elegant gardens	★★★★

central chicago attractions

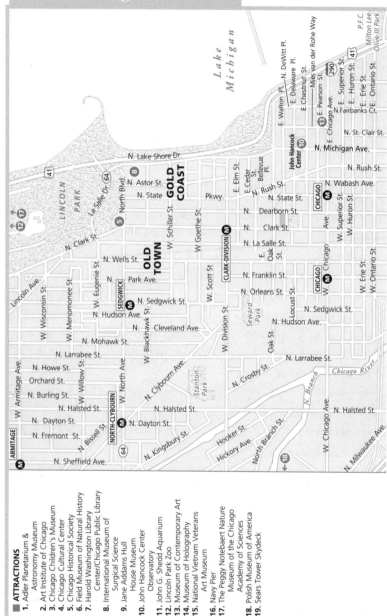

■ **ATTRACTIONS**
1. Adler Planetarium & Astronomy Museum
2. Art Institute of Chicago
3. Chicago Children's Museum
4. Chicago Cultural Center
5. Chicago Historical Society
6. Field Museum of Natural History
7. Harold Washington Library Center/Chicago Public Library
8. International Museum of Surgical Science
9. Jane Addams Hull House Museum
10. John Hancock Center Observatory
11. John G. Shedd Aquarium
12. Lincoln Park Zoo
13. Museum of Contemporary Art
14. Museum of Holography
15. National Vietnam Veterans Art Museum
16. Navy Pier
17. The Peggy Notebaert Nature Museum of the Chicago Academy of Sciences
18. Polish Museum of America
19. Sears Tower Skydeck

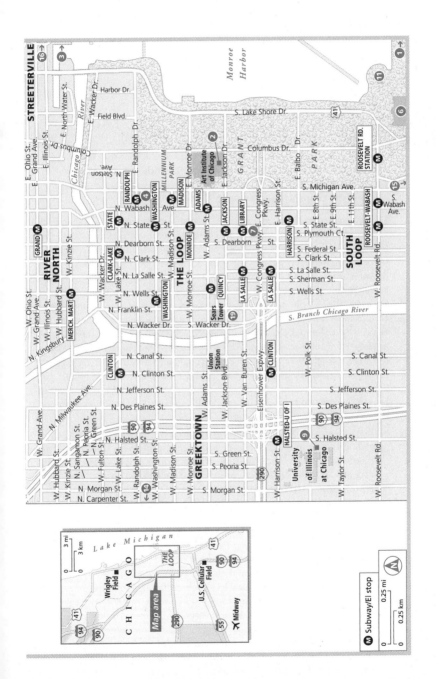

OTHER THINGS TO DO NEARBY Oak Park, hometown of Ernest Hemingway and Frank Lloyd Wright, is a few miles east of the Brookfield Zoo on the Eisenhower Expressway. Take I-290 east to Harlem Avenue (Route 43 north), then turn right on Lake Avenue to Forest Avenue and the visitor center. In addition to snack bars in the zoo, there's fast food on the road linking the zoo and the Eisenhower Expressway.

Chicago Botanic Garden ★★★★

APPEAL BY AGE	PRESCHOOL ★★★	GRADE SCHOOL ★★★	TEENS ★★★
YOUNG ADULTS ★★★★	OVER 30 ★★★★		SENIORS ★★★★★

LOCATION **Northern Suburbs; 1000 Lake-Cook Road, Glencoe. From Chicago, take Sheridan Road north along Lake Michigan, or I-94 (the Edens Expressway) to Lake-Cook Road. The gardens are about 15 miles north of the Loop; ☎ 847-835-5440; www.chicagobotanic.org**

Type of attraction 18 formal gardens that feature collections showcasing plants of the Midwest (including plants being tested for their performance in the Chicago area) and native and endangered flora of Illinois; guided and self-guided tours. Admission Free. Parking is $12, $7 for seniors on Tuesday. Hours Daily, 8 a.m.–sunset; closed Christmas. When to go June through August to see the most plants in bloom. Yet staffers say the gardens are gorgeous year-round—and especially after a heavy snowfall. Avoid summer afternoons on weekends, when crowds are at their heaviest; come in the morning and leave by 1 p.m. to miss the worst crowds. Special comments Prohibited activities include bicycling (except on designated bike routes), inline skating, or other sports activities such as Frisbee throwing, skiing, fishing, or skating; collecting plants and flowers; climbing on trees and shrubs; standing or walking in garden beds; and feeding wildlife. No pets are allowed except guide and hearing dogs. A stunning collection of beautifully designed gardens, pathways, ponds and pools, and outdoor sculpture. How much time to allow Half a day.

DESCRIPTION AND COMMENTS This living museum is a 300-acre park of gently rolling terrain and water that contains 23 garden areas brimming with plants. Other collections include an herbarium of 5,000 dried plants, rare books, and an art collection of plant-related prints, drawings, sculpture, and decorative objects.

Among the most popular areas are the Japanese, English Walled, Naturalistic, Prairie, and Rose gardens. Linking the formal gardens are paths that wander past lakes, ponds, and greens that are meticulously groomed and provide impressive views. The Orientation Center near the parking lots features an audiovisual presentation, exhibit panels, computers, and a wall map to help visitors plan their visit. Food is available in the Gateway Center, and a picnic area is located between parking lots 1 and 2.

TOURING TIPS Narrated tram tours lasting 45 minutes are offered from April through October; the tours depart every 30 minutes from 10 a.m. to 3:30 p.m. Tickets are $5 for adults, $4 for seniors, and $3 for children ages 3 to 15.

If you're short on time and want to see the garden's highlights, cross the footbridge from the Gateway Center and turn left at the Heritage Garden. Then visit the Rose, English Walled, Waterfall, and Japanese gardens.

Combine a visit with a workout: The North Branch Bicycle Trail starts at Caldwell and Devon avenues in Chicago and continues north 20 miles along the North Branch of the Chicago River to the Chicago Botanic Garden. Bring a lunch and eat it at the picnic area between parking lots 1 and 2.

OTHER THINGS TO DO NEARBY Ravinia, the summer home of the Chicago Symphony Orchestra, is on Sheridan Road; it's only a few minutes away. Sheridan Road follows Lake Michigan and is one of the best scenic drives around Chicago. Take a left onto Lake-Cook Road; it becomes Sheridan Road at the third traffic light.

kids Chicago Children's Museum ★★

| APPEAL BY AGE | PRESCHOOL ★★★★★ | GRADE SCHOOL ★★★★★ | TEENS ★ |
| YOUNG ADULTS ★ | | OVER 30 ★ | SENIORS ★ |

LOCATION **Near North Side; Navy Pier, 700 East Grand Avenue (just north of the Chicago River on the lakefront); ☎ 312-527-1000; www.chichildrensmuseum.org**

Type of attraction A high-tech playground and engaging interactive exhibits for children up to age 12; a self-guided tour. **Admission** $8 adults and children, $7 seniors; free for infants under age 1; free first Monday of every month (age 15 and under; free family night, Thursday, 5–8 p.m. (all ages); closed Thanksgiving and Christmas. **Hours** Sunday–Wednesday and Friday, 10 a.m.–5 p.m.; Thursday and Saturday, 10 a.m.–8 p.m. **When to go** During the summer, on weekends, and on school holidays, arrive when the museum opens at 10 a.m. During the school year, come in the afternoon to avoid school groups that arrive in the morning. **Special comments** This isn't a babysitting service. While activities are supervised by the museum staff, all children must be accompanied by someone age 16 or older. Nirvana for youngsters through age 12; for other age groups, not so much. **How much time to allow** Half a day.

DESCRIPTION AND COMMENTS This $14.5-million, 60,000-square-foot "museum"—it's really a high-tech playground for ankle biters and children through the fifth grade—provides an active play and learning environment spread across three levels of Navy Pier. A dozen exhibits provide a range of age-appropriate activities that captivate toddlers as well as older children. One of the most popular is Waterways, where kids don raincoats (provided) and pump, squirt, and manipulate water (they can shoot a stream of water 50 feet into the air). In the Inventing Lab, children can build and launch gliders from a 50-foot tower. In Treehouse Trails and PlayMaze, toddlers can explore an indoor "nature park" (featuring a hiking trail, pond, waterfall, trees, log cabin, and animal homes) and play in a working bakery, service station, construction site, and the Play It Safe exhibit, which teaches safety at home and in the the environment.

TOURING TIPS Start a visit with the Climbing Schooner, a three-story replica of a sailing ship that lets kids burn off energy by climbing the rigging up 35 feet to the crow's nest and then sliding down a ladder. Then explore the rest of the museum.

OTHER THINGS TO DO NEARBY Make a day of it by exploring Navy Pier. Take a scenic cruise on Lake Michigan, relax in the IMAX theater, ride the Ferris wheel and carousel, eat lunch in the food court, or simply take a stroll to enjoy the Chicago skyline and Lake Michigan stretching out to the horizon.

Chicago Cultural Center ★★★½

| APPEAL BY AGE | PRESCHOOL ★★ | GRADE SCHOOL ★★ | TEENS ★★★ |
| YOUNG ADULTS ★★★ | | OVER 30 ★★★★ | SENIORS ★★★★ |

LOCATION **The Loop; 78 East Washington Street; ☎ 312-346-3278; www.cityofchicago.org/Tourism/CulturalCenter**

Type of attraction A huge neoclassical structure containing eclectic art and a free visitor-information center; a downtown refuge for weary tourists; a self-guided tour. Admission Free. Hours April 1–October 31: Monday–Thursday, 8 a.m.–6 p.m.; Friday, 8 a.m.–6 p.m.; Saturday, 9 a.m.–6 p.m. and Sunday, 10 a.m.–6 p.m. November1–March 31: Monday–Thursday, 10 a.m.–7 p.m.; Friday, 10 a.m.–6 p.m.; Saturday, 10 a.m.–5 p.m. and Sunday, 11 a.m.–5 p.m., closed Thanksgiving and Christmas. When to go Anytime. Special comments Free building tours are offered on Wednesday, Friday, and Saturday at 1:15 p.m. An impressive building with a little bit of everything. How much time to allow An hour for a quick run-through. Because of its convenient location and free admission, plan to stop here throughout your visit.

DESCRIPTION AND COMMENTS The nation's first free municipal cultural center served as Chicago's central library for nearly 100 years. Today it dispenses culture the way it once loaned books. Highlights of the building are spectacular stained-glass domes located in the north and south wings, which originally served as skylights. They were later enclosed in copper and backlighted to fully reveal and protect their beauty; the 38-foot dome in Preston Hall is thought to be the world's largest Tiffany dome, with a value estimated at $38 million. Preston Bradley Hall was renovated in the 1970s into a performance hall and hosts free weekly classical music concerts; the G.A.R. Rotunda and Memorial Hall will intrigue Civil War buffs.

First-time visitors to Chicago should take advantage of the Visitor Information Center in the main lobby and the Welcome Center, which provides orientation to the city and downtown. The coffee bar can inject a caffeine boost and give respite to weary feet. A number of nearby corridors serve as art galleries showcasing established and emerging artists. The Grand Staircase features multicolored mosaics set in the balustrades, while the fourth floor of the Cultural Center boasts nearly 13,000 square feet of art-exhibition space.

TOURING TIPS Plan to stop at this prime example of 19th-century Beaux Arts architecture early in your visit; the Visitor Information Center in the lobby dispenses free information and touring advice. Then head up the Grand Staircase to view the Tiffany stained-glass dome on the third floor. From there, walk to the fourth-floor exhibition hall to see what's on display. Then take a peek into the beautiful Preston Bradley Hall.

OTHER THINGS TO DO NEARBY The Art Institute of Chicago is two blocks south on Michigan Avenue; the Loop is a block to the west. Directly across from the Art Institute on South Michigan Avenue is the Chicago Architecture Foundation, the starting point of not-to-be-missed daily walking tours of the Loop. For a great view, walk three blocks north to the Michigan Avenue Bridge and look up.

Chicago History Museum ★★★
(formerly Chicago Historical Society)

APPEAL BY AGE	PRESCHOOL ★	GRADE SCHOOL ★★★	TEENS ★★★
YOUNG ADULTS ★★★★		OVER 30 ★★★★	SENIORS ★★★

LOCATION **Clark Street at North Avenue, North Side; ☎ 312-642-4600; www.chicagohistory.org**

Type of attraction A spacious 20,000-square-foot museum highlighting Chicago history, from early frontier days to the present; a self-guided tour. Recently rehabbed and renamed to get with the 21st century. Admission $12 adults, $10 seniors (over age 65) and students (ages 13–22). Free for children age 12 and under. General admission free on Monday. Hours Monday–Saturday, 9:30 a.m.–4:30 p.m.; Sunday, noon–5 p.m. When to go Weekdays during the school year; plan your visit in the afternoon after the school field trips are over. Special comments In the past a visit here was as stuffy as the former name. Known for years as the Chicago Historical Society, the museum was closed for nearly a year to reconfigure with a more contemporary vibe. It is now a better museum. Parking Spaces for disabled visitors provided in the adjacent lot. There's also a parking garage at Clark and La Salle that charges $6; enter on Stockton Drive. How much time to allow 2 hours.

DESCRIPTION AND COMMENTS Visitors enter off Clark Street, walking through expanses of gridded glass. The clean and modern interior features high ceilings and plenty of elbow room for perusing the many exhibits. The revamped museum includes a new five-sensory gallery devoted to children and a temporary space featuring the work of contemporary Chicago artists.

There are also galleries hung with paintings, glass cases filled with artifacts (in the tradition of Victorian collecting), and a seemingly endless procession of static displays explaining the city's past. The new museum even includes artifacts from the Chicago White Sox 2005 World Series championship. (Winning baseball championships are truly historic events in Chicago: the White Sox broke an 88-year drought in 2005, and the Cubs haven't won a World Series since 1908.) Other exhibitions include a real steam locomotive and miniature scenes depicting Chicago's rapid growth in the 19th century.

TOURING TIPS The centerpiece of the $27.5 million renovation is the new permanent exhibit *Chicago: Crossroads of America,* which dissects the city's defining moments. Visitors can see the city's first elevated train car, purchased in 1892 in order to take tourists to the World's Columbian Exposition of 1893, and items from Riverview Park, which was Chicago's version of Coney Island. There's also *City in Crisis,* which uses artifacts from events such as the 1871 Chicago Fire and *My Kind of Town,* which celebrates the city as a cultural and entertainment center. Chicago blues legend Buddy Guy even performed at the museum's grand reopening.

The museum's critically acclaimed American-history galleries, with artifacts from the Revolutionary and Civil wars, are being moved, reconfigured, and enlarged. They won't open to the public until 2008. Hungry? The Big Shoulders Cafe on the first floor gets rave reviews from local diners. The museum also features an excellent Chicago-centric gift shop.

OTHER THINGS TO DO NEARBY The Lincoln Park Zoo is within easy walking distance. Head west on North Avenue to find a selection of fine restaurants and fast-food restaurants. Or take the pedestrian bridge over Lake Shore Drive to take a look at Lake Michigan.

David and Alfred Smart Museum of Art ★★★

| APPEAL BY AGE | PRESCHOOL ★ | GRADE SCHOOL ★★ | TEENS ★★★ |
| YOUNG ADULTS ★★★ | | OVER 30 ★★★ | SENIORS ★★★ |

LOCATION **South Side; 5550 South Greenwood Avenue (on the University of Chicago campus); ☎ 312-702-0200; www.smartmuseum.org**

Type of attraction A collection of art objects spanning five millennia, including works by Albrecht Dürer, Auguste Rodin, Frank Lloyd Wright, Walker Evans, and Mark Rothko; a self-guided tour. Admission Free. Hours Tuesday–Friday, 10 a.m.–4 p.m.; Saturday and Sunday, 11 a.m.–5 p.m.; closed Monday and holidays. When to go Anytime. Special comments All the galleries are on 1 level and are wheelchair accessible. Free parking is available in the lot on the corner of 55th Street and Greenwood Avenue on weekends. A sparkling white series of rooms featuring an eclectic array of art; you're sure to find something you like. How much time to allow 1–2 hours.

DESCRIPTION AND COMMENTS The art on display ranges from ancient Greek to outrageous modern works culled from a permanent collection of more than 7,000 objects. In addition, the museum schedules eight special exhibitions each year. The feel of the place, like the campus around it, is serious, cerebral, and highbrow.

TOURING TIPS Don't miss the furniture on display designed by Frank Lloyd Wright, "Dining Table and Six Chairs," a prime example of the Chicago architect's spare, modern style. (And you thought the Wizard of Oak Park only designed houses you can't afford.) The Smart, a museum named for the founders of *Esquire* magazine, is a compact and easy gallery to explore. The bookstore features art books, posters, cards, children's books, and jewelry. A cafe offers sandwiches, salads, pastas, and other goodies.

OTHER THINGS TO DO NEARBY The Oriental Institute Museum and the DuSable Museum are close. If the weather is nice, stroll the beautiful University of Chicago campus; look for the Henry Moore sculpture (placed on the site of the first self-sustaining nuclear reaction on December 2, 1942) across from the Enrico Fermi Institute. The massive Museum of Science and Industry is on 57th Street. Join the locals for lunch at Valois, at 1518 East 53rd Street.

DuSable Museum of African American History ★★★½

APPEAL BY AGE	PRESCHOOL ★★	GRADE SCHOOL ★★★	TEENS ★★★
YOUNG ADULTS ★★★	OVER 30 ★★★★		SENIORS ★★★★

LOCATION **South Side; 740 East 56th Place (57th Street and Cottage Avenue near the eastern edge of the University of Chicago); ☎ 773-947-0600; www.dusablemuseum.org**

Type of attraction A collection of artifacts, paintings, and photos that trace the black experience in the United States; a self-guided tour. Admission $3 adults, $2 students, $1 children ages 6–12; free on Sunday. Hours Tuesday–Saturday, 10 a.m.–5 p.m.; Sunday and Monday, noon–5 p.m.; closed Thanksgiving, Christmas, and New Year's Day. When to go Anytime. Special comments The large main-floor gallery hosts permanent exhibits; check the *Chicago Reader* or call before visiting to find out what's on display in the museum's temporary exhibits on the upper levels. Fascinating stuff, including, on our visit, an eye-opening show on the everyday lives of slaves in the antebellum South. How much time to allow 1–2 hours.

DESCRIPTION AND COMMENTS This museum, which once served as a park administration building and a police lockup, is named after Jean-Baptiste Point du Sable, a Haitian of mixed African and European descent who was Chicago's first permanent settler in the late 18th century. Exhibits include paintings by African Americans, displays that vividly portray the lives of blacks in pre–Civil War days, and a room dedicated to black hero Joe Louis.

TOURING TIPS Avoid weekday mornings, when large school groups schedule visits; Sundays, when admission is free, are also crowded. The gift shop features jewelry, fabrics, and arts and crafts created by African Americans.

OTHER THINGS TO DO NEARBY Outside the DuSable Museum, the beautiful lawns of Washington Park beckon in nice weather. The nearby University of Chicago campus is a great place to stroll; places to visit include the Oriental Institute Museum and the Smart Museum of Art. The immense Museum of Science and Industry is on 57th Street. Valois, a cafeteria where locals hang out, is located at 1518 East 53rd Street. Don't venture too far from the campus, though; it's only a marginally safe neighborhood.

Ernest Hemingway Museum ★★

APPEAL BY AGE	PRESCHOOL ★	GRADE SCHOOL ★	TEENS ★★
YOUNG ADULTS ★★	OVER 30 ★★		SENIORS ★★

LOCATION **North Central–O'Hare Airport; in the Oak Park Arts Center, 200 North Oak Park Avenue, Oak Park; ☎ 708-848-2222; www.ehfop.org**

Type of attraction A small collection of exhibits featuring rare photos of the Nobel laureate, his childhood diary, letters, early writing, and other memorabilia focusing on the writer's Oak Park years; a self-guided tour. Admission $7 adults, $5.50 seniors and students, free for children under age 5; fee covers admission to both museum and birthplace. Hours Daily, 1–5 p.m.; Saturday, 10 a.m.–5 p.m. When to go Anytime. Special comments Hemingway's Birthplace is about a block and a half away on the other side of Oak Park Avenue. A *very* narrow slice of the great writer's life that will be best appreciated by hard-core fans. **How much time to allow** 30 minutes.

DESCRIPTION AND COMMENTS   A handful of display cases in the basement of a former church house this small collection of Hemingway memorabilia. Artifacts on view range from photos, diaries, and family items to a violin and typewriter once owned by the writer, whom many critics consider the greatest American author. A six-minute video recalls Hemingway's upper-middle-class high-school years . . . but doesn't mention that he left town for good at age 20 and, unlike most famous writers from Chicago, wrote very little about his hometown.

TOURING TIPS   There's one gem to be found in this smallish collection: the "Dear John" letter Hemingway received from Agnes Von Kurowsky, the nurse who tended his wounds in Italy after he was injured while serving as a volunteer ambulance driver during World War I. "For the rest of his life Hemingway was marked by his scars from battle and by an abiding distrust of women," the exhibit notes. Hem got his revenge, though; check out the ending of *A Farewell to Arms*—the beautiful nurse who tended the wounded hero croaks in the last chapter. What you *won't* find is any reference to his alleged remark that Oak Park is a town of "broad lawns and narrow minds."

OTHER THINGS TO DO NEARBY   The Frank Lloyd Wright Home and Studio is only a few blocks away. Unity Temple, a National Historic Landmark designed by Wright in 1905, is located at 951 Chicago Avenue; it's considered a masterpiece and is open weekdays 10:30 a.m. to 3:30 p.m. for self-guided tours ($12 for adults and $10 for seniors and children under age 18), and on weekends for guided tours at 12, 1, and 2 p.m. Downtown Oak Park has a selection of dining and fast-food options. Brookfield Zoo is a few miles west off the Eisenhower Expressway (take Route 171 south).

kids Field Museum of Natural History ★★★★★

APPEAL BY AGE PRESCHOOL ★★★★★	GRADE SCHOOL ★★★★★	TEENS ★★★★★
YOUNG ADULTS ★★★★★	OVER 30 ★★★★★	SENIORS ★★★★★

LOCATION   **South Loop; East Roosevelt Road at Lake Shore Drive (in Grant Park); ☎ 312-922-9410; www.fieldmuseum.org**

Type of attraction One of the largest public museums in the United States, with more than 9 acres of exhibits; a self-guided tour. **Admission** $12 adults, $7 seniors, $4 children ages 3–11 and students (includes one special exhibit); *Discount days:* January–March 7, April 24–May 23, and September 11–October 31. *Gold package:* Monday and Tuesday, $7 adults, students, and seniors; $4 children ages 3–11; $15 parking (north garage). **Hours** Daily, 9 a.m.–5 p.m.; closed Christmas and New Year's Day. **When to go** Anytime. **Special comments** If someone in your party needs to make a pit stop while touring the special exhibits, go to the Dinosaur Hall exit and speak to a Visitor Services Representative (in a red jacket). This world-renowned institution draws on more than 20 million artifacts and specimens to fill its exhibits. If you can't find something you like here, it's time to get out of Chicago. **How much time to allow** 2 hours for a brief run-through; all day for a more leisurely exploration (but even then, you won't see it all).

Descriptions and Comments Founded in 1893 to create a permanent home for the natural history collections gathered in Chicago for the World's Columbian Exposition, the Field Museum today is one of the great institutions of its kind in the world, focusing on public learning and scientific study of the world's environments and cultures. For visitors, it's a chance to explore a mind-boggling assortment of the world's wonders.

While much of the museum reflects the Victorian mania for specimen collecting—aisle after aisle of wood-and-glass display cases and dioramas are filled with items from around the world—much of what you find here includes newer, more dynamic exhibits. Many emphasize hands-on fun and thematic exhibits, such as "Africa," "Forbidden City," "Underground Adventure", "Inside Ancient Egypt," "Into the Wild," "Gems," "Traveling the Pacific," and "Life over Time," a high-tech journey that takes visitors through 3.8 billion years of the history of life.

"Life over Time" picks up where the dinosaur show leaves off. Fossils, dioramas, a nine-foot-tall walk-in hut built of mammoth bones, and videos in the 7,000-square-foot exhibit explore climatic change and mammal evolution during the Ice Age.

TOURING TIPS Folks with youngsters in tow or with a strong interest in dinosaurs should make their way to the second level to explore "Life over Time." It's a kid-oriented exhibit that's heavy on education, hands-on science stuff, and TV monitors showing "newscasts" by suit-clad anchors "reporting" on the beginning of life a billion years ago. It all ends up in a huge hall filled with dinosaur fossils and reconstructed skeletons. It's pure bliss for the Barney crowd.

After exploring the world of dinosaurs and mammoths (including Sue, the largest, most complete fossil of *T. rex* yet discovered), check your map and pick something of interest. Here's some help: Tots will enjoy the play area on the second floor, while older folks can check out exhibits of gems and jades also on the second floor. The popular Egyptian tomb (complete with mummies) is on the first floor, as are exhibits on Native Americans, Africa, birds, reptiles, a re-creation of a wilderness, and a "nature" walk. The ground floor features places to grab a bite to eat and exhibits on bushmen, sea mammals, prehistoric people, and ancient Egypt. Finally, an indoor parking garage provides spaces for 2,500 cars (across McFetridge Drive); $15 per day.

OTHER THINGS TO DO NEARBY The Shedd Aquarium and Adler Planetarium are both within easy walking distance on the new, traffic-free Museum Campus. Fast food is available inside the museum, but anything else requires taking a cab or bus downtown.

Frank Lloyd Wright Home and Studio ★★★★

APPEAL BY AGE	PRESCHOOL ★	GRADE SCHOOL ★★	TEENS ★★
YOUNG ADULTS ★★★	OVER 30 ★★★★		SENIORS ★★★★

LOCATION **North Central–O'Hare Airport; 951 Chicago Avenue, Oak Park. If you drive, park in the garage next to the Oak Park Visitor Center at 158 Forest Avenue. The center is open daily from 10 a.m. to 5 p.m. and centrally located, within easy walking distance to all the Wright and Hemingway attractions in town; purchase your tickets and pick up a map and more information inside. The visitor center is closed Thanksgiving, Christmas, and New Year's Day. Parking in the garage is free on weekends; ☎ 708-848-1976; www.wrightplus.org**

Type of attraction The Oak Park home of famed architect Frank Lloyd Wright and the birthplace of the Prairie School of architecture; guided and self-guided tours. Admission $12 adults, $10 seniors and children under age 18; Forest Avenue walking tours (self-guided by audio cassette): $9 plus deposit; guided Forest Avenue walking tours: $12 adults, $10 seniors and children. Hours 45-minute guided home and studio tours begin at 11 a.m., 1 p.m., and 3 p.m. Monday–Friday and about every 20 minutes 11 a.m.–3:30 p.m. on weekends; closed Thanksgiving, Christmas, and New Year's Day. Self-guided audiocassette tours of the exteriors of 13 Wright-designed houses along nearby Forest Avenue are available 10 a.m.–3:30 p.m. daily. Guided walking tours of the neighborhood take place at 11 a.m. and 4 p.m. weekends, March–October. Tours begin at noon, 1 p.m., and 2 p.m., November–February. When to go Anytime. For the walking tours, bring an umbrella if it looks like rain. Special comments The house tour involves climbing and descending a flight of stairs. A fascinating glimpse into the life of America's greatest architect. How much time to allow 1 hour.

DESCRIPTION AND COMMENTS Between 1889 and 1909, this house with prominent gables, window bays, and dark, shingled surfaces served as home, studio, and architectural laboratory for young Chicago architect Frank Lloyd Wright. Today it offers a permanent visual record of the beginnings of his continuous exploration of the relationship of light, form, and space. This is where Wright established the principles that guided his life work and launched a revolution that changed the architectural landscape of the 20th century. Yet this house that Wright built with $5,000 borrowed from his employer doesn't reflect his Prairie School of design, the first distinctly American style of architecture featuring low, earth-hugging dwellings. That would come later.

TOURING TIPS What's fascinating about the tour—and what you should watch out for—are glimpses of early examples of elements that would become hallmarks of a Wright-designed home: large rooms that flow together, unity of design, minimal form, functionality, and the fusion of art and design elements. The tour guides do a good job of pointing them out.

The studio, which ends the tour and was added to the house by Wright in 1898, is a stunner, with walls supported by chains and a two-story octagonal drafting room. Here, working with 15 apprentices, Wright completed about 150 commissions and refined his Prairie School principles.

OTHER THINGS TO DO NEARBY The Ernest Hemingway Museum and the Hemingway Birthplace are only a few blocks away; both destinations are pleasant walks when the weather is nice. Unity Temple, a National Historic Landmark designed by Wright in 1905, is located at 875 Lake Street;

it's considered a masterpiece and is open weekdays 10:30 a.m. to 4:30 p.m. for self-guided tours ($6 for adults and $5 for seniors and children under age 18; phone ☎ 708-383-8873 for more information). Downtown Oak Park offers several places to grab something to eat.

Garfield Park Conservatory ★★★

APPEAL BY AGE	PRESCHOOL ★★★	GRADE SCHOOL ★★★	TEENS ★★★
YOUNG ADULTS ★★★		OVER 30 ★★★	SENIORS ★★★

LOCATION **North Central–O'Hare Airport; 300 North Central Park Avenue; ☎ 312-746-5100; www.garfield-conservatory.org**

Type of attraction Four and a half acres of grounds and 5,000 species and varieties of plants, most of them housed under the glass of a landmark 1907 structure; self-guided tours. Admission Free; $2 suggested donation for flower shows. Hours Daily, 9 a.m.–5 p.m. (until 8 p.m. Thursday); 10 a.m.–5 p.m. during major flower shows. When to go Anytime. Special comments Garfield Park is located in a high-crime area. But stick close to the conservatory and you'll be okay; the free parking lot is only a few steps away from the entrance. Some really big plants (many dating from 1907) and plenty of interior space promote a feeling of serenity. How much time to allow 1 hour (or longer if you've got a green thumb).

DESCRIPTION AND COMMENTS Four times larger than the conservatory in Lincoln Park, the Garfield Park Conservatory offers a world-class collection of botanical gardens for visitors to enjoy. The Palm House displays a variety of graceful palms, while the Cactus House encloses one of the nation's finest cactus displays (including giant saguaro) arranged in a typical Southwestern desert motif. A quiet visit here is soothing after a hectic morning of shopping on the Magnificent Mile or sightseeing in the Loop.

TOURING TIPS Horticulture hounds and home gardeners can quiz the trained personnel that staff the conservatory about house plants and gardening in general. If you can't make it in person, call in your questions at ☎ 312-746-5100. The conservatory hosts major flower shows throughout the year; see "A Calendar of Festivals and Events" in Part Two, Planning Your Visit to Chicago (page 25).

OTHER THINGS TO DO NEARBY The Peace Museum (see page 172) is located in the Garfield Park Gold Dome, two blocks south of the conservatory. Garfield Park is one of the areas of green linked by the city's network of boulevards.

Harold Washington Library Center ★★★

APPEAL BY AGE GROUP	PRESCHOOL ★	GRADE SCHOOL ★★	TEENS ★★
YOUNG ADULTS ★★★		OVER 30 ★★★	SENIORS ★★★

LOCATION **The Loop; 400 South State Street; ☎ 312-747-4999; www.chipublib.org/001hwlc/001hwlc.html**

Type of attraction The world's second-largest public library (after the British Library in London); guided and self-guided tours. Admission Free. Hours Monday–Thursday, 9 a.m.–6:30 p.m.; Friday and Saturday, 9 a.m.–4:30 p.m.; Sunday, 1–4:30 p.m. When to go Anytime. Special comments The library isn't very visitor friendly: From the enclosed lobby on the first floor, take the escalators to the third floor, which serves as the main entrance to the library proper. From there, elevators and escalators provide access to the other seven levels. Conversely, to leave the building, you must return to the third floor and take the escalators down to the exit level (elevators are available for disabled folks). What a pain. Though a trip to the library isn't on most travel itineraries, consider making an exception in Chicago. It's definitely worth a stop. **How much time to allow** An hour; consider joining a free public tour beginning at 2 p.m., Monday through Sunday. The guided tour lasts an hour and starts in the third-floor Orientation Theater.

DESCRIPTION AND COMMENTS This neoclassical building with elements of Beaux Arts, classical, and modern ornamentation opened in 1991 and cost $144 million. Named after the late Chicago mayor (a notorious bookworm), the 750,000-square-foot Harold Washington Library Center serves as the Loop's southern gateway.

Inside are housed more than 2 million volumes; an electronic directory system that displays floor layouts, book locations, and upcoming events; a computerized reference system; more than 70 miles of shelving; a permanent collection of art spread over ten floors; and lots of nooks for curling up with a book.

TOURING TIPS Several not-to-be-missed attractions include the ninth-floor glass-enclosed Winter Garden; the Harold Washington Collection (an exhibit located next to the Winter Garden); and the Jazz, Blues, Gospel Hall of Fame (eighth floor).

Folks with time and interest should visit the eighth-floor Listening/Viewing Center, where patrons can watch videos and listen to music from the collection's 100,000 78 rpm records, LPs, and CDs. Selections are particularly plentiful in popular music, jazz, and blues. Hours are Tuesday through Thursday, 1 until 6 p.m.; Friday and Saturday, 1 p.m. until 4:30 p.m.; closed Sunday. You don't have to be a Chicago resident to take advantage of the free service, although all patrons are limited to one session per day; there is a one-hour time limit if other people are waiting. Since the Center relies on a large array of electronics, it's often closed for maintenance; call ☎ 312-747-4850 before going.

In addition, the library presents a wide range of special events throughout the year, including films, dance programs, lectures, storytelling sessions for children, concerts, special programs for children, art exhibits, and more. See the *Chicago Reader* (a free "alternative" paper) to find out what's happening during your visit.

OTHER THINGS TO DO NEARBY The Loop is a block to the north; hang a right to head toward Grant Park and the Art Institute of Chicago. Turn left at the elevated tracks to reach the Chicago Board of Trade and the Sears Tower. Eating and shopping establishments abound throughout the heart of downtown.

Hemingway's Birthplace ★½

APPEAL BY AGE	PRESCHOOL ★	GRADE SCHOOL ★	TEENS ★★
YOUNG ADULTS ★★	OVER 30 ★★		SENIORS ★★

LOCATION **North Central–O'Hare Airport; 339 North Oak Park Avenue, Oak Park; ☎ 708-848-2222**

Type of attraction The partially restored Victorian house where Ernest Hemingway was born in 1899; a guided tour. **Admission** $7 adults, $5 seniors and students, free for children under age 5 with an adult; fee covers admission to both museum and birthplace. **Hours** Sunday–Friday 1–5 p.m.; Saturday, 10 a.m.–5 p.m. **When to go** Anytime. **Special comments** One short but rather steep flight of stairs leads to the second floor. Strictly for die-hard Hemingway fans. **How much time to allow** 45 minutes.

DESCRIPTION AND COMMENTS Open since the fall of 1993, this fine Victorian house has a long way to go before it becomes fully restored—and even then, it will only interest folks seeking a glimpse of upper-middle-class life in turn-of-the-19th-century Oak Park. Hemingway lived here for five years as a child, and only a few of the items on display are original. Upstairs, visitors can look into (but can't enter) the lavishly restored room where the writer was born.

TOURING TIPS Look for the embalmed muskrats (at least, that's what the docent and I guessed they are) that Hemingway and his doctor father stuffed when the great writer was a boy. Unfortunately, visitors are subjected to a much-too-long video (15 minutes, actually) that tells them more than they'll ever want to know about the Nobel Prize winner's grandparents. Unless you've got an abiding interest in Hemingway's genealogy, plead a tight schedule and try to skip the film.

OTHER THINGS TO DO NEARBY The Ernest Hemingway Museum is down the street; the Frank Lloyd Wright Home and Studio is only a few blocks away. Unity Temple, a National Historic Landmark designed by Wright in 1905, is located at 951 Chicago Avenue; it's considered a masterpiece and is open weekdays 10:30 a.m. to 3:30 p.m. for self-guided tours ($12 for adults and $10 for seniors and children under age 18). Downtown Oak Park offers several dining and fast-food options. Brookfield Zoo is a few miles west, off I-290.

International Museum of Surgical Science ★★½

APPEAL BY AGE	PRESCHOOL ★	GRADE SCHOOL ★★	TEENS ★★
YOUNG ADULTS ★★★	OVER 30 ★★★		SENIORS ★★★

LOCATION **Near North Side; 1524 North Lake Shore Drive; ☎ 312-642-6502; www.imss.org**

Type of attraction Exhibits from around the world trace the history of surgery and related sciences; a self-guided tour. **Admission** $6 adults, $3 seniors and students; free on Tuesday with a suggested donation of the regular admission; free guided tours on Saturday (reservation required). **Hours** *October–April:* Tuesday–Saturday, 10 a.m.–4 p.m.; *May–September:* Tuesday–Sunday, 10 a.m–4 p.m.; closed Monday. **When to go** Anytime. **Special comments** Though the truly squeamish should avoid this place like the plague, there's actually very little on display that's overtly gory or upsetting. The museum is located on the #151 bus route, and limited parking is available in a small lot behind the building; additional parking is located in

Lincoln Park and at North Avenue Beach. It's a short, pleasant stroll away from North Michigan Avenue. A must-see for folks in the medical field; otherwise, it's a nice fill-in spot when exploring the Gold Coast on foot. **How much time to allow** 1 hour for most folks; half a day for those with a keen interest in medical science.

DESCRIPTION AND COMMENTS The mysteries, breakthroughs, failures, and historic milestones of surgical science are on display in this unusual museum housed in an elegant mansion facing Lake Michigan. Implements on display range from the truly horrifying (2,000-year-old skulls with holes bored into them and tin-and-wood enema syringes from the 1800s) to the quaint (such as an X-ray shoe fitter from the early 1950s). The first floor features a re-creation of a 19th-century pharmacy and an early-20th-century dentist's office.

TOURING TIPS Start on the first floor and explore displays of antique medical instruments, then work your way up to the fourth floor. The second floor's Hall of Immortals features 12 eight-foot statues representing great medical figures in history, while the third floor includes an exhibit of antique microscopes and early X-ray equipment. Look for Napoleon's original death mask and more ancient medical instruments on the fourth floor. A guided tour is offered on Saturdays at 2 p.m.; call ☎ 312-642-6502, ext. 3130, for a reservation.

OTHER THINGS TO DO NEARBY Explore Chicago's opulent Gold Coast neighborhood on foot. It's only a few blocks south to the Magnificent Mile, which features expensive shops, malls, department stores, and a knock-your-socks-off view from the 94th-floor observatory in the John Hancock Center (when it's not raining).

Jane Addams Hull-House Museum ★★½

APPEAL BY AGE	PRESCHOOL ★	GRADE SCHOOL ★★	TEENS ★★★
YOUNG ADULTS ★★★		OVER 30 ★★★	SENIORS ★★★

LOCATION **South Central–Midway Airport; 800 South Halsted Street, on the campus of the University of Illinois at Chicago; ☎ 312-413-5353; www.uic.edu/jaddams/hull**

Type of attraction The restored 1856 country home that became the nucleus of the world-famous settlement-house complex founded by Jane Addams (a Nobel Peace Prize winner) at the end of the 19th century; a self-guided tour. **Admission** Free. Parking $2–$9. **Hours** Tuesday–Friday, 10 a.m.–4 p.m.; Sunday, noon–4 p.m.; closed Monday and Saturday. **When to go** Anytime. **Special comments** Park across the street in the University of Illinois parking lot. An oasis of dignity, this restored museum is all that remains of a once-vibrant ethnic melting pot served by the Nobel laureate. **How much time to allow** 1 hour.

DESCRIPTION AND COMMENTS This square brick 19th-century house in the shadow of the University of Illinois at Chicago is where Jane Addams and Ellen Gates Starr began the settlement work that helped give immigrants a better shot at the American dream. The lush Victorian interior includes Addams's desk, an old Oliver typewriter, photos of the staff, and several rooms of rich furnishings.

TOURING TIPS Start your tour upstairs in the Residents' Dining Hall with the 15-minute slide show on the settlement house movement. The tour ends in the restored mansion.

OTHER THINGS TO DO NEARBY Sample some pasta in Little Italy, southwest of the University of Illinois campus. Greektown and more great ethnic dining is north on Halsted, just past the Eisenhower Expressway. The Loop is a few blocks to the northeast.

 John Hancock Center Observatory ★★★★★

APPEAL BY AGE   PRESCHOOL ★★★★★   GRADE SCHOOL ★★★★★   TEENS ★★★★★
YOUNG ADULTS ★★★★★   OVER 30 ★★★★★   SENIORS ★★★★★

LOCATION **Near North Side; 875 North Michigan Avenue; ☎ 888-875-VIEW or ☎ 312-751-3681; www.hancock-observatory.com**

Type of attraction A 39-second elevator ride leading to a spectacular 94th-floor view of Chicago; a self-guided tour. Admission $9.95 adults, $7.50 seniors, $6 children ages 5–12, free for children under age 4; individual sky tours, $3 with admission. Hours Daily, 9 a.m.–11 p.m. (no tickets sold after 10:45 p.m.). When to go Anytime. Special comments This is an excellent alternative to the Sears Tower Skydeck, where the lines can be very long. In fact, most Chicagoans say the view is better. If the top of the building is hidden in clouds, come back another day. A stunning view, especially at sunset or at night. How much time to allow 30 minutes.

DESCRIPTION AND COMMENTS This distinctive building with the X-shaped exterior crossbracing is the 14th-tallest structure in the world. Although the 94th-floor observatory is nine floors lower than the Sears Tower Skydeck, some folks say the view is better here, perhaps due to its proximity to Lake Michigan.

TOURING TIPS The ideal way to enjoy the vista (you're 1,030 feet above Michigan Avenue) is to arrive just before sunset. As the sun sinks lower in the west, slowly the city lights blink on—and a whole new view appears.

OTHER THINGS TO DO NEARBY The 95th and 96th floors of the John Hancock Center house the highest restaurant and lounge in the city. (You can relax with a drink for about the same cost as visiting the observatory, but there's no guarantee you'll get a seat with a view.) Or return to street level and shop till you drop along chi-chi North Michigan Avenue; the Water Tower Place shopping mall is next door.

kids **John G. Shedd Aquarium** ★★★★★

APPEAL BY AGE   PRESCHOOL ★★★★★   GRADE SCHOOL ★★★★★   TEENS ★★★★★
YOUNG ADULTS ★★★★★   OVER 30 ★★★★★   SENIORS ★★★★★

LOCATION **South Loop; 1200 South Lake Shore Drive; ☎ 312-939-2438; www.sheddaquarium.org**

Type of attraction The world's largest indoor aquarium; the Oceanarium, the world's largest indoor marine mammal facility, re-creates a Pacific Northwest coastline; a self-guided tour. Admission *Aquarium and Oceanarium:* $23 adults,

$16 seniors and children ages 3–11. *Aquarium only:* $8 adults, $6 seniors and children. Aquarium is free on Mondays and Tuesdays, September–November. **Hours** Monday–Friday, 9 a.m.–5 p.m. (until 6 p.m. in summer); closed Christmas and New Year's Day. **When to go** Before noon during the summer and on major holidays. A time-ticket system is in effect for visitors to the extremely popular Oceanarium and tickets are often sold out by 3 p.m.; if you get a ticket, waits of 2–3 hours are not uncommon on busy days. (If you're waiting, tour the aquarium or other attractions.) Try to time your visit to coincide with the aquarium's Caribbean reef feedings—a diver enters the circular 90,000-gallon exhibit and hand-feeds an assortment of tropical fish; kids love it. Feeding times are 9:30 a.m., 11 a.m., 12:30 p.m., 1:30 p.m., 3 p.m., and 3:30 p.m. daily. **Special comments** Three continuous nature slide shows lasting about 30 minutes are featured in the Phelps Auditorium. The seats are comfortable, and it's a great place to chill out when crowds are heavy. Whales breaching the surface with Lake Michigan in the background are an unforgettable sight. **How much time to allow** 2 hours.

DESCRIPTION AND COMMENTS Not only does the Shedd Aquarium house more than 6,000 aquatic animals, the building itself is an architectural marvel, featuring majestic doorways, colorful mosaics, and wave and shell patterns on the walls. For most folks, however, the highlight of a visit is the Oceanarium, which treats visitors to a wide array of sea mammals—both from the surface and underwater through glass windows. The huge exhibit, which features a Lake Michigan backdrop, is quite spiffy.

In the aquarium, cool and dark rooms are lined with tanks filled with a wide assortment of creatures, including a huge alligator, snapping turtle, electric eels, piranhas, and an especially creepy-looking green moray eel (which, we're sad to report, is actually blue; its skin appears green because it's coated with thick yellow mucus—yuck). The Amazon Rising exhibit features 250 species in a re-creation of the Amazon River Basin.

TOURING TIPS Purchase a ticket that includes admission to the Oceanarium; from the foyer, head left around the circular Caribbean Reef Exhibit to the entrance. After touring both levels of the sea-mammal emporium, return to the aquarium for a leisurely stroll past the many tanks; don't forget about the feedings in the coral reef (see above for times).

OTHER THINGS TO DO NEARBY The Adler Planetarium and the Field Museum of Natural History are both within walking distance on the traffic-free Museum Campus. If it's late in the afternoon and the sun's about to set, stick around; the Chicago skyline is about to do its nighttime thing. It's a view you won't soon forget.

kids Lincoln Park Zoo ★★★

| APPEAL BY AGE GROUP | PRESCHOOL ★★★★ | GRADE SCHOOL ★★★★★ | TEENS ★★★★★ |
| YOUNG ADULTS ★★★★ | | OVER 30 ★★★ | SENIORS ★★★★ |

LOCATION **North Side; 2200 North Cannon Drive (Lincoln Park, off Lake Shore Drive at Fullerton Avenue north of the Magnificent Mile);** ☎ **312-742-2000; www.lpzoo.com**

Type of attraction The most visited zoo in the nation, featuring more than 1,600 animals, birds, and reptiles; a self-guided tour. **Admission** Free; parking $12–$22. **Hours** Daily, 9 a.m.–6 p.m. (until 7 p.m. in summer on Saturday, Sunday, and holidays); buildings open at 10 a.m. **When to go** Anytime, except weekday mornings from mid-April to mid-June, when as many as 100 school buses converge on the zoo; by 1:30 p.m., the hordes of youngsters are gone. Weekend afternoons during the summer also attract big crowds. **Special comments** Don't rule out a visit on a rainy or cold day: a lot of the animals are housed indoors. Interestingly enough, neighbors residing in nearby high-rises report they can hear wolves howling on warm summer nights. Alas, this stately, old-fashioned zoo isn't in the same league as newer animal parks springing up around the nation. But it's still a refreshing oasis in the heart of bustling Chicago. **How much time to allow** 2 hours.

DESCRIPTION AND COMMENTS Beautifully landscaped grounds, Lake Michigan, nearby high-rises, and the Chicago skyline in the distance are the hallmarks of this venerable but smallish park. Plus, the stately old buildings that house many of the zoo's inhabitants lend a Victorian elegance. Adults and especially children won't want to miss the Farm in the Zoo (a farm featuring chickens, horses, and cows) and a children's zoo where the kids can enjoy a collection of small animals at eye level.

TOURING TIPS If you're pressed for time, the most popular exhibits at the zoo are the polar bear, elephants, and (hold your nose) the Primate House, where great apes cavort behind thick panes of glass. Before or after your visit, stop by the Lincoln Park Conservatory, three acres of Victorian greenhouses built in 1891 that provide a lush rain-forest setting for flora and fauna from around the world. Seasonally, the Christmas poinsettias and Easter lilies draw huge crowds.

The conservatory is just outside the zoo's northwest entrance (near the elephants), and it's free. The restored Café Brauer serves salads and sandwiches; the Penguin Palace Ice Cream Shoppe dishes up ice cream during the summer.

OTHER THINGS TO DO NEARBY The Chicago History Museum (and its acclaimed cafe) is an easy stroll from the zoo. A walk west for a block or two leads to a number of fast-food restaurants. Or take the pedestrian bridge across Lake Shore Drive and watch the waves crash against the Lake Michigan shoreline.

Mexican Fine Arts Center Museum ★★★½

APPEAL BY AGE	PRESCHOOL ★	GRADE SCHOOL ★	TEENS ★★★
YOUNG ADULTS ★★★★	OVER 30 ★★★★		SENIORS ★★★★

LOCATION **South Central–Midway Airport; 1852 West 19th Street;** ☎ **312-738-1503; www.mfacmchicago.org**

Type of attraction The only Mexican museum in the Midwest features permanent and temporary exhibits by local, national, and international artists; a self-guided tour. **Admission** Free. **Hours** Tuesday–Sunday, 10 a.m.–5 p.m.; closed Monday and major holidays. **When to go** Anytime. **Special comments** All the exhibition space is on 1 level. The galleries are attractive and well lit; the

Day of the Dead exhibit shown during our visit was an entertaining collection of colorful, funny, and bizarre folk art. **How much time to allow** 1 hour.

DESCRIPTION AND COMMENTS When approaching Harrison Park in the Pilsen neighborhood, there is no doubt as to which building is the Mexican Fine Arts Museum (there's an Aztec design in the brickwork along the top of the structure). There are five different areas inside the museum: the permanent collection, the interactive room, the temporary art exhibits, the museum store, and the performing arts theater. The permanent collection offers a walk-through tour of Mexican history. Starting in Ancient Mexico, you then visit colonial Mexico, the Mexican Revolution, and the Mexican experience in the United States. Each exhibit displays artifacts, social structures, and significant developments along with the people that brought them about. An abundance of information accompanies each display (written in both English and Spanish). At the end, a large-screen display runs a short movie about the Mexican experience. After leaving the permanent collection, the interactive room offers touchscreen computers that provide a look into other Mexican traditions as well as the opportunity to hear indigenous music. Most computers are set up for standing interaction, but there are a few terminals on a small desk for children. The temporary collection displays artwork from local, national, and international artists in a spacious gallery. Call ahead for a schedule of upcoming exhibits and performances, or visit the museum's Web site.

TOURING TIPS The large gift shop offers an extensive selection of Mexican items, such as handicrafts, posters, toys, and books. Free guided tours are offered every Sunday at noon (English) and 1 p.m. (Spanish). In addition to changing exhibits by Hispanic artists, the Mexican Fine Arts Center Museum presents an ongoing series of readings, performances, and lectures. To see what's going on during your visit, pick up a free copy of the *Chicago Reader*.

OTHER THINGS TO DO NEARBY Pilsen, located along 18th Street between Canal and Damen streets, is a thriving Hispanic neighborhood with signs in Spanish and lots of spicy smells (good ethnic eateries, too). The Jane Addams Hull-House Museum is about two miles northeast of the museum on Halsted Street (at the University of Illinois at Chicago). On weekends and holidays, the Blue Line does not stop at the museum; however, the city has provided a free trolley service to the museum that runs every 20 minutes on these off-days. More information on the other locations visited by the free trolley can be found by visiting **www.877chicago.com** or by calling ☎ 877-CHICAGO.

Morton Arboretum ★★★½

APPEAL BY AGE	PRESCHOOL ★★★	GRADE SCHOOL ★★★	TEENS ★★★
YOUNG ADULTS ★★★★	OVER 30 ★★★★		SENIORS ★★★★

LOCATION **Western Suburbs; Route 53 (just off I-88) in Lisle (25 miles west of the Loop); ☎ 630-719-2400 and ☎ 630-968-0074**

Type of attraction A 1,700-acre landscaped outdoor "museum" featuring more than 3,000 kinds of trees, shrubs, and vines from around the world; guided and self-guided tours. **Admission** $7 adults, $5 seniors, $4 children ages 3–12; Wednesdays: $4 adults, $3 seniors, $2 children ages 3–12. **Hours** April–October, daily, 7 a.m.–7 p.m.; November–March, daily, 7 a.m.–5 p.m. On major holidays, the grounds are open but the buildings are closed. **When to go** Spring and fall are the most beautiful seasons to visit, although the arboretum is worth a look year-round. May and October weekends are the busiest; come in the morning to avoid the heaviest crowds. **Special comments** If throngs are packing the arboretum during your visit, head for the trails in Maple Woods at the east side of the park; most visitors don't venture far from the visitor center. You don't have to be a tree hugger to appreciate this unusual and beautiful park. **How much time to allow** An hour for a scenic drive; half a day to explore by foot.

DESCRIPTION AND COMMENTS In 1922, Joy Morton, the man who started the Morton Salt Company, founded this arboretum, a large park honeycombed with 25 miles of trails and 12 miles of one-way roads for car touring. Terrains here include native woodlands, wetlands, and prairie. The visitor center provides information on tours, trails, and places of special interest, such as the Plant Clinic, and houses a free library with books and magazines on trees, gardening, landscaping, nature, and other plant-related subjects.

The park, approximately four miles long and a mile wide, is divided into two segments bisected by Route 53; the visitor center is located on the east side. By car or on foot, visitors can explore a wide range of woodlands ranging from Northern Illinois and Western North American forests to collections of trees from Japan, China, the Balkans, and Northeast Asia. Interspersed between the woods are gently rolling hills and lakes.

TOURING TIPS Driving the 12 miles of roadway takes about 45 minutes without stopping. Good places to park the car and stretch your legs include Lake Marmo on the west side (park in lot P23) and the Maple Woods on the east side (lot P15). Foot trails range from pavement to wood chips, mowed paths, and gravel.

One-hour open-air tram tours of the grounds are offered spring through fall from the visitor center. In May and October, the busiest months, tours start at 10:30 a.m., noon, 1:15 p.m., 2:45 p.m., and 4 p.m. on weekends, and at 10:30 a.m., noon, 1:15 p.m., and 2:30 p.m. on weekdays. Tickets are $4 adults, $3 children.

OTHER THINGS TO DO NEARBY Argonne National Laboratory, one of the nation's largest centers of energy research, is about five miles south of the Morton Arboretum. Saturday tours are available and advanced reservations are required; call ☎ 630-252-5562. If you're heading back to Chicago on I-88 to I-290 (the Eisenhower Expressway), both the Brookfield Zoo and Oak Park are convenient stopping-off points.

Museum of Contemporary Art ★★★★½

APPEAL BY AGE	PRESCHOOL ★★★	GRADE SCHOOL ★★★	TEENS ★★★
YOUNG ADULTS ★★★★	OVER 30 ★★★★★		SENIORS ★★★★

LOCATION **Near North Side; 220 East Chicago Avenue; ☎ 312-280-2660; www.mcachicago.org**

Type of attraction An art museum dedicated to the avant-garde in all media; a self-guided tour. **Admission** $10 adults; $6 students and seniors; free for children age 12 and under; free for all Tuesday, 5–8 p.m. **Hours** Wednesday–Sunday, 10 a.m.–5 p.m.; Tuesday, 10 a.m.–8 p.m.; closed on Monday, Thanksgiving, Christmas, and New Year's Day. **When to go** Anytime. **Special comments** Paid parking is available in the museum's parking garage; the MCA has wheelchair-accessible entrances, elevators, and restrooms. Bright, cheerful, and filled with paintings and sculpture, as well as some other difficult-to-categorize artwork. A not-to-be-missed destination for anyone who enjoys art that's both beautiful and challenging. **How much time to allow** 1–2 hours; dyed-in-the-wool culture vultures should figure on at least half a day.

DESCRIPTION AND COMMENTS   This five-story art museum opened in 1996 and provides a major world-class showcase for the MCA's permanent collection of late-20th-century art. Bright and airy on the inside, the new building doesn't overwhelm visitors like, say, the huge Art Institute. Most of the art is displayed on the fourth floor, with two smaller galleries on the second floor dedicated to special and traveling exhibitions. With lots of seating, carpeting, and sunlight streaming in through large windows, the MCA is an easy place to visit.

The permanent exhibit shows off paintings, sculpture, prints, and a wide variety of art utilizing a mind-boggling range of materials: acrylics, video, sound, neon, an inflatable raft, flashing lights. . . . Kids, perhaps unsaddled with preconceptions of what defines "art," seem to especially enjoy the MCA's eclectic offerings. The artists represented include Andy Warhol, Roy Lichtenstein, Robert Rauschenberg, Alexander Calder, Marcel Duchamp, Franz Kline, René Magritte, and Willem de Kooning.

TOURING TIPS   From either the ground-floor entrance or the second-floor entrance at the top of the stairs facing Michigan Avenue, take the elevator to the fourth floor. Free 45-minute tours depart from the second floor at 1 p.m. and 6 p.m. on Tuesdays, 1 p.m. on Wednesdays and Fridays, and 11 a.m., noon, 1 p.m., 2 p.m., and 3 p.m. on Saturdays and Sundays. The bilevel book and gift shop features a wide selection of art books and kids' stuff, such as games, stuffed animals, T-shirts, and toys. The high-ceilinged cafe, which overlooks the outdoor sculpture garden and Lake Michigan, is comfortable and offers a European-style menu with prices in the $10 range. Restrooms are located on the ground floor near the entrance.

OTHER THINGS TO DO NEARBY   The MCA is only a block off the Magnificent Mile, Chicago's shopping mecca; the Water Tower Place shopping mall (and its huge food court) is only a stone's throw away. The John Hancock Observatory and a wide array of restaurants are within easy walking distance. Children will enjoy NikeTown at 669 North Michigan Avenue, which features an actual basketball court on the second floor and a 22-foot-long aquarium.

Museum of Holography ★★½

| APPEAL BY AGE | PRESCHOOL ★★ | GRADE SCHOOL ★★ | TEENS ★★★ |
| YOUNG ADULTS ★★★ | | OVER 30 ★★★ | SENIORS ★★★ |

LOCATION **North Central–O'Hare Airport; 1134 West Washington Boulevard; ☎ 312-226-1007; www.holographiccenter.com**

Type of attraction A small gallery exhibiting holograms, laser-produced photographic images that are three-dimensional and often feature movement, color change, and image layering; a self-guided tour. **Admission** $4 adults, $3 children 6–12, free for children under age 6. **Hours** Wednesday–Sunday, 12:30–5 p.m.; closed Monday and Tuesday. **When to go** Anytime. **Special comments** Located just west of the Loop in an otherwise-drab neighborhood of warehouses; one flight of stairs. Images are at adult eye level, so small fry will need a lift to get the full effect. Not high art, but fascinating—sometimes startling—images. **How much time to allow** 30 minutes to 1 hour.

DESCRIPTION AND COMMENTS It would probably take a physics degree to really understand how holograms are created, but the results are fascinating just the same. The museum, the only one of its kind in the United States, features stunning 3D images, such as a microscope that leaps off the surface; when you look into the "eye piece" you're rewarded with the sight of a bug frozen in amber!

Other holograms produce a motion-picture effect as you move your head from left to right in front of the image. Though the museum is small—it's essentially four small galleries (150 holograms) and a gift shop—the stuff on display is unusual, to say the least.

TOURING TIPS The gift shop offers a wide array of holograms for sale, ranging from bookmarks and cards to framed images. Prices range from a few bucks to several hundred dollars for large, framed holograms. Most, however, are four-by-six-inch images that start at $60 (including the frame). *Note:* Before purchasing a hologram, keep in mind that to get the full effect at home, it needs to be illuminated by an unfrosted incandescent bulb mounted at a 45-degree angle to the image.

OTHER THINGS TO DO NEARBY Nothing within walking distance, but the Loop is only a few blocks to the east.

kids Museum of Science and Industry ★★★★★

APPEAL BY AGE	PRESCHOOL ★★★★★	GRADE SCHOOL ★★★★★	TEENS ★★★★★
YOUNG ADULTS ★★★★★		OVER 30 ★★★★★	SENIORS ★★★★★

LOCATION **South Side; 57th Street and Lake Shore Drive; ☎ 773-684-1414 or ☎ 800-GO-TO-MSI; www.msichicago.org**

Type of attraction 14 acres of museum space housing more than 2,000 wide-ranging exhibits (many of them hands-on), an Omnimax Theater, the Henry Crown Space Center, and a replica of a coal mine; a self-guided tour. **Admission** Museum: $11 adults, $9.50 seniors, $7 children ages 3–11; combination tickets for museum and Omnimax Theater: $17.50 adults, $14.50 seniors, $12 children. Free on Monday and Tuesday, fall–winter (except December; call or check Web site for an exact schedule). **Hours** Memorial Day–Labor Day and on holidays: daily, 9:30 a.m.–5:30 p.m.; Sunday, 11 a.m.–5:30 p.m.; weekends and rest of year, 9:30 a.m.–4 p.m.; Sunday, 11 a.m.–4 p.m.; closed Christmas Day. **When to go**

Monday–Wednesday are the least crowded days, except in winter, when Monday and Tuesday attract the most visitors, because admission is free. Weekends are usually packed, but Sundays are generally less crowded than Saturdays. **Special comments** Expect to get lost (well, disoriented) while exploring this immense—and often bewildering—museum. The public-address system, by the way, is reserved for summoning the parents of lost children. Can there be too much of a good thing? Probably not, but this huge place comes close. Anyway, you'll find one full-sized wonder after another, plus plenty of hands-on fun that makes other museums seem boring by comparison. **How much time to allow** Even a full day isn't enough to explore the museum in depth. First-time visitors should figure on spending at least half a day and plan to come back.

DESCRIPTION AND COMMENTS   It might be easier to catalog what you *won't* find in this mega-museum, which once held the distinction of being the second-most-visited museum in the world (after the National Air and Space Museum in Washington, D.C.) before it started charging admission in 1991. Even with its rather steep admission price, the place still attracts nearly 2 million visitors a year.

Full-size exhibits include a real Boeing 727 jetliner, a Coast Guard helicopter, World War II German fighter planes—all suspended from the ceiling; the Apollo 8 command module that circled the moon in 1968; a mock-up of a human heart you can walk through; exhibits on basic science and, of all things, plumbing; and re-creations of 19th-century living rooms. Visitors can also thrill to a film in the domed Omnimax Theater, which boasts a five-story, 72-foot-diameter screen and a 72-speaker, 20,000-watt sound system.

TOURING TIPS   Unless you've got all day and feet of steel, do some homework. Grab a map at the entrance and make a short list of must-see attractions. Just make sure you walk past the information booth to the rotunda and the eye-popping view of that 727 docked at the balcony overlooking the main floor.

To get to the Henry Crown Space Center and the Omnimax Theater, walk through the Food for Life exhibit near the main entrance and descend to the ground floor near the U.S. Navy exhibit. The space exhibit features lunar modules, moon rocks, and a mock-up of a space shuttle. Nearby is U-505, a German submarine captured on June 4, 1944; on busy days the wait to tour the interior can last an hour.

At "Navy: Technology at Sea," kids can man the helm of a war ship. Other exhibits include Petroleum Planet, antique cars, bicycles, historic locomotives, computers, an energy lab, dolls, architecture—the list goes on and on and on.

OTHER THINGS TO DO NEARBY   The University of Chicago campus is full of beautiful buildings and interesting museums that offer a nice contrast to the hectic—and sometimes confusing—Museum of Science and Industry. It's a short walk from the museum. For a bite to eat, join the locals at Valois (1518 East 53rd Street), a cafeteria frequented by cops, cab drivers, and students.

National Vietnam Veterans Art Museum ★★★

APPEAL BY AGE	PRESCHOOL ★	GRADE SCHOOL ★	TEENS ★★
YOUNG ADULTS ★★		OVER 30 ★★★	SENIORS ★★★

LOCATION **South Loop; 1801 South Indiana Avenue (in the Prairie Avenue Historic District); ☎ 312-326-0270; www.nvvam.org**

Type of attraction Museum featuring more than 500 works of art (paintings, sculpture, and photographs) created by combat veterans from all nations that fought in the Vietnam War; a self-guided tour. Admission $10 adults and students, $7 under age 16. Hours Tuesday–Friday, 11 a.m.–6 p.m.; Saturday, 10 a.m.–5 p.m.; closed Sunday, Monday, and major holidays. When to go Anytime. Special comments The museum is off the beaten tourist path; if you don't have a car, consider public transportation. From Michigan Avenue, take the bus south to 18th Street, then walk a block east (toward Lake Michigan) to the museum. Spartan and grim—and a potentially wrenching experience for anyone who served in Vietnam, lost a friend or relative in the war, or is old enough to remember the conflict. How much time to allow 1–2 hours.

DESCRIPTION AND COMMENTS Opened in a renovated industrial space in August 1996, this museum—the only one of its kind—is filled with disturbing images of a conflict many Americans would rather forget. But the 130 artists who created the 1,000 works on display can't forget; they all pulled combat duty in Vietnam, and their work is visceral and gut-wrenching. Images of death and dying are a recurrent theme, as are shredded American flags, bombs with dollar bills as fins, a painting of LBJ with an American flag shirt and tie, a GI strung to a post by barbed wire (titled *Waiting for Kissinger*), and a wide array of weapons and artillery displayed as works of art (including a Viet Cong 122mm rocket launcher sitting in front of a painting titled *Rocket Attack*). The bare concrete floors and exposed piping and air ducts add to the no-nonsense, serious tenor of the gallery.

TOURING TIPS Be warned: a visit to this museum is no stroll in the park—it's relentlessly grim and powerful. A good way to start a tour is in the small multimedia theater on the first floor, which continuously shows slide images of the war through the eyes of the soldiers. Many of the images reappear later in the art on display.

OTHER THINGS TO DO NEARBY Next door are the Glessner House Museums, two historic houses that provide visitors a glimpse into Chicago's prairie heritage and later Victorian splendor. Docent-guided tours are offered Wednesday through Sunday, noon to 4 p.m.; the cost is $7 for adults and $6 for students and seniors. For more information, call ☎ 312-326-1480.

 Navy Pier ★★★★

APPEAL BY AGE	PRESCHOOL ★★★★★	GRADE SCHOOL ★★★★★	TEENS ★★★★★
YOUNG ADULTS ★★★★		OVER 30 ★★★★	SENIORS ★★★★

LOCATION **Near North Side; 700 East Grand Avenue (just north of the Chicago River on the lakefront); ☎ 312-595-PIER, ☎ 800-595-PIER (outside the 312 area code), and ☎ 312-595-5100 (administrative offices); www.navypier.com**

Type of attraction A renovated landmark on Lake Michigan with more than 50 acres of parks, gardens, shops, restaurants, a 150-foot Ferris wheel, an IMAX theater, a convention center, a children's museum, and other attractions; a self-guided tour. Admission Free; some attractions such as the Chicago Children's Museum, the Ferris wheel, cruise boats, the Wave Swinger (a 40-foot-high thrill ride), Time Escape (a multisensory ride through Chicago history), and the IMAX theater have separate admission charges. Hours Memorial Day–Labor Day: Sunday–Thursday, 10 a.m.–10 p.m.; Friday and Saturday, 10 a.m.–midnight. Fall: Monday–Thursday, 10 a.m.–9 p.m.; Friday and Saturday, 10 a.m.–11 p.m.; Sunday, 10 a.m.–7 p.m. Spring: Monday–Thursday, 10 a.m.–8 p.m.; Friday and Saturday, 10 a.m.–10 p.m.; Sunday, 10 a.m.–7 p.m. Restaurants are open later throughout the year. When to go Attracting 5 million visitors a year, Navy Pier has catapulted past the Lincoln Park Zoo to become Chicago's #1 attraction—and during warm weather, the place is jammed. Try to arrive before 11 a.m., especially if you're driving and on weekends. Special comments Although 3 on-site parking garages handle more than 1,700 cars, finding a place to put the family car emains a problem at this very popular attraction. Arrive early—or, better yet, take public transportation (the #29, #56, #65, #66, #120, and #121 buses stop at the entrance) or a cab. The view of Chicago's skyline alone makes this a must-see destination. The ultimate is dinner at a window table at Riva or an evening dinner cruise on the Odyssey. How much time to allow Depending on the weather, anywhere from an hour to half a day—or longer if a festival or concert is taking place during your visit.

DESCRIPTION AND COMMENTS A former U.S. Navy training facility and a campus of the University of Illinois, Navy Pier reopened in 1995 after a $196 million face-lift as Chicago's premier visitor attraction. There's something for everyone: a children's museum; a shopping mall and food court; a huge Ferris wheel and a carousel; a six-story-high, 80-foot-wide IMAX theater screen; scenic and dinner cruises on Lake Michigan; a convention center; a beer garden; a concert venue; ice skating in the winter.

Here's the scoop on Navy Pier's most popular attractions: The Ferris wheel is open year-round (weather permitting) and costs $5 for all ages; it's a 7½-minute ride. Long waits in line aren't a problem because it rotates nonstop at a slow speed that lets visitors load and unload almost continuously. The IMAX theater is located near the entrance of the Family Pavilion shopping mall; tickets for the shows start at $10.50 for adults, $9.50 for seniors, and $8.50 for children.

Crystal Gardens (a one-acre indoor tropical garden with fountains and public seating), Festival Hall, Skyline Stage, and the Grand Ballroom feature performances of jazz, blues, rock, theater, and dance, as well as special events such as consumer trade shows, art festivals, miniature golf, and ethnic festivals; most charge admission. The Chicago Shake-speare Theater opened in October 1999. For tickets, call ☎ 312-595-5600. For more information on the popular Chicago Children's Museum, see its attraction profile. Cruise boats depart from Navy Pier's south dock, as does the Shoreline Shuttle, a sightseeing boat that departs every 30 minutes for the Shedd Aquarium.

TOURING TIPS Unless your visit to Navy Pier is midweek during the winter, avoid the hassles and expense of parking (a $19 flat rate on weekends) by arriving via bus or cab. And try to pick a nice day: the Ferris wheel shuts down in the rain, and the view of Chicago's magnificent skyline is what separates this shopping, restaurant, and festival venue from all the others. If you're taking the kids to the Chicago Children's Museum, either arrive when it opens in the morning (when school is out) or in the afternoon during the school year (to avoid school groups that often arrive in the mornings). Before leaving home, call Navy Pier for a sched-ule of special events taking place during your visit.

OTHER THINGS TO DO NEARBY North Pier Festival Market is about two blocks west, offering more shopping and another food court. Kids will enjoy the Battle Tech Center and Virtuality Center game rooms on the third level. You can also stroll the Lakefront Trail or, better yet, rent a bike or inline skates at Bike Chicago (in Navy Pier).

Oriental Institute Museum ★★★★

APPEAL BY AGE	PRESCHOOL ★★	GRADE SCHOOL ★★★	TEENS ★★★★
OVER 30 ★★★★	YOUNG ADULTS ★★★★		SENIORS ★★★★

LOCATION **South Side; 1155 East 58th Street (on the campus of the University of Chicago); ☎ 773-702-9520; oi.uchicago.edu/museum**

Type of attraction A showcase for the history, art, and archaeology of the ancient Near East; a self-guided tour. Admission Free; suggested donation $5 adults, $2 children under age 12. Hours Tuesday and Thursday–Saturday, 10 a.m.–6 p.m.; Wednesday, 10 a.m.–8:30 p.m.; Sunday, noon–6 p.m.; closed Monday, Indepen-dence Day, Thanksgiving, Christmas, and New Year's Day. When to go Anytime. Special comments With galleries devoted to seven ancient Near Eastern civili-zations, from Egypt to Mesopotamia (a region encompassing modern-day Iraq and parts of Iran, Syria, and Turkey), this is an often-overlooked gem that shouldn't be missed. How much time to allow 1–2 hours.

DESCRIPTION AND COMMENTS Most of the artifacts displayed in this stunning collection are treasures recovered from expeditions to Iraq (Mesopotamia), Iran (Persia), Turkey, Syria, and Palestine. The University of Chicago's Ori-ental Institute has conducted research and archaeological digs in the Near East since 1919, and since 1931 has displayed much of its collection in this impressive building. Items date from 9000 BC to the tenth century AD and include papyrus scrolls, mummies, everyday items from the ancient past, and gigantic stone edifices.

TOURING TIPS Not-to-be-missed artifacts on display include a cast of the Rosetta Stone (195 BC), which provided the key for unlocking the meaning of Egyptian hieroglyphics; wall-sized Assyrian reliefs; a striding lion from ancient Babylon that once decorated a gateway; a colossal ten-ton bull's head from Persepolis (a Persian city destroyed by Alexander the Great in 331 BC), and a 17-foot-high statue of King Tut. The museum is a real find for archaeology buffs and anyone interested in ancient history.

OTHER THINGS TO DO NEARBY The DuSable Museum, the Smart Museum of Art, and the rest of the University of Chicago campus are all close—and well worth exploring. The huge Museum of Science and Industry is on 57th Street. For lunch, try Valois, a cafeteria hangout for local gendarmes and residents located at 1518 East 53rd Street.

Peace Museum   *(not rated)*

LOCATION **Near North Side; 100 North Central Park Avenue (2 blocks south of the Garfield Park Conservatory); ☎ 773-638-6450; www.peacemuseum.org**

Type of attraction A museum promoting peace and nonviolence through the arts; a self-guided tour. **Admission** Suggested donation $5 adults, $3 children, students, and seniors. **Hours** Thursday–Friday, 1–6 p.m.; Saturday and Sunday, 12–4 p.m.; closed in summer, reopens September 21. **When to go** Anytime. **Special comments** Take the elevator directly across from the building entrance to the 4th floor and turn right. Because the Peace Museum doesn't have a permanent collection, it's not possible to rate the museum; exhibits change about 4 times a year. **How much time to allow** 30 minutes to 1 hour.

DESCRIPTION AND COMMENTS This essentially one-room exhibit space may be the only museum in the world dedicated to world peace. On our visit, the exhibit was "A Piece of the Peace: Poetry for the Walls," which examined the role of language in making and breaking peace. Some of the original manuscripts on display were by Joan Baez, Bono, and Phil Ochs.

TOURING TIPS To find out what's on display during your visit, pick up a copy of the *Chicago Reader.*

OTHER THINGS TO DO NEARBY The Garfield Park Conservatory is a couple of blocks north.

kids The Peggy Notebaert Nature Museum of the Chicago Academy of Sciences ★★★

APPEAL BY AGE	PRESCHOOL ★★★★★	GRADE SCHOOL ★★★★★	TEENS ★★
YOUNG ADULTS ★★		OVER 30 ★★	SENIORS ★★

LOCATION **The North Side; 2430 North Cannon Drive in Lincoln Park (on the northwest corner of Fullerton Parkway and Cannon Drive); ☎ 773-755-5100; ☎ 773-871-2668 24-hour line with recorded message, including information on bus routes; www.chias.org**

Type of attraction An interactive museum dedicated to nature, from microcosms to wilderness walks, and a children's play gallery with puppets and a beaver lodge. **Admission** $7 adults, $5 seniors and students, $4 children ages 3–12; free for children under age 3. Some exhibits may require an additional charge. **Hours** Monday–Friday, 9 a.m.–4:30 p.m.; Saturday and Sunday, 10 a.m.–5 p.m. **When to go** Anytime. **Special comments** The museum runs special public programs for adult and child education alike. If traveling by car, park on the east side of Cannon Drive only; move your car by 4 p.m. Wheelchair and stroller accessible. Bike lockup is available. Educational for the young and refreshing for adults. **How much time to allow** A good 2 hours for adults, teenagers, and young adults. For families or groups with children, allow at least 3 hours.

DESCRIPTION AND COMMENTS A mellow, kid-centric museum with a beautiful array of photographs and fun, interesting exhibits—including a live haven of butterflies, a wilderness walk, city science environmental center, an active water lab, and children's gallery. A pleasant visit that is full of interesting scientific information. There is a small, comfortable cafeteria that sells slightly pricey but healthy sandwiches and snacks. In the summer, a patio provides a pleasant dining area overlooking the river.

TOURING TIPS Visit the butterfly haven first and enjoy the spectacular beauty of these graceful and docile creatures in their natural environment. Please be sure to respect the do's and don'ts video at the entrance. There is a nature museum shop for souvenir hunters.

OTHER THINGS TO DO NEARBY Head south on Cannon Drive to Chicago's Lincoln Park Zoo or east to Lake Michigan for a bike ride, stroll, or skate. During the summer months, call the museum for trolley tour information.

Polish Museum of America ★★½

| APPEAL BY AGE | PRESCHOOL ★★ | GRADE SCHOOL ★★ | TEENS ★★★ |
| YOUNG ADULTS ★★★ | | OVER 30 ★★★ | SENIORS ★★★ |

LOCATION **North Central–O'Hare Airport; 984 North Milwaukee Avenue; ☎ 773-384-3352; www.pma.prcua.org**

Type of attraction One of the largest and oldest ethnic museums in the United States, featuring Polish and Polish American paintings, sculptures, drawings, and lithographs; a self-guided tour. **Admission** $5 per adult; $4 for seniors (age 65 and over) and students (over age 12); $3 children under 12. **Hours** Daily, 11 a.m.–4 p.m.; closed Thursday. **When to go** Anytime. **Special comments** The museum is on the 2nd and 3rd floors; visitors must climb 2 flights of stairs. An eclectic collection of high-quality art, colorful crafts, and historical items ranging from 17th-century armor to modern paintings. **How much time to allow** 1 hour.

DESCRIPTION AND COMMENTS Located in the heart of Chicago's first Polish neighborhood, the Polish Museum emphasizes the art and history of an ethnic group that maintains a strong national identity; famous Poles include Paderewski, Pulaski, Kosciuszko, Copernicus, Sienkiewicz, Madame Curie, and Chopin. Interesting items on display include a one-horse open sleigh carved from a single log in 1703 that a Polish king gave to his daughter, Princess Maria, who married Louis XV of France.

Other stuff on display here—much of it colorful and reflecting a high degree of craftsmanship—include Polish folk costumes, exquisite hand-decorated Easter eggs, wood sculpture, prints, and paintings. It's not a very large place, but there's a lot to see.

TOURING TIPS   The third floor contains an attractive, well-lit art gallery featuring modern graphic art, paintings, and busts. Check out the stairwell and you'll find a Picasso lithograph and a Chagall etching.

OTHER THINGS TO DO NEARBY   Walk a few blocks north on Milwaukee Avenue to explore the old Polish neighborhood, which still has a few shops and restaurants with signs written in Polish; there's an El station at Ashland and Milwaukee avenues.

kids Sears Tower Skydeck ★★★★★

APPEAL BY AGE	PRESCHOOL ★★★★★	GRADE SCHOOL ★★★★★	TEENS ★★★★★
YOUNG ADULTS ★★★★★		OVER 30 ★★★★★	SENIORS ★★★★★

LOCATION   **The Loop; 233 South Wacker Drive (enter at Jackson Boulevard); ☎ 312-875-9696; www.the-skydeck.com**

Type of attraction Spectacular views into four states from the world's third-tallest building; a self-guided tour. **Admission** $11.95 adults, $9.95 children ages 5–12, $8.50 seniors, free under age 3. **Hours** May–September, daily, 10 a.m.–10 p.m.; October–April, daily, 10 a.m.–8 p.m. **When to go** Early or late on weekends and holidays March–November; waits in line for the elevator ride to the top can exceed 2 hours on busy afternoons. On hot days, go after 6:30 p.m. to avoid the heat and to see the city at sunset or at night. Skip it in inclement weather or when clouds obscure the top of the building. **Special comments** Don't enter the main lobby of the building facing South Wacker Drive; go to the Skydeck entrance on Jackson Boulevard. If the line is long, consider as an alternative the John Hancock Center on North Michigan Avenue. Though not quite as high (it's only the 14th-highest building in the world), it offers a better view, some say, and long waits are rare. Incredible. Part of the fun is looking down on all those other skyscrapers. **How much time to allow** At least 30 minutes once you reach the viewing deck; signs posted at various points in the waiting area in the basement tell you how long you'll stand in line before boarding an elevator.

DESCRIPTION AND COMMENTS   The distinctive 110-story Sears Tower (easily identified by its black aluminum skin, towering height, and twin antenna towers) reaches 1,454 feet; the Skydeck on the 103rd floor is 1,353 feet above the ground. It's a 70-second elevator ride to the broad, wide-windowed viewing area, where you're treated to a magnificent 360-degree view of Chicago, Lake Michigan, and the distant horizon.

TOURING TIPS   Enter the building at the Skydeck entrance on Jackson Boulevard; take the elevator *down* to purchase a ticket. Try to visit the tower on a clear day; or go at night when the crowds are thinner and a carpet of sparkling lights spreads into the distance.

OTHER THINGS TO DO NEARBY   The Chicago Mercantile Exchange is around the corner on Wacker Drive; go downstairs for something to eat from a wide array of eateries. To view more unrestrained capitalism in action, head south toward the Sears Tower, then east on Jackson Boulevard to the Chicago Board of Trade.

Swedish American Museum Center ★★½

LOCATION **North Side; 5211 North Clark Street; ☎ 773-728-8111; www.samac.org**

Type of attraction An attractive store-front museum highlighting Swedish culture and the Swedish immigrant experience; a self-guided tour. **Admission** $4 adults, $3 seniors and children, $10 families. **Hours** Tuesday–Friday, 10 a.m.–4 p.m.; Saturday and Sunday, 11 a.m.–4 p.m.; closed Monday. **When to go** Anytime. **Special comments** All the exhibits are located on the ground floor. Small, but attractive and interesting—and located in a great ethnic neighborhood. **How much time to allow** 30 minutes to 1 hour.

DESCRIPTION AND COMMENTS Swedes were a major immigrant group in 19th-century Chicago, and this museum provides insight into Swedish history and culture and the life of early immigrants. Items on display include jewelry from Lapland, old family Bibles, 19th-century hand tools, and a re-creation of a typical Swedish American home from the early 20th century.

The gallery also exhibits fascinating black-and-white photos, including old pictures of the departed laid out in their coffins before burial: "Death was present everywhere, in a different way than it is today, and the local photographer would often be asked to immortalize deceased persons, both old and young." How things change.

TOURING TIPS The well-stocked and attractive museum shop features a wide range of items such as Swedish videos (including several films directed by Ingmar Bergman), books, road maps of Scandinavia, audio crash courses in Swedish, and traditional handicrafts from the Old Country. The Children's Museum of Immigration tells the story of immigration for youngsters ages 3 to 12.

OTHER THINGS TO DO NEARBY Explore Andersonville, the last ethnic stronghold of Swedes in Chicago. It's a fascinating neighborhood—an unusual mix of Swedish and Middle Eastern—full of interesting shops and inexpensive ethnic restaurants. (See "Exploring Chicago's Neighborhoods," page 116.)

Ukrainian National Museum of Chicago ★

LOCATION **North Central–O'Hare Airport; 2249 West Superior Street; ☎ 312-421-8020; www.ukrainiannationalmuseum.org**

Type of attraction A collection of Ukrainian folk art, embroidery, wood carvings, ceramics, beadwork, and painted Easter eggs; a self-guided tour. **Admission** $5. **Hours** Thursday–Sunday, 11 a.m.–4 p.m.; Monday–Wednesday, by appointment only. **When to go** Anytime. **Special comments** Visitors must climb a set of stairs to reach the entrance. Though some beautiful objects are on display here, this museum is too small and out of the way to recommend a special trip. **How much time to allow** 30 minutes to 1 hour.

DESCRIPTION AND COMMENTS   The Ukraine, a nation of 52 million people that was once part of. the former Soviet Union and an independent state since 1991, is the second-largest country in Europe. Crammed into this tiny but bright museum is a wide variety of folk art, including linens, colorful costumes, exquisitely detailed painted Easter eggs, musical instruments, wood models of native Ukrainian houses, swords, and paintings.

TOURING TIPS   Make this a stop on an ethnic exploration of Chicago; see our description of the Ukrainian Village in "Exploring Chicago's Neighborhoods" earlier in this chapter.

OTHER THINGS TO DO NEARBY   Next door is Sts. Volodymyr and Olha Ukrainian Catholic Church, topped by three gold domes and decorated by rich mosaics over the door. On nearby Chicago Avenue are several Ukrainian eateries and bakeries.

PART EIGHT

DINING *and* RESTAURANTS

by Alice Van Housen

DINING *in* CHICAGO

CHICAGO'S RESTAURANT SCENE IS AT A FULL BOIL, with contenders of all kinds cooking up concepts both classic and contemporary, some with the proverbial twist and others defying categorization. Our geographic dining boundaries continue to expand, with Lincoln Square still booming and, most notably, the South Loop finally getting its due. And beneath the radar of all the "name" and noteworthy newcomers lurk the thousands of funky little ethnic and neighborhood spots for which Chicago is famous—and thanks to which virtually no appetite goes unsatisfied.

ALWAYS MORE FISH IN THE SEA

IT'S ASTOUNDING TO CONTEMPLATE HOW THE SEAS can keep up with our craze for raw fish. Showing no signs of abating, the sushi tsunami has brought us, to name just a few, hipsters **Hachi's Kitchen** in Logan Square (2521 North California Avenue; ☎ 773-276-8080) and **Old Town's Mizu Yakitori & Sushi Lounge** (315 West North Avenue; ☎ 312-951-8880); Uptown's bizarrely decorated **Agami** (4712 North Broadway; ☎ 773-506-1854); Wicker Park's **Aki Sushi** (2015 West Division Street; ☎ 773-227-8080); **Tokyo 21** on the fringe of Lincoln Park (901 West Weed Street; ☎ 312-337-2001); and Roscoe Village's experimental **Kaze Sushi** (2032 West Roscoe Street; ☎ 773-327-4860).

NEW AMERICAN STYLINGS

THE FRESH SEASONAL APPROACH, WITH ITS USE OF LOCAL, often organic ingredients and informed by classic cooking technique, continues to inspire chefs and lure diners to such hot spots as **Sola** (3868 North Lincoln Avenue; ☎ 773-327-3868), owned by chef Carol Wallack (ex-Deleece); Michael Carlson's quirky, teeny-weeny **Schwa** (1466 North Ashland Avenue; ☎ 773-252-1466); **May Street Market**

Newcomers and Other Recommendations

AMERICAN

RL 115 East Chicago Avenue; ☎ 312-475-1100; Gold Coast

Lawry's The Prime Rib 100 East Ontario Street; ☎ 312-787-5000; River North

CHINESE

Emperor's Choice 2238 South Wentworth Avenue; ☎ 312-225-8800; Chinatown

CONTEMPORARY AMERICAN

Avenue M 691–695 North Milwaukee Avenue ; ☎ 312-243-1133; Near West

HB 3404 North Halsted Street; ☎ 773-661-0299; Lakeview

Hot Chocolate 1747 North Damen Avenue; ☎ 773-489-1747; Bucktown

Quince The Homestead Hotel, 1625 Hinman Avenue; ☎ 847-570-8400; Evanston

Schwa 1466 North Ashland Avenue; ☎ 773-252-1466; Bucktown–Wicker Park

Sola 3868 North Lincoln Avenue; ☎ 773-327-3868; Lakeview

CONTEMPORARY ASIAN

Mulan China Place, 2017 South Wells Street; ☎ 312-842-8282; Chinatown

Red Light 820 West Randolph Street; ☎ 312-733-8880; Near West

Shanghai Terrace Peninsula Hotel, 108 East Superior Street; ☎ 312-573-6744; River North

Tamarind 614 South Wabash Avenue; ☎ 312-379-0970; South Loop

CUBAN

Café 28 1800-1806 West Irving Park Road; ☎ 773-528-2883; Lakeview

FRENCH

Ambria Belden-Stratford Hotel, 2300 North Lincoln Park West; ☎ 773-472-5959; Lincoln Park

Oceanique (Seafood) 505 Main Street, Evanston; ☎ 847-864-3435; Evanston

INDIAN

Hema's Kitchen 2411 North Clark Street; ☎ 773-529-1705; Lincoln Park
6406 North Oakley Avenue; ☎ 773-338-1627; Northwest Side

IRISH

Mrs. Murphy & Sons 3905 North Lincoln Avenue; ☎ 773-248-3905; Lakeview

ITALIAN

Il Covo 2152 North Damen Avenue; ☎ 773-862-5555; Bucktown

Quartino 826 North State Street; ☎ 312-698-5000; River North

Rosal's 1154 West Taylor Street; ☎ 312-243-2357; Little Italy

Terragusto 1851 West Addison Street; ☎ 773-248-2777; Roscoe Village

Think Café 2235 North Western Avenue; ☎ 773-394-0537; Bucktown

MEXICAN

Maiz 1041 North California Avenue; ☎ 773-276-3149; Humboldt Park

Zapatista 1307 South Wabash Avenue; ☎ 312-435-1307; South Loop

MIDDLE EASTERN

Maza 2748 North Lincoln Avenue; ☎ 773-929-9600; Lincoln Park

Tizi Melloul 531 North Wells Street; ☎ 312-670-4338; River North

NUEVO LATINO

DeLaCosta 465 East Illinois Street; ☎ 312-321-8933; River North

PIZZA

The Art of Pizza 3033 North Ashland Avenue; ☎ 773-327-5600; Lakeview

Pizza D.O.C. 2251 West Lawrence Avenue; ☎ 773-784-8777; Lincoln Square

Spacca Napoli 1769 West Sunnyside Avenue; ☎ 773-878-2420; Ravenswood

Trattoria D.O.C. 706 Main Street, Evanston; ☎ 847-475-1111; Evanston

SEAFOOD

Fulton's on the River 315 North La Salle Street; ☎ 312-822-0100; River North

Half Shell 676 West Diversey Parkway; ☎ 773-549-1773; Lakeview

SMALL PLATES

Bravo (Tapas) 2047 West Division Street; ☎ 773-278-2727; Wicker Park

del Toro (Tapas) 1520 North Damen Avenue; ☎ 773-252-1500; Wicker Park

Fixture (New American) 2706 North Ashland Avenue; ☎ 773-248-3331;
    Lincoln Park

X/O Chicago (Global) 3441 North Halsted Street; ☎ 773-348-9696; Lakeview

STEAK HOUSES

Custom House Hotel Blake, 500 South Dearborn Street; ☎ 312-523-0200;
    Printer's Row

David Burke's Primehouse The James Chicago Hotel, 616 North Rush Street;
    ☎ 312-660-6000; River North

Tango Sur (Argentinean) 3763 North Southport Avenue; ☎ 773-477-5466;
    Wrigleyville

SUSHI

Hachi's Kitchen 2521 North California Avenue; ☎ 773-276-8080; Logan Square

Meiji 623 West Randolph Street; ☎ 312-887-9999; Near West

Tokyo 21 901 West Weed Street; ☎ 312-337-2001; Lincoln Park

THAI

Spoon Thai 4608 North Western Avenue; ☎ 773-769-1173; Lincoln Square

Thai Pastry 4925 North Broadway; ☎ 773-784-5399; Uptown

TURKISH

Turquoise 2147 West Roscoe Street; ☎ 773-549-3523; Roscoe Village

WINE BARS

The Tasting Room 1415 West Randolph Street; ☎ 312-942-1313; Near West

(1132 West Grand Avenue; ☎ 312-421-5547); and **Avenue M,** with Daniel Kelly (formerly of d.kelly) at the kitchen's helm.

THE GRAZING CRAZE

SNACKABLE, SHAREABLE, SMALL PLATES ARE STILL GROWING in numbers, if not in size. Apparently those who always secretly wished they could order three appetizers are having it their way, with new options including Spanish tapas from **del Toro** (1520 North Damen Avenue; ☎ 773-252-1500), **Bravo** (2047 West Division Street; ☎ 773-278-2727), and **People Lounge** (1560 North Milwaukee Avenue; ☎ 773-227-9339); Italian bites from **Extra Virgin** (741 West Randolph Street; ☎ 312-474-0700); New American noshes from **Fixture** (2706 North Ashland Avenue; ☎ 773-248-3331); and eclectic edibles from **X/O Chicago** (3441 North Halsted Street; ☎ 773-348-9696). And not to be outdone, the portions and/or plates are getting even smaller at spots like **Minnie's** (miniature everything—including airplane-sized booze bottles); 1969 North Halsted Street; ☎ 312-943-9900) and **Take Five** (everything's $5); 3747 North Southport Avenue; ☎ 773-871-5555).

IT'S A STEAK TOWN, AFTER ALL

Morton's, OUR HOMETOWN PRIDE, HAS ADDED a few locations (see profile, page 231), including a Loop outpost that serves lunch. David Burke of Park Avenue Café fame returned to Chicago with **Primehouse,** a swanky steak purveyor in the posh new James Hotel (616 North Rush Street; ☎ 312-660-6000). At press time, Tru's dream team Rick Tramonto and Gale Gand were heading for the North 'burbs (the new Westin Hotel in Wheeling) with a group of restaurants headlined by **Tramonto's Steak & Seafood.** And for those who prefer their steak Carnival style, those Brazilian *churrascarias* keep on coming just like the skewers of meat they serve, with River North receiving **Brazzaz** (539 North Dearborn Street; ☎ 312-595-9000) to challenge the existing **Fogo de Chão,** and Schaumburg shoppers sitting down to **Texas de Brazil** (Woodfield Shopping Center; ☎ 847-413-1600).

SOUTH-OF-THE-BORDER SIZZLE

OUR LANDLOCKED MIDWESTERN STATUS notwithstanding, there's a hot-blooded streak to our collective appetite that welcomes the fiery multicultural offerings from Mexico and the other Americas. Vibrant Mexican and Latin spots have opened up, from the West Loop's **Carnivale** (see profile, page 208) to the South Loop's **Cuatro** (see profile, page 212) and **Zapatista** (1307 South Wabash Avenue; ☎ 312-435-1307), from Andersonville's **Ole Ole** (5413 North Clark Street; ☎ 773-293-2222) to Ravenswood's **Dorado** (2301 West Foster Avenue; ☎ 773-561-3780). And from hot-hot-hot Miami chef Douglas Rodriguez, **DeLaCosta** has invaded River North (465 East Illinois Street; ☎ 312-321-8930).

SAVORING THE SOUTH LOOP

A DECADE BEHIND ALL THE PREDICTIONS, the South Loop has finally popped with a spate of new restaurants to feed a new gentrifying demographic. In addition to Cuatro and Zapatista, the booming area has greeted, among others, Pan-Asian **Tamarind** (614 South Wabash Avenue; ☎ 312-379-0970); the classic-chic deli **Eleven City Diner** (1112 South Wabash Avenue; ☎ 312-212-1112); **Kohan** Japanese steak and sushi (730 West Maxwell Street; ☎ 312-421-6254); and, in the Chinatown district, the superchic, no-sushi Japanese eatery **Mulan** (Chinatown Square, East Gate; 2017 South Wells Street; ☎ 312-842-8282).

WHO WANTS PIE?

NICHE PIZZA PARLORS ARE SLICING THE PIE into specialty subcategories for destination dining, with fanatics flocking to **Frasca** (3358 North Paulina Street; ☎ 773-248-5222); **Spacca Napoli** (1769 West Sunnyside Avenue; ☎ 773-878-2420); **Trattoria D.O.C.** (706 Main Street, Evanston; ☎ 847-475-1111); and **Gruppo di Amici** (1508 West Jarvis Avenue; ☎ 773-508-5565). And at press time, Bistro Campagne's Michael Altenberg had **Crust** in the oven (2056 West Division Street).

TEA TAKEOVER

TEA IS BEING EMBRACED LIKE NEVER BEFORE, WITH destination spots and serious tea programs at existing restaurants. Tea temples include **Tea Geschwender** (2142 North Halsted Street; ☎ 773-525-0671), a cafe-and-retail combo serving 300 varieties, and Chinatown's trendy bubble-tea specialist (75 varieties) **St. Alp's Teahouse,** downstairs from Phoenix (2131 South Archer Avenue; ☎ 312-842-1886). **NoMI** (see profile, page 235) has appointed a tea sommelier for its top-of-the-charts program, and **T-Spot Sushi** (3925 North Lincoln Avenue; ☎ 773-549-4500) hints at its extensive tea selection in its name.

GASTROPUB RUMBLINGS

BB's (22 EAST HUBBARD STREET; ☎ 312-755-0007), descended from the Bud Binyon restaurant legend, purports to be Chicago's first gastropub—which is a bit of a stretch, as many of our modern bars serve more than wraps, poppers, and burgers. Perhaps the first true example is still in the oven, with Blackbird's Paul Kahan cooking up a West Loop gastropub at 845 West Fulton Street, tentatively set for a summer 2007 opening.

RESTAURANTS:
Rated and Ranked

OUR FAVORITE CHICAGO RESTAURANTS: EXPLAINING THE RATINGS

WE'VE DEVELOPED DETAILED PROFILES for what we consider the best restaurants in town. Each profile features an easy-to-scan heading that allows you to check out the restaurant's name, cuisine, star rating, cost, quality rating, and value rating very quickly.

OVERALL RATING The overall rating encompasses the entire dining experience, including style, service, and ambience in addition to the taste, presentation, and quality of the food. Five stars is the highest rating possible and connotes the best of everything. Four-star restaurants are exceptional, and three-star restaurants are well above average. Two-star restaurants are good. One star is used to connote an average restaurant that demonstrates an unusual capability in some area of specialization—for example, an otherwise unmemorable place that has great barbecued chicken.

COST To the right of the star rating is an expense description, which provides a comparative sense of how much a complete meal will cost. A complete meal for our purposes consists of an entree with vegetable or side dish and a choice of soup or salad. Appetizers, desserts, drinks, and tips are excluded.

Inexpensive	$16 or less per person
Moderate	$17–$29 per person
Expensive	$30–$40 per person
Very Expensive	More than $40 per person

A NOTE ON MENUS AND PRICES The better restaurants in Chicago change their menus at least seasonally. Others change them monthly or weekly or even daily. Or with what's available at the market, or at the chef's whim. Anything we tell you is on the menu today might not be there tomorrow. Of course, prices will fluctuate with the menu changes, but not a lot, and they go down as well as up. Just don't be surprised if things aren't quite the same when you get there. In an unprecedented move, in summer 2006 Chicago's City Council banned the serving of foie gras, causing much controversy—and not a little bit of defiance. The long-term fate of the ban was unknown at press time, and some restaurants have continued to serve foie gras despite the edict. Dishes listed herein that include foie gras as an ingredient may no longer be available but are representative of a given chef's culinary vision.

QUALITY RATING The food quality is rated on a scale of one to five stars, with five stars being the best rating attainable. It is based expressly on the taste, freshness of ingredients, preparation, presentation, and creativity of food served. There is no consideration of price. If you want the best food available and cost is not an issue, you need look no further than the quality ratings.

VALUE RATING If, on the other hand, you are looking for both quality and value, then you should check the value rating. The value ratings, expressed in stars, are defined as follows:

★★★★★	Exceptional value, a real bargain
★★★★	Good value
★★★	Fair value, you get exactly what you pay for
★★	Somewhat overpriced
★	Significantly overpriced

PAYMENT We've listed the type of payment accepted at each restaurant, using the following codes: AE equals American Express (Optima), CB equals Carte Blanche, D equals Discover, DC equals Diners Club, MC equals MasterCard, and V equals VISA.

WHO'S INCLUDED Restaurants in Chicago open and close at an alarming rate. So for the most part we've tried to confine our list to establishments with a proven track record over a fairly long period of time. The exceptions here are the newer offspring of the demigods of the culinary world—these places are destined to last, at least until our next update. Newer or changed establishments that demonstrate staying power and consistency will be profiled in subsequent editions. Also, the list is highly selective. Exclusion of a particular place does not necessarily indicate that the restaurant is not good, only that it was not ranked among the best in its genre. Detailed profiles of individual restaurants follow in alphabetical order at the end of this chapter.

THE BEST . . .

Best Beer

- **Bistro Campagne** (see profile, page 203)
- **Chicago Brauhaus** 4732 North Lincoln Avenue, Lincoln Square; ☎ 773-784-4444
- **Chief O'Neill's** (see profile, page 211)
- **Clark Street Ale House** 743 North Clark Street, River North; ☎ 312-642-9253
- **Goose Island Brewing Company** 1800 North Clybourn Avenue, Lincoln Park; ☎312-915-0071; 3535 North Clark Street, Wrigleyville; ☎ 773-832-9040
- **Hopleaf** 5148 North Clark Street, Andersonville; ☎ 773-334-9851
- **Map Room** 1949 North Hoyne Avenue, Bucktown; ☎ 773-252-7636
- **Piece** 1927 West North Avenue, Bucktown; ☎ 773-772-4422
- **Red Lion Pub** 2446 North Lincoln Avenue, Lincoln Park; ☎ 773-348-2695
- **Resi's Bierstube** 2034 West Irving Park Road, North Central; ☎ 773-472-1749

Continued on page 188

The Best Chicago Restaurants

NAME	OVERALL RATING	PRICE RATING	QUALITY RATING	VALUE RATING
AMERICAN				
Green Zebra	★★★★	Exp	★★★★	★★★★
Naha	★★★★	Exp	★★★★	★★★
Prairie Grass Cafe	★★★	Mod	★★★★	★★★★
Park Grill	★★★	Mod	★★★	★★★
Moto	★★★	Very Exp	★★★	★★
Bongo Room	★★½	Inexp	★★★	★★★
Twin Anchors	★★½	Mod	★★½	★★★
Lou Mitchell's Restaurant	★★	Inexp	★★★	★★★★
ASIAN				
Kevin	★★★★	Exp	★★★★	★★
Japonais	★★★	Exp	★★★	★★
Opera	★★½	Mod	★★★½	★★
BREAKFAST				
Orange	★★	Inexp	★★★	★★★★
BREW PUB				
Piece	★★	Inexp	★★★	★★★★
CAJUN				
Wishbone	★★½	Inexp	★★★	★★★★★
CHINESE				
Three Happiness	★★½	Inexp	★★★½	★★★★★
Phoenix	★★	Mod	★★	★★★
COSTA RICAN				
Irazu	★★★	Inexp	★★★★	★★★★★
DELI				
Manny's Coffee Shop & Deli	★★	Inexp	★★★★	★★★
ECLECTIC				
Lula	★★★½	Mod	★★★½	★★★★
FAST FOOD				
Hot Doug's	★★★	Inexp	★★★★★	★★★★★
Superdawg Drive-In	★★	Inexp	★★½	★★

NAME	OVERALL RATING	PRICE RATING	QUALITY RATING	VALUE RATING
FRENCH				
Everest	★★★★★	Very Exp	★★★★★	★★★
Le Francais	★★★★½	Very Exp	★★★★★	★★★
Le Colonial	★★★★	Mod	★★★★	★★★
Bistro Campagne	★★★	Mod	★★★½	★★★★
GERMAN				
Berghoff Café/17 West	★★½	Mod	★★½	★★★
GREEK				
Santorini	★★★	Exp	★★★	★★★
Artopolis	★★½	Inexp	★★★★	★★★★
IRISH				
Chief O'Neill's Restaurant and Pub	★★	Mod	★★	★★★
ITALIAN				
Spiaggia	★★★★★	Very Exp	★★★★★	★★★
Coco Pazzo	★★★★	Very Exp	★★★★	★★
Follia	★★★	Mod	★★★½	★★★
JAPANESE				
Heat	★★★★	Very Exp	★★★★	★★
Mirai Sushi	★★★★	Mod	★★★★★	★★★
KOREAN				
Jin Ju	★★★	Mod	★★★	★★★½
MEDITERRANEAN				
Naha	★★★★	Exp	★★★★	★★★
Avec	★★★	Mod	★★★★	★★★
MEXICAN				
Topolobampo	★★★★½	Very Exp	★★★★★	★★★
Frontera Grill	★★★★	Mod	★★★★½	★★★
Salpicon	★★★	Mod	★★★★½	★★★
De Cero	★★½	Mod	★★½	★★★½

The Best Chicago Restaurants (continued)

NAME	OVERALL RATING	PRICE RATING	QUALITY RATING	VALUE RATING
NEW AMERICAN				
Alinea	★★★★★	Very Exp	★★★★★	★★★
Charlie Trotter's	★★★★★	Very Exp	★★★★★	★★★
Tru	★★★★★	Very Exp	★★★★★	★★★
Spring	★★★★½	Exp	★★★★	★★
Blackbird	★★★★	Exp	★★★★½	★★★
MK	★★★★	Exp	★★★★½	★★★
NoMI	★★★★	Very Exp	★★★★½	★★★
North Pond	★★★★	Exp	★★★★½	★★★
one sixtyblue	★★★★	Exp	★★★★½	★★★
Seasons	★★★★	Very Exp	★★★★	★★
Boka	★★★½	Exp	★★★½	★★★
Bin 36	★★★	Mod	★★★½	★★★
NEW FRENCH				
Kevin	★★★½	Exp	★★★★	★★
Café des Architectes	★★★½	Exp	★★★★	★½
NUEVO LATINO				
Nacional 27	★★★★	Mod	★★★★	★★★
Mas	★★★½	Mod	★★★½	★★★
Cuatro	★★★	Exp	★★★	★★★
Carnivale	★★★	Exp	★★★	★★
SushiSamba Rio	★★★	Exp	★★★	★★
PIZZERIA				
Lou Malnati's	★★½	Inexp	★★½	★★★★
Piece	★★	Inexp	★★★	★★★★
SEAFOOD				
Spring	★★★★½	Exp	★★★★	★★
Scylla	★★★½	Mod	★★★½	★★★
Shaw's Crab House	★★★½	Exp	★★★½	★★

NAME	OVERALL RATING	PRICE RATING	QUALITY RATING	VALUE RATING
SEAFOOD (CONTINUED)				
Santorini	★★★	Exp	★★★	★★★
Joe's Seafood, Prime Steak & Stone Crab	★★★	Very Exp	★★★½	★★
SOUTHERN				
Wishbone	★★★	Inexp	★★★	★★★★★
SPANISH/TAPAS				
Café Iberico	★★★	Mod	★★★	★★★★
STEAK				
Morton's	★★★½	Very Exp	★★★★½	★★
Gibson's	★★★½	Very Exp	★★★★	★★½
Nine	★★★½	Exp	★★★★	★★
Smith & Wollensky	★★★½	Exp	★★★★	★★
Joe's Seafood, Prime Steak & Stone Crab	★★★	Very Exp	★★★½	★★
Chicago Chop House	★★★	Very Exp	★★★	★★
SUSHI				
Heat	★★★★	Exp	★★★★	★★
Mirai Sushi	★★★½	Mod	★★★★½	★★★
SushiSamba Rio	★★½	Exp	★★★	★★
THAI				
Arun's Thai Restaurant	★★★★½	Very Exp	★★★★★★	★★
VEGETARIAN				
Green Zebra	★★★★	Exp	★★★★	★★★★
VIETNAMESE				
Le Lan	★★★★	Exp	★★★★	★★★★
Le Colonial	★★★½	Mod	★★★★	★★★
WINE BAR				
Bin 36	★★★	Mod	★★★½	★★★

Chicago Restaurants by Neighborhood

**SOUTH LOOP–
CHINATOWN**
Bongo Room
Cuatro
Manny's Coffee Shop
& Deli
Opera
Orange
Phoenix
Three Happiness

THE LOOP
Berghoff Café/17 West
Everest
Lou Mitchell's
Morton's
Park Grill

**WEST LOOP–NEAR
WEST–GREEKTOWN**
Artopolis
Avec
Blackbird
Carnivale
De Cero
Follia
Japonais
Moto
Nine
one sixtyblue
Santorini
Wishbone

RIVER NORTH
Bin 36
Café Iberico
Chicago Chop House
River North
Frontera Grill

Joe's Seafood, Prime
Steak & Stone Crab
Kevin
Le Lan
Lou Malnati's
MK
Nacional 27
Naha
Shaw's Crab House
Smith & Wollensky
SushiSamba Rio
Topolobampo

**GOLD COAST–
STREETERVILLE**
Café des Architectes
Gibson's
Le Colonial
Morton's
NoMI
Seasons
Spiaggia
Tru

**OLD TOWN–
LINCOLN PARK**
Alinea
Boka
Charlie Trotter's
Heat
Lou Malnati's
North Pond
Salpicon
Twin Anchors

**BUCKTOWN–WEST
TOWN–WICKER PARK**
Bongo Room
Green Zebra

Irazu
Mas
Mirai Sushi
Piece
Scylla
Spring

**LAKEVIEW–
WRIGLEYVILLE**
Orange
Wishbone

**ANDERSONVILLE–
LINCOLN SQUARE**
Bistro Champagne
Jin Ju

**LOGAN SQUARE–
ROSCOE VILLAGE**
Hot Doug's
Lula

**NORTH CENTRAL–
O'HARE AIRPORT**
Arun's Thai Restaurant
Chief O'Neill's
Lou Mitchell's
Morton's
Superdawg Drive-In

NORTHERN SUBURBS
Le Francais
Lou Malnati's
Morton's
Prairie Grass Cafe
Shaw's Seafood Grill

- **Sheffield's Wine and Beer** 3258 North Sheffield Avenue, Lakeview;
  ☎ 773-281-4989
- **Village Tap** 2055 West Roscoe Street, Roscoe Village; ☎ 773-883-0817

Best Bistros

- **Bistro Campagne** (see profile, page 203)
- **Bistrot Margot** 1437 North Wells Street, Old Town; ☎ 312-587-3660
- **Brasserie Jo** 59 West Hubbard Street, River North; ☎ 312-595-0800
- **Chez Joel** 1119 West Taylor Street, Little Italy; ☎ 312-226-6479
- **Cyrano's Bistrot & Wine Bar** 546 North Wells Street, River North; ☎ 312-467-0546
- **Kiki's Bistro** 900 North Franklin Street, River North; ☎ 312-335-5454
- **La Sardine** 111 North Carpenter Street, West Loop; ☎ 312-421-2800
- **Le Bouchon** 1958 North Damen Avenue, Bucktown; ☎ 773-862-6600

Best Brunch

- **Bongo Room** (see profile, page 206)
- **Brett's** 2011 West Roscoe Street, Roscoe Village; ☎ 773-248-0999
- **Café Selmarie** 4729 North Lincoln Avenue, Lincoln Square; ☎ 773-989-5595; Sunday only
- **Deleece** 4004 North Southport Avenue, Wrigleyville; ☎ 773-325-1710
- **erwin** 2925 North Halsted Street, Lakeview; ☎ 773-528-7200
- **Feast** 1616 North Damen Avenue, Bucktown; ☎ 773-772-7100
- **Frontera Grill** (Saturday only) (see profile, page 215)
- **Ina's** 1235 West Randolph Street, Near West; ☎ 312-226-8227
- **Jane's** 1655 West Cortland Avenue, Bucktown; ☎ 773-862-5263
- **M. Henry** 5707 North Clark Street, Andersonville; ☎ 773-561-1600
- **Magnolia Café** 1224 West Wilson Avenue, Uptown; ☎ 773-728-8785
- **North Pond** (see profile, page 236)
- **Orange** (see profile, page 239)
- **Phoenix** (see profile, page 240)
- **Salpicon** (see profile, page 242)
- **Toast** 2046 North Damen Avenue, Bucktown; ☎ 773-772-5600
  746 West Webster Avenue, Lincoln Park; ☎ 773-935-5600
- **Wishbone** (see profile, page 253)

Best Delis

- **The Bagel** 3107 North Broadway, Lakeview; ☎ 773-477-0300
- **Cold Comfort** 2211 West North Avenue, Bucktown; ☎ 773-772-4552
- **Eleven City Diner** 1112 South Wabash Avenue, South Loop; ☎ 312-212-1112
- **Manny's Coffee Shop & Deli** (see profile, page 228)
- **New York City Bagel Deli** 1001 West North Avenue, Lincoln Park; ☎ 312-274-1278

Best Fast Food

- **Billy Goat Tavern** 430 N. Lower Michigan Avenue, The Loop; ☎ 312-222-1525

Best Fast Food (continued)

- **Byron's Hot Dogs** 1017 West Irving Park Road, Uptown; ☎ 773-281-7474; 1701 West Lawrence Avenue, Lincoln Square; ☎ 773-271-0900; 680 North Halsted Street, River West; ☎ 312-738-0968
- **Hot Doug's** (see profile, page 219)
- **Mr. Beef** 666 North Orleans Street, River North; ☎ 312-337-8500
- **Muskie's** 2878 North Lincoln Avenue, Lakeview; ☎ 773-883-1633
- **Superdawg Drive-in** (see profile, page 248)
- **The Wiener's Circle** 2622 North Clark Street, Lincoln Park; ☎ 773-477-7444

Best Late-night Eateries

- **Avec** (see profile, page 201)
- **Beat Kitchen** 2100 West Belmont Avenue, Roscoe Village; ☎ 773-281-4444
- **Bijan's Bistro** 663 North State Street, River North; ☎ 312-202-1904
- **Coobah** 3423 North Southport Avenue, Lakeview; ☎ 773-528-2220
- **Cru Café & Wine Bar** 25 East Delaware Place, Gold Coast; ☎ 312-337-4001
- **Gibson's** (see profile, page 217)
- **Landmark** 1633 North Halsted Street, Lincoln Park; ☎ 312-587-1600
- **Pepper Lounge** 3441 North Sheffield Avenue, Wrigleyville; ☎ 773-665-7377
- **Quartino** 626 North State Street, River North; ☎ 312-698-5000
- **San Soo Gab San** 5247 North Western Avenue, Northwest Side; ☎ 773-334-1589
- **Tavern on Rush** 1031 North Rush Street, Gold Coast; ☎ 312-664-9600
- **Tempo** 6 East Chestnut Street, Gold Coast; ☎ 312-943-4373
- **Three Happiness** 2130 South Wentworth Avenue, Chinatown; ☎ 312-791-1228
- **Twisted Spoke** 501 North Ogden Avenue, Near West; ☎ 312-666-1500 3369 N. Clark Street, Wrigleyville; ☎ 773-525-5300
- **Wiener's Circle** 2622 North Clark Street, Lincoln Park; ☎ 773-477-7444

Best Outdoor Dining

- **Athena** 212 South Halsted Street, Greektown; ☎ 312-655-0000
- **Bistro Campagne** (see profile, page 203)
- **Café Ba-Ba-Reeba** 2024 North Halsted Street, Lincoln Park; ☎ 773-935-5000
- **Dinotto Ristorante** 215 West North Avenue, Old Town; ☎ 312-202-0302
- **Japonais** (see profile, page 220)
- **Le Colonial** (see profile, page 223)
- **North Pond** (see profile, page 236)
- **Park Grill** (see profile, page 239)

- **Pegasus** 130 South Halsted Street, Greektown; ☎ 312-226-3377
- **Puck's at the MCA** 220 East Chicago Avenue, Streeterville; ☎ 312-397-4034
- **Smith & Wollensky** (see profile, page 246)
- **SushiSamba Rio** (see profile, page 249)
- **Timo** 464 North Halsted Street, Near West; ☎ 312-226-4300
- **Topo Gigio** 1516 North Wells Street, Old Town; ☎ 312-266-9355

Best Pizza

- **Art of Pizza** 3033 North Ashland Avenue, Lakeview; ☎ 773-327-5600
- **Bricks** 1909 North Lincoln Avenue, Lincoln Park; ☎ 312-255-0851
- **Frasca** 3358 North Paulina Street, Lakeview; ☎ 773-248-5222
- **Lou Malnati's** (see profile, page 226)
- **Piece** (see profile, page 241)
- **Pizza D.O.C.** 2251 West Lawrence Avenue, Lincoln Square;
  ☎ 773-784-8777
- **Pizzeria Due** 619 North Wabash Avenue, River North; ☎ 312-943-2400
- **Pizzeria Uno** 29 East Ohio Street, River North; ☎ 312-321-1000
- **Spacca Napoli** 1769 West Sunnyside Avenue, Ravenswood;
  ☎ 773-878-2420
- **Trattoria D.O.C.** 706 Main Street, Evanston; ☎ 847-475-1111

Best Places with Music

- **Bite** *Alternative rock* 1039 North Western Avenue, Ukrainian Village;
  ☎ 773-395-2483
- **Chicago Chop House** *Piano bar* (see profile, page 210)
- **Chief O'Neill's** (see profile, page 211)
- **Cyrano's Bistrot** *Cabaret* 546 North Wells Street, River North;
  ☎ 312-467-0546
- **Green Dolphin Street** *Jazz* 2200 North Ashland Avenue, Lincoln Park;
  ☎ 773-395-0066
- **House of Blues** *Blues, rock* 329 North Dearborn Street, River North;
  ☎ 312-527-2583
- **Joe's Be-Bop Café and Jazz Emporium** *Jazz* Navy Pier, 700 East Grand
  Avenue, Streeterville; ☎ 312-595-5299
- **Nacional 27** *Latin jazz* (see profile, page 232)
- **Pete Miller's Steak House** *Jazz* 1557 Sherman Avenue, Evanston;
  ☎ 847-328-0399
- **Philander's** *Jazz* Carleton Hotel, 1110 Pleasant Street, Oak Park;
  ☎ 708-848-4250
- **Smoke Daddy** *Blues, jazz* 1804 West Division Street, Wicker Park;
  ☎ 773-772-6656
- **Speakeasy** *Cabaret* 1401 West Devon Avenue, Edgewater;
  ☎ 773-338-0600

Best Ribs

- **Hecky's BBQ** 1902 Green Bay Road, Evanston; ☎ 847-492-1182
  1234 North Halsted Street, Near West; ☎ 312-377-7427
- **Leon's Bar-B-Q** 8259 South Cottage Grove Avenue, South Side;
  ☎ 773-488-4556; 1158 West 59th Street, South Side; ☎ 773-778-7828;
  1640 East 79th Street, South Side; ☎ 773-731-1454
- **Lem's BBQ** 311 East 75th Street, South Side; ☎ 773-994-2428
- **Merle's Ribs** 727 Benson Avenue, Evanston; ☎ 847-475-7766
- **The Rib Joint** 423 East 87th Street, South Side; ☎ 773-651-4108
- **Ribs 'n' Bibs** 5300 South Dorchester Avenue, South Side; ☎ 773-493-0400
- **Robinson's #1 Ribs** 655 West Armitage Avenue, Lincoln Park;
  ☎ 312-337-1399
- **Smoke Daddy** 1804 West Division Street, Wicker Park; ☎ 773-772-6656
- **Twin Anchors** (see profile, page 252)
- **Weber Grill** 539 North State Street, River North; ☎ 312-467-9696

Best Soul Food

- **Army & Lou's** 422 East 75th Street, South Side; ☎ 773-483-3100
- **BJ's Market and Bakery** 8734 South Stony Island Avenue, South Side;
  ☎ 773-374-4700
- **Dixie Kitchen & Bait Shop** 825 Church Street, Evanston; ☎ 847-733-9030
  5225 South Harper Avenue, Hyde Park; ☎ 773-363-4943
- **Gladys' Luncheonette** 4527 South Indiana Avenue, South Side;
  ☎ 773-548-4566
- **Heaven on Seven** 600 North Michigan Avenue, River North;
  ☎ 312-280-7774; Garland Building, 111 North Wabash Avenue, 7th Floor,
  The Loop; ☎ 312-263-6443
- **MacArthur's** 5412 West Madison Street, West Side; ☎ 773-261-2316
- **Wishbone** (see profile, page 253)

Elegant Prix-fixe Menus

- **Alinea** (see profile, page 193)
- **Ambria** 2300 North Lincoln Park West, Lincoln Park; ☎ 773-472-5959
- **Arun's Thai Restaurant** (see profile, page 200)
- **Carlos'** 429 Temple Avenue, Highwood; ☎ 847-432-0770
- **Charlie Trotter's** (see profile, page 209)
- **Everest** (see profile, page 214)
- **Green Zebra** (see profile, page 217)
- **Le Francais** (see profile, page 224)
- **Les Nomades** 222 East Ontario Street, Streeterville; ☎ 312-649-9010
- **MK** (see profile, page 230)
- **Moto** (see profile, page 232)
- **NoMI** (see profile, page 235)
- **Seasons** (see profile, page 244)

- **Spiaggia** (see profile, page 247)
- **Tallgrass** 1006 South State Street, Lockport; ☎ 815-838-5566
- **Topolobampo** (see profile, page 250)
- **Tru** (see profile, page 251)
- **Zealous** 419 West Superior Street, River North; ☎ 312-475-9112

Trendy Scene Places

- **Avec** (see profile, page 201)
- **Avenue M** 691–695 North Milwaukee Avenue, Near West; ☎ 312-243-1133
- **Bin 36** (see profile, page 203)
- **Blackbird** (see profile, page 204)
- **Boka** (see profile, page 205)
- **Carnivale** (see profile, page 208)
- **Cuatro** (see profile, page 212)
- **del Toro** 1520 North Damen Avenue, Wicker Park; ☎ 773-252-1500
- **Gibson's** (see profile, page 217)
- **Japonais** (see profile, page 220)
- **Mirai Sushi** (see profile, page 229)
- **Nine** (see profile, page 234)
- **Opera** (see profile, page 238)
- **Red Light** 820 West Randolph Street, West Loop; ☎ 312-733-8880
- **Saltaus** 1350 West Randolph Street, Near West; ☎ 312-455-1919
- **Tavern on Rush** 1031 North Rush Street, Gold Coast; ☎ 312-664-9600

RESTAURANT PROFILES

Alinea ★★★★★

| NEW AMERICAN | VERY EXPENSIVE | QUALITY ★★★★★ | VALUE ★★★ |

**1723 North Halsted Street, Lincoln Park; ☎ 312-867-0110;
www.alinearestaurant.com**

Reservations Highly recommended. **When to go** Midweek, special occasions (reserve early). **Entree range** Degustations only; "tasting" $135 (12 courses), "tour" $195 (20-plus courses). **Payment** AE, D, DC, MC, V. **Service rating** ★★★★. **Friendliness rating** ★★★. **Parking** Valet, $10. **Bar** Limited. **Wine selection** Vast, world-class, well organized, with a strength in old-world gems; $30–$2,700 bottle, $7–$28 glass. **Dress** Jacket suggested. **Disabled access** Yes. **Customers** Foodies, CEOs, well-heeled couples. **Hours** Wednesday–Friday, 5:30–9:30 p.m.; Friday and Saturday, 5–9:30 p.m.

SETTING AND ATMOSPHERE If James Bond opened a restaurant, it might have an entrance like the narrowing hallway that intentionally disorients diners approaching Alinea. Suddenly, an automatic door opens to usher you into another world, one of spare sophistication with Zen touches and reverent
Continued on page 199

river north dining and nightlife

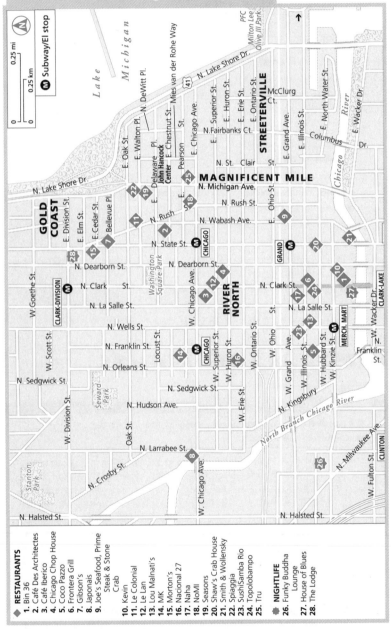

RESTAURANTS
1. Bin 36
2. Café Des Architectes
3. Café Iberico
4. Chicago Chop House
5. Coco Pazzo
6. Frontera Grill
7. Gibson's
8. Japonais
9. Joe's Seafood, Prime Steak & Stone Crab
10. Kevin
11. Le Colonial
12. Le Lan
13. Lou Malnati's
14. MK
15. Morton's
16. Nacional 27
17. Naha
18. NoMI
19. Seasons
20. Shaw's Crab House
21. Smith & Wollensky
22. Spiaggia
23. SushiSamba Rio
24. Topolobampo
25. Tru

NIGHTLIFE
26. Funky Buddha Lounge
27. House of Blues
28. The Lodge

loop dining and nightlife

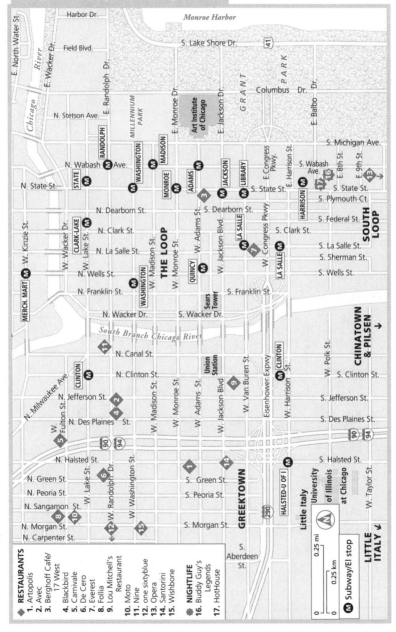

RESTAURANTS
1. Artopolis
2. Avec
3. Berghoff Café/
   17 West
4. Blackbird
5. Carnivale
6. De Cero
7. Everest
8. Follia
9. Lou Mitchell's
   Restaurant
10. Moto
11. Nine
12. one sixtyblue
13. Opera
14. Santorini
15. Wishbone

NIGHTLIFE
16. Buddy Guy's
    Legends
17. HotHouse

Ⓜ Subway/El stop

lincoln park and wrigleyville dining and nightlife

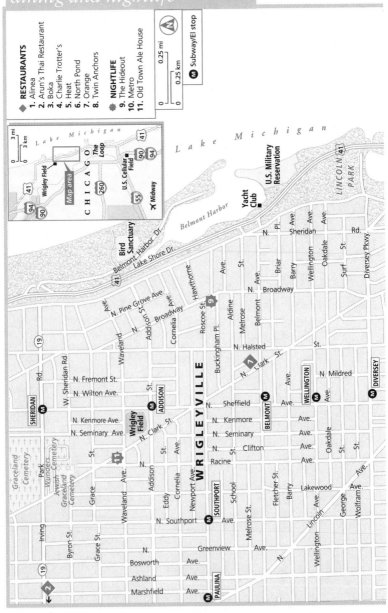

◆ RESTAURANTS
1. Alinea
2. Arun's Thai Restaurant
3. Boka
4. Charlie Trotter's
5. Heat
6. North Pond
7. Orange
8. Twin Anchors

⬣ NIGHTLIFE
9. The Hideout
10. Metro
11. Old Town Ale House

Ⓜ Subway/El stop

0   0.25 mi
0   0.25 km

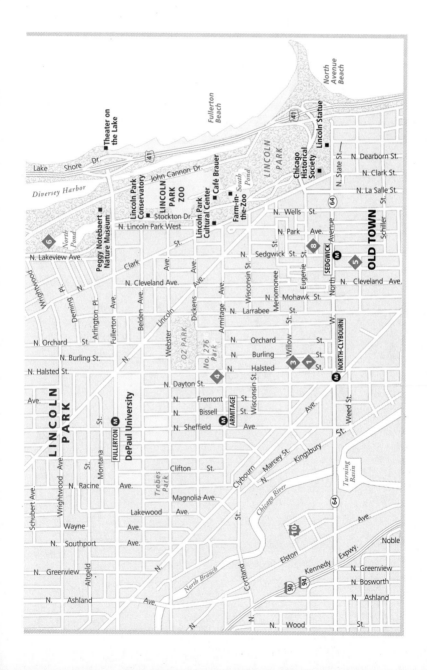

wicker park and bucktown dining

RESTAURANTS
1. Bongo Room
2. Irazu
3. Mas
4. Mirai Sushi
5. Piece
6. Scylla
7. Spring

service—without the hushed, walking-on-eggshells feel of some haute-cuisine temples. Bilevel rooms are all chic modernity, but seating and tables are comfortable and spacious enough for these marathon meals.

HOUSE SPECIALTIES Never one to rest on his laurels (or apparently to rest at all), Grant Achatz perpetually changes his ultracontemporary American menu of deadly serious whimsies—and the outré serving pieces on which they ride in. Things are served on space-age hatpins, grated over your food, and smoked on hot rocks at the table just for the aroma. Humble ingredients like peanut butter and broccoli stem take on whole new identities. It's culinary performance art at its finest, meaning nearly everything tastes out of this world, and the entire sensory experience is as exhilarating as a carnival ride—without seeming silly or overly experimental.

OTHER RECOMMENDATIONS The tasting-only menus maintain the mystery, teasing with succinct ingredient groupings (the marquee ingredient in caps, the complements in lowercase—for example, LOBSTER puffed and seasoned with pollen; SQUAB strawberry, sorrel, long peppercorn). If you don't know your mastic from your yuba or your *verjus* from your *umebashi,* ask lots of questions, or just let it all wash over you. Desserts, once the weakest link in the fantasy, should be more in line now that the indefatigable Achatz has taken those on as well.

SUMMARY AND COMMENTS The whole world has been watching since this protégé of Thomas Keller (French Laundry) and alum of Charlie Trotter's–Trio struck out on his own. Achatz's relative youth notwithstanding, there's mastery in his art and a world-class dining experience in store here—if you can stomach the tariff. If you can, go with sommelier Joe Catterson's wine pairings for the complete experience (they generally add 60 to 70% to the meal cost, with higher-end choices available by request). And plan to spend five hours–plus if you opt for the "tour" (20-plus course), with a few minutes afterwards for a brief glimpse into the clockwork kitchen humming with young chefs cooking their hearts out.

Artopolis ★★½

GREEK	INEXPENSIVE	QUALITY ★★★★	VALUE ★★★★

306 South Halsted Street, Greektown; ☎ 312-559-9000

Reservations Not accepted. **When to go** Weekday lunch. **Entree range** $8–$14. **Payment** AE, DC, MC, V. **Service rating** ★★. **Friendliness rating** ★★★. **Parking** Pay lot, $3; street. **Bar** Full service. **Wine selection** Mostly Greek, Italian, and Californian; $7–$35 bottle, $5–$6 glass. **Dress** Casual. **Disabled access** Yes. **Customers** Urban workers. **Hours** Monday–Thursday, 9 a.m.–12 p.m.; Friday and Saturday, 9 a.m.–1 a.m.; Sunday, 10 a.m.–11 p.m.

SETTING AND ATMOSPHERE The French doors at this Greek cafe and bakery (located in the heart of Greektown) spill onto bustling Halsted Street.

There's a small balcony perched over the cafe tables in the front, and a spacious, dark-oak, copper-trimmed, marble-topped bar in the center divides the back retail area from the dining room. Terra-cotta tile floors are handsomely set off by the rich cherry tables and chairs arranged closely in the cafe seating area.

HOUSE SPECIALTIES   Mediterranean fest appetizer (a sampling of hummus, fava beans, baba ghanoush, tzatziki, and olives); smoky harvest sandwich with oven-roasted vegetables; smoked turkey, tomato, romaine, provolone, and eggplant-garlic spread on kalamata-olive bread; *artopitas* (signature flaky calzone-like stuffed pockets with a variety of fillings, such as spinach and feta; ham and kasseri cheese; crumbled feta, kasseri, and fresh mint; and portobello mushroom and Emmenthaler cheese).

OTHER RECOMMENDATIONS   *Frutti de mare* salad with rock shrimp, octopus, and calamari; *kotosalata* sandwich (mesclun greens topped with chicken salad, pine nuts, green apple, and pesto on walnut bread); roasted lamb with mint aioli sauce; seasonal fresh-fruit tart; all fresh breads.

SUMMARY AND COMMENTS   This Greektown staple brings a French pastry chef's exquisite rustic breads and pastries together with innovative, casual Greek fare. The ambitious staff is eager to please, although lunch is self-service. Wood-fired pizzas and *artopitas* (cheese-, meat-, and vegetable-stuffed pastries) make a nice light lunch, while other specialties are heartier. During nice weather, French doors open for inviting sidewalk dining.

Arun's Thai Restaurant   ★★★½

THAI	VERY EXPENSIVE	QUALITY ★★★★★	VALUE ★★

4156 North Kedzie Avenue, North Central Chicago; ☎ 773-539-1909; www.arunsthai.com

Reservations Recommended. **When to go** Reservations for weekend dinner can be difficult to get, but this is the best time to go. **Entree range** $85 for a multi-course tasting menu. **Payment** AE, D, DC, MC, V. **Service rating** ★★★★. **Friendliness rating** ★★★½. **Parking** Valet, $9 (Fridays and Saturdays only). **Bar** Full service with several Asian beers. **Wine selection** Concise and reasonable list featuring American, French, and Austrian bottles, with several by the glass, $7–$14; by the bottle, $28–$100, with a few reserve bottles near $200. **Dress** Dressy. **Disabled access** Yes. **Customers** Mature patrons, some professionals. **Hours** Sunday–Thursday, 5–10 p.m.; Friday and Saturday, 5–10:30 p.m.

SETTING AND ATMOSPHERE   The nondescript exterior is no indication of the exquisite interior at this upscale Thai restaurant. The tranquil, narrow room is clean and simple, with several semiprivate alcoves and a raised gallery seating area. The mustard-colored walls are trimmed in deep mahogany wood and adorned with Thai artifacts, paintings, and silk panels.

HOUSE SPECIALTIES   Crab spring rolls; spicy roast-duck salad with fresh Thai basil, cilantro, and snap peas in a vinegar-fish sauce; Thai-style sweet-and-sour striped bass with shiitake mushrooms and crispy egg noodles; garlic prawn and sea scallops; musman beef curry; lemongrass ice cream.

OTHER RECOMMENDATIONS Chicken curry soup with soft and crispy egg noodles; steamed assorted mini–rice dumplings filled with chicken or pork;
green curry chicken with Thai eggplant; spicy green papaya salad with
skewers of grilled chicken and hot-chile flakes; lychee sorbet.

SUMMARY AND COMMENTS The Chef's Design Menu leaves the ordering up to
Chef Arun Sampanthavivat, a master of creative and innovative Thai
cooking. Servers inquire about patrons' likes, dislikes, and spice tolerance;
then more than a dozen small tasting courses come streaming out. Arun
has received accolades since he opened in 1985 for his exquisite balance
of flavors, intricate and artistic garnishes, and ability to raise Thai food to
new heights of elegance. Some find it pricey, but most revel in the luxury.

Avec ★★★

MEDITERRANEAN	MODERATE	QUALITY ★★★★	VALUE ★★★

**615 West Randolph Street, West Loop; ☎ 312-377-2002;
www.avecrestaurant.com**

Reservations Not accepted. **When to go** Early evening. **Entree range** $11–$20.
Payment AE, MC, V. **Service rating** ★★★½. **Friendliness rating** ★★★. **Parking**
$10. **Bar** Full service. **Wine selection** Esoteric Southern Italian, French, Austrian,
Portuguese, $17–$98 bottle, $9–$15 glass. **Dress** Casual, downscale chic. **Disabled access** Yes. **Customers** Food-industry locals, young food lovers,
well-dressed theatergoers. **Hours** Daily, 3:30 p.m.–2 a.m.

SETTING AND ATMOSPHERE Communal seating at one of the five eight-person
tables makes the room tight, cozy, and extremely social. It's not a quiet
destination for a romantic date but a place to meet fellow diners. The
light cedar walls, hickory floors, and ceiling are striking in their simplicity, although the hard bench seating can be uncomfortable.

HOUSE SPECIALTIES Whole roasted fish with Swiss chard, mushrooms, and
grilled-ramp vinaigrette; crispy duck leg with plums, watercress, spring
onions, and star anise; wood oven–roasted curried pork shoulder with
lentils, green garlic, leeks, and squash; wood-fired pizza with cured
sardines, shaved lardo, fennel, and arugula; house-made smoked-black-
pepper pasta, garlic sausage, cavolo nero, and Parmesan.

OTHER RECOMMENDATIONS Grilled-squid salad with cannellini beans, peas,
frisée, and lemon vinaigrette; crispy chicken thigh with couscous, preserved lemon, olives, and cilantro vinaigrette; house-marinated olives;
crushed tomato and olive oil–braised octopus, baby spinach, onion
salad, and pancetta vinaigrette.

SUMMARY AND COMMENTS The medley of rustic Mediterranean dishes comes
out of a wood-burning stove that's visible from any seat in the dining
room. The well-selected and unusual wine offerings are top-notch, and
the wait staff makes useful suggestions for food pairings. This sibling to
neighboring Blackbird brings in crowds that snake out the door until
the wee hours of the night, when food-industry veterans flock in. The
late-night scene is something to behold, making it one of the best stops
in town for a midnight snack.

Berghoff Café/17 West ★★½

| GERMAN/NEW AMERICAN | MODERATE | QUALITY ★★½ | VALUE ★★★ |

17 West Adams Street, The Loop; ☎ 312-427-7399;
www.17westchicago.com

Reservations Not accepted. **When to go** Weekday lunch, after work. **Entree range** Cafe $4–$13, bar $10–$16. **Payment** AE, D, MC, V. **Service rating** ★★★. **Friendliness rating** ★★★. **Parking** Lot at 17 East Adams, discount with validation. **Bar** Full service, house beers. **Wine selection** Bargain priced, California focus; $20–$35 bottle, $5–$8 glass. **Dress** Business/travel casual. **Disabled access** Yes. **Customers** Loopers, tourists, families, and seniors. **Hours** Cafe: Monday–Wednesday, 11 a.m.–2:30 p.m. and 4–9 p.m.; Thursday and Friday, 11 a.m.–2:30 p.m.; Saturday, 4–10 p.m. Bar: Monday–Friday, 10:45 a.m.–4 p.m.; Saturday 11:30 a.m.–4 p.m.

SETTING AND ATMOSPHERE After a brief closing and ownership change (within the family), the downstairs level of the beloved Berghoff is once again serving lunch to grateful Loopers, with the same cafeteria-style service and ambience and only minor modifications to the German-American menu. The legendary bar, now expanded, keeps the heritage alive with wood and more wood, stained glass, marquetry murals, castle-worthy light fixtures—and now plush leather barstools.

HOUSE SPECIALTIES Cafe signatures include Wiener schnitzel, sauerbraten, hand-carved sandwiches (corned or roast beef, roast turkey, turkey meatloaf); Cobb salad; German potato salad; beet salad; apple strudel; root-beer float. Updated fare includes a selection of panini (Black Forest ham, grilled portobello-asparagus, pomodoro chicken); Asian chicken salad; Greek salad pocket with hummus; thin-crust pizzas (four-cheese, goat cheese–spinach, pepperoni).

OTHER RECOMMENDATIONS 17 West offers classics like a sausage trio; Jagerschnitzel (pork medallions); the famous creamed spinach; and spaetzles, plus updated items like bourbon-braised beef short ribs; mushroom–goat cheese strudel cigars; Asian pear–Maytag blue cheese salad; Cajun salmon salad; sesame-crusted ahi tuna; pan-seared scallops with bacon-corn risotto.

SUMMARY AND COMMENTS The reformed Berghoff valiantly straddles competing demands for the nostalgic and the new. Lunch or dinner, you can still pack on pounds of heavy German classics or opt for lighter fare. A short-lived effort at "European tapas" in the bar gave way to more traditional menu items by popular demand. And they're still pourin' those Berghoff brews (lager, dark or amber, from Huber of Wisconsin). If you want to soak up the heritage of the historic old main dining room paneled in quarter-sawn oak, hope to get invited to a private party there (or throw your own).

*un*official **TIP**
Carry-out at Berghoff Café/17 West for parties of five or more requires a one-hour advance notice; for 15 or more, give at least two hours' notice.

Bin 36 ★★★

NEW AMERICAN/WINE BAR   MODERATE   QUALITY ★★★½   VALUE ★★★

**339 North Dearborn Street, River North; ☎ 312-755-9463;
www.bin36.com**

Reservations Accepted. **When to go** Weekday lunch or dinner. **Entree range** $15–$45. **Payment** AE, D, DC, MC, V. **Service rating** ★★½. **Friendliness rating** ★★★. **Parking** Valet, $10 weekdays, $12 weekends. **Bar** Full service. **Wine selection** From all wine-producing nations; flights of 4 (2½-ounce) pours, $2.20–$5.65; 49 by the glass, $6–$16.50. **Dress** Casual to chic. **Disabled access** Yes. **Customers** Suburbanites, well-dressed yuppies, showgoers. **Hours** Monday–Thursday, 6:30–10 a.m., 11 a.m.–2 p.m., and 5–10 p.m.; Friday, 6:30–10 a.m., 11 a.m.–2 p.m., and 5–11 p.m.; Saturday, 7 a.m.–noon and 5–11 p.m.; Sunday, 7 a.m.–2 p.m. and 5–9 p.m.

SETTING AND ATMOSPHERE This spacious room has a wall of 30-foot windows draped with rich velvet floor-to-ceiling curtains, a zinc-topped oval bar at center, and a dining room tucked under an overhanging mezzanine used for private parties. The minimalist decor features stark white walls, high ceilings, and lots of glass, lending the feeling of a *Jetsons* space station.

HOUSE SPECIALTIES Herbed rotisserie-chicken sandwich with oven-dried tomatoes, wild arugula, Caesar dressing, and fries; house-smoked salmon with fingerling-potato salad and salmon caviar; pan-seared Alaskan halibut with a trio of spring vegetables, potato puree, pea-tendril salad, and lemon vinaigrette; peppercorn-crusted swordfish with mashed potatoes, onion rings, and sauce bordelaise.

OTHER RECOMMENDATIONS Dijon-crusted lamb steak with flageolets, fava beans, tomatoes, and carrots; lobster club with house-made tomato soup.

SUMMARY AND COMMENTS There are two dining areas in this ultraswanky Marina City restaurant—the full service Cellar dining room and the Tavern tasting area—along with a small wine retail corner and breakfast coffee bar. Though the fare can be hit or miss, the cheese selection is top notch, as is the diverse selection of wine and tasting flights. There's also a raw bar for a late-night snack.

Bistro Campagne ★★★

FRENCH   MODERATE   QUALITY ★★★½   VALUE ★★★★

**4518 North Lincoln Avenue, Lincoln Square; ☎ 773-271-6100;
www.bistrocampagne.com**

Reservations Accepted. **When to go** Weekday dinner; in warm weather for outdoor dining. **Entree range** $10–$19. **Payment** AE, MC, V. **Service rating** ★★★. **Friendliness rating** ★★★★. **Parking** Coin lot across the street; $1 per hour. **Bar** Full service with unique microbrews. **Wine selection** Limited but well selected, mostly French, $26–$78; $7–$12 glass. **Dress** Casual. **Disabled access** Yes. **Customers** Young to middle-aged locals, musicians from neighboring music school. **Hours** Monday–Thursday, 5:30–9:30 p.m.; Friday and Saturday, 5:30–10:30 p.m.; Sunday, 5–9:30 p.m.

SETTING AND ATMOSPHERE The slender room is homey and smart with simple white walls, dark oak trim, and modern works of local art. The garden surrounding the outdoor patio is second to none, with an equal number of tables as the dining room holds.

HOUSE SPECIALTIES *Brandade de morue;* onion soup; Niçoise salad; *croque monsieur;* warm goat cheese and field greens salad with a Dijon vinaigrette; steak frites; roasted organic pork chop with peasant bread salad; sautéed spinach; profiteroles; crème brûlée.

OTHER RECOMMENDATIONS Mussels steamed in Belgian ale; caramelized onion strudel; lamb loin chop with flageolets in a lamb jus; ratatouille-stuffed ravioli with pistou sauce; pan-seared trout in brown butter with almonds and haricots verts; chocolate soufflé.

SUMMARY AND COMMENTS Casual and comfortable, this Lincoln Square French bistro draws a steady crowd for a limited but solid menu of classic bistro fare. The outdoor patio is one of the best in town, and the wine list is well selected. Even the beer offerings were compiled with utmost attention to detail. Don't let the low prices fool you—the expertly prepared organic ingredients used make this one of the best values in town.

Blackbird ★★★★

NEW AMERICAN	EXPENSIVE	QUALITY ★★★★½	VALUE ★★★

**619 West Randolph Street, West Loop; ☎ 312-715-0708;
www.blackbirdrestaurant.com**

Reservations Recommended. **When to go** Weekend evenings. **Entree range** $10–$32. **Payment** AE, D, DC, MC, V. **Service rating** ★★★★. **Friendliness rating** ★★★★. **Parking** Valet, $10. **Bar** Full service. **Wine selection** Mostly French and Californian, some German and Oregonian, $22–$500 bottle; ample by-the-glass options, $7–$16. **Dress** Stylish, chic. **Disabled access** Yes. **Customers** Hip urban dwellers, professionals by day. **Hours** Monday–Thursday, 11:30 a.m.–2 p.m. and 5:30–10:30 p.m.; Friday, 11:30 a.m.–2 p.m. and 5:30–11:30 p.m.; Saturday, 5:30–11:30 p.m.

SETTING AND ATMOSPHERE This minimalist, stark white West Loop hot spot exudes a New York attitude. A diverse and always well-dressed crowd flocks here weekdays through the weekend, making reservations necessary. An exposed kitchen at back is the main visual attraction in the otherwise sparsely decorated space. Tables are extremely close and the noise level often high.

HOUSE SPECIALTIES The ever-changing seasonal menu might feature charcuterie plate with country-style pâté, herbed chicken sausage, celery–red onion slaw, and garnishes; seared Maine diver scallops with brandade, English peas, preserved lemon, toasted garlic, and pea tendrils; grilled Peking duck breast with leeks vinaigrette, tea-poached cherries, baby spinach, and sesame salt; sautéed breast of California squab with bacon, crispy morels, and green garlic–sun-dried-cranberry *agridoux*; roasted Alaskan king salmon and smoked belly with Champagne–Meyer lemon sabayon, sea beans, and purple potato salad; stuffed breast of quail with medjool dates, orange, marcona almonds, smoked bacon and jus; roasted rack of lamb with smoked paprika, artichoke, roasted garlic, lemon confit, and crunchy garnishes;

seared Hudson Valley foie gras with *pain perdu,* rhubarb-turnip marmalade, and muscat syrup; sautéed Alaskan halibut with escargot, french green lentils, mushrooms, and toasted breadcrumbs.

OTHER RECOMMENDATIONS Roasted breast of guinea hen with spring chicories, fingerlings, citrus bone marrow, and green-garlic broth; braised organic pork belly with grilled Illinois ramps, favas, oven-roasted tomatoes, and pickled wax beans; confit of organic veal tenderloin and crispy sweetbreads with *cavolo nero,* roasted-garlic *panisse,* English peas, and caramelized rhubarb; honey-almond *semifreddo* with brioche beignets and oven-roasted rhubarb.

SUMMARY AND COMMENTS Stylish patrons fill this hip eatery located on an offbeat stretch of west Randolph Street. Chef Paul Kahan consistently dazzles diners with his French-rooted, contemporary American fare, which takes full advantage of peak ingredients. The seasonal menu has its share of classic combinations along with just enough innovative dishes to keep it interesting. The wine list is one of the best in town, with hard-to-find selections in a range of prices.

Boka ★★★½

NEW AMERICAN	EXPENSIVE	QUALITY ★★★½	VALUE ★★★

1729 North Halsted Street, Lincoln Park; ☎ 312-337-6070; www.bokachicago.com

Reservations Accepted. **When to go** Weekday or weekend evenings. **Entree range** $15–$38. **Payment** AE, D, DC, MC, V. **Service rating** ★★★. **Friendliness rating** ★★★★. **Parking** Valet, $10. **Bar** Full service. **Wine selection** Californian, French, Australian, Austrian; $32–$500 bottle, $7–$14 glass. **Dress** Modern chic. **Disabled access** Yes. **Customers** Hip young locals, professionals, couples, pre-theater. **Hours** Daily, 5–11 p.m.; bar open until 2 a.m. Sunday–Friday, until 3 a.m. Saturday.

SETTING AND ATMOSPHERE Chic and trendy, the room is done in gunmetal and black but for a huge white-mesh tarp that stretches across the ceiling. A front lounge doubles as dining space, with a bar separating it from the main dining room. There's even a cell phone booth for your privacy, and everyone else's relief.

HOUSE SPECIALTIES Grilled quail with andouille sausage and shrimp Creole dressing; grilled ahi tuna with chanterelle mushrooms, spinach, studded parsnip puree, red-wine sauce, and pistachio oil; grilled calf's liver with crispy Neuski bacon, fried onions, balsamic, and parsley oil; pan-seared grouper with braised oxtail raviolini, wild mushroom ragout, red-wine reduction, and truffle oil; salads of young mesclun greens, field greens, baby spinach, young-leaf romaine and butter lettuces.

OTHER RECOMMENDATIONS Marinated roasted pork chop with Red Bliss potatoes, Brussels sprouts, bacon-and-pomegranate sauce; roasted-chestnut bisque, winter-spiced dried apricots, short ribs, and green onion; mussels steamed with shallots, parsley, brandy cream sauce, and garlic crouton; pan-roasted frog legs with herb butter, *grebiche* sauce, and microgreen salad; pan-roasted mahimahi with shrimp, speck-and-potato hash, and lobster nage.

SUMMARY AND COMMENTS   The neighborhood and pre-theater crowds quickly adopted this combination of swanky ambience, well-executed fare, and amicable staff. The seasonal menu has something to suit most tastes, with a range of cold and hot sharing plates along with more-substantial entrees. The gender-split wine list is another interesting slant, encouraging conversation and smart food-and-wine pairings.

Bongo Room ★★½

AMERICAN	INEXPENSIVE	QUALITY ★★★	VALUE ★★★

1470 North Milwaukee Avenue, Wicker Park; ☎ 773-489-0690
1152 South Wabash Avenue, South Loop; ☎ 312-291-0100;
www.bongoroom.com

Reservations Not accepted. When to go Early weekend, weekday breakfast, lunch. Entree range $5–$14. Payment AE, D, MC, V. Service rating ★★. Friendliness rating ★★★. Parking Street. Bar Brunch drinks, beer. Wine selection None. Dress Come as you are. Disabled access Yes. Customers Hipsters, families, gal-pals, hangovers. Hours Monday–Friday, 8 a.m.–2:30 p.m.; Saturday and Sunday, 9 a.m.–2 p.m.

SETTING AND ATMOSPHERE   Funky-chic surroundings welcome bedheads and stroller-pushers alike—anyone willing to wait a while in crowded surroundings at peak hours. Popularity and a no-reservations policy may play havoc with your plans, and even lunch can be surprisingly busy (they do not serve dinner).

HOUSE SPECIALTIES   Regulars return for the seasonally shifting pancake (for example, banana–Heath bar, Key lime cheesecake) and benedict (such as lobster, lump crab, or roasted red pepper–feta) specialties; ultrafluffy custom omelets from a massive ingredient list; croissant sandwiches; and a hunky breakfast burrito. Lunch sees sandwiches like sliced tenderloin tarted up with Saint Andre cheese, watercress-apple relish, and horseradish aioli; a chicken-pear club; and nice vegetarian options, including a portobello burger.

OTHER RECOMMENDATIONS   Try one of their tantalizing eye-openers like a passion fruit–raspberry sorbet or black raspberry–grapefruit mimosa; a honeydew or cherry Bellini; or a chewy caraway Bloody Mary (great chai, too, which they served before Starbucks).

SUMMARY AND COMMENTS   Brunch is the house specialty, and the Wicker Park location is notoriously frenetic at peak times. Service humps when it has to, slacks when it can. The prevailing wisdom for impatient wouldbe brunchers who've just gotta have their chocolate-tower-French-toast fix is to head to the South Loop location where the wait is usually shorter (and the menu the same).

Café Des Architectes ★★★½

NEW FRENCH	EXPENSIVE	QUALITY ★★★★	VALUE ★½

20 East Chestnut Street, Gold Coast; ☎ 312-324-4000

Reservations Accepted. When to go Weekday lunch, high tea. Entree range $12–$30. Payment AE, D, DC, MC, V. Service rating ★★★. Friendliness rating

★★. **Parking** Pay lot, $22; valet, lunch $10, dinner complimentary. **Bar** Full service. **Wine selection** French and Californian; $32–$92 bottle, $9–$15 glass. **Dress** Business attire, upscale. **Disabled access** Yes. **Customers** Fashion executives, other worker bees, and hotel guests. **Hours** Daily, 6 a.m.–11:30 p.m. High tea served Friday and Saturday, 2–4:30 p.m.

SETTING AND ATMOSPHERE   The dramatically appointed room, situated inside the Sofitel Hotel Chicago Water Tower and designed by Pierre-Yves Rochon, is quite stunning. White walls are highlighted by bright purple high-backed banquettes and brilliant crimson carpeting, with 6-foot-long satin light fixtures affixed to the 30-foot ceilings.

HOUSE SPECIALTIES   Grilled sirloin steak sandwich Parisian-style with french fries and mixed greens with balsamic vinaigrette; grilled fresh tuna with roasted pepper on soft bun with pesto-cilantro spread, *piquillo* vinaigrette, black olives, tomato, onions, lettuce, and hard-boiled egg with mixed greens; pan-seared smoked diver scallops with crab cake, creamed corn, pumpkin seed, and cilantro sauce; chilled yellow tomato soup; chef's flight of French cheeses; shrimp and polenta with *pistou*, crusted herbs, rare tuna, *piquillo* vinaigrette, *brandade* tempura, saffron aioli, and grilled vegetables; smoked salmon purses filled with peekytoe crab salad.

OTHER RECOMMENDATIONS   Papardelle pasta: Manila clams and shrimp, tomato jus, red bell peppers, onion, garlic, almonds, and olive oil; basil-marinated salmon crusted with orange and anise pollen, peppers confit, and fennel emulsion; pan-seared veal tenderloins and cannelloni of sweetbreads, shiitake and porcini mushrooms, cipollini onions confit, rosti potatoes, and jus de Madeira.

SUMMARY AND COMMENTS   The first branch of this ultraluxurious hotel to hit Chicago, the spectacular structure jets into the Gold Coast sky, with the cafe overlooking the street and a main dining room, Cigale, at back. You could just as easily be in Paris when you enter, and the brasserie fare could have come straight from the Place de Vosges. Lovely and sprightly dishes tantalize with innovative combinations of infused oils and grains. Service can be stern, but it makes the place feel more European.

Café Iberico   ★★★

SPANISH/TAPAS	MODERATE	QUALITY ★★★	VALUE ★★★★

739 North La Salle Street, River North; ☎ 312-573-1510; www.cafeiberico.com

Reservations For parties of 6 or more only, Sunday–Thursday. **When to go** Weekday evenings for no waits and a quieter room. **Entree range** Tapas, $4–$7; entrées, $8–$14. **Payment** AE, D, DC, MC, V. **Service rating** ★★. **Friendliness rating** ★½. **Parking** Valet after 5 p.m., $10. **Bar** Full service. **Wine selection** Sangria, $11.95 per pitcher; several sherries; Californian and Spanish wines, $16–$50 bottle, $3.50–$5 glass. **Dress** Casual to trendy. **Disabled access** Yes. **Customers** Loop workers, young lively diners. **Hours** Monday–Thursday, 11 a.m.–11:30 p.m.; Friday, 11 a.m.–1:30 a.m.; Saturday, noon–1:30 a.m.; Sunday, noon–11 p.m.;

SETTING AND ATMOSPHERE The two rooms at this casual, fun tapas bar (plus the basement on busy Wednesday through Saturday nights) get more character from the crowds than from the decor. There's only a few Spanish artifacts along with a tile border to add a splash of color to the otherwise underwhelming space. The food is the main attraction; always fresh, intriguing, and plentiful.

HOUSE SPECIALTIES Roasted veal served cold with raspberry vinaigrette; Spanish cured ham with manchego cheese and tomato bread; grilled squid in olive oil, garlic, and lemon juice; grilled mushrooms; croquetas (chicken and ham puffs with an aioli sauce); paella Iberico with seafood, chicken, pork, and saffron rice.

OTHER RECOMMENDATIONS Spanish potato salad with tuna and peas; tortilla Española (vegetarian Spanish omelet); grilled salmon with green peppercorn sauce; grilled Spanish sausages; Galician white bean and rapini soup.

SUMMARY AND COMMENTS The atmosphere is lively—even rowdy when packed—and the food just right at this River North tapas bar. The menu has more than a dozen each of hot and cold tapas along with a few entrees, the paella Iberico being the best pick. Large parties are common and work best with the tasting menu, meant to be shared. Service can be slow at times and even forgetful, but pitchers of sangria help pass the time painlessly.

Carnivale ★★★

NUEVO LATINO	EXPENSIVE	QUALITY ★★★	VALUE ★★

**702 West Fulton Street, Near West; ☎ 312-850-5005;
www.carnivalechicago.com**

Reservations Accepted. When to go Drinks, night on the town, group dining. Entree range $15–$38. Payment AE, D, MC, V. Service rating ★★. Friendliness rating ★★. Parking Valet, $5. Bar Full service, specialty cocktails. Wine selection moderately priced, mostly Spanish/South American; $20–$275 bottle, $5–$18 glass. Dress Trendy. Disabled access Yes. Customers Singles, 20- and 30-something dates, clubbers. Hours Monday–Thursday, 11:30 a.m.–2:30 p.m. and 5–10:30 p.m.; Friday, 11:30 a.m.–2:30 p.m. and 5–11:30 p.m.; Saturday, 5–11:30 p.m.; Sunday, 5–10 p.m.

SETTING AND ATMOSPHERE Life is a carnival at Carnivale, a Latin-tinged, salsa-soundtracked one with owner Jerry Kleiner's (Marché, Red Light, Opera) unique design and nightclub sensibilities. The cavernous former Drink space retains its multiple environments, a variety of wildly colorful, trippy settings (some bright, some dim) for dining or debauchery (with four bars). Design highlights include modern paintings and photography, oversized furnishings, Kleiner's signature piles of wine, a secluded area with a fireplace, and a catwalk over the dining area.

HOUSE SPECIALTIES Pernil (rum-glazed pork shoulder, Puerto Rican rice and beans, fried plantain); arrachera (grilled skirt steak with chimichurri sauce, rice, and beans); fried whitefish tacos with citrus tartar sauce and tart slaw; ceviche sampler (choices include shrimp, scallop, yellowtail, king crab, and tuna); raspberry mojito; prickly-pear margarita.

OTHER RECOMMENDATIONS Crab–salt cod cake with Venezuelan avocado sauce spiked with horseradish; butternut squash and Swiss chard empanada with mole poblano and squash salad; *ropa vieja* (Cuban braised beef with sweet plantains and spicy mayo); sofrito rice with shrimp, mussels, squid, fish, chorizo, peas, chicken, and lobster broth.

SUMMARY AND COMMENTS Carnivale is sizzling fun for a youthful (or at least young-at-heart) audience. As long as it retains its hot-spot status, expect a touch of cooler-than-thou service attitude and a wait even with reservations. Seclusion seekers be warned: this bustling be-seener is loud (both in decibel level, decor, and staff characters), though there are a few dark corners, some private dining areas, and seasonal outdoor dining.

Charlie Trotter's ★★★★★

NEW AMERICAN   VERY EXPENSIVE   QUALITY ★★★★★   VALUE ★★★

816 West Armitage Avenue, Lincoln Park; ☎ 773-248-6228; www.charlietrotters.com

Reservations Required weeks in advance. **When to go** Any day you can get in; reserve several months in advance. **Entree range** Vegetable degustation menu, $125; grand degustation menu, $145; chef's table, $200. **Payment** AE, D, DC, MC, V. **Service rating** ★★★★½. **Friendliness rating** ★★★. **Parking** Valet, $10. **Bar** Wine only. **Wine selection** Award-winning wine list with over 1,500 French, Italian, Californian, Australian, German, and South African bottles, $25–$19,000; 21 by the glass, $8–$40. **Dress** Jackets required, formal attire. **Disabled access** Yes. **Customers** Tourists, suburbanites, and food aficionados. **Hours** Seatings Tuesday–Thursday, 6–9 p.m.; Friday and Saturday, 5:30–9 p.m.

SETTING AND ATMOSPHERE This attractive Lincoln Park two-flat is easy to miss, tucked behind a billowing trellis of greenery. The three small dining rooms, with a subdued decor in rich tones of burgundy and green (each seating only 30), are quite formal yet intimate with white linens and exquisite stemware and silverware. There's even a kitchen table for four to six guests, allowing a behind-the-scenes view of the masterful kitchen.

HOUSE SPECIALTIES The daily changing menu might include roasted beet risotto with wild asparagus, porcini mushrooms, and toasted almonds; Tasmanian sea trout with radish; rabbit with collard greens and turnip; Millbrook venison loin with rice beans, cumin-infused roasted eggplant, and sage; rhubarb sorbet with spring onion marmalade and manni olive oil; olive oil–poached hamachi, wild watercress, and tamarind orange vinaigrette; buttermilk-poached poularde breast with salsify, chanterelle mushrooms, and thyme-infused consommé; whole roasted squab with cippollini onion and black truffles.

OTHER RECOMMENDATIONS Ragoût of fire beans and dragon tongue beans with fingerling potatoes and garlic-infused mushroom sauce; monkfish liver with lemongrass and ginger root; poached breast of poussin (chicken) with zucchini and hen of the woods mushroom sauce.

SUMMARY AND COMMENTS Early planning is required for a table at the world-renowned Lincoln Park eatery where award-winning chef Charlie

Trotter consistently turns out culinary masterpieces. Trotter's degustation menus, grand and vegetable, are each like a symphony—one petite course (too petite for big-shoulders Chicago types) lays the foundation for the next. All dishes involve impeccably fresh ingredients in innovative preparations and presentations. For a real splurge, the table in the kitchen is the way to go both for an exquisite menu, fine entertainment, and brushing shoulders with the man himself. Service is top notch and the wine list unparalleled, with selections from all wine-producing regions of the world at a range of prices. The selection of large-format wines (such as magnums) is remarkable.

 ## Chicago Chop House ★★★

STEAK	VERY EXPENSIVE	QUALITY ★★★	VALUE ★★

60 West Ontario Street, River North; ☎ 312-787-7100; www.chicagochophouse.com

Reservations Highly recommended. **When to go** Lunch or early dinner. **Entree range** $20–$97. **Payment** AE, DC, MC, V. **Service rating** ★★★. **Friendliness rating** ★★★. **Parking** Valet ($5 lunch, $11 dinner). **Bar** Full service. **Wine selection** 600 bottles, from affordable to heavy-hitters with specialty in American Cabernet verticals; $24–$1,950 bottle, $6–$14 glass. **Dress** Upscale casual. **Disabled access** No. **Customers** Businessmen, politicos, tourists, cigar smokers. **Hours** Monday–Thursday, 11:30 a.m.–11 p.m.; Friday, 11:30 a.m.–11:30 p.m.; Saturday, 4–11:30 p.m.; Sunday, 4–10:30 p.m.

SETTING AND ATMOSPHERE Though it's only been around for 20 years, this non-chain old-boy-network clubhouse in a restored Victorian brownstone is a well-established institution for swaggering carnivores, steak-seeking visitors, politicos, and other people who get things done around here. Quaint, dark, and noisy wood-paneled environs are decorated with more than 1,400 vintage Chicago photographs from the era when "meat-packers, politicians, and gangsters vied for control." Many regulars prefer the even more boisterous bar scene on the lower level, where a nightly piano bar (5 p.m. weeknights, 6 p.m. weekends) adds nostalgic conviviality (and cigar smoke in the back).

HOUSE SPECIALTIES Handcut prime steaks (such as 16- or 24-ounce NY strip; 64-ounce porterhouse); char-grilled 24-ounce prime rib; broiled Alaskan king crab legs; seafood platter (broiled lobster tail, salmon, and french-fried shrimp); potato pancakes; Caesar salad; creamed spinach.

OTHER RECOMMENDATIONS Sautéed lake perch with lemon butter; shrimp de jonghe; clams casino; crab cakes with mustard sauce; mixed grill (lamb chop, veal chop, filet mignon); roast rack of lamb; carrot or chocolate cake.

unofficial **TIP**
If you want a bargain at the Chicago Chop House, try lunch, when entrees run under $25.

SUMMARY AND COMMENTS Don't come here looking for innovation. This is all about classic meat, potatoes, and martinis. Service can be friendly or cavalier, and while tightwads love that dinner includes salad and potatoes (most top-end competitors are all à la carte), it's still an expensive meal.

Chief O'Neill's Pub and Restaurant ★★

IRISH	MODERATE	QUALITY ★★	VALUE ★★★

3471 North Elston Avenue, North Central Chicago; ☎ 773-473-5263; www.chiefoneillspub.com

Reservations Accepted. **When to go** Weekdays during music jam sessions; Sunday, Irish brunch. **Entree range** $8–$20. **Payment** AE, D, DC, MC, V. **Service rating** ★★★. **Friendliness rating** ★★★★. **Parking** Street. **Bar** Full service, with an excellent array of imported and tap beers, $4–$6. **Wine selection** Limited Californian and French; $24–$50 bottle, $6–$9 glass. **Dress** Casual. **Disabled access** Yes. **Customers** Locals, Irish Chicagoans, police, music fans. **Hours** Monday–Friday, 4 p.m.–2 a.m.; Saturday, 10 a.m.–3 a.m.; Sunday, 10 a.m.–2 a.m.

SETTING AND ATMOSPHERE It's all things Irish at this traditional pub, from the Celtic knots on the tin ceiling to the instruments mounted in glass cases around the room. Most of the staff have thick accents. The dark wood-trimmed space is mammoth, especially when the outdoor picnic tables are available.

HOUSE SPECIALTIES Beer-battered Alaskan cod fish and chips; shepherd's pie; Irish fish pot (steamed seafood and fish in a tomato, fennel, and saffron broth); braised lamb shank; Irish breakfast.

OTHER RECOMMENDATIONS Cheddar cheese and Guinness soup; braised mussels; house-cured salmon; corned beef and cabbage.

SUMMARY AND COMMENTS Irish food and music fans are regulars at this huge but homey pub. Live music and jam sessions are staged most nights and pints of beer are the norm. The fare is the real Irish deal as is the Sunday brunch with traditional Irish breakfast, steak and eggs, baked tilapia, omelets and French toast, and eye-opening Bloody Marys. The mostly Irish staff adds to the ambience with cheerful greetings and friendly service.

Coco Pazzo ★★★★

ITALIAN	VERY EXPENSIVE	QUALITY ★★★★	VALUE ★★

300 West Hubbard Street, River North; ☎ 312-836-0900

Reservations Highly recommended. **When to go** Lunch, client and date dinners. **Entree range** $16–$62. **Payment** AE, D, DC, MC, V. **Service rating** ★★★★. **Friendliness rating** ★★. **Parking** Valet, $10 (lunch and dinner). **Bar** Full service. **Wine selection** All Italian, both mainstream and small producers, $32–$790 bottle, $7.50–$16 glass. **Dress** Jacket suggested. **Disabled access** Yes. **Customers** Businessmen, well-heeled couples. **Hours** Monday–Thursday, 11:30 a.m.–10:30 p.m.; Friday, 11:30 a.m.–11 p.m.; Saturday, 5–11 p.m.; Sunday, 5–10 p.m.

SETTING AND ATMOSPHERE This upscale River North haven is at once polished and rustic-chic. The loftlike white-tablecloth setting, done in warm wood and Mediterranean blue, is as simply sophisticated as the food, with polished service worthy of a big deal or momentous rendezvous. The bar is a nice spot to dine alone when traveling.

HOUSE SPECIALTIES Chef Tony Priolo's refined Northern Italian cuisine includes delicacies from a wood-burning oven (notably, seafood like Alaskan halibut and king salmon as well as fresh vegetables) and various forms of fresh pasta, including rags, ribbons, and the house gnocchi. Seasonal ingredients are showcased in a widely acclaimed daily changing risotto and in the eight to ten daily specials. A half rack of lamb is herb crusted and served with fried polenta and market vegetables (perhaps artichokes, peas, and leeks). *Cacciucco alla Livornese* is a traditional Tuscan seafood-shellfish stew in spicy tomato broth and bruschetta.

OTHER RECOMMENDATIONS Lunch creations include a lovely salad of lemon-marinated baby artichokes shaved over arugula and sprinkled with Parmesan. An entree salad brings together pulled braised duck and wood-roasted mushrooms with spinach leaves, croutons, and balsamic dressing. And that wood-burning oven produces some very nice, easy-on-the-wallet pizzas. The efforts of pastry chef Erika Masuda (whose journey includes the Ritz-Carlton and Le Lan) are worth the calories, including the warm flourless chocolate cake with cappuccino ice cream and panna cotta with caramel and berries.

SUMMARY AND COMMENTS Coco Pazzo is a reliable source for a civilized adult meal reminiscent of the home country's modern fine dining—and you pay for it.

Cuatro ★★★

NUEVO LATINO	EXPENSIVE	QUALITY ★★★	VALUE ★★★

2030 South Wabash Avenue, South Loop; ☎ 312-842-8856; www.cuatro-chicago.com

Reservations Accepted. **When to go** Dates, late, Sunday brunch. **Entree range** $13–$38. **Payment** AE, CB, D, DC, MC, V. **Service rating** ★★★. **Friendliness rating** ★★★. **Parking** Street, valet $10 (dinner only). **Bar** Full service, specialty cocktails. **Wine selection** Limited, affordable wine list $16–$52; about 30 by the glass $5–$14; BYO corkage $15. **Dress** Hip casual. **Disabled access** Yes. **Customers** South Loop mix of artsy, business, and hip. **Hours** Monday–Friday, 11:30 a.m.–2 a.m.; Saturday, 5 p.m.–2 a.m.; Sunday, 10 a.m.–midnight.

SETTING AND ATMOSPHERE The mod hacienda building is faced with a wall of garage doors for an airy feel with daytime natural light and city night views when the lighting is low. Saltwater fish tanks add an escapist feel to the clubby environs of exposed brick, open ductwork, urban artwork, and ceiling fans, with a mix of tables, banquettes, and high-tops. Live music Thursday through Saturday and at Sunday brunch introduces that Latin beat.

HOUSE SPECIALTIES Seafood is a primary focus, and there are numerous vegetarian options on the menu. Signature dishes include Brazilian *moqueca do mar* (grouper, shrimp, diver scallops, squid, and mussels in a spicy tomato–coconut milk broth with coconut rice and fried plantains) and a Caribbean-Latin fusion called *chuleta en mole platano macho* (a moist, monolithic double pork chop cured in sugar-cane juice and served with plantain mole). For dessert, don't miss the Oaxacan chocolate-mousse cake filled with tequila cream and plated with sweet-corn ice cream.

OTHER RECOMMENDATIONS Chicken brochettes with tamarind jerk sauce and ensalada Caribe represent limited Caribbean menu accents. Lunchers can take a break from the norm with *tortas gigantes* (hefty warm sandwiches). And brunchers can design an omelet, swoosh tortillas through a variety of egg dishes, or indulge in extra-thick French toast stuffed with vanilla-roasted plantains and farmer's cheese, then drizzled with fresh berries and Vermont maple syrup. The drinks menu lists several intriguing cane-rum cocktails. But if you're of drinking age, we urge you toward the fresh blood-orange margarita—a strong contender for the best cocktail in history.

SUMMARY AND COMMENTS Hip and high-quality, the family-run Cuatro is among a growing breed of swanky (or at least interesting) South Loop adopters. Good-neighbor benefits include online ordering and payment for quicker carry-out, and a night owl–friendly light menu offered Thursday through Saturday till 2 a.m. Oh, and did we mention the blood-orange margarita?

De Cero ★★½

MEXICAN	MODERATE	QUALITY ★★½	VALUE ★★★½

814 West Randolph Street, West Loop; ☎ 312-455-8114

Reservations Accepted. **When to go** Weekend lunch or dinner. **Entree range** $10–$17. **Payment** AE, D, DC, MC, V. **Service rating** ★★★★. **Friendliness rating** ★★★★. **Parking** Valet, $10. **Bar** Full service with extensive fruit and herb margaritas and daiquiris. **Wine selection** Limited Chilean, New Zealand, Portuguese, Argentinean, American; $28–$60 bottle, $7–$9 glass. **Dress** Casual, chic. **Disabled access** Yes. **Customers** Fun, lively, big groups. **Hours** Lunch, Monday–Friday, 11:30 a.m.–2 p.m.; dinner, Monday–Thursday, 5–10 p.m.; Friday and Saturday, 5 p.m.–midnight; closed Sunday.

SETTING AND ATMOSPHERE It's a modern-day taqueria with a hacienda-style room that's sparse but for a few colorful works of Mexican folk art on rustic terra-cotta walls. Wood tables and chairs are generously spaced, except for those lined up against the walls. Noise rebounds off the hard surfaces, making it extremely loud.

HOUSE SPECIALTIES Tres salsas (pico de gallo, verde, and picante) with housemade chips; duck nachos (five housemade tortilla chips served with duck, queso, mashed pinto beans, and crema); sweet-corn soup slightly creamed with sweet corn and poblano peppers and topped with crema; shredded chicken sopes topped with chicken, roasted corn salsa, and served with fresh crema; carne asada (skirt steak marinated in pickled jalapeños, cumin, and garlic, served with mashed pinto beans, basmati white rice, and tortillas);

grilled chicken mole (boneless half chicken grilled and served with mole poblano sauce, basmati white rice, and sautéed greens).

OTHER RECOMMENDATIONS Seviche of rock shrimp and baby scallops with citrus, jalapeño, tomato, and cilantro with housemade chips; charred baby octopus with lime-cumin dressing and fresh tomato; cumin-rubbed ribeye skewers served with avocado crema and smokey tomato salsa; grilled pork chop marinated in tequila served with lime mojo, mashed pinto beans, and basmati white rice; shrimp fajita sautéed with garlic, white onions, and red poblano peppers.

SUMMARY AND COMMENTS The casual Mexican dining room fits right into the industrial chic neighborhood, and the enormous space can accommodate crowds well. One room is strictly devoted to a bar—just right for waiting or lounging over one of the sprightly fruit and herb–blended cocktails. The main dining room has great energy, and the fresh coastal Mexican fare is made with heart and soul, down to the chips and tortillas, both of which are house-made.

Everest ★★★★★

| FINE FRENCH | VERY EXPENSIVE | QUALITY ★★★★★ | VALUE ★★★ |

One Financial Place, 440 South La Salle Street, 40th Floor, The Loop; ☎ 312-663-8920; www.lettuceentertainyou.com

Reservations Required. When to go Special occasions. Entree range À la carte, $27–$46; pre-theater menu, $54; evening tasting menu, $94. Payment All major credit cards. Service rating ★★★★★. Friendliness rating ★★★★. Parking Complimentary valet parking in building. Bar Full service. Wine selection Extensive award-winning list with 1,200 international wines, mostly French, Alsatian, and American; $39+ per bottle; 15–20 selections by the glass. Dress Jacket and tie strongly recommended. Disabled access Wheelchair accessible; call ahead for special accommodations. Customers Upscale professionals, couples. Hours Tuesday–Thursday, 5:30–9:30 p.m.; Friday and Saturday, 5:30–10 p.m.; closed Sunday and Monday.

SETTING AND ATMOSPHERE Everest offers a luxurious, softly lit setting for spectacular dining with a view to match; the twinkling city lights far below your posh perch add a wonderful, far-from-the-madding-crowd element to dining here. The decor blends traditional elegance with modern flash; the table appointments are stunning, with lots of great specialty-serving gewgaws.

HOUSE SPECIALTIES Foie gras terrine with apple and Alsace Tokay gelée; salmon soufflé attributed to Paul Haeberlin of L'Auberge de L'Ill (Chef Jean Joho's mentor); roasted Maine lobster in Alsace Gewurztraminer, butter, and ginger; fillet of halibut wrapped and roasted in potato; poached tenderloin of beef, *pot au feu* style, with horseradish cream.

OTHER RECOMMENDATIONS Cream of Alsace cabbage soup with home-smoked sturgeon and caviar; cold bouillabaisse terrine of seafood and shellfish; mosaic of guinea hen and duck with petite salade; sautéed medallions of venison with wild huckleberry sauce; lemon soufflé parfait with tapioca-almond milk; caramelized banana tart with maple cap mushroom ice cream; warm almond nougatine and roasted figs with cardamom ice milk.

ENTERTAINMENT AND AMENITIES Spectacular view.

SUMMARY AND COMMENTS Everest rides high atop the Chicago Stock Exchange, continuing to enjoy a superlative reputation as one of Chicago's finest. In partnership with Lettuce Entertain You Enterprises, Chef Jean Joho's culinary vision is the true heart of this excellent restaurant as he weaves authentic Alsatian touches into his artful French fare. Joho's pedigree includes an early entry into the business at the age of 13, many subsequent years of European training, and a position as sous chef at a Michelin two-star restaurant at the age of 23. Service is carried out seamlessly by a tuxedoed service team.

Follia ★★★

ITALIAN   MODERATE   QUALITY ★★★½   VALUE ★★★

953 West Fulton Market, West Loop; ☎ 312-243-2888; www.folliachicago.com

Reservations Accepted. When to go Weekend dinner. Entree range $15–$30. Payment AE, D, DC, MC, V. Service rating ★★★. Friendliness rating ★★★. Parking Valet, $10. Bar Full service. Wine selection Californian, Italian, Spanish; $32–$280 bottle, $8–$17 glass. Dress Chic, all black. Disabled access Yes. Customers Fashionable, stylish, well-heeled. Hours Sunday–Thursday, 5–11 p.m.; Friday and Saturday, 5 p.m.–1 a.m.

SETTING AND ATMOSPHERE The front windows of the market district storefront have mannequins in haute couture, giving just a hint at the well-appointed room. Walls and countertops are finished in cool blues and greens with tiny Italian glass tiles and a single work of art—a canvas covered in grass.

HOUSE SPECIALTIES Flat pizza from a wood-burning oven in varieties like *quattro formaggio* (gorgonzola, taleggio, mozzarella, Parmigiano-Reggiano); veal scaloppine with porcini mushrooms; New York strip steak with fresh rosemary; steamed sole with shrimp, tomatoes, and capers.

OTHER RECOMMENDATIONS Antipasti; caprese salad with fresh mozzarella; *tagliolini* with shrimp and zucchini; ziti with tomato sauce and ricotta cheese; daily risotto specials like porcini mushroom and asparagus; veal in lemon sauce with fresh parsley and potatoes.

SUMMARY AND COMMENTS Sandwiched between meat markets on a little-traveled stretch of Fulton Market, the clandestine location makes this chic little eatery even more alluring. The mostly model wait staff strut the floor, greeting customers and serving with sex appeal. The simple food is made from ingredients of the utmost freshness, but there are not too many of them on a given plate.

Frontera Grill ★★★★

REGIONAL MEXICAN   MODERATE   QUALITY ★★★★½   VALUE ★★★

445 North Clark Street, River North; ☎ 312-661-1434; www.fronterakitchens.com

Reservations Accepted only for lunch, or for dinner parties of 5–10. When to go Lunch; early weeknight dinner; Saturday brunch. Entree range $10–$27.

Payment All major credit cards. **Service rating** ★★★½. **Friendliness rating** ★★★. **Parking** Valet, $10; pay lots, street. **Bar** Beer, tequilas, brandy, and margaritas. **Wine selection** Extensive global, 120 selections, $30–$260; 10 by the glass, $11. **Dress** Casual. **Disabled access** Wheelchair accessible. **Customers** Mixed. **Hours** Tuesday–Thursday, 11:30 a.m.–2:30 p.m. and 5–10 p.m.; Friday, 11:30 a.m.–2:30 p.m. and 5–11 p.m.; Saturday, 10:30 a.m.–2:30 p.m. and 5–11 p.m.; closed Sunday and Monday.

SETTING AND ATMOSPHERE With vibrantly colored walls and scene-setting Mexican artwork, Frontera Grill is casual, even boisterous, while still managing to convey an almost reverent sense of commitment to authenticity and quality. This is not your neighborhood chips-and-salsa, refried-beans Mexican joint—not by a long shot.

HOUSE SPECIALTIES Menus evolve constantly. Some evergreen items include: daily tamale specials; *ensalada de jicama* (crunchy jicama salad with oranges, grapefruit, and pineapple, tossed with orange-lime vinaigrette); *sopa de tortilla* (rich tortilla soup with chile pasilla, avocado, and queso fresco); *tostaditas de seviche* (crisp little tortillas piled with lime-marinated marlin, manzanillo olives, tomato, serrano chile, and cilantro); *carne asada* (naturally-raised Limousine rib eye, marinated in spicy red chiles and wood-grilled, served with black beans, fried plantains, sour cream, and guacamole); *tacos al carbon* (wood-grilled meat, poultry, fish, or vegetables sliced and served with roasted pepper rajas, two salsas, frijoles charros, guacamole, and housemade tortillas); *pollo à la Yucateca* (achiote-marinated Gunthorp chicken in roasted tomato-habanero sauce with orange-dressed pea shoots, avocado leaf–flavored black beans, crispy ham, grilled orange, and zucchini).

OTHER RECOMMENDATIONS Examples of changing seasonal dishes include: *sopa de espinacas* (spicy spinach-potato soup with grilled chicken, poblano chiles, roasted carrots, and cilantro); *cazuela de pato y hongos* (Gunthorp duck braised with tomatillos, shiitake mushrooms, and roasted vegetables, over white rice and served with onions and tortillas for making soft tacos); *lobina criolla* (grilled Atlantic striped bass in roasted tomato sauce with chipotle chiles, bacon, pineapple, jícama relish, and plantain-studded red chile rice).

unofficial **TIP**
Frontera Grill chef-owner Rick Bayless's newest venture is **Frontera Fresco,** a quick-service restaurant on the seventh floor of Macy's (formerly Field's) at 111 North State Street (☎ 312-781-4884). Open Monday–Saturday, 11 a.m.-4 p.m.

SUMMARY AND COMMENTS Serving a seductive menu of grilled dishes, moles and chile-thick braises, Frontera Grill ups the ante on casual Mexican cuisine. The fare here is informed by the world-renowned commitment and talents of chef-owner Rick Bayless; there's a lot to explore in the exciting universe of Mexican regional cooking, and Bayless is one of the world's foremost guides through this taste-bud-tantalizing terrain. The adjacent, more formal Topolobampo (see page 250) takes things to an even higher plane. If you've had your fill of omelets and pancakes, try the Saturday-only brunch.

Gibson's ★★★½

STEAK	VERY EXPENSIVE	QUALITY ★★★★	VALUE ★★½

1028 North Rush Street, Gold Coast; ☎ 312-266-8999; www.gibsonssteakhouse.com

Reservations Recommended. **When to go** Weekends for the scene. **Entree range** $10–$129 for surf and turf. **Payment** AE, CB, D, DC, JCB, MC, V. **Service rating** ★★★½. **Friendliness rating** ★★. **Parking** Valet, $10. **Bar** Full service. **Wine selection** American, Italian, New Zealand; $21–$475 bottle, $5–$15 glass. **Dress** Trendy to dressy. **Disabled access** Yes. **Customers** Mature, showy locals; middle-aged singles. **Hours** Monday–Sunday, 11 a.m.–midnight.

SETTING AND ATMOSPHERE The 1940s men's-club decor, with dark-wood wainscoting and trim plus tile floors, continues to draw fans who pack the front bar most nights. There's usually a wait, but patrons don't seem to mind; mingling before dinner is part of the allure. A favorite of the midlife-to-senior social set, Gibson's is one of three Rush Street nightspots collectively known as the "Viagra Triangle" (see Part 11, Entertainment and Nightlife). The crowd is a central-casting mix of "dese and dose" Chicago: singles and preeners, pinky rings and politicos.

HOUSE SPECIALTIES Caesar salad; bone-in sirloin; veal chop; New York sirloin; double-baked potato; sautéed spinach and broccoli with olive oil and garlic; asparagus with hollandaise sauce.

OTHER RECOMMENDATIONS Spicy lobster cocktail; baby back ribs; double-cut lamb chops; Australian and colossal lobster tails; London broil.

ENTERTAINMENT AND AMENITIES Live piano nightly.

SUMMARY AND COMMENTS High-quality steaks and land-of-the-giants desserts are served in obscene quantities, usually in straightforward preparations, at this popular Gold Coast steak house. There's also a limited selection of fish and chicken offered along with classic sides, but fans rave most about the prime, dry-aged beef. It's a happening scene on most nights, with live piano and a bounty of singles with eyes wide open.

Green Zebra ★★★★

CONTEMPORARY AMERICAN/VEGETARIAN EXPENSIVE	QUALITY ★★★★	VALUE ★★★★

1460 West Chicago Avenue, West Town; ☎ 312-243-7100; www.greenzebrachicago.com

Reservations Recommended. **When to go** Weekday or weekend dinner. **Entree range** $11–$17. **Payment** AE, D, DC, MC, V. **Service rating** ★★★★. **Friendliness rating** ★★★★. **Parking** Valet, $10. **Bar** Full service. **Wine selection** French, Italian, Austrian, Alsatian; $23–$110 bottle, $5–$17 glass. **Dress** Casual. **Disabled access** Yes. **Customers** Hip vegetarians and vegans, foodies. **Hours** Tuesday–Thursday, 5:30–10 p.m.; Friday and Saturday, 5–11 p.m.; Sunday, 5:30–9 p.m.; closed Monday.

SETTING AND ATMOSPHERE The sleek, upscale room is done in neutral tones with cool recessed lighting, a stairway on one wall that leads to nowhere, and textured tabletops that resemble reed grass. There are a limited number of tables, so waiting can get crowded at the slender bar up front.

HOUSE SPECIALTIES Crispy sweet-potato dumplings with water chestnuts and dandelion miso broth; crimson lentil cake spiced with shallot and red-pepper jam; chicken breast with new potatoes, crisp skin, and wild honey; roasted halibut with fiddlehead ferns, yellow wax beans, and creamed watercress.

OTHER RECOMMENDATIONS Roasted baby beets with fennel flan and candied beets; buckwheat crepe with escarole, sugar snap peas, and morel mushrooms; grilled trumpet royale mushrooms, roasted white corn, and herb vinaigrette; curry-spiced eggplant soup.

SUMMARY AND COMMENTS This widely acclaimed venture by well-known local chef Shawn McClain (named 2006's Best Midwest Chef by the James Beard Foundation) offers an innovative take on meatless fare. Sharing-size dishes (you'll need more than one) have so much flavor and texture that you don't miss the meat, although there are a very few non-vegetarian options with chicken or fish. The global and reasonable wine list marries well with the menu for a most tantalizing tasting experience.

Heat ★★★★

JAPANESE/SUSHI	VERY EXPENSIVE	QUALITY ★★★★	VALUE ★★

1507 North Sedgwick Avenue, Old Town; ☎ 312-317-9818; www.heatsushi.com

Reservations Recommended. **When to go** Thursday–Sunday, for dinner; weekdays for a prix-fixe lunch. **Entree range** $8–$60. **Payment** AE, D, DC, MC, V. **Service rating** ★★★. **Friendliness rating** ★★★. **Parking** Valet, $8. **Bar** Full service with over 50 varieties of sake, $30–$250 bottle. **Wine selection** Global selections from Alsace (France), New Zealand, Oregon, South Africa, and Australia; $50–$100 bottle; $9–$22 glass. **Dress** Stylish. **Disabled access** Yes. **Customers** Food savvy, young, Asian. **Hours** Monday, Wednesday–Saturday, 11:30 a.m.–2 p.m. and 5–10 p.m.; Tuesday, 5–10 p.m.; Saturday and Sunday brunch, 11 a.m.–2 p.m.

SETTING AND ATMOSPHERE Slate gray and earth tones dominate the subdued swanky room. There's a natural stone backsplash behind the sushi bar along with a 20-foot-long fish tank at knee level, from which live fish are pulled and cooked on the spot. The slender room only fits a dozen tables, making the quarters tight but comfortable.

HOUSE SPECIALTIES Freshly killed spiny lobster, sea urchin, Dungeness crab, blackfish, and grouper, served while still twitching; kaiseki progressive seven-course prix-fixe meal; ultrafresh sushi and sashimi combinations; sake yaki (pan-fried Atlantic salmon with white asparagus and mango miso).

OTHER RECOMMENDATIONS Stuffed Kahaku giant prawn wrapped with tofu tempura skin and topped with macha and marjoram; boiled Pacific snapper served with gobo soy sauce and wasabi-jicama mashed potatoes.

SUMMARY AND COMMENTS It doesn't get much fresher than the sushi and freshly killed fish served at this high-end Japanese eatery. There's barely a sign outside the door, so you're in the know if you find it. Service is quick and precise, and wine suggestions are helpful. Sit at the sushi bar to enjoy the chef's choice menu that will keep coming until you tell them to stop.

 Hot Doug's ★★★

FAST FOOD   INEXPENSIVE   QUALITY ★★★★★   VALUE ★★★★★

3324 North California Avenue, Roscoe Village; ☎ **773-279-9550; www.hotdougs.com**

Reservations Not accepted. **When to go** Lunch, afternoon, or early dinner, as it closes at 4 p.m. **Entree range** $1.50–$7.50. **Payment** Cash. **Service rating** ★★★. **Friendliness rating** ★★★★★. **Parking** Street. **Bar** BYOB. **Wine selection** BYOB. **Dress** Casual. **Disabled access** No. **Customers** Foodies, students, blue- and white-collars. **Hours** Monday–Saturday, 10:30 a.m.–4 p.m.

SETTING AND ATMOSPHERE   Brightly colored and casual, this come-as-you-are "Sausage Superstore and Encased Meat Emporium" has a cultish following that prompts ever-longer lines out the door (friendly, efficient service keeps things moving). There's plenty of Elvis and wiener kitsch, wild music, a larger seating area than the original (pre-fire) location, and easy street parking—but still those frustrating funky hours.

HOUSE SPECIALTIES   Daily specials are the highlight and might include venison, rattlesnake, or alligator. Recent examples include bacon-Cheddar elk sausage with Guinness stout mustard and sage derby cheese; Cognac-infused pheasant sausage with black truffle mustard and foie gras "butter." Even the condiments are special, with four styles of mustard (yellow, spicy brown, honey, and Dijon) and onions raw or caramelized. The french fries are cooked in duck fat on Fridays and Saturdays.

unofficial **TIP**
Hot Doug's takes its leisure seriously, so if you're headed there on even a minor holiday, it pays to call in advance.

OTHER RECOMMENDATIONS   Classic Chicago dog with all the fixin's (steamed, grilled, deep-fried, or deep-fried *and* grilled); bratwurst soaked in beer; vegetarian dog; corn dog; bagel dogs and potato nuggets for kids.

SUMMARY AND COMMENTS   "Gourmet encased meats" may sound like a joke, but in the hands of Doug Sohn, the dog has its day in forms familiar and fantastic. Hot Doug's is a category killer with national recognition and a crazed, beloved genius at the helm. Menu items get silly celeb names (which change on a whim).

 Irazu ★★★

COSTA RICAN/VEGETARIAN   INEXPENSIVE   QUALITY ★★★★   VALUE ★★★★★

1865 North Milwaukee Avenue, Bucktown; ☎ **773-252-5687**

Reservations Not accepted. **When to go** Breakfast, lunch, early-weeknight dinner. **Entree range** $5–$12. **Payment** Cash only. **Service rating** ★★. **Friendliness rating** ★★★★. **Parking** Lot, street. **Bar** BYOB. **Wine selection** BYOB. **Dress**

Neighborhood casual. **Disabled access** Yes. **Customers** Locals, students, Central Americans. **Hours** Monday–Saturday, 10 a.m.–9 p.m.

SETTING AND ATMOSPHERE This cozy little Costa Rican joint is a family-run Bucktown favorite with a warm, if no-frills, ambience. Service is friendly (and kid friendly), and the counter and small dining room are usually buzzing with grateful neighborhood denizens and bargain hunters. There's a bit of sidewalk dining to help with the crowd overflow.

HOUSE SPECIALTIES Traditional *casado* (thin ribeye steak or chicken breast with caramelized onions, white rice, black beans, sweet plantains, an over-easy egg and cabbage salad); vegetarian burrito; *gallo pinto* (breakfast dish of white rice, whole black beans, eggs, and plantains); milk or water "shakes" (such as oatmeal, blackberry, tamarind, corn meal).

OTHER RECOMMENDATIONS Mashed-potato tacos; hearts of palm salad; fried or boiled yucca with garlic oil; *pepito* sandwich (ribeye steak, sautéed onions, cheese, and pinto beans); French toast with sour cream; homemade flan; fresh carrot juice.

SUMMARY AND COMMENTS A few Mexican and American items dot a menu of Costa Rican cooking, including lots of interesting vegetarian items for breakfast, lunch, and dinner. Since the place is very popular—not just for the big portions of oh-so-fresh food but also for the el-cheapo prices—and is walk-in only, try early weeknights for dinner, or call ahead for takeout. Expect slow service from the small kitchen when they're busy.

Japonais ★★★

ASIAN FUSION	EXPENSIVE	QUALITY ★★★	VALUE ★★

600 West Chicago Avenue, Near West; ☎ 312-822-9600; www.japonaischicago.com

Reservations Accepted. **When to go** Weekday dinner. **Entree range** $19–$35. **Payment** AE, D, DC, MC, V. **Service rating** ★★½. **Friendliness rating** ★★★. **Parking** $12. **Bar** Full service with extensive martinis and sake. **Wine selection** Californian, French, Austrian, and German; $42–$510 bottle, $8–$18 glass. **Dress** Casual chic or business casual during day. **Disabled access** Yes. **Customers** Trendy, young; suburbanites on weekends. **Hours** Monday–Thursday, 11:30 a.m.–2:20 p.m. and 5–11 p.m.; Friday, 11:30 a.m.–2:20 p.m. and 5–11:30 p.m.; Saturday, 5–11:30 p.m.; Sunday, 5–10 p.m.

SETTING AND ATMOSPHERE There are two distinct dining areas separated by a limestone waterfall. Step down on the lounge side into a sunken dining room with black granite tables and a large fireplace, or dine in the opposing raised dining area flanked by a sushi bar and banquettes around the room's perimeter. The dream-like downstairs lounge opens to an outdoor patio overlooking the river, attracting a late-night see-and-be-seen crowd.

HOUSE SPECIALTIES Spicy octopus roll topped with spicy tuna and sweet unagi sauce; crab cakes; lobster spring rolls with mango relish and blood-orange vinaigrette; shrimp tempura with a brie fondue sauce; Kobe beef carpaccio; *kani nigiri* (king crab); stir-fried soba noodles with tofu and seasonal vegetables; "Le Quack Japonais" (whole maple-leaf duck with hoisin sauce, mango chutney, and mu shu wraps); soft-shell-crab roll topped with sashimi fluke and ponzu sauce.

OTHER RECOMMENDATIONS Seven-spiced smoked-duck salad with Asian greens in a honey-yuzu dressing; bin cho (marinated sashimi of baby tuna with arugula and shaved daikon in a citrus-sake vinaigrette); fried calamari tossed in a sweet-and-sour sauce with wasabi vinaigrette; Japonais fried rice with chicken, beef, or shrimp; yuzu-almond crème brûlée (home-made creamy citrus custard served with almond tuile cookie).

SUMMARY AND COMMENTS The same stylish team that created the popular Mirai Sushi (see page 229) has expanded on its concept with similar painstaking attention to the decor. The food gets almost as much focus, with intriguing combinations of flavors and textures, along with appealing presentations.

Jin Ju ★★★

KOREAN	MODERATE	QUALITY ★★★	VALUE ★★★½

5203 North Clark Street, Andersonville; ☎ 773-334-6377

Reservations Accepted. **When to go** Any day for dinner. **Entree range** $12–$15. **Payment** AE, D, DC, MC, V. **Service rating** ★★★. **Friendliness rating** ★★★. **Parking** Street only. **Bar** Full service. **Wine selection** Ordinary and limited French, Australian, Californian, Chilean; $24–$45 bottle, $5–$7 glass. **Dress** Casual. **Disabled access** No. **Customers** Young locals. **Hours** Tuesday–Friday, 5–11 p.m.; Saturday and Sunday, 11:30 a.m.–3 p.m. and 5–11 p.m.

SETTING AND ATMOSPHERE The dining room at this Korean establishment feels more like a sushi bar with clean lines, dark oak floors, and black spinning fans overhead. Original tin ceilings remain, but the overall feeling is contemporary—mimicking the style of the food, which puts a new spin on traditional Korean fare.

HOUSE SPECIALTIES Pajun (lightly fried scallion pancake served with a soy dipping sauce); mandoo (Korean dumplings filled with beef, onions, scallions, and tofu); te gim (tempura-style fried shrimp, squid, and veg-etables); crab and cucumber salad; chap chae (vermicelli noodles with beef sirloin, spinach, roasted red peppers, shiitake mushrooms, and scal-lions); kim chee chigae (kim chee soup with pork, tofu, and green chiles); kalbi (beef short ribs marinated in a sweet soy sauce then grilled and served with lettuce and bean paste).

OTHER RECOMMENDATIONS Miyuk soup (mild seaweed soup with scallions in a mussel broth); kim bap (seaweed roll filled with rice, bulgogi, and yellow pickled radish); dol sut bi bim bap (rice bowl with beef, mushrooms, fried egg, and spicy red-pepper paste served in a hot stone pot); o junga bokum (sautéed squid with green chili peppers, onions, and carrots in a spicy red-pepper sauce).

SUMMARY AND COMMENTS It's the first of its kind to bring traditional Korean fare into the mainstream—with killer soju-tinis. The hip room makes tasting this unusual cuisine more palatable, although after an initial introduction, it's not all that intimidating. Flavorful dishes are spiced just hot enough for the American palate, but many still have kick. It's a charming addition to the Asian restaurant scene, situated conveniently in Andersonville.

Joe's Seafood, Prime Steak & Stone Crab ★★★

STEAK/SEAFOOD	VERY EXPENSIVE	QUALITY ★★★½	VALUE ★★

60 East Grand Avenue, River North; ☎ 312-379-5637; www.joesstonecrabchicago.com

Reservations Highly recommended. **When to go** Power lunch, early or late dinner. **Entree range** $14–$45. **Payment** AE, D, DC, MC, V. **Service rating** ★★★. **Friendliness rating** ★★★. **Parking** Valet, $10. **Bar** Full service. **Wine selection** Broad price range, strength in California Cabs; $28–$1,745 bottle, $7–$14 glass. **Dress** Business casual. **Disabled access** Yes. **Customers** Expense accounters, tourists, groups. **Hours** Monday–Saturday, 11:30 a.m.–10 p.m.; Sunday, 4–9:30 p.m. (lounge serves food a half hour later than dining room).

SETTING AND ATMOSPHERE Spun from the Miami mainstay, this Lettuce Entertain You Enterprises concept is more clubby urban steakhouse than seaside getaway; it does have that Lettuce "instant history" in the old-guard masculine decor (dark wood, plush booths, moody vintage photography), but at least it avoids some of that corporate group's over-the-top decorative indulgences—and takes reservations. And this is Chicago—so while stone crab has a season, prime beef does not. Expect an upscale but unstuffy atmosphere with polished, professional service (some tableside) in tuxes and a crowded, boisterous scene.

HOUSE SPECIALTIES Florida stone-crab claws (fresh in season mid-October to mid-May, frozen off-season) with mustard sauce; Alaskan king-crab legs; bone-in prime filet mignon or New York strip; hash browns; fried green tomatoes; cole slaw mixed with relish; pies (key lime, peanut butter, coconut, or banana cream).

OTHER RECOMMENDATIONS Oysters Rockefeller; fried chicken; jumbo lump crab cakes; Parmesan-crusted halibut; grilled swordfish; crab-stuffed sole with lobster sauce; calf's liver with bacon and onions; chopped salad; beef tenderloin salad (lunch only); fried asparagus.

SUMMARY AND COMMENTS Okay, so you're paying the airfare per crab. We may have a lake, but we don't have an ocean—and sometimes nothing but the "sea" in seafood will do. Lunch is calmer and cheaper (but still pricey), and you may experience a long wait, even with reservations.

Kevin ★★★½

NEW FRENCH/ASIAN	EXPENSIVE	QUALITY ★★★★	VALUE ★★

9 West Hubbard Street, River North; ☎ 312-595-0055; www.kevinrestaurant.com

Reservations Recommended. **When to go** Weekend dinner or weekday lunch. **Entree range** $17–$36. **Payment** AE, D, MC, V. **Service rating** ★★★. **Friendliness rating** ★★★. **Parking** Valet, $10. **Bar** Full service. **Wine selection** French and Californian, $32–$450; half bottles, $25–$85; extensive by-the-glass selection,

$7–$25. **Dress** Upscale, dressy. **Disabled access** Yes. **Customers** Business workers at lunch, suburbanites and food lovers for dinner. **Hours** Monday–Thursday,
5:30–10 p.m.; Friday and Saturday, 5:30–11 p.m.

SETTING AND ATMOSPHERE The natural wood room is appointed with various
  stainless-steel details, like a curving wineglass rack and brushed-steel
  bar. Tables can be close, but the room is charming.

HOUSE SPECIALTIES   Menus change daily but have included such dishes
  as grilled asparagus–arugula salad; seared ostrich in aged balsamic vinegar with rosemary-strawberry coulis, toasted walnuts, goat cheese, and
  white-truffle-oil polenta; ragu of lobster and sea scallop on crab risotto
  in chive and citrus dressing with watercress, ginger, and tomato; roasted
  breast of chicken with mushrooms, fingerling potatoes, scallion,
  orange, red potatoes, and watercress; spicy bean–glazed rack of lamb in
  rosemary jus.

OTHER RECOMMENDATIONS Mixed-green salad in sesame vinaigrette with
  grape tomatoes, pickled cucumbers, haricots verts, and wonton crisps;
  sautéed shrimp with pineapple coulis, bok choy, ginger, watercress, and
  crisp shrimp wonton in a spicy shrimp broth; wild-mushroom, goat-
  cheese, pine-nut, and truffle-oil pot stickers.

SUMMARY AND COMMENTS This Asian-inspired New French dining room
  showcases chef Kevin Shikami's lightness of hand with exquisite ingredients. The serene space is comfortable and the service cheerful. An
  extensive and well-selected wine list with ample half bottles and by-
  the-glass pours make it a wine lover's dream.

Le Colonial ★★★½

VIETNAMESE/FRENCH	MODERATE	QUALITY ★★★★	VALUE ★★★

**937 North Rush Street, Gold Coast; ☎ 312-255-0088;
www.lecolonialchicago.com**

Reservations Recommended. **When to go** Weekend evenings, during warm
weather. **Entree range** $15–$26. **Payment** AE, DC, MC, V. **Service rating** ★★½.
Friendliness rating ★★★. **Parking** Valet, $10 weekdays, $12 weekends (dinner
only). **Bar** Full service. **Wine selection** French and Californian, $28–$225 bottle;
6–8 by the glass, $8–$10; Champagne, $10–$12 glass. **Dress** Stylish to dressy. **Disabled access** Yes. **Customers** Older local crowd, well dressed. **Hours** *Lunch:* daily,
11 a.m.–2:30 p.m. *Dinner:* Monday–Wednesday, 5–11 p.m.; Thursday–Saturday,
5 p.m.–midnight; Sunday, 5–10 p.m.

SETTING AND ATMOSPHERE Sultry, French colonial–style room with spinning
  ceiling fans, live palm plants, bamboo shutters, and sepia-toned vintage
  photos of Vietnam. There's an intimate upstairs lounge that's a real
  find, and balcony seating in warm weather.

HOUSE SPECIALTIES *Goi bo* (spicy marinated beef salad); *bo bia* (soft salad rolls
  with julienne vegetables and a sweet apricot dipping sauce); *ca chien
  Saigon* (crisp Vietnamese whole red snapper); *vit quay* (ginger-marinated
  roast duck with a tamarind sauce); *banh uot* (grilled sesame beef rolls with
  lettuce, cucumber, and fresh herbs).

OTHER RECOMMENDATIONS *Ca tim nuona* (spicy basil-lime-grilled eggplant); *com tho ga* (ginger chicken with vegetables and rice in a clay pot); *com chien* (house fried rice with chicken and vegetables); *bahn cuon* (steamed Vietnamese ravioli with chicken and mushrooms).

SUMMARY AND COMMENTS   The appealing, film-set-like dining room at this Rush Street Vietnamese restaurant draws crowds regularly, as does the sultry upstairs lounge. The flavors are quite authentic, and the combinations of warm and cold, sweet and spicy, and soft and crunchy make the fare tasty and sensuous. The food here is approachable enough for a timid American palate—if not overly toned down.

Le Francais ★★★★½

FRENCH	VERY EXPENSIVE	QUALITY ★★★★★	VALUE ★★★

269 South Milwaukee Avenue, Wheeling; ☎ 847-541-7470; www.lefrancaisrestaurant.com

Reservations Strongly recommended. **When to go** Special occasions, big deals, and business lunches. **Entree range** *Lunch:* $21–$23; prix fixe, $35. *Dinner:* Entrees, $35; seven-course degustation, $90; multicourse appetizers and dessert, $8–$14. **Payment** AE, D, DC, MC, V. **Service rating** ★★★★½. **Friendliness rating** ★★½. **Parking** Complimentary valet. **Bar** Full service. **Wine selection** 350 selections, predominantly French and Californian, $30–$3,500; 12 by the glass, $8–$15. **Dress** Jackets suggested. **Disabled access** Wheelchair accessible. **Customers** Older, moneyed crowd. **Hours** *Lunch:* Tuesday–Friday, 11:30 a.m.–2 p.m. *Dinner:* Monday–Saturday, 5:30 p.m.– 9 p.m. Closed Sunday except for private functions and some holidays.

SETTING AND ATMOSPHERE   So many changes, so little time. Redecorated once again under yet another regime (albeit a returning one), the once open kitchen has been enclosed again, robbing patrons of the drama unfolding therein. The hushed, neutral room remains a subdued and civilized setting for the upper-echelon diners who appreciate the comfy banquettes and the finesse of a suited, alert service team that resembles a Secret Service contingent.

HOUSE SPECIALTIES   Poached Maine lobster with diver scallops; Gulf shrimp with Israeli couscous and lobster sauce; Australian lamb côtes rotis with house pickles and au jus naturally scented with sarriette herb; pan-seared breast of Michigan duck with bacon-enriched lentils and Tellicherry green-peppercorn sauce; veal medallions and dry-aged ribeye with farro, cabbage confit, and cèpe sauce; warm apple tart with cassis sorbet and caramel sauce.

unofficial **TIP**
Wallet watchers can enjoy Le Francais's prix-fixe lunch bargain.

OTHER RECOMMENDATIONS   Market fish served *selon l'arrivage;* Greek island wolffish with spring vegetables and red-wine pesto sauce; braised artichokes with sweet-yellow-bell puree, button tomatoes, and D.O.C. balsamico; Maine diver scallops roasted over laurel with beignets of yellow squash, cilantro oil, and *bordelaise au beurre noisette;* flourless almond cake; tapioca soup with Thai basil–coconut sorbet.

SUMMARY AND COMMENTS This one-time prime destination, known for having patrons who flew in by helicopter to enjoy its bounties, has been reeling in Wheeling for several years now. Chef Roland Liccioni departed Les Nomades to return here, where he reigned for several years before the return and subsequent retirement of original chef Jean Banchet, followed by two other takeovers—one with some awful moments, the other merely dimming the glow a bit. Liccioni cooks the sort of classic-with-fresh-touches French that his audience here expects, giving this bastion of fine-dining tradition a chance to get its legs back.

Le Lan ★★★★

VIETNAMESE	EXPENSIVE	QUALITY ★★★★	VALUE ★★★

749 North Clark Street, River North; ☎ 312-280-9100; www.lelanrestaurant.com

Reservations Recommended. **When to go** Weekend dinner. **Entree range** $18–$33. **Payment** AE, D, DC, JCB, MC, V. **Service rating** ★★★★. **Friendliness rating** ★★★. **Parking** Valet, $10. **Bar** Full service. **Wine selection** French, Californian, Austrian, and Alsatian; $28–$275 bottle, $7–$25 glass. **Dress** High end, upscale. **Disabled access** Yes. **Customers** Food fans, suburbanites, visitors. **Hours** Monday–Wednesday, 5:30–10 p.m.; Thursday–Saturday, 5:30–11 p.m.; closed Sunday.

SETTING AND ATMOSPHERE Designed by one of the owners, the room is rich with dark walnut walls, jade-green tile floors, and Vietnamese artifacts. There's an ominous mural of a Chinese dragon painted on the back wall, subtly lit from above and below.

HOUSE SPECIALTIES Sweet-corn soup with marinated oyster and heirloom-tomato salad; *banh cuon* (dumplings filled with tender organic pork and fresh herbs); spicy citrus-noodle salad with wakame-garlic dressing and banana-pepper jardinière; grilled bass with water chesnuts, wild mushrooms, bulgur, grapefruit, and heart-of-palm salad; roasted duck breast with seared foie gras, lemongrass duck rillette, confit of peaches and apricots, creamy polenta, and green-cardamon jus.

OTHER RECOMMENDATIONS Pan-seared red snapper with melted leeks, clams, watercress, and nuage of Yukon Gold potatoes; duo of Vietnamese spring rolls with slow-roasted pork, shrimp, and slaw or veal, chicken, vermicelli, and cucumber salad; roasted rack of lamb with red curried loin, fennel salad, sweet gnocchi, and eggplant chutney.

SUMMARY AND COMMENTS This stylish French-Vietnamese fine-diner is a collaboration between two of Chicago's powerhouse chefs: Roland Liccioni of Le Francais and Arun Sampanthavivat of Arun's Thai. The menu brings the delicate, rich flavors of France together with the spicy and oft-tangy flavors of Vietnam for a unique take on traditional dishes. The room is almost a museum of textiles and art, enhancing the elegance of the dining experience. A well-selected wine list rounds off the nicely executed menu.

Lou Malnati's ★★½

| PIZZA/ITALIAN | INEXPENSIVE | QUALITY ★★½ | VALUE ★★★★ |

439 North Wells Street, River North; ☎ 312-828-9800
958 West Wrightwood Avenue, Lincoln Park; ☎ 773-832-4030
6649 North Lincoln Avenue, Lincolnwood; ☎ 847-673-0800
1850 Sherman Avenue, Evanston; ☎ 847-328-5400 (numerous suburban locations); www.loumalnatis.com

Reservations Not accepted. **When to go** Anytime. **Entree range** $5–$8 (individual); more for pizza. **Payment** AE, D, DC, MC, V. **Service rating** ★★. **Friendliness rating** ★★★. **Parking** Varies by location. **Bar** Full service. **Wine selection** Generic, limited; $18–$25 bottle, $5–$6 glass. **Dress** Casual. **Disabled access** Varies by location. **Customers** One and all. **Hours** Vary by location.

SETTING AND ATMOSPHERE Settings vary widely, from the quaint freestanding Lincolnwood original to the ho-hum frat-dining-room setting of the River North location. Hardly the point, however—you just need a place to sit and someone to cook and bring you your pizza.

HOUSE SPECIALTIES Butter-crust deep-dish pizza; thin-crust pizza; stuffed spinach bread; meatball sandwich; antipasto salad; chocolate-chip "pizza" dessert.

OTHER RECOMMENDATIONS Low-fat cheese pizza; gluten-free, low-carb "crustless" pizza; mostaccioli; chicken club salad; Granny Smith apple pie. There's a kids' menu with chicken nuggets, corn dogs, and the like.

SUMMARY AND COMMENTS In a city of fight-to-the-death pizza partisanship, Lou's perpetually rises to the top with its long-standing consistency and just plain addictive 'za (the house sausage and chunky tomato sauce are noteworthy). You come here for the pizza and perhaps a frosty brew, and everything else—including the other food—is window dressing. You can take home frozen pies for later or to share the sinful goodness of this hometown favorite with others. Or if you get hooked on it while in town, you can have it shipped nationwide for the price of a haute-cuisine meal (visit **www.tastesofchicago.com**).

Lou Mitchell's Restaurant ★★

| AMERICAN | INEXPENSIVE | QUALITY ★★★ | VALUE ★★★★ |

565 West Jackson Boulevard, The Loop; ☎ 312-939-3111
Lou Mitchell's Express, O'Hare Airport, Terminal 5,
5600 North Mannheim Road; ☎ 773-601-8989

Reservations Accepted for parties of 6 or more, Monday–Friday only. **When to go** Breakfast, lunch. **Entree range** $6–$15. **Payment** Cash, checks. **Service rating** ★★. **Friendliness rating** ★★½. **Parking** Public lots, street. **Dress** Casual. **Disabled access** No. **Customers** Loop workers, die-hard fans. **Hours** Monday–Saturday, 5:30 a.m.–3 p.m.; Sunday, 7 a.m.–3 p.m.

SETTING AND ATMOSPHERE Lou Mitchell's celebrates the technological breakthroughs of Naugahyde, Formica, and fake plants. This is lowbrow, high-camp, retro-diner authenticity at its finest, complete with Rat Pack background music.

HOUSE SPECIALTIES Eggs and fluffy, in-the-skillet omelets made with double-yolk eggs (including Greek sausage, tomato, green pepper, and onion, or Michigan sweet apples with old English Cheddar cheese); Belgian malted waffles; grilled French toast; homemade pie. Extensive daily specials run the gamut from corned beef hash and hot turkey sandwiches to chicken pot pie, baked short ribs, and "creamed baked macaroni au gratin."

OTHER RECOMMENDATIONS Pot-roast sandwich with jardinière sauce; club sandwich; baked meat loaf; grilled patty melt; fresh banana pancakes; milk shakes.

SUMMARY AND COMMENTS Head back in time at this legendary diner-restaurant opened in 1923. Lou Mitchell's is notorious for its gruff anti-service, free donut holes for those standing in line and Milk Duds for the ladies, and classic diner schtick. A commitment to freshness is evident in the fresh-squeezed juice, fresh breads, pastries, and marmalade.

Lula ★★★½

ECLECTIC/VEGETARIAN	MODERATE	QUALITY ★★★½	VALUE ★★★★

2537–41 North Kedzie Boulevard, Logan Square; ☎ 773-489-9554; www.lulacafe.com

Reservations Not accepted. **When to go** Early. **Entree range** $8–$25. **Payment** AE, MC, V. **Service rating** ★★. **Friendliness rating** ★★★. **Parking** Street. **Bar** Full service. **Wine selection** Value-priced eclectic; $21–$118 bottle, $5–$14 glass. **Dress** Funky-casual. **Disabled access** Yes. **Customers** Hipsters, locals, vegetarians. **Hours** Sunday, Monday, Wednesday, and Thursday, 9 a.m.–10 p.m.; Friday and Saturday, 9 a.m.–11 p.m.

SETTING AND ATMOSPHERE It's a laid-back scene at funky-chic Lula, unless it's packed (which is often). Lucky Logan Square locals don't seem to mind sardine-dining into the small cafe-style dining room with worn wood floors and local artwork, or waiting in the cozy adjoining bar. Off-hours finds neighbors grabbing a barista coffee drink or chilling over a moderately priced meal.

HOUSE SPECIALTIES Bucatini pasta with Moroccan cinnamon, feta, garlic, and brown butter; olive oil–marinated beet bruschetta with arugula and goat cheese; chilled peanut satay noodles with gomae and marinated tofu; three-egg frittata with your choice of ingredients; breakfast burrito; brioche French toast.

OTHER RECOMMENDATIONS Daily specials are a key element in the of-the-moment seasonal cooking here. Examples include mascarpone-stuffed brioche French toast with farm cherries, figs, vanilla anglaise, and graham-cracker strudel; prosciutto omelette with arugula, pecorino, sweet onion, and peach preserves; Nova Scotia lobster soup with new potatoes, watercress, and quail egg; grilled Gunthorp Farms pork loin with shiso-juniper cabbage, glazed carrots, and sweet plum jus.

SUMMARY AND COMMENTS Wonderful organic and vegetarian-vegan options abound on Amalea Tshilds and Jason Hammel's intelligent, eclectic menu. It's a welcoming spot with "hipster hangout" written all over it, but not to the extreme—there's plenty of black and tattoos in evidence, but neither are required to feel at home here. Especially after a rhubarb gimlet or passion-fruit daiquiri.

Manny's Coffee Shop & Deli ★★

DELI/CAFETERIA	INEXPENSIVE	QUALITY ★★★★	VALUE ★★★

1141 South Jefferson Street, South Loop; ☎ 312-939-2855; www.mannysdeli.com

Reservations Not accepted. **When to go** Breakfast, lunch. **Entree range** $6–$12. **Payment** Cash only. **Service rating** ★★. **Friendliness rating** ★★★. **Parking** Street, small lot. **Bar** None. **Wine selection** None. **Dress** Shirt and shoes required. **Disabled access** Wheelchair accessible. **Customers** Blue and white collar. **Hours** Monday–Saturday, 5 a.m.–4 p.m.

SETTING AND ATMOSPHERE This beloved cafeteria-style deli, dishing it up since 1942, oozes authenticity with the fast-paced counter service, no-frills furnishings, water served in paper cones, and cashier station/candy counter selling sweet treats and el cheapo cigars. Down-to-earth, city-of-big-shoulders patrons are here to tie on a serious feedbag.

HOUSE SPECIALTIES Mile-high corned beef and pastrami sandwiches; Reubens; steam-ship round and beef brisket; meat loaf; beef stew; liver and onions; short ribs; knishes; borscht and matzo ball soup.

OTHER RECOMMENDATIONS Corned-beef omelets; lox breakfast; chopped liver. Daily specials include chop suey, fried smelts with mushrooms, and franks and beans.

SUMMARY AND COMMENTS This place is a Chicago institution, and deservedly so. To quote Manny's Web site, "At Manny's you don't diet. You don't snack. You don't nosh. You come to this landmark lunchroom to pile your tray high and eat like there's no tomorrow." Gruff, old-timey counter staff in paper hats sling heavenly, hearty fare; at the end of the line is a time-warp sweets section featuring stewed prunes, Jell-O, rice pudding, and German chocolate cake.

Mas ★★★½

NUEVO LATINO	MODERATE	QUALITY ★★★½	VALUE ★★★

1670 West Division Street, Wicker Park; ☎ 773-276-8700; www.masrestaurant.com/masrestaurant

Reservations Not accepted. **When to go** Weekdays to avoid crowds. **Entree range** $18–$29. **Payment** AE, DC, MC, V. **Service rating** ★★★. **Friendliness rating** ★★★. **Parking** Valet, $8 (Wednesday–Saturday only). **Bar** Full bar specializing in Latin cocktails—caipirinhas, batidas, pico sours, Mas margaritas, and high-end tequilas. **Wine selection** Spanish, Argentinean, Chilean, and Californian, $28–$70 bottle; over a dozen by the glass, $7–$12. **Dress** Casual to trendy. **Disabled access** Yes. **Customers** Local young hipsters. **Hours** Monday–Thursday, 5:30–10 p.m.; Friday and Saturday, 5:30–11 p.m.; Sunday, 11 a.m.–3 p.m. and 5:30–10 p.m.

SETTING AND ATMOSPHERE Tables are close and the room usually crowded at this popular Latin hangout—but nobody seems to mind. Even with a no-reservation policy, the bar is packed with locals, either waiting to eat or just sipping on one of several tasty Latin cocktails.

HOUSE SPECIALTIES Grilled wild salmon with sautéed lentils, salsa criolla, and olive tapinade; seared rare yellowfin tuna with chimichurri and yuca frites; pan-roasted boneless half chicken with fingerling potatoes and poblano rajas with adobo sauce; seared sea scallops and cured duck breast with poha-berry jam and habanero syrup.

OTHER RECOMMENDATIONS Tomatillo-jalapeño–braised pork ribs with pepitas and *queso cotija*.

SUMMARY AND COMMENTS There's never a dull moment at this Nuevo Latin gem; the bar is packed with diners who'll wait over an hour to sample chef John Manion's version of upscale Latin fare. Unique flavor sensations rule in dishes like tuna and papaya tacos, and wild mushroom empanadas. The lights are always dim, the music loud, and the crowd well dressed for a party-like atmosphere, best enjoyed on weekends.

Mirai Sushi ★★★½

JAPANESE/SUSHI	MODERATE	QUALITY ★★★★½	VALUE ★★★

2020 West Division Street, Wicker Park; ☎ 773-862-8500

Reservations Recommended. When to go Dinner (weeknights for less crowding). Entree range $7–$22. Payment All major credit cards. Service rating ★★★. Friendliness rating ★★★. Parking Valet, $7; street. Bar Full service, emphasis on sake. Wine selection 54 global, $34–$106; 13 by the glass, $8–$12. Dress Casual. Disabled access Wheelchair accessible first floor only. Customers Hip urbanites of all ages. Hours Sunday–Wednesday, 5:30–10 p.m.; Thursday–Saturday, 5:30–11 p.m.; upstairs lounge open 5:30 p.m.–1 a.m.

SETTING AND ATMOSPHERE This bustling, bilevel Wicker Park place is a sushi scene, with a bright first-floor restaurant and sushi bar and a dark, sensuous sake lounge upstairs with living-room furniture, dining tables, and bar. Try the house cocktail, a "Red One," comprised of vodka, cranberry juice, fresh passion fruit, and orange and lime juices.

HOUSE SPECIALTIES Daily sushi selection based on season and market (usually several varieties of tuna, salmon, shrimp, and roe); *sakana carpaccio moriawase* (tuna, salmon, and whitefish carpaccio with cilantro, capers, and sesame oil); *hirame usuzukuri* (sashimi of fluke with spicy radish and house ponzu); *kohshyu yaki* (soy-marinated red snapper with sweet-grape reduction); *kushi yaki* (grilled shrimp and squid skewers marinated in sake and garlic sauce).

ENTERTAINMENT AND AMENITIES Live DJ Friday and Saturday.

SUMMARY AND COMMENTS Fresh fish and funky patrons are the allure at this fashionable sushi hot spot. The cut-above Japanese fare is creative and well executed, the sake menu extensive and informative, and the ambience decidedly Wicker Park artsy chic. Focus on the extensive nightly specials for the most intriguing dishes, both sushi and otherwise. Consider reserving a dining spot among the lounge furniture and low tables on the second floor.

MK ★★★★

| NEW AMERICAN | EXPENSIVE | QUALITY ★★★★½ | VALUE ★★★ |

868 North Franklin Street, River North; ☎ 312-482-9179; www.mkchicago.com

Reservations Highly recommended. **When to go** Stylish dinner. **Entree range** $12–$40; 4-course degustation menu, $78–$87. **Payment** AE, D, DC, MC, V. **Service rating** ★★★½. **Friendliness rating** ★★★. **Parking** Valet, $8. **Bar** Full service. **Wine selection** 550 well-chosen international bottles, $29–$700; 12 by the glass, $7–$18. **Dress** Upscale casual to business. **Disabled access** Wheelchair accessible. **Customers** Trendies and power money, nice age mix. **Hours** Sunday–Thursday, 5:30–10 p.m.; Friday and Saturday, 5:30–11 p.m.

SETTING AND ATMOSPHERE Stylish and contemporary without being severe, MK's architectural dining room is spacious and airy, with a pleasantly sophisticated neutral color palette. Plush lounge furniture in the entry area is a great stop for a glass of bubbly before or after.

HOUSE SPECIALTIES Belgian endive salad with French beans, apple, Roquefort cheese, and pecans; lobster soup; prime New York sirloin grilled over hardwood charcoal with red-wine syrup and baby spinach; ahi-tuna tartare with sautéed spinach, shiitake mushrooms, and garlic mashed potatoes; Alaskan halibut with artichokes *en barigoule;* pan-roasted chicken with creamed Tuscan kale, smoked bacon, mushrooms, and Madeira sauce; roasted breast of duck with baby turnips, fava beans, minted farro, and pancetta vinaigrette; roasted rack of lamb with braised lamb cannelloni, ratatouille, cannellini beans, fig jam, and rosemary-scented red wine.

OTHER RECOMMENDATIONS Roasted Maine scallops with littleneck clam–pancetta ragout, oven-roasted tomatoes, and arugula pesto; sliced calf's liver with stone-ground mustard, burnt onions, smoked bacon, and aged balsamic vinegar; sautéed veal sweetbreads with enoki and shiitake mushrooms, miso broth, and scallions; warm banana brioche bread pudding with banana sherbet roasted bananas; peanut-butter mousse with crispy chocolate-peanut-caramel tart and peanut brittle; mocha ice cream, chocolate-mousse cake, toasted meringue, cappuccino dulce de leche, and cashew candy.

SUMMARY AND COMMENTS MK is a mainstay of Chicago's foodie faithful, a restaurant of both style and substance. Expect clean flavor combinations and plate presentations—gratifying without contrivance, handsome without pretense. In the dining room, the staff reaches a fine balance between personable and efficient.

HONORS AND AWARDS *Restaurants & Institutions* magazine Ivy Award for 2006.

Morton's ★★★½

STEAK	VERY EXPENSIVE	QUALITY ★★★★½	VALUE ★★

**9525 West Bryn Mawr Avenue, Rosemont; ☎ 847-678-5155;
www.mortons.com**
1050 North State Street, Gold Coast; ☎ 312-266-4820
65 East Wacker Place, The Loop; ☎ 312-201-0410
1470 McConnor Parkway, Schaumburg; ☎ 847-413-8771
699 Skokie Boulevard, Northbrook; ☎ 847-205-5111

Reservations Recommended. When to go Anytime. Entree range $22–$35.
Payment All major credit cards. Service rating ★★★. Friendliness rating ★★★.
Parking On-site garage (validated). Bar Full service. Wine selection 275 wines,
primarily Californian, French, and German, $28–$3,200; 15 by the glass, $6–$12.
Dress Business casual. Disabled access Yes, all locations. Customers Business
diners, couples. Hours Monday–Saturday, 5:30–11 p.m.; Sunday, 5–10 p.m.

SETTING AND ATMOSPHERE Morton's is renowned for its clubby, masculine
decor; this is quintessential Chicago steak-house territory, complete with photo-lined walls and a discreet entrance reminiscent of a
speakeasy. The main section of the dining room, once a smoker's
refuge, is now nonsmoking thanks to recent law changes—smoking is
allowed in the bar only.

HOUSE SPECIALTIES Jumbo lump crabmeat or shrimp cocktail; Caesar salad;
lobster bisque; double filet mignon, *sauce béarnaise;* 24-ounce porterhouse steak, also available as a 48-ounce double; whole baked Maine
lobster; farm-raised salmon; hash browns; steamed asparagus with
hollandaise.

OTHER RECOMMENDATIONS Blue-point oysters on the half shell; broiled sea
scallops wrapped in bacon with apricot chutney; Sicilian veal chop;
shrimp Alexander, *sauce beurre blanc;* domestic rib lamb chops; Godiva
hot-chocolate cake; soufflé for two (chocolate, Grand Marnier, lemon,
or raspberry).

ENTERTAINMENT AND AMENITIES "See food" menu–cart presentation by the
servers, theatrically displaying enormous cuts of steaks, chops, live
lobsters, and vegetables.

SUMMARY AND COMMENTS Founded by the late, lamented Chicago restaura-
teur Arnie Morton, the Gold Coast location of this steak lover's sanctuary
has spawned a thriving national chain of near-legendary status. This is
the original, a real bastion of old-guard, carnivorous dining delights;
steady as she goes, Morton's delivers quality and consistency without a
hint of highfalutin fussiness—unless you consider the visual "menu" of
football-sized foods over the top.

Moto ★★★

MODERN AMERICAN	VERY EXPENSIVE	QUALITY ★★★	VALUE ★★

**945 West Fulton Market, West Loop; ☎ 312-491-0058;
www.motorestaurant.com**

Reservations Accepted. **When to go** Weekend nights, special occasions. **Entree range** $65–$160. **Payment** AE, D, DC, MC, V. **Service rating** ★★★. **Friendliness rating** ★★. **Parking** Valet, $10. **Bar** Full service. **Wine selection** Californian, French, Italian, Austrian, Spanish; flights from 4-course ($40) to 14-course ($80), $32–$54 bottle, $8–$20 glass. **Dress** All black, ultramodern. **Disabled access** Yes. **Customers** Curious foodies, serious diners. **Hours** Tuesday–Saturday, 5–11 p.m.; closed Sunday and Monday.

SETTING AND ATMOSPHERE Sleek minimalist decor with no clutter in the entire dining room. There are white walls with subtle accents of cinnamon and cocoa in the banquettes and floor covering, plus dim lighting and a waitstaff dressed in black lab coats. "Aromatherapy flatware" is threaded with sprigs of fresh herbs.

HOUSE SPECIALTIES Five-, ten-, and eighteen-course meals might include bass steamed tableside with heart of palm; rice balls injected with sweet-and-sour sauce; fillet of black bass steamed tableside in Pacific oceanic products; sashimi of hamachi or East Coast bluefin with sesame-milk soup; white-truffle ice-cream spaghetti; smoked-watermelon soup; scallop–jalapeño-lime sorbet.

OTHER RECOMMENDATIONS Pear broth with gherkin ice cubes and ham-flavored cotton candy; brown butter–basted bobwhite quail with Swiss chard broth and porcini oil; citrus togarashi sprinkled on lime sorbet; deconstructed egg roll with pull-apart duck; *sous vide* tenderloin of beef with braised oxtail.

SUMMARY AND COMMENTS There's nothing conventional about this far-flung concept, where chef Homaro Cantu holds numerous patents for serving pieces and edible menus, and custom-made silverware threaded with herbs is considered a "course" on the menu. In his favor, he focuses his ever-changing menu on farm-raised meats and organic or artisanal ingredients. Despite the pristine ingredients, dinner here feels more like you're inside an experimental laboratory than in a dining room. If nothing else, the unique experience is a riot of conflicting flavors and textures, along with drama like food injections and savory ice cream and candy. This is Chicago's true representative of the "molecular gastronomy" trend to the nth degree.

Nacional 27 ★★★★

NUEVO LATINO	MODERATE	QUALITY ★★★★	VALUE ★★★

**325 West Huron Street, River North; ☎ 312-664-2727;
www.nacional27.net**

Reservations Accepted. **When to go** After-work cocktails, hot dates. **Entree range** $16–$28. **Payment** AE, D, DC, MC, V. **Service rating** ★★★. **Friendliness**

rating ★★★. **Parking** Nearby lots; valet, $10. **Bar** Full bar, specialty cocktails, Latin beers. **Wine selection** Affordable old and new world, including Spanish and South American; $27–$239 bottle, $4–$14 glass. **Dress** Business, trendy. **Disabled access** Yes. **Customers** After-work, dates, and dancers. **Hours** Monday–Thursday, 5:30–9:30 p.m.; Friday and Saturday, 5:30 p.m.–midnight. Lounge open until midnight on Thursday, until 2 a.m. on Friday, and until 3 a.m. on Saturday.

SETTING AND ATMOSPHERE Despite being a Lettuce Entertain You Enterprises operation, the place offers swanky space that's mercifully lacking in decorative overkill. Sophisticated urban ambience, with earth tones, tiles, massive pillars, and sensuous draping, makes a smart setting for a promising date or deal. Infectious Latin jazz performs Tuesday from 6:30 to 9 p.m., a percussionist Thursday at 8 p.m., and the modern fine-dining mood heats up with salsa dancing on weekends (starting at 11 p.m.).

HOUSE SPECIALTIES Chef Randy Zweiban is a whiz at juggling and blending the 27 national cuisines that make up the menu at this Nuevo Latino hot spot. Seasonal dishes might include a ceviche sampler (shrimp-scallop, hamachi-orange, ahi tuna–watermelon); slow-roasted Gunthorp Farms pork with sweet plantains, black beans, coconut rice, and orange mojo; truffle-crusted filet mignon with three potato-chorizo hash and Malbec reduction.

unofficial **TIP**
Early birds will love Nacional 27's oh-so-Continental "late lunch," a three-course deal including wine or sangria, available daily until 6:15 p.m. for only $29.95.

OTHER RECOMMENDATIONS Pumpkin–goat cheese *croquetas;* chopped-chimichurri shrimp salad with avocado, piquillo peppers, and Champagne vinaigrette; shrimp-and-chorizo paella; ahi-tuna steak with Central American stir-fry and roasted pepper–caper–red-wine vinaigrette; flan.

SUMMARY AND COMMENTS In addition to being one of the few dine-and-dance date options, the place also offers a sexy destination bar and lounge with small bites (such as tiny barbecued-lamb tacos with avocado salsa, and boniato-and-plantain *croquetas* with black-bean salsa and roasted-garlic aioli) and cocktails so clever (for example, pomegranate-ginger-chile mojito, spicy ginger beer–muddled lime–Gosslings rum) they warrant their own "bar chef."

Naha ★★★★

MEDITERRANEAN/AMERICAN   **EXPENSIVE**   **QUALITY ★★★★**   **VALUE ★★★**

**500 North Clark Street, River North; ☎ 312-321-6242;
www.naha-chicago.com**

Reservations Accepted. **When to go** Weekday lunch, weekend dinner. **Entree range** $10–$46. **Payment** AE, D, DC, MC, V. **Service rating** ★★★½. **Friendliness rating** ★★★★. **Parking** Valet, $10. **Bar** Full service. **Wine selection** Mostly French; Rhone Valley, Burgundy, Provence, some New Zealand, Californian, and German; $25–$500 bottle, $7–$30 glass. **Dress** Upscale casual. **Disabled access** Yes. **Customers** Professional, older crowd, with locals by day. **Hours**

Monday–Thursday, 11:30 a.m.–2 p.m. and 5:30–9:30 p.m.; Friday, 11:30 a.m.–
2 p.m. and 5:30–10 p.m.

SETTING AND ATMOSPHERE The contemporary, Zen-like space features walls
of windows on two sides, low-backed chrome-and-leather chairs, and
works of abstract modern art on the cool gray walls. The front bar area
is spacious for waiting.

HOUSE SPECIALTIES Mediterranean Greek salad with warm feta; salmon with
white asparagus, black trumpet mushrooms, and Jerusalem artichokes;
pink snapper with red-rib dandelion, baba ghanoush, fennel, ratatouille,
olive tapenade, saffron-aioli toast, and bouillabaisse broth; lacquered and
aged duck breast with baby turnips, broccoli rabe, dates, black Mission figs,
and port; wood-grilled rib-eye steak with glazed Dutch yellow shallots and
spring ramps, macaroni–goat cheese gratin, oxtail–red-wine sauce, and
fleur de sel; wood-grilled Swiss chard and ragout of applewood slab bacon,
red pearl onions, artichokes, cured tomatoes, and marjoram.

OTHER RECOMMENDATIONS Tartare of Hawaiian yellowfin tuna, cured Tasmanian ocean trout, and golden whitefish caviar with mosaic vegetables,
niçoise garnishes, and aigrelette sauce; sea scallops, caramelized Belgian
endive, blood oranges, and watercress; Alaskan halibut confit of glazed
fennel, onions, olive tapenade, spinach, and red-wine butter.

SUMMARY AND COMMENTS The ever-changing seasonal menu never ceases to
dazzle diners at this Mediterranean-inflected New American restaurant, former home to the venerable Gordon. Service is ultraprofessional
without being intimidating. Wonderful harder-to-find bottles grace the
wine list, and the beautifully presented fare tastes as good as it looks.

Nine ★★★½

STEAK	EXPENSIVE	QUALITY ★★★★	VALUE ★★

440 West Randolph Street, West Loop; ☎ 312-575-9900; www.n9ne.com

Reservations Highly recommended. When to go Early evening for quieter
dining; later and weekends for scene. Entree range $12–$40. Payment AE, DC,
MC, V. Service rating ★★★★. Friendliness rating ★★★½. Parking Valet, $9;
street. Bar Three full-service bars; emphasis on specialty martinis, Champagne
cocktails, and sake. Wine selection Well-chosen, well-rounded list of 150+ selections; emphasis on France and California; large Champagne selection and several
magnums; $45–$1,495 by the bottle, 15–20 wines by the glass, $9–$18. Dress
Officially "casual chic"; unofficially the greatest fashion show in town. Disabled
access Wheelchair accessible. Customers Celebs and beautiful people; all-ages
diners and bar denizens. Hours Monday–Wednesday, 11:30 a.m.–2 p.m. and
5:30–10 p.m.; Thursday, 11:30 a.m.–2 p.m. and 5:30–11 p.m.; Friday, 11:30 a.m.–
2 p.m. and 5 p.m.–midnight; Saturday, 5 p.m.–midnight; closed Sunday.

SETTING AND ATMOSPHERE *Grand, sizzling, spectacular.* Nine calls out the adjec-
tives with its tastefully Vegas-tinged ambience, soaring silver-leaf domed
ceiling, waterfall wall, mirrored pillars, light show, and plushy Ultra-
suede booths. Pose in the cushy lounge; imbibe at the main bar; indulge
at the central Champagne-and-caviar bar; dine in the vast dining room

with ultrasocial sightlines; hold a private party with state-of-the-art audiovisual capabilities; or climb the stairs to the ethereal Ghost Bar, one of the hippest hangouts in town.

HOUSE SPECIALTIES American caviar parfaits (black tobiko, salmon, and whitefish) with crisp potato pancakes; cones of lobster with avocado and Asian tuna tartare; crispy Carolina rock shrimp with two dipping sauces; shellfish platters; 12-ounce filet mignon with béarnaise sauce; 16-ounce New York strip steak; 22-ounce veal porterhouse; roasted whole red snapper; pan-roasted Alaskan halibut with artichokes, leeks, sweet-corn sauce, and pea tendrils; grilled salmon with Chinese-mustard glaze, bok choy, shiitake mushrooms, and ginger vinaigrette.

OTHER RECOMMENDATIONS Cold or steamed Alaskan king crab legs; 24-ounce bone-in rib eye; carpaccio of sliced raw sirloin with endive, radicchio, arugula, Parmigiano, and balsamico; pan-roasted tuna with spinach, oyster mushrooms, red-wine reduction, and garlic mashed potatoes; warm chocolate brownie with banana ice cream and hot fudge sauce; Hershey bar with malted milk ball, Oreo ice cream, and chocolate sauce.

SUMMARY AND COMMENTS When it opened in April 2000, Nine wowed Chicago with its luxury ambience and contemporary-decadent menu and bar offerings. This place is a great scene—with great steak-house-and-beyond food—the perfect place for an evening of well-earned indulgence. The fashionable, often eye-popping crowd is a big part of the action here, but the food assures that Nine goes beyond the "now you're hot, now you're not" fate of many trendy restaurants. Make an evening of it—make a reservation for the Champagne-and-caviar bar before dinner, and head up to the Ghost Bar afterward. Thanks to the Loop location, Nine also does a busy business lunch.

NoMI ★★★★

NEW AMERICAN   VERY EXPENSIVE   QUALITY ★★★★½   VALUE ★★★

800 North Michigan Avenue, Gold Coast; ☎ 312-239-4030;
www.nomirestaurant.com

Reservations Recommended. When to go Weekend evenings. Entree range $19–$39. Payment AE, D, DC, MC, V. Service rating ★★★½. Friendliness rating ★★★★. Parking Valet, $11. Bar Full service with sake selection. Wine selection American, French, Australian, New Zealand, Italian, and Spanish, $30–$3,690 per bottle; 42 wines by the glass, $7–$88. Dress Chic to dressy. Disabled access Yes. Customers Tourists, mature patrons. Hours *Breakfast:* Monday–Friday, 6:30 a.m.–10:30 a.m; Saturday and Sunday, 7 a.m.–10:30 a.m. *Brunch:* Sunday, 11 a.m.–2:30 p.m. *Lunch:* Monday–Friday, 11:30 a.m.–2:30 p.m. *Dinner:* Daily, 5:30–10 p.m.

SETTING AND ATMOSPHERE The spectacular room, designed by Tony Chi and perched on the seventh floor of the Park Hyatt hotel, has fabulous views of North Michigan Avenue (hence the name). The entryway alone is worth a visit; it's a temperature-controlled wine cellar that opens into a handsome adjoining lounge. The white linen–topped tables in the dining room are nicely spaced, there's a small sushi bar with a few tables (an add-on demanded by the owners), and the exposed kitchen is finished in eye-catching iridescent aqua tile. Dale Chihuly–designed light fixtures are suspended above the top tables, those in the "prow" of the restaurant with the massive windows overlooking the historic Water Tower.

HOUSE SPECIALTIES Poached Maine lobster with lemon beurre fondue, duxelles, bone marrow, and *sauce américaine*; milk-fed veal strip loin with truffle polenta, cipollini onions, asparagus, and morel jus; sushi platters of tuna, salmon, eel, prawns, and sea bass; spiced watermelon soup with vanilla, star anise, banyuls vinegar, and lobster croutons; duck breast with Mission-fig tart, confit salad, and pistachio vinaigrette.

OTHER RECOMMENDATIONS New York strip sandwich with caramelized-onion marmalade and horseradish mayo on toasted sourdough with frisée salad; catch of the day with Yukon Gold potato puree, wilted arugula, and *sauce vierge*; porcini-mushroom risotto with mascarpone and natural chicken jus; pan-roasted chicken breast with white-bean ragout and fruit chutney.

SUMMARY AND COMMENTS Classically trained French chef Christophe David executes straightforward fare, highlighting the intrinsic flavors of ingredients in a most artistic and refined manner. The wine list, created in consultation with former Charlie Trotter's sommelier Joseph Spellman, offers affordable gems along with slightly pricier options—but nothing too outrageously priced. Top-shelf tea offerings include rare and limited leaves like vintage Pu-erh and reserve and display teas, as well as pairings of teas and spirits that range from $14 to $700. It's an experience best reserved for a special occasion.

North Pond ★★★★

NEW AMERICAN	EXPENSIVE	QUALITY ★★★★½	VALUE ★★★

2610 North Cannon Drive, Lincoln Park; ☎ 773-477-5845; www.northpondrestaurant.com

Reservations Recommended. **When to go** Weekday evenings. **Entree range** $28–$32; brunch $29 per person. **Payment** AE, D, DC, MC, V. **Service rating** ★★★★. **Friendliness rating** ★★★★. **Parking** Street; valet, $8 (dinner and Sunday). **Bar** Full service with a nice selection of local microbrews and spirits. **Wine selection** Well-appointed list featuring ample American wines from California, Oregon, and Washington, along with a few French sparkling wines; $23–$300 bottle, $7–$14 glass. **Dress** Casual to upscale. **Disabled access** Yes. **Customers** Mix of suburban diners and young neighborhood patrons. **Hours** *Lunch:* June–September, 11:30 a.m.–2 p.m. *Brunch:* Sunday, 11 a.m.–2 p.m. *Dinner:* Tuesday–Sunday, 5:30–10 p.m.

SETTING AND ATMOSPHERE This renovated warming house is perched on the edge of a serene pond in Lincoln Park, with windows covering three wood-trimmed walls. The Prairie-style room harmonizes nicely with the park; the ceiling frescoes depict wild prairie grass, and Arts and Crafts light fixtures illuminate the Frank Lloyd Wright–style tables and chairs. It's sophisticated but still lively and energetic, with a bustling exposed kitchen running the length of one wall.

HOUSE SPECIALTIES Pancetta-wrapped salmon with white grits, glazed knob onions, and pea puree; candied gold, red, white, and Chiogga beets with grape leaf–enrobed goat cheese; grilled honey-glazed pork chop with suckling pig–potato cake, Italian greens, and tart-cherry reduction; sautéed soft-shell crab with English pea–almond bulgur, minted tomato broth, and Bordeaux spinach.

OTHER RECOMMENDATIONS Grilled white sea bass, cornmeal waffle, lemon–French bean timbale, and sweet-corn reduction; roasted eggplant–Parmesan ravioli, grilled fennel, and Provençale vegetables in broth; red butterhead letttuce with citrus and green-shallot vinaigrettes, smoked-salmon-mousse canapé, and radishes.

SUMMARY AND COMMENTS This charming Arts and Crafts–style room is inconveniently located in the heart of Lincoln Park, and parking can be tricky. There's room to wait at the bar and a few dozen additional tables overlooking the pond. The American fare is skillfully executed, incorporating seasonal ingredients in intriguing combinations. The Sunday brunch is a great option. The mostly American wine list is well selected and reasonable. Service has its missteps, but the food and ambience more than make up for it.

one sixtyblue ★★★★

NEW AMERICAN	EXPENSIVE	QUALITY ★★★★½	VALUE ★★★

160 North Loomis Street, West Loop (restaurant); 1400 West Randolph (parking lot); ☎ 312-850-0303; www.onesixtyblue.com

Reservations Recommended. **When to go** Dinner anytime; special occasions and with favored visitors. **Entree range** $18–$40; pre-theater, $49 per person. **Payment** AE, DC, MC, V. **Service rating** ★★★★. **Friendliness rating** ★★★. **Parking** Valet, $7. **Bar** Full service. **Wine selection** Eclectic international list organized by varietals; about 150 selections, from $35 up; 15 by the glass, $9–$14. **Dress** Chic casual to dressy. **Disabled access** Complete. **Customers** Savvy diners of all ages; international glitterati and smart money. **Hours** Monday–Thursday, 5:30–10 p.m.; Friday and Saturday, 5:30–11 p.m.; closed Sunday.

SETTING AND ATMOSPHERE Designed by Adam Tihany, one sixtyblue is a remarkably chic, high-concept restaurant. The color scheme of black, neutrals, and citrus hues manages to be crisp and clean without sterility; table dividers with light boxes provide the illusion of privacy, while allowing for discreet spying on fellow diners.

HOUSE SPECIALTIES Rock-shrimp gnocchi with asparagus, shiitake mushrooms, shaved Parmesan, and lobster-and-tarragon emulsion; sea scallops and smoked sturgeon with corn puree and chanterelle mushrooms with port-wine reduction; Alaskan halibut with black Mission figs, broccoli, puree of shallot, crushed hazelnut, tiny green salad, and balsamic sauce; blue-nose grouper with glazed carrots, cumin, eggplant caviar, crispy parsnips, Moroccan argan oil, and cilantro salad; Amish free-range chicken with asparagus, tempura crayfish, and shellfish emulsion; strawberry-and-rhubarb pie, vanilla ice cream, candied ginger and a shot of strawberry juice, chocolate soufflé with raspberry sorbet.

OTHER RECOMMENDATIONS Foie gras sandwich with peaches, candied lemon, mâche, *pain d'epices,* and banyuls reduction; endive salad with Roquefort, roasted walnuts, and hazelnut vinaigrette; pear cake, crepes, vanilla ice cream, and poached pear with chocolate sauce; roasted pineapple with coconut ice cream.

SUMMARY AND COMMENTS One sixtyblue enjoys an excellent reputation as one of Chicago's best—among many—contemporary American culinary destinations. Chef Martial Noguier's fare is innovative and attractive on the plate, served with polish and precision by a smartly clad service team. Michael Jordan, His Airness himself, is a partner in this gem of a restaurant, anchoring the west end of the Randolph Street restaurant row.

Opera ★★½

ASIAN/AMERICAN	MODERATE	QUALITY ★★★½	VALUE ★★

1301 South Wabash, South Loop; ☎ **312-461-0161;**
www.opera-chicago.com

Reservations Recommended. **When to go** Early evening or late night on busy weekends. **Entree range** $16–$26. **Payment** AE, D, DC, MC, V. **Service rating** ★★½. **Friendliness rating** ★★★. **Parking** $10. **Bar** Full service. **Wine selection** Austrian, Californian, Australian, Alsatian; $32–$157 bottle, $19–$69 half bottles, $9–$14 glass. **Dress** Urban chic. **Disabled access** Yes. **Customers** Hip, loud, young. **Hours** Sunday–Thursday, 5–10 p.m.; Friday and Saturday, 5 p.m.–midnight.

SETTING AND ATMOSPHERE The room is eye candy for the trendy, with odd-shaped light fixtures, colorful silk drapes, pin-cushion, jewel-toned velvet chairs, and opulent room dividers covered in Japanese newsprint. The clientele is equally colorful.

HOUSE SPECIALTIES Foie gras with glazed carrots, English peas, duck confit, mint-and-ginger orange reduction; Belgian endive salad with blue cheese, mixed greens, candied walnuts, basil oil, diced tomatoes, and hazelnut vinaigrette; spinach; fingerling potatoes; mushroom ragout with caramelized pearl onions and parsley; pear tart with almond creme, candied pistachio, and cocoa sorbet.

OTHER RECOMMENDATIONS Szechwan dry-cooked green beans with ground pork; Cantonese roast duck with plum sauce; steamed banana and date pudding with date-cognac ice cream and caramelized banana cream sauce. Vegan menu available.

SUMMARY AND COMMENTS The burgeoning South Loop area is increasingly attracting a high-style, in-the-know crowd. This spot is brimming with action from an energetic crowd and lively staff. The social aspect almost overshadows the food, which is suited for the American palate—large portions, intense flavors, and eye-popping presentations.

Orange ★★

GLOBAL/BREAKFAST	INEXPENSIVE	QUALITY ★★★	VALUE ★★★★

3231 North Clark Street, Lakeview; ☎ 773-549-4400
75 West Harrison Street, South Loop; ☎ 312-447-1000

Reservations Not accepted. **When to go** Weekend breakfast or brunch. **Entree range** $5–$12. **Payment** AE, D, DC, MC, V. **Service rating** ★★. **Friendliness rating** ★★★. **Parking** Street. **Bar** Juice only. **Wine selection** None. **Dress** Casual. **Disabled access** Yes. **Customers** Young local, hungover late-night club hoppers. **Hours** Tuesday–Sunday, 8 a.m.–3 p.m.

SETTING AND ATMOSPHERE   The Lakeview original is a homey, cheerful storefront with orange crates as art, exposed-brick walls, natural floors, and an eye-appealing fresh juice bar.

HOUSE SPECIALTIES   Frushi specialty (rice rolled with fresh fruit in fruit leather); butter-pecan pancakes; green eggs and ham (scrambled eggs with basil pesto, roasted tomatoes, buffalo mozzarella, and diced pancetta); jelly doughnut pancakes with lingonberries.

OTHER RECOMMENDATIONS   French-toast kabobs (coconut-infused French toast skewered and grilled with fresh strawberries and pineapple); hot salmon hash (potatoes, smoked salmon, celery, red onion, roasted red pepper, tarragon, dill, mustard, and two poached eggs).

SUMMARY AND COMMENTS   For a funky, lively early-morning spot, these Lakeview and South Loop gems are just the place. Fresh ingredients are the keys to clever and creative dishes and drinks. Even the coffee gets infused with orange zest. It's one of the most neighborly breakfast haunts in town.

Park Grill ★★★

AMERICAN	MODERATE	QUALITY ★★★	VALUE ★★★

11 North Michigan Avenue, The Loop; ☎ 312-521-7275;
www.parkgrillchicago.com

Reservations Accepted. **When to go** Weekend lunch or dinner. **Entree range** $13–$30; pre-theater menu $40 per person; child's menu $6. **Payment** AE, D, DC, MC, V. **Service rating** ★★. **Friendliness rating** ★★★. **Parking** Underground garage, $8 validation. **Bar** Full service. **Wine selection** Californian, Australian; $26–$275 bottle, $6–$14 glass. **Dress** Casual or business attire. **Disabled access** Yes. **Customers** Tourist, business lunch crowd. **Hours** Sunday–Thursday, 11 a.m.–9:30 p.m.; Friday and Saturday, 11 a.m.–10:30 p.m.

SETTING AND ATMOSPHERE   The enormous 375-seat space overlooks the Millennium Park ice rink (which doubles as spectacular seasonal outdoor seating) for excellent viewing out of the floor-to-ceiling windows. Two big-screen TVs are perched in the raised bar area, and the room is otherwise handsomely appointed with Brazilian wood floors, upholstered banquettes, and richly painted eggplant, moss-green, and burgundy walls.

HOUSE SPECIALTIES   Roasted Atlantic salmon with sweet corn, trumpet mushrooms, and garlic gloves; summer-tomato rigatoni pasta with broccolini, stewed tomatoes, olives, and goat cheese; calamari with roasted goat-horn peppers, caper berries, and Italian parsley; jumbo crab cakes with yellow curry sauce and snow pea–apple salad; chocolate–peanut butter tart with roasted banana and peanut brittle.

OTHER RECOMMENDATIONS Park Grill salad (chopped salad with French green beans, radishes, cucumbers, sweet peppers, onions, potatoes, tomatoes, bacon, artichoke hearts, hearts of palm, and crumbled blue cheese, with Thousand Island dressing and topped with garlic croutons); pizzas topped with tomato and basil, barbeque chicken, spinach, grilled balsamic onions, and fontina cheese, or oven-roasted tomatoes, arugula, and Parmesan cheese; sautéed whitefish with assorted squash and basil-tomato vinaigrette; veal chop with radishes, hedgehog mushrooms, and aged sherry vinaigrette.

SUMMARY AND COMMENTS The best thing about this restaurant is the spectacular view of the Chicago skyline, fronted by the ice rink at Millennium Park. The American fare is somewhat predictable but well prepared and presented with a menu offering something for everyone. Elegant fish dishes can be had alongside a decent burger or a simple appetizer. The materials—floors, wood bar, and furniture—are strikingly beautiful, crafted of natural materials like marble, slate, and Brazilian oak.

Phoenix ★★

CHINESE	MODERATE	QUALITY ★★	VALUE ★★★

2131 South Archer Avenue, Chinatown; ☎ 312-328-0848

Reservations Not accepted. **When to go** Dinner, Saturday dim sum. **Entree range** $10–$36. **Payment** AE, D, DC, MC, V. **Service rating** ★★. **Friendliness rating** ★★. **Parking** Pay lot (discounted with validation). **Bar** Full service. **Wine selection** Limited, moderately priced; $25–$50 bottle, $6 glass. **Dress** Casual. **Disabled access** Yes. **Customers** Groups, families, tourists, students, couples. **Hours** Monday–Thursday, 9 a.m.–10 p.m.; Friday, 9 a.m.–11 p.m.; Saturday, 8 a.m.–11 p.m.; Sunday, 8 a.m.–10 p.m.

SETTING AND ATMOSPHERE Somewhat upscale and plain (low-kitsch) for Chinatown, this clean and spacious Mandarin and dim sum house is a perennial favorite for families, tourists, students, dates—in other words, everyone. Big communal tables are covered with white tablecloths and lazy Susans, and second-floor windows offer panoramic city views. Expect a language barrier with the waitstaff (just point to what you want).

HOUSE SPECIALTIES Dim sum dishes include steamed shrimp dumplings; steamed pork buns; taro "bird's nests"; deep-fried seaweed wrap; silky tofu with sweet syrup; fried crab-claw dumplings; octopus in ginger; fried cuttlefish; fried bean curd; sticky rice in banana leaf; fried sesame balls with red-bean paste; custard tarts; steamed yellow cake.

OTHER RECOMMENDATIONS Main menu dishes include Peking duck; steamed whole sea bass; spicy jellyfish; baked shrimp with spiced salt; Malay-style squid; crispy orange chicken; fresh lobster steamed in Chinese wine; braised bean curd with Chinese mushrooms; Dungeness crab fried with beer; mango pudding.

SUMMARY AND COMMENTS While not up to the standards of some world-traveled dim sum purists, Phoenix aims to please with a big selection and less-grody surroundings than many of its counterparts (perhaps one reason regulars don't mind the slightly higher prices). Especially popular for its daily carts-and-communal-tables dim sum, the 500-seat space is hectic at peak hours, so if you're not into crowds (or waits), go at off-times (but be prepared for a more limited selection; on slow weekdays you might order from a dim sum menu).

 ## Piece ★★

PIZZERIA/BREW PUB   INEXPENSIVE   QUALITY ★★★   VALUE ★★★★

1927 West North Avenue, Wicker Park; ☎ 773-772-4422;
www.piecechicago.com

Reservations Not accepted. **When to go** Weekdays, late night, quick lunch. **Entree range** $12–$18. **Payment** AE, D, MC, V. **Service rating** ★★. **Friendliness rating** ★★★★. **Parking** Valet, $8 after 5 p.m. **Bar** Full bar notable for 7 house-made award-winning brews, plus 10 regional microbrews. **Wine selection** Limited Italian and American; $22–$36 bottle, $6–$9 glass. **Dress** Casual. **Disabled access** Yes. **Customers** Young, urban locals, actors, and athletes. **Hours** Monday–Thursday, 11:30 a.m.–1:30 a.m. (kitchen closes 10:30 p.m. Wednesday and 11 p.m. Thursday); Friday, 11:30 a.m.–2 a.m. (kitchen closes 12:30 a.m.); Saturday, 11 a.m.–3 a.m. (kitchen closes 12:30 a.m.); Sunday, 11 a.m.–1 a.m. (kitchen closes 10:30 p.m.).

SETTING AND ATMOSPHERE Formerly a truck garage, this lofted space still has an industrial feel with poured cement floors and high ceilings with a long glass skylight running the length. That's not to say there aren't any stylish details—a sunken lounge area up front sports blue and green comfy couches and floor-to-ceiling windows which open onto bustling North Avenue. Piece is notorious as having played a role as a *Real World* cast hangout.

HOUSE SPECIALTIES East Coast (New Haven, Connecticut)–style pizza pies topped with traditional ingredients, along with some more adventurous toppings like meatballs, clams, and broccoli rabe. Choose your base: plain (tomato with Parmesan and garlic), white (olive oil with garlic), or red (tomato with mozzarella).

OTHER RECOMMENDATIONS Wild-mushroom quesadillas; salad of candied pecans, pears, and Gorgonzola.

SUMMARY AND COMMENTS It's a natural location for this pizzeria and micro-brewery—right in the heart of the young and happening Wicker Park neighborhood. Not only does their original East Coast–crust recipe come straight from the source, but a former Sierra Nevada brewmaster was installed to supervise the microbrewery attached to this 5,800-square-foot dining room. It all works like a well-oiled machine, and there's space for crowds—even on a major game night when the many TVs are all tuned in.

HONORS AND AWARDS 2006 World Beer Cup Champion Small Brewpub and Brewmaster Award.

Prairie Grass Cafe ★★★

AMERICAN   MODERATE   QUALITY ★★★★   VALUE ★★★★

601 Skokie Boulevard, Northbrook; ☎ 847-205-4433;
www.prairiegrasscafe.com

Reservations Accepted. **When to go** Anytime but prime-time weekend dinner. **Entree range** $12–$28. **Payment** CB, D, DC, MC, V. **Service rating** ★★. **Friendliness rating** ★★★. **Parking** Lot. **Bar** Full service. **Wine selection** Moderately priced mix with American focus, $15–$280 bottle, $7–$12 glass. **Dress** Casual chic. **Disabled access** Yes. **Customers** Couples from the north suburbs, work groups, families. **Hours** Tuesday–Thursday, 11 a.m.–2 p.m. and 5–9:30 p.m.; Friday, 11 a.m.–2 p.m. and 5–10:30 p.m.; Saturday, 9 a.m.–2 p.m. (brunch) and 5–10:30 p.m.; Sunday, 9 a.m.–2 p.m. (brunch) and 5–9 p.m.

SETTING AND ATMOSPHERE Open dining amid a modernized Prairie School milieu sets a casually sophisticated tone that bustles when busy. The room is chic yet warm in stone and wood, with giant hovering light fixtures, and a dividing line of plasma TVs between bar and dining, slow-pulsing random images, including amber waves of grain.

HOUSE SPECIALTIES Slice of Amish blue cheese and grapes rolled in candied walnuts; homemade pâté in a crock with apples and port wine–balsamic reduction; baked feta cheese, spicy banana peppers, and tomatoes; shepherd's pie; moussaka; crispy half boneless chicken; Parmesan-crusted halibut with warm pesto–green bean salad, twice baked with caramelized onions and Gruyère cheese; baked pear in almond cake; Mom's seasonal pie.

OTHER RECOMMENDATIONS Lunch includes a generous selection of entree salads, burgers, and crepes; brunch favorites include yogurt parfait; challah French toast with strawberry compote and ricotta; smoked salmon benedict; large French-style crepes with raspberry cream, fresh berries, and mint sauce, or Greek yogurt and brown sugar with brûléed banana, or balsamic-glazed mushrooms and Gruyère cheese.

SUMMARY AND COMMENTS When top-ranked Ritz-Carlton chefs Sarah Stegner and George Bumbaris headed for the 'burbs to cook comfort food, most of Chicago had culinary whiplash. The results are a solid success showcasing their über-satisfying American cooking (and Sarah's mom's lovely pies)—if you can overlook the sometimes suburban-quality service. Kids can make their own pizzas on Friday nights.

Salpicon ★★★

REGIONAL MEXICAN   MODERATE   QUALITY ★★★★½   VALUE ★★★

1252 North Wells Street, Old Town; ☎ 312-988-7811; www.salpicon.com

Reservations Recommended. **When to go** Lively weekend dinner. **Entree range** $17–$29. **Payment** AE, D, DC, MC, V. **Service rating** ★★★. **Friendliness rating** ★★½. **Parking** Valet, $8. **Bar** Beer, wine, and tequila drinks only. **Wine selection** French, American, Australian, Chilean, Austrian, and German, $22–$400 bottle; several by the glass, $8–$17. **Dress** Chic to casual. **Disabled access** Yes.

Customers Urban workers, mature locals. **Hours** Sunday–Thursday, 5–10 p.m.; Friday and Saturday, 5–11 p.m.; Sunday brunch, 11 a.m.–2:30 p.m.

SETTING AND ATMOSPHERE The lively two-room storefront space is splashed with color, from the brightly painted walls to the large Mexican canvases and artifacts. Tables are tightly spaced, making it feel inordinately crowded at times.

HOUSE SPECIALTIES Jalapeños rellenos de queso *capeados* (jalapeños stuffed with Chihuahua cheese, dipped in light egg batter, sautéed, and served with black-bean sauce); three corn tamales: one with queso fresco, serrano chiles, mocajete salsa, and crema; another with black beans, rajas, Chihuahua cheese, and black-bean puree; and another with zucchini and chipotles; *costillitas de borrego con salsa de chile pasilla y tomatillos* (rack of baby lamb encrusted with pumpkinseeds and served with pasilla-tomatillo sauce, sautéed fingerling potatoes, and spinach).

OTHER RECOMMENDATIONS *Pescado al carbón* (fillet of seasonal fish, charcoal-grilled and served with salsa and white rice); chef's seven-course tasting menu ($60; subject to availability, so check when reserving).

SUMMARY AND COMMENTS Chef Priscila Satkoff prepares the Mexican cuisine of her homeland in an elegant, upscale manner. Dishes can be spicy, so it's best to inquire before ordering. The menu features clean, authentic flavors from the indigenous ingredients, like chipotle chiles, mangos, tomatillos, and her fabulous homemade mole. An on-site wine cellar houses over 800 bottles of wine for an outstanding selection, not to mention a killer premium tequila list.

Santorini ★★★

GREEK/SEAFOOD	EXPENSIVE	QUALITY ★★★	VALUE ★★★

800 West Adams Street, Greektown; ☎ 312-829-8820; www.santorinichicago.com

Reservations Accepted. **When to go** Before United Center events. **Entree range** $11–$39. **Payment** AE, D, DC, MC, V. **Service rating** ★★★½. **Friendliness rating** ★★★. **Parking** Valet, free. **Bar** Full service. **Wine selection** Greek, French, Californian, and Italian; $17–$250 bottle, $5–$12 glass. **Dress** Casual to dressy. **Disabled access** Yes. **Customers** Mixed crowd; professionals by day, families and suburbanites by evening. **Hours** Sunday–Thursday, 11 a.m.–midnight; Friday and Saturday, 11 a.m.–1 a.m.

SETTING AND ATMOSPHERE This upscale Greektown eatery has a wood-burning fireplace in the center of the dining room, with various Mediterranean artifacts and baskets scattered about. It's rustic, homey, and comfortable.

HOUSE SPECIALTIES Roasted whole fish (red snapper or black sea bass), prepared simply with olive oil and lemon juice; Kamari beach calamari char-grilled with garlic, lemon juice, and olive oil; lemon sole; seafood platter (lobster, shrimp, oysters, and fish).

OTHER RECOMMENDATIONS Char-grilled octopus; tzatziki; *kolokithakis* (fried zucchini with garlic sauce); Florida grouper.

SUMMARY AND COMMENTS This cozy yet bustling addition to Greektown specializes in seafood, with Mediterranean-style whole fish that's a standout. Service is professional and attentive, accommodating sports fans on their way to a game. Family-style multi-course dinners are offered for large parties at a rate of $19 to $39 per person.

Scylla ★★★½

SEAFOOD/MEDITERRANEAN	MODERATE	QUALITY ★★★½	VALUE ★★★

1952 North Damen Avenue, Bucktown; ☎ 773-227-2995;
www.scyllarestaurant.com

Reservations Recommended. **When to go** Dinner, special occasions. **Entree range** $6–$18. **Payment** AE, D, DC, MC, V. **Service rating** ★★★½. **Friendliness rating** ★★★. **Parking** Valet, $8. **Bar** Full service. **Wine selection** Limited, global, moderately priced; $32–$115 bottle, $7–$15 glass. **Dress** Upscale casual, trendy. **Disabled access** Yes. **Customers** Foodies, trendies, locals. **Hours** Tuesday–Thursday, 5:30–10 p.m.; Friday and Saturday, 5:30–11 p.m.; Sunday, 5–9 p.m.

SETTING AND ATMOSPHERE Subtle sea-monster references, whimsical metalwork and paintings, funky colors, and glossy mahogany accent this little Bucktown seafood house in a converted 1879 brownstone. Tables are cozy; there's a lounge bar upstairs and patio dining in season.

HOUSE SPECIALTIES Seasonal dishes might include lobster caprese salad with tomato sorbet, basil gelée, and lobster espresso; sautéed diver scallops with braised pork belly, fruit-and-vegetable ratatouille, and arugula salsa verde; pan-roasted halibut with escargot-stuffed black Mission figs, pancetta, and pine nut–roasted-garlic sauce; grilled jumbo shrimp with shredded ham, white beans, roasted tomato, picholine olives, ricotta salata, and sorrel vinaigrette.

OTHER RECOMMENDATIONS Landlubbers can try dishes like goat cheese "lasagna" with eggplant-and-fennel caponata and heirloom-tomato sauce; roasted Muscovy duck breast with apricot-and-confit crepes and grilled sweet corn in gingered ale sauce; pan-roasted quail with white polenta and apricot–brown ale sauce.

SUMMARY AND COMMENTS Stephanie Izard (veteran of Spring and Vong) has made a name for herself cooking Mediterranean-tinged, seasonal seafood of all sorts (with a smattering of meat and vegetarian dishes), with creative preps, smashing presentations, and hip, knowledgeable servers sealing the deal. She plays fast and loose with conventional sweet-and-savory thinking—in both the main and dessert creations—so read the menu carefully if you're averse to offbeat combinations.

Seasons ★★★★

NEW AMERICAN	VERY EXPENSIVE	QUALITY ★★★★	VALUE ★★

120 East Delaware Place, Gold Coast; ☎ 312-649-2349;
www.fourseasons.com/chicagofs/dining.html

Reservations Highly recommended. **When to go** Big moments, big business. **Entree range** $32–$46; 5-course tasting menu $86, 8-course grand tasting menu

$105. **Payment** AE, CB, D, DC, MC, V. **Service rating** ★★★★. **Friendliness rating** ★★. **Parking** Lot (hourly or $27 for 24 hours; restaurant validation discount); valet (hourly or $40 for 24 hours). **Bar** Full service. **Wine selection** Fine, extensive, California-centric; $32–$670 bottle, $9–$24 glass. **Dress** Jacket suggested. **Disabled access** Yes. **Customers** Business travelers, sedate couples, celebrants. **Hours** Daily, 6:30 a.m.–10 p.m.

SETTING AND ATMOSPHERE   This civilized aerie above the Gold Coast offers a traditional, tasteful setting of plush carpets, mahogany walls, chandeliers, and oversized upholstered chairs—all enhanced by views of Michigan Avenue and Gold Coast goings-on. It's a grand, classy setting for a deal, be it business or romance.

> *unofficial* **TIP**
> The top-dollar brunch at Seasons is best for hotel guests who don't feel like leaving the property.

HOUSE SPECIALTIES   Representative seasonal dishes have included organic carnaroli risotto with green garlic and Burgundy hazelnut snails; surf-and-turf tartare of American Kobe beef with violet-mustard ahi tuna, wasabi sorbet, and tamari soy gelée; Alaskan halibut cooked in a clay pot with Kaffir lime–scented broth, Chinese sausage, forbidden black rice, and Thai basil; farmer's egg ravioli with celeriac and white-truffle sauce; smoked paprika–crusted duck with persimmon gastrique, duck confit agnolotti, and creamed Brussels sprouts.

OTHER RECOMMENDATIONS   The buffet lunch and high tea in Seasons Café are both delightful and a better value than Seasons, though hardly the caliber of dining, of course. Depends on what you're looking for.

SUMMARY AND COMMENTS   While chefs come and go here and the resulting output hovers between three and a half and five stars, Seasons delivers a quality New American dining experience with formal pampering on the side. There's a time for this sort of dining—and Seasons is a good place for it. Expense accounters should take advantage of the great wine list.

Shaw's Crab House ★★★½

SEAFOOD	EXPENSIVE	QUALITY ★★★½	VALUE ★★

**21 East Hubbard Street, River North; ☎ 312-527-2722; www.shawscrabhouse.com/chicago.html
Shaw's Seafood Grill, 1900 East Higgins Road, Schaumburg; ☎ 847-517-2722**

Reservations Recommended. **When to go** Anytime. **Entree range** $12–$57. **Payment** All major credit cards. **Service rating** ★★★½. **Friendliness rating** ★★★½. **Parking** Valet, $9. **Bar** Full service. **Wine selection** 175+ domestic selections, $19–$280; 20 by the glass, $6–$15. **Dress** Business casual, dressy. **Disabled access** Wheelchair accessible. **Customers** Professionals, tourists, and seafood lovers. **Hours** Monday–Thursday, 11:30 a.m.–2 p.m. and 5:30–10 p.m.; Friday, 11:30 a.m.–2 p.m. and 5–11 p.m.; Saturday, 5–11 p.m.; Sunday, 5–10 p.m.

SETTING AND ATMOSPHERE   Upscale and clubby, with rich woods and all the accouterments of fine dining.

HOUSE SPECIALTIES Fresh oysters, generally seven regional selections plus a sampler plate; seasonal crab (for example, chilled Florida stone-crab claws, Alaskan "red" king-crab legs, Alaskan Dungeness); Shaw's crab cakes; fresh Maine lobster, whole or stuffed.

OTHER RECOMMENDATIONS Fried oyster Caesar salad; sautéed yellow perch with tartar sauce; grilled red grouper with asparagus and pepper–caper relish; grilled and sesame-crusted yellowfin tuna with Asian salad and sashimi sauce; planked whitefish with potatoes; sautéed sole with green beans and tomato-herb butter.

SUMMARY AND COMMENTS Though the tariff is high, this is the price we pay for fresh seafood in the Midwest. The quality and selection are there for lovers of the bounties of the sea, and the clubby atmosphere is suitably toney. Service is polished and professional. The adjoining Blue Crab Lounge is more casual (as is Schaumburg's Oyster Bar), with a great East Coast oyster bar feel and occasional live music.

Smith & Wollensky ★★★½

STEAK	EXPENSIVE	QUALITY ★★★★	VALUE ★★

318 North State Street, River North; ☎ **312-670-9900;**
www.smithandwollensky.com/LOC-Chicago-Hours.asp

Reservations Suggested. **When to go** Deals and dates. **Entree range** $16–$51. **Payment** All major credit cards. **Service rating** ★★★. **Friendliness rating** ★★★. **Parking** Valet, $10. **Bar** Full service. **Wine selection** 200+ selections, mostly Californian, French, Italian, and German, $19–$2,800; 20 by the glass, $6–$15. **Dress** Casual, business. **Disabled access** Yes. **Customers** Older power money, professionals, and upscale diners. **Hours** Daily, 11:30 a.m.–11:30 p.m.; grill open until 1:30 a.m.

unofficial **TIP**
Wollensky's Grill, below Smith & Wollensky's main dining room, has lower prices on dishes that are comparable to those at the main restaurant.

SETTING AND ATMOSPHERE Smith & Wollensky has one of the most beautiful, inviting buildings and locations in town, with a grand entrance and clubby steak-house atmosphere of dark wood, marble, creamy walls, and globe light fixtures. The pomp is punctuated with a whimsical collection of American folk art, including a group of antique carved bears commemorating Chicago Bear greats. Great outdoor dining on the Chicago River in warm weather.

HOUSE SPECIALTIES Smoked pastrami salad; Wollensky's salad; split-pea soup; Maryland crab cakes; filet au poivre; sirloin steak; crackling pork shank with firecracker applesauce; "angry" lobster.

OTHER RECOMMENDATIONS Caesar salad; Maine lobster, steamed or broiled; veal chop; mustard-crusted tuna; lemon-pepper chicken; creamed spinach; Cape Cod lobster and shrimp roll (lunch only).

SUMMARY AND COMMENTS This pedigreed New York import gives great steak and great steak-house ambience, making it a great place to satisfy those carnivorous cravings. It has the feel of a classic, though it's only been around a few years.

Spiaggia ★★★★★

ITALIAN	VERY EXPENSIVE	QUALITY ★★★★★	VALUE ★★★

**980 North Michigan Avenue, Gold Coast; ☎ 312-280-2750;
www.levyrestaurants.com**

Reservations Required Friday and Saturday nights, recommended at other times.
When to go Big deals, special occasions. **Entree range** $17–$40. **Payment** All major
credit cards. **Service rating** ★★★★½. **Friendliness rating** ★★★½. **Parking** Lot in
building, $14 (validated). **Bar** Full service; numerous grappas, brandies, and *amari*
(*digestivi*). **Wine selection** 600–700 Italian varietals and prestige cuvée Champagnes,
$35–$2,000; 10 wines by the glass, $8–$20. **Dress** Jacket required for dinner, recommended for lunch; tie optional; no jeans or gym shoes. **Disabled access** Wheelchair
accessible. **Customers** Mature couples, international business types, upscale special-
occasion celebrants. **Hours** Monday–Thursday, 6 p.m.–9:30 p.m.; Friday and Saturday, 5:30 p.m.–10:30 p.m.; Sunday, 6 p.m.–9 p.m.

SETTING AND ATMOSPHERE Spiaggia's ultrasophisticated ambience is dramatically enhanced by looming 40-foot windows overlooking the
fashionable intersection of Oak Street and Michigan Avenue. The multi-
tiered, architectural dining room is done in subtle neutrals with
spectacular light fixtures, black-marble pillars, and topiary. Tables are
sumptuously appointed. The cheese "cave" storage system harbors
wonderful postprandial delights.

HOUSE SPECIALTIES Raw tuna and yellowtail with osetra caviar, citrus, and
2005 Cappezzana extra-virgin olive oil; veal-filled pasta with fennel
pollen and braised veal breast; wood-roasted filet mignon with sunchoke
puree–veal reduction, black trumpet mushrooms, and handcrafted
black spaghetti with scungill, tomatoes, and basil.

OTHER RECOMMENDATIONS Wood-roasted sea scallops with fennel puree, summer vegetables, and chef's garden micro rapini; fire-roasted summer eggplant with warm tomino cheese, wild arugula, and lemon marmelatta.

SUMMARY AND COMMENTS Spiaggia has long been known as Chicago's finest
Italian restaurant. Chef Tony Mantuano has a deft hand with luxury
ingredients and simply beautiful presentations, with fine wines and gra-
cious service rounding out a superlative Italian-dining experience.

Spring ★★★★½

SEAFOOD/NEW AMERICAN	EXPENSIVE	QUALITY ★★★★	VALUE ★★

**2039 West North Avenue, Wicker Park; ☎ 773-395-7100;
www.springrestaurant.net**

Reservations Required. **When to go** Weekday dinner to avoid long waits. **Entree
range** $31–$50. **Payment** AE, D, MC, V. **Service rating** ★★★★. **Friendliness
rating** ★★. **Parking** Valet, $9. **Bar** Full service. **Wine selection** French, Califor-
nian, Italian, and Austrian; $36–$250 bottle, $21–$85 half bottles, $8–$14 glass.
Dress Casual chic. **Disabled access** Yes. **Customers** Trendy young locals and suburbanites. **Hours** Tuesday–Thursday, 5:30–10 p.m.; Friday and Saturday, 5:30–
10:30 p.m.; Sunday, 5:30–9 p.m.; closed Monday.

SETTING AND ATMOSPHERE Formerly a Roman bath house, the subterranean pool area is now the dining room with a Zen garden at the entrance and minimalist decor. The feng shui space has tables zigzagging down the center, separated by high banquets for privacy. Pistachio-colored walls are illuminated by recessed lights, making the room glow.

HOUSE SPECIALTIES Fresh Hawaiian hearts of palm and green papaya salad with Maine lobster, shrimp, fresh mint, and a ginger dressing; lemongrass and coconut soup with red Thai curry and cellophane noodles; Dungeness crab salad with caviar, avocado, and cucumber; sea scallop and potato "raviolis" with mushroom broth and truffle essence; baramundi with grilled trumpet royale mushrooms, parsley root purée, and white asparagus; poached pear strudel with walnuts, *cajeta* ice cream, and port-wine caramel.

OTHER RECOMMENDATIONS Maine lobster tempura with buckwheat soba noodles and apple-ginger broth; roasted red snapper with lobster and crabmeat risotto and lobster-vanilla reduction; sturgeon with roasted fingerling potatoes, horseradish sauce, and pickled beet relish; parsnip cake with cream-cheese ice cream.

SUMMARY AND COMMENTS It didn't take this elegant newcomer long to make a splash in the dining scene. It's already highly touted as one of the best new restaurants in town, and reservations can take months to secure. But the serene space—combined with the exquisitely prepared and executed dishes, fabulously broad wine list, and professional servers—make it no wonder. It's garnering just attention for the innovative Asian-inspired fare, which incorporates layers of ingredients in innovative combinations.

kids Superdawg Drive-In ★★

FAST FOOD	INEXPENSIVE	QUALITY ★★½	VALUE ★★

6363 North Milwaukee Avenue, North Central Chicago;
☎ **773-763-0660; www.superdawg.com**

Reservations Not accepted. **When to go** For a junk food or nostalgia fix. **Entree range** $4–$9 (fries included). **Payment** Cash only. **Service rating** ★★. **Friendliness rating** ★★★★. **Parking** Lot. **Bar** None. **Wine selection** None. **Dress** Casual. **Disabled access** Yes. **Customers** Dawg lovers of all stripes. **Hours** Sunday–Thursday, 11 a.m.–1 a.m.; Friday and Saturday, 11 a.m.–2 a.m.

SETTING AND ATMOSPHERE The kitsch factor and old-timey, tray-on-the-window carhop service set this landmark hot-dog haven apart from the pack. That, and the adorable little boxes with fetching wienie graphics, and the hilarious he-man/cutie-pie costumed hot dogs on the roof.

HOUSE SPECIALTIES Superdawg (pure-beef hot dog with mustard, piccalilli—aka fluorescent relish, kosher dill pickle, chopped Spanish onions, and hot peppers); Whoopskidawg (Polish sausage with special sauce and grilled onions); Whoopercheesie (fresh ground 100% beef double cheeseburger in a single bun); Superonionchips (chip-shaped chunks of battered onions); ice-cream sundaes and malts.

OTHER RECOMMENDATIONS Supershrimp (fried-shrimp boat with toasted bun); Superchickenmidgees (battered chicken strips); Superveggies (mixed battered vegetables); pineapple shakes.

SUMMARY AND COMMENTS Okay, it's junk food, and it's beyond out of the way. And there's—gasp!—no celery salt. And the fat crinkle fries are more limp than crispy. But somehow it all works. And if you want a slice of vintage Americana with your Chicago dog, you can't beat this time-warped slice of the 1940s.

SushiSamba Rio ★★½

LATINO NUEVO/SUSHI	EXPENSIVE	QUALITY ★★★	VALUE ★★

504 North Wells Street, River North; ☎ 312-595-2300; www.sushisamba.com

Reservations Accepted. **When to go** Weekend evenings. **Entree range** $12–$43. **Payment** AE, D, DC, MC, V. **Service rating** ★★. **Friendliness rating** ★★. **Parking** Valet, $10. **Bar** Full service with dozens of sake varieties, plus martinis, mojitos, and caipirinhas. **Wine selection** Californian, French, Austrian, German; $24–$325 bottle, $8–$14 glass. **Dress** Hip and modern. **Disabled access** Yes. **Customers** Trendy club-hoppers. **Hours** Sunday–Wednesday, 11:45 a.m.–12 a.m.; Thursday and Friday, 11:45 a.m.–1 a.m.; Saturday, 11:45 a.m.–2 a.m.; Sunday brunch, 11:45 a.m.–3:30 p.m.

SETTING AND ATMOSPHERE The dizzying room, designed by David Rockwell, is like the Cirque du Soleil of restaurants, with glittering beads hanging, reflective light fixtures suspended from the ceiling, backlit panels on the walls, and raised seating areas along the perimeter. A 20-seat sushi bar centers the room, surrounded by wavy patterns of tables, all surrounded by thumping Latin tunes. The covered outdoor dining area is one of River North's hottest seats in warm weather.

HOUSE SPECIALTIES Raw regional oysters; a variety of seviches (which come on a tasting platter); braised pork belly with roasted Peruvian potatoes; miso-marinated black cod; Brazilian churrascos of barbecued pork, chorizo, rib eye, and hanger steak; Chi-Town roll with spicy tuna and crispy salmon skin with hazelnut ponzu sauce; *moqueca mista* (a paella-like collection of nicely handled seafood with coconut milk and rice).

OTHER RECOMMENDATIONS Sushi and maki in dozens of varieties; shrimp tempura; *sawagani* (tiny Japanese river crabs flash-fried and salted); citrus-cured lobster seviche presented in hollowed lobster shell with spicy balsamic-mango sorbet; *anticuchos* (skewered meats), including cubes of grilled beef with mild red chile paste, or teriyaki-seasoned chicken livers, served on a bed of Peruvian white corn niblets.

SUMMARY AND COMMENTS The room and the music are quite loud at this branch of the chain (other incarnations are in New York and Miami). Japanese, Brazilian, and Peruvian food meet at a crossroads on the extraordinarily large menu. The food isn't fusion—rather, the menu is neatly separated into sections representing each cuisine. The front bar is frequently packed with those waiting, sometimes for up to an hour, for a coveted table in the main dining room, although the full menu can be had at the bar as well.

Three Happiness ★★½

| CHINESE | INEXPENSIVE | QUALITY ★★★½ | VALUE ★★★★★ |

209 West Cermak Road, Chinatown; ☎ 312-842-1964

Reservations Accepted. **When to go** Busy for lunch, crowds on weekend evenings. **Entree range** $8–$20. **Payment** AE, D, DC, MC, V. **Service rating** ★★★. **Friendliness rating** ★★★★. **Parking** Pay lot, $1.50 (will validate). **Bar** Full service. **Wine selection** Limited, but sake and plum wine also served. **Dress** Casual. **Disabled access** Yes. **Customers** Diverse crowd; university and Loop workers. **Hours** Daily, 9 a.m.–2 a.m.

SETTING AND ATMOSPHERE The simple, small room isn't fancy, but it's clean and efficient, and the friendly staff and owner help make it comfortable. Simple linoleum floors, a red Tsing Tao paper dragon hanging from the ceiling, and booths lining the perimeter of the room complete the decor. The family-style dining with revolving lazy Susans at most tables makes for lively conversation both at lunch and dinner.

HOUSE SPECIALTIES Spare ribs with black-bean-and-garlic sauce; Szechwan diced chicken; shrimp lobster-style; pork chop Mandarin-style; seaweed soup; Buddhist delight (vegetarian medley of stir-fried vegetables).

OTHER RECOMMENDATIONS Pan-fried prawn in the shell; five-spice soy chicken; beef with ginger and scallion; various dim sum dishes served all day long, such as pan-fried taro root cake; rice in lotus leaf with pork and chicken; *kow wong* (chicken and bean sprouts in rice pancake).

SUMMARY AND COMMENTS As the oldest establishment in Chinatown, this small storefront (easily confused with—but unrelated to—the prosaic, larger "New Three Happiness" on the corner) maintains high-quality fare. Lunch is a real bargain—$3.95 for a meal soup-to-nuts—but dinner or à la carte ordering allows for sampling of more interesting dishes from the incredibly broad menu. Dim sum, the small dishes normally served for a unique brunch, is available all day, every day. It's a midweek delight for adventurous nibblers.

Topolobampo ★★★★½

| REGIONAL MEXICAN | VERY EXPENSIVE | QUALITY ★★★★★ | VALUE ★★★ |

445 North Clark Street, River North; ☎ 312-661-1434; www.fronterakitchens.com

Reservations Accepted for parties up to 8. **When to go** Weeknight dinner. **Entree range** $16–$40; chef's 5-course tasting menu, $75, $115 with wine pairing. **Payment** All major credit cards. **Service rating** ★★★★. **Friendliness rating** ★★★½. **Parking** Valet, $10; public lots; street. **Bar** Extensive premium tequila list, margaritas, brandies, and beer. **Wine selection** Extensive global, 120 selections, $30–$260; 10 by the glass, $6–$11. **Dress** Casual. **Disabled access** Wheelchair accessible. **Customers** Upscale locals and travelers, professionals, and couples. **Hours** Tuesday–

Thursday, 11:30 a.m.–2 p.m. and 5:30–9:30 p.m.; Friday, 11:30 a.m.–2 p.m. and 5:30–10:30 p.m.; Saturday, 5:30–10:30 p.m.; closed Sunday and Monday.

SETTING AND ATMOSPHERE   Jeweled blues and sun-drenched hues of oranges and golds; colorful, evocative Mexican folk and fine art. Though more formal than the more casual Frontera Grill adjacent, the Topolobampo dining room tempers its sophistication with a sense of fun.

HOUSE SPECIALTIES   The menu of Mexican celebratory dishes, game, and little-known regional specialties changes every two weeks, and no single dish is considered a house specialty. Sample items might include *ensalada de chayote* (tender, delicate chayote salad dressed with Spanish sparkling-wine vinaigrette, housemade goat-milk queso fresco, Neuske bacon, water-cress, and pickled red onions); *langosta en crema de calabaza* (super-sweet roasted Maine lobster in ancho-tinged pumpkin cream with mushroom and chard–stuffed delicata); *cochinita adobada* (Maple Creek Farm pork slow-roasted in banana leaves with *guajillo* chile marinade, served with rich pan juices, grilled acorn squash, and braised greens).

OTHER RECOMMENDATIONS   A few lunch items remain constant, including *pollito en mole verde* (roasted, marinated free-range baby chicken with classic green pumpkinseed mole, Mexican greens, and heirloom beans); *Milanese de puerco* (crunchy-coated pork tenderloin, panfried in olive oil, with a spicy salsa of tomatoes, habañeros, onions, and sour orange with baby lettuces and pickled red onions); *chilaquiles verdes* (tangy tomatillo sauce simmered with crispy tortillas, topped with grilled chicken, thick cream, and jicama); *cuatro cositas* (a sampler plate of chicken enchilada in roasted tomatillo sauce; griddle-baked quesadilla of Jack cheese, duck, and peppers; tostada of marinated cactus salad; and black beans); lime tart.

SUMMARY AND COMMENTS   Considered by many the nation's forerunner of fine Mexican dining, Topolobampo opens up a whole new world of soulful flavors from the regions of Mexico. Owner Rick Bayless is a true culinary artist and a dedicated scholar of Mexican cuisine (author of several cookbooks, he is also the host of *Mexico: One Plate at a Time* on PBS). The ever-changing menu creates a sense of unfolding seasonal pageantry that keeps loyalists returning frequently for another trip to Mexican culinary heaven. Make reservations well in advance. The adja-cent sister restaurant, Frontera Grill, offers a less formal (and less expensive) variation on Bayless's trailblazing regional-Mexican theme.

Tru ★★★★★

NEW AMERICAN   VERY EXPENSIVE   QUALITY ★★★★★   VALUE ★★★

676 North St. Clair Street, Streeterville; ☎ 312-202-0001; www.trurestaurant.com

Reservations Highly recommended. **When to go** Dinner. **Entree range** Prix-fixe "collections" only: 3 courses, $90; 6 courses, vegetable, $100; 7 courses, chef, $110. **Payment** All major credit cards. **Service rating** ★★★★½. **Friendliness rat-ing** ★★★. **Parking** Valet, $10; nearby lots and garages. **Bar** Full service. **Wine**

selection 1,700 wines, diverse with an emphasis on France and California, $32–$2,300; 17 wines and Champagnes by the glass, $9–$45. **Dress** Jackets required for men; ties requested. **Disabled access** Wheelchair accessible. **Customers** Power money, Michigan Avenue denizens, creative professionals. **Hours** Monday–Thursday, 5:30–10 p.m.; Friday and Saturday, 5–11 p.m.; closed Sunday.

SETTING AND ATMOSPHERE The dining room is ultracontemporary, stark, and simple with a few original artworks (Warhol, Mapplethorpe); the buzz of the patrons and the plushy blue-velvet purse stools keep the space from feeling sterile. The restaurant's signature whimsy appears in touches like a "Zen garden" of handmade lollipops in sugar "sand." Don't miss the gravity-defying bathroom sinks.

HOUSE SPECIALTIES With a constantly changing menu, regular items are few. Some mainstays include the caviar staircase, a sculptural glass spiral staircase dotted with various caviars and fixin's; a tasting of various exquisite soups in eye-popping Gianni Versace cappuccino cups; any of chef Rick Tramonto's various foie gras preparations; Gale Gand's roasted-pineapple carpaccio with coconut-cilantro dressing and buttermilk-key lime sherbet; bittersweet chocolate tarte with malt vanilla crème brûlée and espresso madeleine; and her house-made animal crackers and *mignardises* (petits fours).

OTHER RECOMMENDATIONS Sample menu items might run along the lines of roasted Scottish salmon; braised endive with porcini and scallion crema; roasted veal tenderloin; veal sweetbread ragoût with sauce supreme; grilled beef with potato purée and bone-marrow foam; chocolate-mousse crepe with banana bisque and candied mint; carrot cake with cream cheese crottin; peanut-butter-and-banana-bread pudding.

SUMMARY AND COMMENTS Stunning Tru represents another collaboration between Rich Melman's Lettuce Entertain You and established, high-end chef talent. The high-concept fare is renowned for its contemporary creativity with touches of humor leavening the sophistication (like a dish served perched on a "fishbowl" with live tropical fish). This is très chic—and très lengthy—dining, so plan to make an evening of it, especially if you want to experience the full spectrum of the larger collection menus (choices also include vegetarian and seafood). European-style team service; no smoking, and no cell phones in the dining room.

 Twin Anchors ★★½

| AMERICAN/RIBS | MODERATE | QUALITY ★★½ | VALUE ★★★ |

1655 North Sedgwick Street, Old Town; ☎ 312-266-1616; www.twinanchorsribs.com

Reservations Not accepted. **When to go** Weekend lunch, early dinner. **Entree range** $11–$24. **Payment** AE, CB, D, DC, MC, V. **Service rating** ★★. **Friendliness rating** ★★★. **Parking** Street, valet $7. **Bar** Full service. **Wine selection** Extremely limited, generic; $25–$35 bottle, $6–$9 glass. **Dress** Casual. **Disabled access** No. **Customers** Locals, characters, rib lovers. **Hours** Monday–Thursday, 5–11 p.m.; Friday, 5 p.m.–midnight; Saturday, noon–midnight; Sunday, noon–10:30 p.m.

SETTING AND ATMOSPHERE Raucous, casual, and comfy, this Chicago neighborhood classic has the kind of history that restaurant developers are always trying to fake. A Frank Sinatra hangout in the old days and the setting for the film *Return to Me,* this divey Wisconsin-like saloon opened in 1932 (in an 1881 building). The mood is set by Old Town memorabilia, perpetual sports on TV, an eclectic jukebox heavy on the nostalgia, and, yes, two big anchors. The notorious "Positively no dancing" sign was posted in the disco days, when Travolta wannabes were interfering with service. Nice patio, too.

HOUSE SPECIALTIES Barbecued baby-back ribs and chicken; chili; burgers; baked beans; onion rings; dark rye bread; cheesecake.

OTHER RECOMMENDATIONS Caesar salad; New York strip steak; fish fry; giant grilled shrimp; vegetarian sloppy joe.

SUMMARY AND COMMENTS While fanatics debate the relative merits of the original sweet sauce ("zesty" is available) and fall-off-the-bone texture, the long waits here speak for themselves. But, actually, the thing people seem to love most about this ribs-and-a-cold-one institution is that it stays the same. Service can be brusque. Carryout is a good option, and you can ship their ribs if you get hooked.

unofficial **TIP**
Lots of celebs have visited Twin Anchors, with prime seats being Booth 7 (Frank Sinatra) and Booth 5 (John Belushi and Dan Aykroyd). Kids get their own menu items, games, and crayons.

kids Wishbone ★★½

| CAJUN/SOUTHERN | INEXPENSIVE | QUALITY ★★★ | VALUE ★★★★★ |

3300 North Lincoln Avenue, Lakeview; ☎ 773-549-2663
1001 West Washington Boulevard, West Loop; ☎ 312-850-2663;
www.wishbonechicago.com

Reservations Required at lunch for parties of 6 or more. **When to go** Brunch, casual dinner. **Entree range** $5–$15. **Payment** AE, D, DC, MC, V. **Service rating** ★★. **Friendliness rating** ★★★. **Parking** Valet, $6; street. **Bar** Full service. **Wine selection** Limited, $14–$26; 13 by the glass, $5–$8. **Dress** Casual. **Disabled access** Wheelchair accessible. **Customers** Come-as-you-are locals, families. **Hours** (Lincoln) *Brunch:* Saturday and Sunday, 8 a.m.–2:30 p.m. *Breakfast:* Monday–Friday, 7 a.m.–3 p.m. *Lunch:* Monday–Friday, 11 a.m.–3 p.m. *Dinner:* Wednesday, Thursday, and Sunday, 5 p.m.–9 p.m.; Friday and Saturday, 5 p.m.– 10 p.m. (Washington) *Brunch:* Saturday and Sunday, 8 a.m.–3 p.m. *Breakfast:* 7 a.m.–11 a.m. *Lunch:* Monday–Friday, 11 a.m.–3 p.m. *Dinner:* Tuesday–Thursday, 5 p.m.–9 p.m.; Friday and Saturday, 5 p.m.–10 p.m.

SETTING AND ATMOSPHERE This funky-casual, warehouse-style restaurant is a big, exposed brick room with lots of windows and whimsical chicken-and-egg art. There's a cafeteria-style counter for quick, inexpensive meals.

HOUSE SPECIALTIES Menu specialties change daily. Possibilities include shrimp sautéed with bacon, mushrooms, and scallions, served over cheese grits; blackened chicken pan-seared in Cajun spices and served with coleslaw garnish; blackened catfish (fresh farm-raised catfish fillet, blackened with Cajun spices); red eggs (two eggs over corn tortillas with black beans, cheese, chili ancho sauce, scallions, sour cream, and salsa); and French toast dipped in cornflakes.

OTHER RECOMMENDATIONS Louisiana chicken salad (enormous salad with blackened chicken breast and corn muffin); North Carolina crab cakes; hoppin' John or hoppin' Jack (vegetarian black-eyed peas or black beans on rice with Cheddar cheese, scallions, and tomatoes).

SUMMARY AND COMMENTS The casual-dining and tousled brunch crowds head here for "Southern reconstruction cooking" that's hearty and inexpensive, though hit or miss. There are numerous vegetarian options, as well as full-pint Bloody Marys. This is a prime destination for families with kids—there's a children's menu for breakfast, lunch, and dinner (till the 7 p.m. "adult swim"). On Thursday nights, the Lincoln Avenue location has traditional Irish music by performers with puppets from 6:30 to 9 p.m.

PART NINE

SHOPPING *in* CHICAGO

by Laurie Levy

◼ "NOTHING *Like It* BACK HOME"

VISITORS WHO COME TO CHICAGO TO SHOP expecting Second (or Third) City are overjoyed. Time was, fashion was the resultant mélange of trends that blew in from the Coast (either one). No more. Said mélange floated down "Boul Mich" (that is, Michigan Avenue), blew west across the Loop, fanned north and south, and became Chicago Style. Suddenly, the world sat up and took notice.

And it only gets better.

The City of the Big Shoulders still takes the best of the West, combines it with the best of the East, imports every possible plum from abroad, adds the dash that is all its own, and comes up with the formula that puts the *chic* in Chicago. As a clever copywriter for the former Marshall Field's said so succinctly long ago, "There's nothing like it back home."

Still true, though Field's is now Macy's. More on *that* later.

The savviest locals will tell you that style has nothing to do with how much you spend, but with how you spend it. *Chic, élan, verve,* and all those natty synonyms are rooted in curiosity and vitality, indigenous to Chicago. Style has nothing to do with what's In or Out and everything to do with aesthetics (and fun). Great taste means it would be nice to own an original Cézanne, but you can still stir the senses with a stunning litho created by a local artist and purchased at a local gallery.

The question is, where should you look in a city this size? There's always the obvious Michigan Avenue, but what about those neighborhood boutiques that are the natives' well-kept secrets? Sorry, natives, it's time to divulge the wheres and how-to-find-its.

THE WHERE OF IT

CHICAGO SHOPPING IS CENTERED DOWNTOWN. First, bordered by the Chicago River on both the north and west is the **Loop,** a 35-block cornucopia of limited retail action circumscribed by elevated train tracks; it's the home of the giant aforementioned **Macy's/Field's.** The triumphant arrival of gorgeous lakefront **Millennium Park** has revitalized the Loop, including the fabled **Block 37.** The latter has ceased being a winter skating rink and is finally under construction, projected to open in 2008, with a four-story retail base and three towers, one of which will be the new CBS studio facing Daley Plaza. The retailers have not yet been named. The new **Joffrey Building,** at the corner of State and Randolph streets, will house the Joffrey Ballet but will also contain retailing at its base; completion is projected before 2008.

The biggest news to hit the Loop is the loss of **Carson Pirie Scott** at its historic State Street store. The famed Louis Sullivan building, designated as a landmark, has undergone a $60 million restoration and is to be converted into a mix of retail, office, school, and entertainment uses. There will be stores, but none will be Carson's, the ownership of which has announced that it will surface somewhere else—could be Michigan Avenue, could even be elsewhere in the Loop. (It is also true that all of Carson's 25 other stores in the region will remain.) As Field's green awnings become Macy's red and black, the look of State now changes. But as the *Chicago Tribune* recently reported, "State Street is still standing, and very much open for business." Stay tuned.

It should be mentioned, additionally, that the area is a busy theater district. South of the river are several of the city's best museum stores (but more on those later).

Moving north of the river is the so-called **Magnificent Mile,** where grand malls and opulent boutiques flank both sides of Michigan Avenue. The **Near North Side**—known for streets that fan east and west of the Magnificent Mile, including the "tree" streets: Maple, Chestnut, Oak, and so on—is home to small pockets of eclectic shopping pleasures. Off the north end of Michigan Avenue, heading west, **Oak Street** is a shopping venue in its own right. Ritzy, upscale, exclusive, and generally expensive, Oak's single block is designer-fashion headquarters, with four of the city's top jewelers within steps of each other. **River North,** on the west side of Near North, is the epicenter of Chicago's art, antique, and designer-furniture scene.

Moving beyond Near North and River North and away from downtown are **Lincoln Park** and the ever-burgeoning **Bucktown–Wicker Park** area. The latter district, west of downtown, is filled with shopping, gallery hopping, and great dining, too, since some of the city's most interesting restaurants are nearby. Even farther west, more galleries, restaurants, and a few shops make up the area known as **West Town.** Some may call it the Near West Side, while still others consider it just an extension of the West Loop. Whatever the case, property values are rising.

Lincoln Park's parallel streets of **Webster** and **Armitage** are such fun they warrant time of their own, though neither has shopping areas that are all that large. Because many of these shops are mom-and-pop operations, with the owners usually on site, they provide an antidote to any impersonality you might find on Boul Mich. In this same area, the north–south streets of **Halsted, Clark,** and **Southport** amble for miles, sometimes in drab fashion, occasionally glowing with a shop or two (especially Southport) and restaurants to rival top areas in the city. **Lincoln Avenue,** slanting northwest from Lincoln Park, is less likely to glow, but an occasional charmer can refute that theory.

Cut east and head north along the lake into **Evanston.** When you've finished trooping the Northwestern University campus, avail yourself of some of the town's good shopping. North of Evanston are affluent and shopping-rich communities such as **Wilmette, Winnetka, Glencoe, Northbrook, Highland Park,** and **Lake Forest.** To the north is **Milwaukee,** but before you leave Illinois, stop at **Gurnee Mills** in Gurnee for your PhD in outlet shopping.

To the west, suburban communities such as **Schaumburg, Oak Brook, Oak Park, Hinsdale, Naperville, Geneva,** and many others offer often-awesome browsing (at both shopping centers and boutiques).

THE HOW OF IT

AS MUCH AN ATTRACTION AS A REPOSITORY OF GOODS, **Michigan Avenue** is a browser's paradise. No shopping list or agenda is required—simply set off to walk the Magnificent Mile, and some article or item will thrust itself upon you and insist that you buy it. The aggregation of merchandise is so vast that you generally don't need to concern yourself with its availability. If it can be sold in a store, you'll find it on Michigan Avenue.

In discussing the other downtown and Greater Chicago shopping venues, however, the territory is immense and the stores geographically dispersed. Off Michigan Avenue it's more important, and sometimes necessary, to define what you're shopping for. When we talk about shopping in the myriad stores of the Loop, Oak Street, Near North, River North, and beyond, we organize our discussion around specific genres of merchandise. Some Michigan Avenue stores not incorporated in malls are also included in these categories.

unofficial **TIP**
Because people shop Michigan Avenue as if it's one huge consolidated shopping center, that is the way we've presented it. Block by block, we describe the malls and the stores in and between them without attempting to organize what's available into specific categories of goods and services.

MICHIGAN AVENUE:
The Magnificent Mile

FROM THE CHICAGO RIVER NORTH along Michigan Avenue is America's largest concentration of upscale shopping, known collectively as the "Magnificent Mile" or "Miracle Mile." Leading department stores anchor a dazzling array of chain stores, boutiques, and malls. It is a place where department stores are grander and boutiques more specialized, and where even chain habitués of suburban malls are enticingly packaged. Many stars in this shopping galaxy are neatly integrated into malls tucked away inside huge buildings. Imagine ducking into a streetside shop that opens unexpectedly into canyons of retail concourses. To shopping junkies, the discovery of these merchandise cities is akin to passing through the looking glass. And the malls are fairly gorgeous: **Chicago Place, Water Tower Place,** and **900 North Michigan,** just to name three.

It is no secret that Oprah loves Michigan Avenue (and Chicago shopping in general). Another long-ago talk-show host, Jenny Jones, who arrived from L.A. to set up in Chicago, confided that she was dazzled by the proximity of so many great stores. "Everything in L.A.," she lamented, "is a car ride away."

Still true. Add five B's (**Bloomingdale's, Barneys, Burberry, Brooks Brothers,** and **Bulgari**) to **Macy's, Saks Fifth Avenue, Neiman Marcus, Chanel, Ralph Lauren,** and dozens more, sometimes within a two-block area, and it's shopper's paradise.

MICHIGAN AVENUE'S GRAND MALLS

UNTIL SEPTEMBER 2000, while there was some shopping on Michigan Avenue between the river and Ohio Street, most of the primo shops were concentrated in the nine blocks from Ontario north to Oak. This changed when the "mall" at 520 North Michigan, known originally as North Bridge and housing the city's first **Nordstrom** (☎ 312-464-1515), opened (though suburban Nordstroms were already ensconced). The four-level, 271,000-square-foot fashion specialty store is strong on cosmetics, departments called "style stations," men's bath and spa shops, fitting rooms to accommodate persons with disabilities, outstanding kid stuff on level three, a concierge desk, and two restaurants.

THE SHOPS AT WESTFIELD NORTH BRIDGE For general information, call the concierge desk at ☎ 312-327-2300. The shops include 50 other retailers, such as **Tommy Bahama** (sportswear), **Oilily** (vivid fashions for women and children), **A/X Armani, F. Carriere** (apparel), **Aris** jewelry, **The Go! Game Store, Sabon** soaps and skin care, **Premiere Collection Fine Art Gallery, Lucky Brand Dungarees, Vosges Haut-Chocolat, C.D. Peacock** (another big-name Chicago-area jeweler), **Benetton** (women and children), and girlhood rave **Sanrio's Hello Kitty. Sephora** (grooming aids and women's designer cosmetics by the ton) is also here, and on the fourth level are 20 Chicago-style eateries, including **Relish, Tuscany Café, Mezza, Café Typhoon, Potbelly Sandwich Works, Max Orient,** and others.

540 NORTH MICHIGAN This block houses a **Virgin Megastore**

shopping: magnificent mile and the loop

MAGNIFICENT MILE
1. The Shops at North Bridge
2. 540 North Michigan
3. 600 North Michigan
4. Chicago Place

5. Neiman Marcus
6. Water Tower Place
7. 900 North Michigan
8. One Mag Mile

THE LOOP
9. Macy's

Ⓜ Subway/El stop

(☎ 312-645-9300) for music, movies, games, and more, plus a **Kenneth Cole** store (☎ 312-644-1163) for clothing, shoes, and accessories.

Also included in this nine-block area are such stores as **Harley Davidson Downtown** (66 East Ohio Street; ☎ 312-274-9666) for clothing, not cycle parts; **Bose** audio-video equipment (55 East Grand Avenue; ☎ 312-595-0152); and the expanded **Room & Board** furniture (55 East Ohio Street; ☎ 312-266-0656). Restaurants to consider in this area include **Weber Grill** and **P.F. Chang's**.

Among chains of note, there's a great **Gap** (555 North Michigan Avenue; ☎ 312-494-8580) that covers every member of the family: Gap Kids, Gap Baby, Gap Men's, Gap Women's, and Gap Maternity. Nearby **Guess?** (605 North Michigan Avenue; ☎ 312-440-9665) may attract a younger crowd.

600 NORTH MICHIGAN This mall houses a new **Home Element,** a sleek contemporary-furnishings store with 13,000 square feet on the third floor and an entrance on Ontario Street (☎ 312-787-3358), next to **Linens & Things** (☎ 312-867-3822). Here, too, is **Levi's, The Original Store** (☎ 312-642-9613), where women can buy "customized" Levi's (thanks to the store's unique Personal Pair jeans-that-fit service). Also in this mall are **Marshalls** (☎ 312-280-7506), **Cineplex Odeon** theaters (entrance at the corner of Rush and Ohio streets; ☎ 312-255-9340), **Ann Taylor** (☎ 312-587-8301), and **H20 Plus** (☎ 312-397-1243).

CHICAGO PLACE This eight-level shopping center at 700 North Michigan has one of the nation's prettiest **Saks Fifth Avenue** stores and some 45 specialty stores, including **Ann Taylor; Talbots** (☎ 312-944-6059), with clothes from petites to slightly larger sizes; terrific togs at **Tall Girl Shops** (☎ 312-649-1303); and the original **Home Element** (☎ 312-587-8752), a spacious fifth-floor grouping of contemporary furniture with an outstanding collection of Asian antiques sprinkled throughout. Here, too, are art galleries such as the famed **Chiaroscuro** (☎ 312-988-9253), where the wares of 300 artists and artisans are shown (including jewelry, glass, furniture, and mixed media). This is a truly fun store, where any gift for any person is guaranteed. A few feet away is **Abby & Yanni** (☎ 312-988-7188), with stylish furs from around the world. In the international mode, **Russian Creations** (☎ 312-573-0792) may or may not be the only place in Chicago where you can find some of the iconic, brilliantly painted Russian nesting dolls called *matryoshka,* at $35 and up.

The last word goes to glossy **Saks Fifth Avenue** (☎ 312-944-6500). The retailer has been on the avenue since 1929, and this is one of its showcase stores—everything always sparkles here. Find traditional and cutting-edge designers, a children's department, and a home section on the sixth floor. Across the street at 717 North Michigan Avenue, the **Saks Men's Store** also dispenses fine wares. There is also a beauty of a Saks store in Highland Park. The low-end (one hesitates to say "cut-rate" about anything Saks-ish) **Off 5th Saks Fifth Avenue**

Outlet stores are in Schaumburg (☎ 847-413-8803) and Gurnee Mills (☎ 847-662-0988).

NEIMAN MARCUS Just down the avenue from Chicago Place is this nonmalled titan at 737 North Michigan (☎ 312-642-5900). Suburbanites (who adore the store at Northbrook Court in Northbrook) swear that Neiman's is the only reason they trek into the city. Says one, firmly: "This is Michigan Avenue's best store. I can find evening wear there and designer jewelry I can't find anywhere else." Also noteworthy are the great gift-wrapping, with ornamentation of packages a specialty; the **Zodiac** restaurant, known for signature popovers; a superb designer-shoe salon; a limited fourth-floor home-furnishings area; and unique home-decor items in their gift galleries. All this plus cosmetics, beauty, and bath items—some hard to find—on the first floor. The price range varies (one of the best and most costly skincare names here is Natura Bissé from Barcelona, Spain).

WATER TOWER PLACE At 835 North Michigan is this seven-level marble palace, anchored by **Macy's.** The first two floors of former anchor store **Lord & Taylor** will be occupied by **American Girl Place** (a mix of other specialty stores will fill the remaining L&T space), a hugely popular destination for girls and their moms (or dads or grandmas) featuring rooms full of of the famed American Girl dolls and their accessories. There's also a theater for the AG revue and a cafe for munching (plus seating for dolls). Until autumn 2008, when the move to Water Tower Place happens, the doll paradise is still at 111 East Chicago Avenue (☎ 312-943-9400).

Once past the mall's beautiful entrance (the bubbling waterfall is soothing), you may think this is chainsville, but some of the retailers may surprise you: of the more than 100 specialty shops at Water Tower Place, some are exclusive to Chicago. In apparel, there are kids' things at **Abercrombie & Fitch** and **Limited Too,** as well as clothing stores for women such as beauteous **Eileen Fisher** (☎ 312-943-9190) on level two, **Chico's** on level three (☎ 312-943-2442), and **J. Jill** (the first J. Jill in Chicago; ☎ 312-712-9940) on level six. Other attractions include **C.O. Bigelow** (☎ 312-642-0551) on level four, for body and bath supplies, and **Crabtree & Evelyn** (☎ 312-787-0188), also on level four, for more beauty-related goodies.

One of the more interesting aspects of this shopping center is the vast food court called **Foodlife** (☎ 312-335-3663) on the mezzanine, where you can dig in to (or take out) almost anything, from tacos to freshly baked pies. Ensconced here, lounging amid the fake greenery while forking pasta, you may forget you're in the middle of a huge city. Foodlife even has a market where you can run in and pick up a bottle of wine, beautiful breads, sauces, home-cooked meals (macaroni and cheese, poached salmon, you name it). Tucked into a space behind the food court is a restaurant called **Mity Nice Grill** (☎ 312-335-4745); filled with some mighty nice edibles, it's one of the mall's best-kept secrets. Got a sweet tooth? Run up to **Lindt Chocolates** (☎ 312-440-3986) on level seven.

900 NORTH MICHIGAN This formidable shopping venue houses beautiful **Bloomingdale's** (☎ 312-440-4460), gorgeous **Gucci** (☎ 312-664-5504), silvery **Pavillon Christofle** (☎ 312-664-9700), and a city mall of laid-back charm that makes it easy to shop. Bloomie's is full of surprises, offering a range of prices. Find shoes (divine rip-offs of styles attempted by only top designers, featured right along with shoes by the latter), a **David Yurman** boutique, a remodeled **B Now** (bridge fashions), and a first-floor visitor center. After you've found inexpensive jeans, you can go up a floor or two and find the priciest of import gowns, or furs to die for at Bloomie's **Maximilian** salon. The first-floor cosmetics department offers extraordinary abundance.

On 900's fifth floor, **Galt Toys + Galt Baby** has items for kids who have a lot (but would always like a little more, such as outstanding English prams); tiny **Glove Me Tender** (☎ 312-664-4022) is the place to buy gloves (natch) as well as hats. Other clothing stores include the very major **MaxMara** (☎ 312-475-9500); **bebe** (☎ 312-943-2323); **Yolanda Lorente** (☎ 312-867-0900), whose gowns have long adorned international fashionables; and **Club Monaco** (☎ 312-787-8757). Here, too, is the fifth U.S. location of **Lalique** (☎ 312-867-1787), where you can pick up crystal, along with perfume and porcelain. This store is known for its commitment to Lalique's accessories collection (how about a crystal ring?). While on the first level, check out the china at **Bernardaud** (☎ 312-751-1700); the watches, pens (note the gorgeous Virginia Woolf ballpoint), and butter-soft leather goods at **Montblanc** (☎ 312-943-1200); and the divine shoes at **Stuart Weitzman** (☎ 312-943-5760). Then waltz off to the fifth level to dine on Italian goodies at **Tucci Benucch** (☎ 312-266-2500). Or skip the food and schedule an appointment at **Equinox Fitness Club** (☎ 312-254-2500) on the lower level. At level four is a new favorite at 900: **The Goldsmith,** (☎ 312-751-1986), where Sherry Bender, one of the city's top gold artisans, works her magic with a variety of unusual stones and settings. This award-winning designer and her jewel-box setting are well worth a visit. Another don't-miss is the spacious **Silk Trading Company** on level three, for home accessories.

MORE MAG MILE Across the street from 900 to the east are choice retailers: the beautiful **St. John Boutique** (919 North Michigan Avenue; ☎ 312-943-1941), **Louis Vuitton** next door (☎ 312-944-2010), and the midwestern outpost for the Roman jeweler **Bulgari** (909 North Michigan Avenue; ☎ 312-255-1313). Across the street from 900 to the north, at 970 North Michigan, is another marble palace, dubbed **One Mag Mile** by the developer, but it's primarily residential except for **Manrico Cashmere** (☎ 312-649-1114), a fine Italian cashmere house. After you've finished your sweater spending, go upstairs and have a glass of Pinot Grigio at **Spiaggia,** one of the city's best Italian restaurants (see page 247). At

980 North Michigan is a stunning store housing the furs of **Dennis Basso** (☎ 312-640-9500); they're modern, sexy, and flattering for all ages, and the salon is making a big splash for fashionistas into fur. More shopping is in evidence across the street, where you'll find **Chanel, Georg Jensen,** and a mini-cluster of other retailers housed at the **Drake Hotel.**

EAST OF MICHIGAN

PERENNIAL TOURIST FAVORITE **Navy Pier** (600 East Grand Avenue on the lake; ☎ 312-595-PIER for info) is home to one of the best places in the city to take the kids: the **Chicago Children's Museum,** with hands-on exhibits. Afterward, take them for a ride on the pier's Ferris wheel or to the Crystal Gardens for a snack. If you want to take a dinner cruise (ships depart from Navy Pier), you can choose from among *Spirit of Chicago* cruises (☎ 312-836-7899), **Mystic Blue Cruises** (☎ 877-299-7854), or the more expensive *Odyssey* cruises (☎ 800-947-9367). Also at Navy Pier: the **IMAX Theater,** the terrific **Chicago Shakespeare Theater,** and the **Smith Museum of Stained Glass Windows** (☎ 312-595-5024), where you'll find contemporary and vintage stained glass. Trinket shopping and snacks are available throughout the Pier premises.

The LOOP'S LANDMARK DEPARTMENT STORE

SOUTH OF THE CHICAGO RIVER and just west of Michigan Avenue is the **Loop,** circumscribed by elevated train tracks. As concerns shopping, this area falls into the "obvious" category. Nevertheless, even many locals don't realize just how interesting **Macy's**—formerly **Marshall Field's,** and the leading Loop treasure house—is. The cliché for tourists, some say, is to avoid this extraordinary department store, so do the opposite. Even though this stunning new incarnation can't obscure the fact that the Loop's glory comes and goes, visitors to the city, influenced by natives who shop only boutiques (whether they be Armani or thrift shops), may pass up a chance to investigate, thus failing to bask in the light of this star and learn that the glory never fades. So don't listen. Tell naysayers you know the star hasn't gone Out, it's In.

MACY'S

THE 7I-TON CLOCKS (at the Randolph and Washington street corners) that tower over this granddaddy of Chicago stores (111 North State Street; ☎ 312-781-1000) signal your arrival. Ongoing renovations include the ever-fabulous **beauty department** under a Tiffany ceiling that arcs seven stories above the selling floor. The fragrance area features glass art, and there has been a beautiful flower shop in the past (and might be again) where you could pick a bouquet before trying cosmetics from Fresh to Yves Saint Laurent. Grab a sandwich

unofficial **TIP**
At this writing, the former Field's on State Street is in great transition as Macy's takes over. The information presented here is subject to change in the future, but though the basic departments may be switched around, they will no doubt continue to exist.

at the **Marketplace Food Court** on the so-called lower level (all basements should look like this). Of all the floors, chock-full of goods, Macy's high-fashion **28 Shop** is a stunner, as are its children's and accessories departments.

This is arguably the most beautiful department store in the country. As Field's, it was a source of firsts: first to establish a European buying office (in England, in 1871); first to open a dining room in a department store; first to delight customers with lavish window displays; and first U.S. store to institute a bridal registry. Also notable is the Christmas-season **Great Tree,** which towers 45 feet and still delights patrons as much as they enjoy viewing the holiday windows.

This is probably the only store of its kind that burned down twice in its history—once, when it was Field & Leiter, during the great Chicago Fire of 1871, and again in 1873. Leiter retired in 1881, and the store became Marshall Field & Co., reigning in this fashion almost a century until it became part of the department-store division of the Dayton Hudson Corporation in 1990, then Target Corporation, and now Federated Department Stores, whereupon it has become Macy's.

Think of shopping here as not unlike exploring a small village. There's a huge store for men on two, featuring the **shirts and ties** of such designers as **Thomas Pink, Ike Behar,** and **Alexandre Savile Row,** some with their own shops. Other designers found here are **Kenneth Cole, Hugo Boss,** and **Burberry for Men.** On two are **men's suits and coats** from designers like **Giorgio Armani** and **Polo Ralph Lauren.** Women enjoy designer wares on three as well at **Select** (free personal shopping). Among the many boutiques on three are **French Connection U.K., Mimi Maternity, Kate Spade,** and **Burberry.** On four is the **women's shoe department** (now 16,000 square feet) and the full-service **Bridal Salon.**

Five is for **petites, children's clothes,** and fun, educational toys at **Creative Kidstuff.** Also here are **intimate apparel,** the **Premier beauty salon,** and **Women's Way** plus-size fashions.

The highlight of six is the **home store,** with crystal galleries, silver, a shop for designer bed linens, and more than 500 china patterns on display (but thousands may be ordered). The hot **Steuben crystal gallery** brings together huge collections of **Hoya, Orrefors, Baccarat, Waterford, Swarovski,** and **Lalique. Christofle** offers more china and crystal, and there are also departments here for quilts, lamps, and corporate gifts. Plus, this is the place to find dinnerware from **Pickard,** known for making china for U.S. embassies.

The seventh floor is largely dedicated to **food.** A recent renovation has created and updated fine attractions. The famed **Walnut Room** has a center fountain, and both natives and tourists like to come here at Christmas to gape at the Great Tree. The **Frango Café** is a 140-seat restaurant featuring soups, salads, sandwiches, ice-cream delights, a children's menu, and a dessert bar. An open atrium area houses the **7 on State Gourmet Food Court,** seating 450 people and offering goodies ranging from soups to noodles. We had a panini seven floors up (the crispy Autostrada, with mortadella, salami, provolone, and capicolla, is delish) at the **La Brea** bakery booth; you'll swear you were in Milan. A **Visitor Services Center and Archives** is on the seventh floor as well.

On the lower level, the newly remodeled **Marketplace Food Court** includes a deli for salads, grilled foods, sushi, and other homemade dishes; a bakery; a sports bar; and other highlights, such as a renovated candy department (there is also a Culinary Studio on the seventh floor). The eighth floor is earmarked for **furniture,** including such lines as **Thomas O'Brien** and **Baker,** plus the 2,000-square-foot **Trend House** rooms. On the ninth floor is what is claimed to be (who knows?) the largest **Oriental-carpet collection** of any American department store. A final pleasure, on the first floor when we last checked, is the **Baccarat Boutique**—the first such boutique in Chicago—carrying jewelry, handbags, watches, corporate gifts, chandeliers, and, of course, gorgeous crystal.

CARSON PIRIE SCOTT

CARSON'S IS GOING OUT OF BUSINESS in its present location, though a smaller version is scheduled to reopen elsewhere in the city. With the loss of the flagship store, it should be reiterated that there are 25 Carson's stores (including furniture galleries) in the Chicago area. At this writing, other locations include Harlem–Irving Plaza on the North Side and at 120 South Riverside Plaza (near Union Station). There are also stores at suburban malls, including Chicago Ridge, Ford City, Stratford Square, Spring Hill, Lincoln Mall (Matteson), Randhurst, North Riverside, Orland Square, Edens Plaza (take the Lake East exit on the Edens Expressway), and the Streets of Woodfield in Schaumburg. But check before you go, because things may change.

WHERE *to* FIND . . .

IF YOU CHOOSE NOT TO SHOP at a Michigan Avenue mall or a huge Loop department store, there is a distinct possibility that you are looking for something specific. We've therefore chopped the remainder of the Chicago shopping iceberg into neat little categories to make it easy to find what you want.

ART AND FINE CRAFTS

IN THE LOOP Be sure to take a look-see at one of the city's most tasteful (and too-little-known) galleries: the **Illinois Artisans Shop** (100 West

Randolph Street; ☎ 312-814-5321), at the State of Illinois building, Suite 2–200. Everything here is handmade by Illinois artists: jewelry, glass, ceramics, handwoven wearable art, quilts, baskets, dolls, woodworking, ironwork, prints, paintings, sculpture, and photographs. Hours are Monday through Friday, 9 a.m. to 5 p.m. Newly situated in the Loop is **Malcolm Franklin** (79 East Van Buren Street; ☎ 312-337-0202), purveyor of 17th- and 18th-century furniture and accessories.

At the south end of Michigan Avenue is the **Chicago Architecture Foundation Store** (224 South Michigan Avenue; ☎ 312-922-3432), another gem full of architecture and design books, decorative items, and top-quality Chicago memorabilia. (The foundation also does superb city tours.) While we're moving south, move even farther to the Hyde Park area, where famed **Harper Court** houses **Artisans 21** (5211 South Harper Avenue; ☎ 773-288-7450), a co-op gallery run by 21 artists and craftsmen who create everything from ceramics to jewelry to oil paintings. While you're in the vicinity, stop in at the **Museum of Science and Industry Store** (5700 South Lake Shore Drive; ☎ 773-684-1414, ext. 2781), housing everything from science experiments to IMAX movies on DVD, with special sections on space, trains, rocks, and other interesting items.

Several fine galleries have gone into what's sometimes known as **West Loop Gate,** west of the Loop. Notable among them is **Donald Young Gallery** (933 West Washington Blvd.; ☎ 312-455-0100), displaying such contemporary artists as Bruce Nauman, Sol LeWitt, Martin Puryear, Robert Mangold, and others in a 6,000-square-foot space. Nearby, other fine galleries have set up shop, like **Vedanta Gallery** (835 West Washington Boulevard; ☎ 312-492-6692) and others mentioned later in this section.

ON NORTH MICHIGAN AVENUE   There was a time when Michigan Avenue not only was the retail repository of the Midwest's best but also was dotted with some of the city's finest art galleries. Many of the latter have moved to the River North area, but among those remaining are the **Richard Gray Gallery** (875 North Michigan Avenue, John Hancock Building, Level 25; ☎ 312-642-8877), one of Chicago's outstanding dealers in fine art; **Galleries Maurice Sternberg** (875 North Michigan Avenue; ☎ 312-642-1700), a fine-art dealer since 1945; and **Valerie Carberry Gallery** (875 North Michigan Avenue; ☎ 312-397-9990).

When you say "art in Chicago," your number-one thought should be the **Art Institute of Chicago,** the magnificent institution south of the Chicago River (on Michigan Avenue at Adams) that consistently outpaces the finest museums in the world. Also extraordinary is the **Art Institute Museum Shop** (☎ 312-443-3583), which was one of Chicago's best-kept secrets for too long. Find the Midwest's best art books, posters, T-shirts, and note cards—everything from a Monet-inspired paperweight to Impressionist-inspired scarves, unique Baltic amber jewelry, Monet prints, even umbrellas, such as a scenic one by "urban Impressionist" Gustave Caillebotte called "Paris Street, Rainy Day" ($36; there's also a collapsible size at $24, one of the most popular items ever carried in the store). Hours: Monday, Tuesday, and Wednesday, 10:30 a.m. to 5 p.m.; Thursday, 10:30 a.m. to 8 p.m. (summer, 10:30 a.m. to 9 p.m. from the first Thursday of June through Labor Day); Friday, 10:30 a.m. to 5 p.m. (summer, 10:30 a.m. to 9 p.m.); Saturday and Sunday, 10 a.m. to 5 p.m.; closed Thanksgiving, Christmas, and New Year's Day. (You need not be admitted to the museum to get into the shop.)

Another beauteous store, generously trimmed in oak, is a highlight of the **Museum of Contemporary Art** (220 East Chicago Avenue; ☎ 312-280-2660). Called **The MCA Store,** this light, bright, airy space comprises two levels connected by a sweeping two-story winding staircase under a skylight. You'll find such items as contemporary-art books, experimental-music CDs, mobiles, interesting jewelry, candles, and (a particular strength) home and tabletop gifts. **Puck's at the MCA** is the cafe for lunch. Dine alfresco in good weather on the granite terrace off the sculpture garden; Sunday brunch is very popular. It's just a few feet from Michigan Avenue, but it feels like a world away.

NEAR NORTH Former gallery owner Joy Horwich closed up shop to conduct wonderful tours of art-filled places around the world, from the Getty Museum in California to Bilbao, Berlin, and Prague in Europe to the Milwaukee Museum closer to home. **Joy-Us Jaunts** (☎ 773-327-3366) also takes individuals and families on personalized artistic and cultural forays in Chicago (such as a trip to an auction house or an artist's studio).

The Hart Gallery (64 East Walton; ☎ 312-932-9646) offers contemporary European drawings, paintings, and sculpture, with an emphasis on artists from Eastern Europe and Germany. Just east of Michigan Avenue is **Johnson Antiques** (172 East Walton Street; ☎ 312-440-9466), a lovely shop with a green awning where Phyllis Johnson offers antique jewelry (Georgian to Art Deco) and silver (Georgian to the Arts and Crafts period, fine sterling candlesticks, old Sheffield pieces, and more). The **Kamp Gallery,** an addition to the Drake Hotel (140 East Walton; ☎ 312-664-0090), shows fine historical and contemporary paintings.

Brightening Oak Street is **Aaron Galleries** (50 East Oak Street, second floor; ☎ 312-943-0660), where you'll find 19th- and early-20th-century American paintings and master prints. Another Oak Street gem is **The Colletti Collection** (67 East Oak Street; ☎ 312-664-6767), offering a primarily European collection of posters circa 1880–1940, fine-art ceramics, stunning furniture, wonderful glass pieces, and more. If you're in the market for a Mucha or Toulouse-Lautrec poster, this is certainly the place to find it.

RIVER NORTH Van Gogh might have given his other ear to stroll the hugely expanded **Pearl Art & Craft Supply** (225 West Chicago Avenue;

☎ 312-915-0200). The mostly discount store provides an incredibly wide supply of materials for artisans. Making jewelry? Beads overflow. Want a choice of brushes? Options abound. Staffers get a feel for what you want, whether you're a professional or a hobbyist. Hundreds of new handmade papers come from around the world.

To begin our discussion of the gallery district, we'll attempt a quick summation; then you can go and make up your own mind. One source for antiques is **Christa's Ltd.** (217 West Illinois Street; ☎ 312-222-2520), with Continental antiques from furniture to andirons. Two more antiques sources are **Jay Roberts Antiques Warehouse** (149 West Kinzie; ☎ 312-222-0167) and **Thomas Jolly** (124 West Kinzie; ☎ 312-595-0018), a specialist in early-17th- through 19th-century European antiques.

Robert Henry Adams Fine Art (715 North Franklin; ☎ 312-642-8700) features American modern art circa 1910–1970. The **Zolla/Lieberman Gallery** (325 West Huron; ☎ 312-944-1990) shows contemporary painting, sculpture, and works on paper. The **Aldo Castillo Gallery** (675 North Franklin; ☎ 312-337-2536) specializes in Latin American art.

When you hit Superior Street, the galleries come thicker and faster. It's fun to wander Superior and stop when the feeling (or the gallery) moves you. A good place to begin is **Ann Nathan Gallery** (218 West Superior Street; ☎ 312-664-6622), a long-established yet edgy and right-now spot for paintings, sculpture, even unique furniture pieces. Move on, for fine contemporary art, to **Jean Albano** (215 West Superior Street; ☎ 312-440-0770) and, at the same address and also specializing in fine art, **Maya Polsky Gallery** (☎ 312-440-0055). If you're looking for contemporary glass sculpture, note the **Marx-Saunders Gallery** (230 West Superior Street; ☎ 312-573-1400); check out the museum-like second floor. Also at 230 West Superior is **Schneider Gallery** (☎ 312-988-4033), a great source for contemporary photography by international artists. More fine glass can be found at **Habatat** (222 West Superior Street; ☎ 312-440-0288). In the **300 Building** are **Catherine Edelman** (☎ 312-266-2350) for contemporary photography and the **Judy A. Saslow Gallery** (☎ 312-943-0530) for contemporary artists and a global mix of outsider, self-taught, folk, and ethnographic works.

Another notable is **Steven Daiter Gallery** (311 West Superior Street; ☎ 312-787-3350); photography is special here, especially vintage black-and-white photos. **Printworks** (☎ 312-664-9407), with contemporary prints, drawings, photographs, and artists' books, is also at 311 West Superior, as is **Michael Fitzsimmons Decorative Arts** (☎ 312-787-0496), home of Arts and Crafts–era works in most media. **Perimeter Gallery** (210 West Superior Street; ☎ 312-266-9473) specializes in contemporary fine art (also ceramics, works on paper, sculpture, fiber, and metalwork) by internationally recognized artists.

One of the best galleries in this area is **Roy Boyd** (739 North Wells Street; ☎ 312-642-1606), featuring contemporary painting, sculpture, and works on paper; there are many abstractions but also some surprising exceptions. Nearby is **Carl Hammer Gallery** (740 North Wells Street; ☎ 312-266-8512), with an emphasis on edgy contemporary artists whom some compare to a "punk rock" roster. **Primitive** (706 North Wells Street; ☎ 312-943-3770) and its larger sister gallery (130 North Jefferson Street; ☎ 312-575-9600) both feature four floors of tribal and ethnic displays of authentic international furniture, textiles, rugs, clothing, jewelry, and artifacts. Back on Wells is **Expression Gallery of Fine Art** (708 North Wells Street; ☎ 312-274-9848), where you'll find a mix of master graphics by such stars as Picasso, Miró, and Whistler, as well as more-contemporary lesser-known artists.

Leaving Wells, you might want to stop at the famed **Tree Studios** for a look at the paintings of **Bruce Jefferson** (4 East Ohio Street; ☎ 312-896-3413). Another Tree tenant is **Hildt Galleries** (617 North State Street; ☎ 312-255-0005), which features paintings by British, American, and European artists of the 19th and early-20th centuries.

WEST (AND WEST LOOP GATE)   Most of these galleries are of interest not so much to those looking for decorative mixed-use works as to fine-art collectors seeking the works of edgier, newer, or younger artists. **Aron Packer Gallery** and **Schopf Gallery** have merged at 942 West Lake Street (☎ 312-432-1630); here you'll find contemporary, outsider, and folk art in all media. At 312 North May Street, **Rhona Hoffman Gallery** (☎ 312-455-1990) features contemporary works by Americans and Europeans, both established and less-well-known artists.

At 119 West Peoria is **Bodybuilder & Sportsman Gallery** (☎ 312-492-7261), named for its locale (a former sporting-goods store) and specializing in fine contemporary art by emerging and established nationally recognized artists. A Chicago favorite is **Douglas Dawson Gallery** (400 North Morgan Street; ☎ 312-226-7975), known for ancient and historic ethnic art from Asia, Africa, and the Americas (textiles, furniture, sculpture, stone, and ceramics). Other suggestions in this area include **Thomas McCormick** (835 West Washington; ☎ 312-226-6800) for modern and contemporary American painting; and more contemporary art at **Carrie Secrist Gallery** (835 West Washington; ☎ 312-491-0917). Also at 835 West Washington, **Kraft Lieberman Gallery** (☎ 312-948-0555) presents up-and-coming as well as established artists in bronze, wood, glass, and ceramic sculpture. Finally, don't miss **Flatfile Galleries** (217 North Carpenter; ☎ 312-491-1190) for fine photography and contemporary art.

LINCOLN PARK, CLYBOURN CORRIDOR, AND FARTHER NORTH **Art Effect** (934 West Armitage Avenue; ☎ 773-929-3600) was one of the first stores to feature wearable art, and that's still one of its strong points. National artists' works are displayed here, with attention paid to clothes, jewelry, and items for the home. Several interesting store-galleries can be found in Wicker Park–Bucktown. One of the most enticing is **Pagoda Red** (1714 North Damen; ☎ 773-235-1188), an urban oasis with an Asian garden full of 18th- to 19th-century Chinese furniture and artifacts. **Pavilion Antiques** (2055 North Damen; ☎ 773-645-0924) has 19th- and 20th-century French, Italian, and some American vintage pieces and antiques, with an emphasis on lighting and mirrors.

BABY FURNITURE

SOMETHING NEW AND TINY: **Elizabeth Marie** (3612 North Southport; ☎ 773-525-4100) is a neat place to pick up a personalized something for baby (even wooden blocks). Custom design services for children are offered here. Open Friday through Saturday; other days by appointment only.

When it comes to attractive stores for baby's clothing and gifts (including custom furniture, such as little tables and chairs, decoupage toy chests, and the like), a leader is **The Red Balloon** (2060 North Damen; ☎ 773-489-9800). Here, too, are bedding, wall hangings, and room accessories, as well as wooden toys and classic children's books. A second store is at 5407 North Clark Street (☎ 773-989-8500).

Another important baby-gear outpost is **Design Within Reach** (1574 North Kingsbury Street; ☎ 312-482-8661; and other locations), where the DWRjax line offers baby furniture as well as home goods for adults. Note, too, the charming **Faded Rose** (1017 West Armitage; ☎ 773-281-8161). Here you'll find vintage-inspired furniture and accessories, from doorknobs to dishcloths, along with baby bedding and slipcovers, including treasured patterns by House, Inc. Baby gifts are also here, plus botanicals, gifts, and furnishings for adults. There's a baby registry, too.

BEAUTY AND GROOMING

MICHIGAN AVENUE This probably should be filed under grooming rather than beauty, because it's strictly for men: **Truefitt & Hill** (900 North Michigan Avenue, sixth level; ☎ 312-337-2525) is the perfect man's getaway from everything, including the surrounding shopping mall. In these English club–ish surroundings, he can have a hot-lather shave, haircut, pedicure, boot shine, and all manner of stress-reducing packages.

NEAR NORTH On Oak Street, lined with really beautiful stores, the immaculate and sparkling jewel-box salon of international perfume and cosmetics creator **Marilyn Miglin** (112 East Oak Street; ☎ 312-943-1120) is right up there at the top for any woman. For one thing, this salon smells *so* good. Marilyn's fragrances include Pheromone ("the world's most precious perfume"), and more are available. Her salon is known for its exquisite, high-quality goods and services including facials, nail services, massages, and, of course, makeup applications. On the top floor, the latest addition is **Robert Lucas Salon** (☎ 312-642-6640), a top-rated hairstylist who also excels at hair coloring.

The popular **Channings** (54 East Oak Street; ☎ 312-280-1994), in contrast to the beauty palaces of chrome and glass, is housed in a vintage-y nook, with cozy niches upstairs and down for everything from a fantasy tan to a hot-glove manicure).

Face & Facial (104 East Oak Street; ☎ 312-951-5151) features internationally known facialist Mila Bravi. There are manicurists here, too, who are among the best (but not the most expensive) in the city. Another trained aesthetician with a soothing touch is **Kathleen Peara Studio,** a bit to the north at 534 West Eugenie Street in Old Town (by appointment only; ☎ 312-337-6734), where indulging in an aromatherapy facial, reflexology, or a massage (or all of the above) will have you purring with satisfaction.

Hair salons in the Near North aren't likely to indulge you with bargain prices, but they do deliver the goods. **Charles Ifergan** (106 East Oak; ☎ 312-642-4484) is a trendsetting hair designer who wins national awards for his styles for men and women. The **Anita Russum Salon** (34 East Oak Street, sixth floor; ☎ 312-944-8533) is an oasis of tranquility where hair colorist Anita Russum works her magic. Again, no bargain prices, but Rossum's artistry wins hearts. **Che Sguardo** (161 West Illinois Street; ☎ 312-464-1616) sells notable and unusual cosmetics, and they'll do your makeup and give makeup lessons for a Big Night Out.

Spas are proliferating in Chicago, and followers of the **Elizabeth Arden Red Door Salon** (919 North Michigan Avenue; ☎ 312-988-9191; entrance is on the Walton Street side) are pleased with the beautiful, large environs. Hair colorist Maurice Bonamigo (direct line, ☎ 312-664-6353) is big here. The popular **Kiva** (196 East Pearson; ☎ 312-840-8120) is known for its "am I in Santa Fe?" ambience, but in actuality you're next door to the Ritz-Carlton hotel, enjoying an oasis for body, mind, and spirit, with every type of treatment—from aromatherapy and massages at the spa to pedicures and scalp analysis. The **Four Seasons Hotel** has an outstanding spa as well (120 East Delaware Place; ☎ 312-649-2340). Even if you're not a hotel guest, you can have a lovely Champagne-and-caviar facial (guess what they bring you when the facial is done?). Another fine salon and spa is **Spa Emilia** (21 West Elm; ☎ 312-951-7415), a serene environment where Grace, Elizabeth, and their staff offer manicures and pedicures that people rave about. A new spa with an interesting location near hotels and overlooking Lake Michigan, **Spa 195** (195 North Harbor Drive; ☎ 312-552-9000) offers massages, body wraps, pedicures, manicures, and facials.

Also in the Gold Coast area is **Colette's Salon and Spa** (100 East Walton, Suite 300; ☎ 312-944-8500), a favorite among fashionables for hair, skin care, and other salon services. One of the city's top makeup artists is definitely Diane Ayala at **Mon Ami Coiffeur Chicago** (65 East Oak; ☎ 312-337-4233). Finally, a welcome addition is **Marlena's Factory Outlet Store** (1230 West Washington Boulevard; ☎ 312-943-2626), where you can pick up Marilyn Miglin products, fragrances, makeup, and skin-care products at great prices, all at less than retail.

Before moving north on Halsted Street, you may want to go far south to **Black Passion** (11018 South Halsted; ☎ 773-928-8797), where Nolan Douglas has not only a hair salon but often includes a book-store and dance studio "in tribute to the black community" he serves.

Going north on Halsted Street, you'll find several havens for skin care, cosmetics, and bath products. Loved by many, **Endo-Exo** (2034 North Halsted; ☎ 773-525-0500) has renovated and is expanding; they carry Shu Uemura, Natura Bissé, and the Jo Wood organic product line, for starters. **Fresh** (2040 North Halsted; ☎ 773-404-9776), a crisp, luxe beauty boutique, charms with natural bath supplies (such as eucalyptus–sea kelp soap) and other products. For men, **Guise** (2217 North Halsted; ☎ 773-929-6101) interestingly combines a barbershop with a clothing boutique; the luxurious 30- to 40-minute shaves use three hot towels, essential oils, and Art of Shaving products. Some of the most requested brands in cosmetics and grooming are available at **Bluemercury** (2208 North Halsted; ☎ 773-327-6900).

On Armitage are five must-stops. **Kiehl's** (907 West Armitage; ☎ 773-665-2515) is the famed purveyor of skin- and hair-care products' first freestanding store in Chicago; come sniff the herbal delights. Then there's **L'Occitane** (846 West Armitage; ☎ 773-477-3900). Whether you stop in here or at the 900 North Michigan location, the unique prod-ucts fresh from Provence are winners. Don't miss **Lush Cosmetics** (859 West Armitage; ☎ 773-281-5874). Here, all the products, from soaps to seaweed masks, not to mention foot lotions and dusting powders (there's one called Silky Underwear) are handmade, fresh, and indeed lush (no animal testing, either). A final bastion of beauty in this area is a new perfume salon called **La Maison du Parfum** (701 West Armitage; ☎ 312-944-1747). Fragrances are created in the French perfume coun-try of Grasse and brought to Chicago. You may also cook up your own scent in their lab if you don't find a ready-made one that you like.

The last word goes to neighborhood favorite **Pinky Nail Studio** (3503 North Southport; ☎ 773-248-5080). The mint-colored walls are a backdrop for free back massages given by technicians who've given you superb manicures. It should also be noted that the above listings are hardly all-inclusive. The fact is that new salons and spas are going up all but weekly, so do check neighborhoods to find out what's new (and something will be).

BIKES AND SKATEBOARDS

MANY FOLKS FIND THEIR WAY TO **Turin Bicycle Store** in Evanston (1027 Davis Street; 847-864-7660), but let's stay in the city for bikes.

If we start at North Avenue and work our way north on Ashland, we'll encounter **Quick Release** (1527 North Ashland Avenue; ☎ 773-871-3110). They sell all categories of bikes in small numbers and also offer full-service repair and custom bike construction. Beloved to others: **Kozy's Cyclery** (3712 North Halsted, ☎ 773-281-2263; 1451 West Webster at Clybourn, ☎ 773-528-2700; 219 West Erie, ☎ 312-266-1700; and 601 South La Salle Street; ☎ 312-360-0020). Voted the number-one bike shop in Chicago by *Windy City Sports,* Kozy's carries Giant, GT, Cannondale, Specialized, and Schwinn.

Two recommendations for purchasing skateboards include **Uprise Skateboard Shop** (1820 North Milwaukee Avenue; ☎ 773-342-7763) and **Air Times Snow and Skate Boards** (3317 North Clark; ☎ 773-248-4970). For skateboard apparel, try **Londo Mondo** (1100 North Dearborn; ☎ 312-751-2794), which carries lots of other activewear as well.

BOOKS, CARDS, AND STATIONERY

IN THE LOOP Adam Brent is the son of legendary bookseller Stuart Brent, whose store stood on Michigan Avenue for 50 years. **Brent's Books & Cards, Ltd.,** in the Loop (309 West Washington; ☎ 312-364-0126), is where Adam has won success with his dedication to personal service. His well-read staff reveres books, and the store offers author appearances and a huge selection of titles (including a wide selection of children's books). Adam is out to "match and exceed discounts at the megabookstores," with 10% off some hardcovers and 30% off current *New York Times* bestsellers. The table where he seats authors for signings has a lot of history: Saul Bellow, Tom Wolfe, Nelson Algren, Truman Capote, Gore Vidal, and hundreds of others sat alongside Stuart Brent.

A bookshop that has scored high with literary Chicago is **Barbara's Bookstore** (with locations at Sears Tower, at Northwestern Hospital, at Macy's on State Street, at the corner of Roosevelt Road and Halsted Street, and in Oak Park; **www.barbarasbookstore.com** for more info). In business since 1963, Barbara's often schedules author readings and pays attention to local writers.

ON MICHIGAN AVENUE At Water Tower Place, **Papyrus** (☎ 312-266-9945) sells stationery, custom printing, cards, and gifts (they're also at 10 South La Salle; ☎ 312-201-0902; and at 615 West Diversey; 773-327-9321). When it comes to books, the national-chain titans continue to battle the small independent booksellers around the city, but even among the giant discounters, there are favorites. One of the best is **Borders** (830 North Michigan Avenue; ☎ 312-573-0564), which has won over many readers with a caring staff, a vast supply of tomes (some 200,000 titles), music, a cafe, children's story hours, and exciting author appearances. There are other outstanding Borders at 150 North State, Clark Street and Diversey, Hyde Park, Lincoln Village, 755 West North, and other locations in the city and suburbs.

What are stationery and cards without writing instruments? Find the latter at **Montblanc** (900 North Michigan Avenue; ☎ 312-943-1200), home of limited-edition pens that become coveted collectibles. And while you're here, check out the collection of watches; they're gorgeous, as are the briefcases.

NEAR NORTH Another book giant is **Barnes & Noble** (1130 North State, ☎ 312-280-8155; 659 West Diversey Parkway, ☎ 773-871-9004; 1441 West Webster, ☎ 773-871-3610; and other locations). **Rush Street,** which once housed cabarets, now is home to several unique shops. **Children in Paradise Bookstore** (909 North Rush; ☎ 312-951-5437) is a kids-only first in Chicago, where both children and their parents can browse in happy-making surroundings. A carpeted reading area with pillows is used for weekly story hours (mornings, twice weekly), and children enjoy a large selection of DVDs and books appropriate for ages newborn through middle school.

RIVER NORTH **Paper Source** (232 West Chicago Avenue; ☎ 312-337-0798) is where we've noticed handmade rag papers (in fact, all manner of unusual and special papers and notebooks), specialty books, ribbons, and wax seals. There are also gifts, such as glass pens. In short, shopping here is fun.

OLD TOWN, LINCOLN PARK, CLARK, AND CLYBOURN CORRIDOR In Old Town, find **Pulp & Ink** (1344 North Wells Street; ☎ 312-475-1344), where you can buy (among other items in paper goods and gifts) wedding invitations that embrace color (such as Claudia Calhoun's cards in cranberry or the "Kate" papers in chocolate hues—unique, yet tasteful). Further north in Wicker Park, another popular paper source is **Paper Doll** (1747 West Division Street; ☎ 773-227-6950), the place to find fanciful and funky (sometimes hometown) cards, notepaper, and quirky gifts; they also purvey custom stationery and invitations.

All She Wrote (825 West Armitage; ☎ 773-529-0100; also at 100 East Walton; ☎ 312-274-3470; and in Winnetka) is another great source for stationery and gifts, as well as cards and wrapping paper. Monogrammed items are in demand; you may also find baby gifts and wedding favors. For comic books, including *manga,* head to **Chicago Comics** (3244 North Clark; ☎ 773-528-1983). On Southport, find **Flypaper,** (3402 North Southport; ☎ 773-296-4359). The space is brimming with inexpensive gifty things, paper goods, unusual wrapping paper, and cards.

Farther north, in Andersonville, is a terrific bookstore called **Women & Children First** (5233 North Clark; ☎ 773-769-9299), owned by knowledgeable women who care a lot about the books their customers like and buy accordingly. At the other end of town, out south, **Hyde Park 57th Street Books** (1301 East 57th Street; ☎ 773-684-1300) is also exemplary.

USED BOOKS At 2850 North Lincoln Avenue is a good used-book store, **Powell's** (☎ 773-248-1444), which can also be found at 828

South Wabash (☎ 312-341-0748) and 1501 East 57th Street (the main store) in the Hyde Park neighborhood (☎ 773-955-7780). The South Wabash store is the only Powell's in the Loop, but we like the Lincoln Park location because it has the largest number of art books—and it's usually so quiet, the ghost of Hemingway could be lurking. In Hyde Park, a huge favorite (particularly for antiquarian books) is **O'Gara & Wilson** (1448 East 57th Street; ☎ 773-363-0993). A friend tells us she found a book here that was printed circa 1500. And, for sheer atmosphere, hurry to rambling **Bookman's Alley** (rear of 1712 Sherman Avenue, Evanston; ☎ 847-869-6999); they probably carry most every book printed in this past century.

This is probably the place to mention a real find: **Yesterday** (1143 West Addison; ☎ 773-248-8087). It's a source for rare vintage and antique magazines, newspapers, and posters. A friend found a copy of *The American* magazine from 1923; another unearthed an *Arts & Decoration* magazine from 1931.

CAMERAS

FOR ALL YOUR DIGITAL AND FILM NEEDS, check out **Helix Camera & Video,** where prices are fair and the selection is great. Among their city and suburban locations: the main store at 310 South Racine Avenue (☎ 312-421-6000) and 223 Skokie Valley Road in Highland Park (☎ 847-831-1000). If you're looking for film specialists in this digital age, there are still plenty of options. **Central Camera Company** (232 South Wabash; ☎ 312-427-5580) carries a large, varied selection of cameras, lenses, flashes, and other equipment (film and digital), plus darkroom items. Another top choice is **Calumet Photographic** (1111 North Cherry Street, off Division Street; ☎ 312-440-4920). (Before you buy photo equipment of any kind, it's a good idea to check online resources first; one Web site we recommend is **www.dpreview.com.**)

CLOTHING AND SHOES

IN THE LOOP Pick up flannel shirts at the **Pendleton Woolen Mills Products Store** (120 South Wabash; ☎ 312-372-1699) in the Palmer House Hotel arcade. The store has been here for several decades, offering goods from Pendleton Woolen Mills in Oregon. Choose from scarves, blankets, men's sport coats and slacks, and coats aplenty in winter. You'll also find cotton-knit sweaters, sweatshirts, jewelry, umbrellas, tote bags, and more.

If you travel west on Lake Street, you'll note a chic boutique called **Koros Art + Style** (1019 West Lake; ☎ 312-738-0155), filled with some name brands and some accessories (belts, jewelry), plus art for sale on its brick walls.

La Salle Street houses several men's stores and emporiums dedicated to business accessories (male shoppers involved in law and finance in this area outnumber the women). The suits you buy at **Syd Jerome**

Men's Wear (2 North La Salle Street; ☎ 312-346-0333) will make you someone's best-dressed man, while menswear powerhouse **Brooks Brothers** (209 South La Salle Street; ☎ 312-263-0100) is a favorite of men and women alike. Many prefer the BB at 713 North Michigan Avenue (☎ 312-915-0060), but mall locations are plentiful in the suburbs (Northbrook Court, Old Orchard, Woodfield, and Oakbrook Center).

Another menswear supplier is **Jos. A. Bank Clothiers** (25 East Washington; ☎ 312-782-4432), with several suburban stores in addition to the Loop location. A final men's outfitter to try in this area is **Duru's,** known for its custom-tailored shirts and suits (221 North La Salle Street; ☎ 312-782-4443).

Before we leave the Loop, consider a store for women to the south in the Hyde Park area: **Kimberly Lee & Co.** (1529 East 53rd Street; ☎ 773-643-8040), where accessories (jewelry, watches, and handbags) are appealing.

ON MICHIGAN AVENUE For men, let's begin with an old-time custom tailor recognized for expertise with hand-tailored suits, "architects of fashion for Chicago's living legends": **Lawrence Pucci** (333 North Michigan Avenue, second floor; ☎ 312-332-3759). And while you're cruising the Magnificent Mile, peruse the premises at **NikeTown** (669 North Michigan Avenue; ☎ 312-642-6363); otherwise, people may not believe you've been to Chicago. This is a hotbed for sports enthusiasts—a veritable retail-sports arena of Nike footwear, apparel, accessories, and equipment. There's a lot going on here (video presentations, for example), and the third floor contains a wide-ranging selection of gear for active women.

Speaking of footwear, **Hanig's** shoes for men and women get around: in addition to the emporium at 660 North Michigan Avenue (☎ 312-642-5330), there's a **Hanig's Birkenstock Shop** at 847 West Armitage (☎ 773-929-5568), among other stores.

Fashion reigns at the beauteous **Burberry** (633 North Michigan; ☎ 312-787-2500), even as men and women seek the instantly recognizable camel-and-cream (with a touch of black) plaid that enhances so many raincoats, scarves, and other items. At 645 North Michigan is the local outpost of the great Italian menswear designer **Ermenegildo Zegna** (☎ 312-587-9660).

Extensive is the word for Chicago's flagship **Gap** store (555 North Michigan Avenue; ☎ 312-494-8580), with clothes for the whole family as well as Gap shoes; plus, the sales staff is really friendly. One of the chic names for men to hit the avenue is **Saks Fifth Avenue Men's Store** (717 North Michigan Avenue; ☎ 312-475-9195). Still another national classic is **Polo Ralph Lauren** (750 North Michigan Avenue; ☎ 312-280-1655). This 37,000-square-foot Chicago flagship is said to be the largest Polo Ralph Lauren store anywhere. You'll find the designer's men's, women's, and children's clothing and accessories, plus home furnishings; there's even the chic **RL,** the first Ralph Lauren restaurant (115 East

Chicago Avenue; ☎ 312-475-1100). Within the Georgian facade is every-thing from linens to women's equestrian clothing. Items for the home are presented in unique lifestyle environments. (Word is out, too, of a new **Ralph Lauren Rugby Concept Store** opening at 1000 West Armitage.)

Banana Republic (744 North Michigan Avenue; ☎ 312-642-0020; and other locations) started as a repository for clothes you wished you could afford to buy for camping expeditions; it's graduated to provid-ing really nice sportswear and accessories, but you already knew that. What you may not know is that **Giorgio Armani** is holding court—and charging *molto* for its divine duds—at 800 North Michigan Avenue (☎ 312-573-4220); the more affordable **Armani Exchange** is down the street at 520 North Michigan Avenue (☎ 312-467-5702). Back at 800 North Michigan Avenue, find the posh Park Hyatt Chicago Hotel; the address also houses **Marlowe** (☎ 312-988-9398), a luxe store focusing on ultrachic Italian-made cashmere knitwear, handbags, and leathers. This is Marlowe's first flagship store in the United States.

If we had a separate category in this section for girls age 3 through grade school, **American Girl Place** (111 East Chicago Avenue, across from the Water Tower; ☎ 312-943-9400) would be number one. This was indeed the number-one, and only, location until the popular con-cept went national (as noted earlier, operations will move to Water Tower Place on Michigan Avenue after fall 2008). Girls do truly love the American Girl collection of books, dolls, doll clothes, and other delights, including the latest fashions for real live girls. In addition to a cafe serving lunch, tea, and dinner, there's a theater (call ☎ 877-AG-PLACE for Revue tickets).

Another titan, **Rochester Clothing** (840 North Michigan Avenue; ☎ 312-337-8877), offers top fashions for larger men (notable clients include many pro-basketball players). The emphasis is on the best of Italian designers, from Zanella dress trousers to cashmere coats from Zegna, as well as Calvin Klein, Levi's, a complete Polo casual line, and more.

At 875 North Michigan is the stunning and nearly 100-story-high **John Hancock Building,** which houses the veddy chic men's clothiers **Paul Stuart** (☎ 312-640-2650), which came west from Manhattan; they carry women's clothing, too. While you're there, check out the Hancock's newsy restaurants, little shops below (such as the **Aveda Lifestyle** store; ☎ 312-664-0417), and, of course, the view from the 95th floor.

A word (or more) about **Bloomingdale's** (☎ 312-440-4460) belongs here: Lyman and Joseph Bloomingdale set up a little notions shop in New York, and by 1872 it had become an East Side bazaar. It took until the 1980s for the big B to hit Chicago, at 900 North Michigan Avenue. Bloomie's was first to feature in-store boutiques for international designers, and, it's reported, they introduced the first designer shop-ping bag. Of all the national stores, Chicago has one of the most beau-tiful. There are stores in Old Orchard and Oakbrook Center, too. At

900, out-of-towners can check Bloomie's Visitors' Center (☎ 312-440-4596), on level one near Women's Shoes. Another source for menswear and women's wear is at 900—**Mark Shale** (☎ 312-440-0720)—which has suburban stores as well. Don't leave 900 without stopping at **Max Studio** (on level four; ☎ 312-944-4445) for hot styles that won't decimate your wallet. And you really should check out the bras at **Intimacy** (third level; ☎ 312-337-8366); owner Susan Nethero has appeared on *Oprah* to talk about the importance of fitting bras properly.

Does anyone need a reminder that the north end of Michigan Avenue is Shoe Paradise? Note the before-mentioned **Gucci** and **Stuart Weitzman. Salvatore Ferragamo** has a sparkling store here (645 North Michigan; ☎ 312-397-0464)—the company's first in the Midwest, housing women's and men's shoes, handbags, and clothing, as well as other fine accessories from the Italian master. **Ghurka** (645 North Michigan Avenue; ☎ 312-440-3855) carries leather goods, including small leather items for men and women, from handbags to luggage. And don't forget to peruse the **Chanel** boutique (935 North Michigan Avenue; ☎ 312-787-5500), a lush store filled with internationally renowned clothes, jewelry, and accessories.

ON OAK STREET World-class shopping begins on (no, not Rodeo Drive) Oak Street. Early ambience was strictly beads and wampum. Then the settlers descended. By 1850, Oak was a residential street—among the first to turn to ashes in the Chicago Fire of 1871. By the 1880s, chic mansions gave new meaning to the words "Gold Coast," and this probably set Oak on its lifelong mission to cross sophistication with cozy hospitality. Now, the low-rise, high-fashion city block rimmed by Rush Street and the northernmost end zone of Michigan Avenue has come into its own, evolving into the style center it is today.

In most major cities, visions of the world's most exotic bazaars suddenly crystallize into one prototypical street, teeming with treasures arrayed before the eyes of dazzled shoppers. Surrounded by urban canyons, that single special avenue stands apart, its unique charm inviting, delighting. Such is Oak, Chicago's blockbuster block of fabulous fashion. The Oak Street council carefully keeps the 38 Art Deco street lights new, the 33 trees replaced if winter has been particularly rough, and even its sidewalks colored a distinctive charcoal gray.

unofficial **TIP**

Because parking on Oak is such a nuisance, choose from two solutions: valet parking (an attendant is stationed midblock approximately in front of 101 East Oak) or the 1 East Oak garage (at the corner of Oak and State streets).

What's in store? The ultimate by the world's most prestigious designers, presented with hometown flair. You can go crazy spending money on Oak, from the Michigan Avenue end to the corner of Rush at 25 East Oak Street (where you'll find the newly expanded **Barneys New York;** ☎ 312-587-1700). Designers love it here, including **Sansappelle** (34 East Oak; ☎ 312-642-9642). Founded in 1976, this is a top manufacturer of late-day, evening, casual, and special-occasion fashions for women. But one of Oak's secrets is that you can actually save money at the street's only drugstore: **Bravco, the Beauty Center** (43 East Oak; ☎ 312-943-4305), where you can find anything from false eyelashes to toothpaste.

Oak's most uniquely homegrown high-fashion treasure is **Ultimo** (114 East Oak; ☎ 312-787-1171), known internationally for, as its name implies, the ultimate in high-end clothing for women as well as tomorrow-flavored accessories. Owner Sara Albrecht brings creations from some of the world's top designers here. Speaking of international designers on Oak, you'll also find **Jil Sander** (48 East Oak; ☎ 312-335-0006), for one. A very special Oak Street treasure is the 35-year-old **Glasses, Ltd.** (47 East Oak; ☎ 312-944-6876), a truly mom-and-pop business offering superb frames by designers such as Tom Ford, Gucci, Alain Mikli, Bulgari, and others. This is a full-service business: eyes are examined and lenses made on-site, the frames have tomorrow's look (most don't come cheap, though options for smaller budgets are available, too), and the customer service is exemplary.

International flavor is ever-present on Oak. The French name of renown is **Yves St. Laurent Rive Gauche** (51 East Oak; ☎ 312-751-8995). Two floors (men's on one, women's on two) display ready-to-wear, from shoes, small leather goods, and handbags, to the *beauté* line (the new fragrance for men is L'Homme). Begin your Italian fling at **Prada** (30 East Oak; ☎ 312-951-1113). **Luca Luca** (59 East Oak; ☎ 312-664-1512) presents more Italian women's wear (the colors are lush); **Hermès of Paris** (110 East Oak; ☎ 312-787-8175) deals in exclusive scarves, ties, leather goods, and other goodies *à la française*; and **The Wolford Boutique** (54 East Oak; ☎ 312-642-8787), part of an international chain (originating in Austria), offers fun and fashionable imported hosiery, bodywear, and swimwear. Wolford's goods are pricey, but women like them because they fit, they last, and they're so luxe. Another favorite is **Kate Spade** (101 East Oak; ☎ 312-654-8853), the company's largest freestanding boutique to date, packed with all the Spade bags and shoes, handpicked items to match, and a line of men's accessories (Jack Spade), designed by Kate's husband and business partner, Andy.

Among other shops to peruse are **BCBG Max Azria** (103 East Oak; ☎ 312-787-7395), for young figures; **Nicole Miller** (63 East Oak; ☎ 312-664-3532), with a full line of the New York designer's often whimsical prints and an extensive bridal collection; maternity fashions at **A Pea in the Pod** (46 East Oak; ☎ 312-944-3080); and men's fashions (many by the hand-tailoring genius Pal Zileri) at **Tessuti** (50 East Oak; ☎ 312-266-4949). One of the most right-now bridal salons (specializing in couture gowns) in the country is **Ultimate Bride** (106 East Oak; ☎ 312-337-6300). And juniors make a beeline for hot fashions and accessories at **Sugar Magnolia** (34 East Oak; ☎ 312-944-0885). Another gift to Oak

Street is **Designs by Ming** (70 East Oak; ☎ 312-649-1510), a custom-clothing, alterations, and bridal store.

The last word goes to **George Greene** (49 East Oak; ☎ 312-654-2490) for menswear that is truly exceptional. The designers here are the ones who count.

NEAR NORTH High fashion knows fewer astute practitioners than Marilyn Blaszka and Dominic Marcheschi, whose **Blake** (212 West Chicago Avenue; ☎ 312-202-0047) lives in stunning new quarters. The owners pay attention to knockout and tasteful European lines, such as Dries van Noten, Pierre Hardy, Balenciaga, Marni, Rick Owens, Martin Margiela, and others. Another of the important high-fashion emporiums is **Ikram** (873 North Rush Street; ☎ 312-587-1000)—very special because of owner Ikram's exquisite taste in everything from shoes to vintage jewelry. A fashion spy reports that Ikram was the first in Chicago to carry Jimmy Choo shoes (and *pricey* is a key word).

If you're jonesing for jeans, don't miss **AG Chicago** (48 East Walton Street; ☎ 312-787-7680), which stocks more than 25 styles of denim under the AG label, plus belts and other accessories. Styles range from flared to superskinny, and they'll hem them for you, too, free. The **Denim Lounge of Madison & Friends** (940 North Rush; ☎ 312-642-6403) entices you to wade through the kiddie boutique upstairs and go downstairs to find a huge quantity of many denim brands, from 575 to Shagg.

Also on Rush at 946 is an improbable boutique: **Tender Buttons** (☎ 312-337-7033), which no doubt has that missing button you'd love to resew on your favorite jacket. Choose from men's blazer buttons and imports (including gold buttons from France). Button, button, who's got the button? They do.

A terrific store—because the owner Terri Vizzone is so adept—is **Only She** (719 North State Street; ☎ 312-335-1353). Fashion is the point here, but more specifically, wearable art culled from designers and artisans who know how to dazzle. An unqualified rave.

Beguelin (716 North Wabash; ☎ 312-335-1222) specializes in handmade leathers from Milan; these include handbags, shoes, furniture, and other home accessories. A lot of stunning women think **Mary Walter** (33 West Superior; ☎ 312-266-1094) is their own best-kept secret, but of course they're not alone. In this attractive store, removed from hectic avenue shoppers, you can browse among beautifully chosen suits, jackets, and other delectables for work and leisure, such as hand-painted scarves and jewelry (note the one-of-a-kind pieces). There's also a full-time tailor here. A bit to the north is **Mary Mary** (706 North Dearborn; ☎ 312-654-8100), a fabulous boutique that goes a bit beyond clothing: you'll find everything from shawls to chandeliers. There are wonderful (and affordable) items for the home, a children's gift department, and a ton of lovely surprises.

WELLS STREET At 678 North Wells Street are the French sports wear creations of Marithé and François Girbaud's **Girbaud Boutique**

(☎ 312-787-2022). The address of 1350 North Wells is the spiffy home of **Haberdash** (☎ 312-440-1300), a men's store that achieves a modern spin on a classic haberdashery, reviving the days when men really knew how to dress. They'll find everything here from the British lines of Fred Perry and Ted Baker London to L.A.'s James Perse. At 1706 North Wells is **Handle with Care** (☎ 312-751-2929), famous for up-to-the-second women's fashions. **Fabrice** (1714 North Wells Street; ☎ 312-280-0011) is a must-visit for faux and fab jewelry—the kind featured at the boutique's Paris branch; resin-based and painted, Fabrice's pieces make people say, "Where did you get that?" when you wear them. Here too are accessories, home items, soaps, and other gifts.

LINCOLN PARK–CLYBOURN CORRIDOR West Armitage and Webster avenues house several reasons area clotheshorses don't always have to dash to Michigan Avenue or the Loop. Before we hit these two streets, if you're desperate for something new (if used), note **Cynthia's Consignments** (2218 Clybourn Avenue; ☎ 773-248-7714). Now let's go to Webster:

The Kangaroo Connection (1113 West Webster; ☎ 773-248-5499) carries goods and gear from Australia and animal souvenirs (toy koalas, kangaroos, wombats), as well as stationery, clothing, and jewelry. Owner Kathy Schubert opens the store "by appointment or by chance," filling orders mainly from her Web site at **www.kangaroo connection.com.**

A fine place for lingerie is **Isabella** (1101 West Webster; ☎ 773-281-2352); they also have a Roscoe Village store (2238 West Roscoe; ☎ 773-472-3822). Another of Webster's outstanding shops is **Underthings** (804 West Webster; ☎ 773-472-9291). Don't be embarrassed; this is another store dedicated to (and for) lingerie, carrying everything from robes to bras. But let's back up a bit and go west to **Shopgirl** (1206 West Webster; ☎ 773-935-7467), a sexy, sophisticated boutique with clothes by Trina Turk, Wendy Hil, and Milly, and accessories such as necklaces by Viv & Ingrid, Erin Gallagher, and some Chicago designers. Shopgirl's owner, Kate Prange, has also opened a maternity shop at 1207 West Webster called **Show & Tell** and a darlin' shop for girls, **Spoiled . . . But Not Rotten** (1201 West Webster; ☎ 773-935-1399), with clothing for juniors and sizes 4, 5, and 6, plus shoes, jewelry, and lots of denim.

The highly regarded Italian brand **Furla** has opened a store at 1211 West Webster (☎ 773-525-7420) packed with gorgeous handbags (amazing quality leathers) and some accessories. Another smash hit is **Cotelac** (1159 West Webster; ☎ 773-281-2330), with an accent on superb, carefully edited clothing and shoes. Everything is washable and created by a French designer; this is the first Cotelac in the United States. Nearby is **The Left Bank**—no, we're still on Webster, not Paris (1155 West Webster; ☎ 773-929-7422)—filled with yummy jewelry, great gifts, and candles, but the main stage is reserved for custom-made bridal wear (veils, and so on). A block or so east is **Eskell** (953 West

Webster; ☎ 773-477-9390), where Elizabeth Del Castillo and Kelly Whitesell design their own clothing and sell lots of vintage, too.

Moving to West Armitage Avenue, at 808 you'll find clothes by inventive Chicago designer **Cynthia Rowley** (☎ 773-528-6160). Handmade wearables by national artisans are for sale at **Isis on Armitage** (823 West Armitage; ☎ 773-665-7290); more of their glossy wearables can be found at **Isis on Melrose** (900 North Michigan Avenue; ☎ 312-664-7140). Looking for unique goods by leading artists and craftsmen? **Art Effect** (934 West Armitage; ☎ 773-929-3600) is chockfull of wearable art and jewelry. Having celebrated its 22nd anniversary in the summer of 2006, the Lincoln Park pioneer, owned by Esther Fishman, has jewelry from Jeanine Payer and Me & Ro; Orla Kiely bags; Michael Stars, Three Dots, and Billy Blues clothing; Mor, Archipelago, and Votivo beauty products; and Nigella Lawson, Michael Aram, and Cucina home products.

Nearby, **Jane Hamill** (1115 West Armitage; ☎ 773-665-1102) plies her trade, which is creating women's clothes that are both chic and affordable. With each season, her design talents grow; her accessories are always well chosen, too. **Mint Julep** is new (1013 West Armitage; ☎ 773-296-2997), where Sarah Eshaghy has brought her great fashion sense to women's clothing with contemporary lines and affordable prices.

904 West Armitage is the latest location for **1154 Lill Studio** (☎ 773-477-5455), where you can create your own handbag from their roster of fabrics and ideas. Your next stop should be **Active Endeavors** (853 West Armitage; ☎ 773-281-8100) for lines of jeans and activewear different from the ones you'll see at the chain stores. Peruse **Studio 910** (1007 West Armitage; ☎ 773-929-2400) for upscale women's wear. So many desirables, so little time: they sell Diane von Furstenberg, Da-Nang, Rock & Republic, and jewelry by many local and national designers. A designer who features her own (about 60% of the goods here, 40% other designers) is **Margaret O'Leary** (857 West Armitage; ☎ 773-598-5625), and both men and women may enjoy Euro fashions (casual, career wear) at one of the **Kuhlman** stores (838 West Armitage; ☎ 773-880-5720). Very USA is **American Apparel** (837 West Armitage; ☎ 773-880-9801), where besides hoodies and tees you'll find an interesting tie-on dress (ties make it possible to wear it in different ways); look also for their organic line. Other local stores are at Rush and Walton, on Milwaukee Avenue, and at Broadway and Belmont. Before leaving Armitage, take a peek at the **Paul Frank Store** (851 West Armitage; ☎ 773-388-3122), purveyor of fun and funky women's and men's clothing, bikes, and home furnishings.

Before we hit Wicker Park and Bucktown, it might be advantageous to investigate several stores on North Clybourn; a few are outlet stores, most are not. Three that aren't (but have great sales): the sports-oriented **Patagonia** (1800 North Clybourn; ☎ 312-951-0518), known for outerwear and activewear; **Chico's** (1851 North Clybourn; ☎ 773-472-3722), which offers less-rushed shopping for women's separates and accessories than the Chico's at Water Tower Place and at 948 North Rush Street; and, finally, another in the lineup of **Talbots** (1845 North Clybourn; ☎ 773-472-7510) women's-wear stores (they can fit all sizes from petites to larger sizes).

WICKER PARK–BUCKTOWN This entire area is a booming source for boutiques, especially on Damen Avenue—they're probably proliferating here more than in any other part of town, and some of the most popular have both affordables and "little-bit-moreables." Before heading in that direction, guys who want to hit the latest Bucktown style address should investigate **TK Men** (1909 West North Avenue; ☎ 773-342-9800). Shirts are stacked on a pool table; menswear ranges from $10 sunglasses to cashmere hoodies. Draw a beer while you try on premium denims.

Milwaukee Avenue has many boutiques, but one to love is **Jade** (1557 North Milwaukee Avenue; ☎ 773-342-5233), so named for its green walls and Asian ambience; here, Laura Haberman sells chic women's wear and great jewelry. The smash hit on Milwaukee, though, is **Scoop NYC** (1702 North Milwaukee; ☎ 773-227-9930). Billing itself as "the ultimate closet for men/women," this store has rooms full of kid stuff, hats, clothes, shoes—you name it. There's even a cafe on the premises if you need sustenance while shopping.

Now we'll amble over to Damen and hit a few highlights, starting to the south and working our way north. Shoes and more shoes (great-looking flats and casual shoes for men) reside at **Giraudon New York** (1616 North Damen Avenue; ☎ 866-309-0039); right next door (same address) is **Shebang** (☎ 773 486-3800), for handbags and other accessories (including some great jewelry), many by emerging designers you won't see elsewhere. For young men, a pit stop is **HIM** (1653 North Damen Avenue; ☎ 773-235-3360); there's a motorcycle in the window and a cigar bar across the street at 1648 North Damen. **p.45** (1643 North Damen Avenue; ☎ 773-862-4523) is another terrific (if a bit pricier than most boutiques around here) source for clothes, shoes, jewelry, and other accessories (including those by local talents). A step north, **Helen Yi** (1645 North Damen Avenue; ☎ 773-252-3838) offers some local designers and some national names, such as Theory, Paul Smith, Chloé, Derek Lam, and more; the selection includes clothing, hats, shoes, and thoughtfully selected accessories. Next door is **Belly Dance Maternity** (1647 North Damen Avenue; ☎ 773-862-1133), filled to the brim with the best lines in maternity fashions, workout wear, skin care, and lingerie.

Still on Damen, take a break from shopping at **Silver Cloud** restaurant (1700 North Damen Avenue; ☎ 312-489-6212). Up and coming at 1714 West Damen (just below Pagoda Red's Asian antiques) is the new **Marc by Marc Jacobs,** the designer's first freestanding Chicago boutique, due to open in summer 2007. You'll also love the contemporary clothing and accessories at **Clothes Minded** (1735 North Damen Avenue; ☎ 773-227-3402), where the friendly staff will help you find everything you ever needed. You'll even find gifts for the home. Take a look around **D. Marie Boutique** (1867 North Damen Avenue; ☎ 773-489-3220) for high-quality clothes, belts, and other accessories, and stop at **Michelle Tan** (1872 North Damen Avenue; ☎ 773-252-1888), featuring the Chicago designer's own fashions and her tasteful imported jewelry. This is Tan's first retail store.

Now, a word to the bride. You've set the date and found the dress; now you need other accessories: veils, shoes, gifts, jewelry, and more. Not to worry—they're all at **Urbane Weddings** (1920 North Damen Avenue; ☎ 773-289-3000).

Next, take a look at the superb fashions for the more voluptuous among us, and note the larger (but still very stylish) sizes and well-proportioned accessories that have finally found a fashion home at **Vive La Femme** (2048 North Damen; ☎ 773-772-7429; **www.vive lafemme.com**). At **Saffron** (2064 North Damen Avenue; ☎ 773-486-7753), look for owner Padmaja Manerikar Maryanski's own elegant designs and ready-to-wear, plus the creations of others who love color and fine fabrics. There's everything here from evening gowns to bath-and-beauty indulgences (such as chocolate soap) and even some gourmet-food items (such as artichoke pesto).

The next stop is **Robin Richman** (2108 North Damen Avenue; ☎ 773-278-6150), a visual treat rich with hot clothing, shoes, and accessories by small global designers such as Parisians Marc le Bihan and Elsa Esturgie, New Yorker Gary Graham, Antipast from Tokyo, Maria Calderara from Italy, and more. Here too are antique finds (vintage bags and jewelry) and other treasures. Among the latter: Richman's own hand-knit sweaters.

Then peek into a little shop called **Soutache** (2125 North Damen; ☎ 773-292-9110), the place to find ribbons, braiding, every sort of trimming. And, finally, an unusual find called **G Boutique** (2131 North Damen Avenue; ☎ 773-235-1234) houses lingerie from lines such as Cosabella, Hanky Panky, and others, not to mention even-more-intimate wares (massage oils, sex toys). This might be a good source for bridal gifts, and who knows what else.

Stores keep popping up on West Division, so if you explore the area, you'll probably find more shops that were still on the drawing board when we went to press.

Quality rules at **Public i** (1923 West Division; ☎ 773-772-9088) when it comes to their men's and women's clothing, so expect high-quality, unusual stuff that's not always the most expensive: in menswear, R. Scott French and Isda for Men, and in women's wear, La Rok and Isda for Women. Also check out their travel products, such as Rimowa suitcases.

West Division is also home to two appealing boutiques for shoes, and you probably should check out both to see which you prefer. **Pump**

(1659 West Division; ☎ 773-384-6750) is owned by a true shoe-lover; you can tell because Maureen Longua has found styles you don't see coming and going—brands include Betsey Johnson, Miss Sixty, Charles David, Via Spiga, and many more; some choices are very moderately priced. And while they're on Milwaukee, male and female avant-garde–ists had better pick up their denims at the hot **G-Star Raw** (1525 North Milwaukee; ☎ 773-342-2623). Another option is **Steelo** (1850 West Division; ☎ 773-227-4590), where Monica Yost also has a passion for fabulous shoes as well as women's and men's accessories from handbags to jewelry, so you should probably hot-foot it over to see this place, too. **Saint Alfred** (1531 North Milwaukee Avenue; ☎ 773-486-7159) specializes in affordable (and not-so-affordable) sneakers, including some limited-edition beauties. One last stop to the north is **Silver Moon** (1755 West North Avenue; ☎ 773-235-5797), which excels in vintage clothing, offers bridal-gown reconstruction, and designs gowns based on vintage styling.

ON HALSTED, CLARK, LINCOLN, SOUTHPORT Young women love to shop on North Halsted, thanks to standbys like **Nine West** for shoes and bags (2058 North Halsted Street; ☎ 773-871-4154). Note, too, **Lucky Brand** (2048 North Halsted Street; ☎ 773-975-8168), with clothing as well as jeans; **Betsey Johnson** (2120 North Halsted Street; ☎ 773-871-3961); and a don't-miss: **Calvin Tran** (2154 North Halsted Street; ☎ 773-529-4070), maker of stunning clothes (dresses, gowns, and tops) that can change shape depending on how they're draped and fastened.

Farther north on Halsted is a collection of hot shops where a lot of the natives investigate the goods. They're all just doors from each other, so we'll take 'em as we see 'em. **Barneys New York Co-op** (2209–11 North Halsted; ☎ 773-248-0426) offers fashion that's a bit more affordable than (but just as stylish as) the Barneys on Oak. Next door is **Abercrombie & Fitch** (2215 North Halsted; ☎ 773-281-2148); here, the eardrums of the young take a drubbing thanks to the music (?) in the background, but their fashion sense is heightened with the best in casual wear for kids from grammar school to college. Across the street is the **Blues Jean Bar** (2210 North Halsted; ☎ 773-248-5326)—strictly jeans, tons of brands. If you're looking for a unique style, this is the place. At **Club Monaco** (2206 North Halsted; ☎ 773-528-2031), find high style at good prices in togs for women.

Clark Street fashion stores, most of them for women, include trendsetting sportswear and edgy accessories (handbags and jewelry, especially) at **Panache** (2252 North Clark Street; ☎ 773-477-4537); this is a neighborhood fave with a variety of prices and sizes. Two **Express** stores, one for women's separates and accessories (☎ 773 871-2738) and another for men's sportswear (☎ 773-868-4670), are at the corner of Clark and Belden. Across the street is **Nonpareil** (2300 North Clark Street; ☎ 773-477-2933), where you're likely to see incredibly eclectic goods: fashions as well as table treasures, silk jackets, trinkets, expensive imported jewelry, and more. There's also a large **Urban Outfitters** (2352 North Clark Street; ☎ 773-549-1711), where some things are real finds and others real *junque,* both in clothes and home design. And while you're hopping about this neck of the woods, slip north to **Soupbox** (2943 North Broadway; ☎ 773-935-9800) and take out (or eat in) some of the best soup you've ever had. They have ices in the summer months, too.

We're going a few blocks west now to Southport Avenue, where you'll find the superb **Krista K** (3458 North Southport Avenue; ☎ 773-248-1967). Owner Krista Meyers carries only the most chic women's wear, accessories such as jewelry by local designers Coco Plumb and Sway, and handbag lines by Kooba and Luba J. A second location at 3530 North Southport (☎ 773-248-4477) carries only maternity fashions, such as those by Liz Lange.

Southport, in fact, is increasingly attracting young (and not so) shoppers for everything from plates to pleated skirts. After a look inside **Dilani Shoes** (3440 North Southport; ☎ 773-598-1501) for stylish and affordable styles, pop into a fun store called **Red Head Boutique** (3450 North Southport Avenue; ☎ 773-325-9898), specializing in upscale, unusual clothing for women, accessories, and jewelry (not inexpensive). Across the street is **Flirt** (3449 North Southport Avenue; ☎ 773-935-4789), with merchandise that matches its name: date togs, career separates, and inexpensive jewelry. Another attractive boutique is **She One** (3402 North Southport Avenue; ☎ 773-549-9698), where Jennifer Crotty offers clothing (including unique sweaters) and accessories at reasonable prices; we noticed pieces by several local designers. Need a leather coat? Laura Villa travels way, way south to find coats of Argentinean leather ($365 to $600), as well as leather handbags and other wares, to display at **Xksito Boutique** (3453 North Southport; ☎ 773-525-8785). After a manicure at **Pinky Nail Studio** (3503 North Southport; ☎ 773-248-5080), you owe it to your stylish self to stop at **Trousseau** (3543 North Southport; ☎ 773-472-2727). Of course, they have a bridal section, but there's much more: bras by the dozens, swimsuits (ditto), candles, soaps, and more, all unusually tasteful in this fun-to-shop environment. A final stop is **Shane** (3657 North Southport; ☎ 773-549-0179), where men and women can find a lot of denim and other casual styles.

Back to Clark Street: head to **Hubba-Hubba** (3309 North Clark Street; ☎ 773-477-1414) for the best in vintage-inspired fashion (that means new and trendy clothes with a retro twist). **The Alley Stores** are popular, too (one central number, ☎ 773-883-1800, will give you store extensions). The original store, **The Alley** (3228 North Clark Street), is popular; one teen shopper told us, "They have really neat jewelry and those hard-to-find Chicago-cop leather jackets." They also have a vast number of T-shirts emblazoned with the name of your favorite band. The other Alley Stores are **Blue Havana** (858 West Belmont), a cigar and tobacco-accessory shop; **Silver District** (858 West Belmont), which sells jewelry and watches; **Taboo Tabou** (854 West Belmont), a source for adult novelties and lingerie; **Jive Monkey** (854 West Belmont, second floor), which offers some vintage wear but mostly custom T-shirts and accessories; **Tragically Hip** (850 West Belmont), a shop selling clothing (mostly junior sizes) and accessories at reasonable prices; the **John Galt Gallery** (3222 North Clark), for eclectic art; and **Architectural Revolution** (3224 North Clark), dealing in Asian-flavored home decor.

Another vintage source is **Vintage Deluxe** (1846 West Belmont; ☎ 773-529-7008)—they seem to have everything, even vintage eyewear, their specialty. Yet another trove of great vintage and thrift buys is at 812 West Belmont: **Hollywood Mirror** and (top floor and basement) **Ragstock** (☎ 773-868-9263; the latter is also at 1433 North Milwaukee Avenue; ☎ 773-486-1783).

An outlying addition to specific clothing needs that's north and west is **Chicago Tennis & Golf** (3365 North Drake; ☎ 773) 489-2999), where you can pick up great sportswear, including warm-ups, shoes, headbands, vests, hats—everything you need for tennis and golf. (This membership club also has services for restringing racquets and same-day regripping of golf clubs.) A bit west is **Marky Exclusive European Shoe Boutique** (3919 North Lincoln Avenue; ☎ 773-248-1500), where some great Italian and Spanish designs are on tap.

BEYOND WICKER PARK Do costumes belong in the clothing category? Why not? **Fantasy Headquarters** (4065 North Milwaukee Avenue; ☎ 773-777-0222 or 800-USA-WIGS) is the place to buy and rent costumes and wigs (both crazy and serious), makeup, and party props. Here's an entire area with "1,001 gags" (talking, singing skeletons for Halloween and whenever you need 'em), plus a magic section. If you're in need of a Santa Claus suit, characters from Harry Potter to Easter bunnies, a cow mask, or a vegetable (tomato, carrot) mask, it's here. This is the largest costume and wig store in the Midwest.

Further north in Andersonville is **Studio 90** (5239 North Clark Street; ☎ 773-878-0097), owned by two women sensitive to the clothing needs of the slightly older fashionista who wants comfort as well as style. Studio 90 is their own line, but they also purvey designs in clothing and accessories by other designers, such as remakes of vintage shoes. **Trillium at the Landmark** (5245 North Clark Street; ☎ 773-728-5301) has some great wearable art (and, in colder months, some toasty Icelandic sweaters), as well as styles for all ages. And while you're north, note that **Chicago Dance Supply** (5301 North Clark Street; ☎ 773-728-5344) has ballroom-dancing shoes, jazz pants, children's ballet togs and shoes, plus clothing and shoes for bellydancing and dance videos. At the opposite end of town, **Motion Unlimited** (218 South Wabash Avenue, eighth floor; ☎ 312-922-3330) is a super supply store for dancers and wannabes. A great place to pick up new pointe shoes.

IN GLENCOE, WINNETKA, AND BEYOND When it comes to women's clothes, people from the city drive to **Shirise** in Glencoe (341 Park;

unofficial **TIP**
Many locals prefer the Northbrook Court Neiman Marcus (☎ 847-564-0300) to the one in downtown Chicago; there's a huge parking lot, for one thing, and the sales force tends to be the shoppers' neighbors, dedicated to the fine art of Finding Something.

☎ 847-835-2595) for snazzy shoes, and while they're in that suburb they never miss **Nicchia** (688 Vernon; ☎ 847-835-2900) for gorgeous sportswear (including great knits) for men and women. A new favorite in Winnetka is **Neapolitan** (715 Elm Street; ☎ 847-441-7784), with an all-star roster of designer names like Philosophy, Tuleh, Chloé, Etro, Carolina Herrera, TSE, Narciso Rodriguez, and Zac Posen. Another favorite in the high-style category is Winnetka's **Frances Heffernan** (810 Elm; ☎ 847-446-2112), sporting Akris, Bogner, Piazza Sempione, Maria Pinto (a super hometown designer), Carmen Marc Valvo, and several younger designers at adjacent **Frannie** (808 Elm; ☎ 847-446-5508).

Northbrook Court—in the suburb of Northbrook, bordering Highland Park and Deerfield—is perhaps more fun to shop than most malls, thanks to its size (not too excessive) and goods (upscale but not desperately pricey). There's also a good small shopping center in downtown Highland Park (1849 Green Bay Road) called **Renaissance Place** with, among other stores, a pretty **Saks Fifth Avenue, Ann Taylor, Talbots, Pottery Barn, Restoration Hardware,** and more. Among other Highland Park designers, **Sandra Joy, Inc.** (1760 Cloverdale Avenue; ☎ 847-831-2318; by appointment only) is hot for high-end, one-of-a-kind antique framed handbags and frames of sterling silver, bakelite, and the like, with fabrics such as beaded lace, silk, satin, and leathers; each is a collector's (read: expensive) item.

Finally, wardrobe consultant **Jane Miller**, who specializes in fashions for the over-40 set, says, "I look for designers you don't see elsewhere." She produces shows in different locations and works by appointment; call ☎ 773-472-3027.

DISCOUNT CLOTHING AND SHOES

IN THE LOOP   Designer Resale of Chicago (658 North Dearborn; ☎ 312-587-3312) offers mostly high-end fashion (Chanel, Versace). A second Designer Resale shop, offering sportswear and accessories, is at 2260 North Clark (☎ 773-472-6022). **The Daisy Shop Women's Couture Resale** (67 East Oak; sixth floor; ☎ 312-943-8880; **www.daisyshop.com**) carries gently worn current and vintage items. The way Chicagoans have embraced Boston's **Filene's Basement** (1 North State; ☎ 312-553-1055), you'd think it was a native operation. Clothes here occasionally surprise you: cut-rate DKNY, great shoes, and wedding dresses. There are other FB stores out north and west in the suburbs, as well as in Designerland (that is, on Michigan Avenue; see below).

ON MICHIGAN AVENUE   Above Borders Bookstore at 830 North Michigan is the first "discount" store to hit the avenue, which the powers that be determined couldn't open on the ground floor. Therefore, **Filene's Basement** (☎ 312-482-8918) opened on the third and fourth floors in a 50,000-square-foot shop that's a bit glossier than most FBs (as befits Michigan Avenue) but still offers bargains aplenty. Another top source for inexpensive goods is the classic **H&M** (840 North Michigan Avenue; ☎ 312-640-0060), where Cinderella can pick up, if not a ballgown, just about everything else for her castle closet. And if you think Michigan Avenue is solely for the Gucci crowd, think again: high fashion had to move over for a **Payless ShoeSource** (444 North Michigan Avenue; ☎ 312-755-0482).

LINCOLN PARK–CLYBOURN CORRIDOR   A top outlet store is **Fitigues Outlet** (1535 North Dayton; ☎ 312-255-0095), offering distinctive looks for women and children. Sportswear buys here are excellent but a season later than you might find in their fashion stores. Look for seasonal sales twice a year (February and July) for special values. If you're hunting for menswear, head west (five to ten minutes) to Elston Avenue, then just north to Fullerton (east of Interstate 94). At 2593 North Elston Avenue is the **Mark Shale Outlet** (☎ 773-772-9600). Shale does women's wear, too, on the tailored side. You'll find clothes at 30% to 70% off, much of it private-label Shale merchandise; men can also find Calvin Klein, Joseph Abboud, and dozens more designers. Look for summer and winter sales, around the time of the Fourth of July and New Year's, respectively, with discounts of 50% to 75% off already marked-down goods. Blowout sales happen in August and February.

   Lori's Discount Designer Shoes (824 West Armitage Avenue; ☎ 773-281-5655) does exactly what it says: gives you discount prices on shoes sold elsewhere for more (can we put it more succinctly?). They're always up to the minute, with a vast stock; the emphasis is on variety, with a shoe for every style. We've seen great-looking bags in here, jewelry, hosiery, and socks, too. (There are also stores in Highland Park, Lincolnshire, Naperville, and Northfield.)

ON HALSTED, CLARK, AND LINCOLN   A New York women's clothier is a favorite savings stop here: **Fox's** (2150 North Halsted; ☎ 773-281-0700), with kicky women's wear (new things every day) from 4% to 70% off. There's also a Fox's at 9444 Skokie Boulevard in Skokie (☎ 847-673-8516). There are two consignment boutiques to visit: **Buy Popular Demand** (2629 North Halsted; ☎ 773-868-0404), with clothes (some new) for women to buy and sell; and **Selections** (2152 North Clybourn Avenue; ☎ 773-296-4014), with low, low prices.

   Finally, we hear you can find a good selection and save 20 to 80% off regular department-store prices at **DSW Shoe Warehouse** (3131 North Clark Street; ☎ 773-975-7182), in Lincoln Park at the Pointe, where Clark and Halsted streets meet.

IN THE SUBURBS   North (several blocks East off the Edens Expressway) in Lincolnwood is **Suits 20/20** (4560 West Touhy Avenue;

☎ 847-676-2020), with good prices on menswear: suits, sport coats, tuxedos, trousers, shirts, coats, ties, shoes, and sweaters by recognizable designers. Alterations are done on the premises.

A number of outlet malls are described in Suburban Shopping Centers, Discount Malls, and Shops later in this chapter.

CRYSTAL, CHINA, AND KITCHEN ITEMS

ON MICHIGAN AVENUE *Major* is the word for **Crate & Barrel**'s flagship store (646 North Michigan; ☎ 312-787-5900); it's as luminous at night as an ocean liner. Contemporary furniture and decorative items are provided at mostly moderate prices. You may run across finds like Mexican glass, Danish teak, or Italian pottery. There's another C&B at 850 North Avenue (☎ 312-573-9800), though it's not to be confused with the **CB2** stores at 800 West North Avenue (☎ 312-787-8329) and out north at 3745 North Lincoln (☎ 773-755-3900), where the goods are arranged with a younger, less pricey feel.

Lalique is the crystal palace at 900 North Michigan (☎ 312-867-1787). Though you can find Lalique pieces all over town, this is the one place that gathers them all together. You can spend less than $100 for a tabletop item or find a crystal dining table for $100,000 (!)—and everything in between. Also at 900 North Michigan are two exquisite sources for crystal, china, and flatware, both on level one: **Bernardaud** (☎ 312-751-1700) and **Pavillon Christofle** (☎ 312-664-9700).

LINCOLN PARK–CLYBOURN CORRIDOR If you're looking for bargains on housewares, it may pay to drive north to browse at **Krasny & Company** (2829 North Clybourn Avenue, Damen and Diversey area; ☎ 773-477-5504). There's everything for the tabletop (miles of glassware and professional cookware, plus some spices and herbs). Heavy-duty commercial frying pans and stainless-steel stockpots can be found here below retail.

Two finds are **Tabula Tua** (1015 West Armitage Avenue; ☎ 773-525-3500) and **Faded Rose** (1017 West Armitage Avenue; ☎ 773-281-8161); they're next-door neighbors but not connected. Tabula Tua (which means "your table") uses the slogan "beautiful wares," and that's the truth. Half the tablewares are imported, such as pottery from Deruta (Italy), and half are American, such as a hand-painted pear dish. There are tables, picture frames, and other home accessories; prices are mixed. Faded Rose carries everything from doorknobs to dishcloths, with an emphasis on beautiful bedding for baby (the House collection is here).

Those searching for kitchenware, woks, electric rice cookers, knives, and other implements used to cook Asian foods will find the **J. Toguri Mercantile Company** (851 West Belmont Avenue; ☎ 773-929-3500) a treasure. Here, too, are nonperishable foods, as well as goods from kimonos to lacquered trays to sushi items.

WILMETTE The Crystal Cave (1141 Central; ☎ 847-251-1160) features a master artisan who custom-designs in crystal (they've created award pieces for the Olympics and many corporate pieces); they also do repairs and carry dozens of china and crystal patterns.

FLORISTS

A TRULY UNIQUE CHICAGO FLORIST is **A New Leaf** (1645 North Wells Street; ☎ 312-642-1576), packed with fresh posies to adorn your hotel room or take to a lucky hostess. We've seen things here that nobody else seems to stock, including lilacs in the springtime. Three other locations: 1818 North Wells (☎ 312-642-8553); 700 North Michigan Avenue, lobby (☎ 312-649-7008); and 312 South Dearborn (☎ 312-427-9097).

That Flower Shop (537 South Dearborn Street; ☎ 312-341-0808) also shines. Owners Peter and Michelle Daut use fresh-cut Holland flowers to create natural designs (they're in demand a lot by celebrities). The shop also sells dried flowers, candles, unusual French wire baskets, and an all-natural line of bath products.

Finally, a word about the very best flower source for weddings and parties. She has no retail shop, but she's acknowledged as the top— pricey, too, but you get what you pay for, don't you? The name is **Virginia Wolff** (1332 West Lake Street; ☎ 312-226-1777; **www.virginiawolff.com**).

FOOD AND WINE

IN THE LOOP If you miss the Rue Cler in Paris, now is your moment. Just be in the Loop in the summer months, and shop at the **City of Chicago Farmer's Markets,** one of the biggest of which is held at Daley Plaza. The city sponsors these merry markets (overflowing with trucked-in *fleurs,* fruits, and vegetables) at some 27 locations several times weekly. The Farmer's Market on Saturdays at Armitage (off Halsted) is very popular, but others are equally so. To check on the Loop market and other whens and wheres, call ☎ 312-744-3315. Additionally, an independent organization sponsors what's known as the **Green City Markets,** Wednesdays and Saturdays from mid-May through the end of October in Lincoln Park (between Clark Street and Stockton Drive), from 7 a.m. to 1:30 p.m. The Winter Green City Market is held at the Peggy Notebaert Nature Museum, 2430 North Cannon Drive (off Fullerton) in November and December, again on Wednesdays and Saturdays. For exact Green City Market times and dates, call ☎ 847-424-2486. This is the only independent private market to support local farmers who utilize sustainable and organic practices.

Chocoholics should know about the fulfilling **Godiva Chocolatier** (10 South La Salle Street; ☎ 312-855-1588; 845 North Michigan; ☎ 312-280-1133). A big hit is the **Ghirardelli Chocolate Shop & Soda Fountain** at 830 North Michigan Avenue (☎ 312-337-9330), and at 822 North Michigan Avenue is **Hershey's Chicago** (☎ 312-337-7711). Here, an interactive chocolate-factory experience grants kids kisses, Reese's candies, minis, ice creams, and more (there's even a singing cupcake-baker).

Two additions to the **Tree Studios** are terrific. In foodstuffs, delectable **Oil & Vinegar** (619 North State Street; ☎ 312-986-3422) is a culinary find, with 450 products, including 30 olive oils and vinegars, handpicked olives from Spain, a lavender-vinegar tapenade from Provence, and much, much more. Then there's **Pops for Champagne,** which has not only opened its Jazz Bar but also the Pops Shop (605 North State Street; ☎ 312-266-7676), selling sparkling wines and Champagnes.

The object of hometown raves (including kudos from local food columnists) is the caramel-and-cheese popcorn made by **Garrett Popcorn** (670 North Michigan Avenue, 26 West Randolph Street, 2 West Jackson Boulevard, and 4 East Madison Street; ☎ 888-476-7267; **www.garrettpopcorn.com**). Their secret recipe assures hot-air-popped (no oils or fat) premium-quality popcorn; choose from plain, buttered, CheeseCorn, CaramelCrisp (with or without nuts), or the aforementioned caramel-cheese combo. As noted in the *Chicago Tribune,* writer Monica Eng advises that the best place to find Yorkshire pudding in the Loop is the English pub **Elephant & Castle** (111 West Adams; ☎ 312-236-6656). A short cab ride from the Loop is **Greek Islands** (200 South Halsted; ☎ 312-782-9855), which not only has top Greek dishes but sells its own fabulous honey and olive oil, along with wines from an award-winning Greek boutique vineyard called Monemvassios. Liesel Bennett has brought her once–North Side shop, **Bennett Wine Studio,** to the West Loop (802 West Washington Street; ☎ 312-666-4417). Handily, for a nominal fee, you may taste six superb wines and buy what you like; you can find exceptional wines for under $10.

MICHIGAN AVENUE To the east of the avenue is **Fox & Obel** (401 East Illinois Street; ☎ 312-379-0146), home of gourmet foods; the emphasis is on freshness, and chefs prepare an array of delectables (the breads and cheeses are among the best in town). Another notable shop is **Kensington Fine & Rare Wines** (465 East Illinois Street; ☎ 312-836-7855), just west of Navy Pier. Owned by Chicago actress Jennifer Laks, this is the only retailer associated with a fine-wine auction division.

On South Michigan Avenue is **Caffé Baci** (332 South Michigan Avenue; ☎ 312-420-4991), an upscale yet moderately priced place to grab a quick lunch while shopping. Still south of the bridge, find **Moonstruck Chocolate Co.** (320 North Michigan Avenue; ☎ 312-696-1201) for good hot chocolate in winter and shakes in summer. Sweet treats abound at **Long Grove Confectionery** (500 West Madison; ☎ 312-441-0263), an offshoot of the popular original in the village of Long Grove. The exotic-truffle emporium **Vosges Haut-Chocolat** (☎ 312-644-9450) has joined the roster of **The Shops at North Bridge** (520 North Michigan Avenue). This shop creates some of the most luscious chocolates in the world (the owner having trained at the Paris-based Le Cordon Bleu). Chocolates may contain flowers as well as rare spices; prices range from $1.50 for a single piece to $10 for a four-piece box, and up. Yum. Also at the Shops at North Bridge (third floor) is the new **Ta-Ze** (☎ 312-527-2576), stocked with all things olive, including oils, from Turkey's famed olive-oil firm, Tarus. A tiny chocolate shop called **Teuscher** (900 North Michigan Avenue, level five; ☎ 312-943-4400) brings chocoholics happiness with yummy truffles, not to mention exquisite packaging.

NEAR NORTH The place to find fresh mozzarella is **L'Appetito** (30 East Huron Street; ☎ 312-787-9881), along with many imported Italian goodies; there's a second location on the ground floor of the John Hancock Building (875 North Michigan Avenue; ☎ 312-337-0691). The divine breads from **The Corner Bakery** (516 North Clark Street; ☎ 312-644-8100) are much praised. Among the many other Corner Bakeries in the city are one at the Field Museum and one at the Chicago Cultural Center, as well as locations throughout the suburbs. All have delish sandwiches, pizzas, and muffins.

A cozy cafe that has gone beyond its good coffee and food to become a wine bar as well—all with a hometown flavor—is **The 3rd Coast** (1260 North Dearborn Street; ☎ 312-649-0730).

A new Gold Coast hot spot for foodies is **The Goddess & Grocer** (25 East Delaware; ☎ 312-896-2600; also at 1646 North Damen; ☎ 773-342-3200). Gourmet sandwiches, salads, and pastries add spice.

LINCOLN PARK–CLYBOURN CORRIDOR At 2121 Clybourn Avenue is **Market Square.** "Market" refers to a huge **Treasure Island** (☎ 773-880-8880); some consider this grocery chain the city's best, and this location in particular the best of all; others like the TIs at 1639 North Wells (☎ 312-642-1105) and 75 West Elm (☎ 312-440-1144). To the west, take Elston south till you reach North Avenue; you'll soon bump into **Stanley's** (1558 North Elston; ☎ 773-276-8050), notable for good fruits and veggies. Some prefer **Whole Foods** (1000 West North Avenue; ☎ 312-587-0648), where you'll find everything from health aids to top-notch meats and poultry and many rave about the huge salad bar (it's one of few places that has diced celery).

The terrific **Trader Joe's** (1840 North Clybourn; ☎ 312-274-9733) is the place to pick up anything (at fair prices) from gazpacho to daisies to Pinot Gris (but if you've had too much of the latter, don't try the up-ramp into the parking area). A tip: their refrigerated half-sour kosher dill pickles beat out every other deli pickle in town, and this is probably one of the few places you can find a one-pound bag of walnut halves and pieces for $4.29. There's another Joe's at 3745 North Lincoln Avenue (☎ 773-248-4920), and there will soon be a third in the city at 44 East Ontario.

Near Whole Foods on North Avenue, look for **Sam's Wines & Liquors** (1720 North Marcey; ☎ 312-664-4394). This is a place beloved by many Chicagoans, who know they can pick up the best wines for the best prices. Staffers here know how to advise you, so listen—you may come in for a California Cabernet and walk out with a Piemontese

Barolo. You won't be sorry. Also check out the **House of Glunz** (1206 North Wells Street; ☎ 312-642-3000), wine merchants with a very broad range thanks to their extensive cellar. Shoppers from certain (few) states may order their selections by mail and have them shipped sans Illinois sales tax. **The Chopping Block,** which also houses cooking schools at its Merchandise Mart Plaza (Suite 107; ☎ 312-644-6360) and Lincoln Square (4747 North Lincoln Avenue; ☎ 773-472-6700) locations, purveys appealing cookware and fine foodstuffs (such as a walnut mustard from France that's out of this world).

Pastoral (2945 North Broadway; ☎ 773-472-4781) was named one of the top cheese shops in the United States by *Saveur* magazine. This gourmet retailer is a great stop for breads, condiments, and, of course, cheeses. They make up picnic packs, too.

Time for dessert? To the north, edging Lincoln Park, is a lovely pastry shop called **Bittersweet** (1114 West Belmont; ☎ 773-929-1100). You can pick up yummies here from mini–fruit tarts to homemade truffles to scones to custom-ordered cakes, and if you need space in which to consume them, there's a cafe on the premises, too.

We've also entered cupcake territory: check out **Cupcakes** (613 West Briar Place; ☎ 773-525-0817), Lincoln Park's **Mandy B's** (1208 West Webster; ☎ 773-244-1174), and the highly creative **Sensational Bites Bakery** (3751 North Southport; ☎ 773-248-2271). After a film at the Music Box Theater, stop here for coffee and . . .

Finally, let's give a quick nod to a place the kids seem to like: **Jimmy John's World's Greatest Gourmet Sandwiches.** We tried a Country Club (turkey, ham, and more) for $4.99 at 2206 North Clybourn (☎ 773-477-0077), though they're spreading (and so will your waistline).

IN EVANSTON, WILMETTE, AND GLENVIEW If you hate to cook, stop at **Foodstuffs** (2106 Central Avenue, Evanston; ☎ 847-328-7704) or farther north in Glencoe (338 Park Avenue; ☎ 847-835-5105). Both stores have huge delis, bake their own pastries, feature fish (Glencoe) or meats and fish (Evanston), and offer gift baskets and catering (both are excellent). In Wilmette, the best take-out place is **A La Carte** (111 Green Bay Road; ☎ 847-256-4102). All their homemade foods are marvelous, but special mention must go to their soups (try the mushroom-barley), salads, and desserts. You can also eat here, in the small lunchroom and, in summer, outdoors. More raves go to the seafood at **Burhop's Fisheries** (1515 Sheridan Road, at Plaza del Lago, Wilmette; ☎ 847-256-6400), where everything from soups to crab cakes is terrific. Back in Evanston, additional treats include the coffees roasted on the premises at **Casteel Coffee** (2924 Central Avenue; ☎ 847-733-1187). Many prefer these to the (let's keep it nameless) chain stores' blends; a fave here is Decaf Sumatra. Another Evanston attraction is the original **Spice House** (1941 Central; ☎ 847-328-3711). This is the last word in everything from Back-of-the-Yards garlic pepper to Saigon cinnamon. People came from miles around for these extraordinary spices until, happily, they opened a fragrant store in Chicago, too (1512 North Wells Street; ☎ 312-274-0378).

FURS

THE **Chicago Fur Mart** HAS MOVED TO 700 North Michigan Avenue (☎ 312-951-5000). Meanwhile, on the edge of the Lincoln Park area is a satisfying source for new and "gently used" furs called **Chicago Fur Outlet** (777 West Diversey Parkway; ☎ 773-348-3877), the "home of the furry godmother." They have furs for both men and women, as well as shearlings and leathers. Of course, if you're interested in higher-end furs, see **Maximilian at Bloomingdale's** (900 North Michigan Avenue; ☎ 312-337-8882), or longtime Chicago favorite **S. Garber Furs** (also at 900 Michigan; ☎ 312-6442-6600), where 50% of the fur coats are private label. One of the city's best fur departments is on the third floor of the former Marshall Field's, now **Macy's,** on State Street; opened in 1859, the original fur salon is perhaps the oldest fur business in Chicago and was the first in a Chicago department store. This is a very large, pretty, full-service salon, offering sales, remodeling, repair, cleaning, and storage. There are tons of minks but they have everything from beaver to sable and chinchilla (not too practical except as trim—tsk!). If you can't find what you want, they'll make it for you. And we can't say another word about furs without mentioning one of the best: **Abby & Yanni** (700 North Michigan Avenue, fourth level, in Chicago Place; ☎ 312-988-7188), where a plethora of top international designers is displayed in a plush setting. Finally, in the suburb of Elmhurst, an all-around favorite is **York Furrier** (107 North York Road, Elmhurst; ☎ 630-832-2200), where they're as likely to do a full-length sable as a denim jacket lined with mink.

GARDEN AND LANDSCAPING

A HOUSE-AND-GARDEN FORCE IS **Jayson Home and Art Source** (1915 and 1911 North Clybourn; ☎ 773-525-3100), a warehouse holding varieties of indoor and outdoor furnishings. This place is a must-stop.

Alhambra (3737 North Southport; ☎ 773-435-0202) is a cavernous source of fine wrought-iron outdoor furniture (lots of O. W. Lee), patio lighting, garden accessories, and, in the back of the store, a full urban-style nursery.

Finally, a terrific attraction is **The Wild Pansy** gift shop at Gethsemane Garden Center (5739 North Clark Street; ☎ 773-878-5915), where you can find anything from a watering can to a sun hat with a moisture-wicking headband.

HOME FURNISHINGS, LINENS, AND BATH SUPPLIES

ON MICHIGAN AVENUE See "Crystal, China, and Kitchen Items" (page 290) for more details on **Crate & Barrel** stores.

WEST OF THE LOOP The West Loop is a growing source of furniture and home-furnishings sources; sometimes they run into each other in certain districts. Most of the stores are farther east than **Modern Times** (2100 West Grand Avenue; ☎ 312-243-5706), a fount of 20th-century modern furnishings, including the collectibles of Charles and Ray Eames. To look into more of their diverse items, consult **www.modern timeschicago.com.** Nearby, **European Furniture Importers** (2145 West Grand; ☎ 312-243-1955) is also worth the trek. They offer modern classics and contemporary furniture for all home needs. Not as far west on Grand at 1139–43 is **Design Inc.** (☎ 312-243-4333), founded by interior designer Bill Bruss, with a fine collection of offbeat artisan-made furniture and other goods he has found while roaming the world. In the Loop at 401 North La Salle (corner of Kinzie) is **Michaelian & Kohlberg** (☎ 312-467-1490), home of fine Oriental rugs and an equally fine collection of fanciful treasures from Southeast Asia and Africa.

ON OAK STREET One of the city's top home-furnishings emporiums is **Elements** (102 East Oak; ☎ 312-642-6574). Tabletop accessories can be found here, along with everything from picture frames to men's and women's jewelry and wedding gifts. The owners have been on the scene for years and select their goods with wisdom; what you buy will be a knockout.

Posh bed, bath, and table linens come with love (and great taste) from Italy at **Pratesi Linens** (67 East Oak; ☎ 312-943-8422). They're not inexpensive, but the quality is high. Another favorite is the fabled Italian linens emporium **Frette** (41 East Oak; ☎ 312-649-3744), fresh from Milan with the company's signature linens, fragrances (scented candles and sachets), and an at-home clothing line lush with cashmeres. They're best known for their jacquard-print bedding of 300- to 600-thread-count Egyptian cotton and linen. Pricey, but you can always pop in for a divine sachet.

NEAR NORTH Definitely a place to browse, **Cambium** (119 West Hubbard; ☎ 312-832-9920) offers furniture, kitchen items, and some wonderful home and tabletop gifts. **Le Magasin** (408 North Clark Street; ☎ 312-396-0030) shows off its French flair in furniture, tableware, and decorative accessories (table linens, painted furniture from Provence, candles, soaps, and a few antiques). The stock is chic, fresh, and not at all frou-frou, with goods by talented independents. For contemporary lighting (and one of the largest showrooms around), try **Lightology** (215 West Chicago; ☎ 312-944-1000); they stock goods from 400 manufacturers.

The **Morson Collection** (100 East Walton Street; ☎ 312-335-9417) is impressive, with European contemporary furniture, area rugs, lighting, and accessories. At **Material Possessions** (704 North Wabash; ☎ 312-280-4885), eclectic spirit is combined with a sense of humor in showcasing a unique selection of original home furnishings. Furniture includes custom tables starting at $1,800. Tabletop and custom-made dinnerware are specialties as well, plus linens and other one-of-a-kind decorative accessories from around the world. This is a must-see for the discerning shopper.

A bit west of Michigan Avenue: If you're into "faded, classical slip-covered furniture," slip into **Shabby Chic** (46 East Superior Street; ☎ 312-649-0080). A transplant from Southport Avenue is **POSH** (Tree Studios, 613 North State Street; ☎ 312-280-1602). Interesting items run rampant here: vintage hotel silver and commercial china (manufactured for hotels and country clubs but unused), Victorian ivory-handled fruit knives, coffee mugs with Chicago-skyline designs created for Posh, English guest towels, and so much more. This place is fun. Also at the Tree Studios is the showroom of **Thos. Moser** (607 North State Street; ☎ 312-751-9684), a highly respected maker of solid wood handcrafted furniture. Superlative craftsmanship is a trademark of these pieces known for graceful lines that echo the traditions of Shaker, Arts and Crafts, Mission, and other cultural influences in design.

RIVER NORTH Along with many of the city's best galleries are some of its most cherished home-decor emporiums. There are, in fact, so many of them, it's not easy to pick and choose. The problem is, of course, that what one person detests another will adore. We'll try to give you a quick summary; then you can go and make up your own mind.

The scene here began with a few furniture and antiques galleries that first moved west from La Salle to cluster around Superior and Huron streets (wags dubbed the area "SuHu," after New York's SoHo, but it didn't take). Today, the area is larger, extending in spots to Clark Street on the east and south of Grand Avenue as far as Illinois, Hubbard, and Kinzie, in some cases. The cutoff point is usually Chicago Avenue to the north, but then again, rules are made to be broken.

Dazzling goods await at **Champagne Furniture Gallery** (65 West Illinois Street; ☎ 312-923-9800), and at the **Golden Triangle** (Clark at 72 West Hubbard Street; ☎ 312-755-1266) you might find a teak-and-cane plantation chair from Thailand or Burmese wooden puppets. **Sawbridge Studios** (153 West Ohio Street; ☎ 312-828-0055) is a gallery of custom-made designs by craftspeople from across the United States. Furniture (from Shaker to traditional to Prairie) is predominant, and, considering the high cost for custom-made pieces, it's affordable. Many other craft items are also here, including pottery, glass, quilts, hand-painted rugs, and a fine assortment of lamps. Plus, Sawbridge features one of the largest collections of handblown crystal by craftsman Simon Pearce of Vermont.

Asian House (159 West Kinzie; ☎ 312-527-4848) boasts a complete line of Oriental furniture and accessories, such as cloisonné vases and animals, bronze statues, porcelain fishbowls, Korean furniture, antique Chinese pieces, Coromandel screens, and more. On Hubbard Street, contemporary furniture by international designers reigns at **Roche-Bobois** (222 West Hubbard; ☎ 312-951-9080). And on La Salle, at the

Kreiss Collection showroom (415 North La Salle Street; ☎ 312-527-0907), find the latest Kreiss family designs; the family manufactures its own elegant pieces, and you can pick out the finishes, fabrics, and accessories right here. Farther west, **Design Studios** (225 West Hubbard; ☎ 312-527-5272) offers contemporary home furnishings.

The name **Rita Bucheit** (449 North Wells Street; use the Illinois Street entrance; ☎ 312-527-4080) is synonymous with one of the finest collections of authentic Empire, Neoclassical, Biedermeier, Vienna Secession, and Art Deco antiques, fine art, and decorative arts in North America. Since 1988, the gallery has specialized in museum-quality European antiques from the 18th to 20th centuries.

Also on Wells, 501 is the number to look for if you want exquisite floor tiles. At **Ann Sacks Tile & Stone** (501 North Wells Street; ☎ 312-923-0919) you'll also see gorgeous stone flooring at a variety of price points. At the corner of Wells and Ohio is the showroom of **Mig & Tig** (549 North Wells Street; ☎ 312-644-8277), with a fine furniture mix: upholstered pieces, some wood, wrought iron from Mexico, and other imports that fit in all settings, from contemporary to country.

Nearby is **Arrelle Fine Linens** (445 North Wells Street; ☎ 312-321-3696). Bargain shoppers, take note: this is not the place to come if you're looking for Fieldcrest on sale. Rather, you'll find a gorgeous Italian sheet, silky as gelato, that might set you back a bit. At least look at the table linens and beautiful bed settings by Anichini, Sferra, Ann Gish, Yves Delorme, Anali, and Graziano. (Maybe you can afford pillowcases?)

An extraordinarily artful collection of furniture and furnishings (half the pieces are Italian; some are designed by the owner-architect) is at **Manifesto** (755 North Wells Street; ☎ 312-664-0733). If you peruse the three floors, you'll see dining tables, sofas, benches, lounge chairs, vases, lighting, and some accessories. **Luminaire** (301 West Superior Street; ☎ 312-664-9582) is a 30,000-square-foot showroom that began as a fine-lighting emporium and graduated into retail. Everything is top-flight here; find the very best international designers, from Philippe Starck to a Boffi kitchen center on the third level to the largest B&B Italia retailer in the world.

The **Spicuzza Collection** (Merchandise Mart, Suite 150; ☎ 312-661-1459) is the showroom for furniture designer and interior architect Martin Spicuzza. He specializes in high-end custom interiors, providing complete project management; you'll find his woods beautiful and adornments (from fab fabrics to drawer and door pulls) impressive. The owners of **Orange Skin** (223 West Erie; ☎ 312-335-1033) have changed direction and now work with the city's best designers. Represented in their showroom are top furniture manufacturers such as Minotti, Kartell, Magis, and Arper.

A final plum to pick in this area: **Svenska Mobler** (516 North Wells Street; ☎ 312-595-9320), the place to find hot, vintage Swedish furniture. The collection features Swedish Functionalism, Art Deco,

Jungendstil, Biedermeier Revival, and Art Moderne designs, all personally selected in Sweden by owner Andrew Wilder. Midcentury pieces from Argentina have also been added.

LINCOLN PARK–CLYBOURN CORRIDOR Right next door to Jayson Art Source at 1915 North Clybourn is **Jayson Home** (1911 North Clybourn; ☎ 773-525-3100), which has become one of the hottest retail stores in the Lincoln Park area (also see page 295). In vintage warehouses, you'll find treasures that interestingly combine old and new, domestic and imported. Unusual gifts include heirloom photo albums; opulent sofas, chairs, and ottomans; and Euro bath luxuries. For the garden, there are plants, fresh flowers, and outdoor furniture, among other goodies.

A furnishings gallery called **Symmetry** (1925 West Division; ☎ 773-645-0502; **www.symmetryshowroom.com**) is the place to pick up a stunning Tibetan rug (they have quite a collection), or lamps from the Philippines, or a pedestal from Thailand. Farther west is **Black Walnut Gallery** (2135 West Division; ☎ 773-772-8870), where owner Robert Wayner displays his own beautiful woods and those of others. All the wood-based pieces here are enhanced by the art for sale on the walls.

A charming source for antiques and reproduction pine furniture is **Pine & Design** (511 West North Avenue; ☎ 312-640-0100), with an in-house cabinetry shop and a gift boutique of eclectic accessories, from photography to antique sconces. Farther west is one of the top storage and organization leaders in the housewares industry, **The Container Store** (908 West North Avenue; ☎ 312-654-8450). They have everything for storage—every type of shelving from bookcases to entertainment centers, and storage containers for kitchens, bathrooms, and every room in the house, including closets. They also have stores in several suburbs.

Findables, Inc. (907 Armitage; ☎ 773-348-0674) is a treasure trove of items past, present, and future. You're as likely to see antique beads or a piece of old crystal or silver as a new woolen throw from Italy or table linens from France. Here, too, are unique books, decorative dinnerware and home furnishings, and sumptuous bath items, including body lotions and scented soaps. Findables is truly a find. As is, further west, **Verde** (2100 West Armitage; ☎ 773-486-7750), where designer Michele Fitzpatrick offers high-quality custom furniture—pick a fabric and she'll design the piece you want. She also displays local artwork.

ON HALSTED, CLARK, AND LINCOLN Halsted has so much to offer, not the least of which are galleries full of decorative furnishings, but let's start with one on Lincoln. One of the best is way-north **Gallimaufry** (4712 North Lincoln Avenue; ☎ 773-728-3600), where you'll find unique art glass, kaleidoscopes, perfume bottles, pottery, scarves, some great music boxes and jewelry boxes, and jewelry to put in them.

If contemporary furniture is your thing, head to **Pauline-Grace** (1414 North Kingsbury Street; ☎ 312-280-9880), a showroom that represents top lines such as Directional, Altura, and Della Robbia. It looks like a loft, and the stock is sleek. Back on North Halsted, a store that sets the style for sleepyheads is **Bedside Manor Ltd.** (2056 North Halsted; ☎ 773-404-2020), with beds, beautiful linens, and fluffy down comforters. They also have stores in several suburbs. A northside find is **Antique Resources** (1741 West Belmont; ☎ 773-871-4242)—not your ordinary antiques store, because this two-story showroom excels in fine furniture, chandeliers (tons of them, from Art Nouveau to Victorian treasures), oil paintings, clocks, and accessories, all unearthed by owner Richard Weisz, and all at reasonable prices.

The **Broadway Antique Market** (6130 Broadway; ☎ 773-868-0285) is an unlikely setting, but it's a good place to shop (though there are more vintage items—1950s and 1960s—than true antiques). Some furniture, some Russell Wright and Eva Zeisel pottery, some vintage clothes and posters—it's all here.

I.D. (3337 North Halsted Street; ☎ 773-755-IDID) is a superb design emporium. Co-owned by Steven Burgert and Anthony Almaguer, this contemporary-lifestyle store is a source for Artifort and Gus modern furniture, Ameico tabletops, titanium eyewear, and Santa & Cole lighting. We hear nothing but raves when it comes to shopping here. **Aiko's Art Materials Import** (3347 North Clark Street; ☎ 773-404-5600) would properly be listed under paper goods (handmade Japanese paper in 500 different varieties) but for the fact that they also offer some interesting folk-art pottery.

Interesting is also the word for **Splendor** (3717 North Southport; ☎ 773-244-2444), a neat boutique where the stock is eclectic as can be, from paper goods to pottery. The owner, who concentrates on artisanal goods from smaller vendors, has an eye for vintage pieces such as flowered plates. You can find everything from oilcloth, curtain panels with smocking, pillows, and throws to washable rugs from France.

Last—but certainly not least to the budget-conscious urban tastemakers who frequent it—let's add a few words about the 6,000-square-foot **CB2** (3745 North Lincoln Avenue; ☎ 773-244-1188), the cool design offspring of Crate & Barrel. The product mix is contemporary and full of priced-right furniture (futon sofas), hip accessories (Chinese wall clocks), home office gadgets, and storage objects.

IN BUCKTOWN AND WICKER PARK In Wicker Park, go see the French-flavored **Porte Rouge** with the red door at 1911 West Division Street (☎ 773-269-2800). There's a nice collection of antique furniture and au courant housewares like Staub cast-iron cookware. The upholstered pieces at **Embelezar** (1639 North Damen; ☎ 773-645-9705) cast it into the furniture category, but that doesn't do the place justice. A browse-through revealed hand-painted Fortuny lights, Tibetan cabinets, stunning Asian pieces made using the same centuries-old traditions as found in Tang-style ceramic horses, and a treasure house of goods that range from drawer pulls to antiques.

Many shoppers love the furniture (desks, coffee tables, and more) and leather goods at **Stitch** (1723 North Damen Avenue; ☎ 773-782-1570); you'll find terrific leather handbags here, too. When it comes to antiques, put **Pagoda Red** (1714 North Damen Avenue; ☎ 773-235-1188) high on your list. It's notable for unusual furniture and artifacts from China, Tibet, and Southeast Asia, and if you're looking for something as utilitarian as it is decorative, this is the place. Items range from fireplace mantels to 18th-century calligraphy brushes. While you're on Damen, stop in at **Climate** (1702 North Damen Avenue), a neat little gift shop with things for hostesses, holidays, cards, and the like.

The new location of **Wow and Zen** is at 1912 North Damen (☎ 773-269-2600). You'll find Asian country antiques for a song; the owners travel a lot and pick up multiples of cultural objects like Chinese tea boxes and Mongolian toy chests. At **Kachi Bachi** (2041 North Damen; ☎ 773-645-8640) find pillows, duvet covers, and window treatments; at **Pavilion** (2055 North Damen Avenue; ☎ 773-645-0924), Deborah Colman and Neil Kraus specialize in all things French and Italian. How about lighting by Angelo Brotto, French ceramics by Georges Jouve, and French 1970s metal design?

Note the Victorian English and French antique tableware and furniture at **The Painted Lady** (2128 North Damen Avenue; ☎ 773-489-9145). The accent here is on hand-painted antique furniture, plus an array of bedding, linens, tabletops, rugs, and artwork. While you're trying to figure out why some stores in the area out-achieve others, stop in for a cup at **Caffe De Luca** (1721 North Damen; ☎ 773-342-6000); then head to **Virtu** (2034 North Damen; ☎ 773-235-3790), probably one of the most interesting shops on Damen, offering a potpourri of wonderful handmade crafts, from teapots to local artist Dahlia Kanner's sterling rings. Nearby, **Jean Alan** (2134 North Damen Avenue; ☎ 773-278-2345) is a find: designer Alan reworks vintage furniture and custom-designs pillows, draperies, and much more. With so many stores in this area, it's fun to just take off and walk, walk, walk!

OFF THE BEATEN PATH Discover **Vintage Pine** (904 West Blackhawk; ☎ 312-943-9303), a 13,000-square-foot showroom overflowing with current custom, antique, and vintage looks in both furniture and accessories. It's two blocks south of North Avenue and two blocks west of Clybourn Avenue. The goods here range from shipments of English pine armoires, farm tables, chairs, and silver pieces to items sold by on-site galleries that deal in antiques and more-contemporary home furnishings. At 4727 North Damen is **Ravenswood Antique Mart** (☎ 773-271-3700), a great source for mod midcentury finds.

Off the Bolt (1333 North Kingsbury; ☎ 312-587-0046) is owner Norene Fremont's dream come true: high-end, highest-quality textiles for interiors at mill-direct prices, immediately available. In one locale, you won't believe your eyes: silks, chenilles, mohairs, tapestries, and a wall of shimmering taffetas that seems as fluid as a waterfall.

If you continue north, you'll arrive at **Architectural Artifacts** (4325 North Ravenswood; ☎ 773-348-0622), an extraordinary outlet for furniture and decorative items from around the world. In this huge warehouse, find everything from garden furniture to old (and sometimes beautiful) fireplace mantels. There's even a big events space for weddings. Another sprawling warehouse stocked with retro and just plain old artifacts from long-ago buildings, **Salvage One** (1840 West Hubbard Street; ☎ 312-733-0098) is reported to have some 250,000 items (many of them treasures), including stained-glass windows, odd cornices, bathtubs, garden ornaments, and hardware. North on Lincoln, **Homey** (3656 North Lincoln Avenue; ☎ 773-248-0050) is full of affordable globetrotter goods, from beaded pillows to Balinese masks.

JEWELRY

IN THE LOOP A big Loop attraction for those who must have baubles, bangles, and beads is a series of jewelers (both wholesale and retail) at the renovated **Jewelers' Center** at the Mallers Building (5 South Wabash Avenue; ☎ 312-853-2057). It's worth a look just to see how beautifully one of the oldest buildings in the Loop was redesigned, and there are reputed to be more than 200 jewelers in the building to lure you. If you need an independent gemologist, call on Lorraine Oakes at the **Chicago Gem Lab** on the 14th floor. **Wabash Jewelers Mall** (21 North Wabash Avenue, street level; ☎ 312-263-1757) also entices with good values.

ON MICHIGAN AVENUE At 900 North Michigan Avenue glows **The Goldsmith** (☎ 312-751-1986), where Sherry Bender does every kind of commission, from updating a fun heirloom to creating a spectacular diamond necklace. The Midwest's only **Bulgari** is a dazzling outpost of the Italian designer at 909 North Michigan (☎ 312-255-1313). All of the contemporary classics are here, from Tubogas (hand-wrapped flexible-band designs) to the double-stone ring called the Doppio Buccellato. Here, too, you'll find Bulgari fragrances for men and women (some with green tea), scarves, handbags, and sunglasses. One of the most exclusive boutiques in the country is **Cartier** (630 North Michigan Avenue; ☎ 312-266-7440), where you can pick up anything from a silver cup for baby to an engagement ring. At 636 North Michigan, **Van Cleef & Arpels** brings its posh baubles to your wondering eyes. And you mustn't slight **Tiffany & Co.** (730 North Michigan Avenue; ☎ 312-944-7500), where you can find a crystal vase, stainless-steel flatware, picture frames, and all manner of gems to take home in that unmistakable blue box. In the John Hancock Building is the private jeweler **Manny B. & Co** (875 North Michigan Avenue, suite 2644; ☎ 312-337-5275; by appointment only). This interesting gentleman manufactures his own very high-end pieces and deals primarily with clients by referral. The basis of his business is engagement rings, but he'll find a stone for anything you want.

Just west of Michigan Avenue is **Sidney Garber** (118 East Delaware Street; ☎ 312-944-5225), a creative jeweler here since 1945 who deals in fine watches as well as diamonds and pearls. Garber goes directly to his sources all over the world for stones, and he designs his own pieces. He does a huge pearl business, too.

The Drake Hotel houses **Georg Jensen** (959 North Michigan; ☎ 312-642-9160), with a mélange of gorgeous jewelry and tabletop items. Note a Danish artist (all the designers featured here seem to be Danish) named Viviana Torun, who does superb silversmithing.

ON OAK STREET Jewelry is unbeatable on Oak. A longtime Chicago standby is master designer **Lester Lampert** (57 East Oak; ☎ 312-944-6888), offering three floors of custom-made contemporary and classic designs, estate jewelry, and a huge selection of fine watches. Another local star, **Trabert & Hoeffer** (111 East Oak; ☎ 312-787-1654), has operated since 1937, most of that time over on Michigan Avenue. Fine gemstones and custom designs are the rule here; you're not bombarded by lots of jewelry cases, and they bring items to you, somewhat in the style of an extra-haute fashion house. Don't be intimidated: the gems are expensive, but the staff here can make buying them pleasant. The fluid style of New York star **Judith Ripka** (129 East Oak; ☎ 312-642-1056) incorporates interchangeable components (an earring can be a stud or evolve into a pendant drop on a French wire), and whether she's working in gold or platinum, people like Hillary Clinton have been known to crave her creative work. A more recent newcomer to Oak is the international powerhouse **Graff** (103 East Oak; ☎ 312-604-1000). The company's first U.S. location is striking enough to rival those in London, New York, Palm Beach, and Monte Carlo, among other Graff outposts, and this is probably one of the most impressive jewelry stores anywhere. They're known for such treasures as the Idol's Eye (70.21 carats) and the Windsor diamonds, for starters, and they do it all themselves, from gathering rough gemstones to the finished jewelry. As if all this magnificence weren't enough, the rumor is that this area may soon welcome a Chicago outpost of **Harry Winston.** His stones may be sparkling within the next year or two.

OFF THE BEATEN PATH In the Lincoln Park area, a boutique not to be missed is that of **Ani Afshar** (2009 North Sheffield Street; ☎ 773-477-6650). Nationally known as a jeweler who works exclusively with beads, Afshar creates stunning pieces sold at such outposts as the Asia Society of New York and Harrods of London, as well as here. (For customizing, call her at ☎ 773-645-8922.) In Bucktown, find **Gem,** (1710 North Damen Avenue; ☎ 773-384-7700), where owner-designer Laura Kitsos sells beautifully handcrafted one-of-kind pieces. You'll also find fun jewelry among the interesting accessories at **Robin Richman** (2108 North Damen; ☎ 773-278-6150) and pieces made by artisans at **p.45** (1643 North Damen; ☎ 773-862-4523). Way off the beaten path, in the suburb of Lincolnwood, is one of the prime showrooms in all of Chicagoland for fine watches and jewelry: **Smart Jewelers** (3350 West Devon Avenue; ☎ 847-673-6000). They claim to have more watch lines than anyone, and the selection is *huge.*

LUGGAGE

IN THE LOOP Emporium Luggage (128 North La Salle Street; ☎ 312-372-2110; also at Westfield North Bridge; ☎ 312-832-0363) offers Tumi, Hartmann, Kenneth Cole, Zero Halliburton aluminum briefcases, and much more. Their discount store is **Irv's Luggage Warehouse** (820 West North Avenue; ☎ 312-787-4787). Both stores also have messenger bags, backpacks, travel-related merchandise, and accessories; Irv's has Kenneth Cole, Gravis, Hobo, and Timbuk2 at prices 10% less than competitors'.

Deutsch Luggage Shop (40 West Lake; ☎ 312-236-2935) is a family-owned source for fine luggage, leather goods, business cases, and gifts. Among many national brand names are Tumi, Hartmann, Briggs & Riley, Travel Pro, and Swiss Army. They also have an Oak Brook store. **City Traveler** (50 East Randolph; ☎ 312-984-3514) carries most luggage brands and some less pricey varieties in briefcases and handbags. You can find all manner of upscale leather goods, from belts to handbags to handmade leather travel bags (these can be as pricey as $2,000) at **Henry Beguelin** (716 North Wabash Avenue; ☎ 312-335-1222). As you head near north, **Flight 001** (1133 State Street; ☎ 312-944-1001) sells luggage, passport cases, space-saver garment bags, and more in a boutique interior-designed to resemble the fuselage of a 747.

MICHIGAN AVENUE A lot of stores carry **Tumi** goods, but you may want to go straight to the source at Water Tower Place (835 North Michigan Avenue; ☎ 312-274-0824). You can find a $200 backpack or any number of carry-ons. As for that name, all we know is that Tumi was a Peruvian god. Another don't-miss is beautiful **Ghurka** (645 North Michigan Avenue; ☎ 312-440-3855), home of upscale, classic luggage as much enjoyed by women (handbags and totes) as by men (reversible laptop cases). Ghurka also is available at Macy's. The merchandise is high-end as well at **Louis Vuitton** (919 North Michigan Avenue; ☎ 312-944-2010), another impressive store that purveys luggage along with clothing and accessories. And of course there's **Hermès,** the oh-so-pricey home of the Kelly (named for Grace) bag. If you can't afford a travel tote, think about picking up a scarf (maybe).

LINCOLN PARK–CLYBOURN CORRIDOR Kaehler Travelworks has multiple Chicago locations, including one at Water Tower Place, but one of the best is at 2070 North Clybourn Avenue (☎ 773-404-1930). The store specializes in luggage, leather goods, and gifts, and there are some terrific buys here. And **Stitch** (1723 North Damen Avenue; ☎ 773-782-1570) has travel bags, duffels, laptop cases, and more that are sleek, sturdy, and stylish.

MUSICAL INSTRUMENTS AND RECORDED MUSIC

IN THE LOOP With the dispersal of music stores at the onetime Chicago Music Mart, you'll find pianos downtown at **Macy's in the Piano Gallery** (☎ 312-781-4050); they also sell digital pianos, keyboards, and organs. There are additional Piano Galleries in the suburbs of Naperville, Forest Park, and Niles. **The Saxophone Shop** and **Evanston Band & Orchestra** (4819 Main Street, Skokie; ☎ 847-673-3812) have combined to sell band and orchestra instruments.

"One of the best places in Chicago to find an acoustic guitar"—this is how author and singer-songwriter Jeff Libman describes **Different Strummer** (Old Town School of Folk Music, 4544 North Lincoln Avenue; ☎ 773-728-6000). "The people there are very friendly, it's a welcoming place with a fantastic assortment." A second location is at 909 West Armitage (☎ 773-751-3410); this is the children's branch of the store, where kids can find a beginner guitar, violin, sheet music, or CDs. Libman also recommends **Make'n Music** (1455 West Hubbard; ☎ 312-455-1970). They've been in business for decades and carry 150 to 200 high-end boutique acoustic guitars, plus electric guitars, amps, basses, and more. **Andy's Music** (2300 West Belmont; ☎ 773-868-1234) is the last word in percussions. In the basement of this simple storefront are drums of every type—Jamaican steel drums, Peruvian drums, and more. At **Selected Works** (3510 North Broadway; ☎ 773-975-0002), a super used-book store, Keith Peterson sells used sheet music (some vintage).

ON MICHIGAN AVENUE Another recommendation is **Sherry-Brener** (226 South Michigan Avenue; ☎ 312-427-5611), selling violins and other string instruments, bagpipes and pan pipes, mandolins, guitars handmade in Spain, used guitars, and more. This is also the place for violin lessons.

The futuristic **Sony Gallery** (663 North Michigan Avenue) is now history, but you can purchase any of their electronic wonders by calling ☎ 877-865-7669.

NEAR NORTH Not far from Michigan Avenue close to North Bridge, **Bose** (55 East Grand Avenue; ☎ 312-595-0152) is a great place to look for great sound, from radio/CD players to headphones to computer speakers and home-theater technology. A block south of Grand Avenue at the edge of the Loop—and a must if you're feelin' groovy—is **Jazz Record Mart** (444 North Wabash Avenue; ☎ 312-222-1467), which bills itself as the world's largest jazz-and-blues shop. Featured in the movie *High Fidelity*, **Reckless Records** (1532 North Milwaukee Avenue; ☎ 773-235-3727) specializes in emo, punk, electronica, and more. If you seek blues memorabilia, check out the **Blue Chicago Store** (534 North Clark Street; ☎ 312-661-1003) for everything from CDs to limited-edition art reproductions.

ORIENTAL RUGS

NEAR NORTH One of the best names to note is **Oscar Isberian** (122 West Kinzie Street; ☎ 312-467-1212). There are also showrooms in Evanston (1028 Chicago Avenue; ☎ 847-475-0000) and Highland Park (3330 Skokie Boulevard; 847-266-1515). At 401 North La Salle is

Michaelian & Kohlberg (☎ 312-467-1490), home of an impressive collection of handmade Oriental rugs and some fanciful treasures (such as handpicked Tibetan cabinets) from the regions where these new (but made in the age-old way) rugs are dyed, spun, and knotted.

ON HALSTED, CLARK, AND LINCOLN Check out **Peerless Rug Co.** (3033 North Lincoln; ☎ 773-525-9034). Riches include Oriental rugs and unusual European tapestries, skillful reproductions of centuries-old designs. The motto here is "It's worth the trip," and if you're looking for carpets, indeed it is. In Wicker Park, **Symmetry** (1925 West Division; ☎ 773-645-0502) carries the Tibetan Collection, consisting of custom Himalayan wool or silk rugs.

OUTDOOR GEAR

ON MICHIGAN AVENUE The North Face (875 North in the John Hancock Center; ☎ 312-337-7200) is newsworthy, with great skiwear and ski equipment, as well as climbing and other outdoor gear.

ON HALSTED, CLARK, AND LINCOLN What started as a discount army-navy surplus store has graduated to a sporting goods, camping, and travel emporium where you can pick up anything from a pea coat to mountain-climbing gear. **Uncle Dan's Army-Navy, Camping & Travel** (2440 North Lincoln Avenue; ☎ 773-477-1918) is nothing fancy, but it's very service-minded. They're also in the suburbs, including Highland Park. A fine addition to the outdoor-clothing scene is the California-based chain **Patagonia** (800 North Clybourn; ☎ 312-951-0518).

SPORTS CARS AND VINTAGE AUTOMOBILES

A DAY TRIP TO THE NORTHERN SUBURBS takes you to two sources for vintage cars and other antique-car collectibles, which may be why some international shoppers find Chicago a hub for these auto prizes.

Chicago Classic Cars is in Gurnee, Illinois (3555 West Grand Avenue, Route 132; ☎ 847-336-1930). Owned by Charles Kuhn, the family business features antique and collectible cars: vintage sports cars, classics from the 1920s through 1950s, and racy 1960s muscle cars with big 1960s engines. "New cars depreciate in value," says Kuhn. "These cars are viewed as an investment to drive." Cars are shown by appointment only.

Not far from there is the **Volo Auto Museum,** on 30 wooded acres (27582 Volo Village Road, near Routes 12 and 120; ☎ 815-385-3644). Here you'll find more than 250 collector cars, all for sale (values range from $17,000 to $3 million). Choose from antique, brass-era, classic, milestone, muscle, exotic, and sports cars, both domestic and foreign, from the early 1900s through the 1980s. Owned and operated by the second- and third-generation Grams family (Greg Grams and sons Jay and Brian, and Greg's brother Bill), the museum is a guest exhibitor at the annual Chicago Auto Show every February. There are other sources for collector cars, but this is the largest. The

American Classics Gift and Book Shop carries auto-related gifts. There are also three separate but connected (not auto-related) antiques malls representing more than 300 established antiques dealers. The museum and malls are open daily, 10 a.m. to 5 p.m.

TOYS, GAMES, CLOTHES, AND GIFTS FOR CHILDREN

ON MICHIGAN AVENUE A favorite is the **LEGO Store** (520 North Michigan; ☎ 312-494-0760); there are additional stores with children's goods at the same address. Two are the upscale **Jordan Marie** (☎ 312-670-2229) and **Oilily** (☎ 312-527-5747). Just off Michigan is **Madison & Friends** (940 North Rush Street; ☎ 312-642-6403). Pass the fish tanks in front, and you'll find lots of adorable clothes for the kids whose moms shop Oak Street, a side room full of strollers, and, in the basement, a jeans empire. A great source for toys is **Galt Toys + Galt Baby** (900 North Michigan Avenue, fifth level; ☎ 312-440-9550). This place has exceptional things like a child-sized toy truck, unique Papo toy soldiers (Napoleon on a horse!), and a fine stroller and pram selection.

ON HALSTED, CLARK, AND LINCOLN Full of toys and clothes (for kids to age 6), **Psycho Baby** (1630 North Damen Avenue; ☎ 773-772-2815) is the choice of many moms. **The Red Balloon Company** (2060 North Damen Avenue; ☎ 773-489-9800) has imported furniture and accessories for kids, along with some antique and one-of-a-kind gifts. **The Gymboree Store** (1845 North Clybourn; ☎ 773-525-2080) has clothes for newborns up to size 9 for girls and size 7 for boys. And when it comes to kids' shoes, note **Piggy Toes** (2205 North Halsted; ☎ 773-281-5583), shoes for first walkers all the way up to juniors. Look for **The Children's Place** stores scattered throughout the city and suburbs; they often have hot looks and fair prices. **Uncle Fun** (1338 West Belmont Avenue; ☎ 773-477-8223) has everything from jelly beans to toys. Out south, the choice of thinking parents is **Toys Et Cetera** (5211-A South Harper Avenue; ☎ 773-324-6039), with fine educational toys.

IN EVANSTON, **Wild Child** (612 Davis Street; ☎ 847-475-6225) always manages to come up with unique baby and little kids' clothes you don't find anywhere else, from hats to shoes. And to the west in Naperville, a broken doll can seek treatment at **Angelic Creations Doll Hospital** (816 West Washington; ☎ 630-369-2522). This is also a fine toy store and a great source for doll collectibles.

WESTERN WEAR

Out of the West (1021 West Armitage Avenue; ☎ 773-404-9378) also sells contemporary sportswear, but we've included it here because of its lifestyle appeal. Savvy buying is obvious in the various categories of goods, which range from silver jewelry and belt buckles to contemporary jeans (such as Seven and AG), racks of urban-focused sportswear, and decorative home items.

Way out west is **Alcala Western Wear** (1733 Chicago Avenue; ☎ 312-226-0152), definitely the place to be if you're in the market for 10,000 pairs of boots (including exotic skins), some 3,000 hats, and heaven knows how many belts. There are lots of leathers and Native American jewelry, too. It's a five-minute cab ride from the Loop.

SUBURBAN SHOPPING CENTERS, DISCOUNT MALLS, *and* SHOPS

SOME CHICAGO-AREA MALLS ARE MUSTS, a few are recommended if you happen to be in the area, and some don't warrant a visit even if you're visiting relatives in that suburb.

Most shoppers—whether they're from Lucca in Tuscany or Las Vegas in Nevada—know that a Gap store is a Gap store, Saks Fifth Avenue is SFA, Osco is Osco, and a rose is a rose. Sometimes, however, a mall store will surprise; those are the ones you want to hear about.

If you're driving past the beautiful Bahá'í House of Worship on Sheridan Road into Wilmette, you may want to stop at the second-oldest shopping center in the United States, **Plaza del Lago** (☎ 847-256-4467). The distinctive style of a romantic Spanish courtyard serves as a backdrop for 30 stores—everything from **Crate & Barrel** to a fine fish store called **Burhop's** (they not only sell fish and basics as well as gourmet foods, but they make wonderful soups and crab cakes, too). With so many places to shop here, you'll get hungry, so stop at **Convito Italiano** (☎ 847-251-3654) for lunch. Convito features Italian foods (their take-out counter and retail food-and-wine counters are always packed).

One of the biggest shopping centers on the north shore is **Westfield Old Orchard** (Skokie Boulevard and Old Orchard Road, Skokie). Westfield also owns **Hawthorn,** a large mall in far-north Vernon Hills, as well as the aforementioned North Bridge complex on Michigan Avenue. Some 12 miles from Chicago, Westfield Old Orchard serves an upscale clientele, anchored by **Nordstrom, Bloomingdale's, Macy's,** and **Lord & Taylor,** plus some 130 stores like the **Apple Store, Armani Exchange, Banana Republic, Coach, Lacoste, Sisley, Sony Style, Tiffany & Co.,** and more. Two theaters (13 screens) are here, along with every type of dining from the **Corner Bakery** and **Maggiano's Little Italy** to the **Cheesecake Factory** and **California Pizza Kitchen.**

An equally busy, beautiful, and somewhat smaller indoor shopping center is **Northbrook Court** in Northbrook (☎ 847-498-1770). In addition to anchors **Neiman Marcus, Lord & Taylor,** and **Macy's,** you'll find dozens of other stores, from chains to one-of-a-kinds: **Gap, Williams-Sonoma, Abercrombie & Fitch, Polo Ralph Lauren, Coach, Max Mara, Land of Nod, The Love Sac** (ultraplush beanbag chairs), **Burberry, Louis Vuitton,**

BCGB Max Azria, Monograms Today, Wet Seal, Pac Sun, Tommy Bahama, Nicole Miller, Mark Shale, and many more, plus a very active food court and the only **Palm Restaurant** this side of Chicago. A huge separate **Crate & Barrel** is nearby.

Woodfield Shopping Center in Schaumburg (about 40 minutes northwest of Chicago and not far from O'Hare; ☎ 847-330-1537; **www.shop woodfield.com**) has been joined by a handful of other shopping centers in the area. Add the **Barrington Ice House** in Barrington (☎ 847-381-6661), the folksy charm of **Long Grove Shopping Village,** and several small malls in Schaumburg to Woodfield, and you've got Greater Woodfield's 4 million square feet of retail (and what we last heard was nearly 500 stores). Whew.

*un*official **TIP**
Woodfield Shopping Center is one of the largest malls in the United States (nearly 300 stores), so wear comfy shoes to walk its miles of indoor track.

Woodfield Shopping Center itself is anchored by **Nordstrom, Lord & Taylor, Macy's, Sears,** and **JCPenney.** Other nifty stores vary from **Abercrombie & Fitch, H&M, Anthropologie,** and **Hanna Andersson** to **Build-A-Bear Workshop** (☎ 847-517-4155), where kids can make their own teddy bears; **Armani Exchange; Coldwater Creek; J. Jill;** and **Iridesse** (Tiffany's pearl concept). Kids will love the **Rainforest Café** (☎ 847-619-1900), a Disneyesque restaurant set in a faux jungle, complete with android animals, while grown-ups can catch an act at the mall's outpost of the famed **Improv Comedy Club** (☎ 847-240-2001). Or sample the skewers at **Texas de Brazil,** a Brazilian-style steak house (☎ 847-413-1600).

While you're out west, it's an excellent idea to investigate the stores in historic **Geneva** (visit **www.genevachamber.com**). On Third Street, check out **Cocoon** (☎ 630-232-8340) and **Past Basket** (☎ 630-232-4191) for home and bath accessories; **One Fine Art Gallery** (☎ 630-262-0800); **Paper Merchant** (☎ 630-232-1880); **Graham's Chocolates and Ice Cream** (☎ 630-232-6655); **The Perfect Setting,** (☎ 630-232-6655), a tabletop-accessories and gift shop; and **Bella Ragazza** (☎ 630-232-9580), a boutique selling designer women's wear, jewelry, and cosmetics. Then jog to State Street and visit **Lily of the Valley** (☎ 630-232-6685), a flower and gift shop; **Les Tissus Colbert** (☎ 630-232-9940), a purveyor of antiques and fine furniture; **Nature's Gallery** (☎ 630-208-9970), the Midwest's largest selection of log furniture and rustic accessories; and **Valley Golf** (☎ 630-232-1177). **Dick's Sporting Goods** (☎ 630-943-4100) leads the lineup at **Geneva Commons** shopping center. While you're visiting Geneva, it's a great idea to stay at the beautiful **Herrington Inn & Spa** (15 South River Lane; ☎ 630-208-7433); their fine-dining restaurant is **Atwater's.**

While we're on the subject of day-tripping, the following destinations may add further incentive to hit the road, shopping bags poised for purchasing. All are an hour or two from the city (one-way), so allot enough time. In many cases, however, the savings can be sky-high.

Gurnee Mills Mall (Illinois Route 132, Gurnee; ☎ 800-937-7467; **www.gurneemills.com**), the Midwest's largest value retail and manufacturer outlet mall at the intersection of I-94 and Grand Avenue, is bigger than Soldier Field and attracts more visitors than Graceland. Among the 200-plus retailers are the **Bass Pro Shops Outdoor World** (which is more of an environment than a store, fishing included), **Marshalls MegaStore, T.J. Maxx, American Eagle Outfitters, Circuit City, Fuzziwig's Candy Factory, Auntie Anne's Pretzels, Off 5th Saks Fifth Avenue Outlet, JCPenney Outlet, H&M,** and so many more. Representing the nonoutlet stores in the mall are **Sears Grand** and **Kohl's.**

Take I-94 and State Highway 50 to Exit 344 in Kenosha, Wisconsin, and you're at the **Original Outlet Mall** (7700 120th Avenue; ☎ 262-857-7961): 100 outlet stores include **Eddie Bauer, Carter's** (the kidswear is great), **Oneida, Hush Puppies Factory Direct, Pendleton, KB Toys, Koret, NordicTrack,** and **Pfaltzgraff.**

Prime Outlets at Pleasant Prairie (I-94, Exit 347, Kenosha; ☎ 262-857-2101) has more chic names than the other centers. Their big draws are seldom attached to the word *outlet:* **Waterford Wedgwood, Restoration Hardware, Coach, Guess?, St. John, Ann Taylor,** and tons of others. More bargains can be found at the **Prime Outlets at Huntley** (11800 Factory Shop Boulevard; ☎ 847-669-9100), way out west in Huntley, Illinois. Among the 50 outlet stores are **BCBG Max Azria, Guess?, Anne Klein, Borders, Nine West, Banana Republic, Nautica,** and **OshKosh B'Gosh,** just to name a few.

And to all, a good buy!

PART TEN

EXERCISE, RECREATION, *and* SPORTS

CHICAGOANS WORK HARD AND PLAY HARD.

Their extreme ethic mirrors the weather. Chicago is a city of great contrasts when it comes to climate, and natives are willing to bring it on. In the summer, humidity is intense and temperatures often climb to about 90°F by midafternoon, making outdoor exercise and recreation problematic unless you plan to lounge on a Lake Michigan beach or go for a swim. Winter, on the other hand can be positively Arctic in intensity, especially in January and February, when cold temperatures and icy blasts off the lake plunge wind-chill factors to well below zero.

The idea in the summer is to exercise early, before the sun and humidity make conditions outdoors too hot and muggy. In the winter, only hearty outdoor types such as cross-country skiers will want to brave the cold and wind; everyone else should plan to exercise indoors. The rest of the story is that spring and fall are usually fine for enjoying the outdoors.

> *unofficial* **TIP**
> Regardless of the season, understand that Chicago's weather can change in minutes. Keep that in mind before setting out on an all-day outing, and take along appropriate raingear and/or warm clothing.

Chicago is one of America's best cities in terms of recreation and sports options. Local sports fans are loyal despite decades of being frustrated by mediocre product (with the exception of Michael Jordan's run with the Bulls). One of the reasons Theodore Thomas founded a symphony orchestra in Chicago was that "he understood the excitement and nervous strain that everyone, more or less, suffered from living there." So relax. And take a deep breath.

INDOOR ACTIVITIES

A QUINTESSENTIAL CHICAGO EXPERIENCE

BUILT IN 1906, THE **Division Street Russian and Turkish Baths** (1916 West Division; ☎ 773-384-9671) is the only traditional bathhouse left in Chicago and one of only several that remain in the United States. Chicago authors Nelson Algren and Saul Bellow incorporated the baths into their writing, and John Belushi featured them in his hit film *The Blues Brothers*. Mobster Sam Giancana allegedly used to come here; these days you might run into the Reverend Jesse Jackson and/or assorted Chicago aldermen. (It's hard to define status when you're sitting in a sauna, wrapped in a hot sheet like a butt-naked burrito.) For $20, men and women visitors have access to a large whirlpool, cold pool, eucalyptus-scented steam bath, granite-stone heat room, and oak-leaf brooms. Invigorating Swedish massage is extra. A small lunch counter serves salads and sandwiches. The baths are open daily from 8 a.m. to 10 p.m. Don't miss this Chicago legend.

FREE WEIGHTS AND EXERCISE MACHINES

MOST OF CHICAGO'S MAJOR HOTELS have either spas or fitness rooms with weight-lifting equipment on-site, or have arrangements with nearby health clubs that extend privileges to hotel guests. For an aerobic workout, most of the fitness rooms offer stationary bikes, stair-climbers, or rowing machines. Many clubs are also open to men and women and accept daily or short-term memberships. The **Chicago Fitness Center** (3331 North Lincoln Avenue at Belmont; ☎ 773-549-8181) offers a weight room with 50 pieces of equipment, including free weights and Nautilus and Universal fixed-weight machines. Aerobic equipment includes StairMasters, treadmills, and exercise bikes. The daily fee is $10; bring a lock. **World Gym Fitness Center** (909 West Montrose at Sheridan; ☎ 773-348-1212) offers free weights and Nautilus fixed-weight machines, StairMasters, exercise bikes, NordicTracks, and steam and sauna rooms. The cost is $15 a day. And **Equinox** has three city locations: the Loop (200 West Monroe; ☎ 312-252-3100); the Gold Coast (900 North Michigan; ☎ 312-254-2500), and Lincoln Park (1750 North Clark Street; ☎ 312-254-4000). All offer studio cycling, yoga, Pilates, a spa, and a pool. The cost for guests is $25 a day, but you must find a member to bring you in. Just hang around the parking lot.

EXERCISING IN YOUR HOTEL

YOU WORK OUT REGULARLY, but here you are, stuck on a rainy day in a hotel without an exercise room. Worse, your game is off from overeating, sitting in airplanes, and not being able to let off steam. Don't despair: unless your hotel is designed like a sprawling dude ranch, you can put on your workout clothes and find a nice interior stairwell, which all hotels are required to have in case of fire.

Because it's important for your step workout to be consistent with your fitness level, we've provided two different plans. Here's the first one, from Bob Sehlinger, creator of the *Unofficial Guide* series (for a ten-story hotel):

From your floor, descend to the very bottom of the stairwell. Walk up ten flights and down again to get warmed up. Then, taking the stairs two at a time, bound up two floors and return to the bottom quickly, but normally (that is, one step at a time). Next, bound up three floors and return. Add a floor after each circuit until you get to the top floor. Then reverse the process, ascending one less floor on each round trip: nine, eight, seven—you get the idea. Tell somebody where you'll be in case you fall down the stairs. Listen to your body, and don't overdo it. If your hotel has 30 stories, don't feel compelled to make it all the way to the top.

Now here's coauthor Dave Hoekstra's plan:

Sit in the stairwell on the fourth-floor landing with a six-pack of Old Style and a slice of deep-dish pizza, and laugh at Bob every time he chugs past. Or just lie down on your hotel-room floor, hook your feet under some furniture, and knock out 50 sit-ups.

OUTDOOR ACTIVITIES

WALKING

CHICAGO IS A FANTASTIC TOWN FOR GETTING AROUND by foot: as flat as an Illinois cornfield yet as ambitious as a shark at sea. If you mentally break up the city into discrete portions—the Loop, River North, the Magnificent Mile, and such—and you don't overextend yourself, walking is the best way to learn about Chicago. It keeps you on your toes. Every step requires a decision. Folks who are fit and enjoy using their own two feet should bring comfortable walking shoes and regularly give themselves a rest by occasionally taking a taxi, a bus, or the El.

Along the Lake

Serious walkers and people in search of great scenery and prime people-watching as they stretch their legs should head for Chicago's premier walking destination, the **Lakefront Trail** along Lake Michigan. The 20-mile paved path is flat, clean, well lit—and usually crowded with other people whose boots are made for walkin'. You really haven't done Chicago unless you've experienced the Lakefront Trail.

City Walks

Other good destinations for a scenic stroll include the **Gold Coast** (a neighborhood of sumptuous mansions and town houses located just above the Magnificent Mile), **Lincoln Park** (featuring 1,200 acres of greenery, three museums, and a free zoo), and **Oak Park,** a Near West suburb where strollers can

unofficial **TIP**
The stretch of the Lakefront Trail from McCormick Place south to Hyde Park is tough turf; stay to the north in daylight hours and you'll be okay. Pedestrian tunnels under Lake Shore Drive make it possible to reach the trail without getting hit by a car on the busy drive.

explore a shady neighborhood full of homes designed by Frank Lloyd Wright. Ambitious walkers with the Wright step will want to head to the South Side and take in the row houses at 3213–19 **South Calumet.** These are the only Wright-designed row houses ever built.

In late 1996, the northbound lanes of Lake Shore Drive were relocated to the west of the Field Museum. Landscaping created a new traffic-free **Museum Campus** consisting of the Field Museum, the Shedd Aquarium, and the Adler Planetarium. Other pedestrian-friendly amenities at the ten-acre park include rows of elm trees; a large, sloping lawn in front of the Field Museum and to the west of the Shedd Aquarium; and a series of decorative plazas linked by walkways between the museums. A pedestrian concourse underneath Lake Shore Drive at Roosevelt Road serves as an entranceway to the Museum Campus, which hearty Chicagoans always come to by foot—it's more convenient than trying to find a parking place. The planetarium sits on a former island in Lake Michigan that's now linked to the shore by a half-mile peninsula. From this point—one of the city's most romantic spots—the view of the Chicago skyline is tremendous.

Another outstanding place to walk is the beautiful Gothic campus of the **University of Chicago** in Hyde Park, south of downtown. Don't miss the 12-ton abstract sculpture *Nuclear Energy* by Henry Moore; it's located on the spot where Enrico Fermi and other UC scientists split the atom and achieved the first self-sustained nuclear chain reaction in 1942. This may be one of the most important spots in America.

Farther afield, more great walking destinations include **Brookfield Zoo** (14 miles west of the city but easily accessible on the Metra train line); the **Morton Arboretum** (25 miles west of the Loop in Lisle, with 1,500 acres of native woodlands and 25 miles of trails); and the **Chicago Botanic Garden** (300 acres of landscaped gardens and island located 18 miles north of downtown).

RUNNING

NOT JUST CHICAGO'S FAVORITE WALKING PATH, the **Lakefront Trail** is also where the city's most serious runners come to work out. And runners, without handlebars sticking out or the need to weave like inline skaters, have it easier when it comes to penetrating the throngs who crowd the path when it's nice outside. The trail is most crowded between 6 a.m. and 10 a.m. in good weather. Folks looking for more elbowroom can head a little north of downtown and run on the section of trail between Belmont Harbor and the northern neighborhood of Edgewater. While the same holds true for the six-mile stretch starting south of McCormick Place, it's not nearly as safe.

Good news for runners who prefer training on a soft surface instead of asphalt: Chicago is surrounded by a network of forest preserves that are easy to reach by car. To run in a sylvan setting, head to **Palos Forest Preserve District** in southwest Cook County, about

20 miles from downtown. The nation's largest forest preserve (nearly 14,000 acres) features 80 miles of multipurpose trails, which are ten feet wide and covered with gravel or grass. For more information on Palos and other forest preserves, call ☎ 773-261-8400.

TENNIS

THE 150 PARKS OF THE **Chicago Park District** incorporate close to 700 outdoor tennis courts. Some of them are convenient to visitors staying downtown; the better ones are along the lakefront. The nets go up in mid-April and usually stay up through October. Reservations aren't required for most courts—just put your racquet by the net, and the other players using the court will know you want to use it next. Other courts must be reserved by phone.

Daley Bicentennial Plaza, downtown at 337 East Randolph Street (between Columbus and Lake Shore drives), features 12 lighted courts. For reservations, call ☎ 312-742-0377 after 10 a.m. the day before you plan to play. Hours are 7 a.m. to 10 p.m. weekdays and 8 a.m. to 5 p.m. weekends; the fee is $7 an hour.

Another 12 lighted courts are available in **Grant Park** (900 South Columbus Drive; ☎ 312-742-7648). Reservations aren't accepted; courts are free during the day, and there's a nominal charge after 5 p.m. **Lake Shore Park** (808 North Lake Shore Drive, across from Northwestern University; ☎ 312-742-7891) has two lighted courts; no reservations are accepted. Hours are 7 a.m. to 11 p.m. daily, and there is no charge to use the courts.

Waveland, located in popular Lincoln Park (4000 North Lakeshore Drive; ☎ 312-742-8515), features 20 lighted courts. Reservations are required; cost is $7 an hour.

McFetridge Sports Center (3843 North California Avenue), on the Far Northwest Side, has six indoor tennis courts. Weekday rates are $16 per person per hour from 7 a.m. to 4 p.m., $24 from 4 to 10 p.m. Weekend rates are $24 from 7 a.m. to 7 p.m., $22 from 7 to 10 p.m. Call ☎ 773-478-2609 for reservations.

GOLF

Small Ball ·

Even most locals are unaware there's an 18-hole "putting" course tucked away in downtown Grant Park. The **Green at Grant Park** is strictly for putting on a true-to-form 18-hole putting course. The course looks like it's made from real grass; however, the grounds are filled with sand and made with synthetic material (real grass cannot be used because of heavy foot traffic). The Green at Grant Park is just west of Lake Shore Drive at 352 East Monroe (☎ 312-642-7888; **www.thegreenonline.com**). The fee (includes putters and balls) is $8 for an 18-hole round; kids pay $6. The Green also has a full-service restaurant and patio that is open from 10 a.m. to 10 p.m. daily.

Longer Shots

The **Chicago Park District** boasts six public courses managed by Kemper Golf Management. Affordable, accessible, and well maintained, they inspired *Golf Digest* magazine to call Chicago "a likely candidate for best golf city in America." The courses are open mid-April through November from dawn to dusk. Make reservations at least a week in advance on Kemper's helpful automated phone tee-time-reservation system (☎ 312-245-0909), which provides directions to and descriptions of all six courses. Have a credit card handy, and remember that no rain checks and refunds are issued.

The **Sydney R. Marovitz Golf Course** (usually called Waveland, the course's former name) is the crème de la crème of Chicago's public courses. Located near the ritzy Gold Coast and Lake Michigan, it offers great views and a design modeled on that of Pebble Beach. Not a lot of trees, but the fairways are fairly long (3,290 yards) compared with those of other municipal courses.

Waveland is the place to go to impress a client—and you won't be alone. The nine-hole golf course handles about 400 golfers a day, so figure on three hours to play a round. Hold your bets if you bump into noted golfer Michael Jordan. Fees for adult nonresidents are $20 on weekdays and $23 on weekends. The course is at Waveland Avenue and the lakefront in Lincoln Park. There's also a restaurant. Call ☎ 312-742-7930 for more information.

South Shore Golf Course, located at the South Shore Cultural Center (7059 Lake Shore Drive), is a public nine-holer that's fairly short (2,903 yards). The holes are well designed and moderately challenging, and South Shore is considered an undiscovered gem. The setting on the lake means that every hole is a visual feast, whether it's the waves off of Lake Michigan crashing along the fairway or spectacular views of the city. This is the only municipal course that rents driving carts ($12 to $16 per round). Fees for adult nonresidents are $15 on weekdays, $16 on weekends. Call Chicago Parks (☎ 312-256-0986) for more information.

Robert A. Black Golf Course (2045 West Pratt Street, near the lakefront and the city's northern boundary, a good choice if you're staying in Evanston), is a nine-hole, 3,200-yard course with no water hazards (it does have 21 bunkers, or sand traps, however). Adult nonresident fees are $16 on weekdays, $18 on weekends. Call ☎ 312-742-7931 for more information.

Chicago's only 18-hole municipal course is at **Jackson Park** (near the southern terminus of Lake Shore Drive at 63rd Street and Stony Island Avenue). It's a moderately difficult 5,538-yard course with lots of trees, but not much sand or water. Fees for adult nonresidents are $23 on weekdays, $26 on weekends; club rental is $14. Call ☎ 773-667-0524.

Marquette Park Golf Course (6700 South Kedzie Avenue at 67th Street, near Midway Airport), a nine-holer, offers wide fairways and water on seven holes. The 3,300-yard course is rated as fairly easy.

Adult nonresident fees are $15 on weekdays, $16 on weekends. Call ☎ 312-245-0909 for more information.

Located west of downtown near Oak Park, **Columbus Park Golf Course** (5700 West Jackson Boulevard at Central) is recommended for novices. The 2,832-yard course presents wide, open fairways and large greens. Fees for adult nonresidents are $15 on weekdays, $16 on weekends; for seniors and kids learning to golf, fees are $7 on weekdays, $8 on weekends. Call ☎ 312-746-5573 for more information.

ROAD BICYCLING AND INLINE SKATING

CHICAGO IS TO BIKES what Sturgis, South Dakota, is to bikers. Mayor Daley and community groups are driving to make Chicago a bike-friendly city. There's even a heated 300-space indoor bicycle-parking facility at the new Millennium Park. One downside of this biking-for-the-masses philosophy is the sense of entitlement many native bikers have developed. Along with bike messengers, most regular Chicago bicyclists ignore traffic signals and oncoming cars (though city streets have clearly marked bike lanes), zigging in and out of traffic like the late Bears running back Walter Payton.

unofficial **TIP**
If you're a recreational rider, stay off Chicago's mean streets. The same goes for inline skaters.

So where's the best place to ride a skinny-tire bike or skate the black ice? You guessed it—the **Lakefront Trail**—which is already chock-full of joggers (see the Running and Walking sections of this chapter). Any excursion on the paved path along Lake Michigan is an out-and-back endeavor, so try to figure out which way the wind blows before starting out. Then ride or skate into a headwind, which becomes a helpful tailwind on the return trip. If you want to avoid the worst of the crowds, try riding or blading north of downtown between Belmont Harbor and the Edgewater neighborhood. The six-mile stretch of trail south of McCormick Place is considered unsafe, in spite of beefed-up bike-mounted police patrols, but if you ride with a friend and go early, you should be okay.

Renting Bikes and Inline Skates

Bike Chicago rents bikes and gear at Millennium Park, Navy Pier, North Avenue Beach, and at far-north Foster Beach, and offers free maps, group guided tours, and delivery to your hotel. For more information, check out **www.bikechicago.com.** For inline skates, your best bet is **Bike & Roll** located at North Avenue Beach (☎ 773-327-2709); rental fees are $9.75 per hour and $34 per day (8 a.m. to 10 p.m.). Closer to downtown, **Londo Mondo** (1100 North Dearborn; ☎ 312-751-2794; **www.londomondo.com**) is Chicago's oldest inline-skate shop.

Road Rides

Local roadies who like to go the distance say the best riding is out **Sheridan Road** and north along **Lake Michigan** to **Kenosha, Wisconsin,**

unofficial **TIP**
Although Sheridan Road is scenic and even has a couple of gentle hills, it's not very bicycle friendly—there's no bike lane and often not much shoulder, and traffic is heavy—so it's a route best left to experienced road cyclists.

a 115-mile round trip, if you're up for it. A shorter option is to drive to Evanston, park at Northwestern University, and ride north to Sheridan Road and **Fort Sheridan,** about a 30-mile round-trip.

MOUNTAIN BIKING

EVEN THOUGH IT'S PAVED, THE **Lakefront Trail** is Chicago's top fat-tire route. But what if you want the feel of mud between your knobbies? Mountain biking has taken Chicago by storm (just as it has everywhere else), but, unfortunately, challenging single-track trails are scarce around the Chicago plains. Bicycles are restricted to designated single-track trails in the immensely popular 14,000-acre **Palos Forest Preserve,** a ravine-sliced forest 20 miles southwest of the city, and the best place around for dedicated fat-tire fanatics to get down in the dirt. Call ☎ 708-771-1330 for a free map showing trails that are okay to ride.

Easy Riding

Other off-road options close to Chicago are considerably tamer than the challenging trails in Palos. Forty miles west of the city, the beautiful **Fox River Trail** provides relative solitude and easy pedaling on a 37-mile stretch of asphalt and crushed limestone that follows the river between Aurora (near Naperville) and Elgin (Metra trains go to Aurora and Geneva along the Fox). **Mill Race Cyclery** in Geneva (11 East State Street; ☎ 630-232-2833) rents hybrid and mountain bikes for use on the trail. Rates are $6 an hour (two-hour minimum) and $25 a day on weekends. During good weather, stop in for a riverfront drink and snack at the Mill Race Inn gazebo across the street.

The **Busse Woods Bicycle Trail** is an 11-mile scenic bike path weaving through the woods and meadows of the 3,700-acre Ned Brown Preserve, located in northwestern Cook County about 20 miles from the Loop. The **North Branch Bicycle Trail** starts at Caldwell and Devon avenues in Chicago and continues 20 miles along the North Branch of the Chicago River to the Chicago Botanic Garden. Pack a lunch and picnic in the gardens; freshwater wells can be found along the trail.

For the Hard-core

Local hammerheads say the most adventurous, varied, and accessible single-track action is found at **Kettle Moraine** in Wisconsin, about a 90-minute drive from Chicago. A system of trails originally designed for hikers (and now legal for mountain bikes) features some steep and narrow stuff that will thrill experienced mountain bikers, but might put off first-time riders. For more information, call ☎ 262-594-6200. To get there, take I-94 to Wisconsin Highway 50 to US 12. Park at the La Grange General Store, and pick up sandwiches and maps; then head down to County Road H one mile to the main parking area. The parking fee is $10, and there's a $4-per-person trail-use fee (bikers must be 16 or older).

SWIMMING

The Lake Michigan shore is lined with 31 sand beaches for sunning and swimming. These free public beaches are manned with lifeguards daily from June to September, from 9 a.m. to 9 p.m. Lockers are available at the major beaches.

Oak Street Beach, the closest to downtown and only a credit card's throw away from Bloomingdale's, is called the St. Tropez of the Midwest. It's also the most crowded of the lakefront beaches, as perfect-10 models, bodybuilders, jet-setting flight attendants, all-American Frisbee-tossing frat brothers and sorority sisters, Eurotrash, and ordinary folk blanket the sand on steamy summer weekends. Don't go if you're offended by skimpy clothing. Pedestrians can arrive safely via the underpass across from the Drake Hotel at Michigan Avenue and Oak Street.

In more family-oriented contrast to the nightclub-by-day vibe at Oak Street Beach, **North Avenue Beach** stretches north for a mile, from just above North Avenue to Fullerton Avenue. Farther north, **Montrose Avenue Beach** offers great views of the Chicago skyline.

> *unofficial* **TIP**
> Rule of thumb: the crowds at the popular beaches tend to thin out—and tummies tend to expand—the farther north you go.

Unabashed swimmers of all types flock to **Pratt Boulevard Beach** for illegal skinny-dipping in the wee hours. Separated by a seldom-used park, a wide beach, no spotlights, no high-rises, no searchlights, and even a little hill to block views, the dark, sandy beach near Morse Avenue is a good place to take it all off and dive into the surf.

Practical note: Lake Michigan water can be cold, even in August. So check out the Chicago Park District's 50 outdoor and 42 indoor pools. **Portage Park**'s Olympic-size outdoor pool, for example, was constructed for the 1954 Pan-American Games. For a complete list of pools, visit **www.chicagoparkdistrict.com.**

PADDLING

FOR FOLKS IN SEARCH OF WILDERNESS SOLITUDE, the best bet for achieving it in lakebound Chicago is by water. While powerboat traffic can make Lake Michigan a misery of chop, noise, and exhaust on summer afternoons, tranquility in a canoe or kayak can be found early in the morning or late at night. On the main branch of the Chicago River, canoeing is one of the most popular ways of enjoying the architectural delights of the city, while a canoe trek on the North Branch of the river reveals an astounding amount of wildlife for an urban stream. For background and seasonal trips (that include canoe rentals for $45), visit **Friends of the Chicago River** (☎ 312-939-0490;

www.chicagoriver.org). Headquarters for paddling information and rentals in Chicago is **Chicagoland Canoe Base** (4019 North Narragansett Avenue; ☎ 773-777-1489; **www.chicagolandcanoebase.com**), one of the finest canoe shops in America. Patient owner Ralph Frese aims to please, sharing nature stories and pointing you to area secrets like the Skokie Lagoons, an urban jewel where boaters can eavesdrop on deer, coyote, fox, and blue heron. The Canoe Base schedules more than 100 organized free trips a year, including an annual New Year's Day paddle down the Chicago River, rain, shine, or snow. Canoe rentals are $45 the first day and $25 each additional day; kayak rentals are $55 the first day and $35 each additional day. Fees include a car-top carrier, paddles, and personal flotation devices, and Ralph and his staff will even load the boat on your car for you.

WINDSURFING

THE WINDY CITY EARNS ITS EPITHET with nine-mile-an-hour average winds on Lake Michigan. Hey, it ain't Oregon's Columbia River Gorge, but Chicago's boardsailors aren't complaining. **Montrose Beach** is rated Chicago's safest point, with the **South Side Rainbow Beach** next in popularity. Never tried windsurfing? **Windward Sports** (3317 North Clark Street) offers a two-day certification course that will teach you all you need to know for $120. Lessons are given at Greenwood Beach in Evanston, just north of Chicago, where there's a good northeast wind, and sometimes at Wolf Lake, south of Chicago near the Indiana state line; the safe, controlled environment lets novices concentrate on learning skills. Board rentals, offered June through August by Windward Sports at Montrose Beach, are $35 a day. For more information, call the shop at ☎ 773-472-6868. To get a marine weather forecast, call the National Weather Service at ☎ 815-834-0675. Keep in mind that Chicago's quick-change weather can leave novices stranded far from home.

ICE SKATING

Daley Bicentennial Plaza (337 EAST RANDOLPH) features an outdoor 80-by-135-foot rink with superb views of Lake Michigan and the Loop. The season for the prepared rink (which is equipped with chillers) starts in November and runs through mid-March. That's a long winter. Hours are 10 a.m. to 10 p.m. Monday through Friday and until 5 p.m. weekends. Admission is $2 for adults, $1 for children under age 14; skate rental is $2 for adults, $1 for children. For more information, call ☎ 312-742-7648.

The newest and most popular rink in Chicago is the **McCormick Tribune Ice Skating Rink** at Millennium Park (55 North Michigan), where scores of pedestrians catch a glimpse of the stars on ice. At this 16,000-square-foot outdoor rink, skaters waltz around to taped music. There's also a warming house and a nearby cafe. Hours are 10 a.m. to 8 p.m. daily. Admission is free; skate rental is $5 for adults, $4 for children. For more information, call ☎ 312-742-5222.

At **Skate on Skate** (in the Loop at State and Randolph streets), skating is $3 during a season that lasts from November through mid-March. (Did we say that's a long winter?) During the week, two-hour sessions run from 9 to 11:15 a.m., noon to 2 p.m., 2:30 to 4:30 p.m., and 5 to 7:15 p.m. On weekends, shorter sessions run from 9 to 11 a.m., 11:30 a.m. to 1 p.m., 1:30 to 3 p.m., and 3:30 to 7:15 p.m. For more information, call ☎ 312-744-2883.

DOWNHILL SKIING

THE CLOSEST SKI RESORT TO CHICAGO IS **Wilmot Mountain,** about an hour's drive north of O'Hare, just over the Wisconsin state line. The resort features 25 runs with a 230-foot vertical, snowmaking, night skiing until 11 p.m., a pro shop, rentals, instruction, a cafeteria, and a bar. Weather permitting. Wilmot is open from December 1st through mid-March; call its local snow-information line at ☎ 773-736-0787. For directions and a list of local motels, call ☎ 262-862-2301. To hook up with other downhill skiers on the Chicago prairie, visit the Chicago **Metropolitan Ski Council** at **www.skicmsc.com.**

CROSS-COUNTRY SKIING

WHEN MOTHER NATURE LAYS DOWN A BLANKET of the white stuff, a lot of Chicagoans strap on skinny skis and head for the nearest park or forest preserve or northwest Michigan (90 miles away) to enjoy a day of kicking and gliding. **Camp Sagawu,** located about 20 miles southwest of the Loop in the Cook County Palos Forest Preserve District, features a system of groomed cross-country ski trails that traverse a scenic landscape of forest and prairie. The Sag Trail is gentle and ideal for novices, while rolling Ridge Run accommodates intermediate and advanced Nordic skiers. The trails are open whenever there's enough snow on the ground to ski; ski rentals and lessons are also available. Camp Sagawu is on Route 83 east of Archer Avenue at 12545 West 111th Street in Lemont. For more information, a snow report, and directions, call ☎ 630-257-2045.

SPECTATOR SPORTS

A SPORTS-CRAZY TOWN

CHICAGO IS THE MOST PASSIONATE SPORTS TOWN in the United States. Fans aren't as spoiled as New Yorkers, and they're not as rough as those in Boston or Philly. What's more, they're nowhere near as laid-back as fans on the West Coast—heck, Los Angeles doesn't even have an NFL team. Chicago sports fans are renowned for their tenacity, whether it's for the Bears (the most popular team in town), Bulls, White Sox, Cubs, or Blackhawks. The enthusiasm is stoked by a sports culture steeped in tradition and folklore. Consider this: in 1876, the same year General George Custer was shut out by Crazy

Horse and Sitting Bull at Little Big Horn, the team that would evolve in today's Chicago Cubs won the National League Championship in its first season of baseball. Since then, Chicagoans have shown an unwavering passion for pro sports.

Other notable events and personalities from Chicago's sports past include the "Black Sox" betting scandal of 1919; Harry Caray, the late Hall of Fame TV and radio sports announcer, singing an off-key "Take Me Out to the Ballgame" during the seventh-inning stretch, first at Old Comiskey Park, then at Wrigley Field; the Bears' 1985 Super Bowl Championship; and Michael Jordan, the world's most famous athlete, leading the Chicago Bulls to consecutive NBA championships. Washington, D.C., has statues of war heroes. Chicago has statues of Michael Jordan, White Sox legend Minnie Minoso, and even Harry Caray (at Wrigley Field) and fellow announcer Jack Brickhouse (on North Michigan Avenue). That's a sports-crazy town.

For visitors, the quintessential Chicago sporting experience is an afternoon baseball game at **Wrigley Field,** home of the Cubs. It's a place where fans feel like they've stepped back in time. Spectators love the ivy-covered walls, the way errant breezes can turn pop-ups into home runs (usually for the opponent), and the opportunity for first-rate people-watching as all sizes, shapes, and classes of Chicagoans root for the Cubs.

The Chicago area has also become a nationally recognized mecca for minor-league baseball. The **Kane County Cougars** (an Oakland A's affiliate) of the Class A Midwest League play to huge crowds in west-suburban Geneva. Independent Northern League teams prosper in Joliet and northwest-suburban Schaumburg, both accessible by train. The Northern League even has a team in Gary, Indiana, just 35 miles south of Chicago.

The city is also blessed with many colleges and universities, which provide a wide array of spectator sports. For current listings and goings-on of both pro and amateur events, check out the daily sports sections of the *Chicago Sun-Times* and *Chicago Tribune*.

PRO TEAMS

Baseball

Chicago is home to two professional baseball teams: the **Chicago Cubs** (National League), who play at venerable Wrigley Field on the North Side (1060 West Addison, in a neighborhood lined with restaurants and bars), and the **Chicago White Sox** (American League), who play at U.S. Cellular Field on the South Side (333 West 35th Street, in a mostly residential area). The season starts around the first week of April and continues through early October.

The Cubs, as most baseball fans know, are a testament to Chicagoans' unstoppable allegiance in the face of adversity: the team hasn't won a World Series since 1908. The odds of such a futile streak are off the table. No matter—like the Brooklyn Dodgers of yesteryear,

the Cubs (never call them Cubbies) are affection-
ately embraced by Chicago fans, and picture-
perfect Wrigley Field draws nearly 3 million fans
each year for a taste of baseball history. Although
lights were added to the stadium in 1988, a little
less than half the games are still played during the
day; aficionados insist it's still the only way to see a
game at the park. For schedule information, call ☎ 773-404-2827; tickets can be ordered through **www.tickets.com** or by calling ☎ 800-843-
2827 (in Illinois) or ☎ 866-652-2827 (outside Illinois). Get tickets as far
in advance as possible, but you can try your luck at the ticket window or
outside the gates before game time; some fans occasionally sell or give
away extra tickets.

> *uno*fficial **TIP**
> Beware: Scalping is illegal
> in Chicago. The Web site
> **www.stubhub.com** is
> a safer and more reliable
> ticket source.

Street parking around Wrigley Field is restricted during day
games—the city has even installed parking meters that must be fed
on Sunday!—so public transportation is the best way for visitors to
reach the original "house of blues." Take the Englewood-Howard El
line to the Addison Street station.

Geography and family ties divide Cub fans and White Sox fans.
Cub fans are considered more upscale and yuppie, while White Sox
fans are more working class and gritty. White Sox fans wear tattoos.
Cub fans wear scars.

In 2005 the White Sox broke their own 88-year championship
drought by winning the World Series, so tickets can also be hard to
come by at **U.S. Cellular Field.** Unlike Wrigley Field, "the Cell," as Sox
devotees proudly call it, features unobstructed views of the action.
The upper-deck seats have been scaled down in recent years, but the
radical vertical slope should be a point of caution for those scared of
heights. Unlike the early-1990s ballparks of its era (Camden Yards in
Baltimore, Coors Field in Denver, Miller Park in Milwaukee), U.S.
Cellular was built on the cheap. Even the most stalwart White Sox
supporter admits that.

To find out when the White Sox are playing at home, or for tickets, call ☎ 312-674-1000. Legal street parking begins around 29th
Street; the walk several blocks south to the ballpark through old
ethnic neighborhoods is safe and more authentically Chicago than
anything near Wrigley Field. If the Cell is crowded, the official lots
are a nightmare to get in and out of. The El train runs along the Dan
Ryan Expressway two blocks to the east; get off at 35th Street. Large
crowds flocking to and from the game virtually eliminate the chance
of getting mugged on the short walk, but watch out for pickpockets
working the throngs. They may be Cub fans!

Football

Sports tradition in Chicago isn't restricted to baseball. The **Chicago
Bears** point to a football history that goes back to the 1930s. They
also have a bigger fan base than the Cubs or White Sox since they are

the only National Football League team in town. The Bears won the NFL Championship in 1963 before 45,801 fans when they played at Wrigley Field. They also won the 1985 Super Bowl in New Orleans, and members of that team still maintain celebrity status in Chicago.

Pro gridiron action takes place at a renovated **Soldier Field,** where a colonnade of paired 100-foot concrete Doric columns rise majestically behind fans brave enough to endure icy blasts off Lake Michigan. The field is at 425 East McFetridge Drive (at Lake Shore Drive, just south of the Field Museum). For tickets and information on Bears games, call Ticketmaster at ☎ 312-559-1212, Monday through Friday, 9 a.m. to 4 p.m. Alas, subscription sales account for most tickets. Your best bet is to locate a subscriber trying to unload a ticket before the game or try the fan ticket site **www.stubhub.com.** Parking is relatively plentiful and nearby. To get to the game by public transportation, take the #146 State Street–North Michigan Avenue bus downtown or the Red or Orange Line El train to the Roosevelt Road station, and walk east.

Basketball

The National Basketball Association's **Chicago Bulls** almost always sell out. The team plays in the **United Center,** a $170-million arena that seats 21,500 and is outfitted with 217 luxury skyboxes. For game times, call ☎ 312-455-4000; to purchase tickets, call ☎ 312-559-1212. The season starts in October and runs through April— later when the Bulls make the playoffs. Tickets go on sale in September for the season, and some games sell out in a few weeks. You're more likely to get tickets when the Bulls play lower-tier teams. The United Center is located at 1901 West Madison Street, west of the Loop; take the #20 Madison Street bus.

A neat family option is the **Chicago Sky,** the city's new entry in the Women's National Basketball Association. Fans can get up close and personal with the players, and they witness a style of team basketball you sometimes don't see in the NBA. The Sky plays from May to August at the University of Illinois Circle Pavilion (525 South Racine) on the Near West Side. For tickets, call Ticketmaster at ☎ 312-559-1212.

Hockey

Loud, gregarious fans like to watch the **Chicago Blackhawks** of the National Hockey League mix it up on the ice as much as they themselves like to mix it up in the stands. Their devotion to the team is being tested, though—fans are unified in their dislike of team owner Bill Wirtz, and attendance has been dropping for years. The Blackhawks own three NHL championships: 1924, 1938, and 1961. Yes, 1961 was a long time ago.

The Blackhawks share quarters (but not karma) with the Chicago Bulls in the United Center, located at 1901 West Madison Street; take the #20 Madison Street bus. For schedules and game times, call ☎ 312-455-4500; for tickets, call ☎ 312-559-1212. The season runs from October through April.

Many Blackhawks fans love winning hockey so much, they have defected to the **Chicago Wolves,** a successful minor-league team that plays at the **Allstate Arena** (6920 North Mannheim Road in Rosemont, near O'Hare International Airport), sometimes outdrawing its major-league counterpart and usually making the American Hockey League playoffs. The Wolves' season runs from October to May. Tickets are cheaper than those for the Blackhawks; call Ticketmaster at ☎ 312-559-1212.

COLLEGE SPORTS

CHICAGO'S ONLY DIVISION I (BIG TEN) football and basketball representatives are the **Northwestern University Wildcats,** who play in Evanston, just north of the Chicago border. Gridiron action takes place on Ryan Field (1501 Central Avenue; ☎ 847-491-2287). Basketball is played at McGaw Hall–Welsch-Ryan Arena (2705 Ashland Avenue; ☎ 847-491-2287).

Other college basketball teams include the **DePaul Blue Demons,** who play at Allstate Arena (6920 North Mannheim Road in Rosemont; ☎ 312-362-8000); the **Loyola Ramblers,** who provide on-the-court action at Loyola University, in Chicago's Rogers Park neighborhood (6525 North Sheridan Road; ☎ 773-508-2560); and the **University of Illinois at Chicago Flames,** who hold court at the University of Illinois Circle Pavilion (525 South Racine; ☎ 312-413-5700).

HORSE RACING

OUT OF THE ASHES OF THE OLD ARLINGTON PARK RACE TRACK (which burned in 1985) has risen **Arlington International Race Course,** rated as an even bigger and better thoroughbred-racing and entertainment venue. The horses run May through October; the track is located at Euclid and Wilkie roads in Arlington Heights (about 30 miles northwest of the Loop). For more information, call ☎ 847-385-7500.

Hawthorne Race Course in Cicero features harness-racing excitement and thoroughbred racing. The track is at 3501 South Laramie Avenue, about five miles southwest of the Loop. For post times and more information, call ☎ 708-780-3700.

OFF-TRACK BETTING AND RIVERBOAT CASINOS

CHICAGO'S DOWNTOWN OFF-TRACK-BETTING emporiums have closed—the real estate has become too valuable—but folks allergic to real horses and mud can still play the ponies at the excellent **Trackside Chicago** on the Near North Side (901 West Weed Street; ☎ 312-787-9600; **www.tracksideotb.com**). There are dining and beverage options, and the joint is jumping 364 days a year.

Riverboat gambling is as close as an hour away from downtown Chicago. **Hollywood Casino Aurora** features slots, table games, dining, Las Vegas–style entertainment (Frank Sinatra appeared for the last time in the Chicago area here), and movie memorabilia. Hollywood's boat (now permanently docked) is open from 10 a.m. to 4 a.m. on weekdays (until 5 a.m. weekends). Admission is $5. Patrons must be age 21 and older; be prepared to show photo ID. For more information and directions, call ☎ 800-888-7777.

Empress River Casino offers more than 1,000 slots and more than 60 table games plus Empress Off-Track Betting in Hammond, Indiana, 30 miles southeast of downtown. Fourteen gaming sessions are offered daily. Now a permanently docked barge, the casino is open from 10 a.m. to 4 a.m. on weekdays (until 6 a.m. weekends). Admission is $5. Express bus service is only available from downtown hotels to the Hammond location; call ☎ 888-436-7737 for more information.

Harrah's Joliet Casino, docked on the Des Plaines River (151 North Joliet Road, southwest of Chicago), operates daily from 10 a.m. to 4 a.m. on weekdays (until 5 a.m. weekends). Admission is $5. Call ☎ 800-HARRAHS or visit **www.harrahs.com** for more information.

PART ELEVEN

ENTERTAINMENT *and* NIGHTLIFE

▌ CHICAGO *after* DARK

CHICAGO NIGHTLIFE IS FULL OF POSSIBILITIES. You can be wicked or blue, mild or wild. You can laugh and dance and taste romance. The city has a defined work ethic and sports swagger, but when it comes to nightlife, try as it may, Chicago's just not glamorous enough to have attitude. (After all in Chicago, television anchors are regarded as celebrities.) So come as you are. You *will* fit in.

Chicago is a hands-on city. A true Chicagoan plays 16-inch softball—without the glove. A real Chicago woman drinks a 16-ounce beer—from the bottle. An authentic Chicago nightcrawler makes the rounds—without a doubt.

For the maximum Chicago experience, check out neighborhood bars, diners, music clubs, and theater groups. Stay away from chains like the Cheesecake Factory and TGIFriday's. Skip any nightclub where people are waiting in long lines behind velvet ropes. Chicagoans only wait in line for smelt-fishing licenses and Cubs tickets.

Where New York and Los Angeles are about a "scene," Chicago is about a spirit. It's easy to get things done here. The late Irish bartender Butch McGuire redefined the Near North Side of Chicago by opening America's first true singles bar in 1961. Louisiana transplant and blues legend Buddy Guy was one of the first to put a nightclub in the once-seedy South Loop. In recent years, young Russian immigrant Jerry Kleiner regentrified the warehouse districts of the Near West Side and the South Loop with his bars and restaurants. His template? The Chicago speakeasies from 1880 to 1920.

You drink from that gritty spirit in Chicago.

Urban blues, soul, alternative country, and house music began as determined undercurrents of Chicago culture. Today, they are part of America's music lexicon. The **Second City** improvisational troupe, named because of the shadow cast by New York (for all their notorious toughness, Chicagoans still get squirrely about the Big Apple), has become world famous, a direct influence on *Saturday Night Live*—in New York.

Architect Louis Sullivan's beautiful **Auditorium Theatre** tumbled into disrepair for more than 20 years, but in the mid-1960s Chicagoans came together to save the historic palace. In recent years performers like Elvis Costello, Radiohead, and Merle Haggard have appeared at the Auditorium.

In the late 1990s, Chicago's downtown theater district was reborn with the renovation of classic movie palaces like the **Shubert Theatre,** the **Oriental Theatre,** and the **Cadillac Palace**—all within walking distance of each other. The historic **Goodman Theatre** has opened an extravagant two-theater space downtown.

All the city's major sports teams carry storied legacies of coming back from one disaster or another. Even though the Chicago White Sox won the 2005 World Series, their fans still whine about being second fiddle to the Chicago Cubs. Chicagoans aren't shy about their opinions. It is that clarion that generations of them have followed through the night.

LIVE ENTERTAINMENT

THERE'S A FEISTY, ECLECTIC ETHIC at the heart of Chicago's live-entertainment scene, which can be divided into seven categories: rock, jazz, country, blues, cabaret, theater, and classical music. According to the Chicago Music Commission, 250 venues in the city present live acts. The profiles of the clubs that follow focus on live music, dance clubs, and storied neighborhood taverns.

Nightly schedules of live-music clubs, comedy clubs, and theatrical productions, as well as comprehensive listings of movie show times and other events, are printed in the *Chicago Sun-Times*'s Friday "Weekend" section, the *Chicago Tribune*'s "Friday" section, the free *New City* and *Chicago Reader* alternative newspapers, *The Onion*, and *Chicago* and *Time Out Chicago* magazines.

LIVE ROCK

CHICAGO IS THE INDEPENDENT-ROCK CAPITAL OF AMERICA. A slew of critically acclaimed record labels such as Bloodshot, Touch and Go, Thrill Jockey, Minty Fresh, Drag City, Wax Trax, and others have created a scene that filters through the city's live-music clubs. Popular rock figures like Billy Corgan (Smashing Pumpkins), Jeff Tweedy (Wilco), and Jon Langford (Mekons, Waco Brothers) call Chicago home. Liz Phair's career tanked when she left her native Chicago for Los Angeles.

For the last two summers, Chicago's **Grant Park** has hosted the internationally acclaimed **Lollapalooza** festival. At Lollapalooza 2006,

Chicago welcomed home native sons Common and Kanye West as well as popular rock acts like the Red Hot Chili Peppers, the Racounteurs, and Death Cab for Cutie. The 2006 festival also raised $600,000 for the Parkways Foundation, which helped restore a city playground and created day-camp scholarships. (Yet another reason Chicago is called "The City That Works.")

Metro (3730 North Clark Street; ☎ 773-549-0203; **www.metro chicago.com**) is the mother lode for the indie-rock movement. Owner Joe Shanahan has consistently championed up-and-coming bands in his lovingly sleazy theater-cabaret in the shadows of Wrigley Field. Metro is heavily into alternative and grunge with a sprinkling of national acts such as Lucinda Williams, Tom Jones, and even Bob Dylan. Shanahan gave the Smashing Pumpkins their big break, allowing them to open for bands like Jane's Addiction. Demographics slide around as expected: young hipsters for alternative shows, old hippies for Dylanesque gigs. Shanahan also owns the smaller **Double Door** (1572 North Milwaukee Avenue; ☎ 773-489-3160), which is a noisy dump. You're in luck if you go on a night when the young neighborhood crowd is actually listening to the music.

A more connective experience can be had down the street at **Phyllis' Musical Inn** (1800 West Division Street; ☎ 773-486-9862). Portions of the Michael J. Fox–Joan Jett film *Light of Day* were shot in this sweet, ramshackle, 100-seat family-run bar. After World War II and through the early 1960s, West Division Street was known as "Polish Broadway" because more than a dozen nightclubs on the strip featured live polka music. Open since 1954, Phyllis' is the last remnant of that era. The bar features alternative country and rock before an easygoing audience that generally falls into the 20-to-30-year-old age group.

One of the newer entries on the progressive-rock landscape is **The Abbey** (3420 West Grace at Elston; ☎ 773-478-4408; **www.abbey pub.com**). This old-school Irish pub's booking policy ranges from cutting-edge national acts like Pere Ubu and Mark Eitzel to Chicago-based alternative-country and rock bands. Sight lines can get a little fuzzy when the pub fills up, but a balcony affords a better view. The Abbey gets bonus points for live rugby matches broadcast via satellite on Sunday morning and a dinner and weekend breakfast menu. The event dictates the audience—young slackers come for the alt-rock shows; toothless beer drinkers roll in for the Sunday-morning rugby sessions.

During the 1970s and 1980s, the Lincoln Park neighborhood was a focal point of live rock and blues, and the **Wise Fools Pub** was a smart player in that scene. The club has reopened in its original location at 2270 North Lincoln Avenue (☎ 773-929-1300; **www.wisefools.com**). You won't catch many big names playing the 250-seat listening room, but plenty of local pop and rock bands play for a crowd that includes students from nearby DePaul University. You can also catch a sense of history: George Thorogood made his Chicago debut in this room in 1979, and blues queen Koko Taylor used to hold court here.

The Wrigleyville neighborhood (near Wrigley Field, of course) is the home of one of America's oldest live-reggae clubs, **The Wild Hare** (3530 North Clark Street; ☎ 773-327-4273; **www.wildharereggae.com**). Co-owned by former members of the Ethiopian band Dallol, who toured behind reggae superstar Ziggy Marley, this cozy nightclub has presented live music and lots of dancing seven nights a week since 1979. It has evolved into a cultural mecca for transplanted Jamaicans and Africans. And the joint never runs short of Red Stripe and rum.

Just a few blocks south of Wrigleyville is **Schubas Tavern** (3159 North Southport Avenue; ☎ 773-525-2508; **www.schubas.com**), a very comfortable restaurant, bar, and music room that's heavy on acoustic acts and small jazz outfits. American roots artists such as Steve Earle, Steve Forbert, and Alex Chilton have performed for audiences of all ages in the pristine 100-seat club.

Other essential (and deeply intimate) rooms on the alternative rock–pop circuit include **Martyrs'** (3855 North Lincoln Avenue; ☎ 773-404-9494; **www.martyrslive.com**), the grungy **Empty Bottle** (1035 North Western Avenue; ☎ 773-276-3600; **www.emptybottle.com**), and **The California Clipper** (1002 North California Avenue; ☎ 773-384-2547; **www.californiaclipper.com**), a delightfully restored 1940s cocktail lounge that also sails off into live jazz and alternative country.

The Chicago area (don't call it Chicagoland) has several mega- and medium-sized rock-concert venues. Chicagoans love summer because of the temperamental nature of the other seasons, so the big outdoor sheds are very popular. The 28,000-seat **First Midwest Bank Amphitheatre** (formerly the Tweeter Center; 19100 South Ridgeland Avenue at Flossmoor Road in south suburban Tinley Park; ☎ 708-614-1616; **ww.firstmidwestbankamphitheatre.com**) is one of the largest outdoor concert facilities in the country. Acts like Bruce Springsteen, John Mellencamp, and Jimmy Buffett play to full houses here. Bring binoculars—even pavilion seats can be far away.

The **Ravinia Festival,** in the northern suburb of Highland Park (☎ 847-266-5000; **www.ravinia.org**), is older, prettier, and more intimate. The focus is generally on classical music, although light-rock and roots acts pop up. Ravinia has a capacity for 15,000 fans on lawn seating and 3,500 in a rustic pavilion. **Skyline Stage at Navy Pier** (☎ 312-595-7437; **www.navypier.com**) is east of downtown and just off Lake Michigan, which means it isn't a bad idea to bring a windbreaker.

The city and suburbs are sprinkled with diverse indoor concert venues. The home of the Bulls and the Blackhawks, the 22,000-seat **United Center** (1901 West Madison Street; ☎ 312-455-4500; **www.unitedcenter.com**) also books major stadium-rock and pop acts. Built in 1980, the **Allstate Arena** (6920 North Mannheim Road, in Rosemont, next to O'Hare Airport; ☎ 847-635-6601; **www.allstatearena.com**) also

unofficial **TIP**
Don't let the Allstate Arena's suburban location put you off: it's accessible by the Chicago El.

features superstar-caliber acts, including big names in country music. The arena holds up to 18,500 folks for music events.

Several miles west of the Allstate Arena, in Hoffman Estates, is the **Sears Centre,** the Chicago area's newest venue. The 11,800-seat multipurpose arena hosts midsized concerts and is the home of the Chicago Hounds of the United Hockey League and the Chicago Shamrox of the National Lacrosse League. The Sears Centre is between the Illinois 59 and Beverly Road exits from the Northwest Tollway. It's not a Ticketmaster affiliate, so call ☎ 888-SEARSTIX or check out **www.searscentre.com** for ticket info.

The city's newest rock venue—at least in season—is **Charter One Pavilion at Northerly Island** (☎ 312-540-2667; or call Ticketmaster, ☎ 312-559-1212). Situated on a 90-acre peninsula along the shore of Lake Michigan, the two-year-old, 7,500-seat facility comes down during the winter (the site will eventually be developed for parkland). Featured acts have included the likes of Jack Johnson, Willie Nelson, and Tom Petty.

Midrange rock venues include the **Park West** (322 West Armitage Avenue; ☎ 773-929-1322), a former strip club turned elegant 800-seat music room; the 1,200-seat **Vic Theatre** (3145 North Sheffield Avenue; ☎ 773-472-0449), a vaudeville house built in 1912; the cavernous **Riviera Theatre** (4746 North Racine Avenue at Lawrence and Broadway avenues; ☎ 773-275-1012), where the late Warren Zevon fell off the stage into the orchestra pit during his drinking days; and the crazy **Aragon Ballroom** (1106 West Lawrence Avenue; ☎ 773-561-9500). A popular spot for big-band dancing in the 1930s and 1940s, the Aragon has enjoyed a resurgence. During the 1990s it was best known for booking head-banging metal music, but the offerings have recently branched out to reggaetón, norteño music, and even live boxing in air-conditioned comfort. A $1-million renovation has made the 20,000-square-foot ballroom (capacity 5,500) sing again: the Spanish-Moorish stucco and gold-leaf columns have been repainted, and the terra-cotta arches have been repaired. Tickets for shows at all these venues are usually available by phone from Ticketmaster at ☎ 312-559-1212, but be on guard for "service" charges and handling fees.

*un*official **TIP**
Getting to Charter One Pavilion at Northerly Island is almost as hard as remembering its name. There is no parking near the site—fans park by Soldier Field and take shuttle buses or grab a free trolley. But most folks walk from wherever they left their car.

JAZZ

CHICAGO'S LIVE-JAZZ SCENE HAS MADE A LIVELY migration from downtown clubs and hotels into the neighborhoods. The first stop on any jazz lover's tour should be the historic **Green Mill Jazz Club** (4802 North Broadway; ☎ 773-878-5552), the anchor of the funky Uptown neighborhood. Al Capone hung out here; check out the hideaway trapdoor behind the bar. There's also a cemented underground tunnel between the Green Mill and the equally historic Aragon Ballroom. (Old-timers claim Capone's gang ran hooch through here.) Chicago's best-known jazz musicians—like Patricia Barber and Kurt Elling—have held court in this colorful club. A fixture of the South Side, the **Velvet Lounge** has moved from its legendary location on South Indiana up to Chicago's old Motor Row district (67 East Cermak Road; ☎ 312-791-9050). This is actually a better location for visitors, halfway between McCormick Place to the east and Chinatown to the west. Owner Fred Anderson, an influential jazz saxophonist, personally helped move artifacts from the old Velvet, such as the legendary chandeliers, Schlitz signs, and the "Velvet Lady" painting. Sight lines and acoustics in the new club are much better than those in the Velvet's previous century-old digs. Anderson knows what he is doing: he's a founding member of the South Side's respected Association for the Advancement of Creative Musicians.

The most dependable downtown jazz spot is **Andy's** (11 East Hubbard Street; ☎ 312-642-6805), a soulful bar and grill that's known for vibrant after-work sets featuring top local players. This is the only place in Chicago where you can hear traditional jazz. A little farther north, **Green Dolphin Street** (2200 North Ashland Avenue; ☎ 773-395-0066; **www.jazzitup.com**), named after the classic tune "On Green Dolphin Street," features straight-ahead local jazz with occasional salsa and blues. A cool decor is defined by a lofty ceiling, wood paneling, blinds, and white-clothed tables. The club seats around 120 and serves appetizer-type snacks and drinks; there is also an adjacent restaurant.

For something completely different, catch the weekend jazz sets at the **Negro League Café** (301 East 43rd Street; ☎ 773-536-7000; **www.thenegroleaguecafe.info**), a South Side soul-food restaurant and lounge that honors black baseball players. The 5,000-square-foot cafe is on a dicey street corner in the Bronzeville neighborhood, so take a cab here, not public transportation.

COUNTRY AND WESTERN

ALTHOUGH CHICAGO IS MOST CLOSELY IDENTIFIED with blues and jazz, it was once a mecca for country music. During the 1940s and 1950s, country artists from the South were drawn to Chicago since it was the home of WLS Radio's National Barn Dance (1924–1960). For its last 30 years, the live-music show was broadcast from the Eighth Street Theater (now the site of the Conrad Hilton International Ballroom). The hardscrabble aura of the big industrial city attracted a blue-collar population that worked hard and played hard. During the 1950s, the 3000 block of West Madison Street alone (not far from the current United Center) contained five live-country joints with colorful names such as the Casanova Club and the Wagon Wheel. You can still feel this gritty spirit in the working-class Uptown neighborhood by visiting **Carol's Pub** (4659 North Clark Street; ☎ 773-334-2402; open until

4 a.m. Friday through Sunday). Once a late-1960s discotheque, Carol's has been a lovingly seedy honky-tonk since the early 1970s. For a quarter century it was a well-kept secret among Chicago's hard-core country-music community, but in the last couple of years Carol's has been discovered by everyone. The band Diamondback plays straight-ahead country on weekends (no cover). These days it's not uncommon to see a tourist trolley drop people off in front of Carol's. It's safer than it used to be, but the music is still dangerous.

For something a little more slick and alt-country, the **Horseshoe** (4115 North Lincoln; ☎ 773-549-9292) books occasional bluegrass and rockabilly acts. The faux-cowboy atmosphere is accented by chicken wire, wood, and Western kitsch on the walls. Bathroom sinks are set on moonshine stills. There's pool and darts for restless hearts. Barbecue specials like baby-back ribs and smoked chicken are served, and there's a Sunday-morning bluegrass brunch. Smoking, of course, is permitted. The club gets extra points for its popularity with Chicago's roller-derby queens.

It's inconveniently located in the Far North suburbs, but the **Sundance Saloon** (300 Lakehurst Road, Waukegan; ☎ 847-887-0858; **www.sundancesalooon.com**) isn't just another watering hole: it's reportedly the longest-running country-and-western bar in the state of Illinois. Opened in 1975 as Mickey's Honky Tonk, the club recently moved from its longtime location in Mundelein to a bigger space in nearby Waukegan. The new Sundance boasts 62,000 square feet on two levels, a huge stage, and a 4,000-square-foot dance floor, plus two restaurants and a gift shop. The saloon is a half mile off of Interstate 94, just south of Six Flags Great America amusement park; several hotels are nearby. The Sundance opens Tuesday through Friday at 5 p.m. and Saturday at 7 p.m.; no one under age 21 is allowed in the club area.

LIVE BLUES

CHICAGO BLUES ARE AT THE PROVERBIAL CROSSROADS. As young musicians continue to explore rap, hip-hop, and house, the traditional blues scene is faced with a talent void. Clubs have suffered. Among the ones that have closed in recent years is the legendary **Checkerboard Lounge** on East 43rd Street. Once the city's premier blues club for tourists, the Checkerboard was the home base for upstarts like Buddy Guy and Earl Hooker in the late 1950s and early 1960s when they arrived in Chicago. The **New Checkerboard Lounge** has opened in Hyde Park (5201 South Harper; ☎ 773-684-1472), but all it shares with its predecessor is the name. The room is bigger and cleaner, and live jazz and blues are featured. On the walls are pictures of the original Checkerboard, including a photo of the historic evening when the Rolling Stones dropped in to jam with their hero, Muddy Waters. Those days are gone. How do we know? Smoking isn't allowed at the New Checkerboard, which means Keith Richards would be denied admittance.

Any essential live-blues experience still reflects the city's segregated tradition: most whites and tourists go to North Side clubs, most African Americans to South Side clubs. It's been that way since the Hoochie Coochie Man was a kid. Today, though, there aren't as many differences between North Side and South Side shows as there were in the 1960s and 1970s. These days, **Buddy Guy's Legends** is the city's leading blues club, not just because it's owned by the master bluesman, but because its South Loop location attracts fans from all walks of life (see full profile on page 344).

Here's the best of what's left:

Lee's Unleaded Blues (7401 South Chicago Avenue; ☎ 773-493-3477) has replaced the Checkerboard as the definitive South Side blues experience. Known as the Queen Bee until 1983, Lee's has a warm and outgoing crowd. Johnny Drummer and the Starlights, the weekend house band, stretch the definition of the blues by exploring soul, 1950s rock, and country idioms. The joint is small, which means it's always jumping. And the fact that Lee's looks like Christmas 365 days a year—with red carpeting and red tinsel around the 75-seat room—only adds to the merriment. There's ample street parking as well as valet, and while there's no cover, there is a two-drink minimum (the cocktails tend to be watered down, so stick to beer and shots).

Rosa's Lounge (3420 West Armitage Avenue; ☎ 773-342-0452; **www.rosaslounge.com**) celebrates traditional values in the middle of a transitional Hispanic neighborhood. The 150-person-capacity club is owned by Italian blues drummer Tony Manguilo and his mother, Rosa. Their passionate approach to American blues stretches from a tenderly refurbished mahogany bar to a spacious stage and impeccable sight lines. Shows start at 9:30 p.m. on weekdays and at 10 p.m. on weekends. Street parking all around.

B.L.U.E.S. (2519 North Halsted Street; ☎ 773-528-1012; **www.chicagobluesbar.com**) is the longest-running North Side club with the same location and ownership. You can arrive at any time of the night (or morning) and be assured a good shot at the stage, even though the room—which holds 100 people max—is usually crowded. B.L.U.E.S. features top-notch local bands every night of the year, attracting a throng of international and domestic tourists. Trying to find a place to park in this neighborhood might give you the blues, but valet parking is available on weekends. And don't fret: B.L.U.E.S. doesn't stand for anything in particular.

Finally, **Kingston Mines** (2548 North Halsted Street; ☎ 773-477-4646; **www.kingstonmines.com**) draws hard-core fans from B.L.U.E.S.

across the street because it serves liquor later (until 5 a.m. Saturday and 4 a.m. Sunday). Local blues acts alternate on two stages, so there's rarely any dead time. This club has been around for over 25 years in various North Side locations.

COMEDY AND INTERACTIVE THEATER

CHICAGO USED TO BE KNOWN JUST FOR ITS COMEDY CLUBS. But if you can't beat 'em with the shtick, join 'em: interactive theater has become popular in Chicago humor circles as well. Now in its 13th year at the **Pipers Alley Theater** (230 West North Avenue, directly behind The Second City; ☎ 312-664-8844), *Tony 'n' Tina's Wedding* (☎ 312-664-8844; **www.tonylovestina.com**) is a two-hour-and-45-minute production with 32 cast members, a huge set, and an Italian buffet dinner. Audience members ("guests") enter a beautiful chapel for a wedding ceremony, followed by a dinner and dance reception (complete with a live band) that goes haywire. The wedding ceremony is scripted, but the rest of the show is improvised.

Tony 'n' Tina's Wedding features lots of hometown nuance. Many local media and sports figures—the biggest celebrities Chicago has to offer—have appeared in the show, and the occasional big name like Frankie Avalon drops in for a short residency. *Tony 'n' Tina's Wedding* does such a good job of meshing actors with the audience that you can't always tell who's who. Performances are Wednesday and Thursday at 7:30 p.m.; Friday at 8 p.m.; Saturday at 5 and 8 p.m.; and Sunday at 5 p.m. (kids half price); matinees are the first Wednesday of the month at 12:30 p.m. Tickets are $60 to $70 per person.

For more improv, check out **iO** (formerly the ImprovOlympic), just down the street from Wrigley Field (3541 North Clark; ☎ 773-880-0199; **www.iochicago.net**). Founded in 1981, iO has gained fame as a comedy training center and performance venue for long-form improvisation, including the house specialty, the "Harold." Attend a show and you just might see a star in the making; *Saturday Night Live* consistently hires comedians who have trained there, including Mike Myers, Tina Fey, Tim Meadows, Seth Meyers, and Rachel Dratch.

ComedySportz is known for its rat-a-tat-tat improv games performed by two teams in "heated" competition. Be forewarned: the pace can get as dizzy as a Cubs rebuilding plan. ComedySportz performs above Ann Sather's Restaurant (929 West Belmont; ☎ 773-549-8080; **www.comedy sportzchicago.com**). Performances are Thursday at 8 p.m.; Friday and Saturday at 8 and 10 p.m. Tickets are $19.

The *Blue Man Group* (Briar Street Theatre, 3133 North Halsted; ☎ 773-348-4000) is a popular roadside attraction of three cobalt-blue chrome-domed dudes who guide an audience of mostly tourists through a multisensory show of animation, percussive music, art, and vaudeville. Blue Man Group's 1999 debut album *Audio* was nominated for a Best Pop Instrumental Grammy. A must-see if you're into splattering paint, flying mushrooms, and progressive music. Main-floor seats are $59; balcony seats are $49. The gently interactive revue has been a local ritual since 1997. If you can't get a ticket here, other Blue Man groups perform in New York, Boston, Las Vegas, Berlin, Toronto, and London.

DANCE CLUBS

CHICAGO HAS ALWAYS HAD A LEG UP on the rest of the country when it comes to dancing. Popular 1960s soul dances like the Monkey Time and Woodbine Twine came out of Chicago; in the 1980s, spiky-haired punks were pogoing at rank, now long-gone, storefront clubs; and during the 1990s, industrial house music went worldwide after originating on the Near South and West sides.

unofficial **TIP**
Of the dance-oriented clubs mentioned here, some are new, others are standbys. But be aware that the scene is volatile—these clubs go in and out of style more than any other kind of Chicago nightspot, so call ahead.

Over the last few years, the gritty Lake Street corridor has been a breeding ground for cutting-edge dance clubs. Set under the noisy El tracks, this warehouse neighborhood is a cheap cab ride from downtown. That's the only thing you'll find cheap here.

Hippest on the strip is **Reserve** (858 Lake Street; ☎ 312-455-1111; **www.reserve-chicago.com**), a sprawling two-story complex full of attitude. There's not only a rope outside but a second rope inside leading to the upstairs club, which has a dance floor and elevated DJ booth. DJ AM (Adam Goldstein) spins exclusively at Reserve when he is in Chicago. Celebrities like Drew Barrymore and her boyfriend, Fabrizio Moretti of the Strokes, dance here. Michael Jordan and Black Entertainment Television founder Robert L. Johnson toasted their partnership in the NBA's Charlotte Bobcats at Table 501 on the second floor—the only place MJ will sit. Cover prices and drinks vary, but beware of the Ruby Red Cocktail. Served with an actual ruby, it'll set you back $950.

Transit (1431 West Lake Street; ☎ 312-491-8600; **www.transit-usa .com**), an upscale dance club that is part of a 10,000-square-foot complex, features minimalist decor in a maximum setting. DJs deliver heavy doses of funk and R&B with no surrender, and the dense beats can boggle your mind after a few hours. With weekend covers as high as $20, Transit is not cheap—which, of course, keeps out the riffraff.

Several blocks north of Lake Street, **Ohm** (1958 West North Avenue; ☎ 773-278-1009) is the centerpiece of nightlife experience in Wicker Park. It offers progressive micro-house, techno, and drum-and-bass music in a traditional setting. A dark, mysterious mood is set by the clandestine entry from an alley behind the Tavern (formerly Border Line Tap). Ohm consists of three bars and three dance floors, which helps handle overflow weekend crowds. Be warned: it's tough to park in Wicker Park on weekends.

Berlin (954 West Belmont; ☎ 773-348-4975; **www.berlinchicago.com**) is a beloved icon for the gay community, although everyone is welcome. The futuristic storefront dance club has been operating for 18 years in a convenient location just steps from the Belmont El stop (Red Line). Contemporary house, acid jazz, and neo-soul are accented by videos projected on big screens.

Le Passage (937 North Rush; ☎ 312-255-0022) harks back to the days when Rush Street was one of America's premier nightlife districts. The medium-sized club is located down a 1960s cobblestone alley, while the interior is peppered with *Playboy*-esque velvet couches and 14-karat-gold-leaf walls. Le Passage is a popular destination for touring rock stars staying along the Magnificent Mile.

Stepping

A tradition in Chicago's African American community, stepping is a stylized ballroom-dance form—with attitude. A smooth, clearly defined beat is what sets stepping apart from other dances. Classic steppers' songs include "Love's Gonna Last" by Jeffrey and "Windows" by the Whispers. Chicago steppers congregate at the legendary **Fifty Yard Line** (69 East 75th Street; ☎ 773-846-0005), an easy-to-find place (just east off the Dan Ryan Expressway) that mixes a sports theme with a dance theme. The club has 20 television sets and snacks like fried chicken and perch. Smoking is permitted, but jeans and sneakers aren't allowed after 9 p.m. And don't request any Jessica Simpson.

LOOKIN' FOR LOVE

BECAUSE CHICAGO IS A PREDOMINANTLY Catholic city, attitudes toward sex can be conservative. And that means the singles scene can be unpredictable—sometimes friendly and relaxed, other times as uptight as Martha Stewart in a mosh pit. It was Chicago, after all, where Frank Sinatra sang that he actually "saw a man dancing with his own wife." That said, here's a rundown of what's out there.

From the 1950s through the 1980s, **Rush Street** was Chicago's answer to Bourbon Street, with its colorful assortment of jazz clubs, honky-tonks, and strip joints with names like the Candy Store. The city cleaned up the street, and in true Chicago fashion, Rush went south. Only recently has it staged a comeback through a combination of sleek retail and upscale nightclubs that are popular with the 35-to-60 age group.

Three clubs in particular make up what locals jokingly refer to as the "Viagra Triangle." The power player of the bunch is **Gibson's** (1028 North Rush Street; ☎ 312-266-8999; **www.gibsonssteakhouse.com**). The dimly lit bar and restaurant opened in 1989 in what used to be Mister Kelly's nightclub. Known for its killer steaks and even-deadlier martinis (packing four to six ounces of vodka, the popular house martini is $7), Gibson's is a favorite of movie stars and athletes visiting Chicago. Jack

Nicholson and Shaquille O'Neal do the hang here, and Dennis Rodman was a Gibson's regular when he played for the Bulls. That fact alone should tell you not to worry about a dress code.

The swingin' **Jilly's Piano Bar** (1007 North Rush Street; ☎ 312-664-1001; **www.jillyschicago.com**) is across the street from Gibson's. Named in honor of Jilly Rizzo, one of Sinatra's best pallies, the club is loosely modeled after the original Jilly's in New York City, where Sinatra, Johnny Carson, and others held court in the 1960s. This Jilly's has been around for more than a decade. It doesn't play up the Sinatra connection as much as it used to, but it still serves one of the best lemon-drop martinis in town. It's also a good place to watch the sidewalk traffic on Rush Street. No cover.

The third stop on the triangle is another steak house: **Tavern on Rush** (1031 North Rush Street; ☎ 312-664-9600; **www.tavernonrush.com**). Like Gibson's and Jilly's, it's a favorite of older men and women with year-round tans, but it's so far beneath the other two spots on the buzz circuit that Michael Jordan can eat here with minimal hassle.

A few blocks north, a younger crowd descends on **Division Street.** Here you'll find one of the city's most legendary singles bars: **Butch McGuire's** (20 West Division Street; ☎ 312-337-9080). Don't miss Butch's during the holiday season, when more than 200,000 Christmas lights twinkle in two rooms. Not far off Division, the bravest and boldest after-hours customers head to **Gamekeepers** (345 West Armitage; ☎ 773-549-0400), a late-night *Animal House*–type establishment with lots of television sets. If you were born before 1971, you don't belong here.

In **Wicker Park,** known for its live rock 'n' roll and slacker bars, the singles oasis is **Nick's** (1516 North Milwaukee Avenue; ☎ 773-252-1155). Formerly in the DePaul neighborhood, Nick's has found a niche in this part of town. It boasts one of the best jukeboxes in the city, with ample Memphis soul, Chicago blues, and Carolina beach music.

Just blocks north of Wicker Park is the trendy and less Bohemian neighborhood called **Bucktown.** It has several singles bars with singular names (just like Nick's). **Lottie's** (1925 West Cortland; ☎ 773-489-0738) was originally called Busia's Polish Pub. As the neighborhood changed in the late 1980s, it was renamed in honor of the late Lottie Zagorski, who between 1934 and 1967 ran a combination grocery store and tavern at the same location. Lottie caused quite a stir in the working-class neighborhood because she was a "hermaphrodite," in the parlance of the day. Look closely around the bar, and you'll find a black-and-white photograph of Lottie, built like a Bears linebacker but wearing a flower-print dress. Today, Lottie's causes quite a stir because of all the raging 20-something hormones bouncing around in a setting that includes sports on ten television sets and a crummy pool table in the back of the bar. A sedate sidewalk cafe is open in the summer.

A hipper Bucktown space is **Danny's Tavern** (1951 West Dickens; ☎ 773-489-6457), formerly a bookie joint called Art's Tap. Today, the walls are stark and the room is filled with progressive music by the likes of Magnetic Fields and Brand New Heavies. Other times, DJs spin old-school soul, funk, and reggae. The biggest night of the month is generally the first Wednesday, when "Sheer Magic" takes over, with DJs spinning some of the best funk and soul you will hear. The monthly set has even caught the attention of *Rolling Stone* magazine. Scenesters lounge around little tables and sit on high-backed chairs in cozy, dimly lit back rooms filled with candles; points for two bathrooms per gender.

Should you find yourself striking out around the University of Chicago on the South Side, check out **The Woodlawn Tap** (1172 East 55th Street; ☎ 773-643-5516). Since 1948, more than 500 free-thinking UC students have tended bar at this funky working-class tavern. Notable drinkers have included the late bluesman Paul Butterfield, anthropologist Margaret Mead, and poet Dylan Thomas, who once stopped in three different times in one day.

For a late-night taste of the real Chicago, take in the twin spin of **Underbar** and **The Bluelight,** adjacent bars underneath a grisly North Side overpass but across from a police station. Underbar (3243 North Western Avenue; ☎ 773-404-9363) is the more popular joint. It's cleaner, there's an indie-rock soundtrack (played by hipster bartenders), and the room has intimate tables for smooching and arm wrestling. In the wee, wee hours, the Underbar fills with bar and restaurant workers, musicians, and actors from the nearby Viaduct Theater. It's open until 4 a.m. Sunday through Friday and until 5 a.m. Saturday; no cover. The Bluelight (3251 North Western Avenue; ☎ 773-755-5875) is so named because it's popular with policemen. Under different ownership than the Underbar, The Bluelight resembles your uncle's rec room, filled with classic beer memorabilia and neon. The crowd looks rough, but hey, most of them are probably cops. Open nightly, 6 p.m. to 4 a.m. and until 5 a.m. Saturday; no cover.

The city's grand piano bars (without restaurants) include the dark and tiny **Zebra Lounge** (1220 North State Street; ☎ 312-642-5140), done in enticing zebra decor, of course, and the subterranean **Redhead Piano Bar** (16 West Ontario Street; ☎ 312-640-1000), generally full of losers who've struck out in the Viagra Triangle.

Catering to single guys who've totally thrown in the towel, strip clubs have made a comeback in Chicago. This time around, they're called "gentlemens' clubs," following a nationwide trend toward nightspots where scantily clad or nude women are the attractions. The more mainstream gentlemens' clubs are **V.I.P.s** (1531 North Kingsbury; ☎ 312-664-7400), aka "the only topless full-liquor club in downtown Chicago," and **Heavenly Bodies** (1300 South Elmhurst Road; ☎ 847-806-1121) in Elk Grove Village, about ten miles from O'Hare International Airport. Collared shirts and/or nice sweaters are required at Heavenly Bodies after 7 p.m.—for customers, that is. Note that both clubs are topless only (that is, there's no full nudity).

LEGITIMATE THEATER

IN RECENT YEARS, CHICAGO THEATER has been a spawning ground of actors and directors for agents, producers, and casting directors from the East and West coasts. While the Loop (downtown) theaters enjoy success with safe, straight-from-Broadway touring companies—or, in some cases, workshop productions heading to Broadway (such as Mel Brooks's *The Producers* and Eric Idle's *Monty Python's Spamalot*)—a cutting-edge, off-Loop scene has flourished.

The Chicago area features more than 200 theater companies or producing organizations, which range from established institutions to midlevel professional companies to smaller and younger troupes. The **Goodman Theatre** (170 North Dearborn; ☎ 312-443-3800; **www.good mantheatre.org**) is the oldest and largest resident theater in Chicago. Since its founding in 1925, the Goodman had worked out of the rear portion of the Art Institute but in the fall of 2000 moved to a glorious two-theater complex in the heart of Chicago's vibrant North Loop Theater District. The Goodman pioneered regional theater in America. Under artistic director Robert Falls, shows have ranged from experimental Shakespeare to Bertolt Brecht to James Baldwin.

On the Loop commercial front, a Broadway-in-Chicago texture colors the bookings at the **LaSalle Bank Theatre** (formerly the Shubert; 40 West Monroe Street), the **Ford Center for the Performing Arts– Oriental Theatre** (24 West Randolph Street), and the **Cadillac Palace Theatre** (151 West Randolph Street). In recent years, Broadway producers have tried something new and used these theaters as a home for open-ended productions of musicals still playing in New York, most recently *Wicked* and *The Color Purple*. Tickets for all three venues should be ordered through **Ticketmaster** (☎ 312-902-1400; **www.broadwayinchicago.com**).

The LaSalle Bank Theatre, which recently underwent a renovation, opened in 1906 as the Majestic Theatre and as the tallest building in Chicago. Its stature attracted vaudeville acts who performed from 1:30 to 10:30 p.m., six days a week; notable figures gracing the stage included Harry Houdini and Eddie Foy. The Palace and Oriental theaters opened in 1926; the Palace is worth a look-see even if the theater is dark. Designed by noted theater architects the Rapp Brothers, the interior features a spellbinding vision inspired by the palaces of Fontainebleau and Versailles. The lobby is accented with huge decorative mirrors and violet-and-white Breche marble, which sweeps through a succession of foyers. Chicago fun fact: during the mid-to-late 1980s, the Palace was used as a rock venue, and the pop group Frankie Goes to Hollywood had the stage collapse under them during a performance. No one was seriously injured.

All three beautifully restored theaters are a joint venture between Live Nation and the Nederlander Organization, the two largest commercial-theater producers and owners-operators in the United

States. Call or check local listings for performance information. You can also visit **www.chicagoplays.com** for info.

The **Steppenwolf Theatre** (1650 North Halsted; ☎ 312-335-1650; **www.steppenwolf.org**) is one of the pioneers in the Off-Loop movement. Steppenwolf is unique for the consistency of its ensemble; audiences have been able to watch a group of actors develop over the years. It's like a baseball farm system—which is why most Steppenwolf actors are devoted Cubs fans. The original 1976 ensemble included John Malkovich, Gary Sinise, and Laurie Metcalf. Steppenwolf has received international acclaim for its production of John Steinbeck's *The Grapes of Wrath;* it has also staged works by Sam Shepard, Tom Waits, and Tennessee Williams. The immaculate 500-seat main stage and 100-seat upstairs theater are a modest cab ride from downtown.

Some people perceive **The Second City** as simply a comedy club, but it is a legitimate local theatrical institution that started in 1959. Major talents like Ed Asner, John Belushi, Chris Farley, Bill Murray, and George Wendt cut their teeth here. The original founding format is still used. With minimal costuming and props, six or seven actors lampoon life in a torrid series of topical skits. Recent events have raised the bar for actors in critically acclaimed productions like *Thank Heaven It Wasn't 7/11.* Producer emeritus Joyce Sloane has always pledged to keep the theater admission charge ($18 Tuesday through Thursday and Sunday, $24 on Friday and Saturday) in the same ballpark as a movie ticket. The original 300-seat location at 1616 North Wells Street (☎ 312-337-3992; **www.secondcity.com**) also features a 180-seat back room for Second City E.T.C., which is sometimes regarded as more rebellious than its big brother.

unofficial **TIP**
Following every Second City show, the troupe solicits ideas from the audience to improvise new sketches. There is no charge for these late-night sets.

Donny's Skybox Studio Theater is a cabaret space on the fourth floor of Piper's Alley, an entertainment complex adjacent to The Second City. It is used as a classroom and performing venue for Second City Training Center students and alumni. The studio presents various productions each term in the Skybox, including coached ensembles, a Sunday doubleheader, and writing-program revues. The space is named for Don DePollo, who joined the Second City cast in 1974 and went on to become one of the training center's most influential teachers (and biggest Cub fans) until his death in 1995. For listings and tickets, call The Second City or check its Web site.

The **Court Theatre** (5535 South Ellis Avenue; ☎ 773-753-4472) is the third-biggest theater in the city in terms of annual operating budget. It celebrated its 50th anniversary in 2004. The 251-seat theater is just 12 minutes from the Loop on the University of Chicago campus. The critically acclaimed theater features classics such as Oscar

Wilde's *The Importance of Being Earnest*, Edward Albee's *Who's Afraid of Virginia Woolf?*, and Samuel Beckett's *Endgame*.

Another long-established organization is the **Northlight Theatre,** at the North Shore Center for the Performing Arts (☎ 847-673-6300; **www.northlight.org**) in near-north suburban Skokie. For just over 30 years, Northlight has been one of the largest and most innovative theaters in the Chicago area and is an artistic anchor of the northern suburbs. Northlight has won critical acclaim for its production of a wide range of new and contemporary plays and original chamber-size musicals.

The **Chicago Shakespeare Theater** (800 East Grand Avenue; ☎ 312-595-5600; **www.chicagoshakes.com**) resides in a seven-story glass-walled structure on Navy Pier that affords a panoramic view of the lake and the Chicago skyline. On its 500-seat main stage and 200-seat flexible stage are offered cutting-edge productions of the Bard's greatest works, as well as a menu of imported works from Europe and Canada.

The **Victory Gardens Theater** (2433 North Lincoln Avenue; ☎ 773-871-3000; **www.victorygardens.org**), now in a 299-seat home in the renovated Biograph Theater, stages mostly new works by its stable of accomplished playwrights. Visitor bonus points: in 1934, bank robber–Public Enemy Number One John Dillinger was gunned down in the alley adjacent to the Biograph. He had no encores. Victory Gardens will continue to operate in its original location (2257 North Lincoln Avenue), where many of the city's best smaller theater's rent space.

Quality midlevel theater includes the **Lookingglass Theatre Company,** in an immaculate 270-seat space at the downtown Water Tower Water Works (☎ 312-337-0665; **www.lookingglasstheatre.org**); the **Black Ensemble Theatre** (4520 North Beacon Street; ☎ 773-769-4451; **www.blackensembletheater.org**), which stages a lot of shows on dead rhythm-and-blues stars like Jackie Wilson and Howlin' Wolf; the **Mercury Theater** (3745 North Southport Avenue; ☎ 773-325-1700); and the multistage **Royal George Theatre Center** (1641 North Halsted Street; ☎ 312-998-9000). The **Chicago Children's Theatre** (☎ 773-227-0180; **www.chicagochildrenstheatre.org**) stages first-rate productions for the younger set.

One of the hottest midlevel theaters in town is the progressive **Redmoon Theater** (☎ 312-850-8440; **www.redmoon.org)**, one of the only theaters in America that creates large outdoor public spectacles. These events deploy masks, puppets, irreverent mechanical devices, and live music. Redmoon's work can be seen in economically challenged neighborhoods, city parks, and landmarks. The theater group occasionally presents shows from its workshop space at 1463 West Hubbard Street, near downtown.

With the aim to give downtown theatergoers a glimpse of Off-Loop theater, a wide array of notable smaller theaters are invited to perform in two downtown venues sponsored by the Chicago Department of

Cultural Affairs. The **Storefront Theater** (66 East Randolph Street; ☎ 312-742-8497) and the **Studio Theater** in the Chicago Cultural Center (77 East Randolph Street; ☎ 312-742-8497) have seen notable productions by 500 Clown, Tireswing Theatre, the House Theatre, and Plasticene.

The days of Chicago dinner theater are long gone, but to immerse yourself in a total theatrical-tourist experience, check out *The Spirit of Chicago,* a floating dinner theater that cruises Lake Michigan with a mainstream song-and-dance revue. *The Spirit of Chicago* docks at Navy Pier (600 East Grand Street; ☎ 312-836-7899; **www .spiritcitycruises.com**). Advance reservations are recommended.

Apart from the young and experimental theater spaces, most of these shows can be expensive—and many often sell out. The League of Chicago Theatres offers a **Hot Tix** program that sells tickets at half price the day of the performance. Hot Tix booths are at 72 East Randolph Street in downtown Chicago; at the Chicago Water Works Visitor Center, 163 East Pearson Street, near the Water Tower; and at all Tower Records locations. For booth hours, call ☎ 312-554-9800 or check **www.hottix.org.** Many theaters also offer discounts for students, children, senior citizens, the disabled, and armed-forces personnel. Call ahead.

THE CLASSICS

THE WORLD-RENOWNED **Chicago Symphony Orchestra** (CSO; ☎ 312-294-3000; **www.cso.org**) is the touchstone of the Chicago classical-music landscape. Since 1960, the CSO has won 51 Grammy Awards, 23 of them between 1972 and 1991, when the great Georg Solti was music director. Overall, Solti won 31 Grammies—more than any other musical artist, including Michael Jackson. Solti's tradition is consistently celebrated in the CSO's clarity and logic.

The 116-year-old orchestra is based in the 2,251-seat **Symphony Center** (220 South Michigan Avenue). Visiting domestic and international orchestras also appear at the complex's Orchestra Hall as part of the Symphony Center Presents series. In addition, the Symphony Center includes a beautiful gift shop and the **Club at Symphony Center** (☎ 312-294-3333), which features special events such as cabarets and a wine-tasting series.

The Symphony Center is also home to the **Chicago Sinfonietta** (☎ 312-236-3681), a chamber orchestra founded in 1986. The ensemble typically presents five programs a year, including

unofficial **TIP**
The general dress code for Chicago theater is casual. Men need not wear ties, and women don't have to overdress. Jeans, slacks, and nice shirts are perfectly acceptable.

unofficial **TIP**
Book your symphony tickets well in advance. Subscriptions account for roughly 75% of CSO tickets sold, and 2001 attendance filled more than 90% of Orchestra Hall's capacity. Sometimes tickets are available at the last minute, though, so call the box office (☎ 312-294-3000) on the day of the concert.

collaborations with art rockers Poi Dog Pondering and an annual tribute to Martin Luther King Jr.

On a smaller scale, the **Newberry Consort** (☎ 312-255-3700; **www .newberry.org**) is the city's premier early-music ensemble. Its season begins in the fall at various locations in Chicago, Oak Park, and Evanston.

The **Lyric Opera of Chicago** (☎ 312-332-2244; **www.lyricopera.org**) presents the classics with an increased emphasis on progressive works to make opera relevant to younger audiences. Performances take place in the majestic **Civic Opera House** (20 North Wacker Drive), the second-largest opera auditorium in North America. The 45-story Art Deco limestone building was built in the 1920s to one-up the Auditorium Theatre. The entranceways' ornamental masks and musical instruments alone are covered with 2,000 gallons of gold paint.

NIGHTCLUB PROFILES

Buddy Guy's Legends

LIVE BLUES IN A DOWNBEAT, REC ROOM–TYPE SETTING

754 South Wabash Avenue, South Loop; ☎ 312-427-0333
www.buddyguys.com

Cover $8–$15. Minimum None. Mixed drinks $4. Wine $4. Beer $3.50–$5. Dress Everything from tees and sweats to after-work attire. Specials Local record-release parties, spur-of-the-moment bookings such as Eric Clapton, and occasional live recordings, like owner Buddy Guy playing with G. E. Smith of the *Saturday Night Live* band. Food available Southern Louisiana cuisine: ribs, red beans and rice, and "Peanut Buddy Pie," a Buddy Guy–endorsed peanut butter pie. Hours Monday–Friday, 11 a.m.–2 a.m.; Saturday, 5 p.m.–3 a.m.; Sunday, 6 p.m.–2 a.m.

WHO GOES THERE International tourists, more of a racial mix than North Side blues clubs, and sometimes even Buddy Guy, the Chicago guitar great.

WHAT GOES ON A stately approach to booking live local, national, and international blues acts seven nights a week. From 1972 to 1986, local guitar hero Buddy Guy (who influenced Eric Clapton and Stevie Ray Vaughan) ran the Checkerboard Lounge, a South Side blues club that still stands today. In 1989, he reopened in a bigger and safer location as part of Chicago's developing South Loop. The sprawling storefront club is popular with tourists because of Guy's international reputation and its prime location.

SETTING AND ATMOSPHERE Urban roadhouse. Four pool tables are almost always occupied at stage left. Portraits of blues greats like Muddy Waters, Lightnin' Hopkins, and Howlin' Wolf hang throughout the museum-like space. Near the club entrance there's a display case featuring Guy's awards; guitars from the likes of Eric Clapton and Muddy Waters hang above the bar.

IF YOU GO Don't request Britney Spears. This is a blues sanctuary. It's also best to arrive early, as all shows are general admission and often sell out. The

Chicago Nightclubs by Location

NAME	DESCRIPTION	COVER
NORTH SIDE		
The Closet	Classic gay-friendly bar	None
Club Lucky	A quintessential Chicago experience	None
Green Mill Jazz Club	Hepcat speakeasy with live jazz	$3–$8
The Hideout	Eclectic live music in the middle of nowhere	$3–$10
Old Town School of Folk Music	Folk- and world-music mecca	Varies
Weeds	Retreat for Bohemian riffraff	None
NORTH CENTRAL–O'HARE AIRPORT		
Hala Kahiki	Tiki bar to the max	None
NEAR NORTH SIDE		
Davenport's Piano Bar and Cabaret	Find your inner Bobby Short	Varies
House of Blues	Juke-joint opera house	$10–$60
The Lodge	Neighborhood singles bar	None
The Matchbox	Tiny, intimate, friendly tavern	None
Old Town Ale House	From Bach to Bukowski	None
THE LOOP		
Funky Buddha Lounge	Urban-hip dance club and lounge	None–$20
SOUTH LOOP		
Buddy Guy's Legends	Home of the legendary bluesman	$8–$15
HotHouse	Funky arts, music, and performance space	$5–$30
SOUTHERN SUBURBS		
FitzGerald's	Roots-music roadhouse	$5–$20

Southern Louisiana kitchen serves better-than-average bar food. And periodically check out the far west end of the bar. That's Guy's favorite spot.

The Closet

A NEIGHBORHOOD BAR FOR AN ALWAYS-CHANGING NEIGHBORHOOD

3325 North Broadway, North Side; ☎ 773-477-8533

Cover None. **Minimum** 2-drink minimum on Friday and Saturday after 10 p.m. **Mixed drinks** $3–$9. **Wine** $4.50. **Beer** $3–$5. **Dress** Casual. **Specials** Long Island tea specials on Thursday. **Food available** None. **Hours** Monday–Friday, 2 p.m.–4 a.m.; Saturday, noon–5 a.m.; Sunday, noon–4 a.m.

WHO GOES THERE Predominately lesbian crowd, although young, hipster gay men and straight couples are welcome and accepted.

WHAT GOES ON The Closet opened in 1978 and became a popular neighborhood bar for gay men. The Closet is still under original ownership, a remarkable feat for Chicago nightlife. The bar is a staple of what real-estate developers used to call "Newtown" and is now known as "Boystown." Expect music videos by the likes of Janet Jackson, George Michael, and Britney Spears in constant rotation. Karaoke on Thursday.

SETTING AND ATMOSPHERE The Closet only holds about 70 people in a narrow space with a friendly U-shaped bar surrounded by burgundy walls. Lots of bump 'n' grind after 2 a.m. Just about anything goes where women are making out with women, guys making time, boys being boys, and somehow it all makes sense in a hassle-free environment. The Closet holds a late-night liquor license, which is becoming an endangered species in Chicago. There's a small dance floor, plus pinball and darts if you can find the space.

IF YOU GO Don't wear good clothes. The Closet can get smoky, and when it's really crowded, the odds are high that someone could spill a drink on you. Parking is tough, especially on weekends. Cabs and public transportation advised.

Club Lucky

A QUINTESSENTIAL CHICAGO EXPERIENCE IN A CLASSIC NEAR NORTH NEIGHBORHOOD

**1824 West Wabansia, North Side; ☎ 773-227-2300;
www.clubluckychicago.com**

Cover None. Minimum None. Mixed drinks $5.75–$7.75, martinis $6.50–$9.50, espresso and cappuccino are brewed to order. Wine More than 50 Italian wines are offered by the bottle ($27–$46) or glass ($6.50–$12); the reserve wine list focuses on Italy, Sicily, and the Americas. Beer $5–$8. Dress Casually hip; shorts okay in the summer. Smoking Cocktail lounge only. Food available House specialties include Chicken Vesuvio with roasted potatoes and peas and several pastas made on-site with homemade Club Lucky marinara sauce. Hours Food served Monday–Thursday, 11:30 a.m.–11 p.m.; Friday, 11:30 a.m.–midnight; Saturday, 5 p.m.–midnight; and Sunday, 4–10 p.m. Cocktail lounge open late during the week, until 2 a.m. Friday, and until 3 a.m. Saturday.

WHO GOES THERE Residents of the Bucktown neighborhod, downtowners on a ten-minute cab ride, and folks heading out to Chicago Bulls and Blackhawk games.

WHAT GOES ON No-nonsense drinking and eating. Subdued Dean Martin and Frank Sinatra play on a CD jukebox as people roll life's dice along the 35-seat black Formica–topped bar in the cocktail lounge. Feelin' lucky? "That's Life," as the Chairman used to say. Club Lucky's Killer Martini (garnished with three blue-cheese olives) has been voted Chicago's best by the alternative newspaper *New City*.

SETTING AND ATMOSPHERE The corner building that houses the club was built in the 1920s as a hardware store. During Prohibition, it was remodeled to include a speakeasy with a basement entrance. Following Prohibition, the hardware store morphed into a Polish bar and banquet hall with a stage, also called Club Lucky (today's kitchen is where the old stage used to sit). Everyone enters through a 1950s-style cocktail-lounge area with rich red Naugahyde booths, a vintage Chicago back bar, and a barrel ceiling. During good weather, there is seating for 40 on a tree-lined street-side patio. The 135-seat dining room is accented by Art Deco chandeliers replicated from the Empire State Building. The red, black, and cream draperies were silk-screened with a neo-Constructivist design by a neighborhood artist.

IF YOU GO Even Chicagoans don't get jaded about Club Lucky. It's a throw-back experience to find a establishment of this scope wedged in a residential neighborhood. You'll be lucky to feel the vibe of Chicago, and you'll take home a sense of local history.

Davenport's Piano Bar and Cabaret

COME TO THE CABARET, OLD CHUM . . . AND FIND YOUR INNER BOBBY SHORT

1383 North Milwaukee Avenue, Near North Side; ☎ 773-278-1830; www.davenportspianobar.com

Cover Varies for cabaret shows, none for piano bar; reservations highly suggested for cabaret shows. Minimum 2 drinks for cabaret shows. Mixed drinks $7–$9, alcohol-free drinks $3.50–$5.25. Wine $6 (glass)–$38 (bottle). Beer $4.75–$6. Dress Anything but ratty T-shirts. Specials Don't walk away without trying Davenport's "Grown-Up Fountain Drinks" ($8 cocktails), including Cherry Coke (Effen Black Cherry Vodka and Coca-Cola), Chocolate Raspberry Coke (Stoli Razberi Vodka, Godiva Dark Chocolate, and Coca-Cola), Root Beer Float (Kahlúa, cream, IBC Root Beer), and Egg Cream Soda (Kahlúa, cream, and club soda). Food available None. Hours Monday, Wednesday, and Thursday, 7 p.m.–midnight; Friday and Saturday, 7 p.m.–2 a.m.; Sunday, 7–11 p.m.; closed Tuesday nights for private parties.

WHO GOES THERE Serious music fans, gays and straights, young and old.

WHAT GOES ON The cabaret is fashioned after Don't Tell Mama in New York City, where staff not only work but join in to perform. Vocalists such as Karen Mason, Debby Boone, and Julie Wilson have appeared in the cabaret room. Even Bea Arthur has stopped by just to sing at the piano bar. There are also occasional musical revues and comedy. Monday is open-mike night, and female Elvis impersonator Patty Elvis has been a popular Sunday-night booking.

SETTING AND ATMOSPHERE Davenport's opened in 1998 in a shuttered dry-goods store on the blue-collar strip of Milwaukee Avenue. The club consists of an informal piano bar and a cabaret space that seats about 75 people. (Sssssh!) Separated from the piano bar by a soundproof door, the cabaret room features cafe tables, velvet walls, and wood-veneer panels. It is one of the most intimate places in Chicago to hear live music. The piano bar is looser and louder; the bar itself is covered with boldly colored interpretations of cabaret music.

IF YOU GO Remember, this isn't Central Park. Davenport's is in the storied working-class neighborhood of Wicker Park (hardscrabble writer Nelson Algren only lived a few blocks away), but that incongruity only heightens its charm. Don't be shy—the staff won't let you be a wallflower. This is one of Chicago's most unique nightspots, especially in an era where sensationalism generally wins out over style.

FitzGerald's

LIVE AMERICAN ROOTS MUSIC IN A ROADHOUSE CLUB

**6615 West Roosevelt Road, Berwyn (Southern Suburbs); ☎ 708-788-2118
www.fitzgeraldsnightclub.com**

Cover $5–$20. **Minimum** None. **Mixed drinks** $4–$6. **Wine** $5. **Beer** $3–$4.50. **Dress** Casual. **Specials** Occasional smoke-free shows on request of performer, call ahead. **Food available** Occasional event-related fare. **Hours** Tuesday–Thursday, 7 p.m.–1 a.m.; Friday and Saturday, 7 p.m.–3 a.m.; Sunday, 5 p.m.–1 a.m.; closed Monday.

WHO GOES THERE Music lovers of all ages, a hearty portion of Lake Wobegon characters, Near West suburban folks; slacker factor very low.

WHAT GOES ON A family-run operation since it opened in 1980, FitzGerald's is one of the most passionately booked rooms in the Chicago area. Blues legend Stevie Ray Vaughan played the intimate 300-seat club in 1981, long before he hit it big. Other landmark shows that remain indicative of the club's musical mission include appearances from the late zydeco king Clifton Chenier and the Neville Brothers. Ample attention is also given to Chicago blues and folk, and Sunday night sets are generally reserved for traditional and big-band jazz.

SETTING AND ATMOSPHERE American roadhouse: The backwoods feel has even attracted Hollywood. The Madonna jitterbug scene from *A League of Their Own* was filmed here as well as the pool hall shots in the Paul Newman flick *The Color of Money*. Sound and sight lines are top-notch, and space for a dance floor is cleared when appropriate. In recent years the club has expanded to include the Sidebar, an intimate tavern equipped with television sets and a CD jukebox with thousands of selections. The Chicago area's popular Wishbone restaurant also opened up shop directly east of FitzGerald's, serving blackened catfish, Louisiana chicken salad, cheese grits, and other southern Reconstruction specialties. The Gulf Coast has never been this close to Chicago.

IF YOU GO Respect the experience. Over the years, FitzGerald's has cultivated fans who love roots music as well as the roots texture of the room. Rarely do you hear an acoustic performance drowned out by audience chatter. And don't be intimidated by the suburban location. Berwyn is a ten-minute drive from the Loop, and the Congress El goes to Berwyn. Get off at Oak Park Avenue, walk three blocks south and then three blocks east. Or call co-owner Bill FitzGerald and ask him to pick you up. If he has time, he probably will. It's that type of touch that makes FitzGerald's a local treasure.

Funky Buddha Lounge

URBAN-HIP DANCE CLUB AND LOUNGE THAT STANDS THE TEST OF TIME

728 West Grand Avenue, The Loop; ☎ 312-666-1695
www.funkybuddha.com

Cover None early in the week; $10–$20 Friday and Saturday. **Minimum** None. **Mixed drinks** $5–$8. **Wine** $5–$7. **Beer** $4–$8. **Dress** Casually hip; no shorts, no tank tops, no tennis shoes. **Specials** Occasional live African/Brazilian music early in the week. The Funky Buddah prides itself on a smoke-free environment, with huge smoke-eaters positioned throughout the club's three rooms. The Buddah was the first bar in the state of Illinois to be awarded a clean-air certificate. The lounge also features a nonsmoking room. **Food available** None, but La Scarola across the street is one of the city's best Italian restaurants. **Hours** Sunday–Friday, 9 p.m.–2 a.m.; Saturday, 9 p.m.–3 a.m.

WHO GOES THERE An extremely unique group of African American, Asian, Indian, Latino, and white folks ages 21 to 30 that create a collective groove. David Schwimmer of *Friends* visits when in town, and it's a popular post-game hang for NBA stars (it's a cross-court pass away from the United Center, the home of the Chicago Bulls).

WHAT GOES ON One-stop shopping. You can drink, dance to DJs spinning neo-soul, hip hop, and funk, and then make out on exquisite leopard-print sofas.

SETTING AND ATMOSPHERE Loungy Eurotrash. The Buddah consists of three rooms: an upfront bar and lounge, a rear dance club, and a nonsmoking room. Decor is connected with (expensive) antique-store ambience, and lighting is soft and dark. Murals are depictions of vintage Mambo record albums from the 1950s and 1960s. Bass-heavy hip hop can make conversation difficult on weekend nights.

IF YOU GO Make sure you are relatively young. The Buddah has been around for six years, which is a long time on the Chicago club scene. But the Buddah consistently reinvents itself and stays on top of music trends. Anyone over 35 could feel out of place here, unless they are Charles Barkley or Keith Richards.

Green Mill Jazz Club

HEPCAT SPEAKEASY WITH QUALITY LIVE JAZZ

4802 North Broadway, North Side; ☎ 773-878-5552

Cover $3–$8. **Minimum** None. **Mixed drinks** $3–$5. **Wine** $2.50–$3.75. **Beer** $1.75–$4. **Dress** Casual and hip. **Specials** Uptown Poetry Slam, Sunday 5–8 p.m. ($5 cover). **Food available** Bar snacks. **Hours** Sunday–Friday, noon–4 a.m.; Saturday, noon–5 a.m.

WHO GOES THERE Sincere jazz fans, local poets, romantic couples on the last stop before home, 25–ageless.

WHAT GOES ON Top-notch local jazz artists and a steady influx of New York musicians who aren't heard anywhere else in town. The Mill also is the city's premiere joint for late-late jam sessions.

SETTING AND ATMOSPHERE Can't be beat. The dark, seductive Mill opened in 1907 and enjoyed its first run of popularity in the 1920s during the neighborhood's vaudeville heyday. Proprietor Dave Jemilo purchased the club in 1986, and instead of gutting it, he lovingly restored it to its earlier splendor. The only additions were a dance floor and a new stage. The piano behind the bar has always been there, and it's still used on Sunday nights.

IF YOU GO Listen to the music. It's rare that high-quality jazz can be heard at affordable prices in a neighborhood setting.

Hala Kahiki

TINY BUBBLES—LOTS OF THEM

2834 North River Road, River Grove (North Central–O'Hare Airport); ☎ 708-456-3222; www.hala-kahiki.com

Cover None. **Minimum** None. **Mixed drinks** $3.50–$10.50 (for two). **Wine** $5.50. **Beer** $5–$5.50. **Dress** Casual; no hats or tank tops; a Hawaiian shirt and hula skirt are fine. **Food available** Pretzels, pineapple. **Hours** Monday and Wednesday, 7 p.m.–2 a.m.; Thursday, 4 p.m.–2 a.m.; Friday and Saturday, 4 p.m.– 3 a.m.; Sunday, 6 p.m.–2 a.m.

WHO GOES THERE 21–60-year-olds, Chicagoans suffering from intense cabin fever, Jimmy Buffett fans, visitors on layovers from O'Hare International Airport—less than ten minutes north of the Chicago area's biggest tiki bar.

WHAT GOES ON Located in near-west suburban River Grove since 1967, Hala Kahiki (meaning "House of Pineapple") serves almost 75 different tropical drinks, including such bizarre concoctions as Dr. Funk of Tahiti (licorice-flavored Pernod and rum), Skip and Run Naked (a gut-wrenching gin-and-beer mix), and the house favorite, the Zombie, a potent mix of fruit juice and three rums—including 151.

SETTING AND ATMOSPHERE The tiki hut holds more than 200 people in three separate, dimly lit rooms and the bamboo-dominated front bar. The back room features a romantic light-blue water fountain, while the front bar's innocent 1950s feel is accented by seashell-covered lamp shades and a dash of incense. In the back of the nightclub, there is a Hawaiian Seas Gift Shop, replete with Don Ho cassette tapes, Hawaiian shirts, and Kukui nuts (authentic beads worn by Hawaiian royalty). A must-see on any visit to Chicago, the Hala Kahiki is the only full-tilt tropical bar and South Sea shop in the Midwest.

IF YOU GO Don't order beer. Do consider a designated driver. The drinks pack a punch, and getting pulled over wearing a green Hawaiian shirt, a yellow lei, and listening to Don Ho will not help your case.

The Hideout

AN URBAN ROADHOUSE IN THE MIDDLE OF NOWHERE, SURROUNDED BY EVERYTHING

1354 West Wabansia, North Side; ☎ 773-227-4433 www.hideoutchicago.com

Cover $5–$10 for live music; $3 when DJs spin (no cover on Monday). Minimum None. Mixed drinks $2.50–$3. Wine $3.50. Beer $1.50 (Pabst Blue Ribbon)–$5. Dress Very casual. Specials Free bag of pretzels or a shot of Hot Damn! if you mention *The Unofficial Guide to Chicago*. Food available Chips and peanuts. Hours Monday, 8 p.m.–2 a.m.; Tuesday–Friday, 4 p.m.–2 a.m.; Saturday, 7 p.m.–3 a.m.

WHO GOES THERE Local musicians and music-industry folks ages 25 to 35, older blue-collar workers, people trying to maintain a low profile.

WHAT GOES ON   The uncanny ability of The Hideout to reinvent itself is what makes the eclectic live-music room a must-see. Although the tiny building's first deed dates back to 1890 and the club has been called The Hideout since 1934, only since the mid-1990s was the joint discovered by a young alt-country crowd. Popular "Americana" country singers such as Neko Case and Kelly Hogan not only perform at The Hideout, they tend bar there as well. That vibe is what put The Hideout on the map and attracted the attention of national publications such as *Rolling Stone* magazine. National acts such as Wilco and the Mekons have been known to stop in The Hideout for impromptu sets. More recently, The Hideout has branched out to feature harder live rock music, country and soul DJs, and art films, moving ever so slightly away from the country music that put The Hideout in the high life.

SETTING AND ATMOSPHERE   Friendly. Live music is presented in a comfortable back room that resembles a Northern Wisconsin lodge. Adorned with Christmas lights and an efficient stage, the concert space seats about 100 people. The Devil in a Woodpile acoustic blues quartet performs for free every Tuesday in the low-ceilinged front-bar space. The Hoyle Brothers play traditional country music at 5:30 p.m. every Friday, attracting the factory and city workers in the blue-collar neighborhood. Black-and-white pictures of the Chicago Cubs (circa 1969) hang behind the bar. Owners Tim and Katie Tuten found the pictures when they were cleaning up the bar. Tim Tuten is a history teacher in the Chicago public-school system, which accounts for the Hideout's social conscience. There's seating for about 18 people along the bar, and the staff is personal. No jukebox; house tapes.

IF YOU GO   Follow directions. The Hideout is in a hard-to-find industrial neighborhood. Known only by its crooked old-style sign out front, The Hideout is directly west of the City of Chicago Fleet Management parking lot, two blocks north of North Avenue and a block east of Elston Avenue. There's ample free parking, and any decent cab driver can find the place.

HotHouse

THE CITY'S PREMIER PERFORMANCE ART SPACE ACCENTED BY A STEAMY POLITICAL VIBE

31 East Balbo, South Loop; ☎ 312-362-9707; www.hothouse.net

Cover $5–$30. Minimum 2 drinks. Mixed drinks $3.50–$10. Wine $6–$9. Beer $2.50–$5, including Bell's. Dress Stylish. Food available Occasional ethnic food, bigger shows catered by Sinha. Hours Monday–Friday, 7 p.m.–2 a.m.; Saturday, 7 p.m.–3 a.m.

WHO GOES THERE Jazz aficionados, writers, poets, residents of the city's burgeoning South Loop neighborhood.

WHO DOES NOT GO THERE Fraternity guys with backwards baseball caps, Toby Keith fans.

WHAT GOES ON The not-for-profit HotHouse (The Center for Performance and Exhibition) is well into its second decade of offering cultural programming with a deep commitment to international and local artists whose work would otherwise remain under the radar. Besides live jazz, blues, and avant-garde music, the HotHouse space includes a 4,500-square-foot gallery for small group and solo shows, lectures, and month-long exhibitions. Phat Tuesdayz is a weekly showcase of progressive Chicago hip-hop crews.

SETTING AND ATMOSPHERE A very good room to catch the independent vibe of Chicago. The ethnic crowd of all ages is not shy about dancing, smiling, or speaking their mind. The main room's open stage breaks down audience-artist barriers, and a middle-sized bar with several barstools is tucked in the back of the room. The 300-seat room features painted wild japonica, accented by faux wall candles. Large picture windows peer out over the street. Work from local artists hangs on the walls in shows in rotating shows.

IF YOU GO Free your mind. Clubs can become predictable—not so at the HotHouse. The bookings of HotHouse Executive Director Marguerite Horberg include the free jazz of Olu Dara, the Latin Jazz Ensemble, and an annual World Music Festival. HotHouse was the first Chicago-based art organization to bring the Cuban jazz band Los Van Van to the Midwest. Horberg is a founder of the club, and her mission is to respect ethnic diversity while promoting understanding of different traditions and perspectives.

House of Blues

THE BLUES AS A TAP ROOT FOR A COLORFUL MUSICAL TREE

329 North Dearborn Street, Near Rorth Side; ☎ 312-923-2000
www.hob.com

Cover $10–$60, none in restaurant. Minimum None. Mixed drinks $5–$8. Wine $5–$7 by the glass. Beer $4–$6.50. Dress Anything from Bourbon Street to State Street. Specials The extremely popular Gospel Brunch ($15–$43)—seatings at 9:30 a.m. and noon every Sunday; "After 5 Live" concerts, held once a month inside the restaurant. Food available Back Porch restaurant serves Creole/Southern cuisine; dinner until 10 p.m. daily, late-night menu until 2 a.m. weekdays, until 3 a.m. weekends. Hours Sunday–Friday, 8 p.m.–4 a.m.; Saturday, 8 p.m.–5 a.m.

WHO GOES THERE 21 and way over; very few blues fans; the audience demographic depends on the booking; always a smattering of tourists and a hard-core group of Chicago roots music listeners.

WHAT GOES ON Live music seven nights a week. No American concert venue is booked with the adventure and passion of the House of Blues. The Chicago club opened Thanksgiving weekend 1996, and in the first three months of operation, acts as diverse as Soul Brother #1 James Brown, Johnny Cash, jazz guitarist Les Paul, rocker-hunter Ted Nugent, and Cuban salsa singer Celia Cruz all graced the HOB (as locals call it) stage. The 400-room House of Blues hotel with 30 suites is adjacent.

SETTING AND ATMOSPHERE House of Blues owner-founder Isaac Tigrett calls his Chicago music hall a "juke-joint opera house," and it is actually designed from the Tyl Theatre opera house in Prague, Czechoslovakia, where Mozart debuted *Don Giovanni* in 1787. The 1,465-capacity music room is the largest of the House of Blues chain. The four-tiered music hall is adorned with hundreds of pieces of eclectic Southern folk art and closed-circuit television monitors where fans can watch the live music while waiting for a drink. The music room is framed by 12 gold-plated private opera boxes that are sold to support House of Blues–related charities. Sound is impeccable, and sight lines are clear. If you want to sit down, arrive very early. There are a limited number of bar stools near serving areas. Otherwise, it truly is standing room only.

IF YOU GO It took a long time for musically provincial Chicagoans to get over the fact this is not a "blues" bar. *Hello?* Check your attitude at the door and you'll discover this club oozes with warmth and spirit.

The Lodge

IN-YO-FACE DRINKING AND SCHMOOZING IN A NEIGHBORHOOD TAVERN

21 West Division Street, Near North Side; ☎ 312-642-4406

Cover Only for St. Patrick's Day and New Year's throngs. **Minimum** None. **Mixed drinks** $4–$5.50. **Wine** $6.50. **Beer** $3.75–$4.50. **Dress** Anything goes. **Specials** Stoli Sunday, Cuervo Monday, Kettle One Wednesday. **Food available** Shelled peanuts on the floor. **Hours** Sunday–Friday, noon–4 a.m.; Saturday, noon–5 a.m.

WHO GOES THERE Jocks, aging jocks, wannabe jocks, real jocks like Charles Barkley, and conventioneers; curious suburban invasion on weekends.

WHAT GOES ON Open since 1957, this is the longest-running act on Division Street, or what locals call "The Street of Dreams." One of the area's premier singles bars, the Lodge has held its own against evil influences such as disco, punk, and herpes. Its late-night license and 1:1 male-female ratio makes it a popular stop for pro athletes winding down after a game. NBA superstar Charles Barkley and ex–Kansas City Royals infielder George Brett have made the Lodge a regular stop when they're in town.

SETTING AND ATMOSPHERE Less is more. The charm comes in a shoebox-size room resplendent in refined cedar and pseudo-antique paintings, accented by three tottering chandeliers and one of the loudest oldies jukeboxes in Chicago. You can't help but meet someone in this setting.

IF YOU GO Stock up on breath mints, cologne, and perfume. On a busy night, it's like riding an El train at rush hour. And know all the words to Meat Loaf's "Paradise by the Dashboard Light." It's a traditional Lodge sing-a-long.

The Matchbox

SPARKS FLY IN ONE OF THE CITY'S MOST INTIMATE TAVERNS

770 North Milwaukee Avenue, Near North Side; ☎ 312-666-9292

Cover None. **Minimum** None. **Mixed drinks** $5–$9; higher for single-malt scotches, single-barrel bourbons, aged rums, and ports. **Wine** $6.50–$11.

Beer $3–$9; high end is Mad Bitch from Belgium in a 750-ml bottle, and Fin du Monde ("the end of the earth") from Quebec. **Dress** Optional. **Specials** Manhattans, margaritas, vodka gimlets. **Food available** Chips, pretzels, nuts. **Hours** Sunday–Friday, 4 p.m.–2 a.m.; Saturday, 4 p.m.–3 a.m.

WHO GOES THERE A compelling group of characters, including cops, musicians, raconteurs, and folks visiting the INTUIT (The Center for Intuitive and Outsider Art) gallery next door. Chicago can be a segregated city, but you would never know it by spending time at The Matchbox.

WHAT GOES ON The mere size of The Matchbox dictates a sense of community—three feet wide at its narrowest, ten feet at its widest. The friendly bartenders will be the first to tell you that if you don't like being sociable, The Matchbox is not the place for you. The diversity of the crowd can also be attributed to the wide range of drinks, which go as low as a pint of Double Diamond for $3 to a $10 scotch. A high-end tequila selection includes Patron, Porfidio, and Del Maguey Mezcal.

SETTING AND ATMOSPHERE Really friendly. The Matchbox opened in 1995 in a former shot 'n' beer bar and package liquor store of the same name. The back bar contains a collection of poster art, Matchbox toy cars, and a bouquet of flowers brought in every Thursday by a local florist. The cigar fad has passed through Chicago, but The Matchbox still sells Punch, Arturo Fuente, Dunhill, and Montecristos, which means the place can get smoky.

IF YOU GO Arrive early so you can secure a barstool. During late spring and summer months, The Matchbox has sidewalk seating which offers a colorful view of a gentrified Near North neighborhood. No need to wear "Hello My Name Is . . ." tags in this joint, and no need to ask anyone for a light.

Old Town Ale House

FROM BACH TO BUKOWSKI

219 West North Avenue, Near North Side; ☎ 312-944-7020

Cover None. **Minimum** None, nor is there a maximum. **Mixed drinks** $5.25–$6. **Wine** $4–$5. **Beer** $3.75–$5. **Dress** Old raincoated; funky; cigars are welcome. **Specials** None. **Food available** Snacks, but it's okay to bring in fast food. **Hours** Sunday–Friday, noon–4 a.m.; Saturday, noon–5 a.m.; open 365 days a year.

WHO GOES THERE Whoever dares, ages 25 to 70, but a sanctuary for artists, journalists, Second City actors, and late-night waitresses and bartenders.

WHAT GOES ON Serious talking and serious drinking. Classic Chicago writers like Studs Terkel and the late Mike Royko used to pound a few here. The original Ale House opened across the street in 1958. It burned down in 1970, maybe due to negative karma. The original Ale House was run by a German who owned a pack of German shepherds named after Nazi generals. Only the long bar was salvaged from across the street. The Ale House's late-night license makes it a popular stop for nightcrawlers getting off work late.

SETTING AND ATMOSPHERE Sleazy, which is a word even the proprietors use. The jukebox is heavy on jazz, soul, classical, and opera. A cornucopia of crazy artifacts include a gorilla bust that is decorated for appropriate seasons, a crooked "Jurassic Park" sign, and strange newspaper clippings bartenders cut and paste on the wall. Chicago folk singer and humorist Larry Rand best summed up the Ale House as "a fern bar where the customers are often more potted than the plants."

IF YOU GO You won't be sorry. This is as authentic as a Near North Side drinking experience can get. Just don't cross the stray punch lines from the Second City folks, still winding down from their late-night sets across the street.

Old Town School of Folk Music

I'D LIKE TO TEACH THE WORLD TO SING; THE COUNTRY'S PREMIER RESOURCE CENTER FOR FOLK AND WORLD MUSIC IDIOMS

4544 North Lincoln Avenue, North Side; ☎ 773-728-6000
www.oldtownschool.org

Cover Varies. Minimum None. Mixed drinks None. Wine $3.50. Beer $2.50–$3.50. Dress No code; flannel welcomed. Specials Two-day outdoor roots-music festival during July; Latin festival in October; Do-It-Yourself Hanukkah in December. Food available Sandwiches and snacks, $1–$5. Hours Monday–Thursday, 9 a.m.–10 p.m.; Friday and Saturday, 9 a.m.–5 p.m. (for concerts, the school closes at 1 a.m.); Sunday, 10 a.m.–5 p.m.

WHO GOES THERE Everyone between age 8 and 88; people who have either attended or taught here include John Prine, Roger McGuinn of the Byrds, Billy Corgan of Smashing Pumpkins, and Jeff Tweedy of Wilco.

WHAT GOES ON The Old Town School of Folk Music services more than 6,000 adult and youth students weekly in classes as eclectic as Bulgarian singing, flamenco-guitar playing, the songs of Bob Dylan, and Hawaiian hula dancing. Nearly 30,000 people attend Old Town School concerts annually. Singer-songwriter Joni Mitchell christened the Old Town School in the fall of 1998. Other concert regulars include Guy Clark, folk legend Odetta, bluegrass great Del McCoury, roots artist Taj Mahal, and Hungarian folk legends Muzsikah. The Old Town School's previous home (909 West Armitage) remains open as the Old Town School of Folk Music's Children's Center. Some adult classes are offered at the old homestead.

SETTING AND ATMOSPHERE The Old Town School of Folk Music was restored from the 43,000-square-foot Hild Library, an Art Deco treasure built in 1929. The acoustically perfect $2-million concert hall is the crown jewel of the center. With 275 seats on the main floor and 150 in the balcony, no audience member is more than 45 feet from the proscenium stage. The $150,000 sound system features 38 speakers that ring throughout the intimate hall. Vintage acoustic instruments are hung on the hall's 14 pillars to absorb sound. The center also includes 31 teaching spaces. The Different Strummer music store sells instruments and rare recordings (instruments are also rented and repaired).

IF YOU GO This can be one of the most rewarding musical experiences in Chicago. During the day, the concert hall transforms into a cafe area where folk-music fans can relax, talk, and hear impromptu concerts by students. The Old Town School of Folk Music began in 1957 as an off-shoot of the humanist movement in folk music—a notion of bringing people together under the belief that music belongs to the masses.

Weeds

CULTURAL ANARCHY FOR A NEW BEAT GENERATION

1555 North Dayton Street, North Side; ☎ 312-943-7815

Cover None. **Minimum** None. **Mixed drinks** $3–$6. **Wine** $4. **Beer** $2–$4. **Dress** Grateful Deadish. **Specials** Free shot of tequila if it's late enough; a surreal beer garden in season. **Food available** Bar snacks, chips, peanuts, etc. **Hours** Monday–Friday, 4 p.m.–2 a.m.; Saturday, 4 p.m.–3 a.m.; Sunday, noon–9 p.m.

WHO GOES THERE Lovable riffraff between the ages of 21 and 65, artists and/or slackers, newspaper people, cab drivers, strippers.

WHAT GOES ON Just about anything. Monday is poetry night hosted by Gregorio Gomez, artistic director of the Chicago Latino Theater. Tuesday and Wednesday are "Comfort Nights," which means there are no scheduled activities. Some of the city's top jazz players jam on Thursday nights, featured rock bands play on Friday nights, and Saturday nights are reserved for open stage. Never a cover.

SETTING AND ATMOSPHERE Twisted Bohemian. Old bras and unused condoms hang from the ceiling along with the year-round-Christmas-lights thing. Sabbath candles and incense burn along the bar, and a funky beer garden is utilized in season. The bar gets its name from being at the corner of Dayton and Weed streets.

IF YOU GO Owner-proprietor-poet Sergio Mayora—who once ran for mayor of Chicago—wrote of his bar, "A place with a difference; where what you are or who you are is only as important as where you are." Be prepared to rub shoulders with all walks of life, hell-raisers, hillbillies, chicks, and tricks. A once-in-a-lifetime experience.

ACCOMMODATIONS INDEX

Affinia Hotel, 48, 53
Allerton Crowne Plaza, 50, 53
Ambassador East Hotel, 50, 53

Best Western Grant Park Hotel, 51, 53
Best Western Hawthorne Terrace, 51, 53
Best Western Inn Chicago, 51, 53
Best Western O'Hare, 51, 53
Best Western River North, 50, 53
Best Western University Plaza, 50, 53
Blake, 48, 54

Candlewood Suites O'Hare, 49, 52, 54
Carleton of Oak Park, 50, 54
Comfort Inn Downers Grove, 51, 55
Comfort Inn Elk Grove Village, 51, 52, 55
Congress Plaza Hotel & Convention Center,
     51, 55
Courtyard by Marriott Downtown, 49, 54
Courtyard by Marriott Magnificent Mile, 49, 54
Courtyard by Marriott Oakbrook Terrace, 50, 54
Courtyard by Marriott Wood Dale, 50, 52, 55
Courtyard Oakbrook Terrace, 52
Crowne Plaza Chicago O'Hare, 50, 55

Days Inn Lincoln Park North, 51, 55
DoubleTree Downers Grove, 49, 52, 54
DoubleTree Hotel Chicago Oak Brook, 50, 54
DoubleTree Hotel Oak Brook, 52
DoubleTree O'Hare Rosemont, 48, 52, 54
Drake Hotel, 48, 55
Embassy Suites Chicago, 49, 55
Embassy Suites Downtown/Lakefront, 48, 55
Embassy Suites Lombard, 49, 56
Embassy Suites O'Hare, 49, 52, 56
Essex Inn, 51, 56

Fairmont Hotel, 49, 57
Four Points Sheraton O'Hare, 49, 52, 57
Four Seasons Hotel, 49, 57, 271

Gold Coast Hotel, 51, 56

Hampton Inn & Suites Downtown, 49, 56
Hampton Inn Midway Bedford Park, 51, 56
Hampton Inn O'Hare, 50, 52, 57
Hampton Inn Westchester/Chicago, 51, 52, 57
Hard Rock Hotel, 48, 57
Hilton Chicago, 48, 52, 56
Hilton Garden Inn Downtown, 49, 56
Hilton Garden Inn Evanston, 50, 52, 56
Hilton Garden Inn Oakbrook Terrace, 50, 57
Hilton O'Hare, 50, 57
Hilton Suites Downtown, 48, 57
Hilton Suites Oakbrook Terrace, 49, 52, 58
Holiday Inn Chicago City Center, 51, 58
Holiday Inn Elk Grove Village, 50, 52, 58
Holiday Inn Express Downers Grove, 51, 59
Holiday Inn Express O'Hare, 50, 52, 59
Holiday Inn Mart Plaza, 50, 59
Holiday Inn North Shore, 50, 58
Holiday Inn Oakbrook Terrace, 51, 58
Holiday Inn O'Hare International, 77
Holiday Inn Select O'Hare, 50, 52, 58
Hotel Allegro, 48, 59
Hotel Burnham, 48, 59
Hotel Indigo, 48, 59
Hotel Inter-Continental Chicago, 48, 58
Hotel Monaco, 48, 58
House of Blues Hotel, 49, 58
Howard Johnson, 51, 59
Hyatt Regency Chicago in Illinois Center, 48, 59
Hyatt Regency McCormick Place, 42, 49, 59

Hyatt Regency O'Hare, 50, 60, 77
Hyatt Rosemont, 50, 52, 60

James, 48, 60

La Quinta Inn Oakbrook Terrace, 51, 52, 61

Marriott Chicago Downtown, 49, 61
Marriott Fairfield Inn & Suites Downtown, 51, 61
Marriott Oak Brook, 50, 52, 60
Marriott O'Hare, 50, 52, 60
Marriott Residence Inn Downtown, 50, 60
Marriott Suites Downers Grove, 49, 52, 61
Marriott Suites O'Hare, 49, 52, 61
Millennium Knickerbocker Hotel, 50, 61
Motel 6 O'Hare East, 51, 52, 60

North Shore Skokie Hotel, 49, 60

O'Hare Hilton, 82
Omni Chicago Hotel, 48, 60
Orrington Hotel Evanston, 48, 61

Palmer House Hilton, 49, 61
Park Hyatt Chicago, 48, 61
Peninsula, 48, 62
Purple Hotel, 51, 62

Quality Inn O'Hare, 51, 52, 62

Radisson Hotel & Suites Chicago, 50
Radisson O'Hare, 50, 52, 63
Raffaello, 48, 63

Ramada Plaza Hotel O'Hare, 77
Red Roof Inn Downers Grove, 51, 52, 62
Red Roof Inn Downtown, 51, 62
Renaissance Chicago Hotel, 48, 62
Renaissance Oak Brook Hotel, 49, 52, 63
Residence Inn by Marriott O'Hare, 49, 63
Ritz-Carlton Chicago, 48, 63

Seneca, 50, 62
Sheraton Chicago Hotel & Towers, 48, 62
Sheraton Gateway Suites O'Hare, 48, 52, 62, 77
Sleep Inn Midway Airport, 51, 63
Sofitel Chicago O'Hare, 49, 63, 77
Sofitel Water Tower, 48, 63
Solis Chicago Hotel & Spa, 48, 64
Sutton Place Hotel, 49, 64
Swissotel Chicago, 49, 64

Talbott Hotel, 49, 65
Travelodge Chicago O'Hare, 51, 65
Travelodge Downtown, 51, 65

W City Center Hotel, 48, 64
W Lakeshore, 48, 64
Westin Hotel O'Hare, 49, 52, 64, 77
Westin Michigan Avenue, 48, 65
Westin River North Chicago, 48, 65
Whitehall Hotel, 49, 65
Willows Hotel, 51, 64
Wyndham Chicago, 49, 64
Wyndham Drake Hotel Oak Brook, 50, 64
Wyndham Garden Hotel O'Hare, 51, 65
Wyndham O'Hare, 50, 65

RESTAURANT INDEX

Note: Page numbers in **boldface** type indicate restaurant profiles.

A La Carte, 294

The Abbey, 329

Agami, 177

Aki Sushi, 177

Alexander's Steak House and Cocktail Lounge, 131

Alinea, 186, **193, 199**

Al's No. 1 Italian Beef, 125

Ambria, 178, 192

Andy's Deli, 121

Angel's, 117

Ann Sather's Restaurant, 117, 121

Army & Lou's, 131, 192

The Art of Pizza, 179, 191

Artopolis, 185, **199–200**

Arun's Thai Restaurant, 187, **200–201**

Athena, 190

Atwater's, 309

Avec, 185, **201**

Avenue M, 178, 180, 193

The Bagel, 189

BB's, 181

Beat Kitchen, 190

Berghoff Café/17 West, 185, **202**

Bijan's Bistro, 190

Billy Goat Tavern, 189

Bin 36, 186, 187, **203**

Bistro Campagne, 183, 185, **203–4**

Bistro Margot, 189

Bite, 191

Bittersweet, 294

BJ's Market and Bakery, 192

Blackbird, 186, **204–5**

Boka, 186, **205–6**

Bongo Room, 184, **206**

Brasserie Jo, 189

Bravo, 179, 180

Brazzaz, 180

Brett's, 189

Bricks, 191

Bruna's Ristorante, 126

Buddy Guy's Legends, **334–35**

Burhop's Fisheries, 294, 308

Byron's Hot Dogs, 190

Café 28, 178

Café des Architectes, 186, **206–7**

Café Iberico, 187, **207–8**

Cafe Jumping Bean, 127

Café Selmarie, 189

Caffé Baci, 292

Carlos', 192

Carnitas Urupan, 127

Carnivale, 180, 186, **208–9**

Carol's Pub, 332

Charlie Trotter's, 186, **209–10**

Chez Joel, 189

Chicago Brauhaus, 183

Chicago Chop House, 187, **210–11**

Chief O'Neill's Pub and Restaurant, 185, **211**

Clark Street Ale House, 183

Club Lucky, **346–47**

Coco Pazzo, 185, **211–12**

Cold Comfort, 189

Conte di Savoia, 125

Continental, 123

Convito Italiano, 308

Coobah, 190
The Corner Bakery, 293
Cru Café and Wine Bar, 190
Crust, 181
Cuatro, 180, 186, **212–13**
Custom House, 179
Cyrano's Bistrot & Wine Bar, 189, 191

Danny's Tavern, 338–39
David Burke's Primehouse, 179
De Cero, 185, **213–14**
del Toro, 179, 180, 193
DeLaCosta, 179, 180
Deleece, 189
Dinotto Ristorante, 190
Dixie Kitchen & Bait Shop, 192
Dorado, 180

Elephant & Castle, 292
Eleven City Diner, 181, 189
Emperor's Choice, 178
Ennui, 131
Erickson's Delicatessen, 117
erwin, 189
Everest, 185, 192, **214–15**
Extra Virgin, 180

Feast, 189
Ferrara Original Bakery, 125
Fifty Yard Line, 337
Fixture, 179, 180
Fogo de Chão, 180
Follia, 185, **215**
Frango Café, 265
Frasca, 181, 191
Frontera Grill, 185, **215–16**
Fulton's on the River, 179
Furama, 119

Geja's Cafe, 132
Ghirardelli Chocolate Shop & Soda Fountain, 291
Gibson's, 187, **217,** 337–38
Gladys' Luncheonette, 192
Glascott's Saloon, 132
The Goddess & Grocer, 293
Goose Island Brewing Company, 183
Greek Islands, 292
Green Dolphin Street, 191
Green Zebra, 184, 187, **217–18**
Gruppo di Amici, 181

Ha Mien, 119
Hachi's Kitchen, 177, 179

Half Shell, 179
Harold's Chicken, 130
HB, 178
Healthy Food Restaurant, 128
Heartland Café, 131
Heat, **19,** 185, 187
Heaven on Seven, 192
Hecky's BBQ, 192
Hema's Kitchen, 178
Hopleaf, 183
Hot Chocolate, 178
Hot Doug's, 184, **218–19**
House of Blues, 191, **352–53**

Il Covo, 178
Ina's, 189
Irazu, 184, **219–20**

Jane's, 189
Japonais, 184, **220–21**
Jerusalem Kosher Restaurant, 118
Jimmy John's World's Greatest Gourmet
    Sandwiches, 294
Jin Ju, 185, **221–22**
Joe's Be-Bop Café and Jazz Emporium, 191
Joe's Seafood, Prime Steak & Stone Crab, 187, **222**

Kaze Sushi, 177
Kevin, 184, 186, **222–23**
Kiki's Bistro, 189
Kohan, 181

La Brea bakery, 265
La Sardine, 189
Landmark, 190
Lawry's The Prime Rib, 178
Le Bouchon, 122, 189
Le Colonial, 185, 187, **223–24**
Le Francais, 185, **224–25**
Le Lan, 187, **225**
Lem's BBQ, 192
Leon's Bar-B-Q, 192
Les Nomades, 192
Long Grove Confectionery, 292
Lottie's, 338
Lou Malnati's, 186, **226**
Lou Mitchell's Restaurant, 184, **226–27**
Lula, 132, 184, **227–28**

M. Henry, 189
MacArthur's, 192
Magnolia Café, 189
Maiz, 178

Manny's Coffee Shop & Deli, 184, **228**
Map Room, 183
Mario's Lemonade Stand, 125
Marketplace Food Court, 264, 265
Mas, 186, **228–29**
May Street Market, 177, 180
Maza, 179
Meiji, 179
Merle's Ribs, 192
Mi Tsu Yun, 118
Mila's Restaurant and Bakery, 126
Minnie's, 180
Mirai Sushi, 185, 187, **229–30**
Mr. Beef, 190
Mity Nice Grill, 261–62
MK, **230**
mk, 186
Moonstruck Chocolate Co., 292
Morton's, 180, 187, **231**
Moto, 184, **232**
Mrs. Murphy & Sons, 178
Mulan, 178, 181
Mundial Cocina Mestiza, 127
Muskie's, 190

Nacional 27, 186, **232–33**
Naha, 184, 185, **233–34**
Negro League Café, 130, 332
New York City Bagel Deli, 189
Nine, 187, **234–35**
No Exit Café, 131
NoMI, 181, 186, 192, **235–36**
North Pond, 186, **236–37**
The Northside, 122

Oceanique, 178
Odyssey cruise, 113–14
Old Town Ale House, 124
Old Town School of Folk Music, **355–56**
Old Town's Mizu Hakitori & Sushi Lounge, 177
Ole Ole, 180
one sixtyblue, 186, **237–38**
Opera, 184, **238**
Orange, 184, **239**

Palm Restaurant, 309
Panaderia Nuevo Leon, 127
Park Grill, 184, **239–40**
Pegasus, 191
People Lounge, 180
Pepper Lounge, 190
Pete Miller's Steak House, 191
Philander's, 191

Phoenix, 184, **240–41**
Piece, 183, 184, 186, **241**
Pizza D.O.C., 179, 191
Pizzeria Due, 191
Pizzeria Uno, 191
Polo Cafe, 128
Prairie Grass Cafe, 184, **242**
Primehouse, 180
Puck's at the MCA, 191, 267
Pump Room, 124

Quartino, 178, 190
Quince, 178

Rainforest Café, 309
Red Apple, 121
Red Light, 178, 193
Red Lion Pub, 183
Resi's Bierstube, 183
The Rib Joint, 192
Ribs 'n' Bibs, 192
RL, 178
Robinson's #1 Ribs, 192
Rosal's, 178

St. Alp's Teahouse, 181
Salaam Restaurant & Bakery, 131
Salpicon, 185, **242–43**
Saltaus, 193
San Soo Gab San, 190
Santorini, 185, 187, **243–44**
Schwa, 177, 178
Scylla, 186, **244**
Seasons Restaurant, 186, **244–45**
7 on State Gourmet Food Court, 265
Shanghai Terrace, 178
Shaw's Crab House, 186, **245–46**
Sheffield's Wine and Beer, 188
Siam Country, 120
Smith & Wollensky, 187, **246**
Smoke Daddy, 191, 192
Sola, 177, 178
Spacca Napoli, 179, 181, 191
Speakeasy, 191
Spiaggia, 185, **247**
Spoken Word Cafe, 130
Spoon Thai, 179
Spring, 186, 187, **247–48**
Sundance Saloon, 333
Superdawg Drive-In, 184, **248–49**
SushiSamba Rio, 186, 187, **249–50**
Svea Restaurant, 117
Swedish Bakery, 117

Take Five, 180
Tallgrass, 193
Tamarind, 178, 181
Tango Sur, 179
The Tasting Room, 179
Tavern on Rush, 190, 193
Tea Geschwender, 181
Tempo, 190
Terragusto, 178
Texas de Brazil, 180, 309
Thai Pastry, 179
Think Café, 178
Three Happiness, 184, 190, **250**
Timo, 191
Tizi Melloul, 179
Toast, 189
Tokyo 21, 177, 179
Topo Gigio, 191
Topolobampo, 185, **250–51**
Tramonto's Steak & Seafood, 180
Trattoria D.O.C., 179, 181, 191

Tru, 186, **251–52**
T-Spot Sushi, 181
Tufano's Restaurant, 125
Turquoise, 179
Twin Anchors, 124, 184, **252–53**
Twisted Spoke, 190

Vernon Park Tap, 125
Viceroy of India, 118
Village Cafe, 123
Village Tap, 188

Weber Grill, 192
The Wiener's Circle, 190
Wishbone, 184, 187, 189, **253–54**

X/O Chicago, 179, 180

Zapatista, 178, 180
Zealous, 193
Zodiac Restaurant, 261

SUBJECT INDEX

Accommodations, 33–65.
    See also separate Accommodations Index
    alphabetical listing of, 53–65
    bed and breakfast, 39
    for business travelers, 41–44
    characteristics of, 44–47
    condos, 39
    from consolidators, 38–39
    for conventions, 41–44, 75–77
    corporate rates for, 36–37
    costs of, 42–43, 48–65
    discounts for, 36–39
    fitness facilities in, 312
    good deals in, 36–39
    half-price programs for, 37–38
    by locations, 46–47
    package deals in, 39–40
    parking at, 36
    preferred rates for, 38
    quality ratings of, 48–65
    rating/ranking of, 48–51
    reservations for, 41
        bed and breakfast, 39
        condominiums, 39
        for conventions, 42–43
        services, 37
        telephone numbers for, 43
    selection of, 33, 36
    top 30, 47, 52
    travel agent help with, 40–41
    weekend rates for, 36
    from wholesalers, 38–39
Addams, Jane, Hull House Museum, 12, 160–61
Adler Planetarium and Astronomy Museum, 95, 138–39
Aerobics, facilities for, 312

African Americans, 30, 130–31, 153
Airport(s)
    Midway, 28, 75, 79, 84–86
    O'Hare International, 28, 75, 79–84
    transportation to/from McCormick Place, 75
Airport Express, 81–82, 86
Alcohol, 97. *See also* Entertainment and night life
Allstate Arena, 325
American Girl Place, 134, 258, 277
American Sightseeing tours, 111–12
Amtrak service, 28, 86–87
Amusement parks, 134, 169–71
Andersonville, 30, 117
Animals. *See* Zoos
Antique Coach & Carriage Company, The, 114
AON Centre, 22
Aquariums, 137, 161–62
Arboretums, 164–65
Architecture, 16–22
Art Deco, 20
    Carson Pirie Scott, 265
    Chicago School, 17
    classical, 17, 20
    after fire, 17
    International Style, 20–21
    Loop, 256
    mansions
        Gold Coast, 124
        Hyde Park, 128–29
        Pullman, 132–33
        South Shore, 130–31
        Uptown, 118
        Wicker Park, 122–23
    postmodern, 21–22
    Prairie School, 20, 155–56
    skyscrapers, 22, 143

Art Deco. (*continued*)
tours, 22, 30, 110–12. *See also* Neighborhoods, sightseeing in
Wright, Frank Lloyd, 20, 30, 111, 155–56, 314
Arie Crown Theater, 72
Arlington International Race Course, 325
Art
murals, 126–27
outdoor sculptures, 22–23
shopping for, 265–70
Art Deco architecture, 20
Art Institute of Chicago, 20, 139–40
disabled visitor access to, 95
shopping in, 266–67
Art museums
African-American, 153
American, 267
Art Institute of Chicago, 20, 95, 139–40, 266–67
contemporary, 165–66, 267
disabled visitor access to, 95
Near East, 171–72
eclectic, 152
holography, 166–67
Mexican, 126, 163–64
oriental, 171–72
peace, 172
Polish, 173–74
shopping in, 266–67
Ukrainian, 175–76
Vietnam veterans, 169
Asian community, 118–19, 124–25
Attractions, 138–76
chart of, 142–45
by locations, 144–45
profiles of, 136–76
Automatic teller machines, at airport, 83

Balzekas Museum of Lithuanian Culture, 140–41
Banking services, 83
Bars. *See* Entertainment and night life
Baseball, 321–23
Basketball, 324, 325
Bathhouses, 311–12
Beaches, 319, 320
Bed and breakfasts, 39
Beer, 183, 188
Betting, 325–26
Bicycling
mountain, 318–19
road, 317–18
Boat(s)
recreation in, 319–20
tours in, 109–12
Bridgehouse tours, 112

Bridgeport, sightseeing in, 127–28
Brookfield Zoo, 96, 141–42, 148, 314
Buckingham Fountain, 111, 134
Bucktown, 122–23, 300–301
Buildings. *See* Architecture; *specific buildings*
Burnham, Daniel H., 12–13, 17, 20
Buses, 28–29, 105–6
to/from McCormick Place, 74–75
tours in, 108–9, 112–13
wheelchair accessible, 96
Business travelers, 41–44, 66. *See also* Conventions and trade shows
Busse Woods Bicycle Trail, 318

Cabs, 106–7
crime avoidance in, 98–99
to/from McCormick Place, 75
to/from Midway Airport, 86
to/from O'Hare International Airport, 81–82
tipping for, 93
to/from Union Station, 86
Calendars
convention, 68–69
special events, 29–32
Camp Sagawau, 321
Canoes, recreation in, 319–20
Car(s). *See* Driving; Parking
Carriage rides, 114
Carson Pirie Scott & Company, 17, 256, 265
Casinos, riverboat, 325–26
Chicago Architecture Foundation, 110–12
Chicago Board of Trade Building, 20
Chicago Botanic Garden, 96, 136, 148–49, 314
Chicago Children's Museum, 149–50
Chicago Cultural Center, 20, 91, 150–51
Chicago Fire of 1871, 11–12, 110, 126
Chicago History Museum, 95, 151–52
Chicago Office of Tourism, 27
Chicago Park District, recreational facilities in, 30, 315, 316
Chicago Place (shopping center), 260–61
Chicago Public Library, 125
Chicago River, 12, 88, 109–12
Chicago River Museum, 112
Chicago Sinfonetta, 343–44
Chicago Symphony Orchestra, 343
Chicago Transit Authority, 82–83, 96, 102–6
Chicago Trolley Company tours, 108–9
Children
activities for, 133–34
bookstore for, 274
gift shopping for, 307
museums for, 149–50, 172–73
playgrounds for, 84, 149–50

Children's Theatre, 342
Chinatown, 124–25
Churches. *See under* Worship, places of
CityPass, 134–35
Clark Street, shopping in. *See under* Shopping
Clothing, shopping for. *See under* Shopping
Clybourn Corridor. *See* Lincoln Park/
    Clybourn Corridor
College sports teams, 325
Comedy, 335–36
Concerts. *See* Music
Condominium rental, 39
Conrad Sulzer Library, 119
Conventions and trade shows, 66–77
    calendar for, 68–69
    at Donald E. Stephens Convention Center,
        68–69, 77
    lodging for, 41–44, 75–77
    lunch alternatives for, 75–76
    at McCormick Place, 42, 66–76
    at Navy Pier, 76–77
Coyote Building, 122
Crime, 97–99
Crowds, avoiding, 26–27
Cruises, river and lake, 109–12
Cultural Center, Chicago, 20, 91, 150–51
Cultural festivals, 29–32
Currency exchange, at airport, 83
Customs, local, 92–94
Cycling
    mountain, 318–19
    road, 317–18

Daley Bicentennial Plaza, 315, 320
Dancing, 336–37, 349
David and Alfred Smart Museum of Art, 152
Department stores, 263–65
DePaul University, 131–32, 325
Devon Avenue, sightseeing in, 117–18
Dining. *See* Restaurants; *separate* Restaurant Index
Dinner cruises, 113–14
Dinner theaters, 343
Disabled visitors, access and services for, 83, 95–96.
    See also specific attractions
Discount outlets, 288–90, 310
Division Street Russian and Turkish Baths, 311–12
Donald E. Stephens Convention Center, 68–69, 77
Driving, 29, 100–102. *See also* Parking
    to/from Donald E. Stephens Convention
        Center, 77
    to/from McCormick Place, 74–75
    to/from Midway Airport, 86
    to/from O'Hare International Airport, 83
    routes for, 78–79

scenic, 136, 164–65
    in subterranean streets, 102
    traffic problems in, 25–26, 90–91, 100
DuSable Museum of African American History, 153

Eating. *See also* Restaurants;
        separate Restaurant Index
    at conventions, 75–76
El (elevated trains), 102–5, 137
Empress River Casino, 325–26
Entertainment and night life, 327–56
    blues, 333–35, 352–53
    classical music, 343–44
    comedy, 335–36
    country-western music, 332–33
    dancing, 336–37, 349
    folk music, 355–56
    gentlemen's clubs, 337–38
    interactive theater, 335–36
    jazz, 31, 331–32, 349–50
    by locations, 345
    piano bars, 338–39, 347–48
    profiles of, 344–56
    rock music, 328–31
    singles bars, 337–39
    theater, 340–43
Ernest Hemingway Museum, 153–54
Ethnic festivals, 29–32
Evanston, shopping in, 257, 294–95, 307
Exercise. *See* Recreation

Farmer's Market, 291
Federal Center Complex, 21
Festival Hall, at Navy Pier, 76–77
Festival of Lights, 137
Field Museum of Natural History, 95, 154–55
Fire of 1871, 11–12, 17, 110, 126
Fitness centers, 312
Flatiron Building, 122
Flower(s). *See* Garden(s)
Food. *See also* Restaurants;
        separate Restaurant Index
    at conventions, 75–76
Football, 323–25
Foreign visitor services, at airport, 83
Forest Preserve, Palos, 314–15, 318

Galleries, art, 265–70. *See also* Art museums
Gambling, 325–26
Gangsters, 14, 113
Garden(s), 31, 136, 142
    Chicago Botanic Garden, 96, 136, 148–49, 314
    disabled visitor access to, 96
    Garfield Park Conservatory, 157

Garden(s). (*continued*)
    Lincoln Park Conservatory, 163
    Morton Arboretum, 164–65
Garfield Park Conservatory, 157
Gentlemen's clubs, 337–38
Geography, of Chicago, 87–88
German community, 119–20
Ghost-related tours, 113
Glencoe, shopping in, 287–88, 294–95
Gold Coast, 89, 124, 313
Golf, 315–17
Grant Park, 88, 137, 315
Greek community, 120

Hair salons, 270–72
Halsted Street, shopping in. *See under* Shopping
Handicapped visitors, access and services for, 83,
    95–96. *See also specific attractions*
Harold Washington Library Center, 21, 157–58
Harrah's Joliet Casino, 325–26
Hawthorne Race Course, 325
Hearing impaired visitors, telephones for, 83
Hemingway, Ernest, 153–54, 158–59
Henry Crown Space Theater, 167–68
Highways, 78–79, 90–91
    scenic, 136
    subterranean, 102
Hispanic community, 126–27
Historic Pullman Foundation, 133
History
    of Chicago, 7–24
    tours related to, 111–12
    History museums, 151–52
    African-American, 153
    Near East, 171–72
    Lithuanian, 140–41
    oriental, 171–72
    Polish, 173–74
Hockey, 324–25
Holidays, calendar of, 29–32
Hollywood Casino Aurora, 325–26
Horse racing, 325
Hotels. *See* Accommodations;
        separate Accommodations Index
Hull House Museum, 12, 160–61
Humboldt Park, sightseeing in, 132
Hyde Park, sightseeing in, 128–29

IBM Building, 21
Ice skating, 320–21
Illinois Institute of Technology, 21
Illinois River, 88
Indian community, 117–18
Information sources, 27, 91–92

Chicago Cultural Center, 20, 91, 150–51
    disabled visitor services, 96
    O'Hare International Airport, 83
    publications, 94–95
    visitor centers, 27
In-line skating, 317
International Museum of Surgical Science, 159–60
Italian community, 125–26

Jackson Park, 316
Jane Addams Hull House Museum, 12, 160–61
Jazz, 331–32, 349–50
Jerry Springer Show, 138
Jewish community, 117–18, 129
John G. Shedd Aquarium, 137, 161–62
John Hancock Center, 22, 136, 161

Kenwood, sightseeing in, 128–29
Kettle Moraine, 318

Lake Michigan, 88
    beaches, 319–20
    boat tours on, 109–12
    running along, 314
    views of, 136–37
    walking along, 313, 314
    water sports on, 319–20
Lake Shore Drive, 79, 88, 136
Lake Shore Park, tennis facilities at, 315
Lakefront Trail, 137, 313, 314, 317, 318
Lakeview, sightseeing in, 120–21
Language services, at airport, 83
Latino community, 126–27
Libraries, 119, 125, 157–58
"Life over Time" exhibit, 154–55
Lincoln Avenue, shopping in. *See under* Shopping
Lincoln Park Conservatory, 163
Lincoln Park Zoo, 162–63
Lincoln Park/Clybourn Corridor, 89
    shopping in. *See under* Shopping
    sightseeing in, 131–32
    walking in, 313
Lincoln Square, 119–20
Liquor, 97. *See also* Entertainment and night life
Little Village, sightseeing in, 126–27
Lodging. *See* Accommodations;
        separate Accommodations Index
Logan Square, sightseeing in, 132
Loop, The
    area west of, 89–90, 269, 296
    attractions, 144–45
    el lines converging in, 102–3
    geography of, 89
    maps of, 257

sculpture in, 22–23
shopping in. *See under* Shopping
walking tours in, 111
Louis, Joe, exhibit on, 153
Loyola University, sports teams, 325
Lyric Opera of Chicago, 344

McCormick Place Convention Center, 66–76
  airport connections with, 75
  Arie Crown Theater, 72
  Business Center, 72–73
  convention calendar for, 68–69
  drawbacks of, 67–68
  exhibit hall designations, 72
  exhibitor move-in and move-out, 74
  Lakeside Center (East Building), 72–73
  layout of, 72–74
  lodging near, 42
  map of, 71
  North Building, 73
  numbering system, 72
  off-site eating alternatives, 75–76
  overview of, 66–67
  parking at, 74
  South Building, 73–74
  transportation to/from, 74–75
McCormick Tribune Bridgehouse, 112
McCormick Tribune Ice Skating Rink, 320
McFetridge Sports Center, tennis facilities at, 315
Macy's, 263–65
Madison Street, 91
Magnificent Mile. *See* Michigan Avenue
Malls, 258–63, 308–10
Mexican community, 126–27
Mexican Fine Arts Center Museum, 126, 163–64
Michigan Avenue (Miracle Mile), 89, 257–63
  bridge on, views from, 137
  maps for, 257
  parking for, 101
  shopping on. *See under* Shopping
Midway, attractions, 145
Midway Airport, 28, 75, 79, 84–86
Mies van der Rohe, Ludwig, 20–21
Milwaukee Avenue, sightseeing in, 121–22
Miracle Mile. *See* Michigan Avenue
Money services, at airport, 83
Montrose Avenue Beach, 319, 320
Montrose Harbor, view from, 137
Morton Arboretum, 164–65, 314
Mosques, 131
Motels. *See* Accommodations;
  separate Accommodations Index
Mountain biking, 318–19
Museum(s), 142–43

archeology, 171–72
art. *See* Art museums
astronomy, 138–39
auto, 306–7
disabled visitor services at, 95
free admission to, 135–36
Hemingway, 153–54
history. *See* History museums
holography, 166–67
Hull House, 12, 160–61
industry, 167–68
Lithuanian, 140–41
natural history, 95, 154–55, 172–73
outdoor, architecture as, 22
peace, 172
Polish, 173–74
science, 154–55, 167–68, 172–73
space, 167–68
surgical science, 159–60
Swedish, 117, 175
Ukrainian, 123, 175–76
Vietnam War, 169
Music
  blues, 333–35, 352–53
  classical, 343–44
  country-western, 332–33
  festivals for, 31, 136, 330
  folk, 355–56
  instruments for, 304–5
  jazz, 331–32, 349–50
  in nightclubs, 344–56
  in parks, 31, 32
  piano bars, 338–39, 347–48
  in public library, 157–58
  radio stations for, 95
  recordings of, shopping for, 304–5
  in restaurants, 191
  rock, 328–31

National African-American History Month, 30
National Vietnam Veterans Art Museum, 169
Nautilus equipment, 312
Navy Pier, 76–77, 149–50, 169–71
NBC Tower, 21
Near North, 144
  shopping in. *See under* Shopping
Neighborhoods. *See also specific neighborhoods*
  crime in, 97–99
  sightseeing in
    Andersonville, 117
    Bridgeport, 127–28
    Bucktown, 122–23
    Chinatown, 124–25
    DePaul, 131–32

Neighborhoods. (*continued*)
  sightseeing in (*continued*)
    Devon Avenue, 117–18
    Gold Coast, 124
    Humboldt Park, 132
    Hyde Park, 128–29
    Kenwood, 128–29
    Lakeview, 120–21
    Lincoln Park, 131–32
    Lincoln Square, 119–20
    Little Village, 126–27
    Logan Square, 132
    Milwaukee Avenue, 121–22
    Old Town, 124
    Pilsen, 126–27
    Pullman, 132–33
    Rogers Park, 131
    Taylor Street, 125–26
    Ukrainian Village, 123–24
    Uptown, 118–19
    Wicker Park, 122–23
    Wrigleyville, 120–21
Neo-Futurarium, 134
Newberry Consort, 344
Newspapers, 94–95
Night life. *See* Entertainment and night life
NikeTown, 134
North Avenue Beach, 134, 319
North Branch Bicycle Trail, 318
North Central/O'Hare, attractions, 144
North Pier, cruises from, 111–12
North Side, 111–12, 144
Northbrook, shopping in, 288
Northwestern University, sports teams, 325

Oak Park
  Visitor Center, 92
  walking in, 313–14
  Wright home and studio in, 155–56
  Wright-designed homes in, 313–14
Oak Street, shopping in. *See under* Shopping
Oak Street Beach, 134, 319
Oceanarium, 161–62
O'Hare International Airport, 28, 75, 79–84
O'Hare region, attractions, 144
Old Town, sightseeing in, 124
Opera, 344
Oprah Winfrey Show, 137
Oriental Institute Museum, 171–72

Package deals, for lodging and travel, 39–40
Palos Forest Preserve District, 314–15, 318
Park(s), 142
  amusement, 134

Grant, 88, 137, 315
Jackson, 316
Lake Shore, 315
music in, 32
Parking, 29, 101. *See also individual attractions*
  commercial lots and garages for, 101
  lodging, 36
  McCormick Place, 74–75
  Michigan Avenue (Miracle Mile), 101
  O'Hare International Airport, 84
  tipping for, 93
  Wrigley Field, 322
Patterson-McCormick Mansion, 124
Peace Museum, 172
Pedways, 107
Peggy Notebaert Nature Museum, 172–73
People mover, O'Hare International Airport, 81
Performance art, 351–52
Pilsen, sightseeing in, 126–27
Planetarium, 95, 138–39
Playgrounds, 84, 149–50
Polish community, 121–22
Polish Museum of America, 173–74
Postal services, at airport, 83
Prairie School of architecture, 20, 155–56
Pratt Boulevard Beach, 319
Precipitation, seasonal, 25–26
Protocols, local, 92–94
Public transportation. *See* Transportation
Publications, for visitors, 94–95
Pullman District, 28, 32, 132–33

Racing, horse, 325
Radio stations, 95
Ravinia Festival, 31, 136, 330
Records, shopping for, 304–5
Recreation, 311–26
  aerobics, 312
  baseball, 321–23
  basketball, 324, 325
  bathhouses, 311–12
  bicycling, 317–18
  canoeing, 319–20
  for children, 133–34
  college sports teams, 325
  fitness centers, 312
  football, 323–24
  gambling, 325–26
  golf, 315–17
  hockey, 325
  horse racing, 325
  ice skating, 320–21
  indoor, 312–13
  in-line skating, 317

in lodging, 312
mountain biking, 318–19
Nautilus equipment, 312
off-track betting, 325–26
publications for, 94–95
riverboat casinos, 325–26
running, 314–15
skiing, 321
spectator sports, 134, 321–26
swimming, 319
tennis, 315
walking, 107, 313–14
weather and, 311
weights, 312
windsurfing, 320
Reliance Building, 17
Reservations, for lodging, 41
bed and breakfast, 39
condominiums, 39
conventions, 42–43
services, 37
telephone numbers for, 43
Restaurants, 177–254. *See also separate* Restaurant
Index
beer in, 183, 188
best, 183–93
bistro, 189
brunches in, 189
deli, 189
dinner cruises, 113–14
dress recommendations for, 92
ethnic, 178–79, 181–87
fast food, 189–90
gastropubs, 181
late-night, 190
by locations, 188
music in, 191
new, 177–80
outdoor, 190–91
pizza, 181, 191
prix-fixe, 192–93
profiles of, 193–254
ribs, 192
small-plate, 180
soul food, 192
steak, 180
sushi, 177
tearooms, 180
tipping in, 93
trendy, 193
River North, shopping in. *See under* Shopping
Riverboat casinos, 325–26
Rogers Park, sightseeing in, 131
Running, 314–15

Safety tips, 97–99, 313
St. Valentine's Day Massacre, 113
Scenic drives, 136, 164–65
Science museums, 167–68, 172–73
natural history, 154–55
surgical, 159–60
Sculpture, in the Loop, 22–23
Sears Tower, 22, 136, 174
Seasons to visit, 25–26
Second City, 327–28, 341
Settlement house complex, 160–61
Shedd Aquarium, 137, 161–62
Sheridan Road, scenic drives on, 136
Shopping, 255–310. *See also* Neighborhoods,
sightseeing in
art, 265–70
autos, 306–7
baby furniture, 270
bath supplies, 295–302
beauty items, 270–72
bikes, 272–73
books, 119, 121, 129, 273–75
boots, 307–8
Bucktown, 300–301
cameras, 275
cars, 306–7
children's gifts, 307
china, 290–91
Clark Street, 117, 257
children's toys and games, 307
clothing, 285–87
home furnishings, 299–300
clothing, 275–90
bridal wear, 279, 284
costumes, 287
at discount outlets, 288–90
furs, 295
high-fashion, 276–77, 280
large-size, 284
menswear, 275–76
western, 307–8
crafts, 265–70
crystal, 290–91
dance supplies, 287
department stores, 263–65
discount outlets, 310
duty free, 83
East of Michigan Avenue, 263
Evanston, 257
children's toys and games, 307
food, 294–95
flowers, 291
food, 291–95

Shopping. (continued)
  furniture, 270
  galleries, 265–70
  games, 307
  garden supplies, 295
  glasses, 279
  Glencoe, 287–88
  Glenview, 294–95
  Halsted Street, 257
    children's toys and games, 307
    clothing, 285–87, 289
    home furnishings, 299–300
    home furnishings, 295–302
  housewares, 290–91
  jewelry, 302–3
  kitchen items, 290–91
  landscaping supplies, 295
  Lincoln Avenue, 257
    clothing, 285–87, 289
    home furnishings, 299–300
    oriental rugs, 306
    outdoor gear, 306
  Lincoln Park/Clybourn Corridor, 257
    art, 269–70
    books, 274–75
    clothing, 281–82, 289
    crystal and china, 290
    food, 293–94
    home furnishings, 299
    jewelry, 303
    luggage, 304
    wines, 293–94
  Lincoln Square, 119–20
  linens, 295–302
  Loop, 255–57, 296
    art, 266–67
    books, 273
    children's toys and games, 307
    clothing, 275–76, 288
    department stores, 263–65
    food, 291–92
    jewelry, 302–3
    luggage, 304
    music-related items, 304–5
  luggage, 304
  malls, 258–63, 308–10
  maps for, 257
  Michigan Avenue (Miracle Mile), 89, 257–63,
      302–3
    art, 266–67
    beauty items, 270
    books, 273–74
    children's toys and games, 307
    clothing, 257–64, 276–78, 288–89

    crystal and china, 290
    food, 292–93
    luggage, 304
    music-related items, 305
    outdoor gear, 306
  music-related items, 304–5
  Navy Pier, 169–71
  Near North, 256
    art, 267
    beauty items, 270–72
    books, 274
    clothing, 280
    food, 293
    home furnishings, 296–99
    music-related items, 305
  Northbrook, 288
  Oak Street, 256
    clothing, 278–80
    home furnishings, 296
    jewelry, 303
  oriental rugs, 305–6
  outdoor gear, 306
  records, 304–5
  River North, 256
    art, 267–69
    home furnishings, 297–99
    stationery, 274
  rugs, 305–6
  saddles, 307–8
  shoes, 276, 278, 284–85, 289
  shopping centers, 308–10
  sports cars, 306–7
  stationery, 273–75
  toys, 307
  Wells Street, 280–81
  western goods, 307–8
  Wicker Park, 122–23, 283–85, 300–301
  Wilmette, 290–91, 294–95
  wines, 293–94
  Winettka, 287–88
Shuttles
  to/from McCormick Place, 74–75
  to/from Midway Airport, 84, 86
  to/from O'Hare International Airport, 81–82
Sightseeing. See Attractions; Tours
Singles bars, 337–39
Six Flags' Great America, 134
Skateboarding, 272–73
Skating
  ice, 320–21
  in-line, 317
Skiing, 321
Sky Theater, 138–39
Skydeck, Sears Tower, 136, 174

Skyscrapers, 22, 143
Smart Museum of Art, 152
Smoking, regulations for, 97
Soldier Field, 324
South Central/Midway, attractions, 145
South Loop, attractions, 145
South Side, 145, 320
Spas, 271–72
Special events calendar, 29–32
The Spirit of Chicago dinner cruise, 343
Sports. *See also* Recreation
 spectator, 321–26
  baseball, 321–23
  basketball, 324, 325
  for children, 134
  college teams, 325
  football, 323–24
  gambling, 325–26
  hockey, 325
  horse racing, 325
  off-track betting, 325–26
  riverboat casinos, 325–26
Springer, Jerry, 138
State of Illinois Center, 21
State Street, 91
Stephens (Donald E.) Convention Center, 68–69, 77
Street layout, 91
Subways, 102–5
Sullivan, Louis, 256, 265
Swedish American Museum Center, 117, 175
Swimming, 319
Symphony Center, 343
Synagogues, 129

Talk show taping, admission to, 137–38
Taxes, 97
Taxis. *See* Cabs
Taylor Street, sightseeing in, 125–26
Telephones, 83, 97
Television, admission to shows, 137–38
Temperatures, seasonal, 25–26
Tennis, 315
Theater, 335–36, 340–43
Time zone, 97
Tipping, 93
Tours, 108–16. *See also specific attractions*
 Andersonville, 117
 architecture, 22, 109–12.
  See also Neighborhoods, sightseeing in
 boat, 109–12
 Bridgeport, 127–28
 Bucktown, 122–23
 carriage, 114

 for children, 133–34
 Chinatown, 124–25
 DePaul, 131–32
 Devon Avenue, 117–18
 driving, 136
 free admission for, 135–36
 gangster-related, 113
 Gold Coast, 124
 for great views, 136–37
 historical, 111–12
 Humboldt Park, 132
 Hyde Park, 128–29
 in-depth, 115–16
 Kenwood, 128–29
 Lakeview, 120–21
 Lincoln Park, 131–32
 Lincoln Square, 119–20
 Little Village, 126–27
 Logan Square, 132
 Milwaukee Avenue, 121–22
 Old Town, 125
 orientation, 108–9
 Pilsen, 126–27
 Pullman, 132–33
 Rogers Park, 131
 South Shore, 130–31
 specialized, 112–14
 Taylor Street, 125–26
 trolley, 108–9
 TV talk show taping, 137–38
 two-day, 114–15
 Ukrainian Village, 123–24
 Uptown, 118–19
 walking, 22, 111
 Wicker Park, 122–23
 Wrigleyville, 120–21
Trade shows. *See* Conventions and trade shows
Traffic, 25–26, 90–91, 100
Trains
 arrival by, 28, 86–87
 elevated, 102–5, 137
 to/from McCormick Place, 75
 to/from Midway Airport, 84, 86
 to/from O'Hare International Airport, 82–83
Transportation, 28–29
 at airports, to/from McCormick Place, 75
 Chicago Transit Authority, 82–83, 96, 102–6
 crime avoidance in, 98–99
 for disabled visitors, 96
 to/from McCormick Place, 74–75
 to neighborhoods. *See* Neighborhoods, sightseeing in
 to/from O'Hare International Airport, 81–83

Travel agents, help from, 40–41
Travel packages, 39–40
Tribune Tower, 20
Trolley tours, 108–9

Ukrainian National Museum, 123, 175–76
Ukrainian Village, 123–24
Union Station, 28, 86–87
University of Chicago, 129, 314
University of Illinois, 125–26, 325
Uptown, tours, 118–19
U.S. Cellular Field, 323

Vietnam Veterans Art Museum, 169
Views, 136–37, 161, 174
Visitor centers, 20, 27, 91–92, 151–52

Walking and walking tours, 22, 107, 111, 313–14
Washington, Harold, 130, 157–58
Water sports, 319–20
Water Tower Place, 261–62
Water Works Visitor Center, 92
Waveland, sports facilities at, 315, 316
Weather, 25–26, 311, 320
Weight lifting, 312
Wells Street, shopping in, 280–81
Westfield North Bridge, 258
Wheelchairs, accessibility with, 95–96
Wicker Park, 122–23, 283–85, 300–301
Wilmette, shopping in, 290–91, 294–95

Wilmot Mountain, 321
Windsurfing, 320
Winettka, shopping in, 287–88
Winfrey, Oprah, 108–9, 137
Worship, places of
    Church of St. Philip Neri, 131
    K.A.M. Isaiah Israel, 129
    Masjid Honorable Elijah Muhammad
        mosque, 131
    Providence of God Church, 127
    Russian Orthodox Holy Trinity Cathedral,
        123
    St. Basil's Greek Orthodox Church, 126
    St. Demetrios Orthodox Church, 120
    St. Hyacinth's Roman Catholic Church, 122
    St. Matthias, 120
    St. Nicholas Ukrainian Catholic Church, 123
    Unity Temple, 156–57
Wright, Frank Lloyd, 20
    furniture designed by, 152
    home and studio, 155–56
    Oak Park homes designed by, 314
    tours, 30, 111
Wrigley Building, 20
Wrigley Field, 120–21, 322
Wrigleyville, sightseeing in, 120–21

Zoos, 142
    Brookfield, 96, 141–42, 148, 314
    Lincoln Park, 162–63

Unofficial Guide Reader Survey

If you'd like to express your opinion about traveling in Chicago or this guidebook, complete the following survey and mail it to:

> *Unofficial Guide* Reader Survey
> P.O. Box 43673
> Birmingham, AL 35243

Inclusive dates of your visit: _____

Members of your party:

	Person 1	Person 2	Person 3	Person 4	Person 5
Gender:	M F	M F	M F	M F	M F
Age:					

How many times have you been to Chicago? _____
On your most recent trip, where did you stay? _____

Concerning your accommodations, on a scale of 100 as best and 0 as worst, how would you rate:

The quality of your room?   The value of your room?
The quietness of your room?   Check-in/checkout efficiency?
Shuttle service to the airport?   Swimming-pool facilities?

Did you rent a car?_____   From whom?_____

Concerning your rental car, on a scale of 100 as best and 0 as worst, how would you rate:

Pickup-processing efficiency?_____   Return-processing efficiency?____
Condition of the car?____   Cleanliness of the car?____
Airport-shuttle efficiency?_____

Concerning your dining experiences:

Estimate your meals in restaurants per day? _____
Approximately how much did your party spend on meals per day? ____
_____

Favorite restaurants in Chicago: _____
_____

Did you buy this guide before leaving? _____ While on your trip?_____

How did you hear about this guide? (check all that apply)

Loaned or recommended by a friend □   Radio or TV □
Newspaper or magazine □   Bookstore salesperson □
Just picked it out on my own □   Library □
Internet □

What other guidebooks did you use on this trip? _____

_____

_____

On a scale of 100 as best and 0 as worst, how would you rate them?

_____

_____

_____

Using the same scale, how would you rate the *Unofficial Guide*(s)?

_____

Are *Unofficial Guides* readily available at bookstores in your area? _____

Have you used other *Unofficial Guides*? _____

Which one(s)? _____

_____

_____

Comments about your Chicago trip or the *Unofficial Guide*(s):

_____

_____

_____

_____

_____

_____

_____

_____

_____

_____

_____

_____

_____

_____

_____

_____

_____

_____